THE OXFORD HANDBOOK OF

POPULATION ETHICS

THE OXFORD HANDBOOK OF

POPULATION ETHICS

Edited by

GUSTAF ARRHENIUS

KRISTER BYKVIST

TIM CAMPBELL

and

ELIZABETH FINNERON-BURNS

OXFORD

UNIVERSITY PRESS

OXFORD
UNIVERSITY PRESS

Oxford University Press is a department of the University of Oxford. It furthers
the University's objective of excellence in research, scholarship, and education
by publishing worldwide. Oxford is a registered trade mark of Oxford University
Press in the UK and certain other countries.

Published in the United States of America by Oxford University Press
198 Madison Avenue, New York, NY 10016, United States of America.

Library of Congress Cataloging-in-Publication Data
Names: Arrhenius, Gustaf, Bykvist, Campbell, and Finneron-Burns editor.
Title: The Oxford handbook of population ethics / [edited by] Gustaf
Arrhenius, Krister Bykvist, Tim Campbell, Elizabeth Finneron-Burns.
Identifiers: LCCN 2021030811 | ISBN 9780190907686 (hardback) |
ISBN 9780190907709 (epub) | ISBN 9780190907693 (pdf) |
ISBN 9780190907716 (online)
Subjects: LCSH: Population—Moral and ethical aspects. |
Population—Political aspects. | Population—Environmental aspects.
Classification: LCC HB849.42 .O84 2021 | DDC 179.7—dc23
LC record available at https://lccn.loc.gov/2021030811

DOI: 10.1093/oxfordhb/9780190907686.001.0001

1 3 5 7 9 8 6 4 2

Printed by Marquis, Canada

ACKNOWLEDGMENTS

WE, the editors, would like to thank the authors of this handbook for their cooperation, dedication, and thoroughness, and for their attempts to make their chapters accessible to a broad audience. In addition, we would like to thank Caleb Althorpe and Jack Rizell for their invaluable assistance in the preparation of this handbook, Peter Ohlin, our editor at Oxford University Press, for his encouragement and help with this handbook at every step of its production, and three anonymous reviewers for helpful comments and suggestions. Finally, we would like to acknowledge generous funding from The Swedish Research Council (421-2014-1037) and from Riksbankens Jubileumsfond (M17-0372:1).

Contents

PART I WAYS OUT OF THE PARADOXES

PART II PHILOSOPHICAL AND METHODOLOGICAL ASSUMPTIONS

PART III APPLICATIONS

About the Contributors

Matthew D. Adler

Matthew D. Adler is the Richard A. Horovitz Professor of Law and Professor of Economics, Philosophy, and Public Policy at Duke University, and is the founding director of the Duke Center for Law, Economics, and Public Policy. Adler's scholarship is interdisciplinary, drawing from welfare economics, normative ethics, and legal theory. His research concerns prioritarianism and its theoretical foundations, implementation as a policy analysis method, and application to a variety of policy domains.
https://law.duke.edu/fac/adler/

Gustaf Arrhenius

Gustaf Arrhenius is a Professor of Practical Philosophy at Stockholm University and the CEO of the Institute for Future Studies in Stockholm. Arrhenius's research concerns moral and political philosophy, specifically intergenerational ethics, population ethics, democratic participation, the structure of value, equality, and power.

Geir B. Asheim

Geir Asheim is a Professor at the Department of Economics at the University of Oslo since 1994. He is a resident researcher at institutes of advanced study in Marseille and Paris. Asheim's primary research interests are game theory, intergenerational justice, and green national accounting.
https://www.sv.uio.no/econ/english/people/aca/gasheim/

Ralf M. Bader

Ralf M. Bader is Professor of Philosophy at the Université de Fribourg in Switzerland, where he holds the chair for ethics and political philosophy. Bader is also a researcher at the Institute for Future Studies in Stockholm. His research is focused on ethics, meta-ethics, metaphysics, Kant, political philosophy, and decision theory.
http://ralf-bader.com/

Walter Bossert

Walter Bossert is Full Professor at the Department of Economics, Université de Montréal. Bossert has taught at the University of British Columbia, the University of Waterloo and the University of Nottingham. Most of his research concerns the analysis of links between the social choice theory and ethics, using mathematical techniques. In particular, he is working on welfare indicators, individual and collective decision theory, and the rationality of economic choices.
https://en.sceco.umontreal.ca/repertoire-departement/vue/bossert-walter/

John Broome

John Broome is Emeritus White's Professor of Moral Philosophy and Emeritus Fellow of Corpus Christi College at University of Oxford. Broome is both a philosophy and economy scholar, and holds visiting posts at Stanford, Princeton, Australian National University etc. His primary areas of research are normativity, rationality, reasoning, and the ethics of climate change.
https://www.iffs.se/forskning/affilierade-forskare/john-broome/

Mark Budolfson

Mark Budolfson is Assistant Professor in Environmental Health Sciences, Population-Level Bioethics, and Philosophy at Rutgers University. He is also an Associate Member of the Princeton University Climate Futures Initiative, and Faculty Affiliate at the University of Vermont Gund Institute for Environment. Budolfson's work is concerned with interdisciplinary issues in ethics, economics, and public policy related to climate change and sustainable development.
http://www.budolfson.com/

Krister Bykvist

Krister Bykvist is a Professor at the Department of Philosophy at Stockholm University and researcher at the Institute for Future Studies. His research areas are intergenerational ethics, populations ethics, the basis of consequentialism, moral uncertainty, and the relationship between preferences, value, and well-being.

Erik Carlson

Erik Carlson is a Professor of Practical Philosophy at Uppsala University and researcher at the Institute for Future Studies in Stockholm. Carlson's main research interests are within axiology and normative ethics specifically concerning consequentialism, moral responsibility, free will, and decision theory. He has also conducted research on metaphysics and epistemology.
https://www.filosofi.uu.se/forskning/seminarier-och-lasgrupper/praktisk-filosofi/

Ruth Chang

Ruth Chang is the Chair and Professor of Jurisprudence at the University of Oxford and a Professorial Fellow at University College, Oxford. Chang is both a philosophy and law scholar. Her research interests concern the nature of normativity, the structure of values and reasons, practical reason, agency, rationality, population ethics, love, commitment, decision-making, and the self.
https://www.ruthchang.net/
https://www.law.ox.ac.uk/people/ruth-chang

Sarah Conly

Sarah Conly is Professor of Philosophy at Bowdoin College. Conly works primarily on ethics and political philosophy, including issues such as liberty, procreation ethics, autonomy, and paternalism.
https://www.bowdoin.edu/profiles/faculty/sconly/

Aisha Dasgupta

Aisha Dasgupta earned her PhD in demography at the University of London in 2015. She is working at the population division (DESA) at the United Nations. Her research interests concern the links between population and environment, specifically fertility, family planning, and population growth.
https://researchonline.lshtm.ac.uk/id/eprint/2124340/1/2014_EPH_PhD__Dasgupta__A_NEW.pdf
https://www.researchgate.net/profile/Aisha_Dasgupta

Partha Dasgupta

Partha Dasgupta is Emeritus Professor and Ramsey Professor Emeritus of Economics at the University of Cambridge. He is also a research Fellow at the British Academy, Royal Society, London School of Economics, and Trinity College (Cambridge). Partha's research interests are environmental economics, the economics of knowledge, the economics of poverty and nutrition, and economic measurement.
http://www.econ.cam.ac.uk/people/emeritus/pd10000

Axel Gosseries

Axel Gosseries is Professeur Extraordinaire at the Université catholique de Louvain in Belgium, where he holds the Hoover Chair in Economic and Social Ethics. He is also Maitre de recherches at the Fonds de la Recherche Scientifique in Brussels and Visiting Professor at the Institute for Futures Studies in Stockholm. Gosseries research is focused on analytical political philosophy, including intergenerational justice, climate change, ethical issues in agriculture, and the political philosophy of information.
https://uclouvain.be/fr/chercher/hoover/presentation.html

Hilary Greaves

Hilary Greaves is a Professor of Philosophy at the University of Oxford and the Director of the Global Priorities Institute. Her current research focuses on moral philosophy, specifically global prioritization, consequentialism, interpersonal aggregation, population ethics, effective altruism, moral uncertainty, and epistemology.
http://users.ox.ac.uk/~mert2255/

Johan E. Gustafsson

Johan E. Gustafsson is a Senior Research Fellow in Philosophy at University of York and Associate Professor in Practical Philosophy at University of Gothenburg. He is also a researcher at the Institute for Future Studies. His work primarily concerns normative ethics, value theory, and political philosophy, but is also concerned with decision theory, moral uncertainty, and metaphysics. (He also designs flags.)
http://johanegustafsson.net/

Elizabeth Harman

Elizabeth Harman is Laurance S. Rockefeller Professor of Philosophy and Human Values at Princeton University, where she has held several positions since 2006. Harman's primary research area is ethics, specifically the ethics of abortion, the concept

of harming, and future persons. She is also interested in epistemology, metaphysics, and political philosophy.
http://www.princeton.edu/~eharman/

Nils Holtug

Nils Holthug is a Professor of Philosophy at the Department of Communication, University of Copenhagen. His areas of research include equality, prioritarianism, multiculturalism, migration, secularism, social cohesion, population ethics, global justice, normative ethics, and personal identity.
https://comm.ku.dk/staff/?pure=en%2Fpersons%2Fnils-holtug(86546289-c002-4f8a-9b71-d4c128139cc5).html

Martin Kolk

Martin Kolk is a researcher and Associate Professor at the Stockholm University Demography Unit (SUDA), Centre for Cultural Evolution (CEK), and Institute for Future Studies (IFFS). Kolk's research interests are intergenerational demography, economic demography, same-sex childbearing, and cultural evolution. He currently studies the demography of kinship and economic demography in contemporary and historical populations.

Jeff McMahan

Jeff McMahan is White's Professor of Moral Philosophy at Oxford University, a distinguished research fellow at the Oxford Uehiro Centre for Practical Ethics and a fellow of Corpus Christi College. McMahan's research concerns areas of both normative and applied ethics such as bioethics, animal ethics, and the ethics of war.
https://www.philosophy.ox.ac.uk/people/jeff-mcmahan

Tim Meijers

Tim Meijers is Assistant Professor of Moral and Political Philosophy at Leiden University. Meijers' research concerns intergenerational justice, sustainability, global justice, the ethics of the family, and reproductive rights. He is also interested in fundamental questions in metaethics such as the nature of value and grounds for moral status.
https://timmeijers.com/

Julia Mosquera

Julia Mosquera is a postdoctoral researcher at the Institute for Future Studies in Stockholm. She earned her PhD in philosophy at the University of Reading 2017 with the dissertation "Disability, Equality, and Future Generations." Her research interests are ethical issues concerning disability, justice, equality, and population ethics.

Serena Olsaretti

Serena Olsaretti is a Research Professor of Philosophy at the Catalan Institute of Research and Advanced Studies, Universitat Pompeu Fabra in Barcelona. Her research interests are theories of justice, the ethics of markets and theories of well-being. She is

currently working on questions of justice involving the family, as well as egalitarianism and libertarianism.
https://w,ww.icrea.cat/Web/ScientificStaff/serena-olsaretti-520

Wlodek Rabinowicz

Wlodek Rabinowicz is Senior Professor of Practical Philosophy at Lund University. He is co-editor for the philosophical journal *Theoria* and Honorary Professor at the University of York and Australian National University in Canberra. Rabinowicz's research concerns value theory, consequentialism, population ethics, and decision theory. He has previously worked on normative ethics and meta-ethics as well as epistemology.
https://www.fil.lu.se/person/WlodekRabinowicz/

M.A. Roberts

Melinda Roberts is Professor of Philosophy and coordinator for the bachelor's program in law at The College of New Jersey. With PhD degrees in both philosophy and law, Roberts' research interests lie mainly in the intersection between moral theory and law. She is also interested in population ethics and other ethical problems related to climate change, future generations, and historical injustice.
https://www.iffs.se/forskning/forskare/melinda-a-roberts/

Dean Spears

Dean Spears is Assistant Professor of Economics at the University of Texas at Austin and Executive Director at Research Institute of Compassionate Economics. He is also visiting economist at Indian Statistical Institute, Delhi Centre, Research Fellow at IZA, Institute of Labor Economics and at Population Research Center, UT-Austin. Spears is an economic demographer and development economist. His research areas include the health, growth, and survival of children, especially in India, climate change, and population dimensions of social well-being.
https://www.iffs.se/en/research/affiliated-researchers/dean-spears/

Larry S. Temkin

Larry Temkin is Distinguished Professor and Chair of Philosophy at Rutgers University. Temkin's research concerns normative ethics, social and political philosophy, meta-ethics, applied ethics, and philosophy of mind. He has focused specifically on issues of inequality and moral reasoning.
https://philosophy.rutgers.edu/people/faculty/details/182-faculty1/faculty-profiles/636-temkin-larry
https://www.practicalethics.ox.ac.uk/people/professor-larry-temkin

Teruji Thomas

Teruji Thomas is a Senior Research Fellow in Philosophy at the University of Oxford, based at the Global Priorities Institute. Thomas also holds a PhD in mathematics from the University of Chicago and has held fellowships at Oxford and Edinburgh. His research is concerned with normative ethics and decision theory, but he is also interested in formal epistemology and the philosophy of mathematics, physics, and so on. http://users.ox.ac.uk/~mert2060/

Stéphane Zuber

Stéphane Zuber is Research Director at the Centre National de la Recherche Scientifique (CNRS) in Paris and Professor at the Paris School of Economics. Zuber's research concerns economic theory, welfare theory and environmental economics, specifically intergenerational equity, and dynamic social choice in relation to environmental issues. https://www.iffs.se/forskning/forskare/st%C3%A9phane-zuber/

INTRODUCTION

GUSTAF ARRHENIUS, KRISTER BYKVIST,
TIM CAMPBELL, AND
ELIZABETH FINNERON-BURNS

WHAT is population ethics? The straightforward answer is that it is the investigation of various ethical issues that arise when we consider how our actions affect both who is born and how many people are born. But, of course, it is more complicated than that.

One complication is that population ethics divides into two forms: the axiological and the normative. The axiological form considers how we ought to *value* different populations, whereas the normative form considers how we *ought to act* in relation to populations, for instance which populations we ought to bring about. There are at least three elements that influence how we value a particular population: (1) the number of people who exist; (2) the well-being of the people who exist; and (3) the identities of the people who exist. Possible populations vary along these lines and the study of population axiology attempts to determine how to rank them, taking account of these differences. For instance, would it be better if one excellent life existed than if two different decent lives existed? Do we make the world better by creating more happy people? Is a world in which many people live with a very low quality of life better or worse than a world in which very few people live with a very high quality of life? (We use the terms "quality of life" and "well-being" synonymously.) The normative form of population ethics, in contrast, asks similar questions but in normative terms. Do we do something wrong when we create a person with a decent life when we could instead have created a different person with an excellent life? Do we have an obligation to create more happy people? Do we have a duty to create many people with a very low quality of life rather than create very few people with a very high quality of life? In order to determine how we ought to govern our actions with respect to different populations, the normative form of population ethics often applies traditional ethical theories—for example, utilitarianism, Kantianism, and contractualism—and then evaluates the results. Exactly how the axiological and normative forms are related is in itself an important issue. Only simple forms of consequentialism would claim that we ought to bring about the best population but there are other more complex theories about the bridge from the axiological to the normative. (As, for example, Arrhenius shows in his contribution to this volume.)

The axiological and normative questions in population ethics are theoretically challenging but they are also directly relevant to many urgent practical decisions and policies. The answers to these questions matter because they affect the moral standing of future people in the decisions we currently make. Future people pose an especially hard problem for our decision-making, since their number and identities are not fixed; rather, they depend on the choices we make. Climate change is a clear example as the increase in temperature makes areas uninhabitable and will kill some people. However, because the increase in temperature will affect people's decisions about where to live, when to have children, and how many children to have, climate change will also affect which particular people come to exist and prevent many possible people from ever existing. Many other policies also influence the size and make-up of the population, both directly and indirectly. For example, many health policies both prevent deaths and affect procreation decisions. Population-control policies, such as China's one-child policy, obviously affect population size. Even taxation policies, such as tax relief for parents, can indirectly affect population size and make up. If we are to adequately assess these policies, we must be able to determine the value of different populations and how we ought to act in relation to them.

1. PARADOXES OF POPULATION ETHICS

Despite these seemingly straightforward questions, what makes the task of formulating an adequate population ethics so difficult is that it is plagued by several very difficult problems and even paradoxes.

1.1. The Non-Identity Problem

Perhaps the most notorious of these problems is the Non-Identity Problem (Parfit 1984). Often when we think about what we owe to future people, we assume that these people will exist at some point in the future, no matter what we do now. We take for granted that it would be wrong to perform actions that would harm them, and that the outcome would be worse if we did (assuming other things are equal). However, the Non-Identity Problem complicates this simple picture, for the existence of some future people depends on what we do now. One small-scale example is procreation (Parfit 1984: 358–359). Suppose that you can either (a) create a child now that, due to your poor financial situation, will have a not especially happy life, although its life will still be worth living or, (b) wait and create a different child later, who will have a much happier, and hence, better life, since by then your financial situation will have improved considerably. Suppose that all other things are equal. It then seems wrong to create the child now, and, furthermore, the outcome of this action seems to be worse than the outcome of postponing the creation. But can we really say that? If you create the child now, it seems that you do not harm her in any way, for she has a life worth living and she does not have it worse than she would have had if she had not been created. If she had not been created, she would not have had any welfare at all, since she cannot have any welfare if she does not exist. How can it then be wrong to create the child now and how can the outcome of the action be worse? No one will be harmed (or so it seems), and it also seems plausible that an action is wrong only if it harms someone, and that an outcome is worse than another only if someone is worse off in the former than in the latter.

There are large-scale versions of the Non-Identity Problem as well (Parfit 1984, 351–355). Suppose you can choose between two policies: conservation of natural resources and depletion of these resources. If we deplete these resources, the quality of life for people over the next few centuries will be slightly higher than it would have been if we had instead conserved. But after the next few centuries, quality of life will fall dramatically and will remain much lower, for many centuries, than it would have been if we had instead conserved. Suppose we decide to deplete the resources. As a result, many millions of people have a quality of life that is much lower than the quality of life that people would have enjoyed if we had instead conserved. However, these millions of people have lives that are worth living. Moreover, if we had chosen the alternative policy, these particular people would never have existed. This is because our choice of policy has certain wide-reaching effects. For example, because of our choice, many people end up living in different places, meeting and procreating with people they would otherwise never have met, and giving their children a different upbringing. This means that while our choice of policy is the reason why many millions of people have a relatively low quality of life, it is also a cause of their existence. *They* would not have existed if we had chosen differently. *Different people* would instead have existed. Hence, the millions of people with a low quality of life cannot plausibly claim that our choice of policy harmed *them* when their existence depended on our choice and in fact they have lives that are worth living. But, surely, we nevertheless would like to say that it is wrong to choose depletion and that the outcome of this action is worse than that of conservation.

The Non-Identity Problem is a challenge to both axiological and normative accounts of population ethics. It seems difficult to avoid the surprising and disconcerting conclusion that our seemingly negligent actions are not wrong, and their outcomes not worse, because they do not make future people worse off than they would otherwise have been. Of course, this is only a problem if we share the intuition that there is something wrong with such actions and something bad about their outcomes. There are some who are willing to bite the bullet and accept that these seemingly wrong actions are in fact permissible (e.g., Boonin 2014), but most disagree and therefore look for alternative ways to "solve" the Non-Identity Problem. One alternative would be to abandon the ideas that an action is wrong only if it harms someone, and that an outcome is worse only if someone in it would be worse off. A more radical solution would be to argue that bringing a person into existence can harm that person even if it is not true that she is thereby made worse off than she would otherwise have been, and even if her life is worth living (Shiffrin 1999).

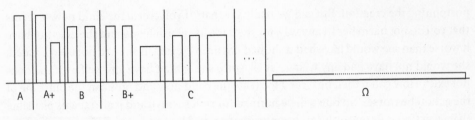

FIGURE I.1

1.2. The Mere Addition Paradox

Another central paradox is the Mere Addition Paradox (Parfit 1984, 419–438). To illustrate, consider the example given in Figure I.1: Population A consists of a small number of individuals, all leading lives with a very high level of well-being. Population A+ consists of all the individuals in A, plus some extra individuals leading lives with a level of well-being that is slightly lower than in A, but still very high. Population B has the same number of individuals as in A+, all leading lives with the exact same level of well-being, that is lower than the level in A and higher than that of the extra individuals in A+. Population B+ modifies B in a parallel way to how A+ modifies A: B+ has all the individuals in B, plus some extra individuals leading lives with a level of well-being that is slightly lower than in B, but still very high. C modifies B+ in a parallel way to how B modifies A+, and so on all the way to population Ω.

Comparing the value of the populations in the sequence leads to the following observations. A+ seems at least as good as A since A+ is a mere addition of positive well-being; it contains some extra people with positive well-being and the well-being of the A population is not affected. More generally, it seems that a mere addition of positive well-being is always at least as good as no mere addition (Parfit 1984). B seems better than A+, since B has higher total and average of well-being and has perfectly equal distribution of well-being. More generally, it seems, an increase of total and average well-being that also creates perfect equality is always an improvement (Ng 1989). Call this Weak Inequality Aversion. Mere Addition implies that B+ is at least as good as B, and Weak Inequality Aversion implies that C is better than B+. Indeed, we can reapply these principles until we reach the conclusion that Ω is better than the immediately preceding population. By the transitivity of the relation "is better than" we must conclude that Ω is better than A. But this result may seem unacceptable. A is a population whose members have very high well-being. Ω is a population whose members have lives barely worth living.

It may seem that, generally, any acceptable theory should avoid the Repugnant Conclusion which (in Parfit's famous version) holds that

The Repugnant Conclusion: for any possible population of at least ten billion people, all with a very high quality of life, there must be some much larger imaginable population whose existence, if other things are equal, would be better even though its members have lives that are barely worth living (Parfit 1984, 388).

But now we have a problem. If we accept Mere Addition, Weak Inequality Aversion, and want to avoid the Repugnant Conclusion, it seems we get a contradiction: A is both better and worse (and hence not better) than Ω. We have to give up one of these compelling principles, if we want to avoid a contradiction. However, as Arrhenius (2000a; 2000b; 2011) has shown, even if we give up one of these principles there are other paradoxes lurking.

1.3. The Repugnant Conclusion

One way to avoid the contradiction is to bite the bullet and accept the Repugnant Conclusion. This is what some advocates of total utilitarianism do. According to this theory, provided the people who exist have lives that are (even just barely) worth living, the existence of a sufficiently large number of such people would have a greater total of well-being, and hence would be better, than the existence of a smaller number of people with very high quality of life.

However, total utilitarianism is not the only theory that has been shown to lead to the Repugnant Conclusion. As shown above, this holds for any theory that accepts Mere Addition and Weak Inequality Aversion (and some other background assumptions, such as that betterness is transitive, that is, if a is better than b and b is better than c, then a is better than c). Many philosophers see avoiding the Repugnant Conclusion as a necessary feature of any satisfactory population ethics and try to find a solution to the problem. Others believe that the Repugnant Conclusion may not in fact be repugnant at all and ought to be embraced or at least grudgingly accepted. Finally, some believe that it is simply impossible to find a population ethics that avoids the Non-Identity Problem (above) and the Repugnant Conclusion and that does not lead to other similarly unpalatable conclusions. All three approaches are represented in this volume.

1.4. The Procreation Asymmetry

Another salient problem arises from two claims that many people seem to accept. The conjunction of these two claims is known as the Procreation Asymmetry:

- (i) That a person would have a life that is worth not living—a life that is worse than no life at all—provides, on its own, a moral reason not to cause that person to exist.
- (ii) That a person would have a life worth living does not, on its own, provide a moral reason to cause that person to exist. (This statement of the Procreation Asymmetry is a slightly altered version of the one given by McMahan 1981, 100.)

To many, each of (i) and (ii) seems, on its own, *prima facie* plausible. Yet it is surprisingly difficult to provide a satisfying explanation of the conjunction of (i) and (ii). Why is it that the fact that a life would be worth not living has reason-giving force *against* creation while the fact a life would be worth living has no reason-giving force *in favor of* creation?

Not all theorists think it is worthwhile to search for an answer to this query, and instead they deny the Procreation Asymmetry. For example, total utilitarians claim that we should maximize total well-being and this can be done not only by refraining from creating lives with negative well-being (lives worth not living) but also by creating lives with positive well-being (lives worth living). Since total utilitarians think we have a duty to increase well-being wherever possible, they would say that if we can increase well-being by creating a worth-living life, we ought to do so.

2. PART I: WAYS OUT OF THE PARADOXES

The question of how to respond to the paradoxes in population ethics has spawned a huge, though largely inconclusive, literature. Part I of this Handbook therefore focuses on different responses to (or "ways out of") these paradoxes. The responses canvassed here are diverse.

Ruth Chang's contribution addresses what are known as *continua* arguments, and in particular, continua arguments for the Repugnant Conclusion. Continua arguments create a continuum of outcomes varying by population size and well-being, such that each successive outcome is better than its predecessor, and because of transitivity, the final outcome is better than the initial outcome. She argues that neither incommensurability, incomparability, indeterminacy, nor Parfit's own proposed "lexical imprecision" view can successfully "break the chain" and provide a solution.

Nils Holtug also confronts the Repugnant Conclusion. He defends a version of prioritarianism that implies this conclusion, as well as several other counterintuitive conclusions. However, he argues that prioritarianism entails more palatable versions of these conclusions than utilitarianism and other rival axiologies. He also argues that different ways of avoiding these conclusions are available to prioritarians, if they are willing to adjust the prioritarian function, but that such adjustments lead to further problems.

Geir Asheim and Stephane Zuber argue that there is a dilemma between assigning "dictatorship" to a single worst-off person, thereby succumbing to a tyranny of non-aggregation, and assigning "dictatorship" to an (unlimited) number of better off people, succumbing to a tyranny of aggregation. They claim that this corresponds to a dilemma between, on the one hand, a Reverse Repugnant Conclusion (a very small number of very well-off people is seen as better than a much bigger population with fairly good lives), and, on the other hand, the Repugnant Conclusion or Sadistic Conclusion. They argue that the dilemma can be resolved by allowing that the evaluation of populations might change with population size, even though the relative distributions of well-being remain unchanged.

Walter Bossert's chapter discusses some important characteristics of critical-level utilitarianism and compares this axiological view to alternative views. He points out that critical-level utilitarianism with a critical level above neutrality can avoid the Repugnant Conclusion but implies what Arrhenius calls the Sadistic Conclusion. Bossert illustrates that it is impossible to obtain a general population axiology that avoids both of these conclusions, provided that some additional plausible requirements are imposed. The chapter illustrates one of the difficult trade-offs in population ethics: embracing the Sadistic Conclusion may be the price that one must pay to avoid the Repugnant Conclusion.

Wlodek Rabinowicz's chapter aims to accommodate *the axiological intuition of neutrality* within a version of neutral-range utilitarianism. The intuition is that there is a range of welfare levels such that adding people with lives at these levels makes the world neither better nor worse. Rabinowicz proposes an interpretation of the neutral range according to which a life within this range is neither good nor bad for the person who has it and is incommensurable with non-existence. The resulting version of neutral-range utilitarianism entails not only that lives are incommensurable with non-existence but also that some lives are incommensurable with each other, and hence, that some lives are not comparable.

John Broome's chapter is a response to Rabinowicz's. Broome argues that if some lives are not comparable, this makes no significant difference to the utilitarian ethics of population. Neutral range utilitarianism can accommodate the same axiological intuitions and will be vulnerable to the same problems that motivated Broome to reject the theory in his book *Weighing Lives* (2004). Furthermore, Broome doubts that Rabinowicz's personalized interpretation of the neutral range can advance our understanding of population axiology, since, Broome thinks, the axiological intuition of neutrality is directly about the general goodness of populations, not about personal goodness.

3. Part II: Underlying Philosophical and Methodological Assumptions

A number of philosophical and methodological assumptions underly the paradoxes discussed in Part I of this volume. Rejecting or revising some of these assumptions may hold the key to formulating an adequate population ethics. The contributions in Part II aim to critically assess some of the most important assumptions in this area.

3.1. The Reliability of Our Intuitions

One important methodological assumption is that our intuitions are reliable guides to axiological and normative truths. For example, if we believe that an adequate population axiology must avoid the Repugnant Conclusion, this is because we find this conclusion deeply unintuitive, and the fact that we find it deeply unintuitive is then taken as strong evidence that it is false.

Yet intuitions are not always reliable. They are subject to various distorting effects and cognitive biases. This might be true of our intuitions about axiological and normative matters. Johan Gustafsson argues in his chapter that our intuitions about the Repugnant Conclusion are unreliable as evidence against total utilitarianism. According to

Gustafsson, there is an insensitivity in our intuitive understanding of the axiologically relevant factors involved in comparisons of different populations, and this insensitivity has its greatest impact when these factors are extremely proportioned in opposite ways, as in the cases used to illustrate the Repugnant Conclusion.

3.2. The Structure of Value and the Betterness Relation

Larry Temkin's chapter argues that the Mere Addition Paradox challenges some of our deepest assumptions about the nature and structure of the good. It distinguishes two opposing views of the goodness of outcomes, an *Internal Aspects View* and an *Essentially Comparative View*, and argues that the latter view underlies our judgments about the comparative goodness of many outcomes, including those featured in the Mere Addition Paradox. An Essentially Comparative View, Temkin argues, challenges the assumption that "all-things-considered better than" is a transitive relation, and has profound implications not only for axiology but also for rationality and practical reasoning.

Gustaf Arrhenius's chapter considers whether the axiological paradoxes translate directly into corresponding paradoxes for normative theories. Perhaps one reason for thinking that they do not is that the axiological paradoxes depend on the transitivity of "better than," and one might think that because there is no convincing analogue to transitivity on the normative level, the paradoxes will not reappear on that level. Arrhenius argues that this claim is false and that the axiological impossibility theorems can be proved without an appeal to the transitivity of "better than."

Erik Carlson's chapter responds to Arrhenius's impossibility theorems and his contention that there is no satisfactory population axiology because plausible adequacy conditions are mutually inconsistent. Carlson argues that if non-Archimedean theories of welfare are not excluded, there are in fact population axiologies that satisfy all of Arrhenius's adequacy conditions and Arrhenius's results therefore fail to conclusively demonstrate that there is no acceptable population axiology.

Teruji Thomas's chapter discusses the principle of *separability*, which says (roughly) that in comparing the value of two possible outcomes one can ignore any people who exist in both and whose welfare is the same in both. The chapter surveys the motivations for separability and its theoretical implications for population ethics. It also systematically explores how axiological theories that satisfy requirements of separability and impartiality can avoid the Repugnant Conclusion.

3.3. Questioning the Status of Claims as Adequacy Conditions

Dean Spears and Marc Budolfson's chapter questions the assumption that avoiding the Repugnant Conclusion is a desideratum for a population axiology. They argue that our aversion to the Repugnant Conclusion derives from an aversion to a more general axiological claim that is implied by "all plausible axiologies," including average, critical-level, and variable-value versions of utilitarianism, prioritarianism, and egalitarianism. This is an important claim, since avoidance of the Repugnant Conclusion is usually the primary motivation for adopting an average, critical-level, or variable-value axiology. If Spears and Budolfson's argument is sound, then these axiologies fail to avoid the *repugnance* of the Repugnant Conclusion, even if they avoid the Repugnant Conclusion as it is stated by Parfit.

3.4. Evaluative Uncertainty and Decision-Making

One assumption that is often implicit in debates in population ethics is that our theories should provide practical guidance for agents facing real-world problems, such as climate change. A natural thought is that we should first discover the correct theory, and then implement whatever policies it prescribes. However, the paradoxes canvassed in Part I of this book present a formidable obstacle for such an approach. They show that we cannot consistently accept all our favorite axiological and normative principles. It may seem that in order to apply theory to practice, we must first decide which of these conflicting principles to abandon. But we are deeply uncertain which principle(s) to abandon, and hence, deeply uncertain which theory is correct. Indeed, given the lack of consensus regarding how the paradoxes should be resolved, our uncertainty may be irresolvable. It may therefore seem that for many real-world issues for which our choice of theory would be relevant, decision-making is paralyzed.

However, some argue that deep evaluative and normative uncertainty need not paralyze decision-making. There are well-established approaches to decision-making under *empirical* uncertainty, and some have sought to develop corresponding approaches to decision-making under evaluative and normative uncertainty. Along these lines, Krister Bykvist's chapter sketches the contours of an approach to rational decision-making under evaluative uncertainty. This approach extends some of the tools of standard decision theory, including certain dominance and expected value maximization principles, to the evaluative setting. Bykvist demonstrates the practical usefulness of the approach by applying these principles to a range of cases in which different axiologies yield conflicting claims regarding the betterness ordering of the agent's alternatives. Given that the agent cares about the value of population changes but is uncertain which betterness ordering (if any) is correct, she can rationally choose an alternative by acting in accordance with one or more of the extended decision theoretic principles.

3.5. Person-Affecting Approaches

Several chapters in this Handbook defend *person-affecting approaches* to population ethics. These approaches attempt to explain the betterness relation between outcomes in terms of a personal betterness relation.

Ralf Bader's chapter rejects impersonal versions of utilitarianism that he claims treat persons as "mere containers" of impersonal good, and considers the theoretical prospects for different person-affecting forms of utilitarianism. It argues that person-affecting total utilitarianism requires metaphysically problematic commitments because it presupposes that existence and non-existence are comparable in terms of personal good. It concludes that same-number person-affecting utilitarianism is the only version of utilitarianism that avoids both objectionable axiological implications and problematic metaphysical commitments.

Melinda Roberts's chapter aims to develop the beginnings of a plausible person-based maximizing consequentialism. According to Roberts, such a theory must not only accommodate the Procreation Asymmetry but also explain how we can have a moral reason to give someone a greater chance of existence with a good life. She proposes a person-based view that satisfies these desiderata, and defends her view against a charge of inconsistency as well as an objection based on the Non-Identity Problem.

Matthew Adler's chapter sets out a conceptual framework that he calls "claims across outcomes." According to this framework, outcome x is morally better than outcome y only if some person has a claim in favor of x over y, and the person has such a claim only if x is better than y with respect to her well-being. In previous work, Adler has defended his framework for fixed population cases. His chapter extends this framework to variable population cases and addresses several objections that arise in this context, including the objection that a person's existence and her non-existence are incomparable with respect to her well-being.

4. PART III: APPLICATIONS

One question in applied population ethics is that of ideal population size and the legitimate role of government in regulating it. Many people believe the world is currently over-populated and the human population ought to be reduced or at least prevented from increasing. There are two related issues here. The first is whether the world really *is* over-populated, and relatedly, what the optimal population size actually is. Hilary Greaves's chapter argues that to answer this question we need a population axiology and an account of which states of affairs are achievable in practice. Assuming a total utilitarian axiology, Greaves surveys economic models of optimum population size at a time and of the optimum population path through time, finding that even the most sophisticated of these models cannot, by themselves, provide quantitative answers to questions of optimal population size. Greaves also considers two important arguments in favor of deliberately reducing the birth rate to bring us closer to the optimal population path. She finds both arguments problematic and inconclusive.

Aisha Dasgupta and Partha Dasgupta's chapter studies some important factors underlying "population overshoot." One concerns the desire for children. The authors criticize demographers' methods of estimating women's desire for children, arguing that these methods fail to account for the social-embeddedness of preferences related to family size. The authors also make use of the estimate of humanity's current ecological footprint to generate their own estimate of how many people Earth can support at a reasonable standard of living without further diminishment of the biosphere.

The second question is, if it is indeed the case that the world is overpopulated, what, if anything, should be done about it? Are individuals morally obliged not to reproduce, or to have only one child even if the incremental harm to others created by their choice is minimal? Serena Olsaretti argues that egalitarian justice demands that even if having children creates burdens for others, everyone should share equally in the costs of providing for them. This is because new generations bring with them societal *benefits* as well as *burdens*. Moreover, Olsaretti argues, the fact that third parties have a complaint against parents for producing too many or too few children presupposes that everyone is entitled to share the benefits of children; but this would seem to imply that everyone must share the costs as well. Sarah Conly's chapter argues that since population increase is one cause of the climate emergency, and, given that voluntary efforts to reduce the fertility rate are ineffective, appropriate government coercion to reduce birth rates is permissible. She argues that individuals have a moral duty to refrain from actions that contribute an increment to a great harm (such as the harm of climate change), and that even if no individual were morally responsible for incremental harms, we could still justify government action to coordinate efforts to avoid the collective harm that overpopulation brings.

Martin Kolk provides an interesting account of how demographic theory can help illuminate certain issues in population ethics. He argues that many population ethicists implicitly assume a Malthusian perspective according to which there is a negative relationship between population size and average welfare. But, as Kolk points out, demographic theory includes a number of alternative perspectives that are often ignored in population ethics. He suggests that population ethicists consider population models that combine these different perspectives, to form a more complete picture of the relationship between population size, population growth, and average welfare. He also describes some implications of demographic theory for intergenerational inequality, reproductive rights, and the risk of human extinction.

Another applied population ethics question is how we ought to consider the value of a possible person's existence in our decisions. Jeff McMahan's chapter argues that causing someone to exist with a good life benefits that person, and that such benefits have moral significance. This result is supported by McMahan's proposed response to the Non-Identity Problem and his view about how to accommodate the first claim of the Procreation Asymmetry (i.e., claim (i) discussed in Section 1.4). McMahan considers how the benefit of bringing someone into existence with a good life weighs against a similarly-sized benefit to an existing person. John Broome's chapter in Part III (his second contribution to the Handbook) notes that one consequence of climate change that is rarely discussed is that it will change the future population. He then considers the "intuition of neutrality" discussed earlier to argue that the impact of climate change must take into account the fact that it will affect population change.

Some issues in applied population ethics intersect with other important issues, both at the level of theory and at the level of practice. For example, Elizabeth Harman's chapter provides an intriguing analysis of gamete donation as a "morally permissible moral mistake"—an act that one ought morally not to do (since it involves isolating one-self from one's biological child) but that is nevertheless morally permissible and morally good (since it gives certain people the opportunity to have and raise children). Based on her discussion of gamete donation, Harman draws out some general lessons about the relationship between *what one is morally obligated to do* and *what one should do, all things considered*, and about the nature of moral reasons.

Julia Mosquera's chapter discusses the relationship between population ethics and the ethics of disability. She argues that while reducing the incidence of disability is desirable in certain important respects, it may also exacerbate inequality. This is be-cause, she argues, as the minority of disabled individuals within a population shrinks, these individuals are subjected to a greater number of pairwise relations of inequality. Egalitarian duties of justice toward disabled individuals may therefore grow stronger as their numbers dwindle.

Finally, most literature in applied population ethics focuses on human populations—but should we not also be concerned about non-human animal populations? Tim Meijers and Axel Gosseries explore how the different theoretical questions and answers in population ethics bear on ethical questions related to our interactions with non-human animal populations. They consider four different hypotheses corresponding to four different ways in which non-human animal population ethics may be thought to be distinctive or special as a subfield. Overall, they suggest, animal and human population ethics may be difficult to distinguish clearly once we abandon our implicitly speciesist commitments.

References

Arrhenius, Gustaf. 2000a. "An Impossibility Theorem for Welfarist Axiology," *Economics and Philosophy* 16: 247–266.

Arrhenius, Gustaf. 2000b. "Future Generations: A Challenge for Moral Theory," PhD diss., Uppsala University.

Arrhenius, Gustaf. 2011. "The Impossibility of a Satisfactory Population Ethics." In *Descriptive and Normative Approaches to Human Behaviour*, edited by H. Colonius and E. Dzhafarov, 1–26. New Jersey: World Scientific.

Boonin, David. 2014, *The Non-Identity Problem and the Ethics of Future People*. New York: Oxford University Press.

McMahan, Jeff. 1981. "Problems of Population Theory." *Ethics* 92: 96–127.

Parfit, Derek. 1984. *Reasons and Persons*. Oxford: Oxford University Press.

Shiffrin, Seana. 1999. "Wrongful Life, Procreative Responsibility, and the Significance of Harm." *Legal Theory* 5: 117–148.

PART I

WAYS OUT OF
THE PARADOXES

CHAPTER 1

....

HOW *NOT* TO AVOID THE REPUGNANT CONCLUSION

....

RUTH CHANG*

IN this chapter, I examine four seemingly promising ways to defuse continua arguments that exploit normative predicates like "stronger reason," "better," "more choiceworthy," "preferable to," "best," and the like in order to generate puzzles or paradoxes of normativity. The most famous of these is Parfit's continua argument for the Repugnant Conclusion (Parfit 1984). According to that argument, we can create a continuum of outcomes varying only by population size and quality of well-being such that each successive outcome is intuitively better than its predecessor until we arrive at an outcome in which there is a very large number of people, each with a life barely worth living. Given the transitivity of "better than," it follows that this world, with vast numbers of people with lives barely worth living, is better than the first world in the continuum, one with a large number of people all of whom are leading excellent lives. This is the Repugnant Conclusion.

Parfit believed his continua argument was significant because it placed a challenging constraint on normative theorizing: the correct normative theory must be able to avoid the Repugnant Conclusion, but it is unclear how it is to be avoided. Indeed, the last paper Parfit published (Parfit 2016), shortly before his unexpected death, was an attempt to answer the challenge he himself had made so famous.

While Parfit's continua argument is the most famous, it is an instance of a more general form of continua argument that has wide application beyond population ethics.[1] That general argument can be given in four steps. First, start with an item that is to be

* This chapter is drawn from my "How to Avoid the Repugnant Conclusion," in *Ethics and Existence: The Legacy of Derek Parfit*, edited by Jefferson McMahan, Tim Campbell, James Goodrich, and Ketan Ramakrishnan (Oxford: Oxford University Press), which was written after this chapter but will, as of this writing, be published shortly before this Handbook. This chapter sets up the problem space to which I then offer a solution in the longer work. Because I discovered that the comprehensibility and attractiveness of my solution depended on the reader being familiar with the problem space, I ended up incorporating this chapter as the first part of the longer work. I am grateful to the editors of both volumes and OUP for permission to do this.

evaluated along two factors, both significant, in determining its overall value. Second, generate a successor item that stands in a transitive comparative relation, R, to the first by diminishing one of the factors slightly and enhancing the other significantly. Continue to generate successive items along a continuum by modifying each predecessor through a small diminution in one respect and a large enhancement in another so that R appears to hold between each item and its predecessor (i.e., so that the third item appears to be R-related to the second, the fourth R-related to the third, and so on). Third, by the transitivity of R, it follows that the last item is R-related to the first item. But, fourth, it is intuitively clear that the last item is *not* R-related to the first item. Hence a puzzle.

A key assumption of all continua arguments with this form is that a small diminution in one contributory factor in conjunction with a sufficient enhancement in the other contributory factor does not make a difference to how the items compare. That is, all continua arguments assume:

> *Uniformity*: The R-relation holds between every item and its predecessor on the continuum because there are no differences between any two adjacent items that makes a difference to whether they R-relate.

I examine four possible "structural" solutions to such arguments. "Structural" solutions deny that Uniformity holds. They maintain that the structural relations among items in the continuum are not as continua arguments suppose; they posit a "break" somewhere along the continuum where there is a difference that makes a difference to how two adjacent items compare. If there is such a break, then the slide to a repugnant conclusion is halted and continua arguments are thereby defused.

The challenge for structural solutions is to specify and defend the supposed change in structure as one proceeds along the continuum. I argue that appeal to any of three natural accounts of structural change, *incommensurability*, *incomparability*, and *indeterminacy*, either fail to avoid the Repugnant Conclusion or suffer from other grave difficulties. A fourth possible explanation, namely Parfit's own appeal to lexical *imprecision*, is also problematic; it fails to provide an answer to some continua arguments, including, arguably, a version of Parfit's own.[2]

None of this is to say that *no* continua arguments, however constructed, can be avoided by appeal to one of four "i" explanations; the point is rather that none of these explanations can provide a general solution to *all* of them. Anyone looking to respond to continua arguments *writ large* must find some other solution.[3] In a sequel to this chapter, I propose such a solution, one which involves thinking about normativity in a nonstandard way (Chang, forthcoming). The aim of the present paper, however, is negative: four seemingly promising ways to defuse such arguments turn out to be ways in which we should *not* attempt to address continua arguments. This conclusion sets the stage for finding a solution elsewhere.

For simplicity, I will focus on Parfit's continua argument in population ethics, but the arguments apply to other continua arguments, such as those that counsel repeated walkings across the grass (Harrison 1953), always having another cigarette, self-torture

(Quinn 1990), and opting for several years of torture over a lifetime of minor pains (Rachels 1998; 2001; Temkin 2012).

1. Parfit's Argument

Parfit's continua argument for the Repugnant Conclusion (Parfit 1984) asks us to consider a continuum of possible worlds or outcomes in which each successive world involves a slight decrease in the well-being of its people but some large addition of people leading lives with that diminished quality of well-being. All else is stipulated as irrelevant or equal. It seems that each successive world is better than its predecessor; after all, surely a sufficiently large increase in the quantity of lives worth living can compensate for the small diminution in quality of life that obtains in each successor world. And if "better than" is transitive, it follows that a world at the end of the continuum, Z, in which there are vast numbers of people whose lives are barely worth living, is better than a world at the beginning of the continuum, A, in which there is a smaller but still significant number of people all leading excellent lives. But that is a Repugnant Conclusion. Parfit's continuum is depicted in Figure 1.1.

There are three assumptions of the argument worth noting, two of which we will reject in order to make continua arguments as broad in scope and as difficult to answer as possible.

First, Parfit—and others who have put forward continua arguments—assume that an increase in quantity of lives at a certain quality maps onto an evaluative difference in quantity. If you add 100 lives at quality q, you add more value than if you add only 80. Talk of an increase in quantity, then, should be understood evaluatively, that is, as an increase in the value that quantity contributes to the overall goodness of the outcome. A large increase in quantity of lives, then, should be understood as a large evaluative increase in the contribution quantity makes to the overall goodness of the outcome. This

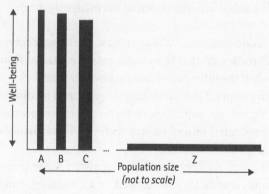

FIGURE 1.1 Parfit's continuum

assumption, although probably not true as a general matter, is not problematic for our purposes and can be granted for the sake of argument.

Second, Parfit sometimes discusses his continua argument as if comparative judgments about the goodness of worlds issue from a god's-eye point of view, impartial goodness, all-things-considered-goodness, or goodness simpliciter. That there is such a viewpoint is highly controversial (and, I believe, deeply mistaken). I suggest that we instead understand comparisons along the continuum as proceeding with respect to an ordinary substantive "covering consideration," call it "V," such as "social well-being," "beneficence," "justice," and so on in terms of which each world is putatively better than its successor. For our purposes, we can simply assume, for the sake of argument, that there is some or other V, understood as a unity or a collection of familiar considerations, in terms of which Parfit's and other continua arguments can proceed.[4]

Third, and in part as a consequence of the second, we should not assume that only consequentialist covering considerations are relevant to assessing how items on the continuum compare, and correspondingly that outcomes are the only items out of which a problematic continuum might be formed. The items forming a continuum might in principle be possible actions or ways of being, differing in terms of deontological V such as "doing one's duty" or in terms of some particular form of perfectionist excellence. You might, for example, have an imperfect duty to give to charity. Facts about the comparative normative significance of giving one amount rather than another are relevant to the determination of what you have a duty to do. More controversially, when duties themselves conflict, they might be said to have respective "strengths" which might stand in comparative relations, especially since it is a mistake to think that comparisons necessarily suppose aggregation, summation, cardinality, rates of tradeoff, or any of the crude representational features with which they are often unfairly saddled (Chang 2016b). At the very least, we should leave open the possibility that continua arguments present a challenge to nonconsequentialist theories (e.g., Arrhenius, this volume).[5]

Whether plausible continua arguments can be generated for a given relation, R, such as "better than with respect to beneficence," depends on at least three conditions, each of which is in principle neutral between different normative theories:

i) the covering consideration, "V," has at least two significant contributory factors that are "bi-directional," that is, in some cases, one factor favors one item on the continuum while the other factor favors the other item;

ii) each successive item on the continuum is generated by diminishing slightly one (particular) significant contributory factor of its predecessor while enhancing greatly the (particular) other in a way such that these changes appear to make it R-related to its predecessor; and

iii) relatively speaking, an "unbalanced" package of these contributory factors of V—for example, one factor instantiated in a nominal (or notable) way relative to the other—is not R-related to a less unbalanced package of these contributory factors.

I restrict my attention to continua that meet these three conditions. Going forward, I will assume that there is always a "V" with respect to which a comparative claim is made even if not explicitly stated and, for simplicity, that "V" has only two relevant contributory components, both of which make important contributions to V-ness. To simplify even further, I will assume that the two factors are quantity of quality of V-ness (though continua could also be generated by two bi-directional *qualities* of V-ness).

Parfit's continua argument meets the three conditions. It proceeds by trading off two bi-directional contributory factors of V: a small diminution in quality of V for a large increase in quantity of V. As we move along the continuum, each item involves a small diminution of quality which, it seems, can be compensated for by a large increase in quantity so that each item is better than its predecessor. At the start of the continuum, world A is, relatively speaking, a "balanced" package of quantity and quality of V-ness— a good number of people leading excellent lives—while Z, at the end of the continuum is, relative to A, an "unbalanced" package of V-ness—a googol of people with lives barely worth living.

As we have said above, structural solutions will deny that each item on Parfit's continuum is better than its predecessor; there will be a "break" somewhere along the continuum where an item is not better than its predecessor. Could the break be given by a single point? Perhaps, depending on how the continuum is constructed. But if the continuum is finely grained, a single break point will be implausible; how could there be a single item along the continuum before which all worlds are better than their predecessors but after which all worlds are not better than their predecessors, or a single item that is not better than its predecessor, but which is followed by worlds each of which is better than their respective predecessors? For any putative structural break point, it seems plausible that we can construct worlds around it that would appear to be part of the structural break, too.

To finesse this issue, I am going to assume that a plausible structural solution will posit a *zone* of items along the continuum that form a break in the structure along the continuum, in principle compatible with there being only two items in "The Zone." In Parfit's continuum, we might suppose that The Zone begins around, say, world P and ends around, say, world S (though of course these are arbitrarily selected). I say "around" because The Zone might, in principle, be surrounded by indeterminacy. Within The Zone, at least one item is not better than its predecessor and thus the slide to the Repugnant Conclusion is halted. The idea of a structural solution positing a zone of break points is depicted in Figure 1.2.

For a structural solution to succeed, it must explain and defend the claim that there must be some world in The Zone, Q, that is not better than its predecessor, P. But there are a number of ways in which this could be so. In the next section, we examine and reject three seemingly natural possibilities.

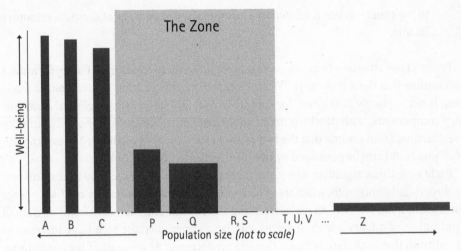

FIGURE 1.2 The Zone

2. THREE STANDARD STRUCTURAL SOLUTIONS TO CONTINUA ARGUMENTS

2.1. Incommensurability

Two items are *incommensurable* with respect to V if there is no common cardinal scale of units by which their V-ness can be represented or measured. For example, the pleasure you get from watching a television sitcom cannot plausibly be measured by a "contribution to well-being unit" that also measures the satisfaction you get from achieving a life-long goal of writing a best-selling novel. A cardinal unit of measure can give rise to either a ratio scale, as the inches or pounds give rise to a scale of length or weight, or an interval scale, as degrees Fahrenheit or Celsius give rise to a scale of temperature. Two items are incommensurable with respect to V if their *V-ness* cannot be measured by either an interval or ratio scale.

Suppose that P is a world with a large population that is doing just fine—"middle class" we might say by way of rough (if icky) shorthand. Q is a world with 50 percent more people, all of whom enjoy very slightly less good middle-class lives than those enjoyed by those in P. Suppose now that Q and P are incommensurable with respect to V: there is no cardinal unit of V by which we might ascertain that the *V-ness* of world P is 4.56 units worse than the *V-ness* of world Q or .876 times better. Is the slide to the Repugnant Conclusion blocked?

The answer is a definitive "no." One might think that some kind of cardinal scale is required to have trade-offs and that all trade-offs must be conceived in numerical terms. But this need not be so. Even if there is no cardinal unit by which achieving a life goal is better with respect to your well-being than watching your favorite television program, achieving the life goal might be better *ordinally*, that is, by a ranking that does not admit of (nonderivative) cardinal differences in your well-being. Similarly, while there may be no ratio or interval scale according to which Q might be more V than P, Q might nevertheless be better than P in V-ness in a merely ordinal ranking. And if Q is better than P, the slide to the Repugnant Conclusion is not halted since Q is better than P, R is better than Q . . . and so on. In short, incommensurability is no solution to continua arguments because incommensurability is compatible with comparability.

This is not to say that incommensurability does not hold in The Zone. It will if there is no numerically specifiable rate of trade-off among the factors that contribute to the comparison of outcomes with respect to V, a condition that will plausibly hold of the continua of interest: could the goodness of the addition of a certain number of good lives really be worth, for instance, 1.214 times the drop in the well-being of the entire population? A structural solution to continua arguments, then, should countenance incommensurability in The Zone. But incommensurability itself is a non-starter as itself a solution to continua arguments.

2.2. Incomparability

If Q and P are *incomparable* (with respect to V), then the slide to the Repugnant Conclusion is halted. Is incomparability the right structural response to continua arguments? Toby Handfield (2014) has suggested so.

Much turns on how we understand "incomparability." We should not, as many economists, philosophers, and decision theorists do, define or assume "incomparability" to be the failure of the one item to be better, worse, or as good as the other (with respect to V). As I've argued elsewhere, what relations exhaust the conceptual space of comparability between two items is a substantive matter open to debate (Chang 1997; 2002a; 2016a). "Better than," "worse than," and "equally good" are three such relations, but there could be more. So we should instead understand "incomparability" neutrally—without prejudging what basic, positive value relations exhaust the conceptual space of comparability between two items—as the failure of *any* basic, positive value relation, whatever those might be—to hold between them.

Are Q and P incomparable with respect to V? It is worth noting, as a first pass, that there is a dearth of strong arguments for the existence of incomparability. As I have argued elsewhere (Chang 1997), the seven arguments in the extant literature each suffer from compelling problems. Of course, it does not follow that there is no incomparability, only that establishing incomparability is not as straightforward as it might seem.

Even if incomparability holds between some items, there is good reason to doubt that it holds between Q and P. Suppose that P is a large number of people with middle-class lives. Q is an even larger number of people with slightly less good lives. (It does not matter how we characterize them so long as they conform to the pattern for generating consecutive items on the continuum, viz., a small diminution in quality of V and a large increase in quantity of V relative to its predecessor). Now consider P+ and Q-. P+ is identical to P in quality of lives but identical to Q in the quantity of lives. Q- is identical to Q in quality but identical to P in quantity. See Figure 1.3.

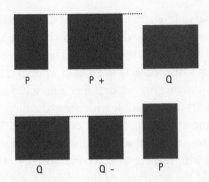

FIGURE 1.3 Against incomparability

P+ is comparable with both P and Q: it is better than each of them as it is identical with each in one respect and an enhancement of each in the other respect (modulo organic unities and the like, but in any case, they are comparable). Similarly, Q- is comparable with both P and Q—it is worse than both of them since it is identical with each in one respect and a diminution of each in one respect. Both P+ and Q- are each comparable with P and Q. So how could P and Q be incomparable with one another? To think that they could is to deny

> *The Small Uni-Dimensional Difference Principle ("Difference Principle"):* A small uni-dimensional (that is, single-factor) evaluative difference between two items cannot trigger incomparability between those items if they are comparable without that difference (Chang 2002a).

Since P+ differs from Q by a small evaluative difference in one contributory factor and P+ is comparable with P, then according to the principle, a small difference in one contributory factor—the difference between P+ and Q—cannot trigger incomparability where before there was comparability. The same goes for Q-. The argument against incomparability proceeds as follows:

1. P is comparable with P+ (modulo organic unities and the like, P+ is better since it is evaluatively identical to P in quality but better in quantity).
2. Q differs from P+ by a small evaluative difference in one contributory factor (Q has a slightly lower quality of well-being than P+).
3. Difference Principle: A small evaluative change in one contributory factor cannot trigger incomparability where before there was comparability.
4. Since P is comparable with P+ (by 1), and the difference between P+ and Q is a small evaluative change in one contributory factor (by 2), and a small evaluative change in one contributory factor cannot trigger incomparability where before there was comparability (by 3), P is comparable with Q.
5. Therefore, P and Q are not incomparable.

The Difference Principle has intuitive support. If the principle did not hold, the continuum would be subject to a very strange pattern of comparison. At the beginning of the continuum, each successor is better than its predecessor. As we progress through the continuum, we reach a zone in which items can no longer be compared with their predecessors. Moving beyond The Zone, the items might then return to the same pattern before, viz., each item is better than its predecessor. The incomparabilist would have us believe that a continuum could display this pattern of comparison even though each item differs from its predecessor in exactly the same way: by only a small diminution in quality and a large enhancement in quantity. A structural solution challenges Uniformity, but incomparability seems to be overkill.

There is a further, more theoretical, reason to think that P and Q are not incomparable with respect to V. It would be natural for there to be a correspondence between a comparative relation that holds between two items on a continuum and an appropriate practical response in a choice situation in which V-ness is all that matters, and one must choose between those items. Of course, comparative merit and choice need not be so connected, but it would be highly attractive if we could "read off" an appropriate practical response to two items from their comparative value and vice versa. I can think of no reason to doubt that there is such a correspondence.

If there were, then we might imagine a god faced with a choice between possible worlds along the continuum, where V-ness is what matters in determining which world to actualize. Since B is better than A, she should actualize B, but since C is better than B, she should actualize C, and so on, working her way through the continuum. Now suppose she reaches P, which is better than O, and Q, which, by hypothesis, is incomparable with P. Which world should she actualize? If two alternatives are incomparable, there can be no justified choice between them; we are stuck with existential plumping rather than rational choosing. But surely a god's choice of which world to create is guided by the value of the worlds she can create. In any case, we can substitute worlds with humdrum alternatives between which we mere mortals choose in the course of leading rational lives. Our choices along such a continuum are not plausibly beyond the scope of justification.

Toby Handfield and Wlodek Rabinowicz (2018) have recently posed a challenge to incomparabilist solutions for a subset of continua arguments, those that posit a lexical relation between the first and last items on the continuum (see also Rabinowicz, forthcoming). We will suggest below that some continua arguments do not satisfy this lexical condition, but at the very least, the Handfield/Rabinowicz argument holds against incomparabilist solutions for *some* continua arguments and is important for that reason.

Handfield and Rabinowicz argue that any incomparability between two adjacent items on the continuum must, if it is to stop the chain of betterness along the continuum, be "radical" and "persistent," that is, it must continue to hold no matter how much the quantity of the successor item is increased. If P is 1,000 people living excellent lives, Q is 2,000 people living slightly less excellent lives, and Q is incomparable with P, then it must remain so no matter how many additional lives we add to Q. This is because if by adding a large number of lives to Q we can make Q better than P, then we will not have broken the chain of betterness—Q so enhanced would be better than P and the continua argument would proceed as usual by following P with enhanced Q.

Is such persistent incomparability implausible? We have already argued that since adjacent items differ by a small diminution in quality and large enhancement in quality, it is implausible to think that they are incomparable. Assuming for the sake of argument that they are, Handfield and Rabinowicz's argument shows that they must be incomparable no matter how much we enhance the quantity of the successor item; the incomparability must be "radical." If P—1,000 people living excellent lives—is incomparable with Q—2,000 people living only slightly less excellent lives—then no matter how many people we add to Q, P and Q must remain incomparable. It is hard to believe, however, that a googol of people leading only slightly diminished excellent lives is incomparable with 1,000 people leading only slightly better lives. "Radical" incomparability is indeed a cost of an incomparabilist solution.[6]

Thus incomparability does not appear to be the right sort of phenomenon to hold in The Zone.

2.3. Indeterminacy

We left open the possibility that The Zone, whatever relations may hold within it, could be surrounded by indeterminacy. But what of the suggestion that indeterminacy holds *in* The Zone? The break in the continuum might consist of items that are indeterminately better (or worse, equal or comparable) than their predecessors with respect to V. This solution has been proposed by Christopher Knapp and Mozzifar Qizilbash (Knapp 2007; Qizilbash 2005; 2014), who draw on work by John Broome (Broome 1997). Perhaps The Zone is a zone of indeterminacy.

It is surprisingly difficult to arrive at an uncontroversial definition of indeterminacy (Greenough 2003; Taylor 2018). We do not have to settle the matter here, although as we will see, indeterminacy has one essential feature that will be important for our purposes.[7]

We can distinguish two sorts of indeterminacy, even though the problem with each of them will be the same. In semantic indeterminacy (due to vagueness), there is indeterminacy in the application of a predicate (or concept); it is indeterminate whether "bald" applies to Herbert, whose cranial hairs, we can imagine, are spare and non-uniformly distributed. Sometimes this idea is taken to be a matter of the sentence "Herbert is bald" being neither true nor false, or the idea that "bald" admits of certain "tolerances," or that there are multiple legitimate "sharpenings" of the predicate not all of which agree that Herbert is or is not bald, or that Herbert is a "borderline" case of being bald, and so on.

If it is semantically indeterminate whether Q is better than P with respect to V, there is vagueness somewhere in the predicate "better than with respect to V" such that the sentence, "Q is better than P" is semantically indeterminate. And if it is indeterminate whether Q is better than P (and perhaps indeterminate whether R is better than Q, and so on), then, as we go along the continuum, we cannot assert "Z is better than A" since the chain of betterness inferences has been interrupted, and thus the slide to the Repugnant Conclusion is halted.

In metaphysical indeterminacy, there is indeterminacy in the way the world is rather than in our words. A property or relation, such as identity or part-whole, may indeterminately hold of an item; it may be indeterminate whether, after undergoing fission or some other operation, the resultant person(s) are identical to me, and it may be indeterminate whether this clump of rock in Tanzania is a part of Mount Kilimanjaro. One way of cashing out the idea holds that there are multiple determinate worlds, some in which this patch of dirt is part of Mount Kilimanjaro and some in which it is not, but it is indeterminate which world is actual. (Or, equivalently for our purposes, there are multiple fully determinate actual worlds, some in which this patch of dirt is part of Mount Kilimanjaro and some in which it is not; Akiba 2004; Barnes 2010; Williams 2008; 2014).

If it is metaphysically indeterminate whether Q is better than P, then although in every world it is determinate whether Q is better than P—in some worlds it is and in some worlds it is not—it is indeterminate which of these worlds is actual. If it is indeterminate whether Q is better than P, Q is not better than P and the slide to the Repugnant Conclusion is halted.

But indeterminacy—whether due to vagueness in our words or indeterminacy in the facts—does not provide a good structural solution to continua arguments. To see why, we start with semantic vagueness. Due to vagueness in the word "bald," it is neither true nor false that Herbert is bald. Suppose that we must *resolve* the indeterminacy; we must sort Herbert into one of two camps—the "bald" or the "not-bald"—and this resolution must be based solely on how Herbert stands to the word "bald." Extrinsic factors, such as the fact that if you resolve the indeterminacy one way rather than another you will receive Herbert's gratitude, must be put aside. Basing our resolution only on facts about how Herbert stands to the semantic item, "bald," we can resolve the indeterminacy only *arbitrarily*. We might "precisify" the word "bald" to include Herbert or we might not. The precisification we choose must be arbitrarily chosen.[8] In short, we can resolve the matter of whether "bald" applies to Herbert by the flip of a coin. But it would be odd to think that continua arguments could be defused by making an arbitrary linguistic stipulation (Chang 2002a; Schoenfield 2015).

The same goes for metaphysical indeterminacy. Suppose it is metaphysically indeterminate whether this clump of rock is part of Mount Kilimanjaro. There are fully determinate worlds in which Kilimanjaro includes within its boundaries the clump of rock and fully determinate worlds in which it does not, but it is indeterminate which world is the actual world. Suppose now that we must draw a map that specifies whether the clump is a part of Mount Kilimanjaro. Again, we stipulate that no extrinsic factors are relevant to the case; we simply need to determine whether this clump of rock is part of Kilimanjaro solely on the basis of the facts about whether the mountain stands in the part-whole relation to the clump of rock. As far as these facts go, there is nothing to be said in favor of drawing the map one way as opposed to another since it is indeterminate whether the clump is a part of the mountain. The resolution of how to draw the map must be *arbitrary*; we are permitted arbitrarily to select a world in which the clump belongs or a world in which it does not belong. Resolution under indeterminacy is, as R.J. Williams puts it, a matter of "randomly and groundlessly" making a judgment (Williams 2016). In short, whether the clump is a part of Kilimanjaro can be settled with the flip of a coin. ·

Now consider Parfit's continuum. Q is a world like P except that there are many more people leading slightly less good lives. Is Q better than P with respect to V? The question is a *substantive* one on which we should bring to bear substantive arguments concerning, for instance, the question of whether a doubling in quantity of lives in P more than compensates for the slight loss in quality of life in P. Suppose P is a world of ten million people leading solidly middle-class lives. If we double the number of people and diminish the quality slightly, do we have a better world? This is a question to be argued over by substantive debate—the kind of debate that forms the bread and butter of first-order normative theorizing. It is not a question to be settled by "random and groundless" fiat. Indeed, if a god had to choose which world to create, it would be odd to think that the choice could be properly resolved by the flip of a coin.

Of course, *some* substantive matters are up for arbitrary resolution: if two items are equally good, then a resolution in favor of one can be determined by the flip of a coin. But P and Q are not equally good: for a quick argument that this is so, try making a small improvement in one of them and see if that necessarily makes the improved world better than the other—it need not (Chang 1997; 2002a).

The problem with indeterminacy as a structural solution to continua arguments is that the question of whether items in The Zone, or for that matter, throughout the continuum, are better than their predecessor is a substantive matter not appropriately resolved by arbitrary stipulation. If we arbitrarily stipulate that Q is not better than P, we are left with "resolutional remainder"—the substantive question at issue remains open rather than settled (Chang 2002a). Things are different when confronted with indeterminacy; it is always permissible to resolve the indeterminacy arbitrarily.

It might be countered that arbitrarily resolving that, say, Q is better than P leaves resolutional remainder only because it is *important* whether Q is better than P; any appearance that the substantive question has not been settled by an arbitrary fiat is due to uncertainty or anxiety over, for instance, whether one has judged the matter correctly (Williams 2016). Perhaps *any* "high stakes" case will leave resolutional remainder in the wake of arbitrary judgment (Constantinescu 2012; Williams 2016).

Resolutional remainder is not psychological anxiety over whether one has employed the right epistemic procedure in coming to a judgment nor is it concern about the fact that epistemic peers may arbitrarily resolve the indeterminacy in different ways. It is the normative fact—left in place after arbitrary fiat—that the substantive question of whether Q *is* better than P remains open. And there may be resolutional remainder even when the matter at hand is trivial and unimportant. Suppose you are to judge which of two poems should win the Woodbury Junior High School poetry prize. Perhaps one poem has great rhythm while the other has an arresting tone. If you flip a coin to decide between them, the substantive question of which is better is not thereby settled. Or you might have to adjudicate the relative aesthetic merits of two tea services, one delicate and muted while the other graphic and bold. If you arbitrarily stipulate that one is more beautiful, you do not thereby settle the question of which is in fact more beautiful—the question remains. You may, of course, arbitrarily stipulate that one is more beautiful than the other on extrinsic grounds—you do not want to waste time working out the substantive truth of the matter—and "settle" the question in a pragmatic sense. But the substantive issue on the merits remains.

The indeterminist might now shift his position, accepting that it is not only high stakes cases that involve resolutional remainder but insisting that *any normative* case will have resolutional remainder after arbitrary resolution (where equality does not hold) (Constantinescu 2012). Normative questions—apart from cases of equality—are not the sort of questions that can be resolved by arbitrary stipulation. Another way to put this point, borrowing from Gallie (1956), is to say that semantic questions about the application of normative predicates and metaphysical questions about the normative facts are *essentially contested* matters that are by their nature always open to substantive debate. Arbitrary stipulation will thus always leave resolutional remainder. But notice that if the indeterminist maintains that there can be indeterminacy about normative matters, such as whether Q is better than P, she has shifted ground by abandoning indeterminacy as it is usually understood. It is essential to indeterminacy, whether semantic or metaphysical, that there can be arbitrary—"random and groundless"—resolution among the permissible ways of resolving the indeterminacy. The permissibility of arbitrary resolution is essential to what indeterminacy *is*.

None of this is to say that normative matters are never vague. It is plausibly vague whether certain things are good—is a life filled with a great deal of suffering and a single moderate achievement a good one? Exactly where we "draw the line" of a good life may be an arbitrary matter. The same goes for many normative predicates; is a shiny beetle beautiful? And, although a trickier matter, there may also be indeterminacy in normative comparisons. It could be indeterminate which of two poems is better; the poems might be identical but for an extra comma that alters the rhythm very slightly—making it not better or worse but just very slightly different. It could be perfectly in order arbitrarily to resolve the indeterminacy by stipulating that one is better. The same goes for "high stakes" cases, although examples of such cases will be more controversial because of the "noise" created by their importance. Indeterminacy in comparison most plausibly holds only if the items are extremely similar in all contributory factors, and yet the difference is so marginal as to make it indeterminate what relation holds. Items on a continuum do not follow this paradigm; while appearing similar in quality, they are very different in quantity.

I suggest that indeterminacy, like incomparability, is not the right sort of phenomenon to defuse continua arguments.[9]

3. Parfit's Solution: Imprecise Lexicality

Some philosophers have suggested that the solution to Parfit's continua argument lies in lexicality: there is a point along the continuum at which an item is lexically superior to each of its successors. At that point, we reach a threshold quality of life such that any diminution in that quality, however small (but not diminishingly so), makes the outcome inferior, no matter the number, even a googol, of people living that quality of life. So, for example, you might think that a world with a sufficient number of people enjoying an upper-class life, say, with the music of Beethoven and the artwork of Picasso, is lexically superior to any number of people leading middle-class lives, say, with the music of Supertramp and some stellar limericks. Or that a world with a sufficient number of people living at subsistence is lexically superior to a world with any number of people living lives below subsistence. Any drop from an upper-class life to a middle-class life, or from subsistence to below subsistence, is so significant a qualitative difference that it marks a lexicality: no number of lives at the lower quality of life can be better (or equal) to a sufficient number of lives at the higher quality.

The trouble with lexicality is a specific version of the problem already encountered in thinking that there could be a single break point along the continuum: it is hard to believe that there is a point on the continuum which is better than all possible successors. Suppose that P is such a point. We can imagine a world, Q, which involves a small diminution in quality of life relative to P and an enormous increase in the number of people leading such lives. It would be hard to maintain that P is better than Q let alone that P is *lexically* better than Q—that is, that P would be better even if there were any, even a googol, number of people leading lives at the slightly lesser quality of life. For any putative point of lexical superiority, it seems that we can generate an item that involves a small diminution in quality of life and a large enhancement in quantity such that it would be hard to believe that the first is lexically superior to the second. It is this implausibility that has led most to abandon lexicality as a solution to continua arguments.[10]

Parfit offers an ingenious response on behalf of lexicalists (Parfit 2016). His defense of lexicality starts with a distinction between two kinds of comparability—precise and imprecise. When things can be compared precisely, there is a cardinal unit—analogous to inches or degrees Celsius—by which you can measure the goodness of each item. In other words, precisely comparable items are commensurable—there is a cardinal scale by which the values of the two items can be measured. When things can only be compared imprecisely, by contrast, there is no "precise" cardinal unit by which their value can be measured. Perhaps there is an "imprecise" cardinal unit, or, what might amount to the same thing, an imprecise cardinal scale with "units" perhaps given by interval ranges or something like probability distributions, which measures the value of items. Imprecisely comparable items are incommensurable but comparable. Parfit did not put things quite this way. He talked instead of a linear scale of value, like a number line, and suggested that imprecisely comparable items cannot be put on such a scale.[11] It is not entirely clear whether Parfit meant to include mere ordinality within imprecise comparability—perhaps merely ordinal rankings are the most imprecise rankings of all—but for present purposes we can set mere ordinality aside since it is not relevant to Parfit's solution. In sum, we can think of Parfit as offering *six* ways two things could be (more-than-merely-ordinally) comparable: precisely better, precisely worse, precisely equal, imprecisely better, imprecisely worse, and imprecisely equal. Whether we have precise comparability or imprecise (sometimes he called it "rough" [Parfit 1984, 461]) comparability depends entirely on whether there is a cardinal ratio or interval scale by which the value of the two items can be measured.

Parfit thought that lexicality is the right sort of solution to the continua argument he made famous, but not lexicality as it is ordinarily understood. Assuming precision in comparisons, if P is lexically superior to Q, there is some number representing the value of P (or more accurately, some function unique up to affine transformations), say 100, such that a diminution in the quality of life in Q, however small, cannot be compensated for by an increase in the quantity of such lives in Q, no matter how large. But how could this be, Parfit thought, if, as is plausible, the addition of lives worth living in Q each adds value to Q? With enough such lives, Q's value should surpass 100. The same holds for any putative point of lexicality. Parfit thought that the presumed precision is the problem. Once we give up the idea that the value of P could be represented by some number on a cardinal scale, we can save lexicality.[12]

We should, Parfit argues, understand comparisons along the continuum as *imprecise* rather than precise. As we move along the continuum, each item is imprecisely better than its predecessor. Eventually we reach a point, P, which, while imprecisely better than its predecessor, O, is also *imprecisely lexically better* than every item beyond The Zone—U, V . . . Z. An item x is imprecisely lexically better than an item y just in case x is imprecisely better than y and no increase in the quantity of y, even a googol, could change this fact. But the transition from P, the lexically superior item, to U, a lexically inferior item, is not implausibly sharp. In between, there are a number of items comprising The Zone in which each item is *imprecisely equally as good* as its predecessor. Presumably two items are imprecisely equally good when they are equally good, but their respective values cannot be measured by any cardinal scale of value.[13] Thus, there is a gradual transition from P, the lexical threshold, to U, the first item beyond The Zone, through a series of items that are imprecisely equally as good as their immediate predecessor. And, Parfit adds, there can be indeterminacy around The Zone. Since the chain of betterness is broken, the slide to the Repugnant Conclusion is halted.[14] Parfit's solution is depicted in Figure 1.4.

Though there is much to say about Parfit's solution, here I simply raise one general worry about its scope.[15]

If imprecise lexicality and imprecise equality exist and are not mere chimeras, *some* continua arguments could surely be constructed that surreptitiously exploit this fact, and thus pointing out an imprecise lexical threshold with a buffer zone of imprecisely equally good items could defuse such arguments. But lexicality, whether

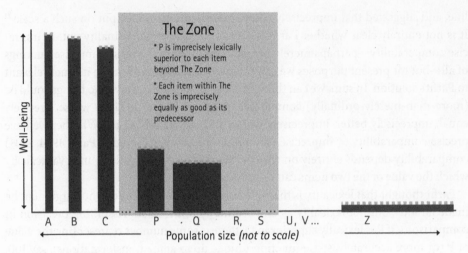

The Zone

* P is imprecisely lexically superior to each item beyond The Zone

* Each item within The Zone is imprecisely equally as good as its predecessor

Well-being

A   B   C   ...   P   .   Q   R,   S   U, V...   Z

Population size *(not to scale)*

FIGURE 1.4 Parfit's imprecise lexicality solution

precise or imprecise, as a solution to continua arguments has limited scope. This is because lexicality is a very strong condition, and continua arguments can be generated without it.

Parfit's argument begins with a world, A, with a large number of people living excellent lives and ends up with a world, Z, with a googol people leading lives barely worth living. What gives the appearance that lexicality is relevant to avoiding the Repugnant Conclusion is that it is plausible to think that A is lexically superior to Z—it does not matter how many people there are with lives barely worth living, a world with a sufficient number of exquisite lives will always be better. The same goes for the Rachels/Temkin continua arguments involving pain—a sufficient amount of torture is plausibly lexically inferior to any number of years of mosquito bites—and Quinn's self-torturer argument—mild pain for any length of time is plausibly lexically superior to some period of excruciating pain. Apparent lexicality between the first and last items on the continuum has been so common a feature of continua arguments that some authors treat it as a fixed feature of such arguments (Handfield and Rabinowiciz 2018).

Might it be possible to generate continua arguments without apparent lexicality? One strategy might be to take standard continua and simply remove all items that appear to stand in lexical relations. In some cases, there would be nothing left, if, for instance, each item on the continuum represents one seemingly lexical superior item relative to its successor. In most cases, however, a continuum could remain that leads to a false, if perhaps not repugnant, conclusion. Continua leading to false conclusions need avoiding, too. Appeals to lexicality thus will not help. Once we recognize that we need some other solution for such continua arguments, we might also see that this alternative solution holds even in continua where there is apparent lexicality. Or so I will suggest in the final section.

It is difficult to generate continua that *clearly* lead to false conclusions while at the same time not relying on lexicality because all such continua trade on controversial substantive claims. But we can offer an example and an abstract argument for thinking that such continua exist.

Suppose world A_1 contains 1,000 people leading upper-class lives. Its successor, A_2, involves a slight diminution in quality of life but also one extra life. If the diminution is sufficiently small, it can be traded off against the value of a whole extra life. Everyone in A_2 leads nearly as good lives as they do in A_1, and there is a whole extra person enjoying that excellent level of well-being. Thus, we suppose, A_2 is better than A_1. (If you don't agree, jigger the numbers until you do.[16]) A_3 then involves a slight diminution in the quality of life in A_2 and the addition of another life such that A_3 is better than A_2. The same for A_4 until we arrive at A_{50}, which involves, suppose, 1,050 people leading lower-class lives. In fifty small steps we move from an upper-class to a lower-class quality of life, but with each successive world containing an extra life. Since the change in quality of lives is so slight, each successor is better than its predecessor. By the transitivity of "better than with respect to V," 1050 people leading lower-class lives is better than 1,000 people leading upper-class lives. While perhaps not exactly repugnant, the conclusion seems false. Could fifty extra people leading lower-class lives make A_{50} better than a world where nearly everyone is leading significantly better upper-class lives? Suppose our covering consideration, V, is beneficence. It seems more beneficent for a god to create world A_1 with 1,000 people leading excellent upper-class lives than to create world A_{50}, a world with an extra fifty people but everyone leading much worse lower-class lives. Nonetheless, it does not seem correct to think that A_1 is lexically superior to A_{50}; a sufficiently large, perhaps a googol, number of people leading lower-class lives is clearly better than a mere 1,000 people leading upper-class lives. A god would be a snob if she thought otherwise. If these claims are correct, we have a continua argument leading to a false conclusion but no lexicality between any of the items along the continuum.

There is a general, abstract argument for thinking that there are many such continua, despite the fact that any given continuum will be open to challenge and controversy. Suppose a covering consideration, V, admits of hierarchical categories of quality of V-ness. Take, for instance, the very general categories of quality: excellent, very good, good, mediocre, and poor—most naturally understood as occupying some region on some (perhaps imprecise) cardinal scale. Some things might be of an excellent quality with respect to V while others might be a poor quality with respect to V. Now perhaps some sufficient amount of the excellent will be lexically superior to some amount of the poor; that is, a sufficient amount of the excellent will always be better than any, even a googol, amount of the poor (though the plausibility of this will depend on the "V" at stake). But it is less plausible to think that a sufficient amount of the excellent will always be superior to any amount of the very good or the mediocre. Lexicality does not plausibly hold between the excellent, on the one hand, and the very good or even the mediocre, on the other.

When a continuum is generated by having successive items move from one qualitative category to a hierarchically near one, lexicality is less plausible. At the same time, such a continuum could plausibly lead to a false conclusion; for example, some relatively small quantity of mediocrity is better than some sufficiently large quantity of excellence. These considerations suggest that, insofar as there are many such Vs with hierarchical qualitative categories, there could be many continua arguments that do not involve apparent lexicality.

If this is right, then lexical solutions, whether precise or imprecise, will not cover all possible continua arguments. For Parfit's solution to work across all continua arguments, there must *always* be some qualitative feature of some items on a continuum that, in sufficient quantity, lexically beats any item of a lower quality. But as we've seen, this is a high standard to demand of all continua in continuum arguments. Even in Parfit's own, it seems doubtful that lexicality—whether precise or imprecise—is the right solution (Chang 2016c).

The point here is not that Parfit's appeal to imprecise lexicality is mistaken. It is rather that it puts too stringent a condition on a solution to continua arguments, a condition that plausibly fails to hold in at least some continua that lead to false, if not repugnant, conclusions. As such, it will not provide an answer to the general problem raised by continua arguments.

4. CONCLUSION

A structural solution to continua arguments posits a break in the chain of betterness relations that putatively holds throughout the continuum: somewhere along the continuum betterness between an item and its predecessor no longer holds. We have examined and raised significant difficulties for four such solutions: incommensurability, indeterminacy, incomparability, and imprecise lexicality. Some of these solutions cannot help us avoid continua arguments (incommensurability); others provide formal solutions but suffer from serious substantive flaws (indeterminacy and incomparability); and some may successfully defuse only a small class of continua arguments (imprecise lexicality).

This conclusion is not intended to be a skeptical one. There is, I believe, a structural solution to continua arguments, but it requires shedding some unreflective assumptions we make about the nature and structure of value. And that is a story for another day.[17]

ACKNOWLEDGMENTS

Thanks to Tim Campbell for helpful comments and to Laura Callahan, Carolina Flores, and Stacy Topouzova for invaluable research assistance.

NOTES

1. Strictly speaking, Parfit's argument is not a "continuum" argument, since it does not involve mathematical continua, but we can follow Parfit in his looser use of "continua" to cover a family of different kinds of arguments. Since some of the arguments I consider below apply also to genuine continua arguments, and out of deference to Parfit's stature as the modern godfather of such arguments, I adopt Parfit's nomenclature. Although I believe that the arguments of this paper apply to many non-normative continua arguments, my focus is primarily on normative continua arguments and on Parfit's Repugnant Conclusion puzzle in particular.

2. A fifth possible "i" explanation is *ignorance*; perhaps there is some point along the continuum at which two adjacent items are not R-related, but we just do not know where. I am sympathetic to this solution as far as it goes, but the interest lies in the question of what is the phenomenon about which we are unaware. In this chapter I argue that it is not any of four "i" explanations. I have also argued elsewhere against the idea that ignorance of whether one item is better, worse, or equal to another can do work of this sort (Chang 2002a).

3. There may be *non*structural "solutions" to continua arguments. Two main ones have been proposed.

   First, Rachels (2001) and Temkin (2012) have suggested that "better than, simpliciter" or (what is treated synonymously) "all-things-considered-better-than" are nontransitive relations. I believe that there are two issues that can be raised about their arguments:

   i) There is no genuine *substantive* relation, "better than, simpliciter" or "all-things-considered-better-than," whose transitivity we should expect. Such relations are, I have proposed instead, "placeholder relations"—not themselves substantive relations but formal relations that hold the place of *substantive* relations, such as "better than with respect to justice" or "better than with respect to honoring/maximizing social well-being" (Chang 1997; 2004a; 2004b). As placeholders for substantive relations, they cannot properly be thought to be in themselves transitive or nontransitive. See also Kamm (1996, fn 34, pp. 350ff) and Thompson (2001).

   ii) Even if, as both Rachels and Temkin suggest, there *is* some stipulated, substantive as opposed to placeholder, nontransitive "better than simpliciter" relation, we require an argument for thinking that this relation does work that *cannot* be done by more familiar substantive relations such as "better than with respect to some particular V." While we may in everyday practical reasoning appeal to "all-things-considered betterness" as a conceptual rubric or placeholder for the particular substantive betterness judgments we make with respect to particular V across different choice situations, it seems that the work that they think this putative relation does can also be done by the placeholder relation in conjunction with the specific relations relativized to particular V. If we instead understand Rachels' and Temkins' arguments as arguments about betterness with respect to some particular V, they fall within the target group of the arguments of this chapter.

   Second, Gustaf Arrhenius (2011) has argued for an impossibility result—there is no way of resolving problems raised by continua arguments without giving up certain plausible assumptions. The "solution," then, is that the paradox is genuine, admitting of no solution. If I have understood Arrhenius correctly, one his assumptions is what I call *Trichotomy*, the view that it two items are comparable with respect to some V, one must better than it, worse, or the two must be equally good. I believe that we should give up this assumption and that if we do, an attractive solution to continua arguments becomes available.

4. Although I assume a suitable V for Parfit's argument, if you find this assumption problematic, you can throughout substitute a paradigmatic continuum involving painful experiences with the covering consideration being "painfulness."

5. Compare Boonin-Vail (1996) who argues that the continuum argument holds only for values and not duties. Note that theories that eschew normative comparative assessment *altogether* would be immune from continua arguments, but such theories are patently implausible. So long as a theory allows notions such as trumping, being more significant than, being less important than, and so on, it may be open in principle to continua arguments. I have argued that comparisons transcend the usual divide between axiology and deontology and that the question of value and the question of what one ought to do can be treated under the same rubric of comparisons with respect to an appropriate— deontological or axiological—covering consideration (Chang 2016b).

6. This conclusion must be understood carefully. As I argue in Chang (forthcoming), the Handfield/Rabinowicz argument against incomparability hits its mark only on the assumption of "Trichotomy," the view that if two items are comparable with respect to some V, one must be better than the other, worse than it, or the two must be equally good with respect to V. If instead we accept "Tetrachotomy," which allows for a fourth possible *sui generis* relation to hold between two items, the failure of the usual trichotomy of relations, while persistent in The Zone in the way Handfield and Rabinowicz point out, is not implausibly so.

7. Kit Fine has proposed a novel account of indeterminacy as a global and not local phenomenon (Fine 2017). His account does not have the essential feature upon which I rely in criticizing indeterminacy as a solution to continua arguments, but it avoids my criticism at what I believe to be a significant cost. Fine must deny that the idea of resolving the question of how two consecutive items relate in The Zone even *makes sense*. This is because he rejects classical logic and thinks that indeterminacy holds only globally—for a region of a continuum—and not between any two given items on it. Like those who have offered continua arguments and solutions to them, I assume classical logic and that talk of indeterminacy between two adjacent items makes sense.

8. Indeterminists who go in for degrees of truth might suggest that it could be "more true" that Herbert is bald than that he is not bald if, say, there are more sharpenings that favor his being bald. But appealing to a ratio of possible sharpenings to resolve the indeterminacy is to appeal to something extrinsic to the facts about how Herbert stands to the word "bald," such as "majority rule."

9. Against indeterminacy, there is also the Handfield and Rabinowicz argument that any indeterminacy must be "radical," that is, persist no matter how much the quantity of an item is increased. I am less certain about the persistence of indeterminacy being a problem, and indeed, Rabinowicz's suggested solution to the radicality of the failure of "better than," "worse than," and "equally good" to hold between two adjacent items, seems to me best suited to the case of indeterminate rather than determinate failure. See Rabinowicz, forthcoming. I believe that the nature of indeterminacy, and in particular, the arbitrary resolution that is permissible in the face of indeterminacy, presents a deeper problem for indeterminists in presenting a plausible solution to continua arguments, but any readers who disagree can help themselves to the Handfield/Rabinowicz argument instead.

10. Note that if the arguments in the previous section are correct, an appeal to indeterminacy will not help the lexicalist with this difficulty.

11. Here is what Parfit writes: "Many people assume that, when there are truths about the relative goodness of different things, these truths must be precise, though we may not know what these truths are. There is one way of thinking which can make this seem the only possible view. If things of some kind can be better or worse than others, and by more or less, it may seem that the goodness of these things corresponds to their positions on some line or scale of value. On this *Linear Model*, truths about goodness must be precise because positions on a line are precise . . . But when two things are qualitatively very different, that could not be true. So when we think about the goodness of such things, we should reject this Linear Model. Nor could the goodness of such things correspond to different real numbers, since such numbers are also precise. Nor could some of these things be better than others by some imprecise amount or to some imprecise degree, since the concepts of an amount or a degree also imply precision. We should think only about *differences* between the value of these things, since the concept of a difference does not imply precision" (Parfit 2016, 114). It is perhaps worth noting that over years of conversation with Parfit, it became clear to me that Parfit's key point in introducing imprecise or rough comparability was that the value of an individual item could not be located on a linear scale of value. This seems to me a very important point. The last two sentences of Parfit's explanation may seem jarring to the reader as Parfit moves from a claim about measuring the goodness of individual items to a claim about *differences* between items. When Parfit was preparing for his Schock Prize lecture, he asked me whether he thought he should add in this paper reference to *differences* between items since he knew that I understood the related idea of "parity" in terms of evaluative differences. I urged him to do so in order to 1) make clear that his concern was not with mere ordinality, 2) move imprecise comparability away from the difficult idea of "imprecise" cardinal units, and 3) bring the idea of imprecise equality closer to parity. Still, for Parfit, the foundational idea concerns how to represent the value of individual items, and the upshots for evaluative differences come down the road. I have suggested that this explanatory priority should be reversed: we should understand comparisons between incommensurables in terms of features of the *differences* between items first, and what follows about how to represent the value of individual items being compared is of less importance (Chang 1997; 2002b; 2016a). Other differences between parity and imprecise equality are explored in Chang (2016c), the main one being that Parfit is still thinking "trichotomously," that is, that "better than," "worse than" and "equally good" form the foundation of comparisons, while I favor "tetrachotomy."

12. It is unclear why Parfit did not take seriously the possibility that each additional life in Q has diminishing marginal value. In that case, while each additional life in Q adds value, the overall V-ness of Q might only asymptotically approach the value of P. Insofar as this possibility is plausible, it may remove some of the motivation for Parfit's introduction of imprecision to save lexicality. Another, perhaps less plausible, possibility is that the increase in value of each additional life beyond a certain point is infinitesimal.

13. Or we might say that their values can be measured by every cardinal scale; they have the same value on each such cardinal scale.

14. An alternative interpretation of Parfit's solution holds not that one item, P, is lexically superior but that every item in The Zone is lexically superior to every item beyond The Zone. I am unclear as to which interpretation of Parfit is correct. In Chang (2016c), I consider this alternative interpretation—that P *and* all items in The Zone are lexically superior to every item beyond The Zone. I argued that such a view would be open to the challenge that it is quite plausible that there could be an item further along the continuum that was *not*

lexically inferior to *every* item in The Zone. If, for example, The Zone is characterized by middle-class qualities of life, it seems quite plausible that there could be some sufficiently large number of lower-class quality lives beyond The Zone that is better than some package of quantity and quality of a middle-class life. And this intuition could be generalized, *mutatis mutandis*, for any quality of life above subsistence: for any quality of life within some range of quantity likely to appear in The Zone, there could be some larger number of people at some close neighboring quality of life that might be better. Although Parfit, who kindly read the penultimate draft of the paper, did not object to this characterization of his view, I now think Parfit need not be committed to thinking that every item in The Zone is a lexical threshold and so could avoid the objection I posed in (Chang 2016c). Thus, in the present chapter, I consider the interpretation of Parfit's view according to which there is a single item, P, that is imprecisely lexically superior to all items beyond The Zone, where The Zone of imprecise equality serves as a buffer between an item P and the items U, V, . . . Z to which it is supposedly lexically superior. The scope issue I raise below applies to both interpretations of Parfit's solution.

15. A more detailed examination of Parfit's solution is in Chang (forthcoming). A consideration of how imprecise equality differs from what I call "parity" can be found in Chang (2016c).

16. Jiggering the numbers in any way will not necessarily lead to a plausible continua argument, however. The claim is existential; there are *some* continua arguments that don't involve even apparent lexicality between the first and last items of the continua.

17. See Chang (forthcoming) for an argument and defense of the idea that the structural break along a continuum is explained by "parity," a basic way two items can be compared even though neither is at least as good as the other.

REFERENCES

Akiba, Ken. 2004. "Vagueness in the World." *Nous* 38, no. 3: 407–429.

Arrhenius, Gustaf. 2011. "The Impossibility of a Satisfactory Population Ethics." *World Scientific Review* 20, no. 54: 1–26.

Barnes, Elizabeth. 2010. "Ontic Vagueness: A Guide for the Perplexed." *Nous* 44, no. 4: 601–627.

Boonin-Vail, David. 1996. "Don't Stop Thinking About Tomorrow: Two Paradoxes About Duties to Future Generations." *Philosophy and Public Affairs* 25, no. 4: 267–307.

Broome, John. 1997. "Is Incommensurability Vagueness?" In *Incommensurability, Incomparability, and Practical Reason*, edited by Ruth Chang. Cambridge, MA: Harvard University Press, pp. 67–89.

Chang, Ruth. 1997. "Introduction." In *Incommensurability, Incomparability, and Practical Reason*. Cambridge, MA: Harvard University Press, pp. 1–34.

Chang, Ruth. 2002a. "The Possibility of Parity." *Ethics* 112: 659–688.

Chang Ruth. 2002b. *Making Comparisons Count*. New York: Routledge.

Chang, Ruth. 2004a. "All Things Considered." *Philosophical Perspectives* 18 (2004a):1–22.

Chang, Ruth. 2004b. "Putting Together Morality and Well-Being." In *Practical Conflicts*, edited by Monika Betzler and Peter Baumann. Cambridge: Cambridge University Press, pp. 118–158.

Chang, Ruth. 2016a. "Parity: An Intuitive Case." *Ratio* 29, no. 4: 395–411.

Chang, Ruth. 2016b. "Comparativism: The Grounds of Rational Choice." In *Weighing* Values, edited by Errol Lord and Barry Maguire. New York: Oxford University Press, pp. 213–240.

Chang, Ruth. 2016c. "Parity, Imprecise Comparability, and the Repugnant Conclusion." *Theoria* 82: 183–215.

Chang, Ruth. Forthcoming. "How to Avoid the Repugnant Conclusion." In *Ethics and Existence: The Legacy of Derek Parfit*, Oxford: Oxford University Press, edited by Jefferson McMahan, Tim Campbell, James Goodrich, and Ketan Ramakrishnan, Oxford: Oxford University Press.

Constantinescu, Cristian. 2012. "Value Incomparability and Indeterminacy." *Ethical Theory and Moral Practice* 15, no. 1: 57–70.

Fine, Kit. 2017. "The Possibility of Vagueness." *Synthese* 194, no. 10: 3699–3725.

Gallie, W. B. 1956. "Essentially Contested Concepts." *Proceedings of the Aristotelian Society* 56: 167–98.

Greenough, Patrick. 2003. "Vagueness: A Minimal Theory." *Mind* 112, no. 446: 235–281.

Handfield, Toby. 2014. "Rational Choice and the Transitivity of Betterness." *Philosophy and Phenomenological Research* 89: 584–604.

Handfield, Toby and Wlodek Rabinowicz. 2018. "Incommensurability and Vagueness In Spectrum Arguments: Options for Saving Transitivity of Betterness." *Philosophical Studies* 175: 2375–2387.

Harrison, Jason. 1953. "Utilitarianism, Universalisation, and Our Duty to be Just." *Proceedings of the Aristotelian Society* 53: 105–134.

Kamm, Frances. 1996. *Morality, Mortality*, vol. 2. Oxford: Oxford University Press.

Knapp, Christopher. 2007. "Trading Quality for Quantity." *Journal of Philosophical Research* 32: 211–234.

Parfit, Derek. 1984. *Reasons and Persons*. Oxford: Oxford University Press.

Parfit, Derek. 2016. "Can We Avoid the Repugnant Conclusion?." *Theoria* 82, no. 2: 110–127.

Qizilbash, Mozzafar. 2005. "Transitivity and Vagueness." *Economics and Philosophy* 21: 109–131.

Qizilbash, Mozzafar. 2014. "'Incommensurability' and Vagueness: Is the Vagueness View Defensible?" *Ethical Theory and Moral Practice* 17, no. 1: 41–54.

Quinn, Warren. 1990. "The Puzzle of the Self-Torturer." *Philosophical Studies* 59, no. 1: 79–90.

Rabinowicz, Wlodek. Forthcoming. "Can Parfit's Appeal to Incommensurabilities in Value Block the Continuum Argument for the Repugnant Conclusion?". In *Ethics and Existence: The Legacy of Derek Parfit*, Oxford: Oxford University Press, edited by Jefferson McMahan, Tim Campbell, James Goodrich, and Ketan Ramakrishnan, Oxford: Oxford University Press.

Rachels, Stuart. 1998. "Hedonic Value." PPE Dissertation, Oxford University.

Rachels, Stuart. 2001. "A Set of Solutions to Parfit's Problems." *Nous* 35, no. 2: 214–238.

Schoenfield, Miriam. 2015. "Moral Vagueness is Ontic Vagueness." *Ethics* 126, no. 2: 257–282.

Taylor, David. 2018. "A Minimal Characterization of Indeterminacy." *Philosophers Imprint* 18 no. 5: 1–25.

Temkin, Larry. 2012. *Rethinking the Good*. Oxford: Oxford University Press.

Thompson, Judith Jarvis. 2001. *Goodness and Advice*. Princeton, NJ: Princeton University Press.

Van der Burg, Wibren. 1991. "The Slippery Slope Argument." *Ethics* 102, no. 1: 42–65.

Williams, J. Robert. 2016. "Indeterminacy, Angst and Conflicting Values." *Ratio* 29: 412–433.

Williams, J. Robert. 2014. "Decision Making Under Indeterminacy." *Philosopher's Imprint* 14: 1–34.

Williams, J. Robert. 2008. "Ontic Vagueness and Metaphysical Indeterminacy." *Philosophy Compass* 3, no. 4: 763–788.

CHAPTER 2

PRIORITARIANISM AND POPULATION ETHICS

NILS HOLTUG

1. INTRODUCTION

PRIORITARIANISM is a principle of distributive justice, according to which we should give priority to the worse off. The worse off an individual is, the greater the value of a further benefit to her, morally speaking. I shall define prioritarianism with greater precision in the next section, but for now this brief characterization will suffice. While a great deal has been written about prioritarianism since Derek Parfit first introduced the concept in his 1991 Lindley Lecture, "Equality or Priority?",[1] there are but a few discussions of the implications of this principle in population ethics (which include Adler 2009; Arrhenius 2000; Brown 2007; Holtug 1999 and 2010: Ch. 9; Nebel 2017). Indeed, while Parfit not only introduced the concept of prioritarianism but also in many ways pioneered the contemporary debate about population ethics, he himself did not write much about the implications of the former for the latter.

One of the main virtues of prioritarianism, according to many of its proponents, is that it introduces distribution-sensitivity without being vulnerable to the so-called levelling down objection. Since prioritarianism gives priority to the worse off, it is sensitive to how a given sum of benefits is distributed. In this respect, it is like egalitarianism but unlike, for example, utilitarianism. However, unlike egalitarianism, it does not imply that levelling down, that is, reducing the level of some and increasing the level of none, can make an outcome in any respect better. I elaborate on these points in the next section, when I have given a more formal definition of prioritarianism.

Nevertheless, like other distributive principles, prioritarianism seems to have implausible implications in the sphere of population ethics. Thus, prioritarianism seems to imply the so-called Repugnant Conclusion and several other rather counterintuitive conclusions.

In the following, I first provide a more formal account of prioritarianism. Then I turn to the question of whether prioritarianism applies to possible individuals. I argue that denying that it does leads to certain difficulties and that, in any case, we should explore its implications before we make a final judgment. In the following section, I outline a number of such implications and point out how some of them may seem rather troubling. I then go on to consider whether there are modal restrictions on the categories of individuals that morally matter that can be imposed on prioritarianism such as to avoid these implications. Finally, I consider whether the prioritarian function can be modified in ways that would enable us to avoid these troubling conclusions.

2. PRIORITARIANISM

In the following, I restrict myself to axiological versions of prioritarianism and, more precisely, to versions that order outcomes with respect to their moral value. Furthermore, I assume that welfare is the currency of prioritarian justice, that is, is what an individual needs to be worse off in terms of in order to be entitled to priority. And finally, I assume a whole lives account of prioritarianism, according to which it is an individual's lifetime welfare that determines the value of a further unit of welfare to her. That is, what determines the moral value of a further benefit accruing to me now is not how well off I now am, or how well off I am in the present period of my life, but how well off I am in my life as a whole (or, rather, would be if this further benefit did not now accrue to me). Neither of these assumptions is uncontroversial, but they allow me to simplify my discussion while teasing out the implications of the core elements of the prioritarian doctrine in the rest of the chapter.

Consider, then:

> *Axiological Prioritarianism*: An outcome is non-instrumentally better, the larger the sum of weighted individual benefits it contains, where benefits are weighted such that they gain a greater value, the worse off the individual is to whom they accrue.

Here, benefits refer to units of welfare. More formally, Axiological Prioritarianism (henceforth: prioritarianism) can be represented as follows:

$$G = f(w_1) + f(w_2) + \ldots + f(w_n),$$

where w_1 is the welfare level of the first individual, w_2 the level of the second individual, and so on, and f is an increasing and strictly concave function of individual welfare. For clarity, I shall refer to G as the "prioritarian function," and to f as the "prioritarian weighting function." Since f is increasing and strictly concave, it gradually assigns less weight to increases in welfare, the better off the recipient is, as illustrated in Figure 2.1:

FIGURE 2.1 The prioritarian weighting function

Like utilitarianism, then, prioritarianism states that moral outcome value is an additive function of individual welfare but differs in that it weights benefits according to how badly off the beneficiary is, whereas utilitarianism applies the same weight to each unit of welfare that accrues to an individual. To illustrate, consider the following prioritarian function, where f is fixed as square root:

$$G^* = \sqrt{w_1} + \sqrt{w_2} + \ldots + \sqrt{w_n}$$

According to this function, the value of the first unit of welfare that accrues to an individual is $\sqrt{1}=1$, the value of the first two units is $\sqrt{2}=1,41$, the value of the first three units $\sqrt{3}=1,73$, and so on. As transpires, each additional unit contributes less to the overall value than the previous one. Another way of putting this is that welfare has diminishing marginal moral value (which is not to be confused with the diminishing marginal utility of resources such as money). Adding a further unit of welfare to an individual who is at a level of, say, 10, will contribute more to the overall value of an outcome than giving this unit to an individual who is at a level of 11.

It will be helpful to further characterize prioritarianism in terms of a number of structural features. Prioritarianism satisfies the Pareto Principle, according to which two outcomes are equally good if they are equally good for everyone, and one is better than another if it is better for some and at least as good for everyone. Thus, an extra benefit to an individual, holding the welfare of others constant, always increases the value of an outcome (although the size of the increase depends on this individual's welfare level). I can now explain more formally why prioritarianism is not vulnerable to the levelling down objection. Compare the following two outcomes, (2, 1) and (1, 1), where the numbers refer to individual welfare levels. The Pareto Principle implies that (2, 1) is better than (1, 1). Thus, whereas (axiological) egalitarianism implies that (1, 1) is in at least one respect better, since it is more (in fact, perfectly) equal, prioritarianism has no such implication.

Another structural feature of prioritarianism is that is satisfies strong separability (see also Teruji Thomas' chapter on separability in the present volume). An ordering is strongly separable if and only if the ordering of the welfare level of any subset of individuals is independent of the levels of others (Broome 1991, 69). Since it satisfies strong separability, prioritarianism does not allow the ordering to be impacted by unaffected individuals. To illustrate, compare outcomes A–D:

$$A = (2, 2, 2, 2, 2, 2, 2) \quad B = (4, 1, 2, 2, 2, 2, 2)$$
$$C = (2, 2, 1, 1, 1, 1, 1) \quad D = (4, 1, 1, 1, 1, 1, 1)$$

Strong separability implies that A is better than B if and only if C is better than D. This is because only the two first individuals are affected by the move from, respectively, A to B and C to D, and are identically situated in, respectively, A and C, and B and D. Thus, with respect to these two individuals, the move from A to B is identical to the move from C to D, and on the assumption that unaffected individuals do not impact the ordering, A is better than B if and only if C is better than D. It can easily be seen from the prioritarian function, G, that unaffected individuals do not impact the ordering, because the contribution of each individual to outcome value is independent of the contributions of others.

Like prioritarianism, utilitarianism also satisfies both the Pareto Principle and strong separability. However, these two principles differ in that only prioritarianism satisfies the Pigou-Dalton Principle of Transfer. According to the Pigou-Dalton Principle, shifting a fixed sum of welfare from a better off individual to a worse off individual, holding other individuals' levels constant, increases the value of an outcome, assuming that the former remains better off after the transfer than the latter was before. Thus, (4, 2) is better than (5, 1). Utilitarianism, on the other hand, implies that these two outcomes are equally good.

Like prioritarianism, egalitarianism also satisfies the Pigou-Dalton Principle, but unlike the former, it satisfies neither the Pareto Principle nor strong separability (although, of course, the concern for equality may be combined with a concern for efficiency, but the concern for equality does not in itself satisfy the Pareto Principle). It is also worth pointing out a further similarity between prioritarianism and egalitarianism. They both imply that the best possible distribution of a fixed sum of welfare is a perfectly equal distribution. Nevertheless, they provide different reasons for finding these equal distributions better. Compare (9, 1) and (5, 5). Egalitarianism implies that (5, 5) is better because it is more equal. Prioritarianism, on the other hand, does not assign non-instrumental value to equality. Rather, prioritarians find (5, 5) better because they give priority to the worse off, and so consider an increase from 1 to 5 more important that a decrease from 9 to 5.

Finally, prioritarianism (like egalitarianism and utilitarianism) satisfies an important condition of impartiality, namely anonymity, according to which the value of an outcome is not affected by the permutation of welfare over individuals. So, for example, (2, 1) is equal in value to (1, 2). Prioritarianism secures anonymity by assigning the same weight function, f, to each individual's welfare.

While the prioritarian weight function secures impartiality by being identical across individuals, there is nevertheless ample room for disagreement between prioritarians about the precise weights to be applied. Indeed, prioritarianism can be seen as a family of distributive principles that differ with respect to the weights attached to benefits, and so with respect to the degree of priority assigned to the worse off. Thus, depending on the prioritarian weight function, f, prioritarianism can get infinitesimally close to utilitarianism, at one end of the spectrum, and to leximin at the other. (Leximin is the principle that an outcome, x, is better than another outcome, y, if and only if x is better for the worst-off individual or, in case of equal benefits of the worst-off individuals in x and y, x is better for the second worst-off individual, and so on.) If almost no priority is given to benefits to the worse off (that is, if almost the same weights apply to benefits irrespective of the level at which they fall), prioritarianism is close to utilitarianism, whereas if extreme priority is assigned, prioritarianism is close to leximin. However, given that f is increasing, continuous, and strictly concave, as represented in Figure 2.1, there are no versions of prioritarianism that coincide with either of these two alternative principles.

3. Prioritarianism and Possible Individuals

I can now turn to the question of the implications of prioritarianism in population ethics. First, we need to distinguish between different kinds of comparisons that are made within this field. Thus, comparisons are made between outcomes that contain only the very same individuals, some (or all) of which may be future individuals. Let us call these "fixed identity comparisons." Furthermore, comparisons are made between outcomes that include distinct, but nevertheless the same number of individuals. Let us call these "fixed number comparisons." Finally, comparisons are made between outcomes that contain different numbers of individuals (that, therefore, are neither fixed identity nor fixed number). Let us call these "different number comparisons."

To which of these kinds of comparisons does prioritarianism apply, if any? First, it is worth pointing out that prioritarianism can be applied to fixed identity and fixed number comparisons without having implications that prioritarians are likely to find troubling or are of the kind that have generally worried population ethicists. Consider first fixed identity comparisons. Such comparisons may involve both actual individuals, that is, individuals who either have existed, do exist, or will exist in the future, and merely possible individuals, that is, individuals who might have existed but in fact won't. Suppose we are comparing two outcomes consisting of the same actual future individuals. Applying prioritarianism to such comparisons seems rather straightforward. For simplicity, compare again (9, 1) and (5, 5). Prioritarians prefer the latter of these two outcomes, and thus the second of these two individuals being much better off. And it does not seem intuitively awkward to maintain this judgment, even if these individuals are actual *future* individuals. Even though they do not yet exist, they will exist, and it is better that the welfare is distributed more equally between them.

Now suppose that these two individuals are not actual, but merely possible future individuals. While these individuals are merely possible, they are nevertheless necessary in the sense that they exist in both the outcomes compared. Again, applying prioritarianism to the comparison and on that basis judging that (5, 5) is better than (9, 1) seems rather straightforward. Even if neither of these individuals will ever exist, we may believe that if they had come about, it would be better if the welfare were distributed equally between them, to the benefit of the second individual.

Now consider fixed number comparisons. Here, the compared individuals are not necessary but contingent, since they do not exist in all the outcomes compared. Compare, for example, (9, 1, *, *) and (*, *, 5, 5), where "*" refers to the nonexistence of a particular individual in a given outcome. Thus, there is no individual that exists in both of the outcomes compared. Suppose also that all of these individuals are merely possible. Prioritarians may well think that the latter outcome is better, because it would be better if one group of people existed and shared the welfare equally, than if another group existed and experienced a very unequal distribution of the same sum. This may be so even if, as it happens, neither of these two groups will ever exist.

Nevertheless, it may be argued that prioritarianism cannot apply to fixed number comparisons. This is because such comparisons involve contingent individuals, where the welfare that may be bestowed on them consists in the welfare that accrues to them if they come into existence. The problem is that, arguably, they do not have a welfare level independently of this welfare, on the basis of which the welfare that accrues to them if they come into existence can be weighted. Remember that, according to prioritarianism, benefits should be weighted on the basis of the welfare level at which they fall. According to this line of argument, there is a difference between comparing (9) and (0) and comparing (9) and (*). In the former case, the benefit of nine units of welfare falls at a level of 0, whereas in the latter case there is no independent welfare level at which the benefit falls. Or, to put it differently, prioritarianism is about giving priority to the worse off, but in the second comparison, the individual to whom nine units may accrue would not otherwise be worse off but nonexistent.

However, it is arguable that a welfare value can in fact be ascribed to nonexistence on the basis of which an individual's welfare in a world in which she exists can be weighted. To see this, consider the following argument for why existence can be better (or worse) for an individual than never existing (Holtug 2010: Ch. 5; 2016). Consider a world in which a given individual, *a*, exists, and has a life worth living. In this world, the following triadic relation will obtain: the state that *a exists* is better for *a* than the state that *a does not exist*. In this world, the first relata, *a exists*, obtains, and the second relata, *a*, exists. The third relata, *a does not exist*, however, does not obtain. Nevertheless, arguably, the third relata exists (as an abstract entity) in this world, which is all that is required for the triadic relation to obtain (see also Arrhenius and Rabinowicz 2015). Just as other relations may obtain even though not all their relata do, for example, the state that *the Allies win the war* is better than the state that *the Nazis win the war*. Furthermore, this is not only an argument for why existence can be better (or worse) for an individual than never existing, it can also be invoked to justify the claim that nonexistence has a value on the basis of which an individual's welfare can be weighted in the prioritarian function. In the world where *a* comes into existence, arguably, the state that *a does not exist* has zero value for *a*. After all, it contains neither good nor bad for her. Note that in making this claim, I am not ascribing a property to her in a world in which she does not exist, only in a world in which she does exist. The difference between the zero level and the welfare level she enjoys in this particular world in which she exists can then be described as the benefit to her of coming into existence and leading a particular life.[2] Furthermore, the zero level can provide the basis for weighting the units of welfare that accrue to her in this life.

Thus, when I go on to consider various challenges to prioritarianism in population ethics, it is worth remembering that some types of comparisons within this field may raise few or even no worries for prioritarians. Indeed, it is when we turn to different number comparisons that the real trouble begins. I shall engage with these difficulties in much greater detail in the following section, but for now it suffices to point out that when outcomes containing different numbers of individuals are compared, questions arise of what reasons we have to create people and of how to weight the quality of peoples' lives against the number of people living them. Thus, if we compare an outcome in which an individual is caused to exist and live a happy life and outcome in which she is not caused to exist, does her welfare in the former outcome give us a reason to prefer this outcome and perhaps even an obligation to bring it about, everything else being equal? Note that this is different from a fixed number comparison, in which we are assuming that someone will exist and asking whether it is better that it is this individual rather than that.

Furthermore, if we compare an outcome in which fewer individuals exist and experience a high level of welfare and an outcome in which more individuals exist but at a lower level, can the quantity of the welfare in the latter outcome compensate for the quality, or higher level, of the welfare in the former? These are of course general questions that any theory in population ethics will have to grapple with. However, some concerns are specific to prioritarianism, and perhaps a few other distributive theories. Suppose, for example, that we can either bestow, say, ten units of welfare on an individual who already exists and has a life worth living or create a new individual who will then enjoy ten units in her life. Assuming, as I argued above, that the ten units falling in the latter individual's life fall at a level of zero, whereas the ten units in the former individual's life fall at a positive level, prioritarianism would seem to imply that it is better to create a new individual than to benefit the person already in existence.

Prioritarians can avoid problems such as this by restricting the scope of the principle, such that it applies only to fixed identity and fixed number comparisons. At one point, Parfit (2004, 257) thus suggested "quarantining" different number comparisons in the application of our distributive principles. And indeed, usually, discussions of prioritarianism proceed within a framework of fixed populations. However, this is not as straightforward a solution as it may initially seem. Many of the most urgent problems we need to address in distributive justice involve different number comparisons, including global poverty and global warming. Thus, our choices about how to try to eradicate global poverty and what policies to implement to reduce global warming are likely to have implications for how many children people have, not least the globally poor and those most exposed to the resulting changes in weather and rising sea levels. Therefore, it is unfortunate if our distributive principles cannot be applied to such choices.

In the following, then, I focus on versions of prioritarianism that do aim to cater for different number comparisons. And here, we should distinguish between person-affecting and impersonal theories. According to person-affecting theories, outcomes are better or worse than other outcomes in virtue of these outcomes being better or worse for individuals. Such theories rely on the idea that welfare is good because it is good for individuals (Parfit 1984, 393–394). According to impersonal theories, on the other hand, welfare is good, period, and this is why it is good that welfare accrues to individuals. Thus, according to impersonalism, the moral importance of individuals is that they are "containers" of welfare (see also Ralf Bader's chapter in the present volume). Some theorists argue that our theory in population ethics should take a person-affecting form (Holtug 2010, 162–163). Consider an individual, b, who has a life with overall negative value, that is, a life worth not living. Arguably, it would have been better if b had not been caused to exist, everything else being equal. And if we hold a person-affecting view, we will say that this is because existence is worse for b than never existing. The badness of the outcome in which he exists is tied to the *badness for him* of existing. This seems plausible, because it is after all for his sake that we should prefer the outcome in which he does not come into existence. According to an impersonal theory, on the other hand, it does not in itself matter that it is worse for him to exist, the outcome in which he exists is worse because it renders the world, or this part of the world, worse.

This, of course, is a general reason why we might want to espouse a person-affecting theory. It is general in the sense that it applies quite generally to distributive theories; if we are utilitarians, we should be person-affecting utilitarians, if we are prioritarians, we should be person-affecting prioritarians, and so on. However, there is also a reason to adopt a person-affecting account that is more particular to prioritarianism. Thus, as we have seen, many prioritarians consider their distributive principle superior to egalitarianism because, unlike egalitarianism, prioritarianism is not vulnerable to the levelling down objection. While (1, 1) is more equal than (2, 1), this does not therefore give prioritarians a reason to think that (1, 1) is in any respect better. There are different possible explanations of the force of the levelling down objection, but one of them relies on a person-affecting account of morality (Holtug 2010, 181–192; Temkin 1993, Ch. 9). Along this line of argument, (1, 1) cannot be in any respect better than (2, 1), because there is no one *for whom* it is better.

Nevertheless, it may be objected that person-affecting accounts generate various problems in population ethics. Thus, consider the following more precise statement of the person-affecting principle:

The Narrow Person-Affecting Principle: An outcome, O_1, cannot be better (or worse) than another outcome, O_2, if there is no one for whom O_1 is better (or worse) than O_2.

Furthermore, consider the Non-Identity Problem, as illustrated in Figure 2.2. Here, A and B are outcomes, p, q, and r are distinct groups of individuals, and the width of a column represents how many individuals are in a group, whereas its height represents their level of welfare. In the Non-Identity Problem, most of us want to say that A is worse than B. However, this judgment is ruled out by the Narrow Person-Affecting Principle. After all, there is no one for whom A is worse. It is clearly not worse for p, because they are better off in A than in B. Nor is it worse for q, since their lives are after all worth living in A and they do not exist in B. Finally, A is not worse for r, since they do not exist in A. On this basis, it may be argued that the Narrow Person-Affecting Principle should be rejected.

There are, however, other person-affecting principles available that prioritarians may appeal to (for a person-affecting approach to prioritarianism in population ethics, see also Matthew Adler's contribution to the present volume). Consider:

The Wide Person-Affecting Principle: An outcome, O_1, cannot be better (or worse) than another outcome, O_2, if, were O_1 to obtain, there would be no one for whom O_1 would be better (or worse) than O_2 and, were O_2 to obtain, there would be no one for whom O_2 would be worse (or better) than O_1.

Unlike the Narrow Person-Affecting Principle, this principle is compatible with the claim that A is worse than B. This is because, were B to obtain, r would exist and A would indeed be worse for them than B. This follows from the above account of how existence can be better/worse for individuals than never existing. Person-affecting prioritarians can thus argue that they are entitled to invoke the welfare of r when explaining why A is worse and B better. And the prioritarian function then straightforwardly implies that B is better because the loss to p and q in B is outweighed by the gain to r.

Furthermore, to provide a person-affecting account of what is troubling about levelling down, prioritarians need only extend the Wide Person-Affecting Principle slightly. Thus, they can appeal to:

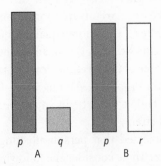

FIGURE 2.2   The Non-Identity Problem

The Strong Wide Person-Affecting Principle: An outcome, O_1, cannot be *in any respect* better (or worse) than another outcome, O_2, if, were O_1 to obtain, there would be no one for whom O_1 would be *in any respect* better (or worse) than O_2 and, were O_2 to obtain, there would be no one for whom O_2 would be *in any respect* worse (or better) than O_1.

Since there is no one for whom (1, 1) is in any respect better than (2, 1) and no one for whom (2, 1) is in any respect worse, and this is so independently of whether (1, 1) or (2, 1) obtains, this principle rules out that (1, 1) can be in any respect better. And so prioritarians may appeal to the Strong Wide Person-Affecting Principle in their explanation of what is troubling about levelling down if they so desire (Holtug 2010: 184-8).

4. REPUGNANT CONCLUSIONS

I now turn to some of the implications of prioritarianism in population ethics, assuming that this principle applies not only to fixed identity and fixed number comparisons, but also to different number comparisons. Consider, first, what Parfit (1984, 388) has labelled:

The Repugnant Conclusion: A world populated by individuals, every one of whom has a life barely worth living, would be better than a world populated by, for example, ten billion individuals all of whom have very worthwhile lives—as long as the former population is sufficiently large.

These two worlds can be illustrated as in Figure 2.3.

The Repugnant Conclusion is implied by a number of distributive principles, including total utilitarianism. Thus, if only there are enough individuals in B, B will have a higher total sum of welfare than A, even though everyone living in B has a much worse life than everyone living in A. In a sense, quantity compensates for quality. This is also the case according to prioritarianism. If there are enough individuals in B, the sum of

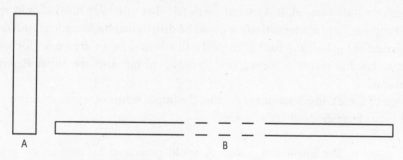

FIGURE 2.3 The Repugnant Conclusion

weighted welfare in this outcome will exceed the sum of weighted welfare in A. Thus, prioritarianism implies the Repugnant Conclusion.

Indeed, because of the prioritarian weighting function, this principle implies an even stronger version of the Repugnant Conclusion (Holtug 1999, 33; 2010, 254):

> *The Super-Repugnant Conclusion*: A world populated by individuals, every one of whom has a life barely worth living, would be better than a world populated by (for example) ten billion individuals, all of whom have very worthwhile lives, even if the former population has a lower total sum of welfare—if only the former population has an appropriate size.[3]

The reason why prioritarianism implies the Super-Repugnant Conclusion is that, on average, the welfare units that fall in B have a higher prioritarian value than the welfare units that fall in A. This is because, on average, they fall at a lower level. After all, unlike individuals in B, individuals in A are very well off. While the Repugnant Conclusion may seem to be a rather unpalatable implication, the Super-Repugnant Conclusion is even worse. And regarding the latter, prioritarians cannot even console themselves with the thought that at least total utilitarianism has a similar implication.

Indeed, prioritarianism implies:

> *Flattening Out*: For any given amount of welfare, w, the best possible distribution of w on individuals is that as many individuals exist as is compatible with each having the thinnest possible share of w, and that each has this share.

Thus, prioritarianism implies that, for example, $(1, 1, 1, 1)$ is better than $(4, *, *, *)$. However, while Flattening Out may seem rather troubling when it comes to positive welfare, it seems less troubling when it comes to negative welfare. Indeed, here Flattening Out may seem to be a welcome implication for a distributive principle to have. At least, it does not seem counterintuitive to claim that $(-1, -1, -1, -1)$ is better than $(-4, *, *, *)$. Thus, it may not seem fair that one individual should have to suffer a lot when, instead, four individuals could suffer a little each. Of course, some prioritarians may want to generalize this claim. They may claim that, just as it does not seem fair that one individual should have to suffer greatly when four individuals could each suffer a little instead, it does not seem fair that one individual should receive all the happiness when alternatively it could be distributed between four individuals. Why should *she* get all the fun? Ultimately, this would be an argument for why we should accept not only the Repugnant Conclusion, but also the Super-Repugnant Conclusion.

In light of these considerations regarding the implications of prioritarianism for the distribution of negative welfare, consider:

> *The Negative Repugnant Conclusion*: A world populated by individuals, every one of whom has a life barely worth *not* living, would be worse than a world populated by (for example) ten billion individuals, all of whom have extremely

miserable lives (lives very much worth not living)—as long as the former population is sufficiently large.

This conclusion is illustrated in Figure 2.4 (Broome 2004, 213; Carlson, 1998). The line connecting the two columns represents the level where life ceases to be worth living, that is, the zero level. Whereas people suffer greatly in C, they each suffer only a little in D. Both total utilitarianism and prioritarianism imply that, if sufficiently populated, D is worse than C. Like the Repugnant Conclusion, this may seem counterintuitive. But note that there is also a difference between total utilitarianism and prioritarianism as regards the Negative Repugnant Conclusion. It will take more individuals in D to make this outcome worse than C according to prioritarianism than according to total utilitarianism. This is because, on average, the welfare units fall at a lower (negative) level in C than they do in D. This may seem to be a redeeming feature of prioritarianism, as compared to total utilitarianism. After all, if C and D were to hold equal sums of negative welfare, would it not be better if no one had to suffer as terribly as people do in C, even if it meant that the sum would be spread out over many more individuals who would each suffer slightly? If so, it would seem that whereas total utilitarianism fares better as regards the Repugnant Conclusion, prioritarianism fares better as regards the Negative Repugnant Conclusion. Of course, population ethics is not a two-horse race, but it is nevertheless instructive to compare the implications of prioritarianism with those of total utilitarianism.

There is also another implication of prioritarianism in population ethics that is worth mentioning. Some population ethicists, and most notably Jan Narveson (1967, 69–71), have defended:

The Asymmetry: While it detracts from the value of an outcome to add individuals whose lives are of overall negative value, it does not increase the value of an outcome to add individuals whose lives are of overall positive value.

The Asymmetry plausibly implies that it is bad to create an individual who will have a life that consists of nothing but unbearable suffering, everything else being equal. And

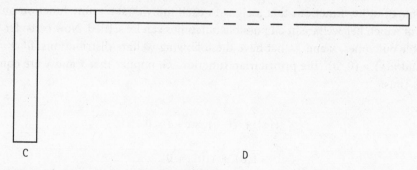

C   D

FIGURE 2.4 The Negative Repugnant Conclusion

yet, it gives us no reason to create an individual simply because this individual will have a life worth living. This may also seem to be a plausible implication (see, for example, Heyd 1992; Narveson 1967; Roberts 1998; Wolf 1997), not least because the opposite claim may imply that we have obligations to create more children, possibly even at the expense of already existing individuals. Thus, according to Narveson (1967; 1976; 1978), our duty is to make individuals happy, not to make happy individuals.

However, the Asymmetry is not as plausible as it may initially seem. Consider, for example, the Non-Identity Problem (Figure 2.2). I suggested that A is worse than B because B is better for r and the increase in r's welfare outweighs the decrease in p's and q's. However, the Asymmetry implies that the existence of r in B cannot add to the value of this outcome. Thus it rules out this kind of person-affecting solution to the Non-identity Problem.

Nevertheless, prioritarianism implies a weaker and more plausible version of the Asymmetry:

> *The Weak Asymmetry*: Everything else being equal, it is better to avoid that an individual comes into existence and has a life worth not living (at level $-w$), than to ensure that an individual comes into existence and has a life worth living (at level w).

Prioritarianism implies the Weak Asymmetry because of the weighting function, where benefits (or avoidance of harms) matter more at lower levels. Furthermore, giving priority to preventing that overall miserable individuals come into existence does not challenge the person-affecting solution to the Non-Identity Problem. In other words, the Weak Asymmetry does not conflict with the claim that, in Figure 2.2, A is worse than B because B is better for r.

I now need to address a further complication. Above, I have assumed that prioritarianism applies to both positive and negative welfare levels. However, as Campbell Brown (2007) has argued, it is by no means a trivial assumption that this principle can simultaneously have both positive and negative levels within its domain. This requires a bit of explaining. Consider Figure 2.5, which represents the prioritarian weighting function applied to both positive and negative welfare levels.

Let a, b, and c be positive numbers such that $f(a) = c$ and $f(-b) = -c$. And let u be a profile of utility functions that assigns to each individual a utility function on the basis of which her welfare in all possible outcomes can be settled. Now consider two possible outcomes, x and y, that have the following welfare distributions: $u(x) = (a, -b)$ and $u(y) = (0, 0)$. The prioritarian function, G, implies that x and y are equally good. Thus:

$$f(a) + f(-b) = c - c = 0$$

$$f(0) + f(0) = 0$$

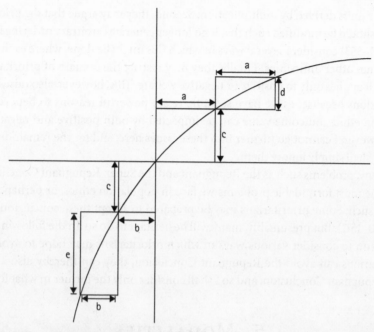

FIGURE 2.5 The prioritarian weighting function

Now suppose that we adopt a new measurement of welfare that simply doubles the unit formerly used. That is, we move from u to u', where, for each possible outcome o, $u'(o) = 2u(o)$. Thus, $u'(x) = (2a, -2b)$ and $u'(y) = (0, 0)$. Note that an increase from a to $2a$ gives rise to an increase in G of d, and that a decrease from $-b$ to $-2b$ gives rise to a decrease in G of e, where $e > d$. The implication is that prioritarianism does not assign equal value to x and y if we assume this new measure of welfare, u'. After all:

$$f(2a) + f(-2b) = (c + d) - (c + e) = d - e < 0$$

$$f(0) + f(0) = 0$$

This is because the decrease from $-b$ to $-2b$ falls at a lower level than the increase from a to $2a$, and since the prioritarian function assigns greater weight to benefits at lower levels, $d - e < 0$. Therefore, the prioritarian ranking of outcomes depends on whether we assume u or u' in our measurement of welfare. The problem is that u and u' seem to provide equally good representations of welfare, given that u' is derived from u simply by multiplying each individual's welfare by two. In other words, it is not clear that there are facts about welfare that would make one representation better than the other. And this, in turn, implies a measure of arbitrariness in the prioritarian ordering.

For prioritarians, there are three possible ways out here (Brown 2007). First, they may argue that, in fact, there is a unit of measurement that better represents welfare than other units derived by multiplication. Second, they may argue that the prioritarian function should be modified such that it no longer generates arbitrary orderings. Brown (2007, 341–353) considers several ways in which this might be done, where each of these faces certain other difficulties. Finally, they may restrict the domain of prioritarianism such that it applies only to positive or negative welfare. This, however, also raises further complications because, as we have seen, there are powerful reasons to believe that in population ethics, outcome value can be impacted by both positive and negative welfare.[4] However, I cannot go further into these issues here, and for the remainder of this chapter, I shall simply ignore them.

For many, problems such as the Repugnant and the Super-Repugnant Conclusion are among the most formidable problems we face in population ethics, or perhaps even in ethics as such. Some prioritarians may be prepared to accept these conclusions (Adler 2009, 1510–1511). But presumably, many will be hesitant to do so. In the following, therefore, I go on to consider various ways in which prioritarians may hope to avoid them. If prioritarians can avoid the Repugnant Conclusion, they can thereby also avoid the Super-Repugnant Conclusion, and so I shall consider only the former in what follows.

5. MODALITIES

The Wide Person-Affecting Principle, discussed above, does not restrict the class of individuals that may contribute to the value of an outcome. As we have seen, it can be applied even to contingent and merely possible individuals. Consider again the Non-Identity Problem (Figure 2.2). And suppose that A is the actual outcome, such that p and q consist of actual individuals, whereas r consists of merely possible ones. Nevertheless, as I have pointed out, A can be claimed to be worse than B because B is better for r. This is so even though r consists of individuals that are both merely possible and contingent. And the Wide Person-Affecting Principle is compatible with this claim because, were B (counterfactually) to obtain, this outcome would be better for r.

Nevertheless, there are other person-affecting principles that do restrict the class of individuals that count when determining outcome value, and in this Section, I consider two such principles. Each aims to bring us closer to Narveson's Slogan, according to which our duty is to make individuals happy, not to make happy individuals. According to the first, we need only take the welfare of necessary individuals into account where, again, necessary individuals are individuals who exist in all the outcomes compared. Consider, then:

> *The Necessary-Person-Affecting Principle*: An outcome, O_1, cannot be better (or worse) than another outcome, O_2, if there is no one who exists in both O_1 and O_2 for whom O_1 is better (or worse) than O_2.

Strictly speaking, this principle does not claim that the welfare of necessary individuals matters for outcome value, but clearly that is part of the underlying rationale. The welfare of necessary individuals matters, whereas the welfare of contingent individuals does not. Therefore, we may add:

> *The Necessary-Person Betterness Claim*: An outcome, O_1, is better than another outcome, O_2, if, within the class of individuals who exist in both outcomes, (a) everyone in O_1 is equally well off, and (b) everyone is better off in O_1 than in O_2.

The Necessary-Person Betterness Claim should be relatively uncontroversial among proponents of the Necessary-Person-Affecting Principle. First, the former principle does not have any implications for comparisons that involve conflicting interests between necessary individuals. Second, indeed, it only implies that an outcome is better than another insofar as the Weak Pareto Principle is satisfied for necessary individuals (where this principle claims that an outcome is better than another if it is better for everyone). Third, while some may hold that efficiency should be weighted against equality, this principle only requires us to judge an outcome better insofar it contains perfect equality as regards the individuals that matter, that is, necessary individuals.

Prioritarians may adopt such a necessary-person-affecting approach, as may of course utilitarians, egalitarians, and proponents of other distributive principles (see also Ralf Bader's chapter in the present volume). Thus, if prioritarians restrict the scope of their principle such that it applies only to necessary individuals, it will satisfy both the Necessary-Person-Affecting Principle and the Necessary-Person Betterness Claim. Before I turn to the implications of this restricted scope version of prioritarianism, let me very briefly point out why some theorists believe that a person-affecting approach can accommodate only necessary individuals. They argue that existence cannot be better (or worse) for an individual than never existing, because that would imply that nonexistence is worse (or better) for them, where nonexistence cannot be worse (or better) for them, because a nonexisting individual cannot have any properties (Heyd 1992, 113; cf. Broome 1993, 77; Parfit 1984, 489). Therefore, an outcome can only be better (or worse) than another for necessary individuals, which is why we should adopt a necessary-person-affecting approach. However, for reasons I have already sketched above, I do not find this a plausible argument. We are entitled to claim that, in a world in which an individual exists, the state that she never exists can be worse (or better) for her than the state that she exists. And this suffices to render the welfare of contingent individuals relevant for outcome value, as transpires from the Wide Person-Affecting Principle.

Nevertheless, let us now consider the implications of a necessary-person-affecting approach in population ethics. If such an approach solves some of the problems we would otherwise have to face, we may have reason to adopt it. Indeed, restricting the scope to necessary individuals may seem to have some plausible implications. Consider again the Repugnant Conclusion (Figure 2.3). Suppose, first, that the individuals that exist in A are also present in B (albeit, at a much lower level of welfare). In that case, the Necessary-Person Betterness Claim implies that A is better than B, and so we avoid the Repugnant Conclusion. Now suppose instead that there is no overlap between the populations of A and B and so that the comparison involves only contingent individuals. In that case, the

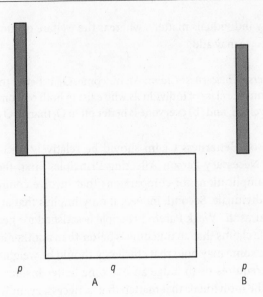

FIGURE 2.6 The problem of sacrifice

Necessary-Person-Affecting Principle implies that B cannot be better than A. These are conclusions that will be welcomed by many.

However, on balance, the necessary-person-affecting approach does not enjoy intuitive support. First, consider that, on the assumption that all the individuals involved in the Repugnant Conclusion are contingent, the Necessary-Person-Affecting Principle implies that A cannot be better than B, which presumably is a less welcome conclusion. Second, consider again the Non-Identity Problem (Figure 2.2). Here, only the p-individuals are necessary and since they are better and equally well off in A, the Necessary-Person Betterness Claim implies that A is better than B. Again, this seems to be the wrong conclusion.

Finally, consider the Problem of Sacrifice (Figure 2.6). Since only the p-individuals are necessary, and since they are better and equally well off in A, the Necessary-person Betterness Claim implies that A is better than B. This is so even though A contains a huge group of people who all suffer terribly. Surely this cannot be right.

There is also a further problem with the Necessary-Person Betterness Claim, over and above its intuitive repugnance. It violates the transitivity of the betterness relation (cf. Broome 1992, 125). Consider Figure 2.7.

The Necessary-Person Betterness Claim implies that C is better than D and that D is better than E. Transitivity then implies that C must be better than E. However, according to the Necessary-Person Betterness Claim, it is rather E that is better than C. Thus, this principle violates the transitivity of the betterness relation.

An alternative person-affecting approach is to restrict the scope of our distributive principles to actual individuals, rather than to necessary individuals. This would involve the claim that only the welfare of actual individuals matters for outcome value

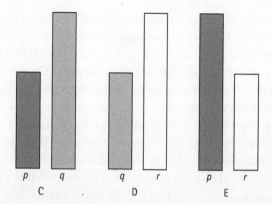

FIGURE 2.7 The problem of transitivity

(cf. Bigelow and Pargetter 1988, 174; Feinberg 1980, 180; Steinbock 1992, 72; Warren 1978, 24). Indeed, it may be asked, why should we be concerned about the welfare of individuals who will, after all, never exist? Consider:

> *The Actual-Person-Affecting Principle*: An outcome, O_1, cannot be better (or worse) than another outcome, O_2, if there is no actual individual for whom O_1 is better (or worse) than O_2.

Just like the Necessary-Person-Affecting Principle, this principle does not explicitly state that the welfare of the favored modal category of individuals contributes to outcome value, and so it may be combined with:

> *The Actual-Person Betterness Claim*: An outcome, O_1, is better than another outcome, O_2, if, within the class of actual individuals, (a) everyone in O_1 is equally well off, and (b) everyone is better off in O_1 than in O_2.

If the scope of prioritarianism is restricted to actual individuals, this principle straightforwardly satisfies both the Actual-Person-Affecting Principle and the Actual-Person Betterness Claim. Now, as was the case for the necessary-person-affecting approach, the actual-person-affecting approach blocks a particular version of the Repugnant Conclusion (Figure 2.3). Suppose that A is the actual outcome, and so all the individuals inhabiting A are actual individuals. Then, irrespective of whether these individuals are also present in B, the Actual-Person Betterness Claim implies that A is better than B. However, now suppose that B is the actual outcome and that A does not contain any actual individuals. In that case, this principle implies that B is better than A. Furthermore, if neither A nor B contains any actual individuals, the Actual-Person-Affecting Principle implies that A cannot be better than B.

This approach has further counterintuitive implications. Suppose that, in the Non-Identity Problem (Figure 2.2), A is the actual outcome. In that case, the

Actual-Person-Affecting Principle implies that B cannot be better than A, as there is no actual person for whom it is better. Then consider the Problem of Sacrifice (Figure 2.6). And suppose that B is the actual outcome, and so p the only actual individuals. Here, the Actual-person Betterness Claim implies that A is better than B. All in all, then, the actual-person-affecting approach generates highly counterintuitive judgments.

The upshot is that restricting the scope of prioritarianism to some favored modal category of individuals does not seem to render this a more plausible principle in population ethics. Of course, there are further person-affecting principles that restrict the significance of selected categories of individuals, but they seem to me not to show much promise either (for a critical discussion of some of them, as well as a more detailed discussion of the necessary-person-affecting and the actual-person-affecting approach, see Holtug 2004; 2010, 263–277).

6. ADDITIVE AND OTHER FUNCTIONS

A different route for the prioritarian to take is to modify the prioritarian function. Indeed, just as prioritarians can make use of various scope-restricting person-affecting principles, there are also a number of suggestions in the literature about functions that may enable us to avoid the Repugnant Conclusion. For illustration, consider the possibility of replacing the additive function with an average function instead, as average utilitarians have proposed. In the case of prioritarianism, this would give us:

$$G_A = \frac{f(w_1) + f(w_2) + \ldots + f(w_n)}{n}$$

It is easy to see how average prioritarianism avoids the Repugnant Conclusion. Clearly, the average level of people's weighted welfare is higher in A than in B in Figure 2.3. However, there are well-known problems with such average views. First, note that average prioritarianism violates several axioms that prioritarians have generally found compelling. Thus, average prioritarianism violates strong separability, assuming that we apply this condition to different number comparisons. Consider the following four outcomes:

$$A = (2, 1) \quad C = (2, 3)$$
$$B = (*, 1) \quad D = (*, 3)$$

Strong separability implies that unaffected individuals do not affect the ordering. Therefore, A is better than B if and only if C is better than D. However, Average Prioritarianism implies that whereas A is better than B, D is better than C. After all, adding an individual with a welfare level of two increases the average level of weighted welfare if the second individual is at one, but decreases the average of weighted welfare if the second individual is at three. For illustration, suppose again that the weighting function is square root. Then:

$$G_A(A) = \frac{\sqrt{2} + \sqrt{1}}{2} = 1,21 \qquad G_A(C) = \frac{\sqrt{2} + \sqrt{3}}{2} = 1,57$$

$$G_A(B) = \frac{\sqrt{1}}{1} = 1 \qquad\qquad G_A(D) = \frac{\sqrt{3}}{1} = 1,73$$

As transpires, $G_A(A) > G_A(B)$ and $G_A(C) < G_A(D)$. Furthermore, Average Prioritarianism violates the Wide Person-Affecting Principle (as well as other person-affecting principles). Consider the following two outcomes: $(-10, *)$ and $(-10, -9)$. Here, Average Prioritarianism implies that the latter outcome is better, although it differs from the former only in that a second individual is added who has an utterly miserable life. Thus, Average Prioritarianism implies that the average weighted welfare is slightly higher in the second outcome. Whether we accept the Wide Person-Affecting Principle or not, this is a very troubling implication. But it is worth also pointing out that this implication contradicts the Wide Person-Affecting Principle. After all, there is no one for whom the second outcome is better, and this is so irrespective of which of these two outcomes obtains.

Finally, Average Prioritarianism implies what Gustaf Arrhenius (2000, 66) has labeled:

> *The Sadistic Conclusion*: It can be better to add individuals who have lives worth not living to an outcome than to add individuals who have lives worth living.

To illustrate, consider Figure 2.8. Here, Average Prioritarianism implies that E is better than F, simply because q detracts less from the average level of weighted welfare in E than r does in F (at least if r is sufficient in size). However, the Sadistic Conclusion is hard to swallow. All in all, Average Prioritarianism does not seem a promising alternative to (total) prioritarianism.

Nevertheless, other modifications of our distributive principles have been proposed to enable us to avoid the Repugnant Conclusion. A number of these are discussed in the present volume, and I cannot discuss them in any detail here. I do, however, want to point out that a number of them are compatible with prioritarianism, or rather prioritarianism suitably modified. According to a variable value view, the value of adding an individual at a given level of welfare to an outcome depends on how many individuals are already included in that outcome (Hurka 1983). The more individuals, the less value this additional individual contributes. Furthermore, for a given level of welfare, adding further individuals to an outcome asymptotically approaches a certain limit as regards outcome value. This allows the variable value view to avoid the Repugnant Conclusion (Figure 2.3). After all, A may have a value that is higher than that which can be asymptotically

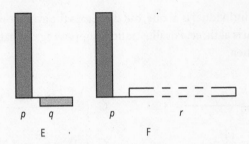

FIGURE 2.8 The Sadistic Conclusion

approached by adding to an outcome more and more individuals with lives barely worth living. Prioritarians may incorporate such a variable value view by claiming that, for a given level of weighted welfare, adding further individuals to an outcome holds increasingly little value, and then apply the usual prioritarian function to fixed identity and fixed number comparisons.

Another proposal is to adopt a critical-level theory. Critical-level theories claim that there is a certain level of welfare, above zero, such that only lives above this level contribute positively to outcome value (Blackorby, Bossert, and Donaldson 1997; see also Walter Bossert's contribution to the present volume). Call this level l. Since lives below l do not contribute positively, the Repugnant Conclusion is blocked. Assuming that l is well above zero, lives barely worth living are below this level, and so an outcome containing (only) such lives cannot outweigh the value of A, no matter how many lives are contained in the former outcome. Now, prioritarians can incorporate a critical-level theory and thus claim that only weighted welfare above a critical level, $f(l)$, contributes positively to outcome value, and thus render themselves invulnerable to the Repugnant Conclusion.

However, such a theory that invokes a critical level (above zero) is not complete unless we know what to do with welfare below the critical level. And here, there are various possibilities. One is to assign negative value to all contributions below the critical level as suggested by Blackorby, Bossert, and Donaldson. The following is a prioritarian version of this view:

$$G_{CL} = \left[f(w_1) - f(l)\right] + \left[f(w_2) - f(l)\right] + \dots + \left[f(w_n) - f(l)\right]$$

A worry about this prioritarian principle is that, just like average prioritarianism (and, for that matter, average utilitarianism and critical-level utilitarianism), it implies the Sadistic Conclusion. A way to try to soften this implication is to argue that the critical level is vague (Broome 2004, 213–214). Alternatively, it may be suggested that adding lives between the critical level and the zero level has no value, positive or negative. However, my aim here is not to assess these particular suggestions, but merely to point out that prioritarians may make use of them if they so desire.

A final suggestion that I want to briefly mention is Parfit's (2016) recent proposal, according to which in different number comparisons, some outcomes are only imprecisely comparable. Parfit argues that this is, at least sometimes, the case when we compare outcomes that differ both in the number of individuals they contain and in the welfare experienced by these individuals. Furthermore, according to Parfit, introducing such imprecision into the betterness ordering enables us to avoid the Repugnant Conclusion. For present purposes, my point is simply that prioritarians may likewise consider some different number comparisons imprecise, and on that basis resist the Repugnant Conclusion.

As it happens, I do not find any of the solutions to the Repugnant Conclusion considered in this section particularly plausible. However, several of them are discussed in much greater detail elsewhere in this volume, and my aim has mainly been to point out that they are also available to prioritarians, insofar as they are willing to adjust the prioritarian function. For those who, like me, remain unconvinced by the proposed solutions, population ethics continues to be a major challenge in ethical theory. Nevertheless, it is worth remembering that prioritarianism seems straightforwardly applicable in fixed identity and fixed number comparisons. And as regards different number comparisons, prioritarians may take some comfort in the thought that other distributive principles seem to face equal challenges.

Notes

1. See, for example, Adler (2012), Adler and Holtug (2019), Arneson (2000), Broome (1991, 216–217), Holtug (2006; 2010; 2015; 2016; 2019), McCarthy (2008a; 2008b), McKerlie (2006), Nagel (1991, 63–74), O'Neill (2012), Otsuka and Voorhoeve (2009), Parfit (1991; 2012), Persson (2008), Rabinowicz (2002), Segall (2016), Tännsjö (2015), Temkin (1993, 247–248), Tungodden (2003, 23–32), and Williams (2012).
2. There is by now a large body of literature on whether coming into existence can be better (or worse) for an individual than never existing, so that individuals can be said to benefit (or be harmed) from coming into existence. The claim that existence can be better (or worse) than never existing has been defended by Arrhenius and Rabinowicz (2015), Bradley (2013), Hare (1993), Holtug (2001; 2010: Ch. 5; 2016), Johansson (2010), Persson (1997), and Roberts (2003). Critics, on the other hand, include Broome (1993), Buchanan et al. (2000), Bykvist (2007), Dasgupta (1995), Heyd (1992), McMahan (2013), Narveson (1967), Parfit (1984), and Visak (2013). Some of the critics, however, hold that while existence cannot be *better* (or worse) than never existing, it can be *good* to come into existence (McMahan 2013; Parfit 1984: 489–490).
3. Here, an "appropriate size" means that the population in the former world would have to be large enough for this world to have a higher prioritarian value than the latter world, but small enough not to have a higher total sum of welfare.
4. Incidentally, it may be worth mentioning that for some, the problem of including both positive and negative welfare in the domain of prioritarianism may suggest adopting a currency of prioritarian justice that, unlike welfare, does not admit of negative levels.

REFERENCES

Adler, Matthew. 2009. "Future Generations: A Prioritarian View." *George Washington Law Review* 77, nos. 5–6: 1478–1520.

Adler, Matthew. 2012. *Well-Being and Fair Distribution. Beyond Cost-Benefit Analysis.* Oxford: Oxford University Press.

Adler, Matthew and Nils Holtug. 2019. "Prioritarianism: A Response to Critics." *Politics, Philosophy & Economics* 18, no. 2: 101–144.

Arneson, Richard J. 2000. "Luck Egalitarianism and Prioritarianism." *Ethics* 110, no. 2: 339–349.

Arrhenius, Gustaf. 2000. "Future Generations: A Challenge for Moral Theory." PhD diss., Uppsala University.

Arrhenius, Gustaf and Wlodek Rabinowicz. 2015. "The Value of Existence." In *The Oxford Handbook of Value Theory*, edited by Iwao Hirose and Jonas Olson, 425–443. Oxford: Oxford University Press.

Bigelow, John and Robert Pargetter. 1988. "Morality, Potential Persons and Abortion." *American Philosophical Quarterly* 25, no. 2: 173–181.

Blackorby, Charles, Walter Bossert, and David Donaldson. 1997. "Critical Level Utilitarianism and the Population-ethics Dilemma." *Economics and Philosophy* 13, no. 2: 197–230.

Bradley, Ben. 2013. "Asymmetries in Benefiting, Harming and Creating." *Journal of Ethics* 17: 37–49.

Broome, John. 1991. *Weighing Goods.* Oxford: Basil Blackwell.

Broome, John. 1992. *Counting the Cost of Global Warming.* Cambridge: The White Horse Press.

Broome, John. 1993. "Goodness is Reducible to Betterness: The Evil of Death is the Value of Life." In *The Good and the Economical*, edited by P. Koslowski and Y. Shionoya, 70–84. Berlin: Springer-Verlag.

Broome, John. 2004. *Weighing Lives.* Oxford: Oxford University Press.

Brown, Campbell. 2007. "Prioritarianism for Variable Populations." *Philosophical Studies* 134: 325–361.

Buchanan, Allen, Dan W. Brock, Norman Daniels and Daniel Wikler. 2000. *From Chance to Choice: Genetics and Justice.* Cambridge: Cambridge University Press.

Bykvist, Krister. 2007. "The Benefits of Coming into Existence." *Philosophical Studies* 135: 335–362.

Carlson, Eric. 1998. "Mere Addition and Two Trilemmas of Population Ethics." *Economics and Philosophy* 14, no. 2: 283–306.

Dasgupta, Partha. 1995. *An Inquiry into Well-Being and Destitution.* Oxford: Oxford University Press.

Hare, Richard M. 1993. "Possible People." In *Essays on Bioethics*, 67–83. Oxford: Clarendon Press.

Feinberg, Joel. 1980. "The Rights of Animals and Unborn Generations." In *Rights, Justice, and the Bounds of Liberty*, 159–184. Princeton, NJ: Princeton University Press.

Heyd, David. 1992. *Genethics: Moral Issues in the Creation of People.* Berkeley: University of California Press.

Holtug, Nils. 1999. "Utility, Priority and Possible People." *Utilitas* 11, no. 1: 16–36.

Holtug, Nils. 2001. "On the Value of Coming into Existence." *Journal of Ethics* 5, no. 4: 361–384.

Holtug, Nils. 2004. "Person-affecting Moralities." In *The Repugnant Conclusion: Essays on Population Ethics*, edited by Jesper Ryberg and Torbjörn Tännsjö, 71–92. Dordrecht: Kluwer Academic Publishers.

Holtug, Nils. 2006. "Prioritarianism." In *Egalitarianism: New Essays on the Nature and Value of Equality*, edited by Nils Holtug and Kasper Lippert-Rasmussen, 125–156. Oxford: Clarendon Press.

Holtug, Nils. 2010. *Persons, Interests, and Justice*. Oxford: Oxford University Press.

Holtug, Nils. 2015. "Theories of Value Aggregation: Utilitarianism, Egalitarianism, Prioritarianism." In *The Oxford Handbook of Value Theory*, edited by Iwao Hirose and Jonas Olson, 267–284. Oxford: Oxford University Press.

Holtug, N. 2016. "The Value of Coming into Existence." In *The Ethics of Killing Animals*, edited by Tatjana Visak and Robert Garner, 101–114. Oxford: Oxford University Press.

Holtug, Nils. 2019. "Prioritarianism: Ex Ante, Ex Post, or Factualist Criterion of Rightness?" *Journal of Political Philosophy* 27, no. 2: 207–228.

Hurka, Thomas. 1983. "Value and Population Size." *Ethics* 93, no. 3: 496–507.

Johansson, Jens. 2010. "Being and Betterness." *Utilitas* 22, no. 3: 285–302.

McCarthy, David. 2008a. "Utilitarianism and Prioritarianism I." *Economics and Philosophy* 22, no. 3: 335–363.

McCarthy, David. 2008b. "Utilitarianism and Prioritarianism II." *Economics and Philosophy* 24, no. 1: 1–33.

McKerlie, Dennis. 2006. "Egalitarianism and the Difference between Interpersonal and Intrapersonal Judgments." In *Egalitarianism: New Essays on the Nature and Value of Equality*, edited by Nils Holtug and Kasper Lippert-Rasmussen, 157–173. Oxford: Clarendon Press.

McMahan, Jeff. 2013. "Causing People to Exist and Saving People's Lives." *Journal of Ethics* 17: 5–35.

Nagel, Thomas. 1991. *Equality and Priority*. New York: Oxford University Press.

Narveson, Jan. 1967. "Utilitarianism and New Generations." *Mind* 76, no. 301: 62–72.

Narveson, Jan. 1976. "Moral Problems of Population." In *Ethics and Population*, edited by Michael D. Bayles, 59–80. Cambridge, MA: Schenkman.

Narveson, Jan. 1978. "Future People and Us." In *Obligations to Future Generations*, edited by Richard I. Sikora and Brian Barry, 38–60. Philadelphia: Temple University Press.

Nebel, Jacob M. 2017. "Priority, Not Equality, for Possible People." *Ethics* 127, no. 4: 896–911.

O'Neill, Martin. 2012. "Priority, Preference and Value." *Utilitas* 24, no. 3: 332–348.

Otsuka, Michael and Alex Voorhoeve. 2009. "Why it Matters that Some are Worse off than Others: An Argument Against the Priority View." *Philosophy and Public Affairs* 37, no. 2: 171–199.

Parfit, Derek. 1984. *Reasons and Persons*. Oxford: Clarendon Press.

Parfit, Derek. 1991. "Equality or Priority?" The Lindley Lecture, University of Kansas. Reprinted in *The Ideal of Equality*, Matthew Clayton and Andrew Williams (eds.), 81–125. Basingstoke: MacMillan Press Ltd. 2000.

Parfit, Derek. 2004. "Postscript." In *The Repugnant Conclusion: Essays on Population Ethics*, edited by Jesper Ryberg and Torbjörn Tännsjö, 257. Dordrecht: Kluwer Academic Publishers.

Parfit, Derek. 2012. "Another Defence of the Priority View." *Utilitas* 24, no. 3: 399–440.

Parfit, Derek. 2016. "Can We Avoid the Repugnant Conclusion?" *Theoria* 82: 110–127.

Persson, Ingmar. 1997. "Person-Affecting Principles and Beyond." In *Contingent Future Persons*, edited by Nick Fotion and Jan C. Heller, 41–56. Dordrecht: Kluwer Academic Publishers.

Persson, Ingmar. 2008. "Why Levelling Down Could be Worse for Prioritarianism than for Egalitarianism." *Ethical Theory and Moral Practice* 11, no. 3: 295–303.

Rabinowicz, Wlodek. 2002. "Prioritarianism for Prospects." *Utilitas* 14, no. 1: 2–21.

Roberts, Melinda A. 1998. *Child versus Childmaker: Future Persons and Present Duties in Ethics and the Law*. Lanham, MD: Rowman & Littlefield.

Roberts, Melinda A. 2003. "Can it Ever Be Better Never to Have Existed at All? Person-based Consequentialism and a New Repugnant Conclusion." *Journal of Applied Philosophy* 20: 159–185.

Segall, Shlomi. 2016. *Why Inequality Matters: Luck Egalitarianism, Its Meaning and Value*. Cambridge: Cambridge University Press.

Steinbock, Bonnie. 1992. *Life Before Birth*. Oxford: Oxford University Press.

Tännsjö, Torbjörn. 2015. "Utilitarianism or Prioritarianism." *Utilitas* 27, no. 2: 240–250.

Temkin, Larry S. 1993. *Inequality*. New York: Oxford University Press.

Tungodden, Bertil. 2003. "The Value of Equality." *Economics and Philosophy* 19, no. 1: 1–44.

Visak, Tatjana. 2013. *Killing Happy Animals: Explorations in Utilitarian Ethics*. Basingstoke: Palgrave Macmillan.

Warren, Marry A. 1978. "Do Potential People Have Moral Rights?." In *Obligations to Future Generations*, edited by Richard I. Sikora and Brian Barry, 14–30. Philadelphia: Temple University Press.

Williams, Andrew. 2012. "The Priority View Bites the Dust?" *Utilitas* 24, no. 3: 315–331.

Wolf, Clark. 1997. "Person-affecting Utilitarianism and Population Policy; Or, Sissy Jupe's Theory of Social Choice." In *Contingent Future Persons*, edited by Nick Fotion and Jan C. Heller, 99–122. Dordrecht: Kluwer Academic Publishers.

CHAPTER 3

ANONYMOUS WELFARISM, CRITICAL-LEVEL PRINCIPLES, AND THE REPUGNANT AND SADISTIC CONCLUSIONS

WALTER BOSSERT

1. INTRODUCTION

POPULATION principles are used to rank possible states of the world according to their goodness from the moral point of view. Because the identities and the number of those who ever live can differ from one state to another, the principles must be capable of performing variable-population comparisons. A state of the world (a state, for short) contains a full description of everything that may be of relevance for goodness. There are three types of information to be taken into consideration: (1) the set of those who ever live (the population); (2) their levels of lifetime well-being; and (3) all other (non-welfare) information that may be morally pertinent. States of the world can be thought of as full histories, from the remote past to the distant future. Note that, in different states, people may be born or die at different times.

A principle is required to produce a social goodness relation for each possible combination of the above three pieces of information. The term "profile" is used for a triple of a population, a list of utility functions interpreted as indicators of lifetime well-being, and an assignment of non-welfare characteristics to each state of the world. Because a social goodness relation is to be obtained for each possible profile, a multi-profile approach is adopted.

Variable-population welfarism obtains if the principle only uses information regarding the identities of those alive and their lifetime well-beings in two states to rank them. Because people's identities may matter, not all of these principles are impartial—they may treat people differently depending on who they are. An anonymity property can be employed to ensure that only impartial principles are permitted and the use of anonymity can be seen as a solution to Parfit's (1984) non-identity problem. According to the anonymous welfarist principles that result from invoking an anonymity property, an anonymous goodness relation defined on utility distributions is all that is required to rank any two possible states of the world for any underlying profile.

Starting from the notion of a social-evaluation functional (a mechanism that assigns a social goodness relation to each possible profile in this chapter), I successively narrow down the possible population principles by imposing some intuitively appealing conditions. In the first step, the welfarism properties of Pareto indifference and binary independence of irrelevant alternatives explained below are employed to obtain variable-population welfarism. Pareto indifference ensures that unanimous equal goodness within a fixed population is respected by the social relation, and the binary-independence condition imposes a form of consistency on goodness relations across certain profiles. Next, anonymity (requiring equal treatment of equals in terms of lifetime well-being) is added to arrive at anonymous welfarism. The final step consists of imposing the same-people properties of strong Pareto and continuity, along with the variable-population conditions of existence of at least one critical level and existence independence in order to obtain the class of critical-level generalized-utilitarian principles. Strong Pareto is a unanimity condition in the same spirit as Pareto indifference that applies to betterness, and continuity demands that "small" changes in utilities do not lead to "large" changes in the social goodness relation. Existence of at least one critical level guarantees that population size and well-being can be traded off in a non-trivial way, and existence independence is a property that requires only the well-being of those affected to influence social goodness. Critical-level generalized utilitarianism is an extension of fixed-population generalized utilitarianism to a variable-population setting. All of these concepts will be explained in detail once the requisite definitions have been introduced.

Two of the implications that the principles of population ethics should possibly avoid are the Repugnant Conclusion introduced by Parfit (1976, 1982, 1984) and the Sadistic Conclusion defined by Arrhenius (2000). The final part of the chapter analyzes the critical- level generalized-utilitarian principles with respect to these implications.

Although it is possible to work with a temporal framework, approaches that employ an explicit temporal formulation are not covered in this chapter. Within such a setting, population principles that discount the well-being of future people can be defined but they do not treat individuals impartially because they pay attention to their birth dates. See Blackorby, Bossert, and Donaldson (2005, Ch. 8) for a discussion.

2. INDIVIDUAL LIFETIME WELL-BEING

The levels of lifetime well-being experienced by those who ever live are of crucial importance when ranking possible states of the world according to their social goodness.

Because of this, a comprehensive account of well-being (such as that proposed by Griffin, 1986) needs to be employed and, moreover, everyone who may possibly be affected must be considered, including the members of future generations. The term utility refers to an indicator of lifetime well-being, and "lifetime well-being" and "utility" are used interchangeably in this chapter. A well-founded theory of individual utility is especially important when welfarist principles are employed because of their exclusive dependence on lifetime well-being. See, for instance, Broome (2004) and Blackorby, Bossert, and Donaldson (2005).

A neutral life serves as a benchmark to express judgments as to whether a life is worth living. The position taken here is that a person cannot be made better off or worse off by being brought into existence—prior to being in existence, there is no one who can experience any gains or losses (Parfit 1984). It is, however, possible for an existing person to consider her or his life worth living, and this is what the notion of neutrality intends to capture. One possible way to link neutrality to well-being proceeds by asking a fully informed individual whether her or his life, as a whole, is worth living; see also Sumner (1996). If it is, the level of lifetime well-being associated with this life is above neutrality and if it is not, the lifetime well-being of the person is below that of a neutral life. If lifetime well-being is at the neutral level, it is not the case that it is worth living and it is not the case that it is not worth living. Note that, for the purposes of this chapter, it is irrelevant which specific account of neutrality is chosen. The convention adopted here is that individual utilities are assumed to be normalized so that a lifetime well-being level of zero corresponds to a neutral life. The choice of zero for a neutral life is fairly standard in population ethics.

Critical levels of lifetime well-being play a central role in this chapter. For a given state of the world with a given population, consider another state in which an additional person is alive and the well-being of those who live in both states is unchanged. A critical level for the original utility distribution is a level of utility so that the new state is as good as the original. There are population principles for which critical levels do not exist. For instance, for a principle that always declares a larger population to be better than a smaller one, irrespective of the utilities of those alive in the two states, there are no critical levels for any distribution of well-being. Such degenerate principles are ruled out in this chapter by assuming that some minimal trade-off between population size and well-being is possible. If critical levels do exist, they need not be the same for different utility distributions. An example is the average-utilitarian principle that ranks any two states of the world by comparing the average utilities of those alive in them. Adding a person with average utility does not change the average of a given population and, therefore, the critical level for any distribution is given by the average utility of the original distribution. Total (or classical) utilitarianism employs a common critical level that is equal to zero (neutrality) for all possible utility distributions. This move is not without its problems, however, and there are other possibilities that will be explored and advocated later on in this chapter.

3. Population Principles as Social Goodness Relations

Population principles rank possible states of the world in terms of their social goodness. The symbol X is used to indicate the set of all possible states, and the description of a state of the world contains three types of information.

The first of these three types consists of the set of those who are alive (that is, those who ever live) in the state under consideration. This set is also referred to as a population and, for simplicity, we assign natural numbers to its members. It is assumed that, for every possible population, there are at least three states of the world with that population. The set of all possible people is represented by the set of all natural numbers 1, 2, ... Whereas there is an infinity of possible people, the list of those that are actually alive in any state of the world is assumed to be finite. A population function N assigns a finite population $N(x)$ to each possible state x in X. If, for example, individuals 763, 3, and 82 ever live in state x, the value of this function for x is given by the set $N(x) = \{763, 3, 82\}$.

The second type of information contains, for each individual, her or his lifetime well-being as recorded by means of a utility function. Individual utility functions assign a level of lifetime well-being to each state in which the person in question is alive. Thus, an individual utility function is an indicator of lifetime well-being. A utility profile $U = (U_1, U_2, . . .)$ is a collection of individual utility functions, one function for each possible individual. For a state x in X and its associated population $N(x)$, we use $U(x)$ to indicate the lifetime utilities of those who ever live in x.

Finally, there is all the remaining information that does not pertain to individual well-being, which is called "non-welfare" information. This category (which could include information on desert or diversity, for instance), in turn, is composed of two components. First, there is non-welfare information that is relevant for society as a whole, and second there is non-welfare information that is concerned with individual non-welfare characteristics. Parallel to information on well-being, a non-welfare-information function specifies non-welfare information for society and for each person in the list of those alive. In analogy to a utility profile, a non-welfare profile is a collection $K = (K_0, K_1, K_2, . . .)$ composed of one non-welfare-information function for society, K_0, and one non-welfare-information function for each possible individual, K_1, K_2, ... For a given state of the world x in X with population $N(x)$, we write $K(x)$ for the values of the social and individual non-welfare information associated with x and the individuals who ever live in x.

The three types of information introduced above can be combined into a triple (N, U, K) of a population function, a utility profile, and a non-welfare profile. Such a triple is referred to as a profile. The purpose of a population principle is to rank states with respect to their social goodness. A multi-profile approach is adopted: a social goodness relation is to be established for any possible profile (N, U, K); see Blackorby, Bossert, and Donaldson (2005, Ch. 3). Following the convention used in social-choice theory, we use the term social-evaluation functional for a mechanism that assigns a social goodness relation $R_{(N,U,K)}$ to each possible profile (N, U, K). An unlimited-domain assumption is implicit in this definition because the process that assigns social goodness relations to profiles is assumed to be well-defined for any possible profile. This is merely a simplification of the standard definition according to which the unlimited-domain condition is explicitly imposed as a formal property and, in general, a social-evaluation functional may be defined on a smaller class of profiles. Because the unlimited domain is the only domain considered in this chapter, the formulation used here does not involve any loss of generality.

Using the social goodness relation $R_{(N,U,K)}$ associated with the profile (N, U, K), the statement $x \, R_{(N,U,K)} \, y$ means that, given the profile (N, U, K), the state x in X is at least as good as the state y in X according to the social-evaluation functional. The betterness relation corresponding to $R_{(N,U,K)}$ is represented by the symbol $P_{(N,U,K)}$ so that $x \, P_{(N,U,K)} \, y$ means that, under the profile (N, U, K), state x is better than state y. Equal goodness is denoted by $I_{(N,U,K)}$, that is, $x \, I_{(N,U,K)} \, y$ means that the states x and y are equally good for the profile (N, U, K). (Although the relation under consideration is a goodness relation and not a preference relation, the symbols P for betterness and I for equal goodness are chosen because they are ubiquitous in much of the literature, where they stand for "(strict) preference" and "indifference," respectively.)

All goodness relations considered in this chapter are orderings—that is, they are reflexive, complete, and transitive. Reflexivity means that any state is at least as good as itself so that we have $x \, R_{(N,U,K)} \, x$ for each possible state of the world x in X. Completeness ensures that any two distinct states x and y in X can be compared so that at least one of the statements $x \, R_{(N,U,K)} \, y$ or $y \, R_{(N,U,K)} \, x$ must be true whenever x and y differ. Finally, transitivity is the well-established requirement that if a state x in X is at least as good as a state y in X and y is, in turn, at least as good as a state z in X, then it must be the case that x is at least as good as z. In terms of the social goodness relation, transitivity is expressed by the requirement that, for any three states of the world x, y, and z in X, the two statements $x \, R_{(N,U,K)} \, y$ and $y \, R_{(N,U,K)} \, z$ together imply that the statement $x \, R_{(N,U,K)} \, z$ is also true.

In the following two sections, I show how (anonymous) welfarism can be obtained from some intuitive properties of the social-evaluation functional. For ease of exposition and accessibility, technical details are not provided here. A more detailed treatment—including formal proofs of the observations stated below—can be found in Blackorby, Bossert, and Donaldson (2005, Ch. 3).

4. Variable-Population Welfarism

A welfarist population principle ranks any two possible states of the world x and y exclusively on the basis of the identities of those in $N(x)$ and in $N(y)$ and their respective levels of lifetime well-being, that is, the values $U_i(x)$ for all individuals i in $N(x)$ and the values $U_j(y)$ for all persons j that are in $N(y)$. As a consequence, a welfarist principle does not depend on non-welfare information represented by the K-component of a profile. It may, however, depend on the identities of those who ever live in each of the two states to be compared.

In a fixed-population setting with multiple utility profiles and a single non-welfare profile, welfarist principles have been studied thoroughly—see, for instance, Guha (1972), d'Aspremont and Gevers (1977), Sen (1977, 1979), Hammond (1979), and Bossert and Weymark (2004). Fixed-population welfarism with a single utility profile and a single non-welfare profile is characterized by Blackorby, Donaldson, and Weymark (1990); see these earlier contributions for details. Although the focus in this chapter is on the variable-population case, most of the fundamentals of welfarist principles have their origins in the fixed-population environment. The remainder of this section illustrates how welfarist population principles result from some intuitive properties.

Pareto indifference is a same-people property that ensures unanimous individual equal goodness to be respected by the social goodness relation. Suppose two states x and y in X have the same population, that is, the sets $N(x)$ and $N(y)$ of those who ever live in x and in y are identical. Moreover, suppose that the lifetime well-being of each of these individuals is the same in both states. Pareto indifference demands that x and y be declared equally good by the social relation $R_{(N,U,K)}$ that corresponds to the profile (N, U, K).

Pareto Indifference: For any two states of the world x and y in X and for any profile (N, U, K), if $N(x) = N(y)$ and $U_i(x) = U_i(y)$ for all i in $N(x)$, then $x\, I_{(N,U,K)}\, y$.

Although the relations considered in this chapter are goodness relations rather than preference relations, the label Pareto indifference is used for this property because it has a long-standing tradition in the theory of social choice. This should not lead to any confusion.

Pareto indifference demands that non-welfare information, as represented by the K-components of a profile, can be disregarded whenever all members of an identical population consider two states of the world x and y equally good. In these cases, social equal-goodness must result, no matter what values the non-welfare-information functions assume. Goodin (1991) provides an appealing argument in favor of the Pareto-indifference property. Goodin's postulate says that, in a situation in which two states x and y have the same population and state x is declared to be socially better than state y, then it must be the case that x is better than y for at least one individual in the common population. This requirement implies Pareto indifference. To see that this is the case, suppose, by way of contradiction, that Pareto indifference is not satisfied. This means that there are two states x and y with a common population $N(x) = N(y)$ such that $U_i(x) = U_i(y)$ for all i in $N(x)$ but, at the same time, x and y are not equally good according to the social goodness relation $R_{(N,U,K)}$. Because social goodness is assumed to be complete, there are two possibilities: either x is better than y, or y is better than x. In either case, a contradiction to Goodin's condition is obtained because there is social betterness without a single instance of accompanying individual betterness. Goodin's requirement is very compelling and provides a forceful argument in favor of the Pareto-indifference property.

The second condition is an independence property that imposes restrictions on the social goodness relations associated with certain different profiles. It is a variable-population requirement that has its origins in Arrow's (1951, 1963) seminal contribution to social-choice theory with a fixed population. Binary independence of irrelevant alternatives demands that the social ranking of any two states x and y depends on the sets of those alive, their utilities and the non-welfare information in the two states under consideration only—the values of any information regarding states other than x and y must be disregarded. Theories that violate this requirement are discussed in, for example, in Arrhenius (2003, 2009).

Binary Independence of Irrelevant Alternatives: For any two states of the world x and y and for any two profiles (N, U, K) and (N', U', K'), if $(N(x), U(x), K(x)) = (N'(x), U'(x), K'(x))$ and $(N(y), U(y), K(y)) = (N'(y), U'(y), K'(y))$, then

$$x\, R_{(N,U,K)}\, y \quad \text{if and only if} \quad x\, R_{(N',U',K')}\, y.$$

Note that binary independence of irrelevant alternatives is a multi-profile requirement; in a single-profile environment, it is not needed to obtain welfarism.

Combined with Pareto indifference, binary independence of irrelevant alternatives has remarkably strong consequences. In the presence of the unlimited-domain assumption implicit in the definition of a social-evaluation functional, Pareto indifference and binary independence of irrelevant alternatives together are equivalent to welfarism, that is, the property that the relative goodness of any two states of the world x and y may only depend on the (possibly different) identities of those alive in x and in y, and on their levels of lifetime well-being achieved in x and in y. The non-welfare information represented by $K(x)$ and $K(y)$ is irrelevant. Moreover, populations, utilities and non-welfare information other than those associated with x and with y must be disregarded when establishing the relative social ranking of x and y.

To state the requisite result, we introduce a convenient way to explicitly keep track of the identities of those who ever live so that every member of a population $N(x)$ can be uniquely identified as the person who experiences a given level of lifetime well-being in $U(x)$. The identities of those who ever live can be determined by using an identities function Π that provides, for each state x in X, a list $\Pi(x)$ of the members of $N(x)$ in ascending order. For example, if $N(x)$ contains the individuals 2, 874, and 17, the corresponding identities list is given by $\Pi(x) = (2, 17, 874)$. The difference between $N(x)$ and $\Pi(x)$ is that the former is a set (which only expresses membership without any reference to an order in which these members appear), whereas $\Pi(x)$ is an ordered list. Because of the convention that the members of a population $N(x)$ are always listed in ascending order in $\Pi(x)$, Π does not represent an additional piece of information—once $N(x)$ is known, $\Pi(x)$ is determined unambiguously. The following result is the variable-population welfarism theorem, a proof of which can be found in Blackorby, Bossert, and Donaldson (2005, Ch. 3):

Theorem 1: A social-evaluation functional with an unlimited domain satisfies Pareto indifference and binary independence of irrelevant alternatives if and only if there exists an ordering R^* on the set of all pairs of identity lists and associated utility distributions such that, for any two states x and y and for any profile (N, U, K),

$$x\, R_{(N,U,K)}y \quad \textit{if and only if} \quad (\Pi(x),\ U(x))\, R^*(\Pi(y),\ U(y)).$$

The result of this theorem simplifies matters considerably when it comes to assessing the relative merits of possible states according to their moral goodness. It states that, in place of the possible very complex goodness relations associated with the possible profiles, a single relation defined on identities and utilities can be employed as long as the principle in question operates on an unlimited domain and satisfies Pareto indifference and binary independence of irrelevant alternatives. The theorem provides an argument in favor of welfarist population principles if the properties of Pareto indifference and binary independence of irrelevant alternatives are accepted. In that case, the relative goodness of any two states of the world x and y can only depend on the respective populations alive in them and on their lifetime well-beings achieved in these states. All other (non-welfare) information must be disregarded, and neither may any population or utility information associated with states other than x and y play any role when ranking x and y according to their social goodness for a given profile. Thus, the relation R^* that is defined for identity-utility pairs can be used to rank states of the world, and all other information contained in a profile is no longer required. Clearly, R^* must be an ordering because all the relations $R_{(N,U,K)}$ are orderings.

The identities function Π is employed in the statement of Theorem 1 rather than the population function N because knowledge of the identities of those who ever live in x and in y is required to avoid any ambiguities regarding the assignment of the utility values in $U(x)$ and in $U(y)$. Note that mere knowledge of $N(x)$ and $N(y)$ is not sufficient because these sets provide information on membership in the requisite populations only.

5. ANONYMOUS WELFARISM

Some of the welfarist population principles identified in the previous section do not treat people impartially. Because the identities of those who ever live may matter, it is possible that the well-being levels of some individuals receive a higher weight than those of others. For instance, the well-being of the members of a privileged class or profession may count more that the well-being of others, an ethically unattractive option. To ensure that this is not the case, this section adds an anonymity property to the conditions introduced earlier. Welfare anonymity demands that everyone's lifetime well-being matters just as much as anyone else's and, as a consequence, only the levels of lifetime well-being experienced in two states are relevant when ranking them; the identities of those who are alive do not influence the relative social goodness of the two states.

In the context of welfarism, an anonymous principle has the property that only the levels of well-being of those who ever live matter but it is irrelevant who they are. This is not a same-people property but, rather, a same-number condition: if the number of those who ever live is the same in two states x and y and each level of lifetime well-being in x is assigned to exactly one person in y, the two states are to be declared equally good for the profile under consideration. Those alive in x need not be the same individuals who ever live in y.

In order to provide a precise definition of the welfare-anonymity property employed here, the notion of a one-to-one reassignment of identities between two equal-sized populations is required. Suppose there are two states of the world x and y with equal-sized populations represented by $N(x)$ and $N(y)$. A one-to-one reassignment of the identities is a function ρ such that, for every i in the population $N(x)$, there is exactly one j in $N(y)$ such that $j = \rho(i)$.

For example, suppose that state x has the population $N(x) = \{3, 82, 763\}$ with utilities $U_3(x) = 5$, $U_{82}(x) = -2$, and $U_{763}(x) = 14$. In state y, we have $N(y) = \{2, 3, 54\}$ and the utilities $U_2(y) = 5$, $U_3(y) = -2$, and $U_{54}(y) = 14$. Using the one-to-one reassignment given by the function ρ with the values $\rho(3) = 2$, $\rho(82) = 3$, and $\rho(763) = 54$, it follows that

$$
\begin{aligned}
U_2(y) &= U_{\rho(3)}(y) = U_3(x) = 5, \\
U_3(y) &= U_{\rho(82)}(y) = U_{82}(x) = -2, \\
U_{54}(y) &= U_{\rho(763)}(y) = U_{763}(x) = 14.
\end{aligned}
$$

Welfare anonymity demands x and y to be equally good according to the social goodness relation that corresponds to the profile (N, U, K). The example generalizes so that the following impartiality condition results.

Welfare Anonymity: For any two states of the world x and y and for any profile (N, U, K) such that the number of those who ever live in x is equal to the number of those who ever live in y, if there is a one-to-one reassignment ρ of identities between $N(x)$ and $N(y)$ such that $U_i(x) = U_{\rho(i)}(y)$ for all individuals i in $N(x)$, then $x\, I_{(N,U,K)}\, y$.

If welfare anonymity is added to the conditions of Theorem 1, it follows that any two states of the world x and y can be ranked for any profile (N, U, K) by means of the utilities in $U(x)$ and in $U(y)$ alone and, in addition to the non-welfare-information values $K(x)$ and $K(y)$, the identities of those in $N(x)$ and in $N(y)$ become irrelevant. Thus, for any possible profile (N, U, K), the social goodness relation ranks any two states x and y in X exclusively on the basis of the two utility distributions $U(x)$ and $U(y)$. A goodness relation R (with associated betterness relation P and equal-goodness relation I) defined on utility distributions of variable size is employed for this purpose. As is the case for the relation R^* identified in the previous theorem, the relation R on the set of utility distributions is an ordering because the relations generated by the social-evaluation functional are orderings. Moreover, R is anonymous as a result of the welfare-anonymity axiom imposed on the social-evaluation functional. This implies that if a distribution u that involves the utilities of n people is considered, there is no loss of generality in assuming that the labels $1, \ldots, n$ are assigned to the n people who ever live. Therefore, an n-person utility distribution is expressed as $u = (u_1, \ldots, u_n)$. As a property of an ordering R defined for utility distributions of variable sizes, anonymity is defined as follows:

> *Anonymity*: For any two utility distributions $u = (u_1, \ldots, u_n)$ and $v = (v_1, \ldots, v_n)$ of the same population size n, if there is a one-to-one reassignment ρ of identities between $\{1, \ldots, n\}$ and $\{1, \ldots, n\}$ such that $v_i = u_{\rho(i)}$ for all individuals i in $\{1, \ldots, n\}$, then $u \, I \, v$.

The version of the variable-population anonymous-welfarism theorem employed in this chapter is stated as follows. A proof and a detailed discussion can be found in Blackorby, Bossert, and Donaldson (2005, Ch. 3):

> *Theorem 2*: A social-evaluation functional with an unlimited domain satisfies Pareto indifference, binary independence of irrelevant alternatives, and welfare anonymity if and only if there exists an anonymous ordering R on the set of all possible utility distributions such that, for any two states x and y and for any profile (N, U, K),
>
> $$x \, R_{(N,U,K)} y \text{ if and only if } U(x) R \, U(y).$$

The anonymous social goodness relation R defined for utility distributions for variable population size is employed in the remainder of this chapter. Although the term is also used for a social-evaluation functional, it should not create any confusion to refer to the ordering R as a population principle. The following two sections introduce further properties of the social goodness ordering R (in addition to the anonymity requirement) to obtain a specific class of critical-level population principles.

6.   SAME-PEOPLE PROPERTIES

Using the class of anonymous welfarist population principles identified in the previous section as a starting point, I now proceed to a characterization of an important subclass. This section introduces two same-people properties, followed by two variable-population conditions in the following section.

The first same-people requirement is strong Pareto. It requires that, in a same-people setting, unanimity be respected in the sense that if everyone is at least as well-off in one state of the world than in another with at least one instance of betterness, the former state is better than the latter.

> *Strong Pareto*: For any two utility distributions $u = (u_1, \ldots, u_n)$ and $v = (v_1, \ldots, v_n)$ with the same population $\{1, \ldots, n\}$, if $u_i \geq v_i$ for all i in $\{1, \ldots, n\}$ with at least one strict inequality, then $u \, P \, v$.

The second same-people property is a continuity requirement. It demands that "small" changes in a utility distribution cannot lead to "large" changes in the goodness relation. In the definition, the notion of a neighborhood is employed. For any population size n, for any utility distribution $u = (u_1, \ldots, u_n)$ and for any positive number ε, the ε-neighborhood of u consists of all utility distributions with n individuals that have a distance from u of less than ε. For instance, consider a two-person example. The ε-neighborhood of a utility distribution $u = (u_1, u_2)$ for $\varepsilon = 1/4$ is given by all distributions that are closer to the distribution u than the points on the circle with center u and radius 1/4. (The same geometric intuition applies to other population sizes.) The notion of a neighborhood allows us to express what it means to be "close" to a distribution: as ε becomes smaller and smaller, the points in the ε-neighborhood of u get closer and closer to u itself. Continuity requires that if a distribution u is better than a distribution v, then all distributions in a neighborhood of u are also better than v, provided that this neighborhood is chosen sufficiently small. A parallel condition applies to the case in which u is worse than v.

> *Continuity*: For any two utility distributions $u = (u_1, \ldots, u_n)$ and $v = (v_1, \ldots, v_n)$ with the same population $\{1, \ldots, n\}$,
> (a) if $u\,P\,v$, then there is a (sufficiently small) positive number ε such that $w\,P\,v$ for all utility distributions w in the ε-neighborhood of u;
> (b) if $v\,P\,u$, then there is a (sufficiently small) positive number ε such that $v\,P\,w$ for all utility distributions w in the ε-neighborhood of u.

Although strong Pareto and continuity are plausible and intuitively appealing properties that are satisfied by most population principles, not all principles possess them. For instance, strong Pareto is violated by the maximin rule because of its sole dependence on the worst-off individual, and lexical principles (such as the lexical extension of maximin) fail to be continuous. Moreover, continuity is not compatible with views that appeal to superiority in value; see Arrhenius (2005) and Arrhenius and Rabinowicz (2015) for discussions.

7. Variable-Population Properties

A critical level for a utility distribution $u = (u_1, \ldots, u_n)$ involving n individuals is a utility level c such that if a person who experiences that level of well-being c is added to the original distribution u, the resulting augmented distribution is as good as the original. If a critical level exists for a utility distribution u with a population of n people, any state with that distribution can be ranked against a state of the world with an added person. Provided that the levels of well-being of the original population are unchanged by the population augmentation, the state with the added person is as good as the original if the utility of the new person is at the critical level. Because the population principles considered here are transitive and satisfy the strong Pareto condition, adding a person leads to a better (worse) state of the world if her or his lifetime well-being is above (below) the requisite critical level. Critical levels need not exist—for instance, a principle that always declares a larger population superior to a smaller population independent of the individuals' lifetime utilities does not have a critical level for any utility distribution. A mild condition that demands the existence of some minimal notion of a trade-off between population size and quality of life is the requirement that there be at least one critical level.

> *Existence of At Least One Critical Level*: There exist a population size $\tilde{n}$, a utility distribution $\tilde{u} = (\tilde{u}_1, \ldots, \tilde{u}_{\tilde{n}})$, and a utility level c such that $(\tilde{u}, c) \, I \, \tilde{u}$.

This property merely requires a critical level to exist for one utility distribution. Critical levels need not exist for other distributions and if they do exist, they may vary from one distribution to another.

The second property introduced in this section is an independence condition. It demands that the social goodness relation depends on affected individuals only. To illustrate the property, consider the following example. Suppose a discovery reveals a previously unknown civilization that existed in complete isolation and became extinct several millennia ago. This ancient society had r members who ever lived and with the lifetime well-being levels given by the utility distribution $w = (w_1, \ldots, w_r)$. The utilities of all other people who ever live are $u = (u_1, \ldots, u_n)$ in one state of the world and $v = (v_1, \ldots, v_m)$ in the other. Without the discovery of the ancient civilization, the task of the population principle is the comparison of the distributions u and v. But once the discovery is made, the requisite distributions are (u, w) and (v, w)—now the utility levels of the long-dead individuals are included. It is very compelling to demand that the relative ranking of (u, w) and (v, w) ought to be the same as that of u and v; it seems difficult to make a case that the discovery of the existence of a group of long-dead individuals should affect how the population principle assesses the relative merits of the requisite states. Note that, in an anonymous setting, the independence requirement cannot be restricted to specific groups—if the long-dead cannot matter, then no unaffected group can matter. The following existence-independence condition captures this intuition:

> *Existence Independence*: For any three population sizes n, m, and, r and for any three utility distributions $u = (u_1, \ldots, u_n)$, $v = (v_1, \ldots, v_m)$, and $w = (w_1, \ldots, w_r)$,
>
> $(u, w) R (v, w)$ *if and only if* $u \, R \, v$.

When combined with the properties introduced earlier, existence independence has powerful implications. First of all, it plays an instrumental role in obtaining the additive structure characteristic of the critical-level generalized-utilitarian principles introduced in the following section. In addition, together with existence of at least one critical level, it implies that critical levels exist for all possible utility distributions (of any possible population size) and, moreover, these critical levels must be identical for all distributions. To see that this is the case, suppose that the population principle satisfies existence of at least one critical level and existence independence. Thus, by definition, there exist a population size $\bar{n}$, a utility distribution $\bar{u} = (\bar{u}_1, \ldots, \bar{u}_{\bar{n}})$, and a utility level c such that

$$(\bar{u}, c)I\bar{u}. \tag{1}$$

Now consider any possible population size n (which can be different from $\bar{n}$) and any possible utility distribution $u = (u_1, \ldots, u_n)$ with n people alive. By existence independence, it follows that

$$(u,c)R \; u \; \textit{if and only if} \; (u,\bar{u},c)R(u,\bar{u}).$$

This is the case because, in the comparison between $(u, \bar{u}, c)$ and $(u, \bar{u})$, the individuals represented by the utility distribution $\bar{u}$ are unaffected and, thus, existence independence applies. Analogously,

$$(u,\bar{u},c) \; R \; (u,\bar{u}) \; \text{if and only if} \; (\bar{u},c)R\bar{u}.$$

Again, this equivalence follows because the individuals represented by the utility distribution u are unaffected. Combining the two equivalences just obtained, it follows that

$$(u,c)R \; u \; \text{if and only if} \; (\bar{u},c)R\bar{u}.$$

Now (1) implies $(u, c) \; I \; u$ so that, by definition, the utility level c is a critical level not only for the distribution $\bar{u}$ but for any possible distribution u, which is the claim that was to be established.

8. CRITICAL-LEVEL GENERALIZED UTILITARIANISM

Many of the commonly discussed population principles are extensions of fixed-population utilitarianism and its generalized counterpart to a variable-population setting. For a population with n members, fixed-population utilitarianism uses the sums of the individual levels of well-being to rank any two distributions $u = (u_1, \ldots, u_n)$ and $v = (v_1, \ldots, v_n)$ of the same size n. That is, according to fixed-population utilitarianism,

$$u \; R \; v \; \textit{if and only if} \; u_1 + \ldots + u_n \geq v_1 + \ldots + v_n$$

for any population size n and for any two utility distributions $u = (u_1, \ldots, u_n)$ and $v = (v_1, \ldots, v_n)$ with n people alive in each.

Fixed-population generalized utilitarianism uses transformed utilities as explained below and, according to this criterion,

$$u \, R \, v \text{ if and only if } g(u_1) + \ldots + g(u_n) \geq g(v_1) + \ldots + g(v_n)$$

for any two distributions u and v with common population size n. The transformation g is increasing and continuous, and it satisfies the equality $g(0) = 0$. Increasingness of g ensures that strong Pareto is satisfied and the transformation is continuous so that the goodness relation is continuous as well. The restriction $g(0) = 0$ does not involve any loss of generality; it merely ensures that the utility level representing a neutral life is not affected by applying the transformation. Utilitarianism is obtained if g is chosen to be the identity transformation, that is, the transformation that assigns $g(t) = t$ to all utility levels t. If a (strictly) concave transformation g is employed, the resulting fixed-population principle exhibits (strict) inequality aversion in well-being.

There are different possibilities to extend generalized utilitarianism to the variable-population framework. Two well-known classes of such principles are total (or classical) generalized utilitarianism and average generalized utilitarianism. According to classical generalized utilitarianism, the social goodness relation R is such that, for any two population sizes n and m and for any two utility distributions $u = (u_1, \ldots, u_n)$ with n people alive and $v = (v_1, \ldots, v_m)$ with a population size of m,

$$u \, R \, v \text{ if and only if } g(u_1) + \ldots + g(u_n) \geq g(v_1) + \ldots + g(v_m).$$

Average generalized utilitarianism uses average utilities and, therefore,

$$\frac{1}{n} [g(u_1) + \ldots + g(u_n)] >= \frac{1}{m} [g(v_1) + \ldots + g(v_m)]$$

for any two n and m and any two $u = (u_1, \ldots, u_n)$ and $v = (v_1, \ldots, v_m)$. Clearly, classical generalized utilitarianism and average generalized utilitarianism produce the same fixed-population rankings: if the population size is the same (that is, $n = m$ is true), both sides of the inequality that defines average generalized utilitarianism can be multiplied by this common population size, and the classical criterion emerges. Of course, if n and m are not the same, the two principles may differ considerably in the way they rank possible states of the world.

A serious shortcoming of the average principle is that its critical levels are given by average transformed utility. This means that if we consider a population in which everyone is extremely miserable (well below neutrality), average generalized utilitarianism recommends the addition of a person with a slightly higher lifetime well-being than this very low transformed average, an ethically unappealing property. Classical generalized utilitarianism has fixed critical levels that are equal to the level of neutrality: adding a person with a lifetime well-being of zero to an existing population (other things being equal) does not change total transformed utility because the contribution of the new person is $g(0) = 0$.

There are principles other than classical generalized utilitarianism that employ fixed critical levels. In particular, according to critical-level generalized utilitarianism, a fixed critical level is employed but this critical level can assume values other than zero. The resulting class of critical-level generalized-utilitarian principles can be expressed by means of a critical-level parameter α that may be zero, positive, or negative. Thus, a social goodness relation R is a critical-level generalized-utilitarian principle if there exists a utility level α such that, for any two population sizes n and m and for any two utility distributions $u = (u_1, \ldots, u_n)$ and $v = (v_1, \ldots, v_m)$,

$$u \; R \; v \text{ if and only if } g(u_1) - g(\alpha) + \ldots + g(u_n) - g(\alpha) \geq g(v_1) - g(\alpha) + \ldots + g(v_m) - g(\alpha).$$

Critical-level generalized utilitarianism is discussed and analyzed in Blackorby and Donaldson (1984) and in Blackorby, Bossert, and Donaldson (2005). Fixed critical levels also appear in Parfit (1976, 1982, 1984). There are other utilitarianism-inspired population principles in the literature that are not discussed in detail here. They include, for instance, number-dampened utilitarianism (Ng, 1986), along with some of its restricted variants (Arrhenius, 2000; Hurka, 2000), as well as principles that employ number-sensitive critical levels (Bossert, Blackorby, and Donaldson, 2005 Ch. 5). See also Hurka (1983), Sider (1991), and Carlson (1998).

The properties introduced in the previous two sections characterize the class of critical-level generalized-utilitarian principles. The following result is proven in Blackorby, Bossert, and Donaldson (2005, Ch. 6):

> *Theorem 3*: An anonymous population principle R satisfies strong Pareto, continuity, existence of at least one critical level, and existence independence if and only if R is a critical-level generalized-utilitarian principle.

The special case of classical generalized utilitarianism is obtained if the critical level is equal to $\alpha = 0$. Clearly, the choice of the critical-level parameter is of crucial importance for the properties of the resulting population principle. Two possible criteria that may be consulted when making this selection are discussed in the following two sections.

9. THE REPUGNANT CONCLUSION

Parfit (1976, 1982, 1984) points out that classical utilitarianism has a property that he calls the Repugnant Conclusion. A population principle leads to this conclusion if, for any state x in which everyone who is alive has a very high level of lifetime well-being, there is another state y with a larger population the members of which all have lives that are barely worth living. If a principle implies the Repugnant Conclusion, it may declare it better to create a situation where everyone has a very low positive level of well-being rather than having a smaller population in which everyone alive has a very high standard of living. The problem with such a goodness ranking is that all those who ever live in the larger population can have lives that are barely worth living. Many authors consider the avoidance of the Repugnant Conclusion an essential property of a population principle; Parfit (1976, 1982, 1984) and Heyd (1992) are two of them. Others, among them Tännsjö (2002), think that the Repugnant Conclusion is not all that repugnant. The Repugnant Conclusion can be formalized as follows:

> *Repugnant Conclusion*: For any population size n, for any positive utility level γ and for any utility level ε such that $0 < \varepsilon < \gamma$, there exists a population size $m > n$ such that $\underbrace{(\varepsilon,...,\varepsilon)}_{m \text{ times}} P \underbrace{(\gamma,...,\gamma)}_{n \text{ times}}$

The reason why classical utilitarianism implies the Repugnant Conclusion is that its critical level is equal to the level of lifetime well-being that represents a neutral life. Combined with the additive structure of utilitarian principles, this means that adding someone with a lifetime well-being above neutrality to a utility-unaffected population is always considered a good thing—no matter how close to neutrality the utility of the added person may be. Thus, adding more and more people above (but arbitrarily close to) neutrality eventually leads to a state with more total utility than any given original state in which everyone alive has an arbitrarily high level of well-being, and the Repugnant Conclusion results. As illustrated below, classical generalized utilitarianism does not fare any better.

In general, all critical-level generalized-utilitarian principles with a non-positive critical level imply the repugnant conclusion. To see that this is the case, suppose that R is a critical-level generalized-utilitarian principle with a critical-level parameter $\alpha \leq 0$. Consider any population size n, any positive utility level γ, and any utility level ε such that $0 < \varepsilon < \gamma$. Choose any population size m that satisfies the inequality

$$m > \frac{n\,[g(\gamma) - g(\alpha)]}{g(\varepsilon) - g(\alpha)}. \tag{2}$$

Because $\alpha \leq 0$, $\gamma > 0$, and $\varepsilon > 0$, the increasingness of g implies that the two differences on the right side of this inequality are positive. Moreover, because $\gamma > \varepsilon$, it follows that $g(\gamma) - g(\alpha) > g(\varepsilon) - g(\alpha)$ and, therefore,

$$\frac{g(\gamma) - g(\alpha)}{g(\varepsilon) - g(\alpha)} > 1.$$

Using this inequality in (2), it follows that $m > n$. Multiplying both sides of (2) by the positive difference $g(\varepsilon) - g(\alpha)$ implies

$$m\,[g(\varepsilon) - g(\alpha)] > n\,[g(\gamma) - g(\alpha)].$$

According to the definition of critical-level generalized-utilitarianism with the critical level α, this inequality means that the m-people distribution in which everyone alive has a utility level of ε is better than the n-person distribution in which all utility levels are equal to γ. Thus, the Repugnant Conclusion is implied.

Conversely, all critical-level generalized-utilitarian principles with a positive critical-level parameter $\alpha > 0$ avoid the Repugnant Conclusion. To establish this claim, suppose that R is a critical-level generalized-utilitarian principle with $\alpha > 0$. Define $n = 1$, $\gamma = 2\alpha$, and $\varepsilon = \alpha/2$. Suppose, by way of contradiction, that the Repugnant Conclusion is implied. Thus, there exists a population size $m > 1 = n$ such that a state of the world in which m people are alive with utility $\varepsilon = \alpha/2$ is better than a state with one person alive with a lifetime utility of $\gamma = 2\alpha$. By definition of the critical-level generalized-utilitarian principles, this means that

$$m\,[g(\alpha/2) - g(\alpha)] > [g(2\alpha) - g(\alpha)].$$

But this is a contradiction because the left side of the inequality is negative and the right side is positive as a consequence of the increasingness of g. Therefore, the Repugnant Conclusion is avoided by any critical-level generalized-utilitarian principle with a positive critical-level parameter.

10. The Sadistic Conclusion

A second criterion that may influence the choice of the critical-level parameter is the Sadistic Conclusion, introduced by Arrhenius (2000). A principle implies the Sadistic Conclusion if it may be better to add people with negative lifetime well-being to a given population than adding (not necessarily the same number of) individuals whose utilities are all positive to the same original population. The Sadistic Conclusion is defined as follows:

Sadistic Conclusion: There exist population sizes n, m, and r, and utility distributions $u = (u_1, \ldots, u_n)$, $v = (v_1, \ldots, v_m)$, and $w = (w_1, \ldots, w_r)$ such that $v_j < 0$ for all j in $\{1, \ldots, m\}$, $w_k > 0$ for all k in $\{1, \ldots, r\}$, and $(u, v)\,P\,(u, w)$.

Arrhenius (2000) argues that the Sadistic Conclusion should be avoided. Among the critical-level generalized-utilitarian principles, the only ones that do so are the classical generalized-utilitarian principles. To see that classical generalized utilitarianism (that is, critical-level generalized utilitarianism with a critical-level parameter of $\alpha = 0$) avoids the Sadistic Conclusion, suppose that three distributions $u = (u_1, \ldots, u_n)$, $v = (v_1, \ldots, v_m)$, and $w = (w_1, \ldots, w_r)$ are such that $v_j < 0$ for all j in $\{1, \ldots, m\}$ and $w_k > 0$ for all k in

$\{1, \ldots, r\}$. Because g is an increasing transformation such that $g(0) = 0$ and, moreover, all components of v are negative and all components of w are positive, it follows that $g(v_j) < 0$ for all j in $\{1, \ldots, m\}$ and $g(w_k) > 0$ for all k in $\{1, \ldots, m\}$. The sum of negative numbers is negative and the sum of positive numbers is positive. Therefore,

$$g(w_1) + \ldots + g(w_r) > 0 > g(v_1) + \ldots + g(v_m)$$

and hence

$$g(w_1) + \ldots + g(w_r) > g(v_1) + \ldots + g(v_m).$$

Adding the sum of the transformed utilities in u to both sides of this inequality, it follows that

$$g(u_1) + \ldots + g(u_n) + g(w_1) + \ldots + g(w_r) > g(u_1) + \ldots + g(u_n) + g(v_1) + \ldots + g(v_m).$$

By definition of classical generalized utilitarianism, this inequality is equivalent to

$$(u, w) P(u, v)$$

and, therefore, it cannot be the case that (u, v) is better than (u, w) so that the Sadistic Conclusion is avoided for critical-level generalized utilitarianism with a critical level of zero.

The Sadistic Conclusion is implied for all critical-level generalized-utilitarian principles whose critical-level parameters are different from zero. Consider first critical-level generalized utilitarianism with a parameter value of $\alpha > 0$. Let γ and δ be two utility levels such that

$$\delta < 0 < \gamma < \alpha.$$

Because $g(0) = 0$ and g is increasing, these inequalities imply that

$$g(\delta) - g(\alpha) < g(\gamma) - g(\alpha) < 0$$

and

$$\frac{g(\delta) - g(\alpha)}{g(\gamma) - g(\alpha)} > 0.$$

Now choose r sufficiently large so that

$$r > \frac{g(\delta) - g(\alpha)}{g(\gamma) - g(\alpha)}. \tag{3}$$

Multiplying both sides of this inequality by the negative number $g(\gamma) - g(\alpha)$ reverses the inequality and it follows that

$$r\,[g(\gamma) - g(\alpha)] < g(\delta) - g(\alpha). \tag{4}$$

Let $n = m = 1$, $u = (\alpha)$, $v = (\delta)$, and

$$w = \underbrace{(\gamma, \ldots, \gamma)}_{r\ times}$$

where r satisfies the inequality in (3). Thus, the single person alive in u has a utility of α, the one person alive in v has utility $\delta < 0$, and all r people alive in w have a lifetime well-being of $\gamma > 0$. By definition, it follows that

$$
\begin{aligned}
{[g(u_1) - g(\alpha)] + \ldots + [g(u_n) - g(\alpha)]} &= n[g(\alpha) - g(\alpha)] = 0, \\
{[g(v_1) - g(\alpha)] + \ldots + [g(v_m) - g(\alpha)]} &= m\,[g(\delta) - g(\alpha)] = g(\delta) - g(\alpha), \\
{[g(w_1) - g(\alpha)] + \ldots + [g(w_r) - g(\alpha)]} &= r\,[g(\gamma) - g(\alpha)].
\end{aligned}
$$

Thus, according to critical-level generalized utilitarianism, it follows that $(u, v)\,P\,(u, w)$ is true if and only if

$$0 + g(\delta) - g(\alpha) > 0 + r\,[g(\gamma) - g(\alpha)]$$

which is true because the inequality in (4) is satisfied. Thus, the Sadistic Conclusion is implied.

The case in which α is negative is analogous: suppose now that R is critical-level generalized-utilitarian with a critical level $\alpha < 0$. Let γ and δ be two utility levels such that

$$\alpha < \delta < 0 < \gamma.$$

Because $g(0) = 0$ and g is increasing, these inequalities imply that

$$g(\gamma) - g(\alpha) > g(\delta) - g(\alpha) > 0$$

and

$$\frac{g(\gamma) - g(\alpha)}{g(\delta) - g(\alpha)} > 0.$$

Choose m sufficiently large so that

$$m > \frac{g(\gamma) - g(\alpha)}{g(\delta) - g(\alpha)}. \tag{5}$$

Multiplying both sides of this inequality by the positive number $g(\delta) - g(\alpha)$, it follows that

$$m[g(\delta) - g(\alpha)] > g(\gamma) - g(\alpha). \tag{6}$$

Let $n = r = 1, u = (\alpha)$,

$$v = \underbrace{(\delta, \ldots, \delta)}_{m \text{ times}}$$

where m satisfies the inequality in (5), and $w = (\gamma)$. Thus, the single person alive in u has a utility of α, all m people alive in v have a lifetime well-being of $\delta < 0$, and the one person alive in w has utility $\gamma > 0$. By definition, it follows that

$$\begin{aligned}
[g(u_1) - g(\alpha)] + \ldots + [g(u_n) - g(\alpha)] &= n[g(\alpha) - g(\alpha)] = 0, \\
[g(v_1) - g(\alpha)] + \ldots + [g(v_m) - g(\alpha)] &= m[g(\delta) - g(\alpha)], \\
[g(w_1) - g(\alpha)] + \ldots + [g(w_r) - g(\alpha)] &= r[g(\gamma) - g(\alpha)] = g(\gamma) - g(\alpha).
\end{aligned}$$

Thus, according to critical-level generalized utilitarianism, it follows that $(u, v)\, P\, (u, w)$ is true if and only if

$$0 + m[g(\delta) - g(\alpha)] > 0 + g(\gamma) - g(\alpha)$$

which is true because the inequality in (6) is satisfied. Thus, the Sadistic Conclusion is implied for negative values of α as well.

11. CONCLUDING REMARKS

An immediate consequence of the observations in the previous two sections is that no critical-level generalized-utilitarian principle can avoid both the Repugnant Conclusion and the Sadistic Conclusion. Essentially, as shown in Blackorby, Bossert, and Donaldson (2005), principles that avoid the Repugnant Conclusion and the Sadistic Conclusion must violate existence independence and, therefore, such principles cannot have the additively separable structure possessed by the critical-level principles discussed in this chapter. The two criteria agree to the extent that both rule out negative critical levels but, beyond that, they are in conflict. Avoidance of the repugnant conclusion requires the critical-level parameter to be positive, whereas the sadistic conclusion can only be prevented if the critical level α is equal to zero, the level of neutrality. There are anonymous welfarist principles that avoid both conclusions, but they cannot be members of the critical-level generalized-utilitarian class. This means that they must violate at least one of the conditions listed in Theorem 3. I consider violations of these fundamental conditions to be difficult to justify and, therefore, my position is that either the Repugnant Conclusion or the Sadistic Conclusion has to be accepted. I am in Parfit's (1976, 1982, 1984) camp in that I consider the Repugnant Conclusion rather unappealing, and I therefore endorse critical-level generalized utilitarianism with a positive critical-level parameter.

A reason why I do not find the Sadistic Conclusion as disturbing as some other authors do is that, from the viewpoint of a critical-level utilitarian who supports the use of a positive critical level, the competing additions of individuals to a given population are not very attractive to begin with. As can be seen from the example used for a positive critical level in the previous section, both population augmentations under consideration are undesirable from the viewpoint of someone who advocates a critical level above neutrality. This is not a mere coincidence—any example of that nature is bound to have this feature. Suppose a social planner has the choice of three options: (1) add people whose lifetime well-being will be below neutrality; (2) add a population in which everyone's utility is above neutrality but below the critical level; (3) leave the existing population unchanged—that is, reject both of the proposed population augmentations. If a critical-level generalized-utilitarian principle with a positive critical level is employed, the planner's choice will be option (3) so that both undesirable states are avoided. Thus, on practical grounds, a positive critical level will prevent both of two ethically unappealing situations—an observation that might lessen the negative impact of the Sadistic Conclusion.

The above-described conflict between avoidance of the repugnant conclusion and avoidance of the Sadistic Conclusion is but an example of the many challenges that emerge in population ethics. These challenges represent some of the most important issues that remain to be confronted in future work.

ACKNOWLEDGMENTS

This chapter is based on joint work with my dear friends Charles Blackorby and David Donaldson. Everything I know about population ethics I learned from Charles and

David during the many years of our extremely enjoyable collaboration. I dedicate this article to them as a small token of my deep appreciation and gratitude. I thank Gustaf Arrhenius, Geir Asheim, David Donaldson, and Julia Mosquera for their thoughtful comments and suggestions.

REFERENCES

Arrhenius, Gustaf. 2000. "An Impossibility Theorem for Welfarist Axiologies." *Economics and Philosophy* 16: 247–266.

Arrhenius, Gustaf. 2003. "The Person-Affecting Restriction, Comparativism, and the Moral Status of Potential People." *Ethical Perspectives* 3–4: 185–195.

Arrhenius, Gustaf. 2005. "Superiority in Value." *Philosophical Studies* 123: 97–114.

Arrhenius, Gustaf. 2009. "Can the Person Affecting Restriction Solve the Problems in Population Ethics?" In *Harming Future Persons: Ethics, Genetics and the Non-Identity Problem*, edited by Melinda Roberts and David Wasserman, 291–316. New York: Springer.

Arrhenius, Gustaf and Wlodek Rabinowicz. 2015. "Value Superiority." In *The Oxford Handbook of Value Theory*, edited by Iwao Hirose and Jonas Olson, 225–248. Oxford: Oxford University Press.

Arrow, Kenneth. 1951, 2nd ed. 1963. Social Choice and Individual Values. New York: Wiley.

Blackorby, Charles, Walter Bossert, and David Donaldson. 2005. *Population Issues in Social Choice Theory, Welfare Economics, and Ethics*. New York: Cambridge University Press.

Blackorby, Charles and David Donaldson. 1984. "Social Criteria for Evaluating Population Change." *Journal of Public Economics* 25: 13–33.

Blackorby, Charles, David Donaldson, and John A. Weymark. 1990. "A Welfarist Proof of Arrow's Theorem." *Recherches Economiques de Louvain* 56: 259–286.

Bossert, Walter and John A. Weymark. 2004. "Utility in Social Choice." In *Handbook of Utility Theory*, vol. 2: *Extensions*, edited by Salvador. Barberà, Peter Hammond, and Christian Seidl, 1099–1177. Dordrecht: Kluwer.

Broome, John. 2004. *Weighing Lives*. Oxford: Oxford University Press.

Carlson, Erik. 1998. "Mere Addition and Two Trilemmas of Population Ethics." *Economics and Philosophy* 14: 283–306.

d'Aspremont, Claude and Louis Gevers. 1977. "Equity and the Informational Basis of Collective Choice." *Review of Economic Studies* 44: 199–209.

Goodin, Robert. 1991. "Utility and the Good." In *A Companion to Ethics*, edited by P. Singer, 241–248. Oxford: Basil Blackwell.

Griffin, James. 1986. *Well-Being: Its Meaning, Measurement, and Moral Importance*. Oxford: Clarendon.

Guha, Ashok. 1972. "Neutrality, Monotonicity, and the Right of Veto." *Econometrica* 40: 821–826.

Hammond, Peter. 1979. "Equity in Two Person Situations: Some Consequences." *Econometrica* 47: 1127–1135.

Heyd, David. 1992. *Genethics: Moral Issues in the Creation of People*. Berkeley and Los Angeles: University of California Press.

Hurka, Thomas. 1983. "Value and Population Size." *Ethics* 93: 496–507.

Hurka, Thomas. 2000. "Comment on 'Population Principles with Number-Dependent Critical Levels.'" Unpublished manuscript, University of Calgary, Department of Philosophy.

Ng, Yew-Kwang. 1986. "Social Criteria for Evaluating Population Change: An Alternative to the Blackorby-Donaldson Criterion." *Journal of Public Economics* 29: 375–381.

Parfit, Derek. 1976. "On Doing the Best for Our Children." In *Ethics and Population*, edited by Michael D. Bayles, 100–102. Cambridge: Schenkman.

Parfit, Derek. 1982. "Future Generations, Further Problems." *Philosophy and Public Affairs* 11: 113–172.

Parfit, Derek. 1984. *Reasons and Persons*. Oxford: Oxford University Press.

Sen, Amartya. 1977. "On Weights and Measures: Informational Constraints in Social Welfare Analysis." *Econometrica* 45: 1539–1572.

Sen, Amartya. 1979. "Personal Utilities and Public Judgements: Or What's Wrong with Welfare Economics?" *Economic Journal* 89: 537–558.

Sider, Theodore. 1991. "Might Theory X Be a Theory of Diminishing Marginal Value?" *Analysis* 51: 265–271.

Sumner, L.W. 1999. *Welfare, Happiness, and Ethics*. Oxford: Clarendon.

Tännsjö, Torbjörn. 2002. "Why We Ought to Accept the Repugnant Conclusion." *Utilitas* 14: 339–359.

CHAPTER 4

··

RANK-DISCOUNTING AS A RESOLUTION TO A DILEMMA IN POPULATION ETHICS

··

GEIR B. ASHEIM AND STÉPHANE ZUBER

1. INTRODUCTION

ONE prominent population ethics view is that there exists a critical level of lifetime well-being which, if experienced by an added individual without changing the well-being levels of the existing population, leads to an alternative which is as good as the original. Combined with a prioritarian criterion where, for fixed population size, the undiscounted sum of the individuals' transformed utilities is maximized, this leads to critical-level prioritarianism (also known in the economics literature as critical-level generalized utilitarianism; Blackorby and Donaldson 1984; Broome 2004; Blackorby, Bossert, and Donaldson 2005).

The standard objection to critical-level generalized utilitarianism is that

- if we set the critical level at or below the individually neutral well-being level (above which life is worth living, and below which it is not), then we get the Repugnant Conclusion (Parfit 1976; 1982; 1984) where, for any population with excellent lives, there is a population with lives barely worth living that is better, provided that the latter includes sufficiently many people,
- if we set the critical level strictly above the individually neutral well-being level, then we get the Very Sadistic Conclusion (Arrhenius 2000a; forthcoming) where, for any population with terrible lives not worth living, there is a population with lives worth living that is worse, provided that the latter includes sufficiently many people.

There are other criteria that avoid the Repugnant and Very Sadistic Conclusions, but they all have their own serious shortcomings. According to average utilitarianism, adding a life not worth living to a population may be socially desirable. According to critical-level leximin, as defined by Blackorby, Bossert, and Donaldson (1996), any population with n persons living excellent lives is worse than a population with $n+1$ persons whose well-being is barely above a critical level. According to leximin, as suggested by Arrhenius (forthcoming, Section 6.8), any population is worse than a population consisting of one individual, provided that the worst-off individual of the former has lower well-being than the single individual of the latter.

Even in a fixed population framework, where there is no difference between the various prioritarian criteria discussed above, and also no difference between the two kinds of leximin criteria, both the prioritarian and the egalitarian (viz. leximin) approaches have shortcomings if there are many present and future people. If one considers a completely egalitarian well-being stream in an intergenerational setting with many future generations, and seeks to evaluate whether the present generation should make a sacrifice leading to a uniform benefit to future generations, then prioritarian and leximin approaches reach opposite and extreme conclusions: according to prioritarianism, the sacrifice should always be made provided that there are sufficiently many future generations, while according to leximin, it should never be made. These have been labeled by Fleurbaey and Tungodden (2010) respectively as the "tyranny of aggregation" and the "tyranny of non-aggregation."

In their paper, Fleurbaey and Tungodden (2010) suggest a class of rank-dependent welfare orderings that do not suffer from the tyranny of aggregation and the tyranny of non-aggregation. Rank-dependent criteria generalize prioritarian ones by adding a weight on transformed utilities that depend on the rank of the individual in the distribution of well-being. In the context of population ethics, Asheim and Zuber (2014) have proposed and axiomatized a family of such rank-dependent criteria, namely the rank-discounted critical-level generalized utilitarianism criteria. They thus showed that they can avoid shortcomings such as the Repugnant and Very Sadistic Conclusions. This chapter studies to what extent other rank-dependent criteria solve dilemmas in population ethics.

In Sections 2 and 3 of this chapter we introduce the framework, present some general desirable properties of social welfare orderings in the variable population framework, and discuss three families of criteria: prioritarian ones, egalitarian ones, and proper rank-dependent criteria. In Sections 4 and 5, we discuss the tyranny of aggregation and the tyranny of non-aggregation. We show that rank-dependent criteria may escape both tyrannies, at the cost of not satisfying a replication-invariance property. We argue that this property may not be so appealing in the variable population context. In Section 6 we consider a related dilemma in population ethics between Repugnant and Sadistic Conclusions, adding new results to those already established by, for example, Blackorby, Bossert, and Donaldson (2004) and Asheim and Zuber (2014, Section 4)). We show that rank-dependent criteria may simultaneously avoid the Repugnant Conclusion, the Very Sadistic Conclusion and the Reversed Repugnant Conclusions. A key condition is that the cumulative effect of adding individuals at a given level of lifetime well-being is bounded. In Section 7 we show how negative results extend to a larger class of prioritarian and egalitarian criteria. Finally, in Section 8 we conclude, while all proofs are contained in an appendix.

2. FRAMEWORK AND BASIC PROPERTIES

Let $\mathbb{N}$ denote the set of positive integers (natural numbers), let $\mathbb{R}$ denote the real numbers, and let respectively $\mathbb{R}_+/\mathbb{R}_{++}/\mathbb{R}_-/\mathbb{R}_{--}$ denote the non-negative/positive/non-positive/negative real numbers.

We consider distributions of (lifetime) well-being within finite populations of variable sizes. We favor the interpretation where the population consists of people that either are alive now or will exist in the future. The set of such distributions is $\mathbf{X} = \bigcup_{k \in \mathbb{N}} \mathbb{R}^k$, with typical element $\mathbf{x} = (x_1, \ldots, x_i, \ldots, x_k)$, and where x_i is the well-being of individual i in this population. Thus a distribution $\mathbf{x}$ of three people with well-being 5, 10, and 20 respectively will be represented by $\mathbf{x} = (5, 10, 20)$, while distribution $\mathbf{y}$ of five people with well-being 1, 17, -4, 15, and 33 respectively will be represented by $\mathbf{y} = (1, 17, -4, 15, 33)$.

Well-being is assumed to be at least level comparable.[1] For every $k \in \mathbb{N}$, and each distribution $\mathbf{x} \in \mathbb{R}^k$, the finite population size in $\mathbf{x}$ is $n(\mathbf{x}) = k$. Following the usual convention in population ethics, a well-being level equal to 0 represents *neutrality*. Hence, well-being is normalized so that above neutrality, a life, as a whole, is worth living; below neutrality, it is not.

For every $k \in \mathbb{N}$ and all $\mathbf{x}, \mathbf{y} \in \mathbb{R}^k$, we write $\mathbf{x} \gg \mathbf{y}$ whenever $x_i > y_i$ for all $i \in \{1, \ldots, n(\mathbf{x})\}$. Similarly, $\mathbf{x} \geq \mathbf{y}$ means that $x_i \geq y_i$ for all $i \in \{1, \ldots, n(\mathbf{x})\}$, and $\mathbf{x} = \mathbf{y}$ means that $x_i = y_i$ for all $i \in \{1, \ldots, n(\mathbf{x})\}$. We write $\mathbf{x} > \mathbf{y}$ whenever $\mathbf{x} \geq \mathbf{y}$ and $\mathbf{x} \neq \mathbf{y}$.

We assume that distributions of well-being can be normatively ranked by a *social welfare ordering* (SWO) $\succsim$. Such a social welfare ordering is a binary relation, which is complete and transitive. For all $\mathbf{x}, \mathbf{y} \in \mathbf{X}$, $\mathbf{x} \succsim \mathbf{y}$ means that the distribution $\mathbf{x}$ is deemed socially at least as good as $\mathbf{y}$. The fact that $\succsim$ is complete means that, for all $\mathbf{x}, \mathbf{y} \in \mathbf{X}$, either $\mathbf{x} \succsim \mathbf{y}$ or $\mathbf{y} \succsim \mathbf{x}$ (or both). The fact that $\succsim$ is transitive means that, for all $\mathbf{x}, \mathbf{y}, \mathbf{z} \in \mathbf{X}$, if $\mathbf{x} \succsim \mathbf{y}$ and $\mathbf{y} \succsim \mathbf{z}$ then $\mathbf{x} \succsim \mathbf{z}$. We let $\sim$ and $\succ$ denote the symmetric and asymmetric parts of $\succsim$. We say that a *social welfare function* (SWF) $W : X \to \mathbb{R}$ represents a SWO $\succsim$ on $\mathbf{X}$ if, for all $\mathbf{x}, \mathbf{y} \in \mathbf{X}$, $\mathbf{x} \succsim \mathbf{y}$ if and only if $W(\mathbf{x}) \geq W(\mathbf{y})$.

For each $\mathbf{x} \in \mathbf{X}$, we let $\mathbf{x}_{[]} = (x_{[1]}, \ldots, x_{[r]}, \ldots, x_{[n(x)]})$. denote the non-decreasing distribution that is obtained by ordering $\mathbf{x}$; that is, for each rank $r \in \{1, \ldots, n(\mathbf{x}) - 1\}$, $x_{[r]} \leq x_{[r+1]}$.

For any real number $z \in \mathbb{R}$ and any positive integer $k \in \mathbb{N}$, we let $(z)_k \in \mathbb{R}^k$ denote the *egalitarian* distribution where all k individual have a well-being level equal to z. For any

$\mathbf{x} \in \mathbf{X}$ and $z \in \mathbb{R}$, $\left(\mathbf{x}, (z)_k\right)$ denotes the distribution $\mathbf{x}$ with k added individuals, all with lifetime well-being equal to $z \in \mathbb{R}$.

We now introduce through axioms some basic requirements that seem appealing for a swo. The first axiom is a principle of impartiality that states all individuals are treated in the same way, so that permuting well-being levels (or permuting the order of people in the list of well-being) leaves the distribution equally good.

Anonymity: A swo $\succsim$ on $\mathbf{X}$ satisfies *anonymity* if, for all $k \in \mathbb{N}$ and all $\mathbf{x} \in \mathbb{R}^k$, $\mathbf{x} \sim \mathbf{y}$ if $\mathbf{y}$ is obtained by reordering the elements of $\mathbf{x}$.

The second principle represents two ideas. First, if we make small mistakes in measuring the well-being of people, this should not radically modify the social assessment so that small changes in distributions do not yield big changes in the social value of the distributions. Second, we want to be able to represent the swo by a swf that is defined across different population sizes. This can be done by endorsing the following principle:

Extended Continuity: A swo $\succsim$ on $\mathbf{X}$. satisfies *extended continuity* if, for all $k, \ell \in \mathbb{N}$ and all $\mathbf{x} \in \mathbb{R}^k$, the sets $\left\{ \mathbf{y} \in \mathbb{R}^\ell \mid \mathbf{y} \succsim \mathbf{x} \right\}$ and $\left\{ \mathbf{y} \in \mathbb{R}^\ell \mid \mathbf{x} \succsim \mathbf{y} \right\}$ are closed in $\mathbb{R}^\ell$.

The two next principles can be viewed as versions of the Pareto principle, namely that a distribution $\mathbf{x}$ should be preferred to a same-population distribution $\mathbf{y}$ whenever all individuals prefer $\mathbf{x}$ to $\mathbf{y}$.

Monotonicity combines Pareto indifference with a weak version of the Pareto principle.

Restricted Dominance requires minimal sensitivity to individual well-being: starting with an egalitarian distribution, if a single individual is made worse off, then the distribution becomes worse.

Monotonicity: A swo $\succsim$ on $\mathbf{X}$ satisfies *monotonicity* if, for all $k \in \mathbb{N}$ and all $\mathbf{x}, \mathbf{y} \in \mathbb{R}^k$, $\mathbf{x} \geq \mathbf{y}$ implies $\mathbf{x} \succsim \mathbf{y}$.

Restricted Dominance: A swo $\succsim$ on $\mathbf{X}$ satisfies *restricted dominance* if, for all $k \in \mathbb{N}$ and all $z, z' \in \mathbb{R}$ with $z > z'$, $(z)_k \succ \left((z')_1, (z)_{k-1} \right)$.

The *Pigou-Dalton* transfer principle requires that we prefer more equal distributions. If well-being is transferred from a better-off person to a worse-off person without reversing their relative ranks, so that the resulting distribution is more equal, then the new distribution is at least as good.

Pigou-Dalton: A swo $\succsim$ on $\mathbf{X}$ satisfies *Pigou-Dalton* if, for all $k \in \mathbb{N}$, all $\mathbf{x}, \mathbf{y} \in \mathbb{R}^k$, all $\delta > 0$, and all $i, j \in \left\{ 1, \ldots, k \right\}$, if (i) $x_h = y_h$ for all $h \in \left\{ 1, \ldots, k \right\}$, $h \neq i, j$, and (ii) $y_i - \delta = x_i \geq x_j = y_j + \delta$, then $\mathbf{x} \succsim \mathbf{y}$.

In this chapter, we will consider both absolute and relative rank-dependent criteria, where absolute criteria require absolute, rather than relative, population size to be significant. To rule out any role for absolute population size, we can use a *Replication Invariance* property. This is also a consistency property across population sizes: if distribution $(1,1)$ is preferred to distribution $(0,2)$ then $(1,1,1,1)$ is also preferred to distribution $(0,0,2,2)$ because we only add a "twin" to each person in the initial distributions.

To formally state this property, we need to introduce the notion of replicas. For all $\ell \in \mathbb{N}$ and all $\mathbf{x} \in \mathbb{R}^k$, let $\ell * \mathbf{x}$ denote the ℓ–replica of $\mathbf{x}$, that is, a distribution giving $\mathbf{x}$ to ℓ disjoint populations of size k.

> *Replication Invariance*: A swo $\succsim$ on $\mathbf{X}$ satisfies *replication invariance* if, for all $k \in \mathbb{N}$, all $\ell \in \mathbb{N}$, all $\mathbf{x}, \mathbf{y} \in \mathbb{R}^k$, $\mathbf{x} \sim \mathbf{y}$ implies $\ell * \mathbf{x} \sim \ell * \mathbf{y}$.

Our last basic axiom is an independence or consistency axiom that holds on ordered ("comonotonic") distributions. A natural independence condition would be that the social ranking of two same-population distributions $\mathbf{x}$ and $\mathbf{y}$ does not depend on the well-being level of individuals who have the same level in the two distributions, provided that we do not change individual ranks. This principle of Independence with respect to Ordered Vectors was introduced by Ebert (1988).[2]

Wakker (1989) and Köbberling and Wakker (2003) have shown that, under mild additional conditions satisfied by all swos discussed in this paper, Independence with respect to Ordered Vectors is implied by a broader condition representing the idea that we have a consistent way to measure transformed well-being. This condition, named the Trade-Off Consistency for Ordered Vectors, states that the cardinal measurement of how changes in well-being affect social evaluation should be consistent: it does not depend on the rank of the individuals (provided we compare people at the same rank). The condition also adds that social evaluation of two same-population distributions is independent of the well-being of individuals who have the same rank and well-being in the two distributions (which is exactly Independence with respect to Ordered Vectors).

To introduce Trade-Off Consistency for Ordered Vectors, we need further notation. Let $\mathbf{x}$ be any distribution, and r be an integer in $\{1,\dots,n(\mathbf{x})\}$ and $z \in \mathbb{R}$ a real number. The distribution $\mathbf{x}_{[-r]}z$, if it exists, is the distribution $\tilde{\mathbf{x}}$ such that $n(\mathbf{x}) = n(\tilde{\mathbf{x}})$, $\tilde{x}_i = x_{[i]}$ for all $i \neq r$ and $r = z$. Hence $\mathbf{x}_{[-r]}z$ is an ordered vector that is a permutation of $\mathbf{x}$ except that the well-being of individual with rank r is now z instead of $x_{[r]}$. Such a vector is *well-defined* only if $x_{[r-1]} \leq z \leq x_{[r+1]}$ (or $r = 1$ and $z \leq x_{[2]}$, or $r = n(\mathbf{x})$ and $z \geq x_{[n(\mathbf{x})-1]}$). Formally, Trade-Off Consistency for Ordered Vectors is written as follows:

> *Trade-Off Consistency for Ordered Vectors*: A swo $\succsim$ on $\mathbf{X}$ satisfies *trade-off consistency for ordered vectors* if, for all $k \in \mathbb{N}$, all $\mathbf{x}, \mathbf{y}, \tilde{\mathbf{x}}, \tilde{\mathbf{y}} \in \mathbb{R}^k$, all $r \ r' \in \{1,\dots,k\}$ and all $z_1, z_2, z_3, z_4 \in \mathbb{R}$ and $z_3' > z_3$, if $\mathbf{x}_{[-r]}z_1$, $\mathbf{y}_{[-r]}z_2$, $\mathbf{x}_{[-r]}z_3$, $\mathbf{y}_{[-r]}z_4$, $\tilde{\mathbf{x}}_{[-r']}z_1$, $\mathbf{y}_{[-r']}z_2$, $\tilde{\mathbf{x}}_{[-r']}z_3'$, and $\tilde{\mathbf{y}}_{[-r']}z_4$ are all well-defined and $\mathbf{x}_{[-r]}z_1 \sim \mathbf{y}_{[-r]}z_2$, $\mathbf{x}_{[-r]}z_3 \sim \mathbf{y}_{[-r]}z_4$, $\tilde{\mathbf{x}}_{[-r']}z_1 \sim \tilde{\mathbf{y}}_{[-r']}z_2$, then $\tilde{\mathbf{x}}_{[-r']}z_3' \succsim \tilde{\mathbf{y}}_{[-r']}z_4$.[3]

In the axiom, $\mathbf{x}_{[-r]}z_1 \sim \mathbf{y}_{[-r]}z_2.$ and $\mathbf{x}_{[-r]}z_3 \sim \mathbf{y}_{[-r]}z_4$ means that the difference in well-being brought by z_1 and z_2 has the same impact on social evaluation as the difference in well-being brought by z_3 and z_4. The axiom says that this difference should not depend on the rank of the individual.

3. Basic Representation Results

With the basic properties introduced in Section 2, we are able to present three representation results. The proofs of these and other propositions are contained in an appendix.

> *Proposition 1*: Assume that a swo $\succsim$ on $\mathbf{X}$ satisfies Anonymity, Extended Continuity, Montonicity, and Restricted Dominance. Then there exist,
> - for each $k \in \mathbb{N}$, a continuous, symmetric and non-decreasing function $e_k : \mathbb{R}^k \to \mathbb{R}$ satisfying $e_k((z)_k) = z$ for all $z \in \mathbb{R}$ and
> - a continuous function $V : \mathbb{N} \times \mathbb{R} \to \mathbb{R}$, which is strictly increasing in its second variable,
>
> such that $W(\boldsymbol{x}) = V\left(n(\boldsymbol{x}), e_{n(\boldsymbol{x})}(\boldsymbol{x})\right)$ represents $\succsim$.

The swos obtained in Proposition 1 decompose the evaluation of well-being distributions in two steps. Functions e_k are the equally-distributed equivalent function: for all $\mathbf{x} \in \mathbb{R}^k$, the well-being level $z \in \mathbb{R}$ determined by $e_k(\mathbf{x}) = z$ has the property that an egalitarian distribution where k individuals have well-being z is socially as good as $\mathbf{x}$.[4] For each k, the function $e_k : \mathbb{R}^k \to \mathbb{R}$ is a SWF that represents the swo $\succsim$ on $\mathbb{R}^k$—the restricted domain of populations of size k—such that for all $\mathbf{x}, \mathbf{y} \in \mathbb{R}^k$, $\mathbf{x} \succsim \mathbf{y}$ if and only if $e_k(\mathbf{x}) \geq e_k(\mathbf{y})$. Hence, the functions e_k embody the principles of justice within populations of the same size. On the other hand, the function V embody the trade-off between population size and equally distributed equivalent well-being in the population.

The following are three examples of swos that are consistent with this decomposition:

- *Critical-level generalized utilitarianism* (CLU) has $V(k,e) = k(\phi(e) - \phi(c))$ for some *critical level* $c \geq 0$ and

$$e_k(\mathbf{x}) = \phi^{-1}\left(\frac{1}{k}\sum_{r=1}^{k}\phi\left(x_{[r]}\right)\right) \tag{1}$$

for some increasing and continuous function $\phi : \mathbb{R} \to \mathbb{R}$ that transforms well-being into transformed well-being, so that the CLU swo $\succsim$ is represented by

$$W(\mathbf{x}) = \sum_{r=1}^{k}\left(\phi\left(x_{[r]}\right) - \phi(c)\right).$$

For consistency with our discussion below we let the index sum according to rank r, but this is clearly immaterial for the CLU SWO. The CLU SWO has a prominent place in the literature on population ethics (Blackorby and Donaldson 1984; Broome 2004; Blackorby, Bossert, and Donaldson 2005).

- *Average generalized utilitarianism* (AU) has $V(k,e) = \phi(e)$ with $e_k(\mathbf{x})$ given by (1), so that the AU SWO $\succsim$ is represented by

$$W(\mathbf{x}) = \frac{1}{k}\sum_{r=1}^{k}\phi\big(x_{[r]}\big).$$

- *Maximin* has $V(k,e) = \phi(e)$ and $e_k(\mathbf{x}) = x_{[1]}$, so that the maximin SWO is represented by

$$W(\mathbf{x}) = \phi\big(x_{[1]}\big). \tag{2}$$

In the presentation of maximin we have chosen (2) instead of the equivalent representation $W(\mathbf{x}) = x_{[1]}$ in order to be consistent with our discussion below.

By imposing that the SWO $\succsim$ on $\mathbf{X}$ satisfies trade-off consistency for ordered vectors and Pigou-Dalton, we obtain a smaller class of SWOs, which contains the set of CLU, AU, and maximin SWOs as special cases. To introduce the general class, we need the following index of non-concavity of a continuous and increasing function ϕ (see Chateauneuf, Cohen, and Meilijson 2005):

$$G_\phi = \sup_{z_1 < z_2 \le z_3 < z_4} \left[\frac{\big(\phi(z_4) - \phi(z_3)\big)/\big(z_4 - z_3\big)}{\big(\phi(z_2) - \phi(z_1)\big)/\big(z_2 - z_1\big)} \right].$$

Proposition 2: Assume that a SWO $\succsim$ on X, in addition to the axioms of Proposition 1, satisfies Trade-Off Consistency for Ordered Vectors and Pigou-Dalton. Then, for each $k \in N$, the equally distributed equivalent of $\mathbf{x} \in \mathbb{R}^k$ is given by

$$e_k(\mathbf{x}) = \phi_k^{-1}\left(\sum_{r=1}^{k} w_r^k \phi_k\big(x_{[r]}\big)\right), \tag{3}$$

where the weights w_r^k, for $r \in \{1,\ldots,k\}$, are non-negative, non-increasing, and sum up to 1, and the function ϕ_k is continuous, increasing and such that

$$G_{\phi_k} \le \min_{r \in \{1,\ldots,k-1\}} w_r^k / w_{r+1}^k.$$

A SWO satisfying the axioms of Propositions 1 and 2 is called a *rank-dependent generalized utilitarian* SWO. We can consider different subclasses of rank-dependent generalized utilitarian SWOs depending on the principles of justice applied for populations with the same size. We will pay particular attention to two subclasses, specified in Definitions 1 and 2.

> *Definition 1*: A swo $\succsim$ on **X** is a *prioritarian* (or generalized utilitarian) swo if it satisfies the axioms of Propositions 1 and 2 with the weights in (3) given by $w_r^k = 1/k$ for all $k \in \mathbb{N}$ and $r \in \{1, \dots, k\}$ and a function $\phi_k = \phi$ for all $k \in \mathbb{N}$.

The prioritarian class includes the CLU and AU swos. However, this class is much richer than these few examples, and can encompass many different ways of trading-off population size and average transformed well-being.

For the prioritarian class, Proposition 2 implies that $G_\phi \leq 1$ so that ϕ is weakly concave. If ϕ is affine, then we obtain (non-generalized) utilitarianism. The utilitarian class is the one that has been most studied in population ethics. A famous example is the *total utilitarian* swo, which is the member of the utilitarian class such that $V(k,z) = kz$ for all $k \in \mathbb{N}$ and $e_k(\mathbf{x}) = \frac{1}{k} \Sigma_{r=1}^k x_{[r]}$. This is a CLU swo with $\phi(z) = z$ and $c = 0$; thus, it is also prioritarian.

The term "prioritarian" suggests that ϕ is a strictly concave transformation of well-being, thereby giving preference to redistribution of well-being from a better-off to a worse-off person. An extreme case of such preference for redistribution is given by equalitarian swos.

> *Definition 2*: A swo $\succsim$ on **X** is an *egalitarian* swo if it satisfies the axioms of Propositions 1 and 2 with the weights in (3) given by $w_1^k = 1$ for all $k \in \mathbb{N}$.

To the best of our knowledge, only a few papers have considered this version of egalitarianism in the population ethics literature.[5] There have been discussions of other versions of egalitarianism that use a leximin rather than a maximin criterion to define e_k.[6] For instance, Blackorby, Bossert, and Donaldson (1996) have argued in favor of Critical-Level Leximin, while Arrhenius (forthcoming, Section 6.8) discusses a version of leximin related to the Positional-Extension Leximin of Blackorby, Bossert, and Donaldson (1996). One issue though is that leximin is not continuous so that we cannot apply Proposition 1 to define a family of leximin criteria. Given that leximin gives priority to the worst-off, like maximin, the conclusions that we would obtain would not be very different from the ones for maximin in the context of the present chapter.

> *Proposition 3*: Assume that a swo $\succsim$ on X, in addition to the axioms of Propositions 1 and 2, satisfies Replication Invariance. Then $\phi_k = \phi$ for all $k \in \mathbb{N}$ and there exists a non-decreasing and concave weighting function $F : [0,1] \to [0,1]$, which is continuous on $(0,1]$ and satisfies $F(0) = 0$ and $F(1) = 1$, such that the weights in (3) are given by $w_r^k = F(r/k) - F((r-1)/k)$ for each $k \in \mathbb{N}$ and $r \in \{1, \dots, k\}$.

A swo satisfying the axioms of Propositions 1, 2 and 3 is called a *relative rank-dependent generalized utilitarian* swo. Both prioritarian and egalitarian swos are in this class. In the case of prioritarianism, we have that the weighting function F is given by

$F(\rho) = \rho$ for all $\rho \in [0,1]$. In the case of egalitarianism, we have that the weighting function F is given by $F(0) = 0$ and $F(\rho) = 1$ for all $\rho \in (0,1]$.

4. Tyranny of Aggregation, Tyranny of Non-Aggregation and Replication Invariance

Fleurbaey and Tungodden (2010) have highlighted a dilemma in social ethics between what they call the "tyranny of aggregation" and the "tyranny of non-aggregation." The tyranny of aggregation means that a tiny gain to sufficiently many well-off people might justify imposing a much larger sacrifice on the worst-off. On the other hand, the tyranny of non-aggregation means that a small gain by the worst-off might be sufficient to justify a sacrifice by a great number of people.

To avoid these two tyrannies, Fleurbaey and Tungodden (2010) have proposed the principles of minimal aggregation and minimal non-aggregation.

> *Minimal Aggregation*: A swo $\succsim$ satisfies *minimal aggregation* if for some $k \in \mathbb{N}$ and for all $\mathbf{x} \in \mathbb{R}^k$, there exist $\delta > \varepsilon > 0$ such that for all $\mathbf{y} \in \mathbb{R}^k$, if (i) for some $i \in \{1, \ldots, k\}$, $0 \leq x_i - y_i \leq \varepsilon$ and (ii) for all $j \neq i$, $y_j - x_j \geq \delta$, then $\mathbf{y} \succsim \mathbf{x}$.

Minimal Aggregation means that for some population, if all individuals except individual i gain sufficiently, then it is tolerable to impose a loss on individual i if the loss is sufficiently small. Note that the loss may be arbitrary low, so that the principle does not seem very demanding.

To introduce minimal non-aggregation, let us introduce for any distribution $\mathbf{x} \in \mathbf{X}$ the set of worst-off and best-off individuals in this distribution:

$$I_W(\mathbf{x}) = \left\{ i \in \{1, \ldots, n(\mathbf{x})\} \mid x_i = \min_{j \in \{1, \ldots, n(\mathbf{x})\}} x_j \right\}$$

and

$$I_B(\mathbf{x}) = \left\{ i \in \{1, \ldots, n(\mathbf{x})\} \mid x_i = \max_{j \in \{1, \ldots, n(\mathbf{x})\}} x_j \right\}.$$

> *Minimal Non-Aggregation*: A swo $\succsim$ satisfies *minimal non-aggregation* if there exist $0 < z < \overline{z}$ and $\delta > \varepsilon > 0$ such that for all $k \in \mathbb{N}$, all $\mathbf{x}, \mathbf{y} \in \mathbb{R}^k$, if (i) for some $i \in \{1, \ldots, k\}$, $i \in I_W(\mathbf{y})$, $y_i \leq z$ and $x_i - y_i \geq \delta$ and (ii) for all $j \neq i$ with $x_j \neq y_j$, it holds that $j \in I_B(\mathbf{x}) \cap I_B(\mathbf{y})$, $y_j \geq \overline{z}$ and $y_j - x_j \leq \varepsilon$, then $\mathbf{x} \succsim \mathbf{y}$.

Minimal Non-Aggregation means that if a worst-off individual is sufficiently badly off and gains enough, there is a small loss that is tolerable for all the best-off, no matter how numerous they are, provided they are sufficiently well-off. Again, the principle does not seem very demanding given that the loss by the best-off may be arbitrary small.

The key remark by Fleurbaey and Tungodden (2010) is that prioritarian swos do not satisfy Minimal Non-Aggregation, while egalitarian swos do not satisfy Minimal Aggregation. Furthermore, in their Proposition 2(i) they establish conditions under which Minimal Aggregation and Minimal Non-Aggregation cannot be combined with Replication Invariance. Our next proposition illustrates this result under conditions that are stronger than those imposed by Fleurbaey and Tungodden (2010, Proposition 2(i)).

Proposition 4: Assume that a swo $\succsim$ on X satisfies the axioms of Propositions 1, 2, and 3. Then $\succsim$ fails either Minimal Aggregation or Minimal Non-Aggregation.

The proof of Proposition 4 shows that the failure of minimal aggregation or minimal non-aggregation depends on the properties of the weighting function F which determines the weights in (3).

(a) The swo $\succsim$ fails minimal aggregation if and only if $\lim_{\rho \to 0^+} F(\rho) = 1$ (so that $\succsim$ is egalitarian).

(b) The swo $\succsim$ fails minimal non-aggregation if and only if $\lim_{\rho \to 0^+} F(\rho) < 1$ (this includes any prioritarian swo).

The upshot of this result is that if we want to satisfy minimal aggregation and minimal non-aggregation, and we want to keep the axioms of Propositions 1 and 2, thus keeping the rank-dependent generalized utilitarian form, then replication invariance must go.

This discussion can be related to Arrhenius's (forthcoming) *general non-extreme priority condition*, capturing the idea that there is some number of people such that a very large loss for them cannot be compensated for by a slight gain for just one person. A swo $\succsim$ satisfying the axioms of Propositions 1, 2, and 3 fails this condition if $\lim_{\rho \to 0^+} F(\rho) > 0$, since then a large loss for many better-off people can be compensated by a slight gain for a single worst-off person if sufficient many people are inserted at intermediate ranks. Hence, by observation (a) above, Minimal Aggregation is weaker than Arrhenius's condition in a setting where these axioms are satisfied.

5. ESCAPING TYRANNIES THROUGH ABSOLUTE RANK-DEPENDENCE

A particular class of swo satisfying the axioms of Propositions 1 and 2, but not necessarily satisfying replication invariance, is obtained by letting weights depend on absolute rather than relative ranks.

Definition 3: A swo $\succsim$ on **X** satisfying the axioms of Propositions 1 and 2 is an *absolute rank-dependent generalized utilitarian* swo if there exist

(i) non-negative and non-increasing *absolute weights* $(a_r)_{r \in \mathbb{N}}$ with $a_1 = 1$ such that, for all $k \in \mathbb{N}$, the weights in (3) are obtained by letting

$$w_r^k = \frac{a_r}{\sum_{r'=1}^{k} a_{r'}}$$

for all $r \in \{1, \ldots, k\}$, and

(ii) a function ϕ such that $\phi_k = \phi$ for all $k \in \mathbb{N}$.

Prioritarian and egalitarian swos are also absolute rank-dependent. In the case of prioritarianism, this is obtained by choosing $a_r = 1$ for all $r \in \mathbb{N}$ as absolute weights. This includes CLU and AU. In the case of egalitarianism, this is obtained by choosing $a_r = 0$ for all $r > 1$. This includes maximin. Hence, prioritarian and egalitarian swos are both relative and absolute rank-dependent generalized utilitarian swos.

Any absolute rank-dependent generalized utilitarian swo satisfies the axioms of Propositions 1 and 2, but is not characterized by these axioms. To obtain absolute rank-dependent swos, we could add an additional independence property (which corresponds to the High Income Group Aggregation Property as defined by Bossert [1990b], and to Top Independence as defined by Pivato [2020]).

Same Population Independence of the Existence of the Best-Off: A swo $\succsim$ satisfies *same population independence of the existence of the best-off* if, for any $k \in \mathbb{N}$, and for all **x**, **y** $\in \mathbb{R}^k$ and $z > \max\{x_{[k]}, y_{[k]}\}$, **x** $\succsim$ **y** if and only if $(\mathbf{x},(z)_1) \succsim (\mathbf{y},(z)_1)$.

Definition 4. An absolute rank-dependent generalized utilitarian swo $\succsim$ on **X** is a *proper* rank-dependent generalized utilitarian swo if the absolute weights $(a_r)_{r \in \mathbb{N}}$ satisfy $a_2 > 0$ and $\sum_{r \in \mathbb{N}} a_r < \infty$.

The restriction that a_2 be strictly positive means that no egalitarian swo is proper rank-dependent, and the restriction that the absolute weights be summable means that no prioritarian swo is proper rank-dependent. If there exists a real number $\beta \in (0,1)$ such that the absolute weights are $a_r = \beta^{r-1}$ for all $r \in \mathbb{N}$, then the swo is proper rank-dependent and called a *rank-discounted generalized utilitarian* (RDU) swo. We will return to this particular subclass in the next section.

One drawback of proper rank-dependent generalized utilitarian swos is that they allow a large loss for many better-off people to be compensated by a slight gain for a single worst-off person. The reason is that the loss of transformed well-being of the many better-off people is discounted below any positive level by inserting sufficiently many people at intermediate ranks. Hence, swos in this class fail Arrhenius's (forthcoming) general non-extreme priority condition (discussed at the end of Section 4).

Definition 5: An absolute rank-dependent generalized utilitarian swo $\succsim$ on **X** is a *regular* rank-dependent generalized utilitarian swo if there exists a positive number $k \in \mathbb{R}_{++}$ such that, for all $k \in \mathbb{N}, a_k \geq k \cdot \left(\sum_{r=k+1}^{+\infty} a_r \right)$.

The restriction imposed by regularity implies in particular that the absolute weights are summable (i.e., $\sum_{r \in \mathbb{N}} a_r < \infty$), but it is stronger than that. Hence no prioritarian swo is regular rank-dependent. On the other hand, the restriction allows weights to be equal to zero from a certain rank r on. Hence egalitarian swos are regular rank-dependent.

As shown by the following result, the absolute rank-dependent generalized utilitarian swo being proper *and* regular is the key to solving the dilemma posed by the requirements of minimal aggregation and minimal non-aggregation.

Proposition 5: Assume that a swo $\succsim$ on **X** is an absolute rank-dependent generalized utilitarian swo. Then $\succsim$ satisfies both Minimal Aggregation and Minimal Non-Aggregation if and only if $\succsim$ is proper and regular rank-dependent.

The proof of Proposition 5 shows that:

(a) If the swo is egalitarian, then $\succsim$ fails minimal aggregation.
(b) If the swo is not regular rank-dependent, then $\succsim$ fails minimal non-aggregation.

The proposition implies that, within the class of absolute rank-dependent generalized utilitarian swos, there must be positive weights on more than the worst-off person, and the sum of the weights must be converging sufficiently fast. This gives a route out of the dilemma posed by Fleurbaey and Tungodden (2010), but at the cost of failing the requirement of replication invariance. Indeed, Fleurbaey and Tungodden (2010, 404) show the existence of a swo satisfying both minimal aggregation and minimal non-aggregation by providing an example of an RDU swo in a form that is actually in the sub-class considered in the subsequent section.

6. Simple Rank-Dependence and Population Ethics

Up to now, the general classes of swos that we have considered in our propositions and definitions have not specified the trade-off between population size and equally distributed equivalent well-being in the population, as embodied by the function V of Proposition 1. We turn now to one particularly natural manner to make this trade-off.

Definition 6. An absolute rank-dependent generalized utilitarian SWO $\succsim$ on **X** with absolute weights $(a_r)_{r\in\mathbb{N}}$ is a *simple rank-dependent generalized utilitarian* SWO if there exists a critical level $c \in \mathbb{R}_+$ such that the function V of Proposition 1 is given by:

$$V(k,e) = \sum_{r=1}^{k} a_r \left(\phi(e) - \phi(c) \right).$$

The term "simple" is appropriate since, any rank-dependent generalized utilitarian SWO $\succsim$ is represented by a SWF $W : \mathbf{X} \to \mathbb{R}$ of the form:

$$W(\mathbf{x}) = \sum_{r=1}^{k} a_r \left(\phi\left(x_{[r]}\right) - \phi(c) \right). \tag{4}$$

The class of simple prioritarian SWO contains only CLU. In particular, the AU SWO is prioritarian, but not simple. The class of simple egalitarian SWO contains only maximin. To the best of our knowledge, only a few papers have considered SWFs similar to the one defined by (4) and that are neither simple prioritarian nor simple egalitarian.

Sider (1991) has proposed principle GV, with similar ideas already discussed by Hurka (1983). Principle GV is related to but incompatible with the form specified by (4). It first divides a population into two ordered sets: one set with the distribution of the people with positive well-being, in order of descending well-being; and another set with the distribution of the people with negative well-being, in order of ascending well-being. For people with negative well-being, principle GV is similar to (4) with decreasing weights a_r, an affine function ϕ, and $c = 0$. For people with positive well-being, principle GV also applies something like (4) with decreasing weights a_r an affine function ϕ, and $c = 0$, but it applies it to the distribution of people ordered in decreasing (and not increasing) order of well-being. Principle GV has been discussed by several papers (Arrhenius 2000a; 2000b; forthcoming; Pivato 2020; the latter paper contains also an axiomatization of a generalized version of the principle). These papers point out that Principle GV implies that, if everyone has positive well-being, it is always socially better to make a (non-leaky) well-being transfer from a poor to a rich. Hence, principle GV does not satisfy Pigou-Dalton.

Asheim and Zuber (2014) have proposed and axiomatized the class of *rank-discounted critical-level generalized utilitarian* (RDCLU) SWOs. They are a special case of the form specified by (4), where there exists a real number $\beta \in (0,1)$ such that the weights are $a_r = \beta^{r-1}$, for all $r \in \mathbb{N}$. The fact that the absolute weights a_r are strictly decreasing implies that a RDCLU SWO may satisfy Pigou-Dalton even if ϕ is not concave: A RDCLU SWO satisfies Pigou-Dalton if and only if $G_\phi \le a_r / a_{r+1} = \beta^{-1}$. Generalizations of rank-discounted critical-level generalized utilitarian SWOs have been discussed by Zuber (2017) and axiomatized by Pivato (2020).

Any simple rank-dependent generalized utilitarian SWO satisfies the axioms of Propositions 1 and 2 but is not characterized by these axioms. To obtain simple rank-dependent SWOs from absolute rank-dependent SWOs, we could add yet another independence property (which is implied by the Low Income Group Aggregation Property as defined by Bossert [1990b]):

Independence of the Well-Being of the Worst-Off: A swo $\succsim$ satisfies the *independence of the well-being of the worst-off* if for all $\mathbf{x}$, $\mathbf{y} \in \mathbf{X}$ and any $z', z'' \in \mathbb{R}$ such that $\max\{z', z''\} < \min\{x_{[1]}, y_{[1]}\}$, $(\mathbf{x}, (z')_1) \succsim (\mathbf{y}, (z')_1)$ if and only if $(\mathbf{x}, (z'')_1) \succsim (\mathbf{y}, (z'')_1)$.

According to Parfit, a social welfare ordering leads to the *Repugnant Conclusion* if:

For any possible population of at least ten billion people, all with a very high quality of life, there must be some much larger imaginable population whose existence, if other things are equal, would be better even though its members have lives that are barely worth living. (1984: 388 [1987])

The repugnant conclusion has caught much attention in the literature on population ethics as most of the literature has discussed ways to avoid such a conclusion. Formally, one can formulate the avoidance of the Repugnant Conclusion as follows:[7]

Avoidance of the Repugnant Conclusion: A swo $\succsim$ on $\mathbf{X}$ *avoids the repugnant conclusion* if there exist $k \in \mathbb{N}$, $y \in \mathbb{R}_{++}$, and $z \in (0, y)$ such that, for all $m \geq \ell \geq k$, $(y)_\ell \succsim (z)_m$.

Although the CLU swo does not avoid the Repugnant Conclusion if the critical level c equals 0, other generalized utilitarian swo, for example CLU with positive c and AU do so. However, they are subject to other difficulties.

On the one hand, CLU with positive c imply that for any distribution with negative well-being there is an egalitarian distribution with low but positive well-being that is worse. This is what Arrhenius (2000a; forthcoming) refers to as the *very sadistic conclusion*. Formally, one can formulate the avoidance of the Very Sadistic Conclusion as follows:

Avoidance of the Very Sadistic Conclusion: A swo $\succsim$ on $\mathbf{X}$ *avoids the very sadistic conclusion* if there exists $\mathbf{x} \in \mathbf{X}$ such that $(z)_k \succsim \mathbf{x}$ for all $k \in \mathbb{N}$ and $z \in \mathbb{R}_{++}$.

One the other hand, AU and maximin lead to the problematic conclusion that for any egalitarian distribution with very high positive well-being, there is a better one-individual distribution with slightly higher well-being. This might be referred to as the *reversed repugnant conclusion* (Arrhenius, forthcoming). Hence, one can formulate the avoidance of the Reversed Repugnant conclusion as follows:

Avoidance of the Reversed Repugnant Conclusion: A swo $\succsim$ on $\mathbf{X}$ *avoids the reversed repugnant conclusion* if there exist $k \in \mathbb{N}$, $y \in \mathbb{R}_{++}$ and $z \in (0, y)$ such that $(z)_k \succsim (y)_1$.

The next result shows that in the class of simple rank-dependent generalized utilitarian swos, being proper is the key to avoiding all these three problematic conclusions.

Proposition 6: Assume that a swo $\succsim$ on **X** is a simple rank-dependent generalized utilitarian swo. Then $\succsim$ satisfies Avoidance of the Repugnant Conclusion, Avoidance of the Very Sadistic Conclusion and Avoidance of the Reversed Repugnant Conclusion if and only if $\succsim$ is proper rank-dependent.

The proof of Proposition 6 shows that:

(a) If the swo is egalitarian, then $\succsim$ entails the reversed repugnant conclusion.
(b) If the swo has non-summable absolute weights, then $\succsim$ entails either the repugnant conclusion (when $c = 0$) or the very sadistic conclusion (when $c > 0$).

Proposition 6 implies that, within the class of simple rank-dependent generalized utilitarian swos, there must be positive weights on more than the worst-off person, and the sum of the weights must be converging, in order to avoid all of the repugnant, very sadistic and reversed repugnant conclusions.

It follows from Proposition 6 and our remark just prior to Definition 5 that any simple rank-dependent generalized utilitarian swo $\succsim$ avoiding the repugnant conclusion, the very sadistic conclusion and the reversed repugnant conclusion must fail Arrhenius's (forthcoming) general non-extreme priority condition.

Remark that, given that proper rank-dependent generalized utilitarian swos satisfy the Pigou-Dalton principle and avoid the repugnant conclusion, they cannot satisfy the famous mere addition principle introduced by Parfit (1984), namely that addition of people with positive well-being is always (at least weakly) socially desirable.

Mere Addition Principle: A swo $\succsim$ on **X** satisfies the *mere addition principle* if for all $z \in \mathbb{R}_{++}$ and all $\mathbf{x} \in \mathbf{X}\,(z, \mathbf{x}) \succsim \mathbf{x}$.

Indeed, Carlson (1998) proved that the mere addition principle and a non-anti-egalitarianism principle (which follows from the Pigou-Dalton principle) imply a violation of our formulation of the avoidance of the repugnant conclusion.

7. ADDITIONAL POPULATION ETHICS RESULTS

Proposition 6 singles out proper rank-dependent swos in the class of simple rank-dependent generalized utilitarian swos. We can more generally compare proper and regular rank-dependent swos to a large class of prioritarian and egalitarian criteria, including those that are not simple. For this purpose we first state a principle generalizing Avoidance of the Very Sadistic Conclusion:

> *Weak Non-Sadism Condition*: A swo $\succsim$ on **X** *satisfies the weak non-sadism condition* if there exist $k \in \mathbb{N}$ and $z \in \mathbb{R}_{--}$ such that for all $\mathbf{x} \in X$, $y \in \mathbb{R}_{++}$ and $\ell \in \mathbb{N}$ $(\mathbf{x},(y)_{\ell}) \succsim (\mathbf{x},(z)_{k})$.

Any prioritarian social welfare ordering will be subject to one of the two problems: either it implies the repugnant conclusion or it cannot satisfy the Weak Non-Sadism Condition.

> *Proposition 7*: A prioritarian swo $\succsim$ on **X** cannot satisfy both Avoidance of the Repugnant Conclusion and Weak Non-Sadism Condition.

Proposition 7 seems to reject prioritarian criteria for population ethics. One could therefore consider egalitarian criteria. However, they are also subject to a population ethics dilemma. They cannot satisfy the weak non-sadism condition if we want to insist on the intuitive principle that we should not create lives with a negative level of well-being.

> *Negative Mere Addition Principle*: A swo $\succsim$ on **X** satisfies the negative mere addition principle if for all $\mathbf{x} \in \mathbf{X}$ and all $z \in \mathbb{R}_{--}, \mathbf{x} \succ (\mathbf{x},(z)_{1})$.

> *Proposition 8*: An egalitarian swo $\succsim$ on X cannot satisfy both Weak Non-Sadism Condition and Negative Mere Addition Principle.

In contrast with these negative results, proper and regular simple rank-dependent swos may escape all the population dilemma we have discussed up to now provided function ϕ is concave and bounded above.

> *Proposition 9*: Assume that a swo $\succsim$ on X is a simple rank-dependent generalized utilitarian swo. Then $\succsim$ satisfies the Weak Non-Sadism Condition and the Negative Mere Addition Principle if $\succsim$ is proper and regular rank-dependent and the function ϕ is concave and bounded above.

Note that, by Proposition 6, we already know that the simple rank-dependent generalized utilitarian swos described in Proposition 9 satisfy Avoidance of the Repugnant Conclusion, Avoidance of the Very Sadistic Conclusion, and Avoidance of the Reversed Repugnant Conclusion. Thus we obtain a family of swos that comply with many population ethics requirements. This family deserves receiving further attention.

8. CONCLUDING REMARKS

In this chapter we have argued that the escape from the tyrannies of aggregation and non-aggregation and the resolution of an important population-ethical dilemma require that we relax the requirement of replication invariance. Thus, the normative evaluation of populations and their well-beings may change as populations and their well-beings are replicated. The RDCLU SWO (Asheim and Zuber 2014) is one example of a population-ethical criterion that offers a solution by relaxing replication invariance. However, as we have shown, a larger class of simple rank-dependent generalized utilitarian SWOS satisfy all the requirements that we have imposed, save replication invariance. In particular, the simple rank-dependent generalized utilitarian SWOS with absolute weights given by $a_r = (R+1-r)/R$ for $1 \leq r \leq R$ and $a_r = 0$ for $r > R$, where $R \geq 2$, are in this larger class.

It is a standard approach in population ethics to associate with the notion of total population not only the people that are alive at any one time, but also people that will ever live and those that have ever lived; in particular, this is the position taken by Blackorby, Bossert, and Donaldson (2005). However, Broome (2004, Ch. 13) and Blackorby, Bossert, and Donaldson (2005, 131–133) argue that it is reasonable to assume existence independence, requiring that the ranking of any two alternatives be independent of the existence of individuals who ever live and have the same well-being levels in both. Existence independence implies that populations principles can be applied to the affected people only.

The relaxation of replication invariance that we promote here is inconsistent with existence independence, and thus it becomes essential to take into account the existence and utility of non-affected people when evaluating population policies with limited scope. In particular, we must consider today the population policies that should be and will be implemented in the far future, and also take into the utilities of people that are dead if we require that the population-ethical criterion be time consistent. We must also depart from the generation-relative population ethics that Dasgupta (2005, 430–431) supports, because the reproductive choices made by future generations will affect the number and well-being of future people, therefore modifying the goodness of changing the population today. This departure from existence independence might have important implications for the conclusions that follow from population ethics.

ACKNOWLEDGMENTS

We thank Gustaf Arrhenius, Walter Bossert, Dean Spears, and Orri Stefánsson for helpful comments. This chapter is part of the research activities at the Centre for the Study of Equality, Social Organization, and Performance (ESOP) at the Department of Economics at the University of Oslo. ESOP has been supported by the Research Council of Norway through its Centres of Excellence funding scheme (project number 179552). Asheim's research has also been supported by l'IMéRA (Institut d'études avancées d'Aix Marseille Université) and CIREQ (Centre interuniversitaire de recherche en économie quantitative—Montréal). Zuber's research has been supported by Agence nationale de la recherche through the Fair-ClimPop project (ANR-16-CE03-0001-01) and the Investissements d'Avenir program (PGSE-ANR-17-EURE-0001).

APPENDIX: PROOFS

Proof of Proposition 1. If the swo $\succsim$ on **X** satisfies Monotonicity and Restricted Dominance, then it satisfies Minimal Increasingness in Blackorby, Bossert, and Donaldson (2005, Ch. 5). To see this, consider the distributions $(z)_k$ and $(z')_k$ with z, $z' \in \mathbb{R}$ satisfying $z > z'$. Construct $\mathbf{x} \in \mathbb{R}^k$ by letting $x_i = z'$ for some $i \in \{1, \ldots, k\}$ and $x_j = z$ for all $j \in \{1, \ldots, k\} \setminus \{i\}$. Then $(z)_k \succ \mathbf{x}$ by Restricted Dominance and $\mathbf{x} \succsim (z')_k$ by Monotonicity, so $(z)_k \succ (z')_k$ by transitivity. Thus, the result follows from Blackorby, Bossert, and Donaldson (2005, Theorem 5.2). ∎

Proof of Proposition 2. From Köbberling and Wakker (2003, Theorem 8), for each population size $k \in \mathbb{N}$, there must exist non-negative weights w_r^k, for $r \in \{1, \ldots, k\}$ and a continuous increasing function ϕ_k such that, for all $\mathbf{x}, \mathbf{y} \in \mathbf{X}$ with $n(\mathbf{x}) = n(\mathbf{y}) = k$,

$$\mathbf{x} \succsim \mathbf{y} \Leftrightarrow \sum_{r=1}^{k} w_r^k \phi_k\left(x_{[r]}\right) \geq \sum_{r=1}^{k} w_r^k \phi_k\left(y_{[r]}\right).$$

Using the definition of equally distributed equivalent, we can take the weights w_r^k summing to one. By the uniqueness result in Köbberling and Wakker (2003, Theorem 8), both the weights and the function ϕ_k are unique after normalization, provided that $w_r^k > 0$ for at least two ranks r.

By Chateauneuf, Cohen, and Meilijson (2005, Theorem 1) (or a similar result in Asheim and Zuber, 2014), for each $k \in \mathbb{N}$ such social orderings satisfy Pigou-Dalton if and only if

$$G_{\phi_k} \leq \min_{r \in \{1, \ldots, k-1\}} w_r^k / w_{r+1}^k.$$

Note that, by Chateauneuf, Cohen, and Meilijson (2005, Proposition 3), $G_{\phi_k} \geq 1$, so that this implies $w_r^k \geq w_{r+1}^k$ for all $r \in \{1, \ldots, k-1\}$: the weights are non-increasing. ∎

Proof of Proposition 3. By Replication Invariance, and by the uniqueness result of functions ϕ_k in Proposition 2, it is easy to show that there must exist a continuous and increasing function ϕ such that $\phi_k = \phi$ for all $k \in \mathbb{N}$, provided that there exist at least two ranks r such that $w_r^k > 0$, for $k \geq 2$ (otherwise, we have $w_1^k = 1$ for all $k \in \mathbb{N}$, and function ϕ_k does not matter: we can take it identical without loss of generality).

Then we can mimic Donaldson and Weymark (1980, Theorem 4) to show that there exists a non-decreasing and concave weighting function F satisfying all the required properties. ∎

Proof of Proposition 4. Case 1: $\lim_{\rho \to 0^+} F(\rho) = 1$. In this case, the weighting function F is given by $F(0) = 0$ and $F(\rho) = 1$ for all $\rho \in (0, 1]$, so that the swo $\succsim$ on **X** is egalitarian. Any egalitarian swo clearly contradicts minimal aggregation since no weight is given any person but the worst-off.

Case 2: $\lim_{\rho \to 0^+} F(\rho) < 1$. To show failure of minimal non-aggregation, we must show that, for all $0 < \underline{z} < \overline{z}$ and $\delta > \varepsilon > 0$ there exist $k \in \mathbb{N}$ and $\mathbf{x}, \mathbf{y} \in \mathbb{R}^k$ with $\mathbf{x} \prec \mathbf{y}$, even though $y_i \leq \underline{z}$ and $x_i - y_i \geq \delta$ for some $i \in I_W(\mathbf{y})$, and it holds that $j \in I_B(\mathbf{x}) \cap I_B(\mathbf{y})$, $y_j \geq \overline{z}$ and $y_j - x_j \leq \varepsilon$ for all $j \in \{1, \ldots, k\}$ with $j \neq i$ and $x_j \neq y_j$.

Choose any $0 < \underline{z} < \overline{z}$ and $\delta > \varepsilon > 0$. Since $\lim_{\rho \to 0^+} F(\rho) < 1$ and $F(\rho)$ is continuous for $\rho \in (0,1]$, we can choose $m \in \mathbb{N}$ sufficiently large so that $F\left(\dfrac{1}{m+1}\right) < 1$, and write $\Delta := 1 - F\left(\dfrac{1}{m+1}\right)$. Construct, for each $\ell \in \mathbb{N}$ with $\ell \geq 2$, $\mathbf{x}^\ell$ and $\mathbf{y}^\ell$ such that $n(\mathbf{x}^\ell) = n(\mathbf{y}^\ell) = \ell(m+1)$, $x_1^\ell = y_1^\ell = y_2^\ell = \underline{z}$, $x_2^\ell = \underline{z} + \delta$, $x_h^\ell = y_h^\ell = \underline{z} + \delta$ for $h = 3, \ldots, \ell$ and $x_{h'}^\ell = \overline{z} - \varepsilon$, $y_{h'}^\ell = \overline{z}$ for $h' = \ell+1, \ldots, \ell(m+1)$. For each $\ell \geq 2$, let

$$\Gamma(\ell) := F\left(\frac{2}{\ell(m+1)}\right) - F\left(\frac{1}{\ell(m+1)}\right),$$

where it follows from our assumptions that $\Gamma(\ell) > 0$ for all $\ell \geq 2$ and $\lim_{\ell \to \infty} \Gamma(\ell) = 0$. Hence, we can choose $\ell' \geq 2$ such that

$$\Gamma(\ell')\big(\phi(\underline{z}+\delta) - \phi(\underline{z})\big) < \Delta\big(\phi(\overline{z}) - \phi(\overline{z}-\varepsilon)\big).$$

By definition of the swos obtained in Propositions 1, 2, and 3, $\mathbf{y}^{\ell'} \succ \mathbf{x}^{\ell'}$, which contradicts minimal non-aggregation.

Hence, either minimal aggregation or minimal non-aggregation fails. ∎

Proof of Proposition 5. Case 1: The swo $\succsim$ on $\mathbf{X}$ is egalitarian. Clearly minimal aggregation is contradicted since no weight is given to any person but the worst-off.

Case 2: The swo $\succsim$ on $\mathbf{X}$ is not regular rank-dependent. Assume that there exist real numbers $0 < \underline{z} < \overline{z}$ and $\delta > \epsilon > 0$ as required in the statement of Minimal Non-Aggregation. Consider any $k \in \mathbb{R}, m \in \mathbb{R}$, with $k < m$. Let $\mathbf{x}, \mathbf{y} \in \mathbb{R}^m$ be such that $x_i = y_i = \underline{z}$ for all $i < k$, $y_k = \underline{z}, x_k = \underline{z} + \delta, x_j = z$ and $y_j = z + \epsilon$ for all $j > k$, where $z > \max\{\underline{z} + \delta, \overline{z}\}$. By definition of an absolute rank-dependent swo, we have:

$$\mathbf{x} \succsim \mathbf{y} \Leftrightarrow a_k \phi(\underline{z}+\delta) + \left(\sum_{r=k+1}^m a_r\right)\phi(z) \geq a_k \phi(\underline{z}) + \left(\sum_{r=k+1}^m a_r\right)\phi(z+\epsilon).$$

This can be written:

$$\mathbf{x} \underset{\sim}{\succsim} \mathbf{y} \Leftrightarrow a_k \geq \frac{\phi(z+\varepsilon)-\phi(z)}{\phi(\underline{z}+\delta)-\phi(\underline{z})}\left(\sum_{r=k+1}^m a_r\right).$$

But denoting

$$\kappa = \frac{\phi(z+\varepsilon)-\phi(z)}{\phi(\underline{z}+\delta)-\phi(\underline{z})},$$

and given that $\underset{\sim}{\succsim}$ is not regular rank-dependent, there must exist $k' \in \mathbb{N}$ such that $a_{k'} < \kappa \cdot \left(\sum_{r=k'+1}^{+\infty} a_r\right)$. This means that there must also exist $m' > k'$ such that $a_{k'} < \kappa \cdot \left(\sum_{r=k'+1}^{m'} a_r\right)$.

So, Minimal Non-Aggregation must sometimes be violated.

Case 3: The swo $\underset{\sim}{\succsim}$ on $\mathbf{X}$ is proper and regular rank-dependent. Let $\lambda \in (0,1)$ be such that $\kappa > \lambda \cdot a_1 / a_2$. By Chateauneuf, Cohen, and Meilijson (2005, Lemma 1), for any x, $y \in \mathbb{R}$, with $x \geq y$:

$$\lambda \cdot G_\phi \geq \frac{\phi(x+\lambda)-\phi(x)}{\phi(y)-\phi(y-1)}.$$

Because the swo $\underset{\sim}{\succsim}$ satisfies Pigou-Dalton, we have

$$G_\phi \leq \inf_{k \in \mathbb{N}} \frac{a_r}{a_{r+1}} \leq \frac{a_1}{a_2}.$$

Therefore, for any $x, y \in \mathbb{R}$, with $x \geq y$:

$$\kappa > \lambda \cdot a_1 / a_2 \geq \frac{\phi(x+\lambda)-\phi(x)}{\phi(y)-\phi(y-1)}.$$

If the swo $\underset{\sim}{\succsim}$ is proper and regular rank-dependent, then it clearly satisfies Minimal Aggregation. Let us show that it also satisfies Minimal Non-Aggregation, where in the statement of this property we take $\underline{z} = 0$, $\overline{z} > 1$, $\delta = 1$ and $\epsilon = \lambda$. Consider any $k \in \mathbb{N}$, and any $\mathbf{x}, \mathbf{y} \in \mathbb{R}^k$ and $i \in \{1,...,k\}$, such that (i) $i \in I_W(\mathbf{y})$, $y_i \leq 0$ and $x_i - y_i \geq 1$; and (ii) for all $j \in \{1,...,k\}$ with $j \neq i$ and $x_j \neq y_j$, it holds that $j \in I_B(\mathbf{x}) \cap I_B(\mathbf{y})$, $y_j \geq \overline{z}$ and $y_j - x_j \leq \lambda$. We need to show that $\mathbf{x} \underset{\sim}{\succsim} \mathbf{y}$. Let $R = \left|\left\{\ell \in \{1,...,k\}: x_\ell \leq x_i\right\}\right|$ the number of individuals with well-being lower than x_i in distribution $\mathbf{x}$; $R' = \left|\left\{\ell \in \{1,...,k\}: y_\ell \leq y_i\right\}\right|$ the number of individuals with well-being lower than y_i in distribution $\mathbf{y}$; $K = \left|\left\{j \in \{1,...,k\} : j \neq i, x_j \neq y_j\right\}\right|$ the number of individuals other than i with different well-being in $\mathbf{x}$ and $\mathbf{y}$. By definition of a proper rank-dependent swo:[8]

$$\mathbf{x} \succsim \mathbf{y} \quad \Leftrightarrow \quad \sum_{r=1}^{R'-1} a_r \phi\left(x_{[r]}\right) + \sum_{r=R'}^{R} a_r \phi\left(x_{[r]}\right) + \sum_{r=R+1}^{k-K} a_r \phi\left(x_{[r]}\right) + \sum_{r=k-K+1}^{k} a_r \phi\left(x_{[r]}\right)$$

$$\geq \sum_{r=1}^{R'-1} a_r \phi\left(y_{[r]}\right) + \sum_{r=R'}^{R} a_r \phi\left(y_{[r]}\right) + \sum_{r=R+1}^{k-K} a_r \phi\left(y_{[r]}\right) + \sum_{r=k-K+1}^{k} a_r \phi\left(y_{[r]}\right)$$

By definition of $\mathbf{x}$ and $\mathbf{y}$, this can be written:

$$\mathbf{x} \succsim \mathbf{y} \Leftrightarrow \sum_{r=R'}^{R} a_r \phi\left(x_{[r]}\right) + \sum_{r=k-K+1}^{k} a_r \phi\left(x_{[r]}\right) \geq \sum_{r=R'}^{R} a_r \phi\left(y_{[r]}\right) + \sum_{r=k-K+1}^{k} a_r \phi\left(y_{[r]}\right)$$

Given that $y_j - x_j \leq \lambda$ for all $j \in \{1,\dots,k\}$ with $j \neq i$ and $x_j \neq y_j$ (and $x_j = x_{[k]}$ for all such j), a sufficient condition to have $\mathbf{x} \succsim \mathbf{y}$ is:

$$\sum_{r=R'}^{R} a_r \left[\phi\left(x_{[r]}\right) - \phi\left(y_{[r]}\right) \right] \geq \left[\sum_{r=k-K+1}^{k} a_r \right]\left(\phi\left(x_{[k]} + \lambda\right) - \phi\left(x_{[k]}\right) \right)$$

But $\displaystyle\sum_{r=R'}^{R} a_r \left[\phi\left(x_{[r]}\right) - \phi\left(y_{[r]}\right) \right] \geq a_R \left[\phi\left(x_i\right) - \phi\left(y_i\right) \right] \geq a_R \left[\phi\left(x_i\right) - \phi\left(x_i - 1\right) \right]$, and

$$\frac{a_R}{\sum_{r=k-K+1}^{k} a_r} \geq \frac{a_R}{\sum_{r=R}^{+\infty} a_r} \geq \kappa > \frac{\phi\left(x_{[k]} + \lambda\right) - \phi\left(x_{[k]}\right)}{\phi\left(x_i\right) - \phi\left(x_i - 1\right)}.$$

It is then the case that $\mathbf{x} \succsim \mathbf{y}$. ∎

Proof of Proposition 6. Case 1: The swo $\succsim$ on $\mathbf{X}$ is egalitarian. Clearly the reversed repugnant conclusion is not avoided.

Case 2: The swo $\succsim$ on $\mathbf{X}$ has non-summable absolute weights and $c = 0$. Consider any $k \in \mathbb{N}$, $y \in \mathbb{R}_{++}$ and $z \in (0, y)$. By definition of a simple rank-dependent generalized utilitarian swo:

$$(y)_k \succsim (z)_m \Leftrightarrow \left(\sum_{r=1}^{k} a_r \right) \phi(y) \geq \left(\sum_{r=1}^{m} a_r \right) \phi(z).$$

But given that the absolute weights are non-summable, there must exist m' such that

$$\frac{\left(\sum_{r=1}^{m'} a_r \right)}{\left(\sum_{r=1}^{k} a_r \right)} > \frac{\phi(y)}{\phi(z)}$$

so that $(z)_{m'} \succ (y)_k$. This contradicts Avoidance of the Repugnant Conclusion.

Case 3: The swo $\succsim$ on **X** has non-summable absolute weights and $c > 0$. Assume that there exists $\mathbf{x} \in \mathbf{X}$ such that $(z)_k \succsim \mathbf{x}$ for all $k \in \mathbb{N}$ and $z \in \mathbb{R}_{++}$. Let $\ell = n(\mathbf{x})$. By definition of a simple rank-dependent generalized utilitarian swo, $\mathbf{x} \succsim (x_{[1]})_n$. Take any $z' \in \mathbb{R}_{++}$ such that $z' < c$. By definition of a simple rank-dependent generalized utilitarian swo:

$$(x_{[1]})_n \succ (z')_k \Leftrightarrow \left(\sum_{r=1}^{n} a_r \right)\left(\phi\left(x_{[1]}\right) - \phi(c) \right) > \left(\sum_{r=1}^{k} a_r \right)\left(\phi(z') - \phi(c) \right).$$

If $x_{[1]} > z'$ then $(x_{[1]})_n \succ (z')_n$, so that by transitivity $\mathbf{x} \succ (z')_n$, which is a contradiction. If $x_{[1]} \le z' < c$ then $\left(\phi\left(x_{[1]}\right) - \phi(c) \right) \le \left(\phi(z') - \phi(c) \right) < 0$ and

$$(x_{[1]})_n \succ (z')_k \Leftrightarrow \frac{\left(\sum_{r=1}^{k} a_r \right)}{\left(\sum_{r=1}^{n} a_r \right)} > \frac{\phi(c) - \phi\left(x_{[1]}\right)}{\phi(c) - \phi(z')}.$$

But given that the absolute weights are non-summable, there must exist k' such that

$$\frac{\left(\sum_{r=1}^{k'} a_r \right)}{\left(\sum_{r=1}^{n} a_r \right)} > \frac{\phi(c) - \phi\left(x_{[1]}\right)}{\phi(c) - \phi(z')}$$

so that $(x_{[1]})_n \succ (z')_{k'}$ and therefore $\mathbf{x} \succ (z')_{k'}$. This contradicts Avoidance of the Very Sadistic Conclusion.

Case 4: The swo $\succsim$ on is proper rank-dependent. Let us check that $\succsim$ satisfies all the required properties.

Because $\succsim$ is proper rank-dependent $a_2 > 0$ and $(a_1 + a_2)/a_1 > 1$. By continuity of ϕ, for any $y \in \mathbb{R}_{++}$ such that $y > c$ there exists $z \in \mathbb{R}_{++}$ such that

$$1 < \frac{\phi(y) - \phi(c)}{\phi(z) - \phi(c)} < \frac{a_1 + a_2}{a_1}$$

so that $(a_1 + a_2)(\phi(z) - \phi(c)) > a_1 (\phi(y) - \phi(c))$. By definition of a simple rank-dependent generalized utilitarian swo, this implies that $(z)_2 \succ (y)_1$. Avoidance of the Reversed Repugnant Conclusion is satisfied.

Because $\succsim$ is proper rank-dependent so that $\sum_{r=1}^{+\infty} a_r < +\infty$, it is also the case that for any $\varepsilon \in \mathbb{R}_{++}$ there exists $\ell \in \mathbb{N}$ such that $\left(\sum_{r=1}^{+\infty} a_r \right)/\left(\sum_{r=1}^{\ell} a_r \right) < 1 + \varepsilon$.

Thus consider $\ell \in \mathbb{N}$, $y \in \mathbb{R}_{--}$ such that

$$\frac{\sum_{r=1}^{+\infty} a_r}{\sum_{r=1}^{\ell} a_r} < \frac{\phi(c) - \phi(y)}{\phi(c) - \phi(0)} = 1 + \frac{\phi(0) - \phi(y)}{\phi(c) - \phi(0)}.$$

Let us show that $(0)_k \succsim (y)_\ell$ for any $k \in \mathbb{N}$. For this to be the case, we need that $\left(\sum_{r=1}^k a_r\right)(\phi(0) - \phi(c)) \ge \left(\sum_{r=1}^\ell a_r\right)(\phi(y) - \phi(c))$ for all $k \in \mathbb{N}$. Given that $0 \le c$, a suffi-

cient condition is then that $\left(\sum_{r=1}^{+\infty} a_r\right)(\phi(c) - \phi(0)) \le \left(\sum_{r=1}^\ell a_r\right)(\phi(c) - \phi(y))$, which is

true by definition of ℓ and y. For any $z \in \mathbb{R}_{++}$ and any $k \in \mathbb{N}$, $(z)_k \succ (0)_k$ and therefore $(z)_k \succ (y)_\ell$. Hence Avoidance of the Very Sadistic Conclusion is satisfied.

If $c > 0$, for any $y > c > z > 0$ and for any $m \ge \ell$, by definition of a simple rank-dependent generalized utilitarian swo, $(y)_\ell \succ (z)_m$ so that Avoidance of the Repugnant Conclusion is satisfied. If $c = 0$ then for any $y > z > 0$, because $\succsim$ is proper rank-dependent, there exists $k \in \mathbb{N}$ such that

$$\frac{\sum_{r=1}^{+\infty} a_r}{\sum_{r=1}^k a_r} < \frac{\phi(y) - \phi(0)}{\phi(z) - \phi(0)} = 1 + \frac{\phi(y) - \phi(z)}{\phi(z) - \phi(0)}.$$

Hence, for all $m \ge \ell \ge k$:

$$\left(\sum_{r=1}^\ell a_r\right)(\phi(y) - \phi(0)) \ge \left(\sum_{r=1}^k a_r\right)(\phi(y) - \phi(0)) > \left(\sum_{r=1}^{+\infty} a_r\right)(\phi(z) - \phi(0))$$
$$\ge \left(\sum_{r=1}^m a_r\right)(\phi(z) - \phi(0)).$$

By definition of a simple rank-dependent generalized utilitarian swo, $(y)_\ell \succ (z)_m$. Hence Avoidance of the Repugnant Conclusion is satisfied. ∎

Proof of Proposition 7. Consider any $\hat{k} \in \mathbb{N}$, $\hat{y} \in \mathbb{R}_{++}$, $\hat{z} \in [0, \hat{y}]$ and $\hat{w} \in (0, \hat{z})$.

Let $z < 0$ be the well-being level in the statement of Weak Non-Sadism Condition, and k the integer in this statement. For $\ell \ge k$, let $\theta_\ell = [(\ell + k)\,\phi\,(y) - k\phi(z)] / \ell$. When ℓ is large enough, θ_ℓ can become arbitrary close to $\phi(\hat{y})$, so that $\phi^{-1}(\theta_\ell)$ is well-defined (ϕ is continuous and increasing and thus invertible). Let $\overline{\ell}$ be an integer such that $\phi^{-1}(\theta_{\overline{\ell}})$ is well-defined and denote $\zeta = \phi^{-1}(\theta_{\overline{\ell}})$.

By definition of a prioritarian swo, $((\zeta)_{\bar{\ell}},(z)_k)) \sim (\hat{y})_{\bar{\ell}+k}$. But, by the Weak Non-Sadism Condition, for any $m \in \mathbb{N}$, $((\zeta)_{\bar{\ell}},(\hat{w})_m) \gtrsim ((\zeta)_{\bar{\ell}},(z)_k)$. However, for m large enough we have:

$$\bar{\ell}\phi(\zeta) + m\phi(\hat{w}) < (\bar{\ell}+m)\phi(\hat{z}),$$

because $\hat{w} < \hat{z}$. Thus, by definition of a prioritarian swo, there exists $\bar{m}$ large enough (and in particular such that $\bar{m} > k$) such that $(\hat{z})_{\bar{\ell}+\bar{m}} \succ ((\zeta)_{\bar{\ell}},(\hat{w})_{\bar{m}})$. By transitivity of social welfare orderings, given that $((\zeta)_{\bar{\ell}},(\hat{w})_m) \gtrsim ((\zeta)_{\bar{\ell}},(z)_k)$ and $((\zeta)_{\bar{\ell}},(z)_k) \sim (\hat{y})_{\bar{\ell}+k}$, we obtain that $(\hat{z})_{\bar{\ell}+\bar{m}} \succ (\hat{y})_{\bar{\ell}+k}$.

In conclusion, for any $k \in \mathbb{N}$, $\hat{y} \in \mathbb{R}_{++}$ and $\hat{z} \in [0, \hat{y}]$, there exists $\bar{m} > \bar{\ell}$ such that $(\hat{z})_{\bar{\ell}+\bar{m}} \succ (\hat{y})_{\bar{\ell}+k}$. This is a violation of Avoidance of the Repugnant Conclusion. ∎

Proof of Proposition 8. By the Weak Non-Sadism Condition, there exist $z < 0$ and $k \in \mathbb{N}$ such that, for any $z' < z$ and $y \in \mathbb{R}_{++}$: $((z')_1,(y)_{k+1}) \gtrsim ((z')_1,(z)_k)$. By definition of an egalitarian swo and transitivity, this implies that $(z')_{k+2} \gtrsim (z')_{k+1}$. This is a violation of Negative Mere Addition Principle. ∎

Proof of Proposition 9. Let us (without loss of generality) normalize function ϕ so that $\phi(0) = 0$.

The simple rank-dependent swo $\gtrsim$ satisfies Weak Non-Sadism Condition. Assume that function ϕ is concave and bounded above and that there exists $\kappa \in \mathbb{R}_{++}$ such that, for all $k \in \mathbb{N}, a_k \geq \kappa \cdot \left(\sum_{r=k+1}^{+\infty} a_r \right)$. Let $\bar{u} := \sup\{\phi(z) : z \in \mathbb{R}\}$. Choose $\hat{z} \in \mathbb{R}_{--}$ such that:[9]

$$-\phi(\hat{z}) > \frac{\bar{u}}{\kappa}. \tag{5}$$

Then, for any initial distribution $\mathbf{x} \in \mathbf{X}$, let r_1 be the highest rank of an individual with well-being strictly lower than $\hat{z}$ and r_2 the highest rank of an individual with well-being strictly lower than 0. By definition of a simple rank-dependent swo, for any and $\ell \in \mathbb{N}$, we have $(\mathbf{x},(0)_\ell) \gtrsim (\mathbf{x},(\hat{z})_1)$ if and only if:

$$\sum_{r=1}^{r_1} a_r \left(\phi(x_{[r]}) - \phi(c) \right) + a_{r_1+1}\left(\phi(\hat{z}) - \phi(c) \right) + \sum_{r=r_1+2}^{n(x)+1} a_r \left(\phi(x_{[r-1]}) - \phi(c) \right)$$

$$\leq \sum_{r=1}^{r_1+r_2} a_r \left(\phi(x_{[r]}) - \phi(c) \right) + \left(\sum_{r=r_1+r_2+1}^{r_1+\ell+r_2} a_r \right)\left(\phi(0) - \phi(c) \right) \tag{6}$$

$$+ \sum_{r=r_1+\ell+r_2+1}^{\ell+n(x)} a_r \left(\phi(x_{[r-\ell]}) - \phi(c) \right)$$

Given that $0 = \phi(0) > \phi(x_{[r]}) \geq \phi(\hat{z})$ for all $r_2 \geq r > r_1$, we have

$$a_{r_1+1}\left(\phi(\hat{z}) - \phi(c)\right) + \sum_{r=r_1+2}^{r_1+r_2+1} a_r\left(\phi(x_{[r-k]}) - (c)\right)$$

$$\leq \sum_{r=r_1+1}^{r_1+r_2} a_r\left(\phi(x_{[r]}) - (c)\right) + a_{r_1+r_2+1}\left(\phi(\hat{z}) - \phi(c)\right),$$

and,

$$\sum_{r=r_1+r_2+2}^{n(x)+1} a_r\left(\phi(x_{[r-k]}) - \phi(c)\right) \leq \sum_{r=r_1+r_2+2}^{n(x)+1} a_r\left(\bar{u} - \phi(c)\right) < \left(\sum_{r=r_1+r_2+2}^{+\infty} a_r\right)\left(\bar{u} - \phi(c)\right).$$

Hence,

$$\sum_{r=1}^{r_1} a_r\left(\phi(x_{[r]}) - \phi(c)\right) + a_{r_1+1}\left(\phi(\hat{z}) - \phi(c)\right) + \sum_{r=r_1+2}^{n(x)+1} a_r\left(\phi(x_{[r-1]}) - \phi(c)\right)$$

$$< \sum_{r=r_1+1}^{r_1+r_2} a_r\left(\phi(x_{[r]}) - (c)\right) + a_{r_1+r_2+1}\left(\phi(\hat{z}) - \phi(c)\right) + \left(\sum_{r=r_1+r_2+2}^{+\infty} a_r\right)\left(\bar{u} - \phi(c)\right).$$

Also, given that $\phi(x_{[r]}) \geq \phi(0)$ for all $r \geq r_2+1$ and $0 \leq c$ (so that $\phi(0) - \phi(c) \leq 0$):

$$\left(\sum_{r=r_1+r_2+1}^{r_1+r_2+\ell} a_r\right)\left(\phi(0) - \phi(c)\right) + \sum_{r=r_1+\ell+r_2+1}^{\ell+n(x)} a_r\left(\phi(x_{[r-\ell]}) - \phi(c)\right)$$

$$> \left(\sum_{r=r_1+r_2+1}^{+\infty} a_r\right)\left(\phi(0) - (c)\right).$$

Hence,

$$\sum_{r=1}^{r_1+r_2} a_r\left(\phi(x_{[r]}) - \phi(c)\right) + \left(\sum_{r=r_1+r_2+1}^{+\infty} a_r\right)\left(\phi(0) - \phi(c)\right)$$

$$\leq \sum_{r=1}^{r_1+r_2} a_r\left(\phi(x_{[r]}) - \phi(c)\right) + \left(\sum_{r=r_1+r_2+1}^{r_1+\ell+r_2} a_r\right)\left(\phi(0) - \phi(c)\right)$$

$$+ \sum_{r=r_1+\ell+r_2+1}^{\ell+n(x)} a_r\left(\phi(x_{[r-\ell]}) - \phi(c)\right)$$

A sufficient condition for inequality (6) to hold is therefore:

$$a_{r_1+r_2+1}\left(\phi(\hat{z})-\phi(c)\right)+\left(\sum_{r=r_1+r_2+2}^{+\infty}a_r\right)(\bar{u}-\phi(c))\leq\left(\sum_{r=r_1+r_2+1}^{+\infty}a_r\right)(\phi(0)-\phi(c)).$$

Given that $\phi(0)=0$, this sufficient condition can be written

$$a_{r_1+r_2+1}\phi\left(\hat{z}\right)+\left(\sum_{r=r_1+r_2+2}^{+\infty}a_r\right)\bar{u}\leq 0.$$

But we know that:

$$\frac{1}{k}\geq\frac{\sum_{r=k+1}^{+\infty}a_r}{a_k}\text{ for all }k\in\mathbb{N},\text{ and }-\phi(\hat{z})>\frac{\hat{u}}{k}.$$

This sufficient condition is thus satisfied.

Therefore we have shown that there exist $z\in\mathbb{R}_{--}$ such that $(\mathbf{x},(0)_\ell)\succsim(\mathbf{x},(\hat{z})_1)$ for any $\ell\in\mathbb{N}$. The Suppes-Sen principle implies that, for any $y\in\mathbb{R}_{++}(\mathbf{x},(y)_\ell)\succ(\mathbf{x},(0)_\ell)$, and by transitivity $(\mathbf{x},(y)_\ell)\succ(\mathbf{x},(z)_1)$.

The simple rank-dependent swo $\succsim$ satisfies Negative Mere Addition Principle. Consider any $\mathbf{x}\in\mathbf{X}$ and any $z\in\mathbb{R}_{--}$. Let r_1 be the highest rank of an individual with well-being strictly lower than z and r_2 the highest rank of an individual with well-being strictly lower than c. By definition of a simple rank-dependent swo $\mathbf{x}\succ(\mathbf{x},(z)_1)$ if and only if:

$$\sum_{r=1}^{r_1}a_r\left(\phi\left(x_{[r]}\right)-\phi(c)\right)+a_{r_1+1}\left(\phi(z)-\phi(c)\right)+\sum_{r=r_1+2}^{r_2+1}a_r\left(\phi\left(x_{[r-1]}\right)-\phi(c)\right)$$

$$+\sum_{r=r_2+2}^{n(x)+1}a_r\left(\phi\left(x_{[r-1]}\right)-\phi(c)\right)\tag{7}$$

$$<\sum_{r=1}^{r_1}a_r\left(\phi\left(x_{[r]}\right)-\phi(c)\right)+\sum_{r=r_1+1}^{r_2}a_r\left(\phi\left(x_{[r]}\right)-\phi(c)\right)+\sum_{r=r_2+1}^{n(x)}a_r\left(\phi\left(x_{[r]}\right)-\phi(c)\right)$$

Inequality (7) can be written:

$$a_{r_1+1}\left(\phi(z)-\phi\left(x_{[r_1+1]}\right)\right)+\sum_{r=r_1+2}^{r_2}a_r\left(\phi\left(x_{[r-1]}\right)-\phi\left(x_{[r]}\right)\right)+a_{r_2+1}\left(\phi\left(x_{[r_2]}\right)-\phi(c)\right)$$

$$<\sum_{r=r_2+1}^{n(x)}(a_r-a_{r+1})\left(\phi\left(x_{[r]}\right)-\phi(c)\right)$$

By definition of r_1 and r_2 the left-hand side of the above inequality is strictly negative, while the right-hand side is non-negative. Hence inequality (7) holds, and therefore $\mathbf{x}\succ(\mathbf{x},(z)_1)$. ∎

Notes

1. We actually need stronger measurement conditions except for maximin, a population-size independent version of the egalitarian criterion introduced in Definition 2.
2. The formal statement of the principle is as follows:

   Independence wrt. Ordered Vectors. A swo $\succsim$ on $\mathbf{X}$ satisfies *independence wrt. ordered vectors* if, for all $k \in \mathbb{N}$, all $M \subseteq \{1,\ldots,k\}$ and all $\mathbf{x}, \mathbf{y} \in \mathbb{R}^k$, $\mathbf{x} \sim \mathbf{y}$ implies $\mathbf{x}' \sim \mathbf{y}'$ whenever $x_{[r]} = y_{[r]}$ and $x'_{[r]} = y'_{[r]}$ for all $r \in M$ and $x'_{[r]} = x_{[r]}$ and $y'_{[r]} = y_{[r]}$ for all $r \in \{1,\ldots,k\} \setminus M$.

3. With $\tilde{\mathbf{x}}_{[-r']} z'_3 \succ \tilde{\mathbf{y}}_{[-r']} z_4$ for any essential rank r' such that there exists an ordered vector for which increasing the well-being of the individual with r' the level of well-being yields a strict social welfare improvement.
4. The axioms of Extended Continuity, Montonicity, and Restricted Dominance imply that such a level exists and is unique.
5. Only Bossert (1990a), Blackorby, Bossert, and Donaldson (2005, Ch. 5), and Arrhenius (forthcoming) mention versions of egalitarianism.
6. The leximin ordering $\succsim^k_{\text{lex}}$ over $\mathbb{R}^k$ is defined as follows. For all $\mathbf{x}, \mathbf{y} \in \mathbb{R}^k$: $\mathbf{x} \sim^k_{\text{lex}} \mathbf{y}$ if and only if $\mathbf{x}_{[\,]} = \mathbf{y}_{[\,]}$, $\mathbf{x} \succ^k_{\text{lex}} \mathbf{y}$ if and only if there exists $r \in \{1,\ldots,k\}$ such $x_{[r]} > y_{[r]}$ and $x_{[\ell]} = y_{[\ell]}$ for all $\ell \in \{1,\ldots,r-1\}$.
7. Other formalizations have been proposed, for instance by Blackorby, Bossert, and Donaldson (2005). The formulation is slightly stronger than the one they have, but we think it is in the spirit of Parfit's initial formulation.
8. We use the convention that $\sum_{r=k}^{k-1} u_r = 0$.

9. There must exist such a $\hat{z} \in \mathbb{R}_{--}$. Indeed $\phi(0) = 0$ and ϕ is concave, so that it is not bounded below on $\mathbb{R}$.

References

Arrhenius, Gustaf 2000a. "Future Generations: A Challenge for Moral Theory." PhD diss. Uppsala University.

Arrhenius, Gustaf 2000b. "An Impossibility Theorem for Welfarist Axiologies." *Economics and Philosophy* 16: 247–266.

Arrhenius, Gustaf. Forthcoming. *Population Ethics: The Challenge of Future Generations.* Oxford: Oxford University Press.

Asheim, Geir B. and Stéphane Zuber. 2014. "Escaping the Repugnant Conclusion: Rank-Discounted Utilitarianism with Variable Population." *Theoretical Economics* 9: 629–650.

Blackorby, Charles, Bossert, Walter, and David Donaldson. 1996. "Leximin Population Ethics." *Mathematical Social Sciences* 31: 115–131.

Blackorby, Charles, Bossert, Walter, and David Donaldson. 2004. "Critical-Level Population Principles and the Repugnant Conclusion." In *The Repugnant Conclusion*, edited by J. Ryberg and T. Tännsjö. Dordrecht: Kluwer Academic Press.

Blackorby, Charles, Bossert, Walter, and David Donaldson. 2005. *Population Issues in Social Choice Theory, Welfare Economics, and Ethics*. Cambridge: Cambridge University Press.

Blackorby, Charles and David Donaldson. 1984. "Social Criteria for Evaluating Population Change." *Journal of Public Economics* 25: 13–31.

Bossert, Walter. 1990a. "Maximin Welfare Orderings with Variable Population Size." *Social Choice and Welfare* 7: 39–45.

Bossert, Walter. 1990b. "An Axiomatization of the Single-Series Ginis." *Journal of Economic Theory* 50: 82–92.

Broome, John. 2004. *Weighing Lives*. Oxford: Oxford University Press.

Carlson, Erik. 1998. "Mere Addition and Two Trilemmas of Population Ethics." *Economics and Philosophy* 14: 283–306.

Chateauneuf, Alain, Cohen, Michèle, and Isaac Meilijson. 2005. "More Pessimism than Greediness: A Characterization of Monotone Risk Aversion in the Rank-Dependent Expected Utility Model." *Economic Theory* 25: 649–667.

Dasgupta, Partha S. 2005. "Regarding Optimum Population." *Journal of Political Philosophy* 13: 414–442.

Donaldson, David and John A. Weymark. 1980. "A Single Parameter Generalization of the Gini Indices of Inequality." *Journal of Economic Theory* 22: 67–86.

Ebert, Udo. 1988. "Measurement of Inequality: An Attempt at Unification and Generalization." *Social Choice and Welfare* 5: 147–169.

Fleurbaey, Marc and Bertil Tungodden. 2010. "The Tyranny of Non-Aggregation versus the Tyranny of Aggregation in Social Choices: A Real Dilemma." *Economic Theory* 44: 399–414.

Hurka, Thomas. 1983. "Value and Population Size." *Ethics* 93: 496–507.

Köbberling, Veronika and Peter P. Wakker. 2003. "Preference Foundations for Nonexpected Utility: A Generalized and Simplified Technique." *Mathematics of Operations Research* 28: 395–423.

Parfit, Derek. 1976. "On Doing the Best for Our Children." In *Ethics and Population*, edited by M. Bayles, 100–102. Cambridge: Schenkman.

Parfit, Derek. 1982. "Future Generations, Further Problems." *Philosophy and Public Affairs* 11: 113–172.

Parfit, Derek. 1984. *Reasons and Persons*. Oxford: Oxford University Press.

Pivato, Marcus. 2020. "Rank-Additive Population Ethics." *Economic Theory* 69: 861–918.

Sider, Theodore R. 1991. "Might Theory X Be a Theory of Diminishing Marginal Value?" *Analysis* 51: 265–271.

Wakker, Peter P. 1989. "Continuous Subjective Expected Utility with Nonadditive Probabilities." *Journal of Mathematical Economics* 18: 1–27.

Zuber, Stéphane. 2017. "Éthique de la population: L'apport des critères de bien-être dépendant du rang." *Revue Économique* 68 : 73–96.

CHAPTER 5

GETTING PERSONAL

The Intuition of Neutrality Reinterpreted

WLODEK RABINOWICZ

ACCORDING to the Intuition of Neutrality, in its axiological version, there is a range of well-being levels such that adding people with lives at these levels does not make the world either better or worse. On the standard interpretation of this "neutral range," it extends from the zero level of well-being upwards, with the upper limit being some positive, though not very high, well-being level. (On the radical interpretation, the range of neutrality still starts at zero but has no upper limit.) Since a life at a positive well-being level is thought to be good for the person who lives this life, the Intuition of Neutrality drives a wedge between what is good for a person and what is impersonally good: adding a person with a life that is good for her but has a well-being level within the neutral range doesn't make the world better, even if no one else is negatively affected by the addition. To this extent then, the Intuition comes into conflict with one of the basic tenets of welfarism.

In Rabinowicz (2009) I discussed the Intuition of Neutrality and defended it against John Broome's challenging objections (Broome 2004). I also sketched a particular axiological theory—neutral-range utilitarianism—that incorporates this intuition. While Broome's criticisms did not target the disparity the Intuition brings in between personal and impersonal goodness,[1] I still thought that it was there the main problem with the Intuition was to be found. Therefore, I also suggested, but did not elaborate in that paper, a reinterpretation of the neutral range that would remove the problematic disparity. On this reinterpretation, a life at a level within the neutral range is not merely impersonally neutral—it does not merely fail to make the world better or worse—but it also is neutral in its personal value: it is neither good nor bad for a person to have such a life. That life's well-being level is neither positive nor negative. A life at this level is thus neither worth living nor worth not living. To put it differently, it is neither better nor worse for its owner than non-existence. Nevertheless, among such personally neutral lives, some might still be personally better or worse than others. Thus, there might be a range of personally neutral well-being levels—some higher and some lower. This is possible provided that lives at these levels can be incommensurable in their personal value with non-existence. Unlike equal goodness, incommensurability is not a transitive relation, which means that a personally neutral life—if it is incommensurable with non-existence—can still be personally better than another personally neutral life.

In this paper, I want to explore some of the implications of this "personalization" of the Intuition of Neutrality. In particular, while such a move might seem to make neutral-range utilitarianism more plausible, I will argue that the appearances are misleading. For one thing, the resulting theory gets considerably more complicated: we need to allow not only for lives that are incommensurable with non-existence but also for lives that are incommensurable with each other. This means that some lives' well-being levels might not be ordinally comparable. Allowing for lives that are incommensurable in personal value makes technical trouble for a utilitarian axiology. One might even wonder whether such an axiology can accommodate incommensurable lives. While this worry, I think, can be dealt with, there is also a substantive issue that neutral-range utilitarianism needs to confront. In my 2009 paper, I pointed out that personalizing the Intuition of Neutrality reinstates the Repugnant Conclusion that neutral-range utilitarianism was supposed to avoid. But I also suggested that this reinterpretation at the same time removes, or at least assuages, the repugnancy of the Repugnant Conclusion. I now think this diagnosis was premature: if the Intuition of Neutrality is reinterpreted on the lines I have suggested, then even a genuinely repugnant conclusion threatens to be reinstated. This poses a challenge to neutral-range utilitarianism. Indeed, on this new picture, the whole landscape of personal value becomes more complicated. Not only must we give up the standard assumption that well-being levels of lives are linearly ordered; as we have seen, we should also allow that these levels need not even be ordinally comparable. In addition, as I am going to show, we can no longer assume that all personally good lives must be better than personally neutral lives. Nor that all personally bad lives must be worse than personally neutral lives. While such implications of this new approach may be surprising, they should be accepted. What also needs to be stressed is that the issues that on this new interpretation arise for the neutral-range utilitarianism do not undermine the personalized Neutrality Intuition itself. The latter can be retained even if the neutral-range utilitarianism were given up.

In Section 1, I will present the standard interpretation of the Intuition of Neutrality and then move on, in Section 2, to neutral-range utilitarianism (NRU). In Section 3, I will describe the personalized version of the Intuition and the way this personalization affects NRU. The picture I will draw will be essentially the same, although more elaborate, as the one I sketched in Rabinowicz (2009). Then, in Section 4, I will consider how this picture changes and gets more complicated, in ways I didn't envisage in my earlier paper, if one allows that different lives might not be commensurable in their personal value.

1. THE INTUITION OF NEUTRALITY: STANDARD INTERPRETATION

As a normative principle of action, the Intuition of Neutrality goes back to Jan Narveson's famous pronouncement: "We are in favour of making people happy, we are neutral about making happy people" (Narveson 1973). A more guarded, less committal formulation of this ethical Intuition is provided by John Brome in *Weighing Lives*:

> We think intuitively that adding a person to the world is very often ethically neutral. We do not think that just a single level of well-being is neutral. (Broome 2004, 143)

Here, following Broome (ibid., 145f), I am going to focus on the axiological version of the Intuition. It can be put as follows:

> *Intuition of Neutrality*: There is a range of well-being levels, call it *the neutral range*, such that adding a person with a life at one of these levels, without affecting the well-being of anyone else, does not make the world either better or worse.

Broome himself was initially attracted to this Intuition, but then eventually felt compelled to give it up, for several reasons that I am not going to discuss in this paper. But see Rabinowicz (2009) for an extended critical discussion of Broome's objections. For Broome's reply, see Broome (2009).

What is supposed to be the scope of the neutral range? On the moderate interpretation, this range begins at the zero level of well-being and extends upwards, to some positive, though not too high, well-being level. On the radical interpretation, it extends from zero all the way up, to infinity. Here I will focus on the moderate interpretation, according to which the neutral range has an upper as well as a lower boundary.[2] On this view, adding bad lives—lives at negative well-being levels—makes the world worse, while adding excellent lives makes the world better. In what follows, I am going to refer to this interpretation of the neutral range as the "standard" one, although I don't want to imply by this label that any dominant view has already developed in this area.

By a bad life I mean a *personally* bad life, that is, a life that is bad for the person who lives it. For that person such a life is "worth not living": It is worse for her than non-existence. I assume that lives at negative levels of well-being are bad in this sense.

Analogously, a good life is a life that is personally good, or worth living: it is a life that is better for the person who lives it than non-existence. A life's well-being level is positive iff the life in question is good in this sense.

In line with this interpretation of positive and negative well-being levels, the zero level of well-being characterizes a life that for the person who lives it has the same value as non-existence.

I will assume that a life's personal value does not depend on the numerical identity of the person who lives this life. Thus, for anyone who would live this life its personal value would for her be the same. I think it is a reasonable assumption, provided we take a person's life to contain everything that characterizes this person—not merely what she does and what happens to her, and not just her external circumstances as they change over time, but also her internal, psychological make-up and internal history. Given this all-encompassing conception of a life, it is plausible to assume that, for anyone who would live it, it would have the same value.[3]

Several philosophers have argued that personal value comparisons between one's life and one's non-existence make no sense. It makes no sense on their view to suggest that it can be better (or worse) for me to live my life than never to live at all. I disagree; I think that comparisons of this kind do make sense, even though they might be difficult to make. (See Arrhenius and Rabinowicz 2010; 2015; cf. also Johansson 2010 and Holtug 2001 for related views. For challenging objections, see especially Bykvist 2007; 2015.) Here I cannot argue this point, but I can at least say something to allay the immediate worry such a claim might invite.

Consider:

(i) It is better for John to have the life he has than not to exist.

This statement implies, according to the critic, that

(ii) If John didn't exist, it would have been worse for him than to have the life he has.

But, if John didn't exist, nothing *could* have been worse, or better, for him, as there would be no him for whom anything could be better or worse. Non-existents cannot have any properties or stand in any relations. Thus, (ii) is absurd, which shows that such claims as (i) have absurd implications.[4]

In my view, this objection is not justified: Contrary to appearances, (ii) does not follow from (i). (i) and the consequent of (ii) state that a certain relation obtains/would have obtained between three relata: John himself and two states of affairs, John having the life he has, and John's non-existence. The former state is better/would have been better for John than the latter state. Now, a relation can only obtain if all its relata exist. Consequently, it couldn't have obtained if John did not exist. Which means that (ii) must be false: if John did not exist, no relation in which he is one of the relata could have obtained. On the other hand, (i) may well be true. If John does exist, the requisite relation between him and the two states of affairs may well obtain.

But, one might wonder, if John does exist, what, then, about the state of his non-existence? Does this state exist in such a case? The answer is yes, if we think of states of affairs as abstract objects. As such (as abstract entities), they exist even when they do not obtain.[5] We may therefore conclude that there is no implication from (i) to (ii): (ii) is necessarily false for the reasons that do not apply to (i).

I will therefore continue to account for the personal value of a life in terms of comparisons with non-existence: For any person, a life L is good (bad, neutral) for that person iff it would be better (worse, neither better nor worse) for her to have life L than not to exist at all.

Let us go back to the main thread. The Intuition of Neutrality together with the standard conception of the neutral range imply that adding a good life need not always make the world better. It will not make it better, or worse for that matter, if the well-being level of that good life lies within the neutral range. Thus, on this view, there is a striking *disparity* between what is good for a person and what is impersonally good: a life might be good for the person who lives it without being impersonally contributively good—without making the world better. This disparity might well be precisely what attracts some philosophers to the Intuition of Neutrality, but at the same time it is a worrying implication from a strictly welfarist point of view. I will return to this issue in Section 3.

How is the neutrality of life additions to be interpreted? If adding a life with a well-being level in the neutral range (while keeping the well-being levels of everyone else unaffected) does not make the world either better or worse, will the world with such an added life be equally as good as the original world? Or will it instead be *incommensurable* with the original world—neither better or worse nor equally as good? It is easy to prove that incommensurability is the only viable alternative.

As a preparation for the proof, let us note that the neutral range is supposed to contain more than just one well-being level. Furthermore, according to the standard conception of the neutral range, the well-being levels are linearly ordered, from higher to lower. Consequently, it follows that *for every well-being level m in the neutral range there is at least one level in that range that is higher or lower than m*. (While the linear ordering assumption will be criticized in Section 4, the italicized claim won't be questioned. And it is only this weak claim that is needed for the proof to follow.)

Let A be the original world and B the world with an added person, call her Barbara, whose life in B is at a well-being level m. Suppose that m lies in the neutral range. By the Intuition of Neutrality, this implies that B is neither better nor worse than A. We want to prove that B is not equally as good as A either. It will then follow that these two worlds must be incommensurable.

Proof:[6] As shown above, there must be at least one level n in the neutral range that is either higher than m or lower than m. Now, consider a world C in which Barbara is added to the original world at well-being level n. Just as in B, no one else in C is affected by this addition.

Case 1: $n > m$. Since it is better for Barbara to live at a higher rather than a lower level of well-being, C is better for her than B. And it is equally as good as B for everyone else. We may therefore conclude that C is better than B. This is implied by the following general principle:

> Suppose that worlds X and Y have the same population, I. (i) If X is better than Y for some individuals in I, while it is equally as good as Y for everyone else in I, then X is better than Y. (ii) If X and Y are equally as good for everyone in I, then X and Y are equally good.

This Pareto-like principle is an important part of the welfarist outlook. It establishes a minimal connection between personal and impersonal good. Following Broome (2004, Section 8.2) we might call it the *Principle of Personal Good*.

This principle is compatible with the Intuition of Neutrality, even though the latter, on the standard interpretation of the neutral range, introduces a disparity between personal and impersonal good. While the Intuition of Neutrality focuses on value comparisons between worlds with partly different populations, the Principle of Personal Good—as stated above—is restricted to comparisons between worlds that have the same population. This restriction is crucial. Without it, the Principle of Personal Good would come into conflict with the Intuition of Neutrality. To see this, note that if $n > m$ and both m and n are in the neutral range that stretches upwards from zero, n must be a positive level of well-being. But then C, in which Barbara's level is n, is better for her than A: It is better for her to live a life at a positive well-being level than not to exist at all. At the same time C is equally as good as A for everyone else. Thus, in the absence of the restriction, the Principle of Personal Good would imply that C is better than A. However, since n lies in the neutral range, the Intuition of Neutrality implies that C is not better than A.

It is an interesting issue whether and how principles such as the Principle of Personal Good can be extended to comparisons between worlds with variable populations. The argument I have just given shows that the straightforward extension of this principle would be in conflict with the Intuition of Neutrality *if* the standard conception of the neutral range is assumed. This argument doesn't go through, however, if the neutral range is reinterpreted as will be done in Section 3. Indeed, the straightforward extension of the Principle of Personal Good will then become possible without it coming into conflict with the reinterpreted Intuition of Neutrality: the restriction to worlds with the same population will be removed.

But let us return to the main proof. Suppose, for *reductio*, that B is equally as good as A. Then C, which by the Principle of Personal Good is better than B, must be better than A. (Betterness is transitive across equal goodness.) But since n just like m lies in the neutral range, the Intuition of Neutrality implies that C is *not* better than A. We must therefore conclude that B and A are not equally good.

Case 2: $n < m$. The Principle of Personal Good now implies that B is better than C. Consequently, if B were equally as good as A, A would also be better than C. But this again is excluded by the Intuition of Neutrality. This completes the proof.

Thus, adding a person with a well-being level that lies in the neutral range creates an incommensurability.[7] But how is this incommensurability to be explained? In the next section I suggest an explanation.

2. ANALYSIS OF VALUE RELATIONS AND NEUTRAL-RANGE UTILITARIANISM

I will start this section with rehearsing my general proposal as to how one might analyze different value relations, including the relation of incommensurability (cf. Rabinowicz

2008; 2012). Then, following Rabinowicz (2009), I will suggest how this account can be applied to the problem at hand.

My account of value relations conforms to the general format of the fitting-attitudes analysis of value (FA-analysis). On this approach, value statements are interpreted as normative assessments of pro- and con-attitudes towards evaluated objects. As for statements of value relations, it is then natural to interpret them as normative assessments of preferences regarding the compared objects. Betterness and equal good-ness are analyzed as follows:

> x is *better* than $y =_{df} x$ ought to be preferred to y.
> x is *equally as good* as $y =_{df} x$ and y ought to be equi-preferred.

Consequently, items x and y are incommensurable iff none of them of them ought to be preferred to the other nor ought they be equi-preferred.

There are two levels of normativity, the strong level of requirement ("ought") and the weak level of permission ("may"). Allowing for weak normativity as regards preferences makes room for further distinctions—further value relations—within the broad cate-gory of incommensurability. In particular, we can define the notion of parity, which is the typical (though not the only) form of incommensurability:

> x and y are *on a par* $=_{df} x$ may be preferred to y and y may be preferred to x.

Thus, in cases of parity, opposing preferences regarding the compared items are permissible.

This approach to value relations can easily be formalized. In Rabinowicz (2008), I proposed the following *intersection modeling*:

The modeling has two components—the domain D of items that are compared and the class K of all permissible preference orderings of this domain.

Betterness is defined as required preference:

> x is *better* than y iff x is preferred to y in every ordering in K.

This is just another way of saying that x ought to be preferred to y: every permissible preference ordering of the domain must incorporate this preference.

Analogously, equal goodness is defined as required equi-preference:

> x and y are *equally good* iff they are equi-preferred in every K-ordering.

In case of parity, opposing preferences are allowed:

> x and y are *on a par* iff x is preferred to y in some K-orderings and y is preferred to x in some other K-orderings.

Betterness is a transitive and asymmetric relation and equal goodness is transitive, reflexive and symmetric. In addition, betterness is transitive across equal goodness.

To guarantee that these conditions hold, we need to impose certain minimal formal constraints on the preference orderings in K. x will be said to be *weakly preferred* to y iff x is either preferred to y or equi-preferred with y. Indeed, we might just as well take this relation of weak preference to be our primitive concept and then define preference and equi-preference as, respectively, the asymmetric and the symmetric parts of weak preference: x is preferred to y iff x is weakly preferred to y but not vice versa; x is equi-preferred with y iff x is weakly preferred to y and vice versa. What we then need to assume about the orderings in K is that in each of them weak preference is reflexive and transitive. This constraint on permissible orderings is what gives us the desired formal properties of betterness and equal goodness.

Now, how can we apply this general modeling to the problem at hand? As the domain D we now take the set of possible worlds. If we accept the basic tenet of welfarism—the view that the value of a world is fully determined by the well-being levels of the individuals in that world—we can, for simplicity, identify each world with a well-being distribution: an assignment of (lifetime) well-being levels to the individuals that exist in this world. The question now is what the class K of permissible orderings of this domain is supposed to look like. Specifying K will determine the value relations that obtain between the possible worlds in D.

To specify K is thus to provide a substantive axiology: more precisely, a substantive population axiology. As is well known, population ethics is haunted by conflicting intuitions and impossibility results (cf. Arrhenius 2000; 2011; 2016, and forthcoming. For a critical discussion, see Carlson, this volume.) It is a fair conjecture that no axiology can accommodate all intuitive judgments concerning value comparisons between worlds with variable populations. Here, I will focus on a utilitarian axiology, not because I find it fully satisfactory, but because it is a relatively plausible and at the same time a very simple form of welfarism. It is a simple and definite theory to work with. However, the kind of utilitarian axiology I want to consider has to make room for incommensurabilities in world comparisons, in order to accommodate the Intuition of Neutrality. In Rabinowicz (2009) I called it *neutral-range utilitarianism*.

Let $w, v, u, \ldots$ stand for lifetime well-being levels. We assume, until further notice, that these levels are measurable on a ratio scale: Thus, only the unit of measurement is arbitrarily chosen. (This strong measurability assumption will be relaxed in Section 3 and then much more relaxed in Section 4.)

Now, one way to think of the neutral range is to view the well-being levels in that range as candidates for permissible "critical levels"—permissible benchmarks—for preference. It is permissible to choose any of them, say level w, as the threshold below which adding new lives to the population is dispreferred and beyond which such additions are preferred. If a well-being level w lies in the neutral range, it can thus be used as a benchmark for determining the position of each world in the preference ordering. This position is obtained by summing up, for all individuals in the world in question, the surpluses and the deficits in their well-being, as compared with the chosen benchmark. Thus, let $I(A)$ be the set of individuals that exist in a world A and let w_{iA} be the well-being level of an individual i in A. The sum of well-being surpluses and shortfalls in A, relative to benchmark w, equals

$$\Sigma_{i\in I(A)}\left(w_{iA}-w\right).$$

The higher this sum is, the higher the world ends up in the preference ordering determined by w. Any two worlds for which this sum is the same occupy the same position in the ordering.

In this way, different preference orderings in K correspond to different choices of critical levels. Different choices of critical levels w from the neutral range (though only from that range) are all admissible and each such w induces a permissible preference ordering P_w on the set of worlds. Note that every P_w is a complete ordering: it contains no gaps. That is, for any two worlds, one of them is preferred in P_w to the other or they are equi-preferred in P_w. Class K might also include gappy preference orderings; it should be permissible to have incomplete preferences between worlds. I will turn to this possibility in a moment. But if we disregard it, we can define the relations of betterness, equal goodness, and parity between worlds as follows:

A world A is *better* than a world B iff for all w in the critical range, A is preferred to B in P_w.

A is *equally as good* as B iff for all w in the neutral range, A is equi-preferred with B in P_w.

A is *on a par* with B iff for some w and v in the neutral range, A is preferred to B in P_w and B is preferred to A in P_v.[8]

To illustrate, consider again the world B in which Barbara is added to the original world A at level m, where m belongs to the neutral range. As we have seen, there must be some level n in that range that is higher or lower than m. Suppose that $n > m$. Then A is preferred to B in P_n but not in P_m. In P_m, A and B are equi-preferred. Analogously, if $n < m$, then B is preferred to A in P_n but not in P_m. Thus, in either case, K will contain preference orderings that differ from each other in how they rank A and B. This means that B is incommensurable with A, neither better nor worse than the latter, nor equally as good. Indeed, if the neutral range contains both levels higher than m and lower than m, A and B are on a par.

What about gappy preference orderings in K? Let W be any non-empty subset of well-being levels in the neutral range. For example, W might be a sub-interval of that range. Let P_W be the set of complete preference orderings induced by the well-being levels in W. Plausibly, the intersection of P_W—the common part of the orderings in P_W—is also a permissible preference ordering of worlds.[9] This intersection $\cap P_W$ will contain gaps if W contains more than one well-being level. Intuitively, $\cap P_W$ represents preferences of someone who is undecided between levels in W as potential benchmarks—someone who has not decided where exactly to draw the line between preferred and dispreferred life additions.

Introducing gappy orderings into K in this way does not affect the extensions of the four typical value relations between worlds: better, worse, equally as good, and on a par. Nor does it affect the incommensurability relationships between worlds. Therefore, in most cases, there is no need to consider these incomplete K-orderings.

The population axiology described above is what I call *neutral-range utilitarianism* (NRU, for short). It combines total-sum utilitarianism with the Intuition of Neutrality. This axiology is formally identical with the theory that has been put forward by Blackorby, Bossert, and Donaldson (1996). They call it the "incomplete critical-level utilitarianism" (ICLU). ICLU is a generalization of the more familiar critical-level utilitarianism (CLU), originally proposed by Blackorby and Donaldson (1984). CLU is a utilitarian theory that picks out a specific non-negative well-being level w as *the* critical level and then lets the value ordering of worlds coincide with P_w. Thus, on CLU, world A is better than world B iff $\sum_{i \in I(A)} (w_{iA} - w) > \sum_{i \in I(B)} (w_{iB} - w)$. If these two sums are equal, the two worlds are equally good. CLU entails that the value ordering of worlds is complete: there are no incommensurabilities. As this completeness of evaluation might well be questioned, ICLU has been proposed as a less categorical option. On ICLU, the value ordering of worlds is taken to be a compromise between different complete value orderings that are generated by different choices of critical levels. As such a compromise, it retains what is common to the alternative complete evaluations and leaves gaps at places where the complete evaluations disagree.

Clearly, even though ICLU and NRU are structurally identical theories, they differ in their philosophical motivations. On ICLU, the ultimate value ordering is a compromise between different complete *value* orderings, while on NRU it is instead the intersection of permissible *preference* orderings. NRU is based on the analysis of value relations in terms of permissible preferences. This anchoring in the FA-format of analysis is absent in ICLU. Indeed, the philosophical motivation for ICLU has never been made very clear by its proponents. It is therefore probably not accidental that in their subsequent publications Blackorby, Bossert, and Donaldson have reverted to CLU as their favoured axiology.

NRU is also structurally identical to Broome's (2004) version of CLU. On this version, while there is just one critical level, its precise location is *indeterminate*. Instead of the neutral range we thus have a zone of indeterminacy—the set of well-being levels such that it is indeterminate which of them is the critical level but determinate that it is one of them. From this zone of indeterminacy, or vagueness, different precisifications of the theory choose different levels as the critical one and offer complete evaluations of possible worlds based on these choices. In the standard supervaluationist manner, what is common to all the precisifications (i.e., what follows from their intersection) is determinately true according to this axiology. Statements that hold on some precisifications but not on others are neither true nor false. They have an indeterminate truth value. Statements that don't hold on any precisification are false. On Broome's proposal, there are thus no incommensurabilities between worlds; instead, we have indeterminacies concerning their mutual value relations. Again, this axiology, in spite of its close structural similarity to NRU, has a different philosophical interpretation.

Let us move on. We have seen how NRU is supposed to work. But how plausible is it as a population axiology?

As is well known, the standard (total-sum) utilitarianism implies the Repugnant Conclusion (see Parfit 1984, Ch. 17):

> *Repugnant Conclusion*: For any world whose inhabitants have excellent lives, there is a better possible world all whose inhabitants have lives barely worth living—lives that are good but only barely so.

Call the former and the latter world the Happy World and the Drab World, respectively. If the Drab World has a sufficiently large population, its total sum of well-being will exceed that of the Happy World. Increases in population size compensate and indeed outweigh losses in life quality.

Unlike total-sum utilitarianism, NRU does not allow for such facile compensations. Barely good lives, i.e., lives at very low positive levels of well-being, have well-being levels within the neutral range. On the standard conception of that range, it stretches from zero upwards to some relatively high (though not too high) level of well-being. Thus, adding lives with low positive levels of well-being to the world does not make it better. On NRU, the Repugnant Conclusion is avoided.

What is not avoided is the Weak Repugnant Conclusion—a claim that is just like the Repugnant Conclusion, but with "better" replaced by "not worse." If the Drab World contains sufficiently many people, then, on NRU, it will be incommensurable with the Happy World. Indeed, the two worlds will be on a par. On some choices of a benchmark w from the neutral range, very close to zero (closer than the level of drab lives), the Drab World will be preferred to the Happy World, while choosing a higher w will yield the opposite preference. While the Weak Repugnant Conclusion might be hard to accept, it is not as outrageous as the original Repugnant Conclusion.

NRU also avoids the so-called Sadistic Conclusion, which plagues CLU, the critical-level utilitarianism (see Arrhenius 2000):

> *Sadistic Conclusion*: For any world whose inhabitants have terrible lives, there is a worse possible world whose inhabitants all have lives worth living (if only barely so).

CLU has this sadistic implication because the well-being levels of some lives worth living are lower than the critical level. Thus, on CLU, each such life detracts from the value of the world. Consequently, if the population of the Drab World is sufficiently large, this world will be worse than the Terrible World.

NRU avoids the Sadistic Conclusion if the neutral range goes all the way down to the zero level of well-being, as the standard interpretation of this range would have it. Low positive well-being levels lie within the neutral range. Therefore, adding lives at such levels does not make the world worse.

But again, NRU does not avoid the Weak Sadistic Conclusion, that is, the claim that is just like the Sadistic Conclusion, but with "worse" replaced by "not better." The Drab

World will not be worse than the Terrible World, but if its population is large enough, it will not be better. It will be incommensurable (on a par) with the Terrible World. It is a worrying and highly implausible implication.

This in itself might be a sufficient reason to consider another, alternative population axiology. But there is a more basic reason as well: as it stands, the Intuition of Neutrality is problematic.

3. THE INTUITION OF NEUTRALITY REINTERPRETED

As we have seen, on the standard conception of the neutral range, the Intuition of Neutrality introduces a disparity, a hiatus, between personal and impersonal goodness. A life might be good for a person who lives that life, better than non-existence, but still the addition of such a life to the world might not be impersonally good: It might not make the world better. It doesn't make it better if the well-being level of the added life lies within the neutral range.

The disparity between what is good for a person and what is good for the world will be seen by some as an appealing feature of the Intuition of Neutrality, indeed, as the reason to adopt it in the first place. But others will consider it highly problematic; they will see it as foreign to the welfarist outlook.

I am now going to consider a reinterpreted Intuition of Neutrality—one that removes the disparity. This new version of the Intuition is obtained by a reinterpretation of the neutral range. The idea is to identify it with the range of well-being levels at which a life is *neither good nor bad* for the person who lives or could live that life—neither better nor worse for her than non-existence. In other words, the *impersonal neutral range*— the range of well-being levels such that additions of lives at these levels do not make the world either better or worse—is now identified with the *personal neutral range*—the range of well-being levels at which a life is neutral for the person who lives (or could live) this life: levels at which this life is neither good nor bad for her. (Cf. Rabinowicz 2009, 390f, for this suggestion. See also Gustafsson 2016, where this suggestion is adopted and elaborated.[10])

Note that this reinterpretation presupposes that personal neutral range exists, that is, that there is more than one well-being level at which a life is personally neutral. In addition, it presupposes that personally neutral lives can be better or worse for us than other personally neutral lives, despite the fact that all such lives are neither better nor worse for us than non-existence. How is it possible? The answer should be obvious by now. It can only be possible if lives at these personally neutral levels are incommensurable with non-existence in their personal value.

The argument for this claim is analogous to the one I have presented in Section 1, in connection with impersonal neutrality. Here I give it in a simplified and condensed version. Thus, suppose that levels m and n are both personally neutral and $m < n$. By assumption, lives at these levels are neither better nor worse for the persons who live them than non-existence. Nor can any of these lives be equally as good for them as non-existence, as the following argument shows. One of these lives, the n-life, is personally better than the other, that is, it is such that it would be better for a person to live this life than to live the other life. But this means that if the m-life were personally equally as good as non-existence, then the n-life would be personally better than non-existence, contrary to the assumption. (The argument here depends on personal betterness being transitive across personal equal goodness.) On the other hand, if the n-life were personally equally as good as non-existence, then the m-life would be personally worse than non-existence, again contrary to the assumption. Thus, both of these lives must be incommensurable with non-existence in their personal value. More generally, if every personally neutral life is better or worse than some other personally neutral life, as it must be if there is more than one well-being level in the personally neutral range and well-being levels are linearly ordered, then every such life must be incommensurable in its personal value with non-existence.

How can such incommensurability in personal value between a life and non-existence be understood? To answer this question, I again need to appeal to the FA-format of analysis, but this time apply it to personal value. There is no clear consensus among FA-analysts as to how personal value—goodness for a person—should be interpreted. I will adopt the view that what is good for a person is what anyone who cares for her ought to wish or desire for her sake.[11] Admittedly, this suggestion is not very precise: both the notion of caring for someone and the notion of wishing/desiring something for someone's sake would need clarification.[12] Hopefully, though, the main idea of this proposal is sufficiently clear. Extending it to personal value relations is straightforward:

> x is better for i than y iff anyone who cares for i ought to prefer x to y for i's sake.
> x is equally as good for i as y iff anyone who cares for i ought to equi-prefer x and y for i's sake.

Incommensurability for i between x and y obtains whenever neither of these items is better for i than the other, nor are they equally as good for i.

Parity for i between x and y—the most typical form of incommensurability in personal value—obtains when it is permissible for anyone who cares for i to prefer x to y for i's sake and likewise permissible for them to have the opposite preference.

The idea is now that this kind of personal parity can obtain between a life and non-existence. For certain well-being levels—the ones in the personal neutral range—it is permissible, for the sake of a person who might live a life at this level, to prefer that she has this life rather than she does not exist and likewise permissible to have the opposite preference—permissible, that is, for anyone who cares for that person.[13]

Normally, in cases of parity, equi-preference with regard to the items on a par is also permissible. If it is permissible to prefer x to y and likewise permissible to have the opposite preference, then it should also be permissible to equi-prefer x and y. This also applies to cases in which a life is personally on a par with non-existence: it should be permissible, for the sake of a person who could live that life, not only to prefer any of these alternatives to the other, but also to equi-prefer them—to be indifferent between her having this life and her non-existence. This point will be of some importance below.

Let me regiment the terminology. I will say that a life is personally better than (worse than, equally as good as) another life iff it is better (worse, equally as good) for a person to have the former life than (as) to have the latter. Analogously, a life is personally better than (worse than, equally as good as) non-existence iff it is better (worse, equally as good) for a person to have this life than (as) not to exist. In the same vein, I will talk about personal incommensurability, or parity, between a life and non-existence, or between one life and another life.

We have three kinds of lives:

A (personally) good life = a life that is personally better than non-existence.[14]
A (personally) bad life = a life that is personally worse than non-existence.
A (personally) neutral life = a life that is neither (personally) good nor bad.

The reinterpreted Intuition of Neutrality only applies to the (personally) neutral lives: according to the Intuition, adding such lives is impersonally neutral; it does not make the world either better or worse. This reinterpretation removes the disparity between personal and impersonal goodness. It is fully compatible with the reinterpreted Intuition that adding good lives (even such that are barely good) always makes the world better, just as adding bad lives always makes it worse. This also means that the reinterpreted Intuition of Neutrality is compatible with the Principle of Personal Good that is no longer restricted to the comparisons between worlds sharing the same population:

Unrestricted Principle of Personal Good: Let $I(X)$ and $I(Y)$ be the populations of worlds X and Y, respectively, and let I be the union of $I(X)$ and $I(Y)$. (i) If X is better than Y for some individuals in I, while it is equally as good as Y for everyone else in I, then X is better than Y. (ii) If X and Y are equally as good for everyone in I, then X and Y are equally good.

Until further notice I continue to assume that well-being levels are linearly ordered, from higher to lower. (This assumption will be given up in the next section, though.) We can thus think of the well-being levels as ordered along a vertical axis, with the personally neutral range located below the levels of good lives and above the levels of bad lives. I can no longer assume, though, that well-being is measured on a ratio scale: there is no longer a non-arbitrary zero level of well-being. A non-arbitrary zero level could be defined as the level of a life that is personally equally as good as non-existence. But, as we have seen, on the current picture no lives are like that. Good and bad lives are, respectively, personally better and worse than non-existence, while personally neutral lives are all personally incommensurable with non-existence. Thus, on this new picture, measurement of well-being on a ratio scale is no longer available. Still, we can continue to assume that well-being is cardinally measurable: well-being levels can be represented on an interval scale, with only the unit and the zero point being arbitrary. Indeed, we have available a scale of well-being that is somewhat stronger than the interval scale but still weaker than the ratio scale: while the zero level of well-being is arbitrarily chosen, this arbitrariness has limits. It is reasonable to require that the zero level should be chosen from the personally neutral range. The reason is that for each well-being level in this range, and only for those levels, it is permissible to have preferences that rank a life at that level equally with non-existence. To put it more precisely: if the life at such level is personally on a par with non-existence, then, as we have seen above, it should be permissible, for the sake of a person who might have this life, to be indifferent between her having this life and her non-existence.[15] In the preference ordering that ranks this life equally with non-existence, its level can therefore be taken as the zero point. In this sense, the levels of personally neutral lives, and only those levels, are permissible candidates for the zero point of the scale.

Indeed, each such permissible scale, with the zero point chosen from the personally neutral range, might be thought of as a *ratio scale* for preferential assessment of lives. This ratio scale specifies a particular permissible configuration of preference strengths for or against different lives, where these preferences are thought of as being held for the sake of a person who could have the lives in question. Thus, instead of a unique ratio scale of well-being, we now have a *set*, call it S, of permissible preferential ratio scales to work with.[16]

This allows us to reinterpret and reformulate *neutral-range utilitarianism* (NRU). Consider any scale s in S. Let $I(A)$ stand for the set of individuals that exist in a world A and, for any individual i in I, let $s(i, A)$ be the measure of preference regarding the well-being level of i's life in A, as measured on scale s. $s(i, A)$ specifies the extent to which i's life in A is preferred or dispreferred, as the case may be, for i's own sake, as compared with her non-existence. We can then determine the total sum of the s-values of all lives in A: $\Sigma_{i \in I(A)} s(i, A)$. The higher this sum is, the higher is the position of A in the preference ordering of worlds induced by s. The NRU-betterness relation on the set of possible worlds can now be defined in terms of these orderings: world A is better than world B iff A is ranked higher than B in all permissible preference orderings of worlds, that is, in all orderings induced by the different scales in S.

What impact does the reinterpretation of the neutral range have on NRU's intuitive appeal? The Sadistic Conclusion is, of course, still avoided: adding bad lives to the world always detracts from its utilitarian value. Indeed, the Weak Sadistic Conclusion is now avoided as well: any world whose inhabitants have good lives is better than a world inhabited by people with bad lives, worth not living. But, on the other hand, this reinterpretation reinstates the Repugnant Conclusion: on the reinterpreted account, good lives, even if they are only barely good, add to the value of the world and these additions do not diminish in value as more and more such lives are being added. Therefore, for any world in which everyone's life is excellent, there will be a better world, with a much larger population, in which everyone's life is still good but only barely so.

However, in Rabinowicz (2009) I pointed out that the repugnancy of this reinstated Repugnant Conclusion now is assuaged, if not altogether eliminated. What in my view made the original Repugnant Conclusion intuitively repugnant was the *short distance* between barely good lives (i.e., lives that wouldn't be good if they were slightly worse) and lives that are positively bad, if only barely so. The former were supposed to be only marginally better than the latter. But, on the reinterpreted conception of the neutral range, the distance between barely good and barely bad lives might well be quite considerable. As I put it: "Lives that are worth living, however modest, cannot be only marginally better than lives that are worth not living, i.e. that are worse than non-existence, if these two kinds of lives are separated by a personal neutral range of non-negligible size" (ibid., 406). Indeed, on this picture, barely good lives might be considerably better than drab lives of "muzak-and-potatoes" variety that Parfit found so unappealing. It is plausible to think that such drab lives are personally neutral rather than positively worth living; arguably, they are neither better nor worse for us than non-existence. But then the Repugnant Conclusion does not seem to be so repugnant anymore.[17]

In the next section, however, we shall see that this reassuring diagnosis might have been premature.

Before concluding this section, I should mention that there is another problem with NRU, which I am not going to discuss in this paper. I have in mind what Broome (2004) calls the "greediness" of neutrality. Suppose that the neutral range contains both level m and some levels lower than $m\text{-}k$, for some $k > 0$. As is easily seen, NRU implies that adding to a world A a person with a life at level m, while at the same time decreasing by k units the well-being of one of the originally existing persons results in a world, B, that is incommensurable with A. For while choosing m as the benchmark gives rise to a preference ordering of worlds in which A is ranked above B, setting the benchmark at a well-being level lower than $m\text{-}k$ yields a preference ordering in which B is ranked above A.[18] Thus, as Broome (2004, 170) puts it: "Incommensurateness . . . is a sort of greedy neutrality, which is capable of swallowing up badness and goodness and neutralizing it. This is implausible."

This problem is exacerbated given my reinterpretation of the neutral range. On this reinterpretation, the life of the person added in B is not even good for her (though it is not bad for her either). But B still is not worse than A, even though it makes life positively worse for one of the originally existing people. This bad thing about B, as compared with A, is swallowed up by B's incommensurability with A. Effects like this might seem implausible, but I am inclined to believe that they should be accepted. They are just part of the package that comes with the existence of a neutrality range. For a critical discussion of the greediness objection, see Rabinowicz (2009).

4. COMPLICATING THE PICTURE: INCOMMENSURABLE LIVES

Let us define a *strictly neutral* life as a life that is personally equally as good as non-existence. Obviously, all strictly neutral lives are neutral, that is, neither personally better nor personally worse than non-existence, but the converse doesn't hold. As we have seen in the preceding section, if a neutral life is personally better or worse than some other neutral life, then it cannot be strictly neutral: the hypothesis that it is personally equally as good as non-existence cannot be upheld, on pain of a contradiction. We can refer to such lives as *weakly neutral*. A life is weakly neutral iff it is incommensurable with non-existence in its personal value.

If strictly neutral lives can exist, along with weakly neutral lives, we must give up the assumption that all lives' well-being levels are linearly ordered. The well-being level of a strictly neutral life cannot be fitted into such an ordering. Unlike weakly neutral lives, a strictly neutral life cannot be personally better or worse than any other neutral life. And it cannot be personally equally as good as any weakly neutral life: by the transitivity and symmetry of equal goodness, it can only be equally as good as other lives that are equally as good as non-existence, that is, it can only have this relation to other strictly neutral lives.

Postulating the possibility of strictly neutral lives along with lives that are weakly neutral thus requires that we allow for the existence of lives that are mutually incommensurable in their personal value. But, on reflection, this is something that we should allow for anyway. Surely, it is implausible to insist that for any two lives with different well-being levels, the well-being level of one must be higher or lower than that of the other life. Life well-being is a *many-dimensional* concept: specifying its level requires characterizing a life with respect to several relevant dimensions. One life might be better than another in some respects, and worse in others. At the same time, different weight assignments to the relevant respects of comparison might be permissible and the all-things considered preference ordering of lives will depend on how these respects are weighed against each other. Consequently, a life L might be preferred to another life L', for the sake of a person who might live one of these lives, given one permissible weight assignment, and dispreferred given another. This would imply that L and L' are incommensurable in their personal value, or—what amounts to the same—that L and L' have different well-being levels even though none of these levels is higher than the other.[19]

Nevertheless, while we should for these reasons be willing to accept that lives might well be mutually incommensurable in personal value, we might still wonder whether to allow for the existence of strictly neutral lives. Gustafsson (2016, Section 5) is unwilling to admit this possibility. He uses a different label for lives of this kind[20] and he does not define them by comparing their personal value with non-existence—indeed, he questions the possibility of such comparisons. But he takes such lives, *if* they exist, to satisfy the following three principles: for any strictly neutral life L and for every life L', (i) L' is good iff it is (personally) better than L, (ii) L' is bad iff it is (personally) worse than L, (iii) L' is strictly neutral iff it is (personally) equally as good as L.[21]

This squares with the definition I have proposed: as is easily seen, the definition of a strictly neutral life as one that is personally equally as good as non-existence entails (i), (ii), and (iii), assuming that the relation of equal personal goodness is transitive and that personal betterness is transitive across this relation.

One potential candidate for a strictly neutral life that Gustafsson (2016) considers, but finally rejects, is a life devoid of any (personally) good or bad components.[22] An example of a life of this kind would, I take it, be a life in a permanent state of unconsciousness.[23] Gustafsson denies, however, that such a life is possible for a person. One is not a person if one is never conscious. Being a person requires having some psychological features and being in some psychological states, but no such states and features can be present if consciousness is permanently absent.

I don't think this shows what it is supposed to show. It doesn't show that a person could not live such a life. It is true that I wouldn't be a person if my whole life were spent in a coma. But it still is true that I—a person—could have had such a life (in which I wouldn't be a person). It is a possible life for me, a person. While it is a popular view that being a person is an essential property of persons, I think this view is mistaken: a person could have had a life in which she hadn't been a person. But then my counterfactual life as a non-person, in a permanent state of unconsciousness, might be for me, a person, equal in value with my (equally counterfactual) non-existence. Consequently, this life might be strictly neutral.

Whether a life in a coma in fact is strictly neutral might of course be questioned. On some views, such a life would be worse for me than non-existence, due to considerations relating to human dignity. Perhaps a better candidate for a strictly neutral life could be found. Or perhaps not. The claim that strictly neutral lives could exist is logically coherent, but it is not clear to me whether such lives really are possible. Perhaps it might be argued that, for any possible life, it is at least permissible to prefer it or permissible to disprefer it (or both) to non-existence, for the sake of a person who could live that life. In such a case, no possible life would be strictly neutral. Let me now, however, consider what it would mean if strictly neutral lives could exist.

A neutral-range utilitarian might find the possibility of such lives quite worrying, as it implies, as we have seen, that lives might be mutually incommensurable in personal value. One might think that such incommensurabilities would make NRU meaningless: it would no longer be possible to determine the total value of a world's population for different choices of benchmarks from the neutral range.[24]

But, as I have pointed out, even if there were no strictly neutral lives to reckon with, we would still have to accept that some lives can be mutually incommensurable in personal value. If it were true that such incommensurabilities make NRU meaningless, then this theory would not be worth serious consideration. I think, though, that this worry can be put to rest: NRU can accommodate incommensurable lives. Let me explain how it can be done.

On the interpretation of NRU I have given in the preceding section, this theory assumes that different permissible preference orderings of worlds are generated by different permissible preferential ratio scales for assessing lives—scales whose zero points are drawn from the neutral range. If life well-being is cardinally measurable, as we have previously assumed, then these scales only differ in their choices of zero from the neutral range, that is, in their choices of the neutral well-being level such that lives on that level are equi-preferred with non-existence on a given scale. (The scales might also differ in their choices of the unit of measurement, but this choice doesn't matter when we do utilitarian calculation in order to compare worlds with each other. And since world comparisons are done independently for each scale, it doesn't matter either if different scales use different units of measurement.) However, if incommensurabilities between lives are allowed, the assumption of cardinal measurability of well-being must be given up.[25] Not only will the choice of zero differ, as before, between different permissible preferential ratio scales, but now some such scales will also differ in their *ordering* of lives: they will differ in how they rank incommensurable lives against each other. For example, if lives L and L' are personally on a par, then some permissible scales will rank L above L', while others will rank it below.[26] The set S of permissible ratio scales will thus be much more varied than it was previously assumed.[27] Class K of permissible preference orderings of worlds will however still consist of the orderings that are generated by the scales in S, as before. For any scale s in S, the position of a world A in the world ordering P_s induced by s is determined by the sum $\Sigma_{i \in I(A)} s(i, A)$. The higher this sum is, the higher is A's position in P_s. The value relations between worlds are then determined by this class K of permissible preference orderings of worlds, in the standard way: world A is better than world B iff it is ranked above B in all permissible orderings; A is equally as good as B iff it is equal-ranked with B in every permissible ordering; A is incommensurable with B iff none of these worlds is better than the other nor are they equally good.[28]

Clearly, on this version of NRU, there will be many incommensurabilities between worlds, many more than if all lives were commensurable in their personal value. But this does not, by itself, undermine a utilitarian axiology.

Nor does this account undermine the basic welfarist principle that all (impersonal) value comparisons between worlds are determined by the well-being levels of the individuals existing in those worlds. However, the well-being level of a life can no longer be represented by a single number. Instead, we can now represent it as a function that assigns to it a numerical value on each scale in S. These values specify how highly a life at this well-being level is assessed on each scale. If all these values are positive, the well-being level is positive; if they are all negative, the well-being level is negative. If neither holds, the well-being level is neutral. In particular, for a strictly neutral life, all the values are zero. Two lives have the same well-being level if they are characterized by the same function of this kind. One well-being level, w, is higher than another, w', iff for all scales s in S, the s-value of the function that represents w is higher than the s-value of the function that represents w'. We can also define what it means that one well-being level is at least as high as the other: this is the case iff for all scales s in S, the s-value for the former level is at least as high as the s-value for the latter level. (Note that, given this definition, a life might be at a well-being level that is at least as high as another life without the level of the former life being higher than or equal to that of the latter life.) As is easy to see, well-being levels are partially ordered by this at-least-as-high-as relation. In other words, the relation in question is reflexive, transitive, and anti-symmetric. (Anti-symmetry means that if level w is at least as high as level w' and w' is at least as high as w, then $w = w'$.)

Thus, the worry that NRU becomes meaningless if strictly neutral lives are allowed and, more generally, if lives are allowed to be incommensurable, is unjustified. It is still possible to define lives' well-being levels and carry out utilitarian calculations in order to determine the value of each world. This value is a function that for each scale s in S specifies the total sum of the s-values of the wellbeing levels of lives of the individuals that exist in the world in question.

It is another issue, however, whether NRU, so interpreted, is an intuitively appealing theory. This might be questioned. To explain why, let me first point out that allowing for strictly neutral lives leads to rather unexpected and unwelcome consequences. Suppose, for definiteness, that a life L, which is wholly spent in a coma, is strictly neutral, and consider a life L^+ that is slightly personally better than L. L^+ might, for example, be a life that also is mainly spent in a coma, apart from a very short period during which its subject is conscious and experiences a moderate sensory pleasure (and nothing else). Since L^+ is slightly (personally) better than L, which is (personally) equally as good as non-existence, it follows that L^+ is slightly (personally) better than non-existence. Which implies that L^+ is a good life, though only barely so: if it were slightly worse, it wouldn't be good. In the same way, we can think of a barely bad life, L^-, which is slightly (personally) worse than L and thus slightly (personally) worse than non-existence. L^- might be a life mainly spent in a coma, apart from a very short period during which its subject is conscious and experiences a moderate pain (and nothing else).

Now, note that the value distance between L^+ and L^- is short: L^+ is only marginally better than L^-. Thus, we now have to accept that there are good lives that are marginally better than bad lives.

But how can this be? Didn't we previously show that well-being levels of good lives are separated from the well-being levels of bad lives by the neutral range, which might be quite extended?

That was then, though, before we gave up the assumption that well-being levels are linearly ordered. On the new picture, things might be different. Indeed, as we already know, a strictly neutral life L, if such a life can exist, is incommensurable in its personal value with all lives that are weakly neutral. And it is arguable that the same applies to L^+ and L^-. The former is slightly better than L and the latter is slightly worse than L. As has been noted by Joseph Raz, it is a "mark of incommensurability" that if this relation obtains between two items, then a small improvement or a small worsening of one of the items need not (and typically will not) remove their incommensurability (Raz 1986, 325f). Thus, since incommensurability obtains between the strictly neutral life L and all lives that are weakly neutral, it might well still obtain when L is replaced by L^+ or by L^-.

This means that on the new picture a good life such as L^+, and a bad life such as L^-, might be incommensurable with a neutral life—a life that is neither bad nor good. Indeed, they might both be incommensurable with all neutral lives that are weakly neutral. Some good lives (such as L^+) need no longer be better than all lives that aren't good and some bad lives (such as L^-) need no longer be worse than all lives that aren't bad. This might be surprising, but it is an implication that we now must accept.

Note also that this surprising implication does not strictly speaking require the possibility of strictly neutral lives. What it does require is the possibility of lives *close to strict neutrality*: lives that are only slightly better or slightly worse than non-existence. Since weakly neutral lives are incommensurable with non-existence, it is to be expected that they will also be incommensurable with lives such as L^+ and L^-.

Thus, the value distance between a barely good life and a barely bad life might be very short. The former might be only marginally better than the latter.[29] L^+ and L^- provide a case in point.[30] But this means that the Repugnant Conclusion which follows from the reinterpreted NRU regains its original repugnance. Just as on the standard total-sum utilitarianism, NRU seems now driven to the conclusion that every world in which everyone has an excellent life is worse than some world in which everyone's life is only marginally better than a life worth not living.

This is bad news for neutral-range utilitarianism. But its adherents might be well-advised to stand fast and hold on to their view. The truly repugnant Repugnant Conclusion crucially depends on the possibility of lives close to strict neutrality. NRU's adherents might persist in denying that strictly neutral lives and lives close to strict neutrality really are possible. Indeed, it can be shown, although I am not going to do it here, that a very natural independence condition on the set S of permissible scales does make them impossible.[31]

However, just as a thought experiment, suppose someone proves to us that strictly neutral lives and lives in their immediate vicinity are possible. Then NRU will have to be given up unless we are willing to accept the repugnant Repugnant Conclusion. But, if we give up NRU, are there some claims from the preceding discussion that we still can we retain?

I think we can retain the Intuition of Neutrality itself, in its reinterpreted, personalized version:

> Adding personally neutral lives to the world is impersonally neutral: It does not make the world either better or worse.

We can also retain the insight that lives can be incommensurable with each other in their personal value. Lives' well-being levels can be accounted for in terms of a set of ratio scales of preferential assessment that make different choices of the zero level from the personally neutral range. So interpreted, well-being levels are not linearly ordered.[32]

Despite this acceptance of incommensurabilities between lives, we can, if we wish, hold on to some of the central tenets of welfarism:

(i) *The Unrestricted Principle of Personal Good,*

and the assumption that

(ii) *Value comparisons between worlds are determined by the well-being levels of the individuals who exist in those worlds.*[33]

Furthermore, if lives close to strict neutrality are possible, we can draw the rather surprising lesson that

A good life need not be better than a neutral life and a bad life need not be worse than a neutral life.

A life that is better (worse) for a person than her non-existence is good (bad), but if it is only slightly better (slightly worse) than non-existence, it need not be better (worse) for her than a life that is incommensurable with non-existence. It might be incommensurable with such a life.

This lesson generalizes: it is potentially applicable to all analyses of "good" and of other monadic value predicates in terms of value comparisons with some *standard*. In this paper, when defining monadic value predicates, the items we have targeted have been lives and the standard we have chosen has been the non-existence of a person whose life is being evaluated. But we can consider other items and choose other standards. Thus, suppose we consider some domain of items, choose a standard σ and adopt the following definitions: for all items x in this domain,

> x is good iff x is better than σ,
> x is bad iff x is worse than σ,
> x is neutral iff x is neither better nor worse than σ,
> x is strictly neutral iff x is equally as good as σ.

Then it does not follow that a good x must, by logical or analytical necessity, be better than a neutral y, or that a bad x must be worse than such a y.[34] These seemingly very plausible entailments do not obtain if y, while neutral, is not strictly so, that is, if y is incommensurable with the adopted standard. In such cases, a good x will typically not be better than y if x is only slightly better than the standard. Likewise, a bad x will typically not be worse than such y if x is only slightly worse than the standard.[35]

Thus, some of the things we have learned have implications that go beyond population axiology.

ACKNOWLEDGMENTS

An early version of this chapter was presented at a conference on formal ethics in York in June 2017 and at a conference on philosophy and economics in Canberra the same year. I am indebted to the participants in these events for several useful suggestions. I also want to thank John Broome, Johan Gustafsson, and Gustaf Arrhenius for their helpful written comments and discussion. Broome's challenging comments, in particular, have caused me to modify some of my conclusions. I also wish to thank Tim Campbell and OUP's copyeditor Tim Rutherford-Johnson, who have put much work into getting this chapter ready for publication.

NOTES

1. Indeed, Broome's own favorite theory in that book, critical-level utilitarianism, also implies such a disparity. In fact, it goes even further in this respect than the Intuition of Neutrality: it implies that what is personally good might be impersonally *bad*. Adding a person with a life that is good for her makes the world worse if the well-being level of the added life, while positive, is lower than the critical level posited by the theory. To be sure, Broome also suggests that the location of the critical level might well be indeterminate. It might even be indeterminate whether this level is higher than zero. This would prevent the implication that adding people with lives at positive levels can make the world determinately worse. Indeterminacy makes the disparity between what's good for a person and what's good for the world less blunt. But it doesn't remove it.

2. Cf. Broome (2004, 144): "Some people think this range is infinitely wide. They think that a person's existence is neutral, however good her life would be if she did exist. It is not neutral if her life would be bad, so there is a lower boundary to the neutral range. But there is no upper boundary. That is one view. A more moderate view is that the range has both an upper and a lower boundary, but there is nevertheless a range of neutral lives in between."

3. But if a life is understood in this encompassing sense and i is a person who leads this life, is it possible for anyone but i to have it? Well, maybe not; it is a question for metaphysicians. But if it is impossible, then it is trivially true that a life would have the same value for anyone who would have it.

4. See Parfit (1984, 395, 489). Cf. Broome (1999, 168): "[I]t cannot ever be true that it is better for a person that she lives than that he should never have lived at all. If it were better for a person that she lives than that she should never have lived at all, then if she had never lived at all, that would have been worse for her than if she had lived. But if she had never lived at all, there would have been no her for it to be worse for, so it could not have been worse for her." In *Weighing Lives*, though, Broome is less categorical: He recognizes that comparing a person's life with her non-existence, in terms of its value for the person in question, might possibly be made sense of after all (see Broome 2004, 63).

5. Note that only if states of affairs can exist without obtaining can there be any relations between states that do not co-obtain. Incompatible states cannot co-obtain. Thus, not even the relation of incompatibility would obtain between them if they couldn't exist unless they obtained. For if one of them obtains, the other does not.

6. In its essentials, this proof is due to Broome; cf. Broome (2004, 146ff).

7. What if we add *several* persons, all with well-being levels within the neutral range, while keeping the well-being levels of everyone else unaffected? Will the resulting world also be incommensurable with the original world? This does not follow from the Intuition of Neutrality as it has been formulated above. If we add to A one person, with a life at a well-being level within the neutral range, the Intuition of Neutrality (together with the Principle of Personal Good) implies that the resulting world, B_1, is incommensurable with A. If we then add to B_1 yet another person, again with a life at a well-being level within the neutral range, the Intuition of Neutrality (together with the Principle of Personal Good) implies that the resulting world, B_2, is incommensurable with B_1. But since the relation of incommensurability is not transitive, we cannot conclude that B_2 must be incommensurable with the original world A. To draw this conclusion, the Intuition of Neutrality would

have to be appropriately strengthened, so as to apply to additions of arbitrary numbers of people with lives at well-being levels within the neutral range. For the case in which all the added people have lives at the same neutral level, such a strengthening would, I think, be very natural, but I abstain from doing it here.

8. In typical cases of parity, there will also be some u in the neutral range such that A is equi-preferred with B in P_u. Indeed, this will hold in all mere-addition cases I here discuss. But in the interest of greater generality I abstain from imposing this condition as part of the definition of parity.

9. In this intersection of P_W, world A is weakly preferred to world B iff A is weakly preferred to B in every ordering in P_W.

10. Gustafsson uses a slightly different terminology, though, and more importantly, he does not define the personal value of a life by a comparison with non-existence.

11. A proposal roughly along these lines was put forward by Darwall (2002). For a competing FA-account, according to which what is good for a person is what *anyone* (and not just those who care for her) ought to favour for her sake, see Rønnow-Rasmussen (2011). (Cf also Rønnow-Rasmussen 2018.) The normative reach of the latter account is much wider than that of the former—too wide, I think. Cf. Taurek (1977, 304): "When I judge of two possible outcomes that the one would be worse (or better) for this person or this group, I do not, typically, thereby express a preference between these outcomes. Typically, I do not feel constrained to admit that I or anyone *should* prefer the one outcome to the other." Although even Taurek would agree, I suppose, that I should have this preference if I care for the person or group in question.

12. Just to give an example of an issue that might need clarification: Can one care for an individual i and desire something for i's sake if i does not exist (but *could* exist)? In principle, it should be possible: i in these locutions appears in an intensional context; neither caring for i nor desiring something for i's sake is a relation in which i is one of the relata. (Just as, say, thinking of Pegasus is not a relation in which Pegasus is one of the relata.) But this would mean that something can be good for i or better for i even if i does not exist, contrary to what I have assumed in Section 1. Should we welcome this implication? It would make personal value comparisons between someone's life and her non-existence even easier than I have previously suggested. On the other hand, caring for someone or desiring something for her sake requires that one is at least able to identify that person, which is difficult in the case of non-existents. So perhaps we should evade this problem and simply add to the analysis of what it means that something is good or better for i an extra condition that i does exist? This would be easy, but rather ad hoc.

13. For a suggestion as to why opposing preferences can be permissible in cases like this, see the next section.

14. This is a context-independent notion of a good life. Ordinarily, when we say that someone's life is good, we implicitly compare it with typical lives that people have in a given social context. Here, though, I aim at a minimal standard of a life's goodness—one that does not vary with social circumstances.

15. Strictly speaking, each level in the personally neutral range will be on a par with non-existence only if this range forms an *open* interval. If this interval is closed, lives at the upper boundary and at the lower boundary of the range still are incommensurable with non-existence, but they aren't on a par with it. It is not permissible to prefer a life at the lower boundary of the range to non-existence, nor to prefer non-existence to a life at the upper boundary. However, lives at these levels are, respectively, permissibly preferred/dispreferred to non-existence, and at the same time even for each of these boundary levels it is permissible to have preferences that rank lives at this level equally with non-existence.

16. Actually, this is not quite right. *S* needn't be that large; it need not contain different scales that only differ by the choice of unit. It is enough if for every maximal set of such permissible scales, *S* contains one representor—one scale drawn from that set.

17. An essentially similar treatment of the Repugnant Conclusion is defended by Gustafsson (2016), who reinterprets the impersonal neutral range in the way I have done in Rabinowicz (2009)—as consisting of the well-being levels of lives that are neither good nor bad for their owners.

18. The same conclusion—that *B* is incommensurable with *A*—can also be established using weaker premises, if one proceeds less directly and considers some other possible worlds as well, along with *A* and *B*. It is then sufficient to rely on the utilitarian balancing of gains and losses only in comparisons between worlds that share the same population. Furthermore, there is then no need to assume my account of incommensurability, in terms of divergent permissible preference orderings. (Cf. Broome 2004, 170, and Rabinowicz 2009.)

19. That some lives (namely, the ones that are weakly neutral) are incommensurable with non-existence in their personal value has a similar explanation, by the way. A life typically has both desirable and undesirable components and its assessment on balance, in comparison with non-existence, might depend on how these components are weighed against each other. Since different weight assignments will normally be permissible, they might give rise to opposing permissible preferences regarding the life in question: it might be permissible, for the sake of the person who could live this life, to prefer it, all things considered, to her non-existence, but it might also be permissible to have the opposite preference, for her sake.

20. He simply calls them "neutral" and refers to lives I call weakly neutral as "blank" (or "undistinguished," in the published version of his draft). In my comments on Gustafsson, I will however, continue to use my own terminology, to avoid confusion.

21. Note that if a life *L* is weakly neutral, it need not satisfy (i) and (ii): a life *L ′* might be better than *L* without being good and it might be worse than *L* without being bad. Rather than good or bad, respectively, *L ′* might itself be weakly neutral.

22. Indeed, if such a life is to be strictly neutral, it should also lack weakly neutral components, that is, it should lack components that it is permissible to prefer it to have (for the sake of the person who could lead this life), but also permissible to prefer it not to have.

23. In Broome's terminology, a life without any good or bad experiences is "blank," and a life spent in a coma is an example of a blank life (Broome 2004, 208f).

24. This is indeed the reason why Gustafsson (2016), who proposes an ethical theory that is very much like NRU (he calls it "critical-range utilitarianism") and who like me works with the personalized neutral range, is so opposed to strictly neutral lives. However, the reasons he offers for rejecting such lives change in the published version of his paper. There, the meaninglessness worry no longer is mentioned. And even in the original paper he eventually suggests a version of critical-range utilitarianism that does allow for incommensurable lives. On that theory, utilitarian aggregation of well-being in a population is done at the level of life moments instead of the whole lives. But he still assumes that, at the level of life moments, there are no incommensurabilities.

25. What is not given up is cardinal measurability of the *strength of preference* for different lives, according to each permissible preferential scale. But a life's well-being, which is characterizable by the position of this life on all the different permissible preferential scales, is no longer cardinally measurable. Nevertheless, lives' well-being levels can still be given a numerical representation, as will be shown below.

26. Note, though, that if strictly neutral lives can exist, they will be placed on all those scales at the zero level. On any such scale, the zero level is the level of lives that are equi-preferred, for the sake of a person who could have that life, with her non-existence. Thus, in one way or another, each scale will commensurate strictly neutral lives with lives that are weakly neutral.

27. As previously, though, it is enough if for each maximal set of permissible scales that differ from each other only by the choice of unit, S contains one representor—one scale drawn from that set.

28. Strictly speaking, class K will also contain incomplete world orderings. But if any such permissible incomplete ordering is the intersection of some set of permissible complete orderings, then adding incomplete orderings to K will not affect the extensions of the relevant value relations between worlds: the relations of betterness, equal goodness, incommensurability, and parity.

29. In private communication, John Broome has suggested that a situation like this will arise if "there are pairs of lives such that one is better than non-existence and one is worse than non-existence, and they are very similar to each other."

30. But if we no longer assume that lifetime well-being is cardinally measurable, how can we say that L^+ is only *marginally* better than L^-? It might be objected that in the absence of cardinal measurement, differences in lifetime well-being cannot be judged to be small or large. I don't think, though, that this objection is compelling. Pockets of cardinality—areas in which size estimates of well-being differences are meaningful—might still exist, even though cardinal measurement no longer is possible in all cases, that is, in all comparisons of lives' well-being levels. Those are the areas in which all the permissible ratio scales in S agree in their assessments of differences between life levels. The difference between two well-being levels is small if it is small on each of the permissible scales.

31. More precisely, this condition stipulates that for every scale s in S and every weakly neutral well-being level w, S contains a scale s' whose zero point is fixed at w but that otherwise differs from s at most by the choice of unit. Actually, just to exclude the possibility of strictly neutral lives, a much weaker condition would suffice: It is enough to require that for some s in S, S contains an order-preserving transform s' whose zero-point differs from s. But we need a stronger condition if we also want to exclude the possibility of lives close to strict neutrality.

32. This of course also applies to levels in the neutral range, and it would apply to them even if there were no strictly neutral lives. Lives that are weakly neutral can be mutually incommensurable. But still, it is reasonable to suppose that for every such level m there is some neutral level that is higher or lower than m. This means that we can continue to uphold the assumption of the proof provided in Section 1. As we remember, that proof was meant to establish that a world in which a person is added at some such level m must be incommensurable with the original world.

33. But, in view of the incommensurabilities between lives, well-being levels no longer can be assumed to be representable by single numbers. Their numerical representation has to be more complicated, as we have seen above.

34. This has already been noted in Gustafsson (2016), though he puts this observation in a terminology that differs from mine.

35. Nebel (2018) argues for what he calls the *Strengthened Principle of Goodness*, according to which if x is good, but y is not, even though it is comparable with x, then x must be better than y. An item is comparable with something good if it belongs to the category of items to

which the predicate "good" in principle is applicable. In other words, if it bears some value, positive, negative, or neutral. What we have seen above is that Nebel's principle is not valid: x might be good, y might be neutral and thus not good but still comparable with x, and yet x need not be better than y. Nebel assumes that whatever is good must be better than something neutral. But we have seen that this need not be the case, if the good item is only slightly better than the standard and the neutral item is not strictly neutral. The same criticism applies, *mutatis mutandis*, to Nebel's *Strengthened Principle of Badmess*, according to which if x is bad, but y is not, even though it is comparable with x, then x must be worse than y. Likewise, it applies to the generalization to all natural-language predicates F: if x is F, but y is not, even though it is comparable with x, then x is F-*er* than y. Dorr, Nebel, and Zuehl (2021) call this generalization *Strong Monotonicity*. They use it to argue that the relation "at least as F as" is complete. But it is an argument that can be turned around. Precisely because we accept incommensurabilities in value and thus deny that the relation "at least as good as" is complete, we can entertain the possibility of items that are neutral without being strictly neutral. And given this possibility, we should reject Strong Monotonicity.

REFERENCES

Arrhenius, Gustaf. 2000. "An Impossibility Theorem for Welfarist Axiology." *Economics and Philosophy* 16: 247–266.

Arrhenius, Gustaf. 2011. "The Impossibility of a Satisfactory Population Ethics." In *Descriptive and Normative Approaches to Human Behavior*, edited by Ehtibar N. Dzhafarov and Lacey Perry, 51–66. Singapore: World Scientific.

Arrhenius, Gustaf. 2016. "Population Ethics and Different-Number-Based Imprecision", *Theoria* 82: 166–181.

Arrhenius, Gustaf. Forthcoming. *Population Ethics: The Challenge of Future Generations*. Oxford: Oxford University Press.

Arrhenius, Gustaf, and Wlodek Rabinowicz. 2010. "Better to Be Than Not to Be?" In *The Benefit of Broad Horizons*, edited by Hans Joas and Barbro Klein, 399–421. Leiden: Brill.

Arrhenius, Gustaf, and Wlodek Rabinowicz. 2015. "The Value of Existence." In *The Oxford Handbook of Value Theory*, edited by Iwao Hirose and Andrew. Reisner, 424–444. Oxford: Oxford University Press.

Blackorby, Charles, Walter Bossert, and David Donaldson. 1996. "Quasi-Orderings and Population Ethics." *Social Choice and Welfare* 13: 129–150.

Blackorby, Charles and David Donaldson. 1984. "Social Criteria for Evaluating Population Change." *Journal of Public Economics* 25: 13–33.

Broome, John. 1999. *Ethics out of Economics*. Cambridge: Cambridge University Press.

Broome, John. 2004. *Weighing Lives*. Oxford: Oxford University Press.

Broome, John. 2009. "Reply to Rabinowicz." *Philosophical Issues* 19: 412–417.

Bykvist, Krister. 2007. "The Benefits of Coming into Existence." *Philosophical Studies* 135: 335–362.

Bykvist, Krister. 2015. "Being and Well-Being." In *Weighing and Reasoning*, edited by Iwao Hirose and Andrew Reisner, 87–94. Oxford: Oxford University Press.

Darwall, Stephen. 2002. *Welfare and Rational Care*. Princeton, NJ and Oxford: Princeton University Press.

Dorr, Cian, Jacob M. Nebel, and Jake Zuehl. 2010. "The Case for Comparability." Unpublished manuscript.

Gustafsson, Johan. 2016. "Population Axiology and the Possibility of a Fourth Category of Absolute Value." Unpublished draft. A revised version has appeared in *Economics and Philosophy* 36 (2020): 81–110.

Holtug, Nils. 2001. "On the Value of Coming into Existence." *Journal of Ethics* 5: 361–384.

Johansson, Jens. 2010. "Being and Betterness." *Utilitas* 22: 285–302.

Narveson, Jan. 1973. "Moral Problems of Population." *The Monist* 57: 62–86.

Nebel, Jacob M. 2018. "The Good, the Bad, and the Transitivity of *Better Than*." *Noûs* 52: 874–899.

Parfit, Derek. 1984. *Reasons and Persons*. Oxford: Clarendon Press.

Rabinowicz, Wlodek. 2008. "Value Relations." *Theoria* 74: 18–49.

Rabinowicz, Wlodek. 2009. "Broome and the Intuition of Neutrality." *Philosophical Issues* 19: 389–411.

Rabinowicz, Wlodek. 2012. "Value Relations Revisited." *Economics and Philosophy* 28: 133–164.

Raz, Joseph. 1986. *The Morality of Freedom*. Oxford: Clarendon Press.

Rønnow-Rasmussen, Toni. 2011. *Personal Value*. Oxford: Oxford University Press.

Rønnow-Rasmussen, Toni. 2018. "Fitting-Attitude Analysis and the Logical Consequence Argument." *The Philosophical Quarterly* 272: 560–579.

Taurek, John. 1977. "Should the Numbers Count?" *Philosophy and Public Affairs* 6: 293–316.

CHAPTER 6

··

LOOSENING THE BETTERNESS
ORDERING OF LIVES:
A RESPONSE TO RABINOWICZ

··

JOHN BROOME

1. INTRODUCTION

THIS chapter is a response to the one that precedes it in this volume, Wlodek Rabinowicz's "Getting Personal: The Intuition of Neutrality Reinterpreted." Rabinowicz's main concern is to incorporate the intuition of neutrality into an account of personal good—of what is good for a person. But he also does something else very interesting. He takes on board an obvious fact about personal good that has so far generally been ignored in the formal theory of value. So far, philosophers have generally assumed in their formal theories that personal betterness is a *tight* ordering, as I shall put it; it contains no indeterminacy, vagueness, or incommensurability. Between any two states of affairs, and for any person, we have assumed that either one of the states is determinately better for the person than the other or they are determinately equally good. This is obviously false. Goodness is a nebulous, imprecise property and betterness is a loose sort of ordering. Rabinowicz takes account of this in his chapter and explores its consequences for the theory of the value of population.

I am more interested in this aspect of his chapter than in Rabinowicz's interpretation of the intuition of neutrality. I am one of those philosophers who made the obviously false assumption that personal betterness is tight. I did so explicitly in my book *Weighing Lives*.[1] I thought it a reasonable simplifying assumption because I thought it would make little difference to the book's conclusions about the value of population. Now Rabinowicz's new work offers me the opportunity of testing whether I was right. Sections 2–6 of this chapter of mine are given over to doing so. I shall hubristically conclude that actually I was right.

In Section 2 I shall formalize the loose ordering of personal betterness. Then in Sections 3–5, I shall outline the conventional utilitarian theory of the value of population. In Section 6 I shall inject into it a loose ordering of personal betterness. In all of this, my methods and conclusions follow Rabinowicz's. Only a minor disagreement will emerge. But I cast the analysis in a significantly different light from his.

Only in Section 7 will I come to Rabinowicz's interpretation of the intuition of neutrality. I am sorry to say that there I shall disagree with him more strongly.

2. A Loose Betterness Ordering

In analyzing betterness, it is best to work with just one primitive relation. If we were to work with two—such as betterness and equality of goodness B we would have to explain why no pair of things ever satisfies both of them. This would be hard if they were truly primitive.

I choose betterness as my primitive relation. It is transitive, reflexive, and asymmetric. I define the relation of being equally good in terms of betterness: two things are equally good when anything that is better or worse than one of them is correspondingly better or worse than the other. This definition ensures that equal goodness satisfies two conditions it must satisfy. First, when two things are equally good then neither is better than the other; it is easy to see that this follows from the definition. Second, the definition also ensures that the relation of being equally good is an equivalence relation.[2]

It is more conventional to take the relation "at least as good as" to be primitive. I do not adopt this convention for two reasons. First, "at least as good as" is plainly not primitive. It is a complex notion equivalent to "better than or equally as good as." Second, it implies an incorrect definition of "equally as good as." Two things are conventionally defined to be equally good when each is at least as good as the other. But two things that satisfy my definition may not satisfy this one: it might be that neither of them is at least as good as the other. In that case, they would conventionally be defined as incommensurable. However, they are not incommensurable. As Rabinowicz notes,[3] the recognized mark of incommensurability is that, if two things are incommensurable, there is a small improvement or a small worsening of one of them that does not remove their incommensurability. Because these two things satisfy my definition of "equally as good as," any small improvement or any small worsening of one of them makes it better or worse than the other. If the two things were incommensurable, it would remove their incommensurability. So this pair of things does not bear the mark of incommensurability. They are in fact equally good, as my definition says.

An objection to my definition is that it is sensitive to changes in the domain of things.[4] Two things that are equally good according to my definition might cease to be equally good if the domain were enlarged. But the domain I am referring to is everything; "anything" in my definition means anything. So the domain cannot change. I stick with my definition.

Like Rabinowicz's, my account of personal betterness and goodness will be an account of personal betterness and goodness among *lives*. Like him, I assume that living a particular life would be just as good for one person as it would be for another person were she to live that same life. This is the way I achieved interpersonal comparability of good in *Weighing Lives*.[5] Mine is an account of *personal* goodness and betterness among lives: when I say one life is better than another, I mean it is better for a person who lives that life. The goodness of a person's life is sometimes called the person's *lifetime well-being*.

I shall develop an account of a loose betterness relation, but I start with a tight one. Imagine initially that the betterness ordering among lives is tight. This implies that if two lives are not equally good, one is better than the other. Imagine also that there is a tight ordering of *pairs* of lives, which is to be interpreted as an ordering of the differences in goodness between pairs. In traditional theory, this ordering of differences is derived from a betterness ordering among gambles on lives.[6] But it could be derived in some other way; it does not matter here. I shall call a betterness ordering of lives together with an ordering of differences of goodness a *cardinal ordering* of lives. Since an ordering of lives is implied by an ordering of differences, there is really only one ordering here. From now on, when I mention an ordering of lives, I mean a cardinal ordering.

A representation theorem tells us that a cardinal betterness ordering between lives can be represented by a goodness measure, which assigns to each life a number that measures its goodness.[7] One life gets a greater numerical goodness than another if and only if it is better. Moreover, the theorem tells us that the goodness measure can correctly reflect the ordering of differences. A goodness measure that does so is called a *cardinal* measure of goodness.

A tight ordering actually has many cardinal measures. If $g()$ is one, then so is any measure $g'()$ that is an *affine transform of* $g()$—that is, if $g'(l) = ag(l) + b$ for all lives l, where a is a positive constant, and b is a positive, negative, or zero constant. The cardinal measures of a tight betterness ordering form a family, each an affine transform of the others. We arbitrarily pick just one of them as the measure to use, standing in for the family. This means that the zero of the measure is arbitrary, and so is the size of the unit in the scale of goodness.

Now I come to a loose betterness ordering. What are the possible relations between a pair of lives k and l? First, it may be that k is better than l. Second, it may be that l is better than k. Third, it may be that k and l are equally good. Fourth, it may be that k is not better than l, and l is not better than k, and also that k and l are not equally good. In this case I say k and l are "incommensurate." (I prefer this term to "incommensurable.") Fifth, there is no determinate answer to the question of whether k is better than l and no determinate answer to the question of whether l is better than k. In this case the relations are vague.

Incommensurateness and vagueness are different sorts of looseness in the ordering. It seems indubitable that betterness is vague to some extent. I am more doubtful that incommensurateness also exists in betterness orderings.[8] But many people including Rabinowicz think it does, so I need to allow for it. It would be possible to allow for both incommensurateness and vagueness together, and at first I tried to do that in this chapter. But I found it led to undesirable complications. I have therefore decided to ignore vagueness in this chapter, as Rabinowicz does in his. So I ignore the fifth possibility.

Not much is lost in doing so. Vagueness can be treated formally in a similar way to incommensurateness. This means that the arguments of this paper can easily be extended to vagueness.

Before coming to a formal treatment, I need to mention a feature of the betterness ordering among lives that will become important in Section 6. Although this ordering is loose, it is locally tight in one particular way. Pick any life l. There is always a better life that is as close to it as you like, and always a worse life that is as close to it as you like. For example, a life is better than l if it is the same as l but has an extra period of good life added in a way that does not damage the rest of the life. This period can be made as short as you like. A life is worse than l if it is the same as l but contains an extra moment of pain at some time, unconnected with anything else that happens in the life. This extra moment can be made as short as you like. These are only examples; there are many ways of improving or degrading a life by a tiny bit.

This local tightness is a feature of betterness among lives in particular. Not all loose orderings are locally tight in this way. For example, I doubt that the ordering of paintings by their beauty is locally tight.

Now the formal treatment of the loose betterness ordering of lives. We treat a loose ordering as a set of tight orderings. No member of the set is the actual betterness ordering, but the whole set together defines the actual ordering. Each member may be called a *proto-betterness* ordering. It describes one way in which betterness might formally be tightened up. I shall call it a *tightening*.

Rabinowicz treats tightenings as permissible preference relations among lives. But there is no need to give them such a substantive interpretation. I take them simply as a formal, theoretical device for describing a loose ordering.

In comparing two lives, the relation between the tightenings and the actual ordering is this. One life is actually better than another if and only if it is better in all tightenings. If neither of two lives is better than the other in all tightenings, the two lives are either incommensurate or equally good. Whether they are incommensurate or equally good is not determined just by the relative position of the two lives in the various tightenings. The definition of equality shows it depends also on their positions relative to other lives.

Because the betterness ordering is locally tight in the way I described, we know that, given any life, there are two lives—each as similar to it as you like—such that every tightening rates one of them proto-better than the given life and the other proto-worse.

I assume that each tightening is a cardinal ordering. Each can therefore be represented by a cardinal measure of proto-goodness. The loose ordering is represented by the set of these measures, one for each tightening. Do not be confused. A single cardinal measure stands in for a family of proto-goodness measures, each an affine transform of the others and each representing the same cardinal ordering. This family is not what I am talking about. Out of the family of functions that represent a single proto-betterness ordering, we arbitrarily pick one as a measure to stand in for the family. Because we have a set of proto-betterness orderings, we end up with a set of measures. These are not affine transforms of each other.

3. Utilitarianism for a Fixed Population

I am now in a position to start formulating the utilitarian theory of goodness. For a moment suppose that betterness among lives is a tight cardinal ordering. Then there is a cardinal measure $g()$ of the goodness of lives. Suppose also for this section that the population of people is fixed. Utilitarianism makes a claim about the relative goodness of different *distributions* of lives across the population. It is the claim that one distribution is better than another that has the same population if and only if the total goodness of lives in the first is greater than the total goodness of lives in the second. It follows that, if two distributions have the same total goodness, they are equally good.

Put differently, utilitarianism makes the claim that the goodness of distributions can be measured by the total goodness of the lives they contain. A distribution can be described by the vector of the people's lives $(l_1, l_2, \ldots l_I)$, where I is the number of people. One person's life is l_1, the next person's l_2, and so on. According to utilitarianism, the total measures the goodness of the distribution:

$$G(l_1, l_2, \ldots l_I) = \Sigma_i\, g(l_i) \tag{1}$$

Goodness and betterness among distributions are *general* rather than personal. When comparing lives, I took their goodness and betterness to be personal: goodness and betterness for the people whose lives they are. But now we come to comparing distributions over many people, we are concerned with general goodness and betterness: goodness and betterness for humanity as a whole. The utilitarian formula (1) is a claim about the relationship between people's personal goodness and general goodness.

To avoid constantly repeating "according to utilitarianism," from here on I shall take the utilitarian theory of goodness for granted.

Because we are assuming there is tight cardinal betterness ordering of lives, there is a determinate answer to the question of whether the total goodness of lives is greater in one distribution than in another. The answer to this question depends only on the information contained in a cardinal measure of the goodness of lives, and we have one. The answer is independent of the zero of this measure of goodness and of the size of the unit. Also, if neither of two distributions has a greater total than the other, they have the same total. The upshot is that a tight cardinal betterness ordering for lives implies a tight ordering of distributions by betterness.

When the betterness ordering of lives is loose, it has a set of tightenings. Each tightening is cardinal and tight. Each therefore implies a tight ordering of distributions by proto-betterness, in the way I have just explained. Take any pair of distributions. It may be that all the tightenings agree that one of them is proto-better better than the other. Then that one is actually better. Or it may be that some tightenings rate one proto-better and some rate the other proto-better. Then neither will be determinately better than the other. So there will be looseness in the actual betterness ordering of distributions. Looseness in the betterness ordering of lives is transmitted to looseness in the betterness ordering of distributions of lives. Nothing else was to be expected.

4. Neutral-Life Utilitarianism with Tight Betterness among Lives

Next, I extend utilitarianism to variable populations. We have to compare the goodnesses of distributions of lives $(l_1, l_2, \ldots l_I)$, where now the total number of people I is not a constant.

As a foundation for this work, I shall simply take for granted *neutral-level utilitarianism*. Arguments for it are to be found in work by Charles Blackorby, Walter Bossert, and David Donaldson[9] and in my *Weighing Lives*.

Once again, I start with a version of the theory that assumes the betterness ordering of lives is tight and cardinal. There is then a cardinal goodness measure of lives $g()$. Neutral-level utilitarianism claims that there is a neutral life n such that the goodness of a distribution is the total—added up across people—of the difference between the goodness of each life and the goodness of the neutral life. That is:

$$G(l_1, l_2, \ldots l_I) = \Sigma_i \left(g(l_i) - g(n) \right) \tag{2}$$

where i ranges over all the lives in the population, whatever its size. This is a goodness measure for the distribution. So long as the betterness of lives is cardinal, it is determinate which distributions are better than which. There is a tight betterness ordering of distributions.

The neutral level referred to in the name "neutral-level utilitarianism" is the goodness $g(n)$ of the neutral life. Without changing the theory, I rename it *neutral-life utilitarianism*. I adopt my name because in Section 6 I shall allow for looseness in the betterness ordering of lives. A loose betterness ordering is described by many tightenings, each of which has a cardinal proto-betterness measure. There is no basis for comparing levels of proto-goodness across these different measures. So tightenings cannot have a neutral level in common. On the other hand, they can have a neutral life in common, and in Section 6 I shall assume they do.

What is the significance of the neutral life? Think about starting from some distribution of lives and adding to it one new person who lives the neutral life. The formula implies that the resulting distribution is equally as good as the original one. This is true also if we add a person who lives any life that is equally as good as the neutral one. In fact, any of these lives is also neutral. A neutral life is neutral in the sense that adding it to a distribution leaves the distribution equally as good as it was before. I call this *strong* neutrality.

Adding a life that is better than the neutral life makes the distribution better and adding a life that is worse makes the distribution worse.

Neutrality is defined in terms of the contribution a life makes to general goodness, not in terms of the person's own good. A neutral life is generally—not personally—neutral.

5. NEUTRAL-RANGE UTILITARIANISM WITH TIGHT BETTERNESS AMONG LIVES

Neutral-life utilitarianism conflicts with something I call "the intuition of neutrality."[10] Many of us have the intuition that adding a person to a population is *typically* neutral. We think intuitively that it is a bad thing to add a person if her life would be full of suffering. Some of us think intuitively it is a good thing to add a person whose life would be wonderful. Others of us think intuitively that adding a person to the population is never a good thing. But most of us think intuitively that there is a wide range of lives— at least from mediocre lives up to very good ones—such that adding them to the population is neutral. That is the intuition of neutrality. Simple neutral-life utilitarianism denies this. It implies that only the single neutral life and other equally good lives are neutral.

The intuition of neutrality is a small-scale intuition about the creation of a single person. It can be reinforced by a pair of large-scale intuitions. The first is this. Take a distribution containing only a large number of very good lives full of happiness. Formula (2) implies that this distribution is worse than one that contains only lives that are a little bit better than the neutral life, provided there are enough of those lives. This conclusion is counter to most people's intuition unless the neutral life is rather good. Derek Parfit calls it "repugnant."[11]

The second intuition is the mirror image of this one. Take a distribution containing only a large number of very bad lives full of suffering. Formula (2) implies that this distribution is better than one that contains only lives that are a little bit worse than the neutral life, provided there are enough of those lives. This conclusion is counter to most people's intuition unless the neutral life is rather poor. It seems impossible to find a neutral life that does not conflict with one or the other of these intuitions. To accommodate the first we need the neutral life to be rather good and to accommodate the second we need it to be rather poor.

However, neutral-life utilitarianism can be extended to accommodate the intuition of neutrality and the large-scale intuitions. Through a means I shall explain, we can say that all the lives from the wide range that are intuitively neutral are indeed neutral. So now we have many neutral lives n^r. I index them by r, where r takes values in some index set R. (R will have at least continuum-many members, and probably more; r is not a natural number.) Not all these lives are equally good; some are better than others in the range.

Making this change comes at a cost. It forces us to adopt a weaker notion of neutrality. Previously a neutral life was one such that adding it to a distribution leaves the distribution equally as good as it was before. These many neutral lives can only be *weakly* neutral, in the sense that adding one of them to a distribution leaves the distribution neither better nor worse than it was before.

The way to extend utilitarianism is to loosen the betterness ordering of distributions. Instead of a single tight betterness ordering, we recognize a set of tight proto-betterness orderings—one for each neutral life. They are indexed by r. Each is given by the same cardinal goodness measure for lives $g()$, but each has its own neutral life n^r:

$$G^r\left(l_1, l_2, \ldots l_I\right) = \Sigma_i\left(g\left(l_i\right) - g\left(n^r\right)\right) \tag{3}$$

One distribution is actually better than another if and only if all these tightenings agree it is proto-better. We now have a loose betterness ordering for distributions, but we retain a tight betterness ordering for lives.

Adding to a distribution a life that is better than all the neutral lives makes the distribution better. Adding a life that is worse than all the neutral lives makes the distribution worse. Adding a life that is neither better nor worse than all the neutral lives makes the distribution neither better nor worse. There is a range of neutral lives that extends from the worst of the neutral lives to the best of them. The resulting theory is *neutral-range utilitarianism*.[12]

This theory accommodates the intuition of neutrality and the large-scale intuitions. However, it suffers from a new problem of its own, which I call the problem of *greediness*. I shall illustrate it using a stylized example of climate change.[13]

Let the goodness of the best neutral life be 40 and the goodness of the worst neutral life 10. (Remember that the scale of goodness is only cardinal, so only differences of levels rather than levels themselves are significant.) Suppose that, were it not for climate change, there would be 10 billion people, and the goodness of everyone's life would be 23.

Suppose that climate change will have two effects. First, it will reduce the goodness of the life of everyone who lives from 23 to 20, either by shortening people's lives or by reducing their quality. This is plainly a bad change.

Suppose, also, that climate change will reduce the size of the population from 10 billion to 8 billion. Since these people would have lived lives at level 23, which is in the range between the worst and the best neutral lives, this change is neutral.

Were it not for climate change, there would have been 10 billion people at 23. Given climate change, there are 8 billion people at 20. To compare the goodness of these distributions, we work out their proto-goodness according to each tightening. It is enough to compare them on the basis of the best and the worst neutral life.

The goodness of the best neutral life is 40 units. On this basis, the proto-goodness of the distribution without climate change is 10 billion times –17. The proto-goodness of the distribution with climate change is 8 billion times –20. The latter is greater.

The goodness of the worst neutral life is 10 units. On this basis, the proto-goodness of the distribution without climate change is 10 billion times +13. The proto-goodness of the distribution with climate change is 8 billion times +10. The former is greater.

So different tightenings order the two distributions oppositely. Therefore, neither distribution is better than the other according to neutral-range utilitarianism.

But this is plainly the wrong conclusion. The distribution with climate change is worse because every person who lives has a worse life. That is a bad thing. It also has a smaller population, which is supposed to be a neutral thing. A bad thing together with a neutral thing should be a bad thing. But the way the theory works, the supposedly neutral change swallows up the bad change and neutralizes the two changes together.

To create neutral-range utilitarianism out of neutral-life utilitarianism, I had to weaken the notion of neutrality. A consequence is that neutrality acquires the power to swallow up good or bad changes and neutralize them. That is why I call this sort of neutrality "greedy." It is not true to the intuition of neutrality. At first, neutral-range utilitarianism seems a way to accommodate the intuition of neutrality, but in the end it fails to do so. The conclusion in the example that the effect of climate change is not bad is not consistent with the intuition.

In the end, in *Weighing Lives* I found no satisfactory way to fit the intuition of neutrality into an acceptable theory of the value of population. I concluded that this intuition has to be rejected.[14]

6. UTILITARIANISM WITH LOOSE BETTERNESS AMONG LIVES

But now we have a new resource that might be able to revive it. I set out neutral-life and neutral-range utilitarianism under the assumption that betterness among lives is tight. Problems emerged. Could it be that recognizing that betterness among lives is loose—as it undoubtedly is—might give us some relief from these problems? I turn now to this question.

So now, instead of assuming that betterness of lives has a single cardinal measure $g()$, I assume it is represented by a set of measures $g^t()$ indexed by t, where t takes values in some index set T. One life is better than another if it is better according to all these measures. To import this loose ordering into utilitarianism for variable populations, I start from neutral-life utilitarianism with tight betterness among lives and amend it as little as possible.

I assume there is a neutral life n such that the goodness of populations is represented by the set of proto-goodness measures

$$G^t\left(l_1, l_2, \ldots l_I\right) = \Sigma_i\left(g^t\left(l_i\right) - g^t\left(n\right)\right) \tag{4}$$

Each of these measures represents a tightening of the betterness ordering among distributions. Tightenings are indexed by t. One distribution is better than another if it is proto-better according to every tightening. We now have a loose betterness ordering for distributions. Although there are many proto-goodness measures of lives, the designated neutral life n is the same for all of them.

One consequence of this theory is that adding the life n to a population leaves the distribution equally as good as it was before. That is to say, the designated neutral life is strongly neutral. This needs to be checked against the definition of equal goodness in Section 2. Let the original distribution be $(l_1, l_2, \ldots l_I)$ and the distribution with the neutral life added $(l_1, l_2, \ldots l_I, n)$. For every tightening t, formula (4) shows that $G^t(l_1, l_2, \ldots l_I) = G^t(l_1, l_2, \ldots l_I, n)$. So any distribution that is proto-better or proto-worse than $(l_1, l_2, \ldots l_I)$ according to t is correspondingly proto-better or proto-worse than $(l_1, l_2, \ldots l_I, n)$ according to t, and vice versa. It follows that any distribution that is actually better or worse than $(l_1, l_2, \ldots l_I)$ is correspondingly actually better or worse than $(l_1, l_2, \ldots l_I, n)$, and vice versa. The definition of equal goodness is therefore satisfied.

Any other life that is equally as good as n is also strongly neutral. Adding a person with a life that is better than n makes a distribution better and adding a life that is worse than n makes a distribution worse.

In all those respects, this new theory matches neutral-life utilitarianism with tight betterness among lives. I count it as a version of neutral-life utilitarianism because it incorporates a life n that is strongly neutral.

However, it also incorporates lives that are incommensurate with n. They are better than n according to some tightenings t, and worse according to others. Adding one of these lives to a distribution makes the distribution neither better nor worse, nor equally good. These lives are weakly neutral in the sense defined in Section 5. Some of them will be better than others. So there is a range of lives—some better than others—that are all weakly neutral. This version of neutral-life utilitarianism therefore imports one feature from neutral-range utilitarianism. It incorporates a sort of neutral range. This is one way in which recognizing the looseness of betterness among lives makes a difference to the axiology of population.

Still, it is an unimportant difference because it goes no way toward solving the problems that motivate neutral-range utilitarianism. Neutral-range utilitarianism is designed to accommodate the intuition of neutrality. But neutral-life utilitarianism with loose betterness among lives does not accommodate this intuition, despite its sort of neutral range.

That is because the betterness ordering of lives, though loose, is locally tight in the way I described in Section 2. Take any strongly neutral life—either n or another one. As close as you like to it is a life that is better than it and another life that is worse than it. These two lives are as similar as you like, yet adding one to a distribution makes the distribution better and adding the other makes it worse. This is strongly counter to the intuition of neutrality, which is the intuition that lives are *typically* neutral. It implies that a wide range of lives lies between any life whose addition makes a distribution better and any life whose addition makes it worse.

Nor does neutral-life utilitarianism with loose betterness among lives accommodate the large-scale intuitions: the repugnant conclusion and its mirror image. A distribution containing only a large number of very good lives full of happiness is worse than one that contains only lives that are a little bit better than n, provided there are enough of those lives. Unless n is rather good, this conclusion is repugnant. Also, a distribution containing only a large number of bad lives full of suffering is better than one that contains only lives that are a little bit worse than n, provided there are enough of those lives. Unless n is rather poor, this is counter to intuition. It seems impossible to find a designated neutral life n that does not conflict with one or other of these large-scale intuitions.

It is possible to accommodate all these intuitions by the same means as I employed in Section 5. We move beyond neutral-life utilitarianism. Instead of a single designated neutral life, we have many neutral lives n^r, indexed by r. We get this set of proto-goodness measures:

$$G^{rt}\left(l_1, l_2, \ldots l_I\right) = \Sigma_i \left(g^t\left(l_i\right) - g^t\left(n^r\right)\right) \tag{5}$$

The index t marks different proto-goodness measures for lives, and the index r marks different neutral lives. To ensure there is a suitable range of neutral lives, not all of them will be equally as good as each other.

They can only be weakly neutral. There can be no strongly neutral life, because if there were it would conflict with the intuition of neutrality and the other intuitions in the way I just described.

Now we have neutral-range utilitarianism with loose betterness among lives. It accommodates the intuition of neutrality and the large-scale intuitions, just as the same move did in developing neutral-range utilitarianism with tight betterness among lives. However, just as the earlier version of neutral-range utilitarianism did, this version brings with it the problem of greediness. This problem is not in any way diminished by loosening betterness among lives.

I conclude that recognizing the looseness of betterness among lives makes no significant difference to the utilitarian ethics of population. Neutral-life and neutral-range utilitarianism each have versions with loose betterness. Whether betterness among lives is tight or loose, the same intuitions arise and can be accommodated in the same way in neutral-range utilitarianism. But this theory suffers from the same difficulty of greediness in either version.

In writing *Weighing Lives*, I thought it a harmless simplification to assume that betterness among lives is tight. I now feel vindicated.

7. GETTING PERSONAL

That deals with my own concern. Rabinowicz has another. He aims to describe a personal betterness ordering that includes nonexistence and use it to dispel a particular difficulty that I shall now describe.

Betterness among lives is personal betterness—betterness for those people who live the lives. Lives are ordered by their personal betterness. Rabinowicz assumes that nonexistence has a place in this ordering. That is to say, he assumes that some lives are personally better for a person than not living at all, and some are personally worse. He works out the consequences of this assumption.

He does so initially on the supposition that the personal ordering of lives together with nonexistence is tight. This implies that all lives, if they are not personally equally as good as nonexistence, are personally either better or worse than nonexistence.

To this supposition, let us add the intuition of neutrality. This is the intuition that there is a range of lives—some personally better than others—that are neutral in the weak sense I defined in Section 5. That is to say, adding one of these lives to a distribution makes the distribution generally neither better nor worse. Since some of these neutral lives are personally better than others, they cannot all be personally equally as good as nonexistence. Therefore, some of them are personally either better or worse than nonexistence. Call these "unequal neutral lives."

Adding a life to a distribution leaves all the existing people with just the same life as they would otherwise have had. So it is personally equally good for all of them. But it gives a life to the person who is added, when otherwise she would not have existed. So adding an unequal neutral life is personally either better or worse for the added person. In sum, adding an unequal neutral life is personally better or worse for one person and personally equally good for everyone else.

This implies that adding an unequal neutral life to a distribution makes the distribution generally either better or worse. That is a consequence of something I have been implicitly taking for granted: that the general goodness of a distribution depends only on the personal goodness of people. This assumption is crystallized in what I call "the principle of personal good," which Rabinowicz supports.[15] One part of it is that, if a change is personally better or worse for one person and personally equally good for everyone else, then it is correspondingly better or worse generally.

I have concluded that adding an unequal neutral life makes a distribution generally better or worse. But the definition of weak neutrality tells us that adding any neutral life makes a distribution generally neither better nor worse.

We have reached a contradiction. It shows that the following four claims are mutually inconsistent:

The principle of personal good.
Nonexistence has a place in the personal betterness ordering of lives.
The intuition of neutrality.
The personal betterness ordering of lives together with nonexistence is tight.

That is the difficulty that concerns Rabinowicz. Rabinowicz likes the first three of these claims, but he argues that the fourth is false. That dispels the difficulty.

Rabinowicz loosens the personal betterness ordering in two ways. Firstly, he loosens the place of nonexistence in it. He stipulates that each neutral life is personally neither better nor worse than nonexistence. Now consider adding a neutral life to a distribution. By the definition of weak neutrality, this makes the distribution generally neither better nor worse. This is now consistent with the principle of personal good. Adding the neutral life is personally equally good for each of the existing people, since it leaves them with the same life as before. By Rabinowicz's stipulation, it is also personally neither better nor worse for the person who lives the added life. It is therefore consistent with the principle of personal good for it to be generally neither better not worse. The difficulty is overcome.

In effect, Rabinowicz gives nonexistence a loose place in the betterness ordering of lives that coincides with the range of neutral lives. A neutral life is defined as neutral on the basis of general betterness; it is generally neutral. But Rabinowicz makes it also personally neutral in the sense that it is personally neither better nor worse than nonexistence. The neutral range is the range of lives that are both personally and generally neutral.

Rabinowicz secondly also loosens the betterness ordering of lives themselves. I have described this move in Section 6. It is not necessary for overcoming the difficulty I described. Loosening the place of nonexistence in the ordering is sufficient for that, whether betterness among lives is tight or loose.

All this passes me by. I do not share Rabinowicz's concern, either with describing a personal betterness ordering that includes nonexistence, or with dispelling the difficulty that arises from doing so. I do not think nonexistence has any place in the personal betterness ordering.

That is because I have a different concept of personal goodness from Rabinowicz's. I take personal goodness to be the good of a person. I take a person's good to be approximately or exactly synonymous with her well-being. It is a quantitative concept, and its quantity varies with varying states of affairs. Using functional notation, we may write it as "$G_s(p)$" or "$G(p, s)$," to be read as "p's good in s," where p is a person and s is a state of affairs. I think both Rabinowicz and I accept the lesson of measurement theory, which tells us that quantities of a property are derived from the corresponding comparative relation. The comparative of the property of a person's good can be written $(p, s)B(q, t)$, to be read as "p would have more good in s than q would have in t" or as "p would be better off in s than q would be in t." This comparative has no meaning unless p would exist in s and q in t.

We often make comparisons where p and q are the same person. Instead of "$(p, s)B(p, t)$", we might use the simplified notation $sB_p t$. This may be read "p would be better off in s than in t," or "s would be better for p than t." However, it is written or read, it has no meaning unless p would exist in both s and t. In this paper I have been concerned with states of affairs that consist in a person's living a particular life, or not living at all. The person would not exist in the latter state of affairs. There is no meaningful comparison to be made between her good were she to live a particular life and her good were she not to live at all.

Rabinowicz outlines his concept of personal goodness in Section 1 of "Getting Personal." He takes goodness to be a property of states of affairs. We can use the notation $G(s)$ for the goodness of a state of affairs s. Measurement theory tells us that quantities of this property are derived from the corresponding comparative relation. The comparative might be written "sBt," read as "s is better than t." Since we are concerned with personal rather than general betterness, we need a comparative that is relativized to a person. We might write it sB_pt, to be read as "s is better for p than t." This comparative sB_pt is a relation that holds between the person and states of affairs. Nothing requires that, if s is better for p than t, the person p exists in either of the states of affairs s and t. Using this concept of personal betterness, it makes sense to say that a particular life is better for a person than not existing. Rabinowicz's concept of personal goodness, which might be written "$G_p(s)$", is derived from this concept of personal betterness.

Goodness as I understand it is a property that a person possesses in a state of affairs. As Rabinowicz understands it, goodness is a relation a person stands in to a state of affairs. Mine might be called an "internal" concept of goodness, and Rabinowicz's an "external" one. Rabinowicz is pushed toward an external concept by his fitting-attitude theory of value. He thinks that for something to be good is for it to be fitting to have a particular favourable attitude toward it. The goodness of a life is a matter of an attitude we take toward the life. The life is evaluated from the outside. I take the goodness of a life to be a matter of what it is like to live the life. It is evaluated from the inside.

Which is the better concept to adopt for the sake of population axiology? The betterness ordering of lives need not differ between the concepts. The significant difference is that the internal concept does not include nonexistence within this ordering, whereas the external concept can include it, so that a life can be better or worse than nonexistence. Furthermore, Rabinowicz assumes there actually are lives that are better or worse than nonexistence. The external concept therefore has more content. In principle, this gives it more analytical power.

Indeed, its extra power creates the potential inconsistency in population axiology that I described. This inconsistency cannot arise if we adopt the internal concept of goodness. In any case, Rabinowicz successfully overcomes it by making sure that the neutral range of lives is personally as well as generally neutral.

Apart from creating this potential difficulty, does the power of the external concept give us extra positive leverage on population axiology? It would do so if it allowed us to bring further intuitions to bear on the subject. For example, because the neutral range is personally as well as generally neutral, it might help us identify the neutral range by bringing to bear our intuitions about which lives are personally better than nonexistence and which are personally worse.

But so far as I can tell, our intuitions relevant to the neutral range are directly about the general goodness of populations and not about personal goodness. Most of us think that adding people to the population is ethically neutral in a wide range of cases; this is a thought about general good. As Jan Narveson puts it, "We are in favour of making people happy, but neutral about making happy people."[16] I do not know of a corresponding intuition about personal good. I have mentioned other relevant intuitions—the large-scale intuitions and the intuition about greediness—and these are also matters of general good. I have not seen intuitions about personal goodness applied to population axiology.

In his paper, I do not find Rabinowicz using the external conception of goodness to make a positive contribution in this way. He brings personal betterness into line with population axiology, rather than the other way round. Given that, I think we are better off with the internal conception. We gain nothing from assuming that some lives are better or worse than nonexistence.

ACKNOWLEDGMENTS

I am very grateful to Wlodek Rabinowicz for perceptive comments. Research for the paper was supported by ARC Discovery Grants DP140102468 and DP180100355.

NOTES

1. *Weighing Lives*, p. 82.
2. *Weighing Lives*, p. 22.
3. "Getting Personal," Section 4.
4. Thanks to Rabinowicz.
5. *Weighing Lives*, p. 95.
6. Starting with von Neumann and Morgenstern, *Theory of Games*.
7. For example, von Neumann and Morgenstern, *Theory of Games*.
8. See my "Is Incommensurability Vagueness?"
9. Blackorby, Bossert, and Donaldson, *Population Issues*.
10. *Weighing Lives*, p. 143ff. My "Climate change and population ethics", in this volume, also contains a fuller description of the intuition of neutrality.
11. *Reasons and Persons*, p. 388.
12. See Rabinowicz, "Getting Personal," Section 2.
13. "Climate change and population ethics" sets out the greediness objection more fully.
14. *Weighing Lives*, p. 205.
15. "Getting Personal," Section 3.
16. "Moral Problems of Population," p. 73.

References

Blackorby, Charles, Walter Bossert, and David Donaldson. 2005. *Population Issues in Social Choice Theory, Welfare Economics and Ethics*. New York: Cambridge University Press.

Broome, John. 1998. "Is Incommensurability Vagueness?" In *Incommensurability, Incomparability, and Practical Reason*, edited by Ruth Chang, 67–89. Cambridge, MA: Harvard University Press.

Broome, John. 2004. *Weighing Lives*. Oxford: Oxford University Press.

Broome, John. 2021. "Climate change and population ethics." This volume, 393–406.

Narveson, Jan. 1976. "Moral Problems of Population." In *Ethics and Population*, edited by Michael Bayles, 59–80. Cambridge, MA: Schenkman. [Originally published in *The Monist* 57 (1973): 62–86].

Parfit, Derek. 1984. *Reasons and Persons*. Oxford: Oxford University Press.

Rabinowicz, Wlodek. 2012. "Getting personal: the intuition of neutrality reinterpreted." This volume, 114–41.

von Neumann, John, and Oskar Morgenstern. 1944. *Theory of Games and Economic Behavior*. Princeton, NJ: Princeton University Press.

PART II

PHILOSOPHICAL AND METHODOLOGICAL ASSUMPTIONS

CHAPTER 7

LESSONS TO BE LEARNED FROM THE MERE ADDITION PARADOX

LARRY S. TEMKIN

1. INTRODUCTION

ON January 1, 2017, Derek Parfit passed away. I was the first graduate student for whom Derek served as the main dissertation advisor. However, Derek was much more than just my teacher and thesis advisor. He was my mentor, my inspiration, my editor, and my long-time colleague. It is no exaggeration to say that I owe my philosophical career to Derek. Beyond all that, Derek was my oldest, and dearest, friend in the profession. This chapter is dedicated to Derek.

In 1977, I took a seminar with Parfit in which he presented an early version of what eventually became Part Four of *Reasons and Persons*.[1] In that seminar, Parfit laid much of the foundation for what we now recognize as the field of population ethics. Parfit asked questions that had never been asked before. He introduced a new methodological approach (at least one new to philosophy)—"box ethics," identified a host of new principles and considerations, and created entirely new terminology for addressing the questions he was raising. In pursuing his questions, Parfit brought a rare combination of argumentative rigor, penetrating insight, and extraordinary originality. Along the way, he also discovered a host of deep puzzles and paradoxes that we are still grappling with forty years later.

In this article, I will restrict my focus to a single paradox to which Parfit introduced us, the *Mere Addition Paradox*.[2] To my mind, this is the richest, and most important, of Parfit's many population puzzles and paradoxes. My aim is to present and develop some of the most important lessons to be learned from the Mere Addition Paradox.[3]

The article is divided into five sections. In Section 2, I introduce the Mere Addition Paradox. In Section 3, I show how the Mere Addition Paradox calls into question the

Axiom of Transitivity and illustrate how this could be possible. In Section 4, I discuss the nature and structure of the good. I distinguish between an *Internal Aspects View* and an *Essentially Comparative View* and note that many of the principles and ideals that people attach value to in assessing the goodness of outcomes, including many of those which underlie our judgments in the Mere Addition Paradox, are essentially comparative. I point out that this has profound implications for many of our deepest assumptions about rationality and practical reasoning. In Section 5, I summarize my main claims and add a brief word about Parfit's extraordinary philosophical legacy.

2. The Mere Addition Paradox

Figure 7.1 represents a version of Parfit's Mere Addition Paradox.[4] It represents four alternative outcomes, A, B, A+, and A-. In each outcome there are either one or two groups of people, x and y, such that the very same people exist in each x group, the very same people exist in each y group, there are 10 billion people in each group with lives of equal duration (say, seventy-five years), and the members of x and y are distinct. A represents an outcome in which only the x group exists, and all of its members are very well-off. B represents an outcome in which both the x and y groups exist, and while all of their members have lives that are more than half as good as the lives of A's members, and are well worth living, they are all worse off than the members of A. A+ represents an outcome containing both the x and y groups, where the members of the x group are exactly as well-off as they would be in A, the members of the y group have lives that are well worth living, but are worse off than they would be in B, and the extent to which the members of y are worse off in A+ than in B is greater than the extent to which the members of x are better off in A+ than in B. A- represents an outcome where the members of the x group are exactly as well-off as they would be in B.

Considering A and B as two possible outcomes, or two possible future states of the world, Parfit argued that A would be better than B. Intuitively, this seems plausible. If we could each have three children, and they would all be exceedingly well-off, or we could each have six children, but the result would be fewer resources for food, education, healthcare, energy, and so on, so that each of our children would be significantly

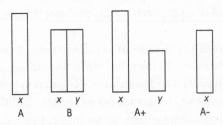

FIGURE 7.1 A version of Parfit's Mere Addition Paradox

worse off, most of us believe that it would be better to have three children rather than six, and we believe this *even if* each of the six children would be more than half as well-off as each of the three children would be, so that the sum total of utility would be greater in the world where we each had six children than in the world where we each had three children.

The judgment that A would be better than B follows from a combination of views that many find plausible. Comparing A with A- in Figure 7.1, it seems clear that A is better than A- in accordance with:

> *The Same Number Quality Claim, or Q*: If, in either of two outcomes the same number of people would ever live, and their lives would be of equal duration, then, if everyone in one outcome would be better off (or have a higher quality of life) than everyone in the other outcome, then the former outcome would be better than the latter.[5]

Indeed, the judgment that A will be better than A- follows from an even weaker (and thereby stronger, which is to say even more plausible and easily defended) claim:

> *The Same People Quality Claim, or P*: If, in either of two outcomes the very same people would ever live, and their lives would be of equal duration, then, if everyone in one outcome would be better off (or have a higher quality of life) than everyone in the other outcome, then the former outcome would be better than the latter.

P is a plausible dominance people for same people cases. It is a particularly weak version of:

> *The Pareto Principle, or PP*: If, in either of two outcomes the very same people would ever live, then, if everyone in one outcome would be at least as well-off (or have at least as high a quality of life) as everyone in the other outcome, and in addition at least one person in the former outcome would better off (or have a higher quality of life) than she would in the latter outcome, then the former outcome would be better than the latter.[6]

Now as it happens, I believe that Q, P, and PP are all too strong, as stated. I believe that they should be qualified to state that if the relevant conditions hold, then the one outcome would be better than the other *in one important respect*, rather than *all things considered*, as their current formulations imply. This allows for the possibility that there are *impersonal* values that are relevant to assessing outcomes that make it possible that one outcome could be better than another *all things considered* despite the antecedents in Q, P, and PP holding.[7] However, in considering A and A- of Figure 7.1, we may presume that none of the relevant impersonal principles that *might* support the judgment that A- is better than A actually does so. That is, we assume an *other things equal clause* in thinking about such outcomes that allows us to focus on how the people in A and A- compare in terms of the quality of their lives, and for *such* comparisons principles like Q, P, and PP all seem to rightly support the judgment that A is better than A-.[8]

Next, consider the view that John Broome has called:

The Neutrality Intuition, or NI: There is a neutral range among possible lives that would be worth living in terms of the quality of people's lives, such that merely bringing people into existence whose quality of lives would lie within that neutral range would not itself make the outcome better, but neither would it make the outcome worse.[9]

Most people find the Neutrality Intuition plausible, at least if one supposes that one would merely be adding more people with lives worth living to an already large population of people who were at least as well-off as the people one would be bringing into existence. It accords with the widely shared view that, in general, if a couple is deciding whether to bring another person into the world, or whether to have three children or six, the mere fact that the child or children would have lives that are worth living does not *itself* provide them with a reason to have the child, or six children rather than three.

Given this, if one supposes that the y people in B would lie within the neutral range, as Parfit does for the purposes of this argument, then the Neutrality Intuition supports the judgment that B is neither better nor worse than A-, since the relation between B and A- is that, relative to A-, B involves merely adding more people, the y group, whose quality of lives lies within the neutral range, to an already large population of people, the x group, all of whom are at least as well-off as the additional new people are. However, if B isn't better than A-, which is clearly worse than A, then it seems plausible to conclude that B is worse than A.[10]

Here, we have in essence presented a line of reasoning that, on the basis of the plausibility of the Same Number Quality Claim, the Same People Quality Claim, and/or the Pareto Principle, together with the plausibility of the Neutrality Intuition, supports:

The Different Number or General Quality Claim, or GQ: If, in either of two outcomes a different number of people would ever live, and have lives of equal duration, then, if everyone in one of the outcomes is better off than everyone in the other (or has a higher quality of life), then the former outcome would be better than the latter.

GQ has great plausibility, at least where very large populations are involved (and perhaps, I add here, where the gap in the quality of lives of the people in the two outcomes is fairly significant, as we suppose it is between A and B[11]). Therefore, in accordance with a properly qualified version of GQ, there is powerful reason to judge that A is better than B and that, indeed, is Parfit's judgment regarding how A and B compare, all things considered.

Next, consider the relation between B and A+. B and A+ involve the very same groups of people, x and y. B is better than A+ with respect to both total and average utility. B is also much better than A+ with respect to equality. In addition, B is better for the members of A+'s worst-off group, the people in y. In accordance with such ideals as Utility, Equality, and Maximin, B is better than A+. To be sure, B is worse off for the members of A+'s better off group, the people in x, and so, depending on the details of the case, which has been under-described, one may also assume than B is worse than A+ regarding the ideal of Perfection. Still, unless one is an Elitist, who thinks it is more important to benefit the best off members of the society by a lesser amount than the worst off by a greater amount, and/or one is a Nietzschean of some sort, who values (substantial) gains or losses in Perfection *more* than (substantial) gains or losses in Utility, Equality, and Maximin *combined*, one will judge that, all things considered, B is better than A+. Most people are not Elitists or Nietzschean-type Perfectionists. Accordingly, reflecting on the outcomes represented by Figure 7.1, and weighing the various considerations that seem relevant to comparing those outcomes, most people judge that B *is* better than A+, all things considered. This is Parfit's view of the matter, as well.

Both intuitively, then, and on reflection, most people judge that, all things considered, A is better than B in Figure 7.1, and B is better than A+. From this, Parfit contends, it follows that A is better than A+, by the transitivity of the "all things considered better than" relation, or, for short:

> *The Axiom of Transitivity*: For any three outcomes, p, q, and r, if, all things considered, p is better than q, and all things considered, q is better than r, then, all things considered, p is (must be) better than r.

However, reflecting on the outcomes represented in Figure 7.1, Parfit finds it difficult to believe that A *is* better than A+. This is because, as Parfit presented the case, A+ involves *Mere Addition*, where, according to Parfit, there is:

> *Mere Addition*: When, in one of two outcomes, there exist extra people (1) who have lives worth living, (2) who affect no one else, and (3) whose existence does not involve social injustice.[12]

As Parfit puts it in a passage from "Future Generations: Further Problems":

> Let us compare A with A+. The only difference is that A+ contains an extra group, who have lives worth living, and who affect no one else . . . it seems [hard] . . . to believe that A+ is *worse* than A. This implies that it would have been better if the extra group had never existed. If their lives are worth living, and they affect no one else, why is it bad that these people are alive?[13]

Here, Parfit's view can be seen as reflecting the Neutrality Intuition, according to which merely adding more people within the neutral zone to an outcome where a large number of people already exist and are at least as well-off—and Parfit is assuming, as part of his example, that the y group in A+ are in the neutral zone—doesn't make the outcome better, but *neither does it make the outcome worse*.

According to Parfit, then, in considering the different outcomes represented by Figure 7.1, most believe that A is better than B, and that B is better than A+, but most believe that A is *not* better than A+. Together, these three judgments are inconsistent, given the Axiom of Transitivity. According to Parfit, therefore, one of the three judgments must go, but it is difficult to see how to give any of them up. This is the *Mere Addition Paradox*.

3. On the Possibility that the Axiom of Transitivity is False

There has been much discussion of the Mere Addition Paradox, and many different arguments presented regarding which of Parfit's three pairwise comparisons—that A is better than B, that B is better than A+, and that A is not better than A+—is least plausible and should be given up. Moreover, the Mere Addition Paradox has led many, including Parfit, to recognize that we should reject Expected Utility Theory's

> *Axiom of Completeness*: All outcomes can be meaningfully compared and ranked, and for any two outcomes, p and q, it must be the case that, all things considered, p is better than q, or p is worse than q, or p and q are exactly equally good.

Furthermore, the Mere Addition Paradox has led many to recognize that beyond the possibility that some outcomes cannot be compared *at all*—the possibility of the *non*-comparability or *in*comparability of certain outcomes—there is the possibility of a *fourth* relation of comparability that can obtain between certain outcomes distinct from the relations of "better than," "worse than," or "equally as good as." This fourth relation is described in various ways as "rough comparability," "not worse than" (where not worse than is *not* equivalent to at least as good as, which means equally as good as or better than), "in the same league as," "on a par with," or "imprecisely equally as good as."[14] For example, in considering how A compares with A+, Parfit thought that it wasn't the case that they were utterly *non*-comparable, or *in*comparable; rather, he thought that they *were* comparable, but that the comparative relation in which they stood was the relation of being roughly comparable, or imprecisely equally good, or on a par, where this implied, and thus licensed us to accurately judge, that neither was better or worse than the other and that they were also not exactly equally good.

There is much to be learned from the various attempts to reject one of the three pairwise judgments that give rise to the Mere Addition Paradox, from the recognition that the Axiom of Completeness should be rejected, and from the further recognition that in addition to the possibility that some outcomes may be incomparable, it is possible that some outcomes may stand in a fourth relation of comparability which is meaningful, and distinct from the three standard comparative relations of better than, worse than, and equally as good as. However, in the space allotted, I cannot pursue those issues here. Instead, I want to suggest that what is *most* interesting and important about the Mere

Addition Paradox is what it reveals about the nature and structure of the good, and certain longstanding assumptions about the nature of practical reasoning.

Consider the reasoning that leads us to judge that A is better than B. We judge that A is better than B, largely, in virtue of such principles as the Same Number Quality Claim, Q, the Same People Quality Claim, P, and the Pareto Principle, PP, which combine with the Neutrality Intuition to generate the Different Number or General Quality Claim, GQ. Such principles have great intuitive plausibility, and they seem both relevant and normatively significant to the judgment that, all things considered, A is better than B. Importantly, however, such principles are limited in scope; they are simply not relevant, and so are of no significance, in comparing B with A+. To determine how B and A+ compare, all things considered, we appeal to how they compare regarding ideals like Utility, Maximin, Equality, and Perfection, and we judge that, as drawn, the extent to which B is better than A+ regarding Utility, Maximin, and Equality outweighs the extent to which B may be worse than A+ regarding Perfection. Thus, the factors that seem relevant and significant for comparing B with A, in order to determine which of those outcomes is better, all thing considered, are *different* from the factors that seem relevant and significant for comparing B with A+, in order to determine which of those outcomes is better, all things considered.

But if the factors that are relevant and significant for assessing the comparative goodness of an outcome, like B, can vary depending on the outcome with which it is compared, like A or A+, then, as I have argued at length elsewhere,[15] there is no particular reason to expect *all things considered better than* to be a transitive relation. Indeed, it could then be the case that the Axiom of Transitivity might *fail*, for the very same reason that in other contexts it *fails to apply*.

Consider the following. A relation, R, is transitive if and only if for any three alternatives, a, b, and c, if aRb and bRc then aRc. "Taller than" is a transitive relation, since for any three people, a, b, and c, if a is taller than b, and b is taller than c, then a is taller than c. By contrast, the "is deeply in love with" relation isn't transitive, as there could be three people, Ishmael, Beejal, and Arun, such that Ishmael is deeply in love with Beejal, and Beejal is deeply in love with Arun, yet Ishmael is not deeply in love with Arun, and indeed intensely hates Arun, his rival for Beejal's affections! So, some relations are transitive, while others are not.

Also, transitivity holds, or fails to hold, only where a *single* relation R is involved. Thus, transitivity simply *fails to apply* across *different* relations. For example, consider two relations, R_1 and R_2, such that R_1 stands for the "being a better tennis player than" relation, and R_2 stands for the "being a better bridge player than" relation. It could then be the case that IR_1B (meaning that Ishmael is a better tennis player than Beejal), and that BR_2A (meaning that Beejal is a better bridge player than Arun), and yet *nothing* would follow at all as to how Ishmael and Arun compared with respect to tennis playing, bridge playing, or anything else! If, in fact, Arun were both a better tennis player and a better bridge player than Ishmael, this would not reveal a *failure* of transitivity, because the relations "being a better tennis player than" and "being a better bridge player than" are simply *different* relations.

Moreover, importantly, what makes it the case that R_1 and R_2 *are* different relations is that the factors that are relevant and significant for being a good tennis player are different from the factors that are relevant and significant for being a good bridge player. This is why it could easily be the case, and would be no surprise, if Ishmael was better than Beejal, giving due weight to *all* of the factors that are relevant and significant for being a good tennis player; and Beejal was better than Arun, giving due weight to *all* of the factors that were relevant and significant for being a good bridge player; and yet Ishmael was not better than Arun, giving due weight to either all of the factors that were relevant for being a good tennis player or all of the factors that were relevant for being a good bridge player. To repeat, transitivity simply doesn't apply across the very different relations of R_1, "being a better tennis player than," and R_2, "being a better bridge player than."

But notice, there *could* be a single relation, R, that obtained when either R_1 or R_2 held. It would then follow that transitivity *failed* for the relation R, *for the very same reason* that it *failed to apply* across relations R_1 and R_2. Consider, for example, the relation, R, "better than with respect to at least one game," where for any two individuals, x and y, xRy if and only if, all things considered, x is better than y regarding at least one game, giving due weight to *all* of the factors that are relevant and significant for being good with respect to the game in question. In that case, it would then be true that IRB (that is, Ishmael would be better than Beejal regarding at least one game), in virtue of the fact that IR_1B (that is, that, all things considered, Ishmael was a better tennis player than Beejal, in terms of all of the factors that were relevant and significant for being a good tennis player), and BRA (that is, Beejal would be better than Arun regarding at least one game), in virtue of the fact that BR_2A, (that is, that, all things considered, Beejal was a better bridge player than Arun, in terms of all of the factors that were relevant and significant for being good a good bridge player), and yet it might not be the case that IRA (that is, that Ishmael is or must be better than Arun regarding at least one game). Thus, the relation R would be nontransitive—which is to say that transitivity would *fail* for the relation R—for the very same reason that transitivity *fails to apply* across two different relations, such as R_1 and R_2.

The preceding reveals how it could be the case that the Axiom of Transitivity is false. If, in fact, the factors that are relevant and significant for assessing whether one outcome is better or worse than another could vary depending on the alternative with which the one outcome is compared, then it could well be the case that there were three alternative outcomes, A, B, and C, such that A was better than B in terms of *all* of the factors that were relevant and significant for comparing *those* outcomes, and B was better than C in terms of *all* of the factors that were relevant and significant for comparing *those* outcomes, and yet it might *not* be the case that A was better than C in terms of *all* of the factors that were relevant and significant for making *that* comparison.

By analogy with the preceding example, there would be one relation, R_1, which holds between A and B in virtue of the set of factors that we believe should be considered in comparing A and B, a second, distinct, relation, R_2, which holds between B and C, in virtue of the set of (different or differently weighted) factors that we believe should be considered in comparing B and C, and a third relation, R, which stands for the "all things considered better than relation," which holds between A and B in virtue of the fact that AR_1B, and which holds between B and C in virtue of the fact that BR_2C. In other words, the very same factors that determine that AR_1B just *are* the factors that we deem relevant and significant for determining that A is better than B all things considered (that is, that ARB), and the different and/or differently weighted factors that determine that AR_2B just *are* the factors that we deem relevant and significant for determining that B is better than C all things considered (that is, that BRC). Thus, we see how it could be the case that the Axiom of Transitivity is false—that is, that the "all things considered better than" relation would be nontransitive—for the very same reason that transitivity fails to apply across distinct relations.

4. On the Nature and Structure of the Good: The Internal Aspect View versus the Essentially Comparative View

The preceding discussion reveals that a *crucial* question regarding the nature and structure of the good is whether, in fact, as reflection on the Mere Addition Paradox seems to suggest, the relevance and/or significance of the factors for assessing how good an outcome is can vary depending on the alternative outcome(s) with which it is compared. I call the view that it can, the *Essentially Comparative View* of Outcome Goodness.[16] I call the view that it cannot, the *Internal Aspects View* of Outcome Goodness, according to which the factors that are relevant and significant for assessing the goodness of an outcome depend solely in its internal features, and do not vary depending on the outcome with which it is compared.[17]

It is difficult to exaggerate the importance of this question. The Axiom of Transitivity has long been regarded as a fundamental principle of rationality.[18] It has long been claimed that anyone with nontransitive preferences was irrational, and that they ought to get their preferences in order. Relatedly, the Axiom of Transitivity is one of the key premises of Expected Utility Theory, which is the most powerfully developed, and widely accepted, model for individual rationality. Expected Utility Theory underlies game theory, decision theory, and much of modern economics. Moreover, we rely on the Axiom of Transitivity in countless everyday practical decisions, often without even realizing it. This is the case, for example, whenever we narrow a list of alternatives on the basis of a series of pairwise comparisons.[19] Finally, the Axiom of Transitivity underlies all forms of maximizing consequentialist reasoning, which tell us that for any set of alternatives, what we ought to do morally, prudentially, or rationally, is to bring about the best outcome (or, at least any outcome which is such that there is no available outcome that is better than it). After all, if the Axiom of Transitivity is false, it might be the case that no matter what outcome we choose, there would be another available outcome that is even better than it, all things considered.[20]

Thus, the stakes for practical reasoning could hardly be higher than they are in the question whether an Internal Aspects View of Outcome Goodness is true, which would support the Axiom of Transitivity, or an Essentially Comparative View of Outcome Goodness is true, which would challenge the Axiom of Transitivity. It is the Mere Addition Paradox that opens our eyes to this issue, when we recognize that the factors that seem relevant and significant for comparing A with B differ in relevance and/or significance from those for comparing B with A+, and/or A with A+. Moreover, as I argue at length in *Rethinking the Good*,[21] once one begins to closely examine the principles and ideals that we appeal to in judging the comparative goodness of different outcomes, we see that many of them have an essentially comparative structure or are limited in scope in ways that support an Essentially Comparative View of Outcome Goodness.

Notice, for example, that in the Mere Addition Paradox, the level of the worse-off group, *y*, seems to be a bad-making feature of A+ *in comparison with* B, but seems *not* to be a bad-making feature of A+ *in comparison with* A. This is because Maximin expresses a special person-affecting concern for how the worst-off members of any outcome fare, a concern that is met by *making those people better off*, as would be the case in B, but which is *not* met by those people *never existing*, as would be the case in A (at least if their lives are well worth living, which we are assuming is the case with the y group in A+). Thus, arguably, the most plausible version of Maximin reflects an Essentially Comparative View, since how good an outcome like A+ is, regarding Maximin, does not depend solely on the internal features of that outcome, but on the outcome to which it is compared.

Likewise, the Neutrality Intuition, which plays a key role in our judgments regarding the Mere Addition Paradox, reflects a particularly plausible person-affecting version of Utility, which is Essentially Comparative. It is the kind of position that Narveson was advancing in contending that "We are in favor of making people happy, but neutral about making happy people."[22] The point for Narveson, and many others, is that if one started with an outcome like A, and one was interested in improving that outcome regarding utility, the way to do that would be to increase the utility of the people in A, not to simply add more people to the outcome. This is why, in the Mere Addition Paradox, it is plausible to think that, where Mere Addition is involved, the fact that B has more total utility than A is not a reason for thinking that B is better than A, since in B, the people in A are actually much worse off, and B's greater total utility is owing to the mere addition of extra people to the outcome. On the other hand, the fact that B has more total utility than A+ *is* a reason for thinking that B is better than A+, since *in the comparison between B and A+*, unlike the comparison between A and B, the extra utility is not owing to the mere addition of extra people with lives worth living, but to the improvement of some of the people who exist in both outcomes. Clearly, then, the kind of Narvesonian person-affecting view of Utility reflected in the Neutrality Intuition and illuminated by the Mere Addition Paradox is an essentially comparative one, as on such a view one cannot evaluate B's utility based solely on B's internal features. To the contrary, the extent to which the utility in B's *y* group is relevant and significant for our evaluation of B's overall (comparative) value depends on whether the alternative to B is A, or A+.

Similarly, principles like the Same Number Quality Claim, the Same People Quality Claim, the Pareto Principle, and the Different Number or General Quality Claim, are not only limited in scope—applying for some comparisons but not others—but also clearly essentially comparative. Such principles do not apply to any given outcome, based solely on the internal features of that outcome; they apply only to certain outcomes *in comparison with others.*

Consider, for example, the Pareto Principle, which many economists regard as a fundamental principle of rationality. The Pareto Principle, as it is normally understood, applies only when comparing outcomes involving the very same people, and it holds that for such outcomes one outcome is better than another if better for one person and at least as good for everyone else. Well, considering again Figure 7.1, the Pareto Principle has nothing to say about how good A is based solely on its internal features, and similarly for B, A+, and A-. Likewise, the Pareto Principle is silent, having no relevance or significance, for comparing A with B, A with A+, or B with A+. But the Pareto Principle *is* relevant and significant for comparing A with A-, supporting the judgment that A is better than A-, since the very same people exist in both A and A-, and A is better for some people (indeed everyone) and worse for no one.

The Pareto Principle has been much discussed, and it has long been recognized that it is limited in scope. But the fact that the *structure* of the Pareto Principle is essentially comparative has not been discussed, nor its fundamental implications for the nature of the good and practical reasoning.

Consider Figure 7.2. A, B, and C represent three possible outcomes, each with three distinct groups of people, *x*, *y*, and *z*. Assume that members of each group are the same for each outcome, so that the very same people exist in each *x* group, in all three outcomes, and similarly for the *y* and *z* groups. In addition, assume that everyone in each group is equally deserving, and that they all deserve to be at the level of A's *y* group from the standpoint of absolute justice. As drawn, A's best-off group is better off than B's and C's best-off groups, which are equally well-off; the middle groups are all equally well-off in A, B, and C; and the worst-off groups are all equally well-off in A, B, and C.

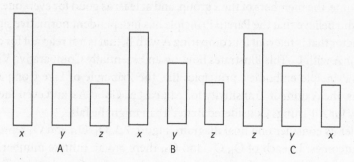

FIGURE 7.2 Illuminating the Pareto Principle

How do A and C compare, all things considered? It is hard to say. By assumption, A is better than C regarding Utility and Perfection, but A is worse than C regarding Absolute Justice and Equality. Assume, for the sake of the argument, that A and C are equally good in all other morally relevant respects. Then, it is *possible* that we should judge C as better than A, all things considered, when we give due weight to all of the factors that are relevant and significant for making *that* comparison. This would be so if the extent to which C is better than A regarding Equality and Absolute Justice is normatively more significant than the extent to which A is better than C regarding Utility and Perfection.

Next, consider how B and C compare. Since each of the best, middle, and worst-off groups in B and C are equally well-off, B and C will be exactly equally good in terms of Utility, Perfection, Equality, and Absolute Justice. So, given the powerful moral norm that we should be impartial between different people, we should regard B and C as equally as good. Does it follow from this that if C is better than A then B must be too, or that B must be at least as good as A? Well, the former *would* follow in accordance with:

> *The Principle of Like Comparability of Equivalents*: For any three outcomes, p, q, and r, if p and q are equally good, then however p compares to r that is exactly how q compares to r.[23]

Likewise, the latter would follow in accordance with:

> *The Axiom of Transitivity of At Least as Good As*: For any three outcomes, p, q, and r, if p is at least as good as q, and q is at least as good as r, then p is (must be) at least as good as r, where one outcome is at least as good as another if and only if it is equally as good as or better than the other.

Moreover, as I have shown in *Rethinking the Good*,[24] both the Principle of Like Comparability of Equivalents and the Axiom of Transitivity for At Least as Good As *will* be true *if* the Internal Aspects View is true.

However, as we have seen, the Pareto Principle is an Essentially Comparative Principle, and this opens up the possibility that A might be better than B, *even if* B and C are equally good, and C is better than A. This is because, when one compares A and B, one sees that A is better than B in accordance with the Pareto Principle, since it is better for some, the members of the x group, and at least as good for everyone else. Thus, for those who believe that the Pareto Principle has independent normative significance, there is a factor that is relevant for comparing A with B, that is not relevant for comparing B with C, or A with C. This illustrates how, on an Essentially Comparative View, which the Pareto Principle embodies, principles like the Principle of Like Comparability of Equivalents, the Axiom of Transitivity for At Least as Good As, and even the Axiom of Transitivity for All Things Considered Better Than might be false.

Finally, let us consider one final diagram, Figure 7.3. O_1, O_2, and O_3 represent three possible outcomes. In each of O_1, O_2, and O_3, there are an infinite number of people, with a different person at each of an infinite number of locations in time, T_n, and each

$$..., \ T_{-3}, \ T_{-2}, \ T_{-1}, \ T_{0,} \ T_{1}, \ T_{2,} \ T_{3}, ...$$
$$..., \ S_{-3}, \ S_{-2}, \ S_{-1}, \ S_{0}, \ S_{1}, \ S_{2}, \ S_{3}, ...$$

$$O_1: \quad ..., \ -3, \ -2, \ -1, \ 0, \ 1, \ 2, \ 3, \ ...$$
$$O_2: \quad ..., \ -3, \ -2, \ -1, \ 0, \ 1, \ 2, \ 3, \ ...$$
$$O_3: \quad ..., \ -3, \ -2, \ -1, \ 0, \ 1, \ 2, \ 3, \ ...$$

FIGURE 7.3 Nontransitive Outcomes

of an infinite number of locations in space, S_n. Also, for each integer, there is a single person in each of O_1, O_2, and O_3 who is at a level of welfare corresponding to that integer. So, for example, in O_1, there is one person at level 0 at a particular location in time, T_0, and a particular location in space, S_0; one person at level 1 at a particular location in time, T_1, and a particular location in space, S_1; one person at level 2 at a particular location in time, T_2, and a particular location in space, S_2; one person at level 3 at a particular location in time, T_3, and a particular location in space, S_3; and so on; and also one person at level -1 at a particular location in time, T_{-1}, and a particular location in space, S_{-1}; one person at level -2 at a particular location in time, T_{-2}; and a particular location in space, S_{-2}; one person at level -3 at a particular location in time, T_{-3}; and a particular location in space, S_{-3}; and so on. The same applies for O_2 and O_3.

How do the different outcomes compare, all things considered? Considering them abstractly, it may seem clear that they are all exactly equally as good. And in accordance with plausible theories of impartiality, I think it is true that *if* the people in O_1 are different from the people in O_2, then O_1 and O_2 *are* equally good. Let's stipulate that that is so. Let's also stipulate that the people in O_2 are different from the people in O_3. In that case, O_2 and O_3 would *also* be equally good. Does it follow from this that O_1 and O_3 must be equally good?

Well, this *would* follow given:

The Axiom of Transitivity for Equally as Good As: For any three outcomes, p, q, and r, if p is equally as good as q, and q is equally as good as r, then p is (must be) equally as good as r.

Moreover, as I have shown elsewhere, the Axiom of Transitivity for Equally as Good As is true *if* the Internal Aspect View is true.[25] However, there is good reason to believe that the Pareto Principle has normative significance, and, as we have seen, the Pareto Principle is essentially comparative, so this opens up the possibility that O_1 and O_3 might *not* be equally good, even *if* O_1 and O_2 *are* equally good and O_2 and O_3 are *also* equally good.

How could that be? Well, by now the reasoning should be familiar. I stipulated that the people in O_1 are distinct from the people in O_2, and that the people in O_2 are distinct from the people in O_3. However, this is compatible with its being the case that the people in O_1 and O_3 are the very same people. Let's suppose that's true. Then let's also suppose that each person, P_n, who exists in O_1 at the temporal location T_n and the spatial location S_n, exists in O_3 at the temporal location $T_{n+1,000,000}$, and the spatial location $S_{n+1,000,000}$. So, the *very same person* who is at level 0 in O_1, is at level 1,000,000 in O_3, the *very same person* who is at level 10,000 in O_1, is at level 1,010,000 in O_3, and more generally, for whatever level n a person is at in O_1, that person is at level $n + 1,000,000$ in O_3. Thus, as described, *the very same people* exist in both O_1 and O_3, and they are *all one million units better off* in O_3 than in O_1. Surely, this provides us with compelling reason to judge that O_3 is better than O_1, in accordance with the Pareto Principle!

Does this give us any reason to change one of our earlier judgments that O_1 and O_2 are equally good, or that O_2 and O_3 are equally good? It does not. After all, the relevant and significant factor that underlies our judgment that O_3 is better than O_1, namely the Pareto Principle, has absolutely *no* relevance or significance for the judgments concerning O_1 and O_2, or O_2 and O_3. This is because the Pareto Principle doesn't even apply to cases involving totally different people.

In sum, a number of plausible principles that seem relevant and significant for assessing the comparative goodness of different outcomes have an essentially comparative structure and/or support an Essentially Comparative View of Outcome Goodness. This raises the serious possibility that, in the end, various plausible, and seemingly compelling principles of rationality may have to be rejected, including, among others, the Axiom of Transitivity for All Things Considered Better Than, the Axiom of Transitivity for Equally as Good As, the Axiom of Transitivity for At Least As Good As, and the Principle of Like Comparability of Equivalents.

There are various responses one might pursue to the arguments I have given, including, among others, abandoning the Internal Aspect View, abandoning the Essentially Comparative View, or seeking ways of preserving the various Axioms of Transitivity and other such principles even on an Essentially Comparative View. Ultimately, however, for reasons that I present in *Rethinking the Good*, I believe that any plausible response to the Mere Addition Paradox will require substantial revision in our understanding of the nature of the good, moral ideals, and practical reasoning, and will have substantial practical and theoretical implications.

5. CONCLUSION

This chapter discussed the Mere Addition Paradox, which I believe is the most important paradox of population ethics. I began by noting some of the reasoning that might lead one to judge that, in the Mere Addition Paradox, A is better than B, and B is better than A+, but A is not better than A+. I noted how one might support the judgment that A is better than B by first noting that A is better than A-, in accordance with principles like the Same Number Quality Claim, the Same People Quality Claim, and the Pareto Principle, then note that B is no better than A-, in accordance with the Neutrality Intuition, and then reasonably conclude that B is worse than A, since B is no better than an outcome, A-, which itself is much worse than A. I noted that B seems better than A+, since, by hypothesis, it is better in three important respects, Utility, Equality, and Maximin, and worse in only one respect, Perfection, and that, as drawn, it is hard to believe that the extent to which B is worse than A+ regarding Perfection outweighs the extent to which it is better in the other three respects combined. Finally, I noted that, in accordance with the Neutrality Intuition, A+ is not worse than A, given the assumption, implicit in Parfit's example, that A+'s y group lies within the neutral range. I further noted Parfit's contention that A+ cannot be worse than A given that, by hypothesis, it involves Mere Addition, since he finds it hard to believe that the Mere Addition of an extra group of people to an outcome could make that outcome worse if their lives are well worth living, if there is no one for whom their existence is worse, and if it involves no social inequality.

I noted how reflection on the Mere Addition Paradox has led some people to recognize that we should reject Expected Utility Theory's Axiom of Completeness, which holds that all outcomes can be meaningfully compared, and for any two outcomes, x and y, either x is better than y, or x is worse than y, or x and y are equally good. I further noted that thinking about the Mere Addition Paradox has led some people to conclude that in addition to the possibility that some outcomes may be *in*comparable, or *non*-comparable, it is possible that there is a *fourth* relation of *comparability* besides the three widely recognized relations of "better than," "worse than," or "equally as good as." The fourth relation has been described in various ways, including "rough comparability," "on a par," and "imprecise equality."

I suggested that there is much to be learned from reflecting on these positions, as well as various possible ways of rejecting one of the three judgments that give rise to the Mere Addition Paradox. However, I claimed that the most important lessons to be gleaned from the Mere Addition Paradox concern what it reveals about the nature and structure of the good, and longstanding fundamental assumptions about practical reasoning.

Parfit assumed that one of the three judgments of the Mere Addition Paradox had to be rejected, because they were inconsistent with each other given the Axiom of Transitivity of the All Things Considered Better than Relation. In holding this view, Parfit assumed—as has virtually everyone else in human history!—that "all things considered better than" is a transitive relation. However, when one carefully explores the *reasoning* that gives rise to the paradox, one sees that the paradox raises the possibility that "all things considered better than" might *not* be a transitive relation.

I pointed out that the factors that seem relevant and significant for assessing how B compares with A are *different* from those that seem relevant and significant for assessing how B compares with A+, and then showed how if this is correct then it *could* be the case that the Axiom of Transitivity for All Things Considered Better Than *failed*, for the very same reason that the Axiom *fails to apply* across distinct relations.

I noted that the Axiom of Transitivity is widely accepted as a fundamental principle of rationality. Indeed, many people, including most economists, assume that people with nontransitive preferences are, in that respect, *irrational*, and that they should "get their preferences in order." I also noted that the Axiom of Transitivity is a fundamental principle of Expected Utility Theory, which is the most widely accepted model of individual rationality, and which is the main theory underlying game theory, decision theory, and much of modern economics. I further pointed out that the Axiom of Transitivity is implicitly relied on in countless cases of everyday practical reasoning, and that all forms of consequentialist reasoning—both moral and prudential—depend on it. The stakes could hardly be higher.

The key question in this area, I argued, concerns the structure of the good. On one view, which I call the Internal Aspects View, the factors that are relevant and significant for assessing an outcome's goodness depend solely on the internal features of that outcome. On another view, which I call the Essentially Comparative View, the factors that are relevant and significant for assessing an outcome can vary, depending on the outcome with which it is compared. If the former is true, then the Axiom of Transitivity for All Things Considered Better Than will also be true, along with a host of other fundamental assumptions commonly made about the nature of practical reasoning. However, if the latter is true, then much of what we commonly assume about practical reasoning is open to doubt, including the Axiom of Transitivity for All Things Considered Better Than.

Reflecting on the Mere Addition Paradox reveals that many of the principles and ideals that people most value in assessing outcomes have an essentially comparative structure or are limited in scope in ways that support an Essentially Comparative View. This turns out to be true of a particularly plausible version of Maximin, a particularly plausible version of Utility, the Neutrality Intuition, the Same Number Quality Claim, the Same People Quality Claim, the Different Number or General Quality Claim, and even the Pareto Principle, which many people have regarded as itself a fundamental principle of rationality.[26] My discussion showed that if principles such as these are genuinely relevant to assessing the comparative goodness of certain outcomes, then we may have to reject the Principle of Like Comparability of Equivalents, which, as noted, holds that for any three outcomes, p, q, and r, if p and q are equally good, then however p compares to r that is exactly how q compares to r. We may also have to reject the Axioms of Transitivity for All Things Considered Better Than, for At Least As Good As, and for Equally as Good As.[27]

Ultimately, one will need to abandon either the Internal Aspects View or the Essentially Comparative View as the sole approach to understanding the nature and structure of moral ideals and outcome goodness. Of course, if one accepts the Essentially Comparative View one might try to reconcile that view with some of our apparently conflicting fundamental assumptions about practical reasoning, such as the Axiom of Transitivity for All Things Considered Better Than. I believe, however, that while such a move is worth pursuing, there is no plausible response to the Mere Addition Paradox which does not have profound implications for our understanding of the good, moral ideals, and the nature of practical reasoning, and which does not have substantial practical and theoretical implications.

Let me end with the following observations. When Parfit first began using his simple rectangular diagrams to explore various issues in population ethics, a common reaction was to ask, "What do *boxes* have to do with ethics?" I think it is safe to say that that question has long since disappeared from the minds of Parfit's readers. However, to my mind, Parfit's work opened up whole areas for philosophical exploration which remain largely underappreciated.

The fact is that Parfit's "box ethics" has ramifications that extend far beyond the topic of population ethics and our obligations to future generations. Indeed, Parfit's curiosity opened up its own Pandora's box of puzzles and problems that remain largely unsolved and deeply perplexing. It is part of Parfit's extraordinary legacy that many future generations of philosophers will need, and want, to contend with the many brilliant insights and complex issues that he has given us. I take some comfort in the thought that through his own unstinting shining example, Parfit, like Pandora herself, has provided us with *hope* that one day, if mankind manages to survive the next few generations, we may finally be up to the task of adequately coming to terms with the brilliant insights and deep paradoxes that he has unleashed upon the world.

ACKNOWLEDGMENTS

I would like to thank the Editors for inviting me to contribute to this volume, and for their efforts in bringing this volume to press. I would especially like to thank Tim Campbell, for his many perceptive and helpful comments on an earlier draft.

NOTES

1. Derek Parfit, *Reasons and Persons* (Oxford: Oxford University Press, 1984).
2. See Chapter 19 of *Reasons and Persons*.
3. This article draws heavily from Chapters 11 and 12 of my book *Rethinking the Good: Moral Ideals and the Nature of Practical Reasoning* (New York: Oxford University Press, 2012). My earliest discussion of these issues appeared in "Intransitivity and the Mere Addition Paradox," *Philosophy and Public Affairs* 16 (1987): 138–187.
4. See Chapter 19 of *Reasons and Persons*.
5. Parfit advocates a view of this sort on page 360 of *Reasons and Persons*. My formulation of the view differs from his. However, I find Parfit's formulation slightly confusing, and I believe that mine accurately reflects the view he was intending to express.
6. Some versions of the Pareto Principle include a second clause, to the effect that if, in either of two outcomes, the very same people would ever live, then, if everyone in the first outcome would be at least as well-off (or have at least as high a quality of life) than everyone in the second outcome, the first outcome would be at least as good as the second. As this second clause plays no role in my ensuing arguments, I have omitted it for the sake of clarity. I am grateful to Tim Campbell for suggesting that I make a note of this.
7. I defend the existence, and importance, of impersonal values and ideals in numerous places. See, for example, "Harmful Goods, Harmless Bads," in *Value, Welfare, and Morality*, edited by R. G. Frey and Christopher Morris (Cambridge University Press, 1993), 290–324;

"Equality, Priority, and the Levelling Down Objection," in *The Ideal of Equality*, edited by Matthew Clayton and Andrew Williams (Houndsmills and New York: Macmillan and St. Martin's Press, 2000), 126–161; "Personal versus Impersonal Principles: Reconsidering the Slogan," *Theoria* 69 (2003): 20–30; and *Rethinking the Good*.

8. One way to put this is that principles like Q, P, and PP (and also another principle that I shall discuss shortly, the *Different Number or General Quality Claim*, GQ) are all plausible, and best regarded, as principles of *beneficence*, rather than as *all things considered* principles.

9. *Weighing Lives*, Oxford: Oxford University Press, 2004, section 10.2, pp. 143-46. The qualifiers "merely" and "itself" reflect the fact that here, and below, I am not discussing any possible *indirect* effects on others from the addition of extra people that might make the outcome better or worse all things considered.

10. This reasoning fits with Parfit's original views regarding the comparison between A and B. In later years, Parfit moved to another position that would block the inference presented here. On Parfit's later views, any two comparisons that differed significantly in population size would only be roughly comparable. I do not pursue this line here, partly because I think it fails to do justice to the true power and significance of the Mere Addition Paradox, partly because it undermines Parfit's own views regarding the Repugnant Conclusion, and partly because it has wildly implausible implications that were independently brought to Parfit's attention by me, Jimmy Goodrich, and Jake Nebel. For example, it implies that a world where everyone is in heaven would *not* be *better* than a world where everyone is in hell, if the populations of the two worlds differed markedly in size. Instead, the two worlds would be roughly comparable, or on a par, or imprecisely equal. I wholly reject such a conclusion; as did Parfit, prompting him to eventually further revise his view along lines that I shall not pursue here, as they are orthogonal to this article's main line of argument. I should add, however, that if "all things considered better than" is not a transitive relation—a possibility that many of my arguments open up—then the claim that the heaven world is *better* than the hell world may not, ultimately, be defensible. A very dismaying thought, indeed.

11. I add this qualification because, in fact, I believe that GQ is actually implausible if the qualitative gap between A and B is *sufficiently* small. My reasons for this are given in Chapter 2 of *Rethinking the Good*; see, especially, my presentation, motivation, and defense of the *First Standard View*.

12. *Reasons and Persons*, 420.

13. *Philosophy and Public Affairs* 11, 1982: 158–159.

14. Parfit presents and motivates the notion of "rough comparability," which he later terms "imprecise equality," in Section 146 of *Reasons and Persons*. Ruth Chang discusses her notion of "on a par" in her introduction to her edited volume *Incomparability and Practical Reasoning* (Cambridge, MA: Harvard University Press, 1997), and also in her articles "The Possibility of Parity," *Ethics* 112 (2002): 659–688; and "Parity, Interval Value, and Choice," *Ethics* 114 (2005): 331–350. I discuss these notions in Chapter 6 of *Rethinking the Good*; see, especially, Section 6.3.

15. See Chapters 6, 7, and 12 of *Rethinking the Good*; also, "A Continuum Argument for Intransitivity," *Philosophy and Public Affairs* 25 (1996): 175–210; "Intransitivity and the Mere Addition Paradox," *Philosophy and Public Affairs* 16 (1987): 138–187; and "Rethinking the Good, Moral Ideals and the Nature of Practical Reasoning," in *Reading Parfit*, edited by Jonathan Dancy (Oxford: Basil Blackwell, 1997), 290–344.

16. See Section 7.7 and Chapter 12 of *Rethinking the Good*.

17. See Section 7.7 and Chapter 11 of *Rethinking the Good*.

18. Strictly speaking, the Axiom of Transitivity that I have been discussing in this article is different from the standard Axiom of Transitivity normally employed by economists and others in discussions of practical reasoning, since my axiom applies to outcomes, and the standard one applies to preferences. However, there is a deep connection between the two, especially for anyone who is a realist about normative reasons. After all, one's preferences often concern the relative merits of different outcomes, and it would be foolish to insist that one's preferences among possible outcomes be transitive, if the betterness relation between those outcomes was not itself transitive. Accordingly, I believe there would be compelling reason to reject the standard Axiom of Transitivity regarding preferences, if, in fact, we were convinced that there was compelling reason to reject the Axiom of Transitivity regarding outcomes. I am grateful to Tim Campbell for suggesting that I elaborate this point.

19. Consider, for example, a typical case where someone is trying to choose between which of ten cars to buy, and there are a number of factors that seem relevant to making that decision, including price, performance, reliability, style, gas mileage, comfort, resale value, color, and so on. Typically, someone might test drive the first two of the ten options, compare them as best she could along each of the many relevant dimensions, and then try to determine which, if either of them, was better all things considered. If she were confident that the first car was better than the second car, all things considered, she would then remove the second car from further consideration, test drive the third car, and then compare the first with the third along each relevant dimension. If the third car was better than the first, she would remove the first from further consideration, and then compare the third car with the fourth, and so on. On this basis, she would conclude what the best alternative was (or at least arrive at an alternative which was such that there was none better than it), on the basis of a series of nine pairwise comparisons. However, this familiar decision procedure *presupposes* the Axiom of Transitivity, as one could not correctly remove the second alternative (in this case the second car) from further consideration solely on the basis of the fact that it was worse than the first alternative (in this case the first car), all things considered, if it *could* be the case that, all things considered, the second alternative was better than one of the other alternatives, which in turn was all things considered better than the first alternative! It is the Axiom of Transitivity that supposedly guarantees that this couldn't ever happen, and so which underlies, and legitimizes, the frequently employed decision procedure of narrowing down a list of options on the basis of a sequence of pairwise comparisons.

20. The qualifier "might" here is important. Failure of transitivity alone does not entail this possibility, which only arises with the possibility of *cycles* (where there is a set of three or more outcomes such that the first is better than the second, the second better than the third, and so on, but the last option is better than the first). However, the same considerations that I have presented which open the possibility that the Axiom of Transitivity fails, also open the possibility of cycles. I am grateful to Tim Campbell for suggesting that I spell this out.

21. See, especially, Chapter 12 of *Rethinking the Good*, and also Chapters 2, 3, 5, and 7.

22. "Moral Problems of Population," 73 and 80.

23. See *Rethinking the Good*, 237.

24. See ibid., Chapter 11.

25. Ibid.

26. Most economists have presumed that it would be *irrational* to prefer a Pareto inferior outcome to a Pareto superior outcome. For the reasons noted in Section 2, and that I argue

for in numerous places, I think this is too strong (see, for example, "Harmful Goods, Harmless Bads," "Equality, Priority, and the Levelling Down Objection," and "Personal versus Impersonal Principles: Reconsidering the Slogan"). Since there are many important *impersonal* ideals, I think it could be rational to prefer a Pareto inferior outcome to a Pareto superior one, as long as the former outcome was sufficiently better in terms of impersonal ideals to outweigh the extent to which it would be worse for people. Still, I think it *is* plausible to give *some* independent weight to principles like the Pareto Principle. The fact that an outcome is *better for some* and *worse for no one* deserves weight in our normative considerations, and not merely because in such a case the one outcome will be better in terms of *utility*. Being better in terms of utility has value, but being better in terms of utility *without anyone's being worse off for the sake of that greater utility* has even greater normative significance. That this is so is suggested by the fact that many people who are not utilitarians are nevertheless strongly attracted to the Pareto Principle.

27. In *Rethinking the Good*, I show that another commonly accepted principle of practical reasoning is also suspect if the Essentially Comparative View is true, and this is the *Independence of Irrelevant Alternatives Principle* (*IIAP*), which holds, roughly, that if A is better than B, all things considered, then A should be better than B no matter how many other alternatives one might also consider other than A and B. Although many objections and worries have been raised to IIAP, there is a particularly plausible version of it which will be *true* if the Internal Aspects View is correct, but false if the Essentially Comparative View is correct (see Chapters 7 and 11–15 of *Rethinking the Good*).

CHAPTER 8

POPULATION PARADOXES WITHOUT TRANSITIVITY

GUSTAF ARRHENIUS

1. INTRODUCTION

Most discussion in population ethics has concentrated on how to evaluate populations in regard to their goodness, that is, how to order populations by the relations "is better than" and "is as good as." This field has been riddled with paradoxes and impossibility theorems which show that our considered beliefs are inconsistent in cases where the number of people and their welfare varies. It is natural to think that the axiological impossibility results directly translate into impossibility results for normative theories since this part of our morality—our theory of beneficence—is consequentialist in nature and thus must be based on an ordering of outcomes in regard to their "welfarist" goodness. However, it is all too hasty to conclude that the axiological impossibility results directly translate into normative ones for two reasons: one can reject the transitivity of "better than" and one can reject consequentialism.

The former idea is that since transitivity of "better than" is presupposed in the axiological impossibility theorems, we can avoid these results by simply giving up on transitivity. What is attractive with this move is that given nontransitivity of "better than" (and thus "at least as good as"), we can stick to our axiological evaluations without any contradiction. We can still, it is hoped, get enough structure in the value ordering of populations to guide our choices via some form of consequentialism.

The latter idea is that we should turn to theories that take welfare into account in a nonconsequentialist manner, that is, theories that take welfare into account directly on the normative level instead of taking the route over an ordering of outcomes in regard to their goodness. Since transitivity plays an important role in the axiological theorems, and since there is no convincing analog to transitivity on the normative level, the theorems will not reappear on the normative level, or so it has been claimed, as we shall see below.

In this chapter, I'll show that this latter claim is unfortunately false. As a corollary, I'll show how we can prove the axiological impossibility theorems without an appeal to the transitivity of "better than." Hence, the idea that we can avoid impossibility theorems in population axiology by just giving up on transitivity of "better than" is unfortunately also false.[1]

2. AN AXIOLOGICAL POPULATION PARADOX

Figure 8.1 illustrates a version of Derek Parfit's well-known axiological population paradox, the Mere Addition Paradox.[2] The diagram shows four populations: A, A', B, and C. The width of each block represents the number of people, and the height represents their lifetime welfare. All the people in the above diagram enjoy positive welfare, or, as we also could put it, have lives worth living.[3] A is a population of people with very high welfare, A' is a population of the same size as A but with even higher welfare, B is a much larger population than A and A' but consisting of people with very low positive welfare. C is a population of the same size as A'∪B (the population consisting of all the lives in both A' and B). Everybody in C has very low positive welfare but they are all better off than the people in B. Moreover, there is perfect equality in C and the total and average welfare in C is higher than in A'∪B.

How should we rank these populations? Consider first populations A and A'∪B. Since the B-people have lives worth living and the A'-people have even higher welfare than the A-people, many would agree that A'∪B is better than A. Here's a principle that expresses this view:

> *Dominance Addition*: If populations A and B are of the same size and everyone in A has lower welfare than everyone in B, then A is worse than a population consisting of the B-lives and any number of lives with positive welfare, other things being equal.[4]

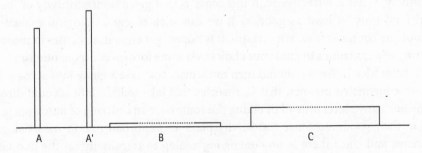

FIGURE 8.1 Parfit's Mere Addition Paradox

What about A'∪B and C? Since there is perfect equality in C and higher total and average welfare in C as compared to A'∪B, it seems reasonable to claim that C is better than A'∪B. Perhaps the following principle captures our intuition:

> *Non-Anti Egalitarianism*: A population with perfect equality is better than a population with the same number of people, inequality, and lower average (and thus total) welfare, other things being equal.[5]

Lastly, how should we rank A and C? Derek Parfit has formulated a conclusion that seems to express most people's intuition about the relative value of A and C:

> *The Repugnant Conclusion*: For any perfectly equal population with very high positive welfare, there is a population with very low positive welfare which is better, other things being equal.[6]

As its name indicates, Parfit finds this conclusion unacceptable. To avoid the Repugnant Conclusion, we could claim that A is better than C, a belief expressed by the following principle:

> *Quality*: There is at least one perfectly equal population with very high positive welfare which is better than any population with very low positive welfare, other things being equal.[7]

By now, we have contradicted ourselves. If C is better than A'∪B, and A'∪B is better than A, then by transitivity of "better than," it follows that C is better than A. But we said that A is better than C, that is, C is not better than A. Hence, these valuations imply a contradiction: C is better than A and C is not better than A.

When faced with an impossibility result like the one just described, a sensible response is to question the principles involved and try to find reasons to reject one of them. One could for example reject Dominance Addition by claiming that A'∪B is worse than A since there is inequality in the former population but not in the latter, or that although the B-people enjoy positive welfare, their presence makes the population worse since people deserve higher welfare than the B-people enjoy, and so forth. I shall not discuss that route here since I have discussed it at length elsewhere and showed that one can construct impossibility results with logically much weaker conditions that are very hard to reject.[8] For example, Dominance Addition could be replaced by a condition according to which, roughly, there is at least some number of horrible lives whose addition makes a population worse than an addition of lives with positive welfare.

Likewise for the other conditions used above. I'm using the above impossibility result not because it involves the logically weakest and most compelling conditions but because it is easy to present and quite well known. The theorems that involve weaker conditions are much more complicated and would unnecessarily complicate the presentation. The simpler Mere Addition Paradox makes my argument take a clearer form.

Moreover, if one can show that it is true, or not true, that the simpler axiological impossibility results translate into normative ones, or can be reformulated without transitivity, then this will also hold for the more complicated ones. I will say more about this in the final section.

3. DO THE AXIOLOGICAL IMPOSSIBILITY RESULTS DIRECTLY TRANSLATE INTO NORMATIVE ONES?

It is natural to think that the axiological impossibility results directly translate into impossibility results for normative theories since, one might argue, this part of our morality—our theory of beneficence—is consequentialist in nature and thus must be based on an ordering of outcomes in regard to their "welfarist" goodness. As a matter of fact, most of the population theories presented in the literature explicitly or implicitly include some form of consequentialism as a bridging principle from the axiological level to the normative level. The most common form of consequentialism is act-consequentialism according to which, roughly, an action is right if and only if it maximizes the good. More exactly, we shall define act-consequentialism as follows:

> *Act-Consequentialism*: An action is right (obligatory) if and only if its outcome is at least as good as (better than) that of every alternative. An action is wrong if and only if it is not right.[9]

Populations can be outcomes of actions, namely populations that consist of all the lives that are part of the outcomes. Which lives are included in the outcome of an action depends, of course, on what we consider the morally relevant outcome of an action. The three most common answers are the possible world that would obtain if the action were performed, the total future state of the world that would obtain if the action were performed, and the causal consequences of the action.[10] These three views correspond to three types of populations, namely populations that consist of all the past, present, and future lives, or all the present and future lives, or all the lives that are causal consequences of the action. Now, there is nothing in the Mere Addition Paradox that rules out that the involved populations are of these types. Moreover, inconsistent evaluations of outcomes are, of course, a devastating problem from a consequentialist perspective, since it will not get off the ground in the first place.

Inconsistent evaluations are not only a problem for pure consequentialists. Such consequentialists assume that all morally relevant factors can be taken into account in the value of outcomes. One might think that certain morally relevant factors cannot be taken into account in such a manner but should be incorporated on the deontic level in terms of actions that are right or wrong by virtue of being of a certain type. Examples are violations of rights, promises, and actions that involve great personal sacrifice for the agent. One may judge actions that involve violations of people's rights or the breaking of promises as wrong, and actions that involve great personal sacrifice as supererogatory, irrespective of how good the consequences of those actions would be.[11] Some of those critics of consequentialism that take this line do take the consequences of actions into account, however, but they think that there are deontic "constraints" that exclude actions of certain types, or deontic "options" that make certain types of actions permissible, irrespective of their consequences. The remaining alternatives are, however, evaluated in a consequentialist manner. They accept what we could call *Ceteris Paribus* Act-Consequentialism:

> *Ceteris Paribus Act-Consequentialism*: Other things being equal, an action is right (obligatory) if and only if its outcome is at least as good as (better than) that of every alternative. Other things being equal, an action is wrong if and only if it is not right.

In other words, if a choice situation doesn't involve actions that are right or wrong by virtue of a certain deontic constraint or option, then the normative status of the actions is determined by the value of their respective outcomes. Assuming that the involved deontic constraints and options don't concern the number and the welfare of lives in populations that are outcomes of actions in the impossibility cases (which is a questionable assumption, however), this view clearly runs into the same problem as pure Act-Consequentialism in respect to the inconsistent evaluations of outcomes. It is all too hasty to conclude from this discussion, however, that the axiological impossibility results directly translate into normative ones for two reasons: one can reject the transitivity of "better than" and one can reject consequentialism.

One can be a consequentialist but reject the transitivity of "better than," a move that has become increasingly popular. The axiological population paradoxes in the literature have presupposed that the relation "better than" is transitive. Some theorists find this a matter of logic, claiming that it is part of the meaning of "better than."[12] One might think otherwise, and argue that the axiological impossibility results actually demonstrate that these relations are not transitive. Among others, Larry Temkin and Stuart Rachels have suggested this.[13] What is attractive about this move is that given nontransitivity of "better than," we can stick to our axiological evaluations without any contradiction. The evaluations involved in the Mere Addition Paradox above and in the other results in the literature exhibit the following structure (substituting outcomes for populations): Outcome A_1 is better than A_2, which is better than $A_3, \ldots$, which is better than A_n, which in turn is better than A_1.[14] With transitivity, we can derive a contradiction from these evaluations, such as that A_1 is both better and worse than A_n, but without it, we cannot. So perhaps there is a possibility for a consequentialist to eschew the impossibility theorems by going nontransitive in the value ordering.[15]

However, a problem with this move is that in cases such as the above involving cyclical evaluations, there is no outcome which is at least as good as all alternative outcomes: it is neither true of any outcome that it is at least as good as all the other outcomes, nor is it true of any outcome that it isn't worse than any other outcome. Consequently, in respect to such cases consequentialism implies, implausibly, that all the available actions are wrong (since an action is right if and only if its outcome is at least as good as that of every alternative, and otherwise wrong). Consequentialism requires some form of acyclicity of the ranking of outcomes in a choice situation to avoid such results.[16] In other words, it doesn't look like abandoning transitivity of "better than" is sufficient to save a consequentialist population morality.

One could claim, however, that what we have here is a plausible interpretation of the Mere Addition Paradox and similar results. In a choice situation involving alternatives like these, we are facing a *moral dilemma*: whatever act we perform we are going to act wrongly.[17] We could claim that the existence of moral dilemmas is part of our moral phenomenology and that it is not surprising that we should face a moral dilemma in situations involving such grand alternatives as are involved in the Mere Addition Paradox. We could stick to our axiological intuitions and use them to guide us in situations that don't involve nontransitive evaluations. Moreover, we would still have something to say about cases like the Mere Addition Paradox: We should avoid putting ourselves in such choice situations since if we do, we will be bound to act wrongly. In other words, nontransitivity (and non-acyclicity) of "better than" doesn't need to spell the end for consequentialism and practical reason as some have feared.

Although I find this a very interesting interpretation of the Mere Addition Paradox and the like, I don't find it satisfactory since I'm skeptical about this type of moral dilemma. As Jan Österberg suggests, any plausible morality is separately satisfiable:

> *Separate Satisfiability*: For any agent and any situation, there is an action such that if the agent were to perform this action, then her action would not be morally wrong.[18]

It is reasonable to claim, I think, that it should at least be logically possible for a person not to do the wrong thing. Normative theories which violate Separate Satisfiability by implying that there are situations in which all the available actions are wrong, or would be wrong were they performed, imply that there are situations where it is not even a *logical possibility* for an agent to do what the theory requires of her.[19] This seems implausible.[20] Consequently, since an adequate morality should be separately satisfiable, the axiological impossibility theorems challenge the existence of an acceptable consequentialist morality.

We could, however, satisfy Separate Satisfiability by slightly reformulating our statement of Act-Consequentialism:

> *Incomplete Act-Consequentialism*: An action is right (obligatory) if and only if its outcome is at least as good as (better than) that of every alternative. An action is wrong if and only if it is not right and there is at least one action that is right.

According to this version of consequentialism, all the involved actions in the Mere Addition Paradox lack normative status, they are neither right nor wrong. This shows that a consequentialist who accepts nontransitivity of "better than" is not committed to endorsing moral dilemmas. Instead, there is a gap in the normative ordering of actions. She could perhaps motivate her position by saying that moral theory has nothing to say about cases that involve cyclical evaluations and that lack a maximal alternative, and that such cases are beyond the scope of moral theory.[21]

One might reasonably consider a theory that does not provide any guidance in situations such as the Mere Addition Paradox unsatisfactory. Moreover, even if one finds this acceptable in the case of the Mere Addition Paradox, there are other similar situations in which this is clearly unsatisfactory. Consider a version of this paradox in which there is also an alternative D available in which everyone has very bad lives. D is clearly worse than A, A′∪B, and C. Hence, it would be clearly better if we were to choose one of those alternatives rather than D and clearly wrong to choose D. Incomplete Act-Consequentialism, however, again yields that all the actions lack normative status, which is clearly implausible.

We could go on and formulate other versions of consequentialism that avoid the drawbacks of the two versions above. Since there are so many possible ways we can formulate consequentialist principles, one might hope that there is one that can handle nontransitive evaluations in a way that satisfies our normative intuitions. Actually, there have been a number of promising proposals in this direction—much more elaborated than the simple principles I have discussed above—in connection with cyclical evaluations in rational choice theory.[22] I shall not discuss these suggestions here, however, since I shall later informally prove that all of these theories have to be deficient in some respect.

Moreover, even if the axiological impossibility results in the end could be shown to be the swansong of consequentialism, this wouldn't suffice to show that they directly translate into paradoxes for all normative theories since we can reject consequentialism. We could instead turn to theories that take welfare into account in a nonconsequentialist manner, that is, theories that take welfare into account directly on the normative level instead of taking the route over an ordering of outcomes in regard to their welfarist goodness. For example, one could claim that it is always wrong to increase a population with lives not worth living when it is avoidable, or that in the choice between giving a small benefit to one person or a great benefit to many people, one ought to do the latter.[23] Since such theories don't rely on an axiological ordering, the axiological paradoxes don't show that these theories are in trouble.

There are also prominent normative theories that take welfare into account in such a different way as compared to consequentialism that it is unclear whether the axiological paradoxes pose a problem for them. Examples are David Gauthier's mutual advantage contractarianism and Richard Arneson's theory of equality of opportunity for welfare.[24]

Actually, David Boonin, who has proposed a nonconsequentialist population morality, suggests that whereas there is no satisfying solution to the axiological Mere Addition Paradox (which he calls "the Goodness Paradox"), the normative version of this paradox (which he calls "the Oughtness Paradox") can be solved and this result deprives the former paradox of its moral significance.[25]

One might object that one cannot deprive the axiological Mere Addition Paradox of its relevance in this way since if we cannot claim that, say, A is better than C, then we cannot justify why we ought to choose A when A and C are the alternatives. Moreover, if we claim that A is better than C, and so forth, then we are going to be faced with the axiological Mere Addition Paradox again. Parfit seems to have an argument like this in mind:

> All we have shown is that . . . we can coherently believe that (4) choosing to produce [C] would be morally worse than choosing to produce A. This does not yet show that (4) is either true, or defensible. Only by defending (4) could we deprive the [axiological] Mere Addition Paradox of its force. . . . The most straightforward [way of defending (4)] would be to appeal to (1) [C], as an outcome, would be worse than A. . . . But . . . this way of defending (4) cannot deprive my paradox of its force. If my arguments were sound, we could not appeal to (1), since this argument would show that [C] could not be worse than A.[26]

I find this objection question-begging since we could claim that A is better than C without committing us to the beliefs that generate the Mere Addition Paradox.

First, there are ways of understanding value-concepts such as "better than" in terms of normative ones such as using "A is better than C" as synonymous with "A ought to be chosen in a situation where A and C are the only alternatives," "A is more choiceworthy than C," and the like. From this understanding of "better than," no axiological Mere Addition Paradox follows since we have explained "better than" in terms of normative concepts and these claims are restricted to pairwise comparisons and there is no plausible analog to the transitivity of "better than" for these normative concepts (more on this below). Hence, one can claim that "A is better than C" without committing oneself to the beliefs that lead to the axiological Mere Addition Paradox.

Second, we could justify our belief that A ought to be chosen when A and C are the alternatives without any appeal to values. We could appeal directly to facts about A and C, for example, that all the people in A enjoy excellent lives whereas all the people in C have lives barely worth living. The belief that these facts give us reason to choose A rather than C when these are the only alternatives don't commit us to the claim that these facts are always decisive since the fact that other alternatives are available, and facts about these alternatives, might provide countervailing reasons.

I therefore agree with Boonin's point regarding the significance of a solution to the Normative Mere Addition Paradox. It is another question, however, whether it is easier to solve than the axiological one, an issue to which we shall now turn.

4. A TRANSITIVITY PRINCIPLE FOR "OUGHT TO BE CHOSEN"?

Consider the Mere Addition Paradox again and assume that our normative evaluations are, as I think many would agree, as follows (assuming now that the populations in question are outcomes of actions): in the choice between population A and A'∪B, it is permissible to choose A'∪B; in the choice between A'∪B and C, we ought to choose C; in the choice between C and A, we ought to choose A; and in the choice among A, A'∪B, and C, we ought to choose A, and it would be wrong to choose A∪B or C. Have we contradicted ourselves? As a matter of fact, we haven't. As long as we don't add any more restrictions on our normative evaluations, there is no contradiction involved in the above evaluation. This suggests, as Boonin believes, that evaluations that are contradictory on the axiological level may not be so on the normative level, the reason being that there is no analog to transitivity on the normative level.[27]

One might think otherwise, however. Gregory Kavka, for example, has suggested the following transitivity principle for moral permissibility: "If it would be permissible to do A if A and B were the alternatives, and would be permissible to do B if B and C were the alternatives, then it is permissible to do A if A, B, and C are [sic] the alternatives."[28] Given this requirement on normative judgements, the above evaluations are inconsistent. Since it is permissible to choose C in the choice between C and A'∪B (if an action is obligatory, it is of course permissible), and permissible to choose A'∪B in the choice between A'∪B and A, it follows from Kavka's principle that it is permissible to choose C in the choice among A, A'∪B, and C. But we said above that in the latter situation, we ought to choose A and it would be wrong to choose C. So we are back in trouble again.

I'm skeptical about Kavka's transitivity principle for moral permissibility, however. Its implication in regard to the Mere Addition Paradox could in itself be used as an argument against it. Here is another counter-example suggested by Parfit. Suppose that a woman at some point faces the following options:

> P: Having a handicapped child.
> Q: Having no child.

As Parfit points out, "[i]f this child's handicap would not be severe, and we make certain other assumptions, we can plausibly believe that it would be permissible for the woman to choose either P or Q."[29] Moreover, this evaluation is, arguably, still plausible if P is replaced by the following alternative:

> R: Having the same child, but in a way that would ensure that she wouldn't be handicapped.

Assume now that all of these three alternatives are available to the woman. According to Kavka's transitivity principle, since P is permissible in the choice between P and Q, and since Q is permissible in the choice between Q and R, it follows that P is permissible in the choice among P, Q, and R. But, as Parfit writes, "[w]e can plausibly believe that, if R were also possible, it would be wrong for this woman to choose P rather than R."[30]

One might think that the problem that Kavka's principle runs into demonstrates an important difference between axiological and normative evaluations. It is usually thought that the intrinsic goodness of an outcome doesn't depend on its relation to other outcomes. If an outcome A is intrinsically good, or intrinsically better than another outcome B, then we usually think that this holds irrespective of whether A and B are alternative outcomes in some choice situation, or whether there are other alternative outcomes available. As it is often put, the intrinsic value of a state of affairs is independent of its relation to other distinct states of affairs. The normative status of actions, however, depends on what other actions are available in a choice situation. For example, it is permissible and obligatory to inflict harm on somebody if the only other alternative is to inflict even more harm, but if harming is avoidable, then it is wrong.

I don't think, however, that this kind of context (in)dependence is the essential difference between axiological and normative concepts. Although axiological concepts such as "good" and "better than" are not context-sensitive as ordinarily understood, there are other ones that are, such as "best" and "worst." Thus the defining difference between axiological and normative concepts cannot be that the latter but not the former are context-sensitive.

Moreover, as I said above, there are ways of understanding value-concepts such as "better than" in terms of normative concepts, such as using "A is better than B" as synonymous with "A is more choiceworthy than B" or "A ought to be chosen in a situation where A and B are the alternatives," and the like. If these normative concepts are context-sensitive in a way that make them nontransitive, which seems probable, then "better than" will be context-sensitive and nontransitive too.

Actually, according to an influential tradition in value analysis, to be valuable is to be a fitting object of a pro-attitude. Value is thus analyzed in terms of the stance that one *ought* to take towards an object. As Franz Brentano writes in *The Origin of Our Knowledge of Right and Wrong*: "When we call one good "better" than another, we mean that . . . it is correct to prefer the one good, for its own sake, to the other." Or as A. C. Ewing, the foremost exponent of this reduction of axiological concepts to deontic ones, writes: "we define 'better' as meaning 'what ought to be preferred.'"[31] Given this analysis, it should come as no surprise that "better than" will be context-sensitive and that transitivity fails, since this will happen for the same reasons that we gave above in regard to the explicitly normative concepts. This possible understanding of value-concepts might explain why some theorists have been willing to abandon the transitivity of "better than."[32]

5. NEUTRALIZING THE CONTEXT DEPENDENCE OF NORMATIVE STATUS

It could of course be the case that whereas only *some* axiological concepts are context-sensitive, this holds for all normative concepts. Be this as it may, this would not suffice to show that Boonin's conjecture regarding the normative paradoxes is correct, since it may still be some normative *relations* among alternative actions that hold irrespective of what other available actions there are in a choice situation. I think this is the case. We can, so to say, neutralize the context dependence of normative status when we formulate normative conditions by partly formulating them in terms of certain features of the choice situation.[33] Consider the following pattern for a normative condition:

(i) If action h_1 is of type G and action h_2 is of type B, and both h_1 and h_2 are available in a certain choice situation, then h_2 is wrong in this choice situation.

The actions P and R in the example earlier, that is, having a handicapped child (P) or having the same child, but in a way that would ensure that she wouldn't be handicapped (R), fit this pattern, as the quote from Parfit suggests. If P and R are both available actions in some situation, then P is the wrong choice.[34] Loosely speaking, we can say that (i) is a normative analog of "better than." We shall formulate the following condition along these lines:

Normative Egalitarian Dominance: If population A is a perfectly equal population of the same size as population B, and every person in A has higher welfare than every person in B, then, in any situation involving a choice between A and B (and possibly other alternatives), it is wrong to choose B, other things being equal.

This condition is, I think, as plausible as its axiological counterpart. The *ceteris paribus* condition involved here is a natural extension of the *ceteris paribus* condition used in the discussion of different axiologies. There are neither any constraints (for example, promise-keeping) nor options (for example, great personal sacrifice for the agent which is beyond the call of duty), nor any non-welfarist values in the outcomes (for example, desert) that give us a reason to (not) choose one or the other of the involved actions. The only reasons for choosing one or the other of the involved actions arise from the welfare of the lives in the involved populations.[35] Consider a situation where you could, at no cost to yourself (you might even be among the beneficiaries), and without violating any other duties or compromising any other values, choose an outcome in which everybody is equally well off, and better off as compared to another outcome involving the same number of people. Surely it would be wrong to choose the latter outcome in this situation.[36]

We could formulate normative versions of all the axiological adequacy conditions involved in the Mere Addition Paradox using this pattern (i). For the result we shall prove, however, it suffices to use the following logically weaker construction which, loosely speaking, can be said to be a normative analog of "at least as good as":

(ii) If action h_1 is of type G and action h_2 is of type B, and both h_1 and h_2 are available in a certain choice situation, and h_1 is wrong in this choice situation, then h_2 is also wrong in this choice situation.

Assume that next Sunday you can help either George or Tony with their gardening, and that they both need your help equally as much and would derive equally as much satisfaction from getting your help. You haven't promised either one of them your help, it is neither George's nor Tony's birthday, nor are there any other circumstances, such as side-effects on other people's well-being, that speak in favor of helping one of them rather than the other.[37] Now, it is reasonable to claim that in a situation involving these two alternatives, if it would be wrong of you to help Tony, then it would also be wrong of you to help George. It could be wrong of you to help Tony if you have promised your elderly aunt to help her next Sunday with the much-needed gardening at her house (assuming that the involved acts are mutually exclusive). If that were the case, however, then it would also be wrong of you to help George.

Here's a normative version of Non-Anti Egalitarianism formulated in this way:

Normative Non-Anti Egalitarianism: For any perfectly equal population A, and any population B of the same size as A but with inequality and lower average (and thus total) welfare, if it is wrong in a certain situation to choose A, then it is also wrong to choose B, other things being equal.

Apart from Normative Egalitarian Dominance, we shall formulate all the normative adequacy conditions used in the normative version of the Mere Addition Paradox below along the lines of pattern (ii). Here are the two remaining conditions, Normative Dominance Addition and Normative Quality:

Normative Dominance Addition: If populations A and B are of the same size and everyone in A has lower welfare than everyone in B, and if it is wrong in a certain situation to choose a population consisting of the B-lives and any number of people with positive welfare, then it is also wrong in this situation to choose population A, other things being equal.

Normative Quality: There is at least one perfectly equal population with very high positive welfare such that if it is wrong in a certain situation to choose that population, then it is wrong in the same situation to choose any population with very low positive welfare, other things being equal.

In addition, we shall require that a plausible population morality is separately satisfiable.

For the purpose of informally proving the theorem, it will be useful to state some terminology more exactly. We shall say that a *population morality* at least assigns the normative status wrong to some actions in some possible choice situations. When we say that an action is "wrong" in a choice situation, then that is short for "wrong or would be wrong if performed."[38] A *choice situation* is a set of at least two mutually incompatible actions available to a certain individual or group of individuals at a certain time.[39]

6. An Informal Demonstration of a Normative Mere Addition Paradox

We shall informally show that the following theorem is true:

> *The Normative Impossibility Theorem*: There is no separately satisfiable population morality which satisfies the normative versions of Quality, Non-Anti Egalitarianism, Egalitarian Dominance, and Dominance Addition.

We shall show that the contrary assumption leads to a contradiction. Consider the situation shown in Figure 8.2. Here we have the same situation as in the axiological Mere Addition Paradox but for population D. Assume that these populations are possible outcomes of actions. Assume further that the only actions available to a certain individual or group of individuals are the actions with either population A, A'∪B, C or D as outcome. These are therefore the only actions available in the choice situation. Again, these populations could consist of all the future lives, or all the lives in some part of the future, that would exist if the respective action were performed.

In Figure 8.2, D is a perfectly equal population of the same size as C, and every person in D has higher welfare than every person in C. Consequently, it follows from Normative Egalitarian Dominance that all the actions that have population C as outcome are wrong.

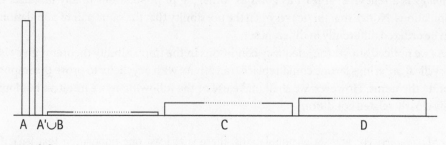

FIGURE 8.2

C is a perfectly equal population of the same size as A'∪B but with higher average welfare. Thus, since the actions with C as an outcome are wrong, Normative Non-Anti Egalitarianism implies that all the actions with population A'∪B as outcome are wrong.

The A'-people are better off than the A-people, and the B-people have positive welfare. Thus, since the actions with A'∪B as outcome are wrong, it follows that all the actions with population A as outcome are wrong.

According to the normative version of Quality, there is at least one perfectly equal population with very high positive welfare such that if it is wrong in a certain situation to choose that population, then it is wrong in the same situation to choose any population with very low positive welfare. We can assume that A is such a high welfare population. Since the actions with A as outcome are wrong, and since D is a population with very low welfare, it follows that all the actions with population D as outcome are wrong.

Since the actions with either population A, A'∪B, C, or D as outcome are all wrong, and these are all of the available actions in the situation, it follows that all the available actions in this situation are wrong. However, according to Separate Satisfiability, this cannot be the case. Hence, the assumption that there is a morality which satisfies all the adequacy conditions entails a contradiction. Thus, the impossibility theorem must be true. In other words, we have showed that a version of the Mere Addition paradox can be reproduced on the normative level.

7. An Axiological Theorem without Transitivity?

One might now reasonably ask: If you can prove the normative theorem without transitivity, why can you not prove the axiological theorem without transitivity?[40] And actually, we can, by using an analogous strategy to the one used in the normative case. Let me first introduce some new terminology. Earlier, we had assumed that a population axiology A is an "at least as good as" quasi-ordering of all possible populations, that is, a reflexive, transitive, but not necessarily complete ordering of all possible populations in regard to their goodness. Since we are going to drop the assumption of transitivity, we shall weaken this definition and define it on sets of populations: a *weak population axiology* is a reflexive "at least as good as" ordering of populations in any finite set of populations. Notice that this leaves open the possibility that the same pair of populations can be ordered differently in different sets.

As we noticed above, the adequacy conditions in the impossibility theorems give rise to cyclical orderings so one could replace transitivity with acyclicity to prove the impossibility theorems. However, we shall make use of the following more intuitive but logically closely related condition:

Maximality: For any set of populations, there is at least one population that isn't worse than any other population in the set.[41]

Maximality can be seen as an axiological analog to Separate Satisfiability. It is reasonable that, in a set of alternative populations, there should be at least one population that isn't worse than another. If not, then for any population one picks, one could have picked a better one. Notice that Maximality is compatible with some or all populations being incommensurable, and cyclical orderings of some of the involved populations (as long as it isn't a top-cycle).

Given Maximality, it is easy to show that the following theorem is true:

> *The Axiological Impossibility Theorem*: There is no weak population axiology which satisfies Quality, Non-Anti Egalitarianism, Dominance Addition, and Maximality.

Assume the opposite and consider again the Mere Addition Paradox depicted in Figure 8.1. By invoking Quality, Non-Anti Egalitarianism, and Dominance Addition, we concluded that C is better than A′∪B, A′∪B is better than A, and A is better than C. Hence, it follows that for each population in the set, it is worse than at least one other population in the set, which is a violation of Maximality. Thus, the impossibility theorem must be true. And we have shown this without any appeal to the transitivity of "better than."[42]

8. Beyond the Mere Addition Paradox

Someone might object to the two impossibility theorems in the following way: "Clearly, one of the conditions must be false since we don't believe that all actions are wrong in the Mere Addition Paradox, or that all involved populations are worse than some other population in that case. Moreover, Dominance Addition is a good candidate for falsehood. So there is no paradox here, just implausible conditions that are not jointly satisfiable."

Of course, one of the conditions must be false since they cannot all be true. However, this objection misses the point of my argument. The point of the above demonstrations is that we now know that we have to reject one of the evaluative or normative conditions or accept the existence of moral dilemmas or situations in which whatever population one picks, one could have picked a clearly better one.[43] We cannot get rid of the paradoxes of population ethics just by giving up the transitivity of "better than," or by rejecting consequentialism and switching to a normative framework. Again, I used the Mere Addition Paradox as an example not because it involves the logically weakest and most compelling condition but because it is easy to present and quite well known.

It is true that Dominance Addition is a questionable condition, but it was the weakest link already in the transitive axiological case. The reasons against the axiological version of this condition work as well as against it in its normative guise. It might also be that we have some further reasons against the normative version of Dominance Addition that have to do with it not being context-sensitive enough.[44] Be this as it may, the point is that we now have a structure for employing the same strategy as we have done in the axiological case: when in doubt over the truth of a condition, try to replace it with a more compelling condition. Now, we can replace Dominance Addition with two conditions which are, I surmise, as hard to deny as Normative Egalitarian Dominance. Here are rough formulations of these conditions:[45]

> *Normative Weak Non-Sadism (roughly)*: There is a number of horrible lives such that if we could instead add some number of people with positive welfare, then it would be wrong to add the horrible lives, other things being equal.

> *Normative Non-Extreme Priority (roughly)*: There is some very large benefit such that in a choice between giving this benefit to a vast number of people and giving a very small benefit to only one person, it would be wrong to do the latter, other things being equal.

As with Normative Egalitarian Dominance, it is hard to imagine any alternatives in a choice situation that would make us doubt the truth of these conditions. Moreover, one can show that there is no separately satisfiable moral theory that jointly satisfies these conditions, Normative Egalitarian Dominance, a version of Quality, and a very compelling egalitarian condition (logically weaker than Non-Anti Egalitarianism).[46]

These results show that the impossibility theorems are a problem for consequentialist and nonconsequentialist alike, transitive and nontransitive value orderings alike. On a more positive note, we now know more clearly where we should and should not look for a possible way, if any, to eschew the impossibility theorems. We have to find a reason to reject one of the evaluative or normative conditions, or a reason to accept the existence of all things considered moral dilemmas or situations in which whatever population one picks, one could have picked a clearly better one.

ACKNOWLEDGMENTS

I would like to thank Vuko Andric, Andrea Asker, Krister Bykvist, John Broome, Tim Campbell, Erik Carlson, Sven Danielsson, Björn Eriksson, Kaj Børge Hansen, Tom Hurka, Mozaffar Qizilbash, Wlodek Rabinowicz, Daniel Ramöller, Don Ross, Joe Roussos, Howard Sobel, Orri Stefánsson, Robert Sugden, Wayne Sumner, and Michael Zimmerman for fruitful discussions and criticism of different ancestors of this paper. An earlier version of this paper was presented at the IFFS's PPE-seminar, January 2019—I would like to thank the participants at this occasion for their useful comments. Financial support from the Swedish Research Council (grant 421-2014-1037) and from Riksbankens Jubileumsfond (grant M17-0372:1) is gratefully acknowledged.

NOTES

1. This paper is an extended and extensively revised version of my Arrhenius (2004). See also Arrhenius (2000b; forthcoming).

2. For a formal proof with slightly weaker conditions, see Arrhenius (2000b, Section 10.6) and Arrhenius (forthcoming). It should be stressed that the above paradox is not identical to Parfit's (1984, 419ff) Mere Addition Paradox since it involves slightly different assumptions (stronger in some respects, weaker in some other respects). This version is similar to the one presented in Ng (1989, 240). A formal proof with slightly stronger assumptions than Ng's can be found in Blackorby and Donaldson (1991).

3. We shall say that a life has neutral welfare if and only if it has the same welfare as a life without any good or bad welfare components, and that a life has positive (negative) welfare if and only if it has higher (lower) welfare than a life with neutral welfare. A hedonist, for example, would typically say that pain is bad and pleasure is good for a person, and that a life without any pain and pleasure has neutral welfare. This definition can be combined with other welfarist axiologies, such as desire and objective list theories. A number of alternative definitions of a life with positive (negative, neutral) welfare figures in the literature. For a discussion of these, see Arrhenius (forthcoming), (2000b) and Broome (1999). For a discussion of this issue in connection to the Repugnant Conclusion, see Fehige (1998), Tännsjö (1998), and Arrhenius (2000b; forthcoming). See also Parfit (1984, 358).

4. The *ceteris paribus* clause means that the compared populations are roughly equal in all other putatively axiologically relevant aspects apart from individual welfare levels. Hence, other values and considerations are not decisive for the value comparison of involved populations. For a discussion, see Arrhenius (2000b; forthcoming).

5. See Ng (1989, 238) for a similar principle. It seems to be unanimously agreed in the literature that inequality aversion of some kind is a prerequisite for an acceptable population axiology. For example, Ng (1989, 239, fn. 4), states that "Non-Antiegalitarianism is extremely compelling" and Carlson (1998, 288); claims that "[r]ejecting NAE [the Non-Anti Egalitarianism Principle] is . . . a very unattractive option." Danielsson (1988, 210) holds that "weak inequality aversion is satisfied by all ethically attractive . . . principles." Fehige (1998, 532), rhetorically asks "if . . . one world contains more welfare than the other *and* distributes it equally, whereas the other doesn't, then how can it fail to be better?." See also Sider (1991, 270, fn. 10). There are, however, reasons for rejecting the Non-Anti Egalitarianism principle. See Arrhenius (2000b, Section 6.2; forthcoming).

6. See Parfit (1984, 388). This formulation is more general than Parfit's except that he doesn't demand that the people with very high welfare are equally well-off.

7. This condition was introduced in Arrhenius (2000b). For simplicity, we are here using a slightly stronger formulation in terms of "better than" instead of "is at least as good as." Likewise for some of the other axiological conditions below.

8. See, for example, Arrhenius (2000a; 2000b; 2011; forthcoming).

9. Carlson (1995, 13). My formulation differs slightly from Carlson's (the brief discussion of consequentialism below draws on Carlson's work). The definition of consequentialism that we have suggested has counter-intuitive implications in cases involving outcomes that are incommensurable in value. I don't think, however, that consequentialism necessarily presupposes a complete ordering of the outcomes in a choice situation. See Carlson (1995, 25, fn. 48) for some suggested revisions of the definition of consequentialism that can handle incommensurable outcomes. There are other versions of consequentialism apart from act-consequentialism, such as rule-consequentialism (see, e.g., Hooker [2000]) according to which an act is right if and only if it can be subsumed under a rule whose general acceptance (or general implementation) would give the best result, which I am not going to discuss. It should be clear, however, that the discussion below applies,

mutatis mutandis, equally well to rule-consequentialism. For example, if our evaluations of outcomes are inconsistent, then we don't have any "best result" to guide our choice of rules under rule-consequentialism.

10. See Carlson (1995, 10–12, and Ch. 4), for an extensive discussion of the morally relevant outcome of an action.

11. It is not clear, however, that such theories cannot be formulated as extensionally equivalent consequentialist theories since it is possible to incorporate a wide range of non-welfarist values in a consequentialist theory. Fred Feldman's (1997) desert adjusted utilitarianism is a case in point. For a discussion of whether any morality can be formulated as a consequentialist morality, see, for example, Brown (2011), Bykvist (1996), Carlson (1995), Danielsson (1988), and Vallentyne (1988).

12. Broome (1991, 11).

13. Rachels (1998), Temkin (1987).

14. The impossibility results in, for example, Arrhenius (2000b; 2011; forthcoming) involve slightly weaker conditions based on the relation "is at least as good as" instead of "better than," but otherwise exhibit the same structure as discussed above.

15. Temkin fears, however, that nontransitivity of "better than" might spell the end for a consequentialist morality and practical reason in general. He suggests that arguments to the effect that "better than" is nontransitive "are [perhaps] best interpreted as a frontal assault on the intelligibility of consequentialist reasoning about morality and rationality. Such reasoning may need to be severely limited, if not jettisoned altogether" (1987, 186, fn. 49). In more recent work, Temkin suggests that nontransitivity "opens the possibility that there would be no rational basis for choosing between virtually any alternatives" (1996, 209), and that therefore the frontal assault on consequentialism would in fact be a frontal assault on "virtually every plausible moral and practical theory" (2012, 513). For an extensive discussion of his views about the relationship between nontransitivity and moral and practical reasoning, see Temkin (2012, 508–520). Many thanks to Tim Campbell for useful discussions of Temkin's view.

16. The acyclicity I have in mind is that if A_1 is better than A_2, A_2 is better than A_3, . . . , A_{n-1} is better than A_n, then A_1 is not worse than A_n. Cf. Sen (1970, 47). For a discussion of cyclical evaluations, see Carlson (1996), Danielsson (1996), and Rabinowicz (2000). Satisfaction of a condition I shall introduce below, Maximality, would also be sufficient for Act-Consequentialism to avoid implying moral dilemmas.

17. Following Vallentyne (1988), we could call a dilemma of the above-mentioned type a "prohibition dilemma." There are also "obligation dilemmas," that is, situations where more than one action is obligatory.

18. See Österberg 1988, 127, 145–146). My formulation is weaker than Österberg's, which is formulated in terms of the possibility of an agent to act morally right. Bykvist (2007) formulates and defends a version of Österberg's condition similar to mine in terms of the possibility of an agent to conform to a normative theory.

19. Österberg (1988, 146) suggests an interesting argument to the effect that his version of Separate Satisfiability is entailed by the common idea that "ought" implies "can." His argument rests, however, on the controversial agglomeration principle that if an agent ought to do each conjunct, he ought to do the conjunction. Moreover, from his argument it only follows that at least one action is not wrong (as in our condition above), not, as Österberg suggests, that at least one action is right (it could be that some actions lack normative status).

20. Some might think that prohibition dilemmas are acceptable if the agent has performed a preceding wrong action. The idea might be that it should be possible to conform to a moral theory but if you have already acted wrongly, then you have deviated from the right path and might end up in a morally impossible situation. To accommodate this point, we can formulate a weaker version which we could call *Weak Separate Satisfiability*: For any agent and any situation such that is hasn't been preceded by a morally wrong action by the agent, there is an action such that if the agent were to perform this action, then her action would not be morally wrong. For the purpose of this paper, the principle could be further weakened in terms of no preceding wrong actions by anyone, that is, complete moral compliance by everyone, but intuitively this seems unnecessarily weak.

21. Notice that there are cases involving cyclical evaluations where there still will be right actions according to Incomplete Act-Consequentialism. Consider a case where B is better than C, C is better than D, D is better than B, and A is better than B, C, and D. In this case, the action with A as outcome is the right action according to Incomplete Act-Consequentialism.

22. Carlson (1996).

23. Jan Narveson's theory is an example of a more developed effort in this direction. He suggests the following principle: "(1) New additions to population ought not to be made at the expense of those who otherwise exist, even if there would be a net increment in total utility considered in person-independent terms. But (2) new additions ought to be made if the benefit to all, *excluding* the newcomer, would exceed the cost to all, *including* him or her, as compared with the net benefit of any alternatives which don't add to population [i.e., if the benefit minus the cost would exceed the net benefit of any alternative]. Finally, (3) within those limits, the decision whether to add to population is up to the individuals involved in its production, provided that if they have a choice of which child to produce they produce the happier one, other things being equal." Narveson (1978, 55–56). Cf. Narveson (1967; 1973).

24. See Gauthier (1986, 299_ and Heath (1997), for the former kind of theory, and Arneson (1989) for the latter. I discuss Gauthier's and Heath's suggestion at length in Arrhenius (1999).

25. Boonin-Vail (1996, 279–280, 307).

26. Parfit (1996, 312).

27. Cf. Boonin-Vail (1996, 285).

28. Kavka (1982, 100, fn. 16). Boonin-Vail (1996, 283), discusses a similar principle.

29. Parfit (1996, 311).

30. Ibid.

31. Brentano (1969, 26); Ewing (1959, 85). Ewing writes further "Bad, I should say, is just what ought to be the object of an unfavourable attitude, as good is what ought to be the object of a favourable." Cf. Scanlon (1998, 97). Extensive discussion of this subject can be found in Rabinowicz and Rønnow-Rasmussen (2004) and Bykvist (2009).

32. For a discussion of some other differences between these kinds of concepts, see von Wright (1993, Ch. 1, Sect. 4), and Danielsson (1999).

33. We are drawing on a suggestion made by Sen (1995, 5), in response to certain criticisms of Arrow's impossibility theorem.

34. Notice that we could formulate an analogous condition for "best": if both P and R are available, then P cannot be the best action in this choice situation.

35. One way in which other things cannot be equal is that at least one of the actions in a choice situation will be an omission and we might think that this is of relevance for an action's moral status. Even if this is sometimes true, there are clear cases where the fact that an action is an omission doesn't affect its deontic status such as when the consequence of the omission is much worse than that of the other alternatives. Consequently, we could restrict the conditions presented above to only concern comparisons between "active" actions and not to cover omissions and then include in the cases we consider a very bad "omission alternative" that is forbidden anyway.

36. One might object here that whether it is morally wrong to choose B depends on the welfare level of its members. If all the lives in this outcome have a very high welfare level, then perhaps choosing outcome A would be supererogatory. However, since these actions don't involve any kind of personal sacrifice for the agent, they don't fit the paradigm description of supererogatory actions, such as someone rushing into a burning house to save its residents at the risk of her own life (see Heyd [2019]). Moreover, it is hard to see any reason for why it should be optional to choose B in the cases that fall under the condition's domain. Hence, I think this objection misses its target. Moreover, for the theorems we shall prove, we could employ a weaker version of Normative Egalitarian Dominance in which the B-people have at most very low positive welfare. With this revision, it is, if possible, even harder to find a reason for considering the choice of the outcome in which everyone is better off a supererogatory action. I'm grateful to Michael Zimmerman for pressing this point.

37. Thanks to John Broome for reminding me that the introduction of another available action can make it wrong to help George rather than Tony because helping George would then have negative side-effects on other people's well-being. Assume that you can also help Howard with his gardening, and Howard's garden is within sight of George's garden but far away from Tony's garden. If you help George rather than Tony, Howard would notice and feel aggrieved at having been neglected. Hence, it is wrong to help George but right to help Tony. Examples such as this show the importance of including the effects on all the involved people's well-being in the specification of the outcomes of the alternative actions, as we indeed do in the statements of the adequacy conditions.

38. The latter is necessary to capture moralities that violate Normative Invariance, such as Normative Actualism, see Arrhenius (forthcoming), section 10.3.

39. For the sake of simplicity, we are assuming that a unique choice situation corresponds to any set of agent- and time-identical actions. There are, of course, a number of problems regarding how to individuate actions, what it means for an action to be available to an agent, or a group of agents, and the like. These problems fall outside the scope of this essay, however.

40. This question was put to me by Wlodek Rabinowicz.

41. Maximality is logically closely related to acyclicity since with an unrestricted domain (or a sufficiently rich domain that guarantees the existence of a subset with a top-cycle), one can derive acyclicity from Maximality. Assume that the unrestricted domain satisfies Maximality but violates acyclicity. Given the latter, there is a cycle in the domain. Given the unrestricted domain, one can pick a subset with a cycle involving all the populations in the set. Then Maximality is violated on this subset. Hence, by reductio, Maximality implies acyclicity given unrestricted domain. Moreover, the adequacy conditions in the impossibility theorems induces a top-cycle on the domain so from a logical perspective, it doesn't make much difference to go for Maximality instead of acyclicity. As we said

above, however, we find the former more intuitive than the latter. I'm grateful to Wlodek Rabinowicz and Orri Stefánsson for a useful discussion of this issue.

42. We could also weaken the involved condition to only yield orderings relative to certain choice situations (or certain sets of populations), analogously to how we did it in the normative case. For example, we could weaken Dominance Addition in the following way: if population A and B are of the same size and everyone in A has lower welfare than in B, and if a population consisting of the B-lives and any number of people with positive welfare is worse than some other population X in a certain situation, then A is worse than X in this situation too, other things being equal. We could then prove an impossibility theorem using such conditions. We shall not pursue this issue further here, however.

43. I'm here setting aside the possibility that one could find a good reason to reject some other background assumption in the theorems, such as the assumption that there are lives with positive and negative welfare or that there are lives with very high and very low positive welfare. For a discussion of these, see Arrhenius (forthcoming).

44. Parfit's example discussed in Section 4 is a case in point. The availability of the option of having the same child without a handicap (R) makes it wrong to have the child with the handicap (P), but it doesn't make it wrong to have no child (Q). In other words, the presence of option R has a wrong-making effect on option P but not on option R. If we add to this the assumption that the parents would be better off if they had a child, then we have a counter-example to Normative Dominance Addition which seems to have to do with it not being context-sensitive enough.

45. For exact formulations of these conditions, see Arrhenius (2000b; 2011; forthcoming).

46. See Arrhenius (2000b; 2011; forthcoming).

References

Arneson, Richard J. 1989. "Equality and Equal Opportunity for Welfare." *Philosophical Studies* 56, no. 1: 77–93.

Arrhenius, Gustaf. 1999. "Mutual Advantage Contractarianism and Future Generations." *Theoria* 65, no. 1: 25–35.

Arrhenius, Gustaf. 2000a. "An Impossibility Theorem for Welfarist Axiologies." *Economics and Philosophy* 16, no. 2: 247–266.

Arrhenius, Gustaf. 2000b. *Future Generations: A Challenge for Moral Theory*, http://www.diva-portal.org/smash/record.jsf?pid=diva2:170236.

Arrhenius, Gustaf. 2004. "The Paradoxes of Future Generations and Normative Theory." In *The Repugnant Conclusion: Essays on Population Ethics*, edited by Jesper Ryberg and Torbjörn Tännsjö, 201–218. Dordrecht: Kluwer Academic Publishers.

Arrhenius, Gustaf. 2011. "The Impossibility of a Satisfactory Population Ethics." In *Descriptive and Normative Approaches to Human Behavior, Advanced Series on Mathematical Psychology*, edited by Hans Colonius and Ehtibar N. Dzhafarov, 1–26. Singapore: World Scientific.

Arrhenius, Gustaf. Forthcoming. *Population Ethics: The Challenge of Future Generations*. Oxford: Oxford University Press.

Blackorby, Charles and David Donaldson. 1991. "Normative Population Theory." *Social Choice and Welfare* 8, no. 3: 261–267.

Boonin-Vail, David. 1996. "Don't Stop Thinking About Tomorrow: Two Paradoxes About Duties to Future Generations." *Philosophy & Public Affairs* 25, no. 4: 267–307.

Brentano, Franz. 1969. *The Origin of Our Knowledge of Right and Wrong*. Edited by Oskar Kraus. London: Routledge.

Broome, John. 1991. *Weighing Goods: Equality, Uncertainty and Time*. Oxford: Blackwell.

Broome, John. 1999. *Ethics out of Economics*. Cambridge: Cambridge University Press.

Brown, Campbell. 2011. "Consequentialize This." *Ethics* 121, no. 4: 749–771.

Bykvist, Krister. 1996. Utilitarian Deontologies? In *Preference and Value: Preferentialism in Ethics*, Wlodek Rabinowicz, 1–16. Lund: Dept. of Philosophy, Lund University.

Bykvist, Krister. 2007. "Violations of Normative Invariance: Some Thoughts on Shifty Oughts." *Theoria* 73, no. 2: 98–120.

Bykvist, Krister. 2009. "No Good Fit: Why the Fitting Attitude Analysis of Value Fails." *Mind* 118, no. 469: 1–30.

Carlson, Erik. 1995. *Consequentialism Reconsidered*. Dordrecht: Kluwer Academic.

Carlson, Erik. 1996. "Cyclical Preferences and Rational Choice." *Theoria* 62, nos. 1–2: 144–160.

Carlson, Erik. 1998. "Two Short Papers on Harm and Value Aggregation." *Uppsala Prints and Reprints in Philosophy* 4: 13–17.

Danielsson, Sven. 1988. *Konsekvensetikens gränser*. Stockholm: Thales.

Danielsson, Sven. 1996. "The Refutation of Cyclic Evaluations." *Theoria* 62, nos. 1–2: 161–168.

Danielsson, Sven. 1999. "The Norm-Value Distinction in 1963." In *Actions, Norms, Values: Discussions with Georg Henrik von Wright*, edited by Georg Meggle, 325–330. Berlin: De Gruyter.

Ewing, A. C. 1959. *Second Thoughts in Moral Philosophy*. London: Routledge and Kegan Paul.

Fehige, Christoph. 1998. A Pareto Principle for Possible People. In *Preferences*, edited by Christoph Fehige and Ulla Wessels, 508–543. Berlin and New York: De Gruyter.

Feldman, Fred. 1997. *Utilitarianism, Hedonism, and Desert: Essays in Moral Philosophy*. Cambridge: Cambridge University Press.

Gauthier, David. 1986. *Morals by Agreement*. Oxford: Clarendon.

Heath, Joseph. 1997. "Intergenerational Cooperation and Distributive Justice." *Canadian Journal of Philosophy* 27, no. 3: 361–376.

Heyd, David. 2019. Supererogation. In *The Stanford Encyclopedia of Philosophy*, edited by Edward N. Zalta, 1–23. Stanford: Stanford University Press. Retrieved from URL https://plato.stanford.edu/archives/win2019/entries/supererogation/.

Hooker, Brad. 2000. *Ideal Code, Real World: A Rule-Consequentialist Theory of Morality*. Oxford: Oxford University Press.

Kavka, Gregory S. 1982. "The Paradox of Future Individuals." *Philosophy & Public Affairs* 11, no. 2: 93–112.

Narveson, Jan. 1967. "Utilitarianism and New Generations." *Mind* 76, no. 301: 62–72.

Narveson, Jan. 1973. "Moral Problems of Population." *The Monist* 57, no. 1: 62–86.

Narveson, Jan. 1978. "Future People and Us." In *Obligations to Future Generations*, edited by R. I. Sikora and Brian Barry, 38–60. Cambridge: White Horse Press.

Ng, Yew-Kwang. 1989. "What Should We Do About Future Generations?" *Economics and Philosophy* 5, no. 2: 235–253.

Österberg, Jan. 1988. *Self and Others: A Study of Ethical Egoism*. Dordrecht: Kluwer Academic.

Parfit, Derek. 1984. *Reasons and Persons*. Oxford: Clarendon.

Parfit, Derek. 1996. "Acts and Outcomes: A Reply to Boonin-Vail." *Philosophy & Public Affairs* 25, no. 4: 308–317.

Rabinowicz, Wlodek. 2000. "Money Pump with Foresight." In *Value and Choice: Some Common Themes in Decision Theory and Moral Philosophy*, 1: 201–234. Boston, MA: Springer.

Rabinowicz, Wlodek and T. Rønnow-Rasmussen. 2004. "The Strike of the Demon: On Fitting Pro-Attitudes and Value." *Ethics* 114, no. 3: 391–423.

Rachels, Stuart. 1998. "Counterexamples to the Transitivity of Better Than." *Australasian Journal of Philosophy* 76, no. 1: 71–83.

Scanlon, T.M. 1998. *What We Owe to Each Other*. Cambridge, MA: Belknap.

Sen, Amartya. 1970. *Collective Choice and Social Welfare*. San Francisco: Holden-Day.

Sen, Amartya. 1995. "Rationality and Social Choice." *The American Economic Review* 85, no. 1: 1–24.

Sider, Theodore. 1991. "Might Theory X Be a Theory of Diminishing Marginal Value?" *Analysis* 51, no. 4: 265–271.

Tännsjö, Torbjörn. 1998. *Hedonistic Utilitarianism*. Edinburgh: Edinburgh University Press.

Temkin, Larry. 1987. "Intransitivity and the Mere Addition Paradox." *Philosophy and Public Affairs* 16, no. 2: 138–187.

Temkin, Larry. 1996. "A Continuum Argument for Intransitivity." *Philosophy & Public Affairs* 25, no. 3: 175–210.

Temkin, Larry. 2012. *Rethinking the Good: Moral Ideals and the Nature of Practical Reasoning*. New York: Oxford University Press.

Vallentyne, Peter. 1988. "Gimmicky Representations of Moral Theories." *Metaphilosophy* 19, nos. 3–4: 253–263.

von Wright, Georg Henrik. 1993. *The Varieties of Goodness*. Bristol: Thoemmes.

CHAPTER 9

....

ON SOME IMPOSSIBILITY
THEOREMS IN
POPULATION ETHICS

....

ERIK CARLSON

AT least since Derek Parfit presented his "Mere Addition Paradox,"[1] the difficulties of formulating a viable population axiology have been widely recognized. Building on Parfit's work, a number of philosophers have proved impossibility theorems, showing that certain plausible adequacy conditions are mutually inconsistent.[2] Perhaps the most important such results are those of Gustaf Arrhenius.[3] His theorems involve more compelling adequacy conditions and weaker assumptions of measurement than earlier work in this area. On the basis of these theorems, Arrhenius is inclined to deny the existence of a satisfactory population axiology.[4]

The aim of this chapter is to show that Arrhenius's impossibility results are not inescapable. I shall mainly focus on his "sixth" theorem, which he considers to be his strongest result. Arrhenius's proof of this theorem requires a certain assumption, as regards the order of welfare levels, which is more contentious than he recognizes. This assumption rules out "non-Archimedean" theories of welfare. If such theories are not excluded, there are, as I shall show, population axiologies that satisfy all the adequacy conditions of Arrhenius's sixth theorem. In the penultimate section of the chapter I shall argue, moreover, that my objection pertains to all of Arrhenius's axiological impossibility theorems.[5] Since non-Archimedean theories of welfare are far from obviously false, Arrhenius's results fail to conclusively show that there is no acceptable population axiology.

1. ARRHENIUS'S SIXTH IMPOSSIBILITY THEOREM AND FINITE FINE-GRAINEDNESS

....

Arrhenius's sixth theorem states that no population axiology satisfies five adequacy conditions, which are informally rendered as follows:

Egalitarian Dominance: If population A is a perfectly equal population of the same size as population B, and every person in A has higher welfare than every person in B, then A is better than B, other things being equal.

General Non-Extreme Priority: For any welfare level A and any population X, there is a number n of lives such that a population consisting of the X-lives, n lives with very high welfare, and one life with welfare A, is at least as good as a population consisting of the X-lives, n lives with very low positive welfare, and one life with welfare slightly above A, other things being equal.

Non-Elitism: For any triplet of welfare levels A, B, and C, A slightly higher than B, and B higher than C, and for any one-life population A with welfare A, there is a population C with welfare C, and a population B of the same size as $A \cup C$ and with welfare B, such that for any population X consisting of lives with welfare ranging from C to A, $B \cup X$ is at least as good as $A \cup C \cup X$, other things being equal.

Weak Non-Sadism: There is a negative welfare level and a number of lives at this level such that [for any population X] an addition of any number of people with positive welfare [to X] is at least as good as an addition of the lives with negative welfare [to X], other things being equal.

Weak Quality Addition: For any population X, there is a perfectly equal population with very high positive welfare, a very negative welfare level, and a number n of lives at this level, such that the addition of the high welfare population to X is at least as good as the addition of any population consisting of the n lives with negative welfare and any number of lives with very low positive welfare to X, other things being equal.[6]

Although some of these conditions may not be entirely perspicuous, I think they are, on reflection, quite plausible. In any case, they will not be questioned here.

Arrhenius's proof proceeds by formulating more exact (and more technical) versions of these conditions and showing that these exact conditions are mutually inconsistent. He thus arrives at:

The Sixth Impossibility Theorem: There is no population axiology which satisfies Egalitarian Dominance, General Non-Extreme Priority, Non-Elitism, Weak Non-Sadism, and Weak Quality Addition.[7]

The main background assumptions of this theorem are as follows. A *life* is individuated by the person whose life it is and the kind of life it is. A *population* is a finite set of lives in a possible world. A *population axiology* is a quasi-order of all possible populations, with respect to their value. (A *quasi-order* is a reflexive and transitive, but not necessarily complete relation.) The relation "has at least as high welfare as," denoted $\gtrsim$, quasi-orders the set L of possible lives. The relations "has higher welfare than," denoted $>$, and "has equally high welfare as," denoted $\sim$, are the asymmetric and the symmetric parts, respectively, of $(L, \gtrsim)$. Some possible lives have *positive* welfare, some have *negative* welfare, and some have *neutral* welfare. Which of these categories a life belongs to is independent of scales of measurement. We assume that L includes a wide range of lives, from ones with very high positive welfare to ones with very low negative welfare. Further, a *welfare level* is an equivalence class of L under $\sim$. Let L be the set of welfare levels, let $(L, \gtrsim)$ be the $\sim$-reduction of $(L, \gtrsim)$, and let $>$ denote the asymmetric part of $\gtrsim$.[8]

By assuming only that $(L, \succsim)$ is a quasi-order, Arrhenius leaves open the possibility that some lives, and the corresponding welfare levels, are incomparable. Thus, there may be welfare levels X and Y, such that neither $X \succsim Y$ nor $Y \succsim X$. In order to simplify the discussion, I shall mostly ignore this possibility, and assume that $(L, \succsim)$ is a complete order. If the sixth impossibility theorem can be shown to be escapable, assuming that $(L, \succsim)$ is complete, it is *a fortiori* escapable if $(L, \succsim)$ is allowed to be incomplete.

A final claim that Arrhenius makes is crucial for the purposes of this chapter. This claim is as follows:

> *Finite Fine-Grainedness*: There exists a finite sequence of slight welfare differences between any two welfare levels.[9]

Arrhenius takes Finite Fine-Grainedness to follow from two assumptions that he makes.

First, he presumes that $(L, \succsim)$ is either "discrete" or "dense," according to the following definitions:

> *Discreteness*: For any pair of welfare levels X and Y, there are only finitely many welfare levels between X and Y.[10]

> *Denseness*: There is a welfare level between any pair of distinct welfare levels, and there are no isolated points.[11]

Since these notions of discreteness and denseness are not entirely standard, let us refer to them as *A-discreteness* and *A-denseness*, respectively.[12]

Second, Arrhenius assumes that $(L, \succsim)$ is "fine-grained." An A-discrete order of welfare levels is taken to be fine-grained iff the difference between any two adjacent levels is "merely slight," in an undefined, intuitive sense.[13] (How fine-grainedness should be understood when it comes to A-dense orders will be discussed in the next section.) If $(L, \succsim)$ is A-discrete, Finite Fine-grainedness follows immediately from the assumption of fine-grainedness.

Arrhenius then argues that if $(L, \succsim)$ is A-dense, it has a fine-grained A-discrete suborder which is comprehensive, in the sense that for any X in $(L, \succsim)$, there is a Y in the suborder, such that the difference between X and Y is merely slight.[14] (In what follows, "suborder" refers to such comprehensive suborders.) In other words, Finite Fine-Grainedness is true.

Finite Fine-Grainedness is necessary for Arrhenius's proof of the sixth theorem, since the proof requires that welfare levels can be represented by integers. There must be an integer-valued function f, such that, for any welfare levels X and Y, $f(X) \geq f(Y)$ iff $X \succsim Y$.[15] Integer representability presupposes A-discreteness, since there are only finitely many integers between any given pair of integers. Arrhenius's proof shows that no population axiology satisfies the exact versions of his five adequacy conditions, given that the order of welfare levels assumed in the proof is fine-grained and A-discrete. Finite Fine-Grainedness implies that, even if $(L, \succsim)$ is not itself A-discrete, the sixth theorem can be proved relative to an A-discrete suborder of $(L, \succsim)$. This suffices to establish the theorem, since for a population axiology to quasi-order the set of finite subsets of L, it must quasi-order every subset of this set.

Suppose, to the contrary, that Finite Fine-Grainedness does not hold. That is, no A-discrete suborder of $(L, \succsim)$ is fine-grained. This implies that every A-discrete suborder $(L^*, \succsim^*)$ contains at least one pair of adjacent welfare levels X and Y, such that $X \succ^* Y$, and X is not merely slightly higher than Y. In Arrhenius's exact version of General Non-Extreme Priority, the locution "one life with welfare slightly above A" is substituted by the assumption that the one life is at the higher welfare level adjacent to A. Similarly, in the exact version of Non-Elitism, the assumption that A is "slightly higher" than B is replaced by the assumption that A is higher than and adjacent to B. Hence, these exact conditions, on which Arrhenius's proof is based, do not reflect the content of the informal conditions, and fail to be intuitively compelling, unless $(L^*, \succsim^*)$ is fine-grained.

Finite Fine-Grainedness is thus essential for Arrhenius's purposes. I shall argue that this claim is insufficiently supported by Arrhenius, and that there are positive reasons to doubt it.

2. Denseness, Fine-Grainedness, and Two Notions of Discreteness

The above criterion for fine-grainedness, in terms of adjacent welfare levels, is not applicable to A-dense orders, since such orders do not contain any pairs of adjacent elements. Arrhenius does not say what fine-grainedness amounts to, as regards A-dense orders. As stated above, however, he argues that any A-dense order has a fine-grained A-discrete suborder:

> If [A-d]enseness is true of $[(L, \succsim)]$, then we can form a [suborder $(L^*, \succsim^*)$ of $(L, \succsim)]$] such that [A-d]iscreteness is true of $[(L^*, \succsim^*)]$, and such that all the conditions which are intuitively plausible in regard to populations which are subsets of L are also intuitively plausible in regard to populations which are subsets of L^*. Given that [A-d]enseness is true of $[(L, \succsim)]$, one cannot plausibly deny that there is such a [suborder $(L^*, \succsim^*)]$] since the order of the welfare levels in $[(L^*, \succsim^*)]$ could be arbitrarily fine-grained even though [A-d]iscreteness is true of $[(L^*, \succsim^*)]$. . . . Hence, given [A-d]enseness, we can be sure that Finite Fine-grainedness is true.[16]

This argument is faulty. Suppose, for example, that $(L, \succsim)$ is isomorphic to the natural order of the real numbers strictly smaller than 0, followed by the real numbers strictly greater than 10. Suppose also that a difference represented by a numerical difference of 10 or more is not merely slight. Under these assumptions, $(L, \succsim)$ is A-dense, but lacks a fine-grained A-discrete suborder. Any A-discrete suborder will include a "gap," in the form of a welfare level represented by a number smaller than 0, immediately followed by a level represented by a number greater than 10.

Is the A-dense order just discussed fine-grained? It is, if fine-grainedness is simply taken to mean that for every welfare level, there is a merely slightly different level. On the other hand, since the order contains a "hole" between welfare levels represented by numbers smaller than 0 and levels represented by numbers greater than 10, it might be denied that it is fine-grained. If it is not, it could still be true that every *fine-grained* A-dense order has a fine-grained A-discrete suborder. An obvious suggestion is that an A-dense order is fine-grained if it lacks holes. Figuratively speaking, an A-dense order without holes is like an unbroken line, with each element of the order corresponding to a point on the line. This seems to constitute a high degree of fine-grainedness. Absence of holes, in an A-dense order, is equivalent to "Dedekind completeness."[17] Applied to $(L, \succsim)$, this amounts to the following. An *upper bound* of a suborder $(L^*, \succsim^*)$ of $(L, \succsim)$ is a welfare level in $(L, \succsim)$ which is at least as high as every level in $(L^*, \succsim^*)$. A *least upper bound* of $(L^*, \succsim^*)$ is an upper bound of $(L^*, \succsim^*)$ that is at least as low as every upper bound of $(L^*, \succsim^*)$. $(L, \succsim)$ is *Dedekind complete* iff every suborder of $(L, \succsim)$ with an upper bound has a least upper bound.

Let us, then, make the plausible assumption that all Dedekind complete A-dense orders should be classified as fine-grained.[18] This puts us in a position to determine whether Finite Fine-Grainedness follows from the supposition that $(L, \succsim)$ is either fine-grained and A-discrete, or fine-grained and A-dense. The answer is negative. To see this, suppose that $(L, \succsim)$ is isomorphic to the Cartesian product of the real numbers, $Re \times Re$, ordered lexicographically. That is, an ordered pair (x, y) of reals is at least as great as an ordered pair (z, w) iff $x > z$, or $x = z$ and $y \geq w$. This means that $(L, \succsim)$ is A-dense and Dedekind complete.[19] Suppose, further, that the difference between two welfare levels, X and Y, is merely slight, in the relevant intuitive sense, only if the first number in the ordered pair representing X is the same as the first number in the pair representing Y. This implies that Finite Fine-Grainedness does not hold. That is, $(L, \succsim)$ has no fine-grained A-discrete suborder. For example, any A-discrete suborder will contain a highest level among those represented by an ordered pair $(1, x)$, for some x, immediately followed by a level represented by an ordered pair (y, z), $y > 1$. The suborder thus has a gap at this point, in the sense of two adjacent levels with a not merely slight difference.[20]

Arrhenius might respond that A-denseness is an unlikely property of $(L, \succsim)$, anyway. In fact, he regards A-discreteness as more probable than A-denseness:

> My own inclination is that [A-d]iscreteness rather than [A-d]enseness is true of [$(L, \succsim)$]. If the latter is true, then for any two lives p_1 and p_2, p_1 with higher welfare than p_2, there is a life p_3 with welfare in between p_1 and p_2, and a life p_4 with welfare in between p_3 and p_2, and so on *ad infinitum*. It is improbable, I think, that there are such fine discriminations between the welfare of lives, even in principle. Rather, what we will find at the end of such a sequence of lives is a pair of lives in between which there are no [lives] or only lives with roughly the same welfare as both of them.[21]

This argument disregards the possibility that $(L, \succsim)$ is neither A-discrete nor A-dense.[22] In particular, Arrhenius does not distinguish between A-discreteness and a logically weaker property we may call *standard discreteness*, or *S-discreteness*, for short:

> *S-discreteness*: For any non-maximal (non-minimal) welfare level X, there is a higher (lower) welfare level Y, such that there is no welfare level between X and Y.

Arrhenius's argument from limited discrimination does not support A-discreteness in particular. At most, it supports S-discreteness.[23]

To see that S-discreteness does not imply A-discreteness, consider the Cartesian product of the integers, $I \times I$, ordered lexicographically. This order obviously satisfies the analog to S-discreteness. For any ordered pair P, there is a greater ordered pair P^*, such that there is no ordered pair between P and P^*. For example, $(1, 2)$ is greater than $(1, 1)$, and there is no ordered pair between these two. The analog to A-discreteness, on the other hand, is not satisfied. For instance, there is an infinite number of ordered pairs between $(1, 1)$ and $(2, 1)$, viz., the pairs $(1, 2), (1, 3), (1, 4) \ldots$, followed by the pairs $\ldots (2, -2), (2, -1), (2, 0)$.

What, then, if we suppose $(L, \succsim)$ to be fine-grained and S-discrete, but not necessarily A-discrete? Presumably, the same criterion for fine-grainedness applies, as in the case of A-discreteness. That is, $(L, \succsim)$ is fine-grained iff the difference between any two adjacent levels is merely slight. If so, fine-grainedness and S-discreteness of $(L, \succsim)$ do not imply Finite Fine-Grainedness. Suppose that $(L, \succsim)$ is isomorphic to the lexicographic order of $I \times I$, and, again, that the difference between X and Y is merely slight only if the first number in the ordered pair representing X is the same as the first number in the pair representing Y. This implies that any A-discrete suborder has a gap.

To sum up, Arrhenius fails to support the assumption that $(L, \succsim)$ is either A-discrete or A-dense, since he does not consider other possibilities. Further, his argument against A-denseness does not support A-discreteness, but only S-discreteness. Fine-grainedness and S-discreteness do not imply Finite Fine-Grainedness. Moreover, he is wrong in claiming that Finite Fine-Grainedness follows from A-denseness and fine-grainedness. Hence, Finite Fine-Grainedness is poorly defended.[24]

3. ARCHIMEDEANNESS AND FINITE FINE-GRAINEDNESS

Finite Fine-Grainedness may of course be true, even though Arrhenius's arguments in its favor are weak. The question, then, is whether there are any positive reasons to doubt its truth. I think that there are, in fact, such reasons. Finite Fine-Grainedness immediately implies the following principle:

> *Proto-Archimedeanness*: For any welfare levels X and Y in $(L, \succsim)$, such that $X \succ Y$, there is a finite sequence of welfare levels $V_n \succ \ldots \succ V_1$ in $(L, \succsim)$, such that $V_n \succsim$

X, Y $\gtrsim$ V$_1$, and, for each pair V$_i$, V$_{i\text{-}1}$, $1 < i \le n$, the difference between V$_i$ and V$_{i\text{-}1}$ is merely slight.

That is, the difference between any two welfare levels is bridged in a finite number of small steps.

Moreover, a stronger condition follows if a difference is taken to be merely slight only if it is not infinitely greater than some other difference between welfare levels in (L, $\gtrsim$).[25] Given that all merely slight differences are spanned by a finite number of arbitrarily small differences, Finite Fine-Grainedness implies:

> *Archimedeanness:* For any welfare levels X, Y, Z, and U in (L, $\gtrsim$), such that X $\succ$ Y and Z $\succ$ U, there is a finite sequence of welfare levels V$_n$ $\succ$ ... $\succ$ V$_1$ in (L, $\gtrsim$), such that V$_n$ $\gtrsim$ X, Y $\gtrsim$ V$_1$, and, for each pair V$_i$, V$_{i\text{-}1}$, $1 < i \le n$, the difference between V$_i$ and V$_{i\text{-}1}$ is roughly equal to the difference between Z and U.

That is, the difference between any two welfare levels is bridged in a finite number of *arbitrarily* small steps.[26]

The derivation of Archimedeanness from Proto-Archimedeanness, in conjunction with the supposition that any merely slight difference is spanned by finitely many arbitrarily small differences, presupposes that the differences between welfare levels are well-behaved in certain ways. I assume, in particular, that if n differences of size d are together at least as great as one difference of size d^*, and m differences of size d^* are together at least as great as one difference of size d^{**}, then $n \times m$ differences of size d are together at least as great as one difference of size d^{**}. This assumption follows from the standard axioms for an "algebraic difference structure."[27]

Many philosophers have expressed views which are incompatible with Archimedeanness, and arguably also with proto-Archimedeanness. Parfit claims that a "century of ecstasy," 100 years of extremely high quality of life, is better than a "drab eternity," an infinitely long life containing nothing bad, and nothing good except muzak and potatoes. "Though each day of the Drab Eternity would have some [constant] value for me, *no* amount of this value could be as good for me as the Century of Ecstasy."[28] This view contradicts Archimedeanness, since it implies that the welfare difference between the century of ecstasy and, say, a life consisting of one day of muzak and potatoes cannot be bridged by adding a finite number of days of muzak and potatoes to the latter life, although each such addition brings a constant increase in welfare level.[29]

In a similar vein, James Griffin suggests that there are examples of

> a positive value that, no matter how often a certain amount is added to itself, cannot become greater than another positive value, and cannot, not because with piling up we get diminishing value . . . , but because they are the sort of value that, even remaining constant, cannot add up to some other value.[30]

Thus, Griffin finds it

> plausible that, say, fifty years at a very high level of well-being—say, the level which makes possible satisfying personal relations, some understanding of what makes life worthwhile, appreciation of great beauty, the chance to accomplish something with one's life—outranks any number of years at the level just barely worth living—say, the level at which none of the former values are possible and one is left with just enough surplus of simple pleasure over pain to go on with it.[31]

Arrhenius is, of course, well aware that many philosophers hold views like those just cited.[32] Nevertheless, he does not seem to recognize the strong tension between such views and Finite Fine-Grainedness. I suspect that this is partly due to the fact that he does not distinguish between A-discreteness and S-discreteness.

A possible response, on the part of Arrhenius, would be to resist the step from Proto-Archimedeanness to Archimedeanness. This amounts to claiming that a difference d between welfare levels can be merely slight, in the relevant sense, even if it is infinitely greater than a certain other difference d^*. That is, no finite number of d^*-differences suffice to make up a d-difference. The trouble with this move is that it threatens to severely weaken the intuitive force of Arrhenius's adequacy conditions. Consider Non-Elitism, and let welfare level A be slightly higher than B, which is very slightly higher than C. For simplicity, let X be the empty population. Non-Elitism implies that there is, for any one-life population A with welfare A, a population C with welfare C, such that a population B of the same size as $A \cup C$, and with welfare B, is at least as good as $A \cup C$. This seems highly debatable, if the difference between A and B, although merely slight, is infinitely greater than that between B and C. Suppose, for example, that an A-life contains a few more happy years than a B-life, whereas the only difference between B and C is that a B-life includes a few more seconds of listening to muzak than a C-life.

4. A NON-ARCHIMEDEAN TOY THEORY OF WELFARE

In order to construct a simple theory of welfare that satisfies fine-grainedness and S-discreteness, but violates Finite Fine-Grainedness, we may suppose that $(L, \succsim)$ is isomorphic to the lexicographic order of $I \times I$, and that all differences between adjacent levels are merely slight. There are, let us imagine, two kinds of welfare components. One of these kinds is "superior" to the other, in the sense that any amount of the superior positive (negative) components contributes more to the total positive (negative) welfare in a life than any amount of the "inferior" positive (negative) components. Assume, further, that superior and inferior welfare is measured on separate additive ratio scales. Any welfare level can then be represented by an ordered pair of integers, (h, l), where h (for "higher") represents a net amount of superior welfare, and l (for "lower") represents a net amount of inferior welfare. We make the following assumptions:

(1) A welfare level X, represented by (h_X, l_X), is *at least as high as* a welfare level Y, represented by (h_Y, l_Y), iff $h_X > h_Y$, or $h_X = h_Y$ and $l_X \geq l_Y$.

(2) A welfare level X, represented by (h_X, l_X), is
positive iff $h_X > 0$, or $h_X = 0$ and $l_X > 0$,
negative iff $h_X < 0$, or $h_X = 0$ and $l_X < 0$,
neutral iff $h_X = 0$ and $l_X = 0$,
very high iff $h_X \geq m$, for a particular positive integer m,
very low but positive only if $h_X = 0$ and $l_X > 0$,
slightly negative only if $h_X = 0$ and $l_X < 0$, and
very negative iff $h_X \leq n$, for a particular negative integer n.

(3) A welfare level X, represented by (h_X, l_X), is *merely slightly higher than* a welfare level Y, represented by (h_Y, l_Y), only if $h_X = h_Y$ and $l_X = l_Y + r, r > 0$.

Under these assumptions, Finite Fine-Grainedness is violated. Any A-discrete suborder of $(L, \succsim)$ contains some pair of adjacent welfare levels X and Y, such that X is very high, whereas Y is not. By (3), therefore, the difference between X and Y is not merely slight. Similarly, any A-discrete suborder of $(L, \succsim)$ contains a pair of adjacent levels Z and U, such that U is very negative, while Z is not. Again, (3) implies that the difference between Z and U is not merely slight.

Moreover, it is easy to see that S-discreteness of $(L, \succsim)$ is not an essential feature of this example. We may instead suppose that $(L, \succsim)$ is isomorphic to $Re \times Re$, and hence A-dense and fine-grained, but retain the other assumptions of the theory. Finite Fine-Grainedness is violated in this case, as well.

5. A Counter-Example to the Sixth Impossibility Theorem

What if Finite Fine-Grainedness is weakened, to merely state that $(L, \succsim)$ has a fine-grained S-discrete suborder? This assumption is trivial, given that $(L, \succsim)$ is itself fine-grained, since the differences between adjacent levels in an S-discrete suborder of $(L, \succsim)$ can, indeed, be arbitrarily small. However, it is not difficult to show that the sixth impossibility theorem is false if Finite Fine-Grainedness is thus weakened.

To this end, let us use our toy theory of welfare, in either its S-discrete or its A-dense variant. Given fine-grainedness, the weakened version of Finite Fine-Grainedness is satisfied. Further, we assume that superior as well as inferior welfare can be added across lives. Thus, letting (h_A, l_A) and (h_B, l_B) represent the total amounts of superior and inferior welfare in populations A and B, respectively, A contains more welfare than B iff $h_A > h_B$, or $h_A = h_B$ and $l_A > l_B$. Finally, we assume that a population is, other things equal, better than another iff it contains more welfare.[33]

Let us verify that this population axiology, which we may label "non-Archimedean totalism," satisfies all of Arrhenius's adequacy conditions. That the axiology satisfies Egalitarian Dominance and Weak Non-Sadism is obvious. To see that Weak Quality Addition is satisfied we need only note that adding any number of lives with very high welfare to a population X always makes the resulting population better than X, according to our axiology, whereas adding lives with very negative welfare plus any number of lives with very low positive welfare always makes the resulting population worse than X. Thus, let (h_X, l_X) be the total welfare in X. An addition of the first kind means adding (m, n), $m > 0$, to (h_X, l_X), while an addition of the second kind means adding (r, s), $r < 0$. No matter what the values of n and s are, $(h_X + m, l_X + n)$ is greater than $(h_X + r, l_X + s)$.

General Non-Extreme Priority is also satisfied. In fact, the condition holds for any number n of lives added to population X. Let (h_X, l_X) be the total welfare in X and let welfare level A be represented by (h_A, l_A). Adding some life or lives with very high welfare and one life at level A to X yields $(h_X + h_A + m, l_X + l_A + r)$, $m > 0$. Adding some life or lives with very low positive welfare and one life slightly above A to X yields $(h_X + h_A, l_X + l_A + u + s)$, $u > 0$. Irrespective of the values of r, s and u, $(h_X + h_A + m, l_X + l_A + r)$ is greater than $(h_X + h_A, l_X + l_A + u + s)$.

It remains to consider Non-Elitism. Let level A be represented by (h_A, l_A), implying that level B is represented by $(h_A, l_A - r)$, $r > 0$. Also, let level C be represented by (h_C, l_C), and let (h_X, l_X) be the total welfare in population X. Let n be the number of people in populations B and $A \cup C$. According to our axiology, BUX is at least as good as $A \cup C \cup X$ iff $\left(nh_A + h_X, n[l_A - r] + l_X\right)$ is at least as great as $\left(h_A + [n-1]h_C + h_X, l_A + [n-1]l_C + l_X\right)$. Canceling out the terms h_X and l_X, this is equivalent to $\left(nh_A, n[l_A - r]\right)$ being at least as great as $\left(h_A + [n-1]h_C, l_A + [n-1]l_C\right)$. Since $h_A > h_C$, or $h_A = h_C$ and $l_A - r > l_C$, this holds for any n.

Thus, if we assume a non-Archimedean theory of welfare, there are population axiologies which satisfy all of Arrhenius's adequacy conditions. Moreover, such an axiology can, as in the case of non-Archimedean totalism, conform to the simple and intuitively appealing idea that a population is, other things equal, better than another iff it contains more welfare.

6. The Plausibility of Non-Archimedean Theories of Welfare

The non-Archimedean toy theory of welfare outlined in Section 4 is rather simplistic. First, it assumes that all welfare levels are comparable. Second, the assumption that there are two kinds of welfare components, such that the smallest amount of the superior kind trumps any amount of the inferior kind is perhaps not very plausible.[34] However, a non-Archimedean theory can be much more sophisticated than our toy model. First, it can allow for incomparability between welfare levels. Second, non-Archimedeanness need not be a simple matter of some welfare components being superior to others. Although the representation of welfare levels by ordered pairs of numbers may naturally suggest such a simple superiority view,[35] this type of representation could be used also for other kinds of non-Archimedean theories. Conversely, non-Archimedean theories, including superiority views, can be mathematically represented in other ways.

On a more complex view, non-Archimedeanness may be a holistic effect, arising from the combination of different welfare components, none of which is in itself superior. To illustrate this possibility, let us assume an "objective list" theory of welfare, akin to the one suggested by Griffin. According to this theory, pleasure, knowledge, friendship, freedom, appreciation of beauty, development of one's talents, purposeful activity, and so on, are positive welfare components. It seems plausible to claim that for a life to have very high welfare, it must contain all or most of these things, to some degree. A life containing just one or two types of welfare components will likely be of an impoverished kind, having at best moderately high welfare. Nevertheless, it appears that an impoverished life can always be slightly improved, by adding more welfare components of the type or types already included in the life. However, such additions can never result in a life with very high welfare. Any finite series of improvements that takes us from an impoverished life to a life with very high welfare must include at least one step at which a welfare component of a new type is added. Such a step, arguably, means an improvement that cannot be arbitrarily slight. Obviously, much work is needed in order to furnish the details of such a holistic non-Archimedean theory of welfare. But the general idea has enough plausibility, I believe, to cast doubt on Archimedeanness.

There are, moreover, putative direct counter-examples to Archimedeanness. Consider an "oyster life," p_1, containing no positive or negative welfare components except one second of mild pleasure. Compared to p_1, a life, p_2, containing nothing but two seconds of the same kind of mild pleasure, seems slightly better. And so on. Thus, each such life, p_i, $i = 1, 2, 3, \ldots$ is a representative of a welfare level X_i, such that $X_{i+1} \succ X_i$. Let us also suppose that the difference between adjacent levels X_{i+1} and X_i is the same, no matter the value of i. That is, an added second of mild pleasure has constant marginal value. Further, let p^* be the best life you can imagine, and let X^* be its welfare level. Probably, p^* contains welfare components of many different kinds, interrelated in diverse ways. It is very plausible to claim that $X^* \succ X_i$, for any i. However, if Archimedeanness is true, the difference between X^* and X_1 is bridged by a finite number of differences, each roughly equal to the difference between X_{i+1} and X_i. Hence, it follows that $X_j \succsim X^*$, for some positive integer j.

The assumption of constant marginal value may be questioned. Perhaps the difference between adjacent levels X_{i+1} and X_i diminishes as i increases. However, the conclusion that $X_j \succsim X^*$, for some j, still follows from Archimedeanness, as long as there is, for any i, some $k > i$, such that the difference between X_k and X_i equals that between X_2 and X_1.[36] To deny that there is such a k is to claim that if a life contains a sufficient number of seconds of mild pleasure (and no other welfare components), *no* extra number of such seconds yields an improvement, in terms of welfare, equal to the improvement from one to two seconds of mild pleasure. This claim does not appear very plausible.

Admittedly, there are structurally similar cases that are apt to evoke opposite intuitions, in favor of Archimedeanness. Again, let p^* be the best life imaginable. Suppose that p^* lasts for n years. Compare p^* to a life p^*_1, lasting for n years plus one second. The last second contains moderate pain, and no positive welfare components. Presumably, p^*_1 is very slightly less good than p^*. Now compare p^*_1 to p^*_2, which is just like p^*_1, except that another moderately painful second is added at the end. It seems that p^*_2 is very slightly less good than p^*_1. And so on. Adding painful seconds to p^* seems eventually to bring us to a life p^*_k, whose welfare level is neutral or even negative. Thus, it appears that the difference in welfare level between an extremely good life and a neutral or bad life *can* be bridged in a finite number of very small steps.[37]

On reflection, however, I find this "added pain" argument much weaker than the oyster life argument *against* Archimedeanness. If, for example, knowledge and friendship are positive welfare components, we must assume that the person loses her knowledge and her personal relationships at the start of the added period. (Maybe she is in a vegetative, barely conscious state, or suffers from severe dementia.) It could be argued that the absence of these welfare components means that even a fairly brief added painful period implies a large decrease in welfare level. Lack of knowledge or friendship may be positively bad for a person, rather than merely neutral.

In response, one may alter the example and allow positive welfare components to be present in the added period but assume that the pain is sufficiently strong to outbalance these positive components. Hence, each added second means a slight net decrease in welfare level. It is not clear that this response solves the problem. Even moderate pain is very distracting, at least for ordinary human beings. Certain positive welfare components, such as knowledge and different kinds of achievement, may therefore be psychologically incompatible with too many instances of pain.[38]

Another worry with the revised added pain case is that many putative welfare components seem to contribute discontinuously over time to a person's welfare level. Suppose that love and accomplishment are positive welfare components and consider the moment when a person meets the love of her life or finishes a great novel. It appears that moderate pain cannot outbalance the positive effect of such moments. One could, of course, give up the assumption that each added second is only moderately painful, and allow some seconds to be extremely painful, in order for the pain to outbalance the effect of positive welfare components. But I can see no intuitive reason to believe that, for any welfare increase stemming from positive welfare components, there is a particular level of pain that just barely outbalances this increase. Furthermore, allowing for extreme pain in the added period aggravates the problem of the compatibility of pain with certain positive welfare components.

Finally, adding a sufficient number of pain episodes to an otherwise very good life is likely to bring about a holistic or threshold effect. This pertains to both versions of the added pain case. If we keep adding moderate pains, it seems that the accumulated pain sooner or later brings about a considerable drop in welfare level, whether or not the pain is accompanied by outbalanced positive welfare components. For sufficiently large numbers n, the disvalue of n episodes of moderate pain seems to be much larger than n times the disvalue of one such episode. It is not nearly as plausible to claim, in the oyster life case, that adding sufficiently many episodes of mild pleasure gives rise to a similar but positive holistic effect.[39]

I shall end this section by briefly considering a general argument for Archimedeanness, recently proposed by Teruji Thomas:

> [W]hatever the nature of well-being, we can find a continuum of possible lives beginning with some drab life and ending with a blissful one. By a "continuum" I mean technically that these lives can be parameterized by a bounded interval of real numbers.... [W]e could ... vary any of the attributes on which welfare depends, such as, at bottom, the configurations of particles or fields across spacetime.... [T]his continuum is required to satisfy two further conditions. First, the lives must get better and better as we go along the continuum. Second, they must do so *continuously*, in the sense that, for any life along the continuum, any other life that is sufficiently close to it along the continuum will differ from it in welfare by only a small amount. The structure of the real numbers ensures that we can get from one end of the continuum to the other in a finite sequence of such sufficiently small steps.[40]

However, Thomas's only argument for the existence of such a continuum is restricted to a simple and, in my view, implausible form of welfare hedonism.[41] He leaves it unclear how to extend this argument to other theories of welfare. The claim that continuous variation of the value-grounding properties gives rise to a value continuum is hardly true for all kinds of value. Literary value seems to be one counter-example. Presumably, the literary value of a text depends on the words it contains and how they are ordered. Must there be, for any text of poor literary quality, a finite sequence of texts, starting with this poor text, and such that (i) each text only differs from its predecessor with respect to a single letter or word, (ii) each text is slightly better than its predecessor, and (iii) the last text is of great literary value? This is surely very implausible, and I can see no obvious reason to accept a corresponding assumption concerning welfare levels.

I think we may conclude, at the very least, that Archimedeanness is not so obvious that it can legitimately be presupposed in an impossibility theorem, purporting to show that there is no acceptable population axiology.

7. Arrhenius's Other Impossibility Theorems

Finite Fine-Grainedness is a background assumption for each of Arrhenius's six axiological impossibility theorems.[42] If Finite Fine-Grainedness is replaced by the weaker assumption that $(L, \succsim)$ has a fine-grained S-discrete suborder, non-Archimedean totalism constitutes a counter-example also to Arrhenius's first, fourth, and fifth impossibility theorems. (This is shown in the appendix.) His second and third theorems, on the other hand, include one adequacy condition that is violated by non-Archimedean totalism. This condition is as follows:

> *Inequality Aversion*: For any triplet of welfare levels A, B, and C, A higher than B, and B higher than C, and for any population A with welfare A, there is a larger population C with welfare C, such that a perfectly equal population B of the same size as A∪C and with welfare B, is at least as good as A∪C, other things being equal.[43]

Non-Archimedean totalism violates this condition if, for example, A is a very high welfare level, while B and C are very low positive levels. However, Inequality Aversion does not appear particularly compelling. Suppose that A is the highest welfare level you can imagine, while B and C are very low positive levels, B being merely slightly higher than C. The only difference between a B- and a C-life, let us assume, is that a B-life contains one extra second of mild pleasure. Inequality Aversion implies that if a population at level C is large enough, it is improved at least as much by giving everyone an extra second of mild pleasure, as by raising a great number of people to level A. This is surely contestable.

In all events, "Inequality Aversion" is a misnomer. If this condition should for some reason be accepted, this cannot essentially have to do with the badness of inequality. Standard, Archimedean total utilitarianism, according to which the total welfare in a population is measured on a real-valued ratio scale, satisfies Inequality Aversion. Since only the total sum of welfare matters for the value of a population, according to total utilitarianism, this theory is "inequality neutral." It neither favors nor disfavors inequality in the distribution of welfare. Non-Archimedean totalism is inequality neutral in exactly the same way. This theory, too, ranks populations exclusively by their total sum of welfare. Hence, it is no less "inequality averse" than standard total utilitarianism.[44]

Actually, Arrhenius acknowledges that Inequality Aversion is intuitively debatable.[45] He nevertheless defends this adequacy condition, by arguing that it follows from the allegedly more compelling Non-Elitism condition.[46] His proof of this implication relies, however, on Finite Fine-Grainedness.[47] Without this assumption, Non-Elitism does not imply Inequality Aversion, as is evident from the fact that non-Archimedean totalism satisfies Non-Elitism but not Inequality Aversion. Finite Fine-Grainedness thus plays an important role also as regards the second and third theorems.

In addition to his axiological theorems, Arrhenius proves two normative impossibility theorems.[48] Roughly, these theorems are designed to show that there are possible situations of choice, with populations as options, in which the agent cannot avoid choosing wrongly. The following condition is an adequacy condition in both of the normative theorems:

Normative Inequality Aversion: For any triplet of welfare levels A, B, and C, A higher than B, and B higher than C, and for any population *A* with welfare A, there is a larger population *C* with welfare C, such that if it is wrong in a certain situation to choose a perfectly equal population *B* of the same size as *A*∪*C* and with welfare B, then it is also wrong in the same situation to choose *A*∪*C*, other things being equal.[49]

If non-Archimedean totalism is combined with the normative principle that one ought always to maximize welfare, the resulting theory violates Normative Inequality Aversion. However, this condition is hardly more compelling than Inequality Aversion. If A is a very high level, while B and C are very low positive levels, one can reasonably claim that one ought to raise a large number of people from level C to level A, rather than raising an even larger number of people from level C to level B. If so, choosing *B* is wrong, but choosing *A*∪*C* is not.

As in the case of its axiological cousin, moreover, Normative Inequality Aversion does not really seem to concern inequality. Standard total utilitarianism satisfies this condition, although it is no more inequality averse than non-Archimedean totalism.

8. Conclusion

Four of Arrhenius's six axiological impossibility theorems presuppose that the order of welfare levels satisfies Archimedeanness. Without this assumption, there are counter-examples to the theorems, in the form of population axiologies satisfying all of his adequacy conditions. The remaining two theorems also rely on Archimedeanness, albeit less directly. Many philosophers have made claims that are incompatible with Archimedeanness, and non-Archimedean theories of welfare do not seem implausible. Hence, Arrhenius's theorems rest on controversial assumptions, and the prospects for finding an acceptable population axiology may not be quite as bleak as he argues.[50]

This does not detract from the significance of Arrhenius's work. By revealing a great number of inconsistencies or tensions among intuitively very plausible claims, his results considerably restrict the room for maneuver, in the search for a satisfactory population axiology.[51]

Acknowledgments

Earlier versions of this chapter were discussed at seminars at Uppsala University in November 2014 and at the University of York in February 2015, as well as at a workshop at the Institute for Futures Studies, Stockholm, in October 2015. I am grateful to the participants for valuable comments. Further, I have benefited from many discussions with Gustaf Arrhenius and Krister Bykvist. Krister also gave me written comments on an earlier draft. Work for this chapter was supported by grant P14-0212:1 from the Bank of Sweden Tercentenary Foundation.

Appendix: Non-Archimedean Totalism and Arrhenius's First to Fifth Theorems

We shall verify that non-Archimedean totalism satisfies the adequacy conditions of Arrhenius's first, fourth, and fifth theorems. The first theorem is as follows:

The First Impossibility Theorem: There is no population axiology which satisfies Egalitarian Dominance, Quality, and Quantity.

As compared to the sixth theorem, two of these adequacy conditions are new:

Quality: There is a perfectly equal population with very high positive welfare which is at least as good as any population with very low positive welfare, other things being equal.

Quantity: For any pair of positive welfare levels A and B, such that B is slightly lower than A, and for any number of lives n, there is a greater number of lives m, such that a population of m people at level B is at least as good as a population of n people at level A, other things being equal.

Non-Archimedean totalism obviously satisfies Quality. To verify Quantity, let levels A and B be represented by (h_A, l_A) and (h_B, l_B), respectively. A and B being positive, and B being slightly lower than A implies that $h_A = h_B \geq 0$, and $l_A > l_B$. Further, if $h_A = h_B = 0$, then $l_B > 0$. Hence, n and m can be chosen so that $mh_B > nh_A$, or $mh_B = nh_A$ and $ml_B \geq nl_A$, implying that the population at level B is at least as good as the one at level A.

Consider next the fourth theorem:

The Fourth Impossibility Theorem: There is no population axiology which satisfies Egalitarian Dominance, General Non-Extreme Priority, Non-Elitism, Weak Non-Sadism, and Quality Addition.

In this theorem, there is only one new condition:

Quality Addition: For any population X, there is a perfectly equal population with very high welfare, such that its addition to X is at least as good as the addition of any population with very low positive welfare to X, other things being equal.

To see that non-Archimedean totalism satisfies Quality Addition, let (h_X, l_X) be the total welfare in X. Adding a population with very high welfare means adding (x, y), $x > 0$, to (h_X, l_X), whereas adding a population with very low positive welfare means adding $(0, z)$, $z > 0$. This implies that $(h_X + x, l_X + y)$ is greater than $(h_X, l_X + z)$, and hence that the former addition is better than the latter.

Let us now turn to the fifth theorem:

> *The Fifth Impossibility Theorem*: There is no population axiology which satisfies Dominance Addition, Egalitarian Dominance, General Non-Extreme Priority, General Non-Elitism, and Weak Quality.

Three of these adequacy conditions are new:

> *Dominance Addition*: An addition of lives with positive welfare and an increase in the welfare of the rest of the population does not make a population worse, other things being equal.

> *General Non-Elitism*: For any triplet of welfare levels A, B, and C, A slightly higher than B, and B higher than C, and for any one-life population A with welfare A, there is a population C with welfare C, and a population B of the same size as $A \cup C$ and with welfare B, such that for any population X, $B \cup X$ is at least as good as $A \cup C \cup X$, other things being equal.

> *Weak Quality*: There is a perfectly equal population with very high welfare, a very negative welfare level, and a number of lives at this level, such that the high welfare population is at least as good as any population consisting of the lives with negative welfare and any number of lives with very low positive welfare, other things being equal.

That non-Archimedean totalism satisfies Dominance Addition is obvious. In Section 5, we showed that it satisfies Non-Elitism. Since that proof is independent of the welfare levels in X, it also proves that General Non-Elitism is satisfied. To see that Weak Quality is satisfied, let (h_A, l_A), be the total welfare in a population A with very high welfare. It follows that $h_A > 0$. The total welfare in a population B of lives with very negative welfare is (h_B, l_B), $h_B < 0$. Adding a number of lives with very low positive welfare to B, yields a population C with a total welfare of $(h_B + 0, l_B + x)$, $x > 0$. Since $h_A > h_B$, (h_A, l_A) is greater than $(h_B + 0, l_B + x)$. Hence, A is better than C.

Let us finally check that non-Archimedean totalism satisfies all the adequacy conditions of Arrhenius's second and third theorems, except Inequality Aversion. The second theorem is this:

> *The Second Impossibility Theorem*: There is no population axiology which satisfies Dominance Addition, Egalitarian Dominance, Inequality Aversion, and Quality.

As already noted, it is obvious that non-Archimedean totalism satisfies these conditions, with the exception of Inequality Aversion.

It remains to consider the third theorem:

The Third Impossibility Theorem: There is no population axiology which satisfies Egalitarian Dominance, Inequality Aversion, Non-Extreme Priority, Non-Sadism, and Quality Addition.

Two of these adequacy conditions are new:

Non-Extreme Priority: There is a number n of lives such that for any population X, a population consisting of the X-lives, n lives with very high welfare, and one life with slightly negative welfare, is at least as good as a population consisting of the X-lives and $n + 1$ lives with very low positive welfare, other things being equal.

Non-Sadism: [For any population X] an addition of any number of people with positive welfare [to X] is at least as good as an addition of any number of lives with negative welfare [to X], other things being equal.

That non-Archimedean totalism satisfies Non-Sadism is evident. To verify Non-Extreme Priority, let (h_X, l_X) be the total welfare in X. Adding n lives with very high welfare to X means adding (x, y), $x > 0$, to (h_X, l_X), yielding at total welfare of $(h_X + x, l_X + y)$. Then adding one life with slightly negative welfare yields $(h_X + x + 0, l_X + y + z)$, $z < 0$. Instead adding $n + 1$ lives with very low positive welfare to X yields $(h_X + 0, l_X + u)$, $u > 0$. Since $x > 0$, $(h_X + x + 0, l_X + y + z)$ is greater than $(h_X + 0, l_X + u)$, implying Non-Extreme Priority.

NOTES

1. Parfit (1984, Ch. 19).
2. See, for example, Ng (1989), Blackorby and Donaldson (1991), and Carlson (1998).
3. For recent statements of Arrhenius's results, see Arrhenius (2011; 2016; forthcoming). (Page references to the last work are to a draft dated June 2018.)
4. Arrhenius (2011, 23; forthcoming, 390).
5. Or at least to all the theorems presented in Arrhenius (forthcoming).
6. Arrhenius (2011, 7–9; forthcoming, 400–403). The purpose of the "other things being equal"-clauses is to leave room for the possibility that other factors than welfare are relevant to the value of a population.
7. Arrhenius (2011, 9; 2016, 178; forthcoming, 351). In the first work, the theorem is simply called "The Impossibility Theorem." The proof is found in Arrhenius (2011, 9–22; forthcoming, 351–358).
8. Arrhenius (2011, 4–6; forthcoming, 300–302). I have slightly reformulated some of the assumptions. The General Non-Extreme Priority condition seems to require that there is no highest welfare level, and hence that L and L are at least countably infinite.
9. Arrhenius (2016, 171; forthcoming, 302).
10. Arrhenius (2011, 5; forthcoming, 302). I have simplified Arrhenius's formulation.
11. Arrhenius (forthcoming, 303). To accommodate the possibility that $(L, \succeq)$ is incomplete, the first conjunct in the *definiens* should state only that there is a welfare level between any

pair of distinct and *comparable* welfare levels. The existence of a welfare level between any pair of distinct levels obviously implies completeness.

12. The standard meaning of "discreteness" corresponds, rather, to the notion of S-discreteness, introduced in Section 2, below. As regards "denseness," a dense order is usually defined as an order that fulfils the first conjunct in Arrhenius's *definiens* (subject to the qualification mentioned in the previous note). The notion of an isolated point is often used to define discreteness and denseness of sets in topological spaces. In the present context, the absence of isolated points implies that, for any welfare level, there are levels close to this level.

13. Arrhenius (2011, 5f; 2016, 171; forthcoming, 302).

14. Arrhenius does not explicitly make this comprehensiveness assumption, but it is implicit in his discussion, as well as necessary for his proof.

15. Moreover, it must hold that $f(X) > 0$ iff X is positive, $f(X) < 0$ iff X is negative, and $f(X) = 0$ iff X is neutral.

16. Arrhenius (forthcoming, 304f). Notation slightly altered.

17. See, for example, Luce et al. (2007, 49f).

18. It is perhaps not very plausible to suggest that Dedekind completeness is a *necessary* condition for fine-grainedness, as regards A-dense orders. Suppose that $(L, \succsim)$ is isomorphic to the rational numbers, naturally ordered, and that differences between welfare levels are ordered in accordance with differences between the representing numbers. In this case, $(L, \succsim)$ intuitively seems fine-grained, although it is not Dedekind complete.

19. Cf. Luce et al. (2007, 50).

20. If $(L, \succsim)$ is A-dense and Dedekind complete, what is required for it to fulfil Finite Fine-Grainedness? A sufficient condition, I conjecture, is that it has a countable suborder $(L^*, \succsim^*)$ which is "order dense" in $(L, \succsim)$. Order denseness means that for every X and Y in $(L, \succsim)$, such that $X \succ Y$, there is a Z in $(L^*, \succsim^*)$, such that $X \succsim Z \succsim Y$. The real numbers have such a countable order dense subset, viz., the rational numbers, while the lexicographic order of $Re \times Re$ lacks a countable order dense subset. See Krantz et al. (2007, 38–40), Roberts (2009, 111f).

21. Arrhenius (forthcoming, 303f; footnote omitted); Arrhenius (2011, 6) contains a nearly identical passage.

22. Arrhenius mentions this possibility in a footnote (forthcoming, 303, n. 4), but he does not pursue the matter.

23. Labeling an order as "S-dense" iff it fulfils the first conjunct in Arrhenius's definition of denseness, we may note that S-discreteness and S-denseness are not jointly exhaustive possibilities. Suppose, for example, that $(L, \succsim)$ is isomorphic to the following infinite order of rational numbers: -1, -1/2, -1/3, -1/4, . . . , 0, . . . , 1/4, 1/3, 1/2, 1. This order is obviously not S-dense. Nor is it S-discrete, since 0 has no next greater (or next smaller) number in the order.

24. Furthermore, Arrhenius does not argue for the assumption that $(L, \succsim)$ is fine-grained. Some adherents of non-Archimedean theories of welfare (see the next section) may want to deny fine-grainedness, and hence Finite Fine-Grainedness. They may argue, for example, that $(L, \succsim)$ is A-dense but contains holes.

25. This assumption introduces a certain degree of "cardinality" into the framework, by presupposing that differences between welfare levels are to some extent comparable. (The term "roughly equal" is meant to allow, though, for some degree of indeterminacy or incommensurability.) This presupposition is implicit, however, in Arrhenius's

informal interpretations of his adequacy conditions. Moreover, the intuitive appeal of the conditions depends crucially on those informal interpretations.

26. Archimedeanness is very similar to a standard Archimedean axiom in the theory of difference measurement, stating that every "strictly bounded standard sequence" is finite. See Krantz et al. (2007, 147) and Roberts (2009, 137).

27. See Krantz et al. (2007, 151) and Roberts (2009, 136).

28. Parfit (1986, 161); italics in the original.

29. I interpret Parfit as claiming that the century of ecstasy contains *more welfare* than the drab eternity. In other words, the welfare level of the former life is higher than the level of the latter life. Parfit could perhaps also be interpreted as holding that the drab eternity contains more welfare than the century of ecstasy, but that the latter life is nevertheless *better* for the person living it. On this interpretation, his view need not violate Archimedeanness with respect to welfare levels. However, it does not matter for our purposes whether or not Parfit, in particular, held a non-Archimedean view. The important point is that such views are possible and at least *prima facie* plausible.

30. Griffin (1986, 85).

31. Griffin (1986, 86).

32. Indeed, he cites Parfit and Griffin, as well as several other authors (Arrhenius 2005, 98; forthcoming, 130), and he even refers to these theories as "non-Archimedean," albeit in a sense that does not correspond exactly to the denial of Archimedeanness, as stated above.

33. Like Arrhenius, I insert an "other things equal"-clause in order not to rule out that other things than welfare can affect the value of a population.

34. Arrhenius (2005, 106) labels this kind of trumping "strong superiority" between welfare components. Further, he defines "weak superiority" as, roughly, the view that *some* amount of the superior welfare components trumps any amount of the inferior components. He is inclined to reject both forms of superiority, since they have implications he finds counterintuitive. However, these implications follow only under the assumption that the relevant welfare components, or composites of such components, can be ordered in a finite sequence, such that the difference in contributive value to a person's welfare, between any two adjacent members of the sequence, is "marginal" (Arrhenius 2005, 107; forthcoming, 412). Arrhenius finds this assumption plausible, but it threatens to beg the question to presuppose it in an argument against superiority, since it is exactly the kind of Archimedean principle that believers in superiority will deny. (Note its similarity to Finite Fine-Grainedness.)

35. According to some superiority views, there may be three or more kinds of welfare components, such that the first kind is superior to the second, the second is superior to the third, and so on. Such a view can be represented in terms of ordered n-tuples of numbers, instead of ordered pairs. For a general development of this idea, not restricted to the measurement of welfare, see Carlson (2010).

36. In other words, the claim that $X^* \succ X_i$, for any i, is compatible with Archimedeanness only if the marginal value of seconds of mild pleasure converges to a finite limit, in the sense that, for any difference d in $(L, \succsim)$, there is a positive integer j, such that, for any $k > j$, the difference between X_k and X_j is smaller than d.

37. This type of case was suggested by Arrhenius, in conversation.

38. I owe this observation to Krister Bykvist.

39. Arrhenius has also suggested a variant of the added pain case, in which the added pain episodes occur *within* the time span of an otherwise very good life (Arrhenius 2016, 172;

forthcoming, 303). This variant seems open to objections very similar to those I have stated.

40. Thomas (2018, 826f); italics in the original, footnote omitted. To be precise, Thomas does not argue exactly for Archimedeanness, as I have defined it, but for a somewhat weaker principle he calls "Small Steps" (p. 815). He considers Small Steps to be essentially identical to Finite Fine-Grainedness (p. 815, n. 13).

41. Ibid., 826.

42. Arrhenius (forthcoming, Ch. 11).

43. Ibid., 311f.

44. This is pointed out by Thomas (2018, 825).

45. Arrhenius (forthcoming, 147). See also Arrhenius's contribution to the present volume.

46. Arrhenius (forthcoming, 150f).

47. For the proof, see Arrhenius (forthcoming, 323–326).

48. Arrhenius (forthcoming, 378–388).

49. Arrhenius (forthcoming, 380).

50. Some philosophers have responded to population-ethical impossibility results by accepting various versions of Parfit's "Repugnant Conclusion" (1984, 388). In the case of Arrhenius's sixth theorem, this would mean rejecting Weak Quality Addition. In my opinion, this is a very implausible response. Sometimes, the rejection of adequacy conditions excluding versions of the Repugnant Conclusion is defended on the grounds that accepting these conditions would force us to deny some other, at least as compelling adequacy condition (Holtug 2004; Huemer 2008; Tännsjö 2002). As we have seen, accepting a non-Archimedean theory of welfare allows us to escape this dilemma, at least as it pertains to Arrhenius's theorems.

51. Thomas (2018), contains criticism of Arrhenius's impossibility theorems that overlaps significantly with mine. In particular, Thomas points out (without submitting proofs) that "total lexic utilitarianism," a population axiology structurally similar to non-Archimedean totalism, satisfies all the adequacy conditions of Arrhenius's first, fourth, fifth, and sixth theorems. As concerns the second and third theorems, Thomas objects, on grounds similar to mine, to Arrhenius's derivation of Inequality Aversion from Non-Elitism. Related objections to Arrhenius's results are also made in unpublished work by Mathias Barra.

References

Arrhenius, Gustaf. 2005. "Superiority in Value." *Philosophical Studies* 123: 97–114.

Arrhenius, Gustaf. 2011. "The Impossibility of a Satisfactory Population Ethics." In *Descriptive and Normative Approaches to Human Behavior*, edited by E. Dzhafarov and L. Perry, 51–66. Singapore: World Scientific.

Arrhenius, Gustaf. 2016. "Population Ethics and Different-Number-Based Imprecision." *Theoria* 82: 166–181.

Arrhenius, Gustaf. Forthcoming. *Population Ethics: The Challenge of Future Generations.* Oxford: Oxford University Press.

Blackorby, Charles and D. Donaldson. 1991. "Normative Population Theory: A Comment." *Social Choice and Welfare* 8: 261–267.

Carlson, Erik. 1998. "Mere Addition and Two Trilemmas of Population Ethics." *Economics and Philosophy* 14: 283–306.

Carlson, Erik. 2010. "Generalized Extensive Measurement for Lexicographic Orders." *Journal of Mathematical Psychology* 54: 345–351.

Griffin, James. 1986. *Well-Being: Its Meaning, Measurement, and Moral Importance*. Oxford: Clarendon Press.

Holtug, Nils. 2004. "Person-Affecting Moralities." In *The Repugnant Conclusion: Essays on Population Ethics*, edited by J. Ryberg and T. Tännsjö, 129–161. Dordrecht: Kluwer Academic.

Huemer, Michael. 2008. "In Defence of Repugnance." *Mind* 117: 899–933.

Krantz, David, R. D. Luce, P. Suppes, and A. Tversky. 2007. *Foundations of Measurement, vol. I: Additive and Polynomial Representations*. Mineola, NY: Dover Publications.

Luce, R. Duncan, D. H. Krantz, P. Suppes, and A. Tversky. 2007. *Foundations of Measurement, vol. III: Representation, Axiomatization, and Invariance*. Mineola, NY: Dover Publications.

Ng, Yew-Kwang. 1989. "What Should We Do About Future Generations?" *Economics and Philosophy* 5: 235–251.

Parfit, Derek. 1984. *Reasons and Persons*. Oxford: Oxford University Press.

Parfit, Derek. 1986. "Overpopulation and the Quality of Life." In *Applied Ethics*, edited by P. Singer, 145–164. Oxford: Oxford University Press.

Roberts, Fred. 2009. *Measurement Theory: With Applications to Decisionmaking, Utility, and the Social Sciences*. Cambridge: Cambridge University Press.

Tännsjö, Torbjörn. 2002. "Why We Ought to Accept the Repugnant Conclusion." *Utilitas* 14: 339–359.

Thomas, Teruji. 2018. "Some Possibilities in Population Axiology." *Mind* 127: 807–832.

CHAPTER 10

··

THE PERSON-BASED INTUITION AND THE BETTER CHANCE PUZZLE

M.A. ROBERTS

1. INTRODUCTION

WE seem to share certain ideas relating to the value of existence. We seem to have certain *existential values* in common.

Thus, the existence I happen to have—here, in the possible world or (we will say) possible *future* that has *actually* unfolded—is of great value to me. To say that is just to say that the actual future is *better for* me than any alternate possible future in which I never exist at all—which seems, at least at first glance, just to say that I have *more well-being* in the actual future than I have in any such alternate possible future.

Even so, it's plausible to think that my worth-having existence doesn't (other things being equal) make the actual future *morally better* than any such alternate possible future. Nor did the fact that my own parents could have predicted that my existence would be worth having (other things being equal) plausibly give rise to a *moral* obligation on their part to bring me into existence.

My existence thus clearly constitutes a *personal* plus, a plus *for me*, but plausibly *doesn't* constitute a *moral* plus.

The idea that *Existence Is Not a Moral Plus* (*ENMP*) is rooted in what is called the *Person-Affecting*, or *Person-Based*, *Intuition* (*PBI*). A seemingly widely shared and deeply held intuition, PBI states that one future is morally worse than another, and a choice made in that one future morally wrong, *only if* that one future makes things *worse for* a person who *does or will exist* in that future.[1] Leaving a person out of existence altogether, according to PBI, can't (other things being equal) make things *worse*. Which means that bringing that same person into existence can't (other things being equal) make things *better*—hence ENMP.

I needn't, of course, have had a worth-having existence. Things could have been otherwise. For any of us, there are possible futures in which we exist and are so thoroughly miserable that it would have been *better for us* never to have existed at all. For any one of us, we could have had, instead of the worth-having existences we in fact have, what in the law is called a *wrongful life*.[2]

Such an existence would clearly constitute not just a *personal* minus but also (other things being equal) a *moral* minus. The addition of a wrongful life to a future (other things being equal) clearly makes that future *morally* worse. And agents (other things being equal) are clearly *morally* obligated *not* to bring such lives into existence.

Wrongful life is one way in which existence can be a moral minus. Are there others? Suppose a person p who is perfectly well off in the actual future is still *better* off in an alternate possible future. We've already said that p's existence plausibly doesn't make the actual future morally *better* than a future in which p never exists at all. But can it make the actual future morally *worse*—worse not just than the future in which p is better off (it obviously does *that*) but also worse than the future in which p never exists at all? Can that which is a personal *plus* also be a moral *minus*?

As we shall see, it is critical that we answer that question in the affirmative. At least: if we want to retain the idea that the worth-having existence isn't a *moral plus*—that is, ENMP; and, with ENMP, PBI—then, as we shall see, we also need to accept the idea that the worth-having existence, even if a *personal* plus, can still be a moral *minus*.

The positions that the additional worth-having existence *isn't* (other things being equal) a moral plus (ENMP) and that the *morally worse* future must be *worse for* at least one person who does or will exist in that future (PBI) seem highly plausible. And, for purposes here, I shall assume that we readily accept ENMP and (depending on how it is constructed) PBI, and argue only briefly why, given those commitments, we must also accept the idea that the worth-having existence is sometimes a moral minus. I then raise the question whether, given that we accept those values, we can consistently accept still one more: the independently compelling idea that, in some sense, the better *chance* of existence can make things morally *better*.

It's that last idea that threatens to upset the apple cart. Suppose that a couple has conceived and given birth to a child. Their earlier choice to undergo a fertility treatment significantly increased their chances of conceiving any child at all. But the treatment itself has predictably caused the child they produced to suffer a mildly burdensome, well-being reducing side effect.

If the child complains to the parents "How could you have done this to me," the parents may respond "Your existence, as it stands, is well worth having, and had we chosen *not* to undergo treatment your chances of ever existing at all would have been *greatly* reduced." That—given that the fertility treatment really was necessary to increase the chances of the couple's conceiving any child at all, that no better treatment was available and that the burden the child bears as a side effect of the treatment truly is mild—seems a perfectly adequate rebuttal of the child's complaint.

But what of *God's* complaint, or the *universe's* complaint, or just the simple unauthored claim that the couple's choice is, though a plus for the child, *morally* wrong?

Those complaints would seem to be rebutted just as nicely. Yes, there may well exist a probabilistically quite remote possible future in which that very same child exists and is better off. And—had we not taken into account the fact that the fertility treatment increased that child's chances of coming into existence—we may well have wanted to say that what the couple did was, accordingly, wrong. But taking those probabilities into account we want to say something else entirely. We want to say that the *better chance* of existence has *made up for* the fact that the existence the child in fact has is *worse for* the child than it might have been.[3]

At the very least, the better chance converts what would otherwise have been a morally *wrong* choice into a morally *permissible* choice. Does it also convert what would otherwise be a morally *worse* future into a future that is not *quite* so bad? Does that better chance, itself embedded in the details of the future that in fact unfolds, also convert that future into a future that is at least as good as the remote possible future in which the child exists and is still better off?

That's less clear (we will come back to that question in section 5.2 below). But whatever we want to say about the *future*, what we've said about the *choice* seems unassailable. The upshot? In at least *some* sense, the better *chance* of existence has made things *morally better*.

And now we have a problem, what I will call the *Better Chance Puzzle*. If the actual *fact* of the worth-having existence (other things being equal) isn't a moral plus and sometimes is a moral minus, how can the better *chance* of existence *ever*, in any sense at all, constitute a moral plus?

To solve the puzzle is to show that we can consistently retain the various existential values we've already assumed *but also accept* the surely correct point that the better *chance* of existence, in at least some sense, can make things morally *better*. If we can't do that, then the puzzle itself can all too easily be reworked to show that we must, after all, disavow the existential values we have assumed.

One purpose of this chapter, then, is to propose a solution to that puzzle: a *genuine* solution, one that allows us to retain *all* the pieces of the puzzle, including the existential values we have assumed *and* the claim that the better chance of existence, in at least some sense, can sometimes make things morally better.

But a genuine solution to the puzzle must take into account still other moral data as well. For our *maximizing* values are just as important as our *existential* values. Indeed, it may well be that we are drawn to certain *existential* values because we understand at some level that those values serve to constrain the scope of our *maximizing* values in morally critical ways. Thus, the goal here will be to solve the puzzle within a framework consisting of principles common to many forms of maximizing consequentialism. The end product will be the start of a plausible *person-based* form of *maximizing* consequentialism.

The framework comes first. I first note some of our maximizing values (Section 2) along with the vocabulary and assumptions we shall need for the purpose of talking about those values. I then articulate our existential values more carefully than I have so far (Section 3). Next, I show why it is critical to say that the worth-having existence can be a moral *minus* if we want to retain the idea that that same worth-having existence isn't a moral *plus*. In that connection, discussions of two objections against PBI are in order (Section 4). On one objection (from John Broome), PBI generates inconsistencies; on the other (from Derek Parfit and Gregory Kavka), PBI is refuted by a certain type of *Non-Identity Problem*.[4] I then turn to the Better Chance Puzzle itself (Section 5). Finally, I note conclusions (Section 6).

2. Our Maximizing Values; Vocabulary; Assumptions

2.1. The Person-Based Intuition (PBI)

The Person-Based Intuition (PBI), along with the idea that existence isn't (other things being equal) a moral plus (ENMP), is assumed for purposes here. Just to note: our maximizing values and our existential values actually aren't entirely at odds with one another. Thus, PBI itself is shaped in part by a value that can only be described as maximizing. No person who does or will exist in a given future is made *worse off*? Each existing or future person's wellbeing has been *maximized*? Then, according to PBI, the future itself isn't deficient in any morally relevant respect; the future isn't morally worse, nor is the choice morally wrong.

2.2. Same-People Pareto; Ordinary Logical Properties

Other principles I assume for purposes here are more obviously maximizing. Where x and y are alternate possible futures and agents in x have the ability, power, and resources to bring about y in place of x—where, that is, y is *accessible* relative to x:

> *Same-People Pareto*: If (i) exactly the same people do or will exist in x and y, (ii) each person in y has at least as much well-being in y as that person has in x, and (iii) at least one person in y has more well-being in y than in x, then y is *morally better* than x.

I assume, moreover, that the *overall moral betterness* relation between futures—*betterness* for short—has its standard semantic and logical features. Thus, by virtue of the meanings of our terms and assuming accessibility, to say that y is *better* than x is just to say that x is *worse* than y; and, if x is better than y for a person p, then y is worse than x for p. And I assume that the betterness relation is *transitive* (if x is better than y and y is better than z, then x is better than z), and the exactly as good as relation is *symmetrical* (if x is exactly as good as y, then y is exactly as good as x).[5] Finally, I assume *trichotomy* (if it's not the case that x is better than y and it's not the case that y better than x, then x is exactly as good as y).[6]

2.3. Connection

For purposes here, I understand the *telic* project (determining when one *future* is morally *worse* than another) and the *deontic* project (determining when a given *choice* is morally *wrong*) to be *closely*—though, as we shall see, not *perfectly*—connected. We should evaluate the permissibility of a given choice on the basis of the *consequences* that choice may bring about, where the consequences of a choice can be spelled out in terms of the futures that unfold from those choices and the futures themselves evaluated by reference to the betterness relation.

Some philosophers separate the telic and deontic projects. And it may be that there is a sense in which one future can be *better though not morally better* than another future in a case in which an agent has the *moral* obligation to make the choice that brings about that other future. Provided, however, that we clearly focus on the relation of *moral* betterness and not some distinct, amorphous relation of betterness-but-not-moral-betterness, the assumption that the two projects are closely—though not perfectly—connected is plausible.

For purposes here, to say that one future is *better*—or *worse*—than another is just to say that one future is *morally* better overall—or *morally* worse overall—than another. Ditto for choice: the permissible choice is just the *morally* permissible choice and nothing more complicated than that.

2.4. Accessibility

It is standard to say that agents are morally obligated to do only that which they *can* do—where *can* here requires not just logical and metaphysical possibility but also *accessibility*, and where *accessible* futures are understood to include only those futures that agents (at the relevant time) have the ability, power, and resources to bring about. Thus, the future in which the sun doesn't rise tomorrow is logically and metaphysically possible but not *accessible*. It isn't a future that agents have the ability, power, and resources to bring about. The laws of science stand in our way.

Accessibility is distinct from *probability*. A future can be accessible even if the odds are that the agent won't implement a given choice in *precisely* the way necessary to bring that future about. Thus, suppose you need to open a safe to disarm a bomb and have no clue what the combination is. The future in which you open the safe is perfectly *accessible* relative to the future in which you instead evacuate the building; nothing in, for example, the laws of science will keep you from turning the dial left and then right and then left again in just the right way to open the safe. It's just that, since you don't know the combination to the safe, it's highly improbable that you will get it right in the few minutes you have before the bomb goes off.[7]

One other note regarding accessibility. We can imagine cases in which a future is barred not in virtue of the laws of science but rather in virtue of the choices of other agents. Thus, my *not* firing my rifle won't bring about a future in which the (wrongly accused) target of the firing squad escapes with his or her life in a case in which nineteen other members of the firing squad will shoot to kill even if I don't. For purposes here, however, I include as *accessible* the future in which the target lives. On what basis? Even if I on my own don't have the power to save the life, the *collection* of agents, whether through collaboration or otherwise, clearly does have the ability, the power, and the resources to bring about just that outcome.

2.5. Well-Being

Starting out, we will assume that one future is *better for* (*worse for*) a given person than another *if and only if* that person has *more well-being* (*less well-being*) in the one future than in the other. I won't try to define *well-being* here. I will just say that it's what makes existence so precious to the one who exists from that person's own point of view. Later in this chapter, however, we will consider the possibility that a person's having *more well-being* may not be all there is to a person's being *better off* (Section 4.2.3 below). When it is not just a person's *well-being*, but also the *probability* of a person's ending up with one well-being level rather than another, that is at stake, we need to consider whether a more robust sense of when things are *better for* that person is in order.

2.6. Nonexistence Comparability

I assume here that we may meaningfully and truthfully compare, for a given person, a future in which that person has a particular existence against a future in which in which that person never exists at all (*Nonexistence Comparability*). Thus: *for me*, the actual future in which I have an existence that includes various well-being-related benefits and burdens is better than any future in which I never exist at all. Still other futures are worse *for me* than futures in which I never exist at all.

I will assume, in addition, that all people—existing, future, and merely possible—have *zero well-being* (zero benefits, zero burdens) in any future in which they never exist.[8]

2.7. Additivity

Our existential values—specifically ENMP and PBI—leave no room for the standard totalist position that betterness between futures is determined by the simple addition of *well-being* levels for each person who does or will exist in the futures that are to be pair-wise compared. But, as Broome and Feldman have argued, there may still be room for *addition*.

Thus what is to be added up, according to Broome, are utilities that are determined under a concept of the *personal good*, which itself may be understood to reflect how well off that person is not just in terms of raw well-being but also in terms of such values as *equality*, *fairness*, and (perhaps) *priority*.[9] For Feldman, the utilities to be added up are determined under the concept of *desert-adjusted value*, which Feldman understands as the value a given future has for a person adjusted in light of considerations of *desert* and *justice*.[10]

For purposes here, I won't be interested in moving from raw well-being (*WB*) to any more ornate concept in order to give voice to the values of equality, fairness, priority, desert, or justice. Rather, my interest in the more ornate concept—which I will call *contributive value* (*CV*)—is limited to whether that concept can be put to work to articulate our *existential* values.[11]

I do not try to decide in this chapter whether we should retain additivity. The important point is rather that, if we do retain additivity, we should understand that the utilities to be added up to decide the overall value of any particular future must be determined not by WB but rather by CV.

Any complete statement of the additive principle will need to include an account of the relation between WB and CV. In some cases it will be obvious how that account should go. For example, where the existence is *less* than worth having—where the life is *wrongful*; where, that is, overall WB is *negative*—and the person could have been left out of existence at no cost to anyone else, that existence will be paired with a *negative* CV.[12]

In some of the cases of interest here, however, the relation between WB and CV may seem—as we shall see—less obvious. Thus, as a reflection of our *maximizing* values we will need to accept that more WB for an existing or future person *often* makes things morally better, which means more CV. But, as a reflection of our *existential* values, we will also need to accept that the existence of an additional person with a positive WB level *doesn't* make things better—that even lots of positive WB *doesn't* translate to even a *little* positive CV. To make it possible to satisfy both desiderata, we'll need to understand that a certain *inversion* of the anticipated CV scale is in order.[13]

3. OUR EXISTENTIAL VALUES

3.1. ENMP

It's plausible to think that the existence of an additional well-off person doesn't (other things being equal) make a future *better*—that Existence Is Not a Moral Plus (ENMP). Thus, where x and y are possible futures and y is accessible relative to x,

> *Existence Is Not a Moral Plus* (*ENMP*): If (i) exactly the same people do or will exist in x and y except that an additional person exists in y and has an existence worth

having in y and (ii) for each person p who does or will exist in x, p has at least as much well-being in x as p has in y, then x is at least as good as y.

In the case where no futures are accessible *beyond* x and y, it's plausible, moreover, to think that it's permissible (other things being equal) for agents not to bring the additional person into existence. Or so Connection, together with ENMP, would immediately imply. Those results seem plausible.

3.2. The Person-Based Intuition (PBI)

3.2.1. *Two Kinds of Losses Case*

ENMP is restricted to the case in which the only distinction between the two futures is the additional worth-having existence—the case in which other things *are* equal. In tradeoff cases, in which other things *aren't* equal, the appeal of the intuition behind ENMP—that is, PBI—can be even clearer.

Consider the *Two Kinds of Losses Case* (Figure 10.1). The choices c1 and c2 lead, with certainty, to f1 and f2, respectively.[14] Anna's existence under c1 is well worth having and comes at the expense of Billy's never existing at all, while c2 brings Billy into an existence that is also well worth having but comes at the expense of Anna's well-being plummeting to zero. (Here and throughout, names in boldface mean that the indicated person does or will exist in the indicated future, and names in italics and asterisked mean that the person never exists in the indicated future.)

The loss of wellbeing Billy sustains in f1 has exactly the dimensions of the loss of wellbeing Anna sustains in f2. But surely these are very different sorts of losses! ENMP itself is silent in this case. But the intuition *behind* ENMP—that is, the intuition that a future isn't worse, or a choice at that future wrong, if *no one* who *does or will exist* in that future has been made worse off; that is, *PBI*—opens the door to a clear distinction. Thus according to PBI Billy's nonexistence in f1 doesn't count *against* f1—nor, by the same token, does Billy's existence in f2 count *in favor of* f2. Consistent with those points, perfectly ordinary moral principles dictate that much has gone wrong in f2—that, given the

	c1	c2
WB	f1	f2
10	Anna	Billy
...		
0	*Billy**	Anna

FIGURE 10.1 Two Kinds of Losses Case

option of f1, it clearly *counts against* f2 that Anna's existence in f2 is just on the edge of an existence *less* than worth having. We easily conclude that f2 is worse than f1, that c1 is permissible, and that c2 is wrong. Any other evaluation of this case—for example, the standard totalist idea that f2 is *exactly as good as* f1; that c1 and c2 are *both* permissible—would seem to be badly misguided.[15]

3.2.2 *Very Narrow Construction of PBI (VNPBI)*

For PBI to remain plausible, it must be constructed *very* narrowly—as a mere *necessary* condition on when a future is *worse* or a choice *wrong*.

> *Very Narrow PBI (VNPBI)*. Where x and y are possible futures and y is accessible relative to x, x is worse than y, and a choice c made at x is morally wrong, *only if* x is worse for a person who does or will exist in x than _____,

where (as noted earlier) we, for the moment, understand that a future is *worse for* a person just in case that person has *less well-being* in that future.

VNPBI is explicitly elliptical. We'll come back to how the ellipsis is to be completed in Section 3.2.3. For now, what is important is what this principle *doesn't* say. It *doesn't* say that x is *better* than y *only if* x is *better for* a person who does or will exist in x.[16] In that respect, the principle is *very* narrow.

It's critical that we understand PBI as *very* narrow in that sense. It is critical, that is, that we understand PBI *not* to provide a necessary condition on when one future is *better* than another.

Why is that? For one thing, we can't otherwise provide a plausible person-based analysis of wrongful life. We need to be able to say that the future in which a person has an existence that is less than worth having is (other things being equal) *worse* than the future in which that person never exists at all. We don't want that result ruled out from the start—which is exactly what the position that the *better* future must be better for some *existing or future* person does.

For another, to reconcile our existential values against one another we are going to need to say—as we shall see in Section 4—that even the worth-having existence can be a moral *minus*: it can make things *worse*. We are going to need to insist that in some cases a person's worth-having existence makes one future *worse* than a second future in which that person never exists at all. But—given that one future can be *worse* than a second only if the second future is *better* than the one—that point won't be one we can consistently insist on if we have already accepted that the *better* future must be *better for* some *existing or future* person or another.

3.2.3. *Expansive Construction of VNPBI (EVNPBI)*

VNPBI states that one future is worse than another *only if* the one future is *worse for* a person who does or will exist in the one future. But worse for that person *than what*? *We haven't said.*

The ellipsis is usually filled in as follows: x is worse than y *only if* x is worse for p *than y is*.

For PBI to remain credible, however, we need a more *expansive* construction.[17] Thus:

> *Expansive Very Narrow Person-Based Intuition (EVNPBI).* Where x and y are possible futures and y is accessible relative to x, x is morally worse than y, and a choice c made at x is morally wrong, *only if* there is a person p and an alternate accessible future z such that
> (i) p does or will exist in x *and*
> (ii) x is worse for p than z (where z may, but need not, be identical to y),

where (as before) we, for the moment, understand that x is *worse for* p than z just in case p has *less well-being* in x than in z.

The usual way of completing the ellipsis is damning for—and question-begging against—PBI. As we shall see in Section 4, PBI remains credible only if we accept that a person p's worth-having existence in x can make x worse than y even though p *never exists* in y. But the usual way of completing the ellipsis bars us from saying anything like that. It thereby blinds us to that *very fact* that would point to a *person-based* moral deficiency in x as compared against y: that x *avoidably* makes things worse for p, that is, makes things worse for p *than z does*.[18]

4. Two Objections Against the Person-Based Intuition

4.1. Broome's Inconsistency Objection

4.1.1. *Broome's Case*

John Broome has argued that what he calls the *Neutrality Intuition*, a principle he (mistakenly, I believe) identifies with PBI, leads to inconsistency. Figure 10.2 (Broome's Case) motivates that argument.

WB	f1	f2	f3
+10			George
+5	George		
+0		George*	

FIGURE 10.2 Broome's Case

It is stipulated that George's existence in the futures f1 and f3 fall in what Broome calls the *neutral range*. Then, according to the Neutrality Intuition, George's existences in f1 and f3 are both morally *neutral*, making each of f1 and f3, under that principle, exactly as good as the future f2 in which George never exists at all. Transitivity and symmetry instruct that f1 is exactly as good as f3. But Same-People Pareto insists that f3 is better than f1. That inconsistency leads Broome to reject the Neutrality Intuition.

4.1.2. *Expansive Account of Broome's Case*

That we must reject the Neutrality Intuition seems exactly right. Ditto the principle that would complete the ellipsis in Very Narrow PBI—VNPBI—in the usual way. For that principle, too, implies that f1, just like f3, is at least as good as f2.

At the same time, *Expansive* Very Narrow PBI—EVNPBI—nicely avoids that result. Given f3, the necessary condition EVNPBI establishes on f1's being worse than f2 is easily satisfied. The principle thus avoids the implication that f1 is at least as good as f2 and opens the door to the result that f1 is *worse* than f2. We can then just note that George's existence in f3 (according to ENMP) doesn't make f3 better than f2, nor does it (according to EVNPBI) make f3 worse than f2. Thus, f2 is exactly as good as f3. Since, under Same-People Pareto, f1 is worse than f3, we may then conclude that f2 is exactly as good as f3 and that f1 is worse than both.

Two notes are in order. First, application of the expansive account to Broome's case reveals a somewhat surprising connection between two seemingly disparate propositions, one quite modest and the other quite extreme: between the idea that George's existence in f1 *doesn't* make f1 *better* than f2 and the idea that George's existence in f1 *does* make f1 *worse* than f2. Thus under the expansive account, it is not enough to *deny* that f1 is *better* than f2—that is, to *accept* ENMP. To do that much while also retaining the principles that we think are clearly correct—e.g., Same-People Pareto—*and* avoiding inconsistency, we find that we are compelled also to *accept* that f1 is actually *worse* than f2.[19] Which is to assert what we can call *Pareto Minus*: the idea that in some cases (Broome's case being a prime example) the additional worth-having existence— even when other things are equal; even when no one else is made worse off in any way— makes things morally worse.

And, second, nothing in the expansive account rules out an additive evaluation *provided* we understand that what is to be added up isn't WB but rather CV. Thus: we immediately concede that the CV of George's existence in f3 is *greater than* the CV of George's existence in f1. But it doesn't follow that the CV of George's existence in f3 (or in f1) is even *slightly* positive. We can instead invert the CV scale and insist that the CV of George's existence in f3 is exactly zero while the CV of his existence in f1 is negative n (for some n). The additive principle then tells us just what we've already established: that f2 is exactly as good as f3 and that f1 is worse than both.

4.1.3. *Two Concerns About the Expansive Account of Broome's Case*

The expansive account of Broome's case that EVNPBI suggests raises two concerns.

(a) The first is that it violates the *Mere Addition Principle*, a principle long embedded in population ethics and one that some theorists even consider axiomatic.

> *Mere Addition Principle*: If (i) exactly the same people do or will exist in x and y except that an additional person has an existence worth having in y and (ii) for each person p who does or will exist in x, p has at least as much well-being in y as in x, then y is at least as good as x.

The Mere Addition Principle implies that f1 is at least as good as f2 and thus forces us to reject a claim critical to the expansive account of Broome's case. Or, to put things the other way around, the expansive account rules out the Mere Addition Principle in favor of *Pareto Minus*: the claim that in some cases—including Broome's—the addition of a worth-having existence, even when other things are equal, makes things morally *worse*.

It's not clear, however, that the fact that the expansive account rules out the Mere Addition Principle should be considered a *problem* rather than a significant *advantage* of that account. The Mere Addition Principle, after all, plays a critical role in generating both the Mere Addition Paradox and the Repugnant Conclusion.[20] On those grounds alone, the principle should be regarded as non-axiomatic and very possibly false. So regarded, the fact that the expansive account violates the Mere Addition Principle cannot credibly be considered on its own to refute that account.[21]

(b) The second concern raised by the expansive account of Broome's case is rooted in the *Independence of Irrelevant Alternatives* (*Independence*). According to that principle, our pairwise comparison of a future x against an alternate future y should proceed *without* reference to facts about any further alternate future z. Our comparison of x against y, in other words, *should not vary* between the case where z *does* exist as an accessible future and the case where z *doesn't* exist as an accessible future.

It is true that the expansive account explicitly relies on the fact that f1 is worse for George than *f3* for the purpose of comparing f1 against *f2*. George's being less well off in f1 than George is in *f3* is what opens the door to the claim that f1 is worse than *f2*. But it doesn't follow from that fact that the expansive account violates Independence. For, under that account, what we are comparing are not denuded distributions of well-being across particular populations but rather possible worlds, or *futures*, in all their detail.

Thus, to say that f3 is *accessible* relative to f1 is to say that agents in f1 have the ability, the power, and the resources to bring about f3. In f1, they could have—they *really* could have; f3 is not just a logical or metaphysical possibility—made things better for George but have instead made things worse. But that fact is itself a feature of f1. If we vary the case and declare f3 *inaccessible* relative to f1, then we in effect shift the reference of "f1."[22]

When, in other words, we say that, given the accessibility of z, x is worse than y, we might just as well say that a *certain feature of x* makes x worse than y, namely, that agents in x have the ability, the power, and the resources to bring about z which they fail to put to work in x.

What that will mean is that the antecedent of Independence is unsatisfied in cases involving shifts in accessibility: it will never happen that, when the comparison is x against y, z will be accessible relative to x in some cases and not accessible relative to x in other cases.[23]

One of the reasons Independence may seem like such a good idea is that it guards against inconsistency. We've already said about Broome's case, a *three* outcome case, that f1, given f3, is worse than f2. But now consider a variation on that case, a *two* outcome case in which f3 *doesn't* exist as an accessible future. Applied to that case, EVNPBI implies that f2 *isn't* worse than f1. But for the reasons already noted there's no inconsistency here. When we say that f3 is *accessible* relative to f1 in the one case and not in the other, we are talking about entirely distinct futures, two distinct "f1s." We thus avoid any hint of inconsistency.[24]

4.2. The Non-Identity Problem

4.2.1. *The Pleasure Pill Case*

The *Non-Identity Problem* has been seen as a significant threat against a person-based approach in ethics. But the expansive construction of the person-based intuition— EVNPBI—opens the door to a credible response to that threat.

The most challenging among the variations on the Non-Identity Problem have two features in common. First, they turn on an evaluation of the relevant probabilities— specifically, on the phenomenon Kavka called the *precariousness* of existence.[25] And, second, they involve choices—the choice to take the teratogenic pleasure pill or sign the slave child contract just prior to conception; the choice of depletion over conservation or the risky policy over the safe policy—that we can easily agree are clearly wrong.[26]

For purposes here, we consider Kavka's case of a parent who takes a teratogenic pleasure pill just prior to conceiving a child. The child—let's say *Gina*—who is then conceived has an existence that is, though well worth having, burdened by a disorder that occurs as a side effect of the parent's choice to take the pleasure pill.

The problem arises when we think about what would have happened had the parent *not* taken the pill. Would *that* have made things better for *Gina* than things in fact are? Very probably not. After all, *any* change in the timing or manner of conception—even one as subtle as the parent's *not* taking the pleasure pill; as subtle as the parent's taking an aspirin, or a sip of water, in place of the pleasure pill—would very likely have left Gina out of existence altogether. Some other child—some child *non-identical* to Gina—perhaps would have existed in Gina's place and been better off. But things would not have turned out any better for *Gina* at all. If anything, things, very probably, would have been *worse*.

Nonetheless, we think that the choice to take the pleasure pill is clearly wrong. But now we have a problem. The future in which Gina in fact exists and is burdened by the effects of the pleasure pill—call it *f1*—is not *worse for* her than any future—call any such future *f2*—in which Gina never exists at all. For Gina doesn't have less wellbeing in f1 than in f2. Nor is f1 worse than f2 for anyone else who does or will exist in f1 (or so we can stipulate). But the whole point of PBI is to insist that *someone*—some person who does or will exist in a given future—must be *worse off* in order for that future to be declared worse than another or for a choice made at that future to be wrong. With that condition—at first glance—failed, PBI may seem immediately to imply that f1 is not, after all, worse than f2, nor is the choice to take the pleasure pill wrong.

4.2.2. *Expansive Account of the Non-Identity Problem*

Thus the Non-Identity Problem. An advantage that EVNPBI has over other constructions of PBI—including the construction that fills in the ellipsis in VNPBI in the usual way—is that it remains completely silent in the face of the facts of the case as stated. Before generating any results at all, EVNPBI demands—rightly, in my view—more information. In particular, before we can apply EVNPBI, we need to know whether there exists any *third* future—call it *f3*—accessible relative to f1 and such that f1 is worse than *f3* for Gina.

But surely there exists *just* such an accessible future. Clearly, a future in which the parent chooses (say) an aspirin in place of the pleasure pill and Gina nonetheless is conceived and brought into existence *unburdened* by the effects of the pleasure pill—a future, that is, in which Gina has more wellbeing than Gina has in f1—is accessible relative to f1.[27]

The necessary condition that EVNPBI establishes is thus satisfied. That, in turn, leaves the door open for still other principles to instruct—just as they did in our account of Broome's case—that f1 is worse than both f2 and f3 and that the choice to take the pleasure pill is wrong.

4.2.3. *But What About the Probabilities?*

The pleasure pill case is among the most challenging of the variations on the Non-Identity Problem that PBI must contend with. As we have just seen, however, EVNPBI nicely avoids the result that f1 is at least as good as f2 as well as the result that the choice to take the pleasure pill is permissible, leaving the door open for us to apply still other person-based principles to determine that f1 is worse than f2 and the choice to take the pleasure pill is wrong.

But it might credibly be argued that EVNPBI isn't all there is to PBI.

The intuition—PBI—that EVNPBI purports to capture is that one future is worse than another, and a choice made in that one future is wrong, *only if* a person who does or will exist in the one future is *worse off* than that person is in an alternate accessible future. And—until now—we have taken it for granted that for one future to be worse for a person than another is for that person to have *less wellbeing* in the one future than in the other. But isn't there more to a person's being *worse off* than just wellbeing? Don't *probabilities* have a role to play as well?

If they do, then it is a problem for EVNPBI that it *ignores* the probabilities at stake in the case. It is a problem for EVNPBI that it takes for granted a narrow and arguably *impoverished* concept of when it is that one future is *worse for* a person than another and thus fails to make the distinction between (i) the case where the particular future that unfolds under a particular choice is highly *probable* given that choice and (ii) the case where the future that unfolds under a particular choice is highly *improbable* given that choice.

But that distinction would seem to be critical to determining whether a given future makes things *worse for*, or alternatively *better for*, Gina in the more robust sense that PBI itself would seem to invoke.

Why is that? Look at things from Gina's own point of view. *If* the future in which the parent chooses the aspirin and Gina has more well-being is (even if *accessible*) highly *improbable* given the choice of the aspirin, and the future in which the parent chooses the pleasure pill and Gina has less well-being is highly *probable* given the choice of the pleasure pill, we can surely agree—the burden Gina bears as an effect of the pleasure pill itself being mild—that it may well make things *better for* Gina—*taking probabilities into account*—for the parent to choose the pleasure pill than for the parent to choose the aspirin.

Accordingly, *if* the case in fact includes the probability-related details just described, then the upshot is that a revised EVNPBI—EVNPBI revised, that is, to take probabilities into account; revised to reflect the more robust sense of when one future is *worse for* a person than another—will generate the same results that we considered problematic before. Given those details, *no one* who *does or will exist* in f1, including Gina, has, after all, been made *worse off*, in that more robust sense, by the parent's choice to take the pleasure pill. The necessary condition established by a revised EVNPBI being failed, that principle will then instruct that f1 isn't, after all, worse than f2 or f3—and that the choice to take the pleasure pill is, after all, perfectly permissible.

But two notes are in order. First, while EVNPBI can be defended against objections based on the pleasure pill case, it now seems that that defense is too narrow to serve as a defense of PBI itself. Now, that that's so doesn't show that EVNPBI is false. Rather, it shows that, for EVNPBI to fully capture PBI, EVNPBI must be extended to take critical distinctions relating to probabilities into account. It is exactly that task we take up when we turn to the Better Chance Case in the next section.

And, second, a far more salient note. It would be a problem for such an extended EVNPBI if it forced us to accept, in the face of the pleasure pill case, that f1 is at least as good as f2 or that the choice to take the pleasure pill is permissible. But such an extended EVNPBI doesn't, in fact, force us to accept that result at all. To see that that's so, let's go back to the point prior to choice and, again, "look at things from Gina's point of view." We at that point asked whether the future in which the parent chooses the pleasure pill is in fact worse for Gina, taking probabilities into account, *if* we were in a case in which Gina's coming into existence is "highly probable" given the parent's choice of the pleasure pill and "highly improbable" given the parent's choice of the aspirin.

But we are not in that case. We can agree, I think, that it is *highly improbable* that Gina herself will be conceived and come into existence given the parent's choice to take the *aspirin*. But the same is so—calculated as of that moment just prior to choice, based on information available to the agent at that time—given the parent's choice to take the *pleasure pill*. Just as the parent taking the aspirin leaves Gina's coming into existence highly "precarious," so does the parent taking the pleasure pill. After all, there's no one way—no one schedule; no one "timing and manner" of conception that the choice to take the pleasure pill secures, any more than there's any one way—any one schedule; any one "timing and manner" of conception—that the choice to take the aspirin secures. Unfolding from *both* choices are a *myriad* of possible futures—and only in a very small number of them, whatever the parent's choice, will it happen that Gina is the person who is in fact conceived and who in fact comes into existence.

The pleasure pill, in other words, is *not* a *fertility* pill. If it were, we would be in a *quite* different sort of case—one in which the choice to take the pleasure pill (aka the *fertility* pill) *increases* the chances of Gina's coming into existence. But as to the actual pleasure pill case—the case in respect of which it was clear to us that the choice to take the pleasure pill was wrong—the probability of Gina coming into existence, *whatever* the parent does, is very small. That, in turn, leaves the analysis to turn on wellbeing alone. When Gina has a very small chance of existing and having a *lower* wellbeing level under one choice and the *same* very small chance of existing and having a *higher* wellbeing under the other choice, it is perfectly clear that the one choice is worse for (even in the more robust sense) her than the other. When the probabilities at stake are a wash, wellbeing is *all* that matters.

The upshot? We can anticipate that EVNPBI, extended to take probabilities into account, will avoid the problem results in the pleasure pill case and thus open the door for other person-based principles to produce the results we intuitively consider correct: that f1 is worse than f2 and that c1 is wrong.[28]

5. THE BETTER CHANCE PUZZLE

5.1. The Better Chance Case

The problem is that the probabilities aren't always a wash.

In the pleasure pill case, the choice to take the pleasure pill—the choice we agree is wrong—doesn't, on closer inspection, give Gina a better chance at existence. But in other cases agents face choices that *do* give the additional person a better chance of existence. And in some of those cases that better chance of existence doesn't just make things *better for the person*, that is, *personally* better. It also makes things, in some sense, *morally* better. Specifically: a better chance of existence can convert what would otherwise be a morally wrong choice into a morally permissible choice.[29] Let's call that the *Better Chance Claim.*

At the same time, ENMP, rooted in PBI, insists that the worth-having existence *doesn't* (other things being equal) make a future morally better. Pareto Minus goes further: the worth-having existence can even (other things being equal) make a future morally *worse*.

	c1 (parent takes fertility pill)		c2 (parent takes aspirin)	
probability of future unfolding, given choice	0.1	0.9	0.0001	0.9999
WB	f1	f2	f3	f4
10			Harry	
8	Harry			
0		Harry*		Harry*

FIGURE 10.3 Better Chance Case

And thus the Better Chance Puzzle: how can a *better chance* of existence make things morally *better*, when the worth-having *existence* itself *doesn't* make things morally better and can even make things morally *worse*?

The Better Chance Case (Figure 10.3) is just one of many that gives rise to the puzzle.

Let's suppose that a parent in that case has taken a fertility pill and that that choice has vastly increased the chances of conception. And let's suppose that Harry is in fact conceived and brought into existence. While the existence itself is well worth having, Harry nonetheless suffers a mildly burdensome, well-being reducing side effect as a result of the parent's choice to take the fertility pill.

We locate all those details in a possible future f1. And we note that, though c1 in our hypothetical has *in fact* been chosen and has *in fact* given rise to f1, c1 does not *guaranty* f1. c1 might have instead ended in f2, where Harry never exists at all. Still, c1 increased Harry's chances of existence as compared against what he would have faced had the parent chosen to take an aspirin instead—had, that is, the parent chosen c2 instead of c1. That is the plus of c1. c2, on the other hand, does not *guaranty* f4; it does not *guaranty* that Harry will never exist at all. Thus, there exists some remote, highly improbable but nonetheless accessible future f3 in which—against all odds—Harry nonetheless exists. Such is the plus of c2: it produces more well-being for Harry if Harry does happen to exist.

On those facts, it seems clear that c1 is—in a robust sense; a sense that takes *both* well-being levels *and* probabilities into account—*better for Harry* than c2. Moreover, that betterness-for-Harry constitutes not just a *personal* plus but a *moral* plus as well. At the very least: it plausibly converts what would otherwise be considered a *wrong* choice into a choice that is *perfectly permissible*.

To solve the Better Chance Puzzle is to explain how the *better chance* of existence can make c1 permissible when c1 would otherwise have been wrong when, as a general matter (and other things being equal), the additional worth-having existence *doesn't* make things morally better and can even make things morally *worse*.

5.2. Probabilities and PBI

The discussion of section 4 concluded with the point that EVNPBI, to capture the full thrust of PBI, must be revised to take distinctions relating to probabilities into account. It shows that EVNPBI revised to take such distinctions into account must capture the idea that c1 in f1 is, after all, morally permissible.

Let's start, then, with a principle that sets aside the question of how the *futures* at play in that particular case compare against each other (the *telic* question) and focuses squarely on what it is about the *choice* c1 that makes c1 in f1 morally permissible (the *deontic* question).

The concept of *expected value* (EV), adapted for a person-based approach, may here seem to have a role to play. The *expected value* for a person of a choice performed at a future is just the summation, for all the futures in which that person exists, of that person's well-being level at each such future multiplied by the probability that that future will unfold under that choice.[30] That concept in mind, we consider the following principle.

> *Expansive Very Narrow Person-Based Intuition + Expected Value (deontic)* (EVNPBI+EV *(deontic)*).
> A choice c performed at x is wrong *only if* there is a person p and an alternate choice c′ at an alternate accessible future z such that
> (i)   p does or will exist in x *and*
> (ii) p has less well-being in x than in z *and*
> (iii) EV of c performed at x for p is less than EV of c′ performed at z for p.

EVNPBI+EV explicitly takes probabilities into account—and thus substitutes, for the arguably ambiguous "better for," the term "well-being," which we understand to reflect how a person fares in a given future and not the chances that that person will fare in that particular way at that future or any other. Applied to the Better Chance Case itself, EVNPBI+EV works well. Since the expected value for Harry of c1 (wherever performed) is *greater* than the expected value for Harry of c2 (wherever performed), the new condition (iii) on c1 being wrong is failed and the principle instructs that c1 is, accordingly, permissible.

It should be noted that the role that EVNPBI+EV assigns to the concept of expected value is very narrow. Thus in keeping with the idea that PBI itself should be constructed very narrowly, EVNPBI+EV *doesn't* imply that c2 is *wrong, notwithstanding* the fact that c2 produces *less expected value* for Harry than c1. Thus, the principle, retaining (while disambiguating) the original condition (ii). Since Harry's wellbeing is maximized in f3 under c2, we infer that c2 in f3 is, just like c1 in f1, perfectly permissible.

What of c1 at f2 and c2 at f4? They too are permissible in virtue of the fact that EVNPBI+EV retains the original condition (i)—that is, the existence condition. Since Harry never exists at all in f2 or in f4, c1 at f2 and c2 at f4 are both permissible.

We thus see clearly how it can be that the better chance of existence can make the choice c1 at f1—a choice that would otherwise look to be wrong—perfectly permissible while the bare fact of the worth-having existence at f1, or even the maximized existence at f3, doesn't make c1 at f2, or c2 at f4, wrong.

Moreover, EVNPBI+EV (deontic) is perfectly consistent with the original telic component of EVNPBI. Again substituting, for the arguably ambiguous "better for," the term "well-being"—and thus making it clear that the comparison of futures in respect of their overall betterness leaves probabilities *out* of the picture, we can assert:

> *Expansive Very Narrow Person-Based Intuition (telic) (EVNPBI (telic))*. Where x and y are possible futures and y is accessible relative to x, x is morally worse than y *only if* there is a person p and an alternate accessible future z such that
> (i) p does or will exist in x *and*
> (ii) p has less wellbeing in x than in z (where z may, but need not, be identical to y).

From that principle in combination with still others (including Same-People Pareto), we can now infer that f2 and f4 are exactly as good as f3 and that f1 is worse than all three.

Should that latter implication disturb us? I don't think so, given that we've already identified c1 at f1 as morally permissible. It would not be impossible to construct a principle that ranks futures taking into account the probabilities that are themselves embedded in the details of those futures. But it is very unclear that, where two futures assign the same wellbeing levels to exactly the same populations, the fact that one future makes that assignment more probable and the other future makes it less probable doesn't, on its own, clearly bear on whether the one future is morally better or worse than the other.

Thus we have a complete picture, one that explains how the better chance of existence can convert a choice that would otherwise have been considered wrong into a perfectly permissible choice, while the bare fact of a worth-having existence, or even a maximized existence, doesn't, on its own, convert an otherwise permissible choice into an obligatory choice or make a future that includes that existence morally better than a future that doesn't.

Is it a picture that undermines our earlier account of Broome's case, the account that supports the idea that the worth-having existence can actually make things worse? Not at all; the account we gave earlier of Broome's case is perfectly consistent with both the telic and deontic versions of EVNPBI provided here.

6. Conclusions

We may remain suspicious of the expected value approach for reasons I shall not try to describe here—reasons grounded in the fact that any standard theory of expected value can generate results that seem clearly false (regardless of one's aversion to risk) in cases that include, among their alternate accessible futures, futures that make very low or very high assignments of wellbeing but that are themselves highly improbable.[31]

For that reason, EVNPBI+EV (deontic) comes with a caveat: there is more work to be done in exploring just how probabilities are to be taken into account within the scope of an otherwise satisfactory, person-based theory of wrongdoing. While it seems that the general outline we have provided is appropriate for resolving the Better Chance Puzzle, the *details* of how probability is itself to be put to work within that case and others are yet, in my view, to be fully settled.

A second point. Combining the forces of EVNPBI+EV (deontic) and EVNPBI (telic) requires some slight loosening of the Connection thesis noted in Section 2.3. Thus, we recognized, in connection with the Better Chance Case, that one future can be *worse* than another (f1 is, that is, worse than f3) even though the choice that is made in the one future (the choice to take the fertility pill) turns out to be perfectly *permissible*. At the same time, Connection will hold tight in cases—like Broome's case—in which probabilities are, for whatever reason, *not* at stake.

And a final point. An implication of EVNPBI+EV (deontic) is that our options cannot always be fully evaluated *prior* to choice. Thus, under that principle, we may not know until the end of the day whether a choice that *looks* to be wrong starting out *really is* wrong. A choice may, for example, *look* to create a very high probability of a future in which an existing or future person has less wellbeing but *in fact* eventuate in a future that is maximizing for p. In that case, that choice will (other things being equal) turn out to be permissible. Ditto if the future eventuates in such a way that the person never exists at all. It is not clear, however, that that is an objection against the person-based I have described here. It may instead simply reflect the way one particular variety of moral risk works.[32]

NOTES

1. For an excellent discussion of different ways in which the seemingly straightforward person-affecting intuition (PBI) can be constructed, as well as the question of whether making things worse must be a matter of making things worse for a *particular* person, see Holtug 2010.

   Misunderstandings of the goals of this chapter are sure to arise without two critical points. First, neither the initial description of PBI offered in this section, nor any of the more detailed formulations of PBI offered in later sections, presuppose or endorse a version of what is sometimes called *moral actualism*. While I will not here review why moral actualism fails (but see, among other discussions, Roberts (2007, 2009)), I will just note that, in my view, the idea that a person's *moral* status is tied to that person's *existential* status (relative either to the *actual* future or to *any other* possible future) clearly fails.

   And, second, the term *person* is to be construed broadly. For purposes here, the term includes many non-human animals (though personhood being signified, in my view, by consciousness, the term will exclude some humans).

2. In the law, *wrongful life* is a cause of action for medical malpractice. It includes the claim that causing the plaintiff to have the unfortunate existence the plaintiff in fact has is to

cause the plaintiff *harm*—to make the plaintiff *worse off*—even in the case in which the plaintiff's only option was never to exist at all.

3. Adapting McMahan's idea that the "goods" of a life can have a "canceling" effect on the "bads," we can say that the better *chance* of existence in effect may have, depending on the details of the case, a *canceling* effect vis-a-vis the loss of well-being. McMahan (2009).

4. In the type of Non-Identity Problem of interest here, claims regarding the relevant probabilities are central and the choices under scrutiny clearly wrong. It includes variations based on Parfit's depletion and risky policy cases (Parfit 1987, 351–379), Kavka's slave child and pleasure pill cases (Kavka 1981, 93–112), historical injustice cases, and environmental cases, including climate change (Broome 1992). Other types of Non-Identity Problems demand other treatments. See Roberts and Wasserman (2016); Roberts (2009, 2007).

5. The assumptions made here have been questioned by Temkin (2012). Temkin has proposed an entirely different methodology than the one put to work here—though one that aims at securing at least certain instantiations of the intuitions that I am interested in securing here.

6. Trichotomy is controversial. My view, however, is that the assumption that it holds is not problematic for the sorts of cases I consider here. For discussion, see Arrhenius (2016); Chang (2015); Rabinowicz (2009).

7. Feldman (1986).

8. Nonexistence Comparability is controversial. For a defense, see Nils Holtug's chapter in this volume. See also Persson (2017), 61; Holtug (2010), 129-150; Roberts (2003b, 2022a, n.d.). Moreover, some of the arguments questioning its cogency do not seem fully persuasive. Thus, Ralf Bader argues that we cannot cogently compare what is good for a person who exists in a certain future and whose well-being has been, for example, maximized against what is good for that person in a future in which that person never exists at all. Why not? Bader writes in the present volume: "It needs to be explained how the betterness relation can hold if one of the relata is missing. The personal betterness relation has lives as its relata. This means that we need two lives that are being compared in order for a personal betterness relation to hold. Yet, there is no life in the case of non-existence."

Bader's argument persuasively establishes that we should not take *lives* to be our relata when engaged in determining whether the one future is better for the person than another. But it is not clear that it establishes that the person who never exists doesn't have a *well-being level* in that future—that it's not cogent to say that that person's well-being level in that future is zero. To say that much, we seem to have the necessary relata: we have the person (in the future in which that person does or will exist), and we have numbers, including zero, which are widely held to exist in all possible worlds.

9. Broome (2015).

10. Feldman (1995), 195 (crediting Brentano); Feldman (2004), 195–197.

11. Indeed, Broome seems to allow for this way of proceeding. Thus, he notes that, if "the presence or absence of alternatives affects the value of a distribution, it can do so only by affecting some person's condition"—that is, what Broome's calls *personal good* and I am calling *contributive value*. "So its effect will show up in the vector of conditions" (Broome 2004, 147). We'll come back to this point in Section 4.1 below.

12. In contrast, where there is a cost to others, negative WB won't necessarily mean negative CV. The case in which the only alternatives are to bring one child into a negative well-being existence or another child into a negative well-being existence is such a case.

13. Feldman suggests such an inversion: "undeserved evils" do not simply "not make the world better"; they can also "make the world much worse" (1995, 195). For further discussion, see Roberts (n.d.).

14. It's understood here and throughout that the displayed futures exhaust the accessible futures and that no one's well-being or existence is at stake other than as explicitly noted in the figure.

15. To determine whether one future is better than another, the standard formulation of the total theory takes the summation of the wellbeing levels for all the people who do or will exist in each of those futures and compares those summations. But it will not just be the standard total view that the Two Kinds of Losses case challenges. Thus Persson's more nuanced view (*inclusive ethics*) and the standard total view deny any distinction between Anna's loss in f1 and Billy's loss in f2. Perhaps concerned about such cases, Persson offers that it is "in general more productive . . . to spend resources directly on benefiting those who are already in a state fit to be benefited than to first add to the stock of these individuals and then set about benefiting the expanded stock of existing individuals." Persson (2017), 101. But that speculative observation does not resolve, but merely side steps, the challenge.

16. Overly broad formulations of PBI are common. See, for example, the "person-affecting principle" from Matthew Adler (this volume) and the "narrow person-affecting principle" from Nils Holtug (this volume). See also Dasgupta (2018); Fleurbaey and Voorhoeve (2015); and many others. Only the *Very* Narrow PBI, in my view, is credible. See Roberts (2015).

17. Only such an expansive construction of PBI in my view, is credible. See Roberts (2015).

18. For discussion of other construction issues relating to the person-based intuition faces, see Roberts (2007; 2009).

19. See Roberts (2003b; 2015; n.d.).

20. See Parfit (1987), 381-390 and 419–441.

21. Others have done exactly that. For discussion, see Arrhenius (2016, 173–174, citing Ng, Blackorby, and Fehige); and Arrhenius, this volume. Cf. Parfit (1987, 429) (in the case where A+ in fact doesn't "change into B," and we set aside the task of evaluating the choice and focus exclusively on the task of comparing A against A+, the "relative goodness of these two outcomes cannot depend on whether a third outcome, that will never happen, [accessibly] might have happened").

22. Possible worlds, after all, have *all* their features necessarily. Thus, when Halstead writes "Z is Z, regardless of whether X is available," he says something that is both true and insensitive to the point that what we call "Z" when X is available and what we call "Z" when X isn't available may be two distinct things (Halstead 2016, 799). Now, Halstead doesn't say what X is, just qualifying it as an "option." If what Halstead has in mind is a simple distribution of well-being across a given population, then the reference of "Z" won't shift as the accessible set is expanded or contracted. My view, however, is that that information alone isn't always adequate to determine moral betterness: sometimes, as in Broome's case, we need to know *more* than how wellbeing is distributed across populations in order to compare one future against another. We need, specifically, to know more about what *further* futures are accessible.

23. I have elsewhere proposed an *Accessibility Axiom*:

   Accessibility Axiom: For any possible futures x and y, if y is accessible relative to x, then *necessarily* y is accessible relative to x.
   Roberts (2022a, n.d.).

24. Broome notes that in presenting his own case he is "not assuming anyone has or could have a choice" among the three alternatives; "these options may be available as choices, or they may not" (Broome 2004, 147). "[W]e must not assume [all three exist] as available alternatives. Nothing says they are" (147).

    In some cases, we may not know what the available alternatives—accessible futures—in fact are. In still other cases, however, we do have that information. Moreover, for purposes of testing, we can divide the cases and stipulate, as we have here, what the accessible futures are (whether, that is, we are in Broome's original three-option case or the revised two-option case).

25. Kavka explicitly attends to the relevant probabilities in articulating his own variations on the Non-Identity Problem (Kavka 1981, 100, n. 15). Other philosophers are more opaque on that point but the cases they describe often turn on probabilities that are, if unmentioned, clearly at stake. For discussion of one of Parfit's variations on the Non-Identity Problem that does *not* involve probabilities, see Persson (2017), 99-100. As noted earlier, the distinct types of Non-Identity Problems demand distinct treatments. See Roberts and Wasserman (2016); Roberts (2009, 2007).

26. But see Boonin (2014).

27. Even if f3 is accessible relative to f1, isn't f3 nonetheless highly improbable, given the parent's choice to take the aspirin in place of the pleasure pill? The answer to that question is yes—and how that fact complicates the discussion is a matter taken up in the next section. For now, it is enough just to note that *accessibility* is not a matter of *probability*. See section 2.4

    Of course, the author of any given variation on the Non-Identity Problem can simply stipulate that no such f3 is accessible relative to f1: that the laws of science dictate it could not accessibly happen that the parent takes the aspirin and Gina nonetheless exists. But that would be a very different sort of case and—to sort out what we would want to say about such a case—we, again, would need to know more. Does, for example, the pleasure pill induce effects in the gametes that, as a *biological necessity*, so changes their genetic structure as to *guaranty* that an entirely distinct person is conceived in place of the one? Interesting case—but not even close to the case at hand, where we are to imagine that a change in the timing and conditions of conception brings it about that one sperm does the inseminating rather than another.

28. Roberts (2007; 2009).

29. Other cases, cases that don't involve probabilities, make a similar point. In the Better Chance Case, it's the better chance of existence that makes up for the lesser existence. In the Tradeoff to Exist Case, it's the necessary tradeoff that makes up for the lesser existence.

30. I have suggested as much in prior work. See Roberts (2007, 2009). I now, however, consider that approach problematic. See Roberts (2022a, 2022b).

31. See Roberts (2022a and 2022b).

32. The final version of this paper owes an enormous debt of gratitude to the editors of this volume, Gustaf Arrhenius, Krister Bykvist, Tim Campbell, and Elizabeth Finneron-Burns, as well as to participants in conferences and workshops organized over the last several months under the auspices of the Institute for Futures Studies (Stockholm) for their comments on earlier versions of this paper and related presentations. Credit is especially owed to Tim Campbell for his many insightful comments that have served to test both the details and the overall framework of the approach proposed here.

REFERENCES

Arrhenius, Gustaf. 2016. "Population Ethics and Different-Number-Based Imprecision." *Theoria* 82: 166–181.

Boonin, David. 2014. *The Non-Identity Problem and the Ethics of Future People.* Oxford: Oxford University Press.

Broome, John. 1992. *Counting the Costs of Global Warming.* Cambridge: The White Horse Press.

Broome, John. 2004. *Weighing Lives.* Oxford: Oxford University Press.

Broome, John. 2015. "General and Personal Good: Harsanyi's Contribution to the Theory of Value." In *The Oxford Handbook of Value Theory*, edited by Iwao Hirose and Jonas Olson, 249–266. Oxford: Oxford University Press.

Chang, Ruth. 2015. "Value Incomparability and Incommensurability." In *The Oxford Handbook of Value Theory*, edited by Iwao Hirose and Jonas Olson, 204–224. Oxford: Oxford University Press.

Dasgupta, Shamik. 2018. "Essentialism and the Nonidentity Problem." *Philosophy and Phenomenological Research* 96 (3) 540–570.

Feldman, Fred. 1986. *Doing the Best We Can: An Essay in Informal Deontic Logic.* Dordrecht: D. Reidel.

Feldman, Fred. 1995. "Adjusting Utility for Justice: A Consequentialist Reply to the Objection from Justice." *Philosophy and Phenomenological Research* 55, no. 3: 567–585.

Feldman, Fred. 2004. *Pleasure and the Good Life.* Oxford: Clarendon Press.

Fleurbaey, Marc and Alex Voorhoeve. 2015. "On the Social and Personal Value of Existence." In *Weighing and Reasoning: Themes from the Philosophy of John Broome*, edited by Iwao Hirose and Andrew Reisner, 95–109. Oxford: Oxford University Press.

Halstead, John. 2016. "The Numbers Always Count." *Ethics* 126: 789–802.

Holtug, Nils. 2010. *Persons, Interests and Justice.* Oxford: Oxford University Press.

Kavka, Gregory. 1981. "The Paradox of Future Individuals." *Philosophy & Public Affairs* 11, no. 2: 93–112.

McMahan, Jeff. 2009. "Asymmetries in the Morality of Causing People to Exist." In *Harming Future Persons*, edited by M. A. Roberts and D. T. Wasserman, pp. 49–68. Dordrecht: Springer.

Parfit, Derek. 1984. *Reasons and Persons.* Oxford: Oxford University Press.

Persson, Ingmar 2017. *Inclusive Ethics:* Extending *Beneficence and Egalitarian Justice.* Oxford: Oxford University Press.

Rabinowicz, Wlodek. 2009. "Broome and the Intuition of Neutrality." *Philosophical Issues (Nous)* 19(1): 389–411.

Roberts, M. A. 2003a. "Can It Ever Have Been Better Never to Have Existed at All? Person-Based Consequentialism and a New Repugnant Conclusion." *Jo. of Applied Philosophy* 20(2): 159–85.

Roberts, M. A. 2003b. "Is the Person-Affecting Intuition Paradoxical?" *Theory and Decision* 55: 1–44.

Roberts, M. A. 2007. "The Nonidentity Fallacy: Harm, Probability and Another Look at Parfit's Depletion Example." *Utilitas* 19: 267–311.

Roberts, M. A. 2009. "The Nonidentity Problem and the Two Envelope Problem." In *Harming Future Persons*, edited by M. A. Roberts and D. T. Wasserman, 201–228. Dordrecht: Springer.

Roberts, M. A. 2011a. "The Asymmetry: A Solution." *Theoria* 77: 333–367.

Roberts, M. A. 2011b. "An Asymmetry in the Ethics of Procreation." *Philosophy Compass* 6, no. 11: 765–776.

Roberts, M. A. 2015. "Population Ethics." In *The Oxford Handbook of Value Theory*, edited by Iwao Hirose and Jonas Olson, 399–423. Oxford: Oxford University Press.

Roberts, M.A. and D.T. Wasserman. 2016. "Dividing and Conquering the Nonidentity Problem." In *Current Controversies in Bioethics*, edited by Matthew Liao and Collin O'Neil, 81–98. London: Routledge.

Roberts, M.A. 2022a. "The Value and Probabilities of Existence." Forthcoming in *Existence and Ethics: The Legacy of Derek Parfit*, edited by Jeff McMahan, Tim Campbell, James Goodrich and Ketan Ramakrishnan. Oxford: Oxford University Press.

Roberts, M.A. n.d. *The Existence Puzzles*. Unpublished manuscript.

Temkin, Larry. 2012. *Rethinking the Good: Moral Ideals and the Nature of Practical Reasoning*. Oxford: Oxford University Press.

CHAPTER 11

PERSON-AFFECTING UTILITARIANISM

RALF M. BADER

The mere notion of *amount* lets philosophers introduce a surrogate for the proper notion of utility—it gives them utilities which are not *someone's*, in the form of quanta of happiness which nobody has but which someone could have. As well as deploring the situation where a person lacks happiness, these philosophers also deplore the situation where some happiness lacks a person. (Bennett 1978, 63–64)

1. INTRODUCTION

TOTAL utilitarianism is meant to be one of the most straightforward moral theories. It assesses the goodness of states of affairs in terms of how much utility they contain. One state of affairs is judged to be better than another iff the former contains a greater amount of utility (= happiness) than the latter. The betterness ordering is strongly separable across persons such that the contribution that the utility of an individual (or a plurality of individuals) makes to the goodness of the state of affairs is independent of the utility of other people. This ensures that the betterness ordering has an additive representation, such that goodness can be aggregated additively. The overall value of a distribution is the sum of the values of the members of the distribution.

$$V(D) \geq V(D') \text{ iff } \sum_{x \in D} V(x) \geq \sum_{x \in D'} V(x)$$

The consequentialist connection between goodness and rightness (which consists in an optimizing function), then ensures that an action is right iff it brings about at least as much utility (or, in the context of uncertainty, expected utility) as all other available alternatives, whereby action ϕ is at least as good as ψ iff the state of affairs that ϕ-ing brings about is as at least as good as that which results from ψ-ing, that is, $D_\phi \geq D_\psi$.

$$C(X) = \left\{ \phi : \phi \in X \wedge \forall \psi \in X (\phi \geq \psi) \right\}$$

Total utilitarianism has a very simple value function, namely $V(D) = \Sigma_{x \in D} V(x)$. This function, however, is in an important sense schematic and underspecified. The problem is that it does not specify what type of value is at issue. That the value of a distribution is the sum of the values of the members of the distribution only specifies the form of the value function, namely that it is an additive function. It does not specify the type of value to which the function applies. We need to be told what kind of value is aggregated. What is it that is being added? Is it the personal goodness of the well-being of different individuals, or is it the impersonal goodness of their well-being? Whether it is personal good or impersonal good determines whether one is dealing with person-affecting utilitarianism or with impersonal utilitarianism.

Total utilitarianism has been much criticized for being an impersonal theory. Most notably, it has been objected that it treats persons as mere containers of utility that are replaceable and do not matter in their own right. For this reason, it has frequently been contrasted with a person-affecting approach that is concerned not with impersonal aggregates but with how persons are affected. Once we distinguish impersonal from person-affecting construals of utilitarianism, we can see that these criticisms do not apply to total utilitarianism per se but only to impersonal versions.

The first part of this chapter argues that impersonal versions of utilitarianism are objectionably impersonal. The problem is that they do not take personal good seriously. They do not attribute ethical significance to personal good but instead (at best) only consider it to be ethically relevant. Although they satisfy a weak (information-theoretic) form of welfarism, impersonal versions do not satisfy a stronger form of welfarism according to which what is good for persons is of ethical significance. This means that they are not operating with the "proper notion of utility," but with a spurious surrogate that leads us to "deplore the situation where some happiness lacks a person." As a result, they end up sub-ordinating and sacrificing personal good for the sake of impersonal good and thereby treat persons as mere containers of impersonal good, which gives rise to troubling implications in the case of variable-population comparisons.

By contrast, person-affecting versions are not objectionable in this way. They operate with the proper notion of utility and assign intrinsic ethical significance to personal good. Instead of being concerned with impersonal aggregates, they are concerned with how persons are affected. The second part evaluates the prospects for person-affecting versions of utilitarianism. It argues that person-affecting total utilitarianism presupposes comparativism, that is, that existence and non-existence are comparable in terms of personal good, and as such involves problematic metaphysical commitments.

Accordingly, same-number person-affecting utilitarianism turns out to be the only version of utilitarianism that neither involves an objectionable axiology nor requires problematic metaphysical commitments.

2. IMPERSONAL UTILITARIANISM

Impersonal utilitarianism is concerned with the impersonal value of the well-being of the various members of the distribution.

$$V_{impersonal}(D) = \sum_{x \in D} V_{impersonal}(x)$$

This approach comes in two forms, depending on whether only impersonal good is countenanced (monistic theories) or whether personal good is also included in the axiology (hybrid theories).

2.1. Monistic theories

The simplest (and most objectionable) version of impersonal utilitarianism is committed to a monistic theory of the good. Defenders of this approach take impersonal good to be basic and try to account for everything else in terms of it. Instead of recognizing an independent notion of personal good, they merely countenance empirical (non-evaluative) claims about happiness. They accept the claim that one life is a happier life than another life and that the former contributes more to the goodness of the world than the latter. However, they reject the claim that the former is better for the person living that life than the latter.

Monistic views either reject the notion of personal good altogether, or they try to construct a substitute for this notion out of facts about impersonal good. For instance, it has been suggested that personal good can be understood in terms of impersonal good that is located in a particular life. On such a view, personal good is derivative and is explained in terms of the location of impersonal good, that is, a state of affairs is good for a person x iff it is (i) impersonally good and (ii) located in x's life. In this way, personal good is nothing but an empirical relativization of impersonal good. Such a conciliatory approach, however, runs into difficulties in trying to construct a notion of personal good out of impersonal good. For instance, there does not seem to be any systematic way of cashing out the "occurring in a life" locution that is consonant with our intuitive judgments (cf. Rosati 2008, 332–345). Accordingly, it would be better for monistic theorists to opt for the strict Moorean line and reject the notion of personal good altogether and do without it.[1]

2.2. Utility containers

The monistic impersonal utilitarian wants there to be happiness. This, however, is not based in a concern for the persons who will experience the happiness in question. The state of affairs in which there is more happiness is not favored for their sake. After all, the monist does not recognize any notion of personal good. Consequently, he cannot want them to be happy on the grounds that being happy is good for them. Instead, he wants them to be happy because this is better from the point of view of the world, because this outcome contains more impersonal good.[2] The impersonal utilitarian is concerned only with how much impersonal good there is in a state of affairs, not with whether and how good that state of affairs is for persons. On this approach, persons are treated as mere containers of impersonal good that are dispensable and replaceable. This form of utilitarianism cares only about an abstract and impersonal form of goodness, not about persons and what is good for them, and consequently does not show adequate concern for persons.[3]

2.3. Hybrid Theories

Given the problematic nature of monistic impersonal utilitarianism, one might opt for a hybrid theory that supplements impersonal with personal good. Unlike monistic theories, which construe well-being entirely in non-evaluative terms (that is, as mere amounts of happiness), hybrid theories accept an evaluative construal of well-being. In addition to recognizing impersonal good, they also recognize an independent notion of personal good that is not reduced to or analyzed in terms of impersonal good. This makes them dualistic theories that countenance two independent and non-derivative types of good. Both personal good and impersonal good are accepted as basic goods—neither of them is constructed out of or reducible to the other. (We will first consider hybrid theories that identify impersonal good with moral good and take personal good to be a form of prudential good. In Section 2.6 we will consider hybrid versions that treat both of them as forms of moral good.)

Hybrid theories allow for two different formulations of the total principle. In terms of impersonal good the hybrid theorist agrees with the monistic impersonal theorist:

$$V_{impersonal}(D) = \sum_{x \in D} V_{impersonal}(x)$$

In addition, the hybrid theorist can formulate the total principle in terms of personal good:

$$V_{impersonal}(D) = \sum_{x \in D} f\left(V_{personal}(x)\right)$$

To connect the impersonal goodness of distributions to the personal good of the members of the distributions, one needs a conversion function f that connects these types of good. Since different types of good involve different units, we cannot end up with an impersonal evaluation by aggregating personal good. In order to arrive at an impersonal evaluation, one first needs to convert personal good into impersonal good. What aggregation does is to get us from restricted or local evaluations to a (relatively) unrestricted or global evaluation, that is, it gets us from evaluations of the components taken separately to an evaluation of them taken together. However, it cannot get us from one type of good to another. That is what conversion functions do. The function f converts personal into impersonal good, that is,

$$V_{impersonal}(x) = f\left(V_{personal}(x)\right)$$

The sum of the impersonal goodness of the well-being of the members of the distribution is thus equivalent to the sum of the converted personal goodness of their well-being. Hybrid theories, in this way, bring out especially clearly the need to be sensitive to units of goodness, as well as the need for conversion functions that specify how units of one type of good can be converted into units of a different type of good.[4]

It is the conversion function that differentiates prioritarianism from hybrid utilitarianism.[5] These theories accept the same value function at the level of impersonal good. However, they disagree about the conversion function between personal and impersonal good. As long as one focuses on the level of impersonal good, utilitarianism and prioritarianism will be indistinguishable. The difference between them only becomes apparent when one also considers personal good, in particular when examining the conversion function connecting these two types of good. Whereas the hybrid utilitarian considers this to be a linear function, the prioritarian deems the function to be strictly concave, such that personal good has diminishing marginal impersonal goodness.[6]

Both prioritarianism and hybrid versions of utilitarianism are dualistic axiologies that are committed to both personal and impersonal good. In each case, the different types of good are connected by a conversion function that specifies the ratios between the different units (without either being reducible to the other). Both theories agree that there are two distinct types of good that stand in a functional relationship, which means that both need to distinguish between how good something is for the person and how much it contributes to impersonal good. The difference between prioritarianism and utilitarianism is simply a matter of what exactly this function is. For the utilitarian they are linearly related. For the prioritarian, by contrast, they are not related by a linear but instead by a strictly concave function.

Critiques of prioritarianism that reject or problematize the distinction between how good something is for the person and how much it contributes to the (impersonal) goodness of the state of affairs (cf. Broome: 1991, McCarthy: 2006) thus turn out to be equally applicable to hybrid versions of utilitarianism.[7] Since hybrid views are dualistic theories, they also have to distinguish between how good something is for the person and how good it is in terms of impersonal good. Once these two separate types of good are recognized, one needs to distinguish evaluations corresponding to these two points of view. Hybrid utilitarianism and prioritarianism thus have analogous commitments.[8] It is only monistic versions of utilitarianism (whether impersonal or person-affecting) that do not need to draw such distinctions.

2.4. Relevance vs. Significance

The hybrid theory has the advantage over the monistic impersonal approach in that it does recognize personal good as an independent type of good. This, however, is not enough. Making room for a notion of personal good that is merely prudential in nature does not suffice for avoiding the deficiencies of the monistic impersonalist approach. Personal good, though not rejected altogether, is not construed in the right manner by this type of hybrid theory. In particular, it is considered to be merely ethically relevant but not ethically significant. Rather than mattering in its own right, it is merely connected via the conversion function to what is taken to matter, namely impersonal good. For hybrid views, the ethical significance of happiness does not consist in the fact that it is good for persons, but in the fact that it makes the world a better place. Happiness is valued because it is good from the viewpoint of the universe, not because it is good for the person and makes his or her life better. As a result, this approach does not show adequate concern for personal good but leads to an unacceptable subordination of personal good.

Intuitively, it seems that we have to take persons as well as personal good more seriously. Persons are not mere containers of impersonal good that matter only in that they are locations where impersonal good can be instantiated. Instead, they are beings that matter and that are ethically significant. We have reasons to help others because it makes their lives go well. Promoting their happiness is something that we have reason to do because their happiness is good for them, not because there being more happiness makes the world a better place. The fact that their lives go well is of direct ethical significance. (This is especially clear in the context of agent-relative theories.) This means that what is good for them is not just ethically relevant because it is connected via a conversion function to something that is ethically significant, insofar as a life that is good for the person is also a life that makes the world a better place. Rather, personal good itself matters and is morally good.[9]

Like the monistic approach, the hybrid theory cares only about impersonal good (when concerned with moral rather than prudential evaluations). Accordingly, it also wants there to be happiness for the wrong reasons. Whilst happiness is recognized to be something that is good for persons, it is not for this reason that the hybrid theorist wants there to be happiness. The utility containers objection thus applies equally to hybrid views. This can be brought out particularly clearly in variable-population cases, since personal and impersonal good can come apart in different-number cases. In such cases, personal and impersonal good diverge and the subordination of the former to the latter leads to personal good being sacrificed for the sake of impersonal good.

The addition of a happy person contributes to the impersonal goodness of the world and makes the world a better place. However, it is not in itself better for anyone. It does not by itself contribute to anyone's happiness and does not make anyone better off. It is for this reason that impersonal versions of utilitarianism lead to Repugnant Conclusions in variable-population cases. Total utilitarianism requires adding persons, as long as doing so has a positive net effect on impersonal good, even if existing persons are made miserable as a result. A world consisting of an extremely large number of lives that are barely worth living will be deemed to be better than one in which a large number of very happy lives are lived. All that matters is the total quantity of goodness independently of the number of containers amongst which it is distributed. As Parfit notes: "The greatest mass of milk might be found in a heap of bottles each containing only a single drop" (Parfit 1984, 388).

This recommendation to expand the distribution is based on neither a concern for existing persons, nor a concern for the non-existing persons to be added. It is neither better for those who exist independently (in fact, it can be considerably worse for them), nor better for those who will exist as a result of expanding the distribution (since existence is not comparable with non-existence for them). Instead, it is based on a concern for impersonal goodness. The hybrid utilitarian considers happiness to matter because it makes the world a better place, not because it is good for persons and makes their lives go better. In this manner, a concern for impersonal goodness becomes detached from a concern for persons and what is good for them. As a result, what should be done out of a concern for what is good for persons can radically diverge from what is required by a concern for impersonal good.[10]

One of the features that renders total utilitarianism susceptible to the Repugnant Conclusion is that it is not sensitive to numbers. All that matters is the aggregate quantity of utility, independently of the number of locations across which it is distributed. Alternative theories, such as critical-level utilitarianism, have been proposed to avoid this problem. These theories are impersonal yet are number-sensitive. Although it is possible to avoid the Repugnant Conclusion by suitably modifying the value function, this does not address the underlying problem with impersonal approaches. Though being number-sensitive, these theories do not care about persons and what is good for them. Instead of being concerned with personal good, they merely build number-sensitivity into the impersonal evaluation. As a result, they are still operating with utility containers. The milk bottle analogy still holds. All that they care about is the total quantity of milk—it simply happens that they try to reduce the number of containers amongst which a given total quantity of milk is distributed as much as possible, since the bottles leak a bit (where the amount of leakage per bottle corresponds to the critical-level parameter).[11]

The fact that a conversion function only ensures ethical relevance is particularly apparent in cases in which the connection between personal and impersonal good is not invariant. This happens for instance when dealing with average value functions. In such cases, personal good and impersonal good can come apart and it becomes clear which of the two types of good is of significance and which one does not matter in its own right but is relevant only as a result of being connected to something that has significance. The ethical significance of an additional life does not correspond to its level of personal good but is instead determined by the impact that it has on the average. A worthwhile life can make things (impersonally) worse if it brings down the average and a miserable life can make things (impersonally) better by improving the average. How good well-being is for the individual then comes apart from how much it matters morally. In these cases, the personal goodness of happiness is intrinsic and invariant. Its contribution to impersonal good, however, is extrinsic and derivative, since it is a function of the relation between the well-being of the individual and that of all the others. What is significant and what determines what is to be done according to such a value function is not whether the life is worth living but how the average is affected. It is the impersonal goodness of the distribution (which is determined by the average principle) that matters and that determines what is to be done, while personal good is merely relevant insofar as it is functionally related to impersonal good.

2.5. Welfarism

The distinction between relevance and significance allows us to distinguish two versions of welfarism. Although all versions of utilitarianism are welfarist theories, in that they are concerned with well-being, there are differences in terms of the significance that they assign to well-being.

Welfarism, understood along the lines proposed by Sen (1979), amounts to an "informational constraint." It requires that information about well-being suffices for evaluating and ordering states of affairs. (As such, it conflicts with impersonal theories that countenance non-person-involving good-makers, such as biodiversity.) Satisfying this informational constraint by insisting that the betterness ordering is purely based on welfarist facts does not adequately address the concerns that have been raised. That well-being plays a role in the theory does not ensure that it enters in the right way. One can be concerned about well-being without caring about persons and what is good for them. In particular, theories that "deplore the situation where some happiness lacks a person" take well-being into consideration but radically misconstrue its significance.

This should be readily apparent, given that the informational constraint can be satisfied by an impersonal monist who rejects the notion of personal good altogether but considers impersonal good to be a function of empirical (non-evaluative) facts about well-being. Even if welfare is understood evaluatively, such that it corresponds to personal good, the welfarist restriction is too weak. This is because it is compatible with a merely functional relation between personal good and what ultimately matters according to hybrid theories, namely impersonal good. Accordingly, it does not ensure that personal good is ethically significant and matters in its own right.

In order to ensure that personal good is not only ethically relevant but ethically significant, a more robust construal, such as the one put forward by Moore and Crisp (1996), is needed. It has to go beyond the information-theoretic characterization and has to build in ethical significance. According to this more demanding characterization of welfarism, impersonal versions of utilitarianism do not classify as welfarist. Theories that are welfarist in this more robust sense consider personal good to be a form of moral good. Personal good then matters in its own right, that is, ethical significance attaches to it and not only to something to which it is functionally connected.

2.6. Non-Subordination Hybrids

So far, we have considered a hybrid theory that accepts both personal and impersonal good as basic notions that are not reducible to each other, but then subordinates personal to impersonal good by construing the former as being merely prudential. This ensures that evaluations of moral goodness will be restricted to impersonal good and that personal good is only at issue in prudential evaluations.

Once it is recognized that personal good has to be ethically significant, the possibility of a non-subordination hybrid theory becomes salient. Such a theory assigns ethical significance to both impersonal and personal good.[12] Although this approach does not suffer from the problem of subordinating personal to impersonal good, it is nevertheless untenable. As a result, one should reject rather than supplement impersonal good.

To begin with, this approach does not generate a version of total utilitarianism. Rather than summing the impersonal value of well-being, both impersonal and personal value will contribute to the overall value of a state of affairs:

$$V(D) = g\left(V_{impersonal}(D), V_{personal}(D)\right)$$

The fact that two kinds of good are countenanced in this way is likely to lead to over-counting. If x's happiness is both good for x and good impersonally, and if both of these types of good are considered to have ethical significance and to give rise to (or at least be connected to) reasons for action, then there will be vast over-counting both in terms of axiological evaluations and in terms of assessments of reasons. While concerns about over-counting can generally be addressed by appealing to the notion of basic value, thereby ensuring that non-basic value is not counted in addition to the basic value from which it derives, this solution is not applicable in the case of hybrid models since both types of value will be basic.

The resulting over-counting gives rise to biases in cases in which personal and impersonal value come apart, that is, when something has impersonal value but no personal value. For instance, adding happy lives counts as an improvement from the point of view of impersonal good, but not from the point of view of personal good (given that one rejects comparativism, cf. Section 3.3). Accordingly, over-counting will privilege improving the life of an existing person by a certain amount over bringing into existence a new person with a level of well-being corresponding to that amount. If $D_0 = (2, \Omega)$ can be turned into $D_1 = (4, \Omega)$ or $D_2 = (2, 2)$, then the former turns out to be preferable since there is a +2 gain in terms of impersonal good as well as a +2 gain in terms of personal good, whereas in the latter case there is only the gain in terms of impersonal good. This ensures that these hybrid axiologies will be strongly biased against non-existent persons.[13]

Additionally, this approach runs into difficulties since one is dealing with two distinct types of values that will be incommensurable. Since there is no common unit of measurement, these values cannot be combined into an overall evaluation. One can only appeal to dominance principles applied over multidimensional value vectors that specify that a distribution D is better than another, D', if D is at least as good as D' with respect to each type of value and strictly better with respect to at least one type. Yet, there will not be any way to trade off the two values against each other and make sense of what is best on balance.

Moreover, since distributions of different sizes are not comparable in terms of personal good (due to the fact that existence is non-comparable with non-existence), dominance principles are not applicable in different-number cases. This is because dominance principles require weak betterness with respect to each dimension of the multi-dimensional value vector, which is not satisfied if the alternatives turn out to be non-comparable along one of the dimensions. Accordingly, the non-comparability with respect to personal good will render the overall evaluation incomplete. The resulting quasi-ordering induced by these dominance principles thus does not yield any determinate verdict when concerned with different-number comparisons.

The inadequacy of hybrid models shows that one cannot address the utility containers objection by supplementing an impersonal theory. Making room for personal good (when this is construed as being ethically significant) is not simply a matter of making a local adjustment to one's axiology. Instead, it requires a radical readjustment that involves switching from an impersonal theory to a person-affecting view that is entirely based on personal good.

3. PERSON-AFFECTING UTILITARIANISM

Person-affecting approaches reject impersonal good and instead only recognize personal good. The betterness ordering of distributions accordingly has to consist in betterness facts for the members of the distributions, which means that the evaluation of distributions has to be reducible to facts about personal good.[14] The total principle in this context requires summing up the personal goodness of the well-being of all the individuals:

$$V_{general}(D) = \sum_{x \in D} V_{personal}(x)$$

This approach can assign ethical significance to personal good and does not succumb to the objection of impersonalism.[15]

In order to end up with a person-affecting total view, one needs: (1) aggregation in order to underwrite same-persons comparisons, (2) impartiality to get same-number comparisons, and (3) comparativism to make sense of different-number comparisons.[16] Whilst (1) and (2) are fine, (3) is objectionable. As a result, person-affecting total utilitarianism is to be rejected. The only defensible version of person-affecting utilitarianism is same-number utilitarianism.[17]

3.1. Aggregation

Person-affecting utilitarianism requires one to aggregate the personal good of different persons. However, it is frequently claimed that it is not possible to make sense of trade-offs of personal good across different persons and that interpersonal aggregation presupposes a commitment to an impersonal point of view:

> when we judge that one person's claim outweighs the claim of someone else we are assuming an impersonal point of view. We are not just looking at things from one person's point of view and registering a loss, and then looking at things from another person's point of view and registering a gain. We make a comparison that includes both people and their points of view. We judge that it is more important to help the first person, and this judgement is not made from any individual's point of view. (McKerlie 1988, 222).[18]

The challenge is thus to make sense of aggregating and trading off personal good. To begin with, it should be noted that the notion of overall or aggregate goodness is not to be confused with impersonal goodness. This should be clear, given that one can aggregate the goodness to be found in different temporal locations from the point of view of personal good to arrive at an overall evaluation that is not restricted to particular times but considers the life as a whole. Likewise, one can aggregate probabilistically discounted personal good to be found in different states of natures to arrive at the expected personal goodness of a lottery. There is hence no problem in general when it comes to aggregating personal good.

What is difficult, though, is making sense of aggregation across different persons. Given that the gains and losses accrue to different persons, there is no person from whose point of view they can be evaluated. The balance of gains and losses is a relation amongst the different personal points of view but does not occur within any such point of view. As such, it seems to transcend the perspective of individuals, which would suggest that a person-affecting view can only make sense of what is better or worse for particular individuals and that trade-offs across persons would consequently be ruled out by a person-affecting approach.

There is, however, no need to invoke an impersonal point of view. One can instead bring in the notion of a plural point of view and argue that to speak of the value of a distribution or world is to speak plurally of the values of the members of the distribution. Facts about general good, in this view, just are plural facts about personal good, and the general betterness relation ends up being a plural comparative. General good is thus not a distinct kind of good. In this way, one stays at the level of personal good when aggregating across persons. One does not bring in impersonal good but simply moves from a singular to a plural evaluation, allowing one to balance gains and losses by comparing them from the point of view of a plurality of individuals (Bader n.d.-a).

3.2. Impartiality

Same-number comparisons that involve different persons require impartiality. This is unproblematic since a person-affecting view can be impartial. Impartiality is not to be confused with impersonality. Instead, it is to be identified with permutation-invariance. This means that permuting the identities of the members of the distribution, whilst holding fixed the structure or value profile of the distribution, does not affect the betterness ordering. Though impersonal goodness is impartial, it is not the case that impartiality requires impersonality.[19] While an impersonal assessment is one that tries to transcend the perspectival nature of evaluation, one that tries to assess a situation independently of how it affects anyone and thus independently of whether it is good or bad for anyone, no such perspective-transcendence is required to achieve an impartial assessment. An impartial perspective need not be impersonal, and the impartial point of view is not to be equated with the impersonal point of view.

Instead, it can be construed as the permutation-invariant point of view. One does not have to adopt a view from nowhere in order to achieve impartiality. Rather than adopting a view from nowhere, one needs to adopt the viewpoint of no one in particular. One needs to detach from one's own perspective by setting aside and abstracting from the particularities of the perspective that one occupies. An assessment that detaches from what is peculiar to particular perspectives will be invariant across perspectives, thereby making the resulting assessment permutation invariant. What holds in such an assessment is not something that transcends and holds independently of perspectival evaluations, but rather something that holds no matter which perspective is adopted.[20]

Since the impartial point of view is not the perspective-transcending impersonal point of view but the perspective-invariant point of view, a rejection of an impersonal betterness relation does not imply a rejection of an impartial betterness relation. An impartial betterness relation does not require a commitment to impersonality. This means that personal goodness can give rise to an impartial ordering that is permutation-invariant.[21]

3.3. Comparativism

Impersonal versions can straightforwardly make different-number comparisons. It can be impersonally better that a happy person exists than that the person does not exist, on the basis that this person's existence makes the world a better place. The situation in which the person does exist is comparable from the point of view of impersonal good with the situation in which the person does not exist.

Difficulties arise, however, when operating with a person-affecting theory. It is far from clear that the two situations are comparable from the point of view of personal good. Comparability only makes sense if one accepts the claim that it is better for a person to live a happy life than to not exist. Unless one accepts comparativism, a person-affecting approach will end up with a failure of completeness and will not be able to make different-number comparisons. In particular, if comparativism is rejected, one cannot compare different-number cases in terms of personal good, that is, $V(D_1)$ will not be comparable with $V(D_2)$ if $|D_1| \neq |D_2|$. This means that a total principle based on personal good presupposes the contentious assumption that comparativism holds for the personal betterness relation. Existence and non-existence have to be comparable from the point of view of personal good. Living a life has to be better/neutral/worse for the person in question than not having lived at all.[22]

Comparativism not only allows one to make different-number comparisons within a person-affecting theory. It also mitigates the objection that the total principle implies the Repugnant Conclusion. This is because comparativism considers coming into existence to be a benefit for a person with a life that is worth living. Since the benefits accruing to those that are brought into existence outweigh the costs of those already in existence, there is no net sacrifice of personal good in moving from a quality to a quantity distribution. Given that the quantity distribution involves a very large number of persons that are slightly benefited, this does not involve any repugnant sub-ordination or sacrifice of personal good.

Comparativism, however, faces serious metaphysical problems. First, it needs to be explained how the betterness relation can hold if one of the relata is missing. The personal betterness relation is a dyadic relation that has lives as its relata. This means that we need two lives that are being compared in order for a personal betterness relation to hold. Yet, there is no life in the case of non-existence. Second, the comparativist needs to provide a supervenience base upon which betterness facts can supervene. This is rather problematic given that a non-existent life does not instantiate any non-evaluative properties that could determine what evaluative properties this life has and how it is to be ordered with respect to various other lives. Comparativism is thus not viable since there cannot be a betterness relation without relata, nor can there be goodness without good-making features (cf. Bader n.d.-c).

If comparativism is rejected, a person-affecting approach precludes ordering distributions by means of the total principle. Instead, it only allows us to generate a quasi-ordering (to which one can apply a maximizing but not an optimizing function) that yields the same results as total utilitarianism in same-number cases but that cannot be extended to different-number cases:[23]

$$D_1 \geq D_2 \text{ iff } |D_1| = |D_2| \wedge \sum_{x \in D_1} V_p(x) \geq \sum_{x \in D_2} V_p(x)$$

3.4. Empty distributions

Total utilitarianism is acceptable within a person-affecting approach if one accepts comparativism. In fact, the total principle that a comparativist can underwrite might be stronger than the one that an impersonal theorist can defend. The (potential) difference between the two total principles comes out when considering empty distributions.

For the comparativist, the empty distribution in which no one exists is as good as a distribution in which there are persons all of whom are living neutral lives. The empty distribution can be assigned a value and is straightforwardly comparable to non-empty distributions. By contrast, the empty distribution might not have value at all for the impersonalist and hence might not be comparable with non-empty distributions.

Distributions in the impersonal approach are the analogs of lives in the person-affecting approach, which makes the empty distribution the analog of non-existence. In the same way that it is a substantive question whether existence is comparable with non-existence with respect to personal good, so it is a substantive question whether non-empty distributions are comparable with the empty distribution with respect to impersonal good. Adding a time-slice makes the life better without being better from the perspective of that time-slice. Likewise adding a person makes the distribution better without being better for that person. An empty life (that is, one without any time-slices) is not a life and hence, according to the non-comparativist, is not comparable with non-empty lives. One only has a life in one of the cases but not in the other and hence does not have the two relata that are connected by the personal betterness relation. Analogously, an empty distribution (that is, one without any members) is not a distribution and hence, according to the non-comparativist, is not comparable with non-empty distributions. One needs two (non-empty) distributions as relata of the impersonal betterness relation. This means that there is a substantive question as to whether we have comparability in terms of impersonal good. As a result, the impersonal approach might differ extensionally from the person-affecting total view when it comes to the empty distribution.

4. CONCLUSION

Total utilitarianism has deeply problematic axiological commitments. By adopting an impersonalist approach, one ends up with an objectionable theory that either eschews any independent notion of personal good altogether, or that recognizes personal good but is willing to sacrifice and sub-ordinate personal good for the sake of impersonal good. Such theories can at best assign ethical relevance but not ethical significance to personal good and thus operate with the spurious notion of "utility" that Bennett warned us about. They do not show adequate concern for personal good but consider persons as mere containers of impersonal good. This type of theory is committed to various repugnant conclusions and does not take seriously the idea that what matters is how well peoples' lives go.

Alternatively, a person-affecting version of total utilitarianism that is not subject to the charge of subordinating and sacrificing personal good requires a commitment to comparativism. Such a theory operates with the proper notion of "utility," but is nevertheless to be rejected, since the claim that existence is comparable with non-existence from the point of view of personal good runs into insurmountable metaphysical difficulties. Moreover, this type of theory can underwrite neither the neutrality intuition nor the asymmetry.

In order to avoid this predicament, one has to reject comparativism along with impersonalism and accept same-number person-affecting utilitarianism (considered as an axiological theory). This is an impartial theory that completely orders populations of the same size in terms of their total utility, but that renders populations of different sizes non-comparable. Such a theory neither has the problematic metaphysical commitments nor the objectionable ethical implications from which the various versions of total utilitarianism suffer.

ACKNOWLEDGMENTS

For helpful comments, I would like to thank Roger Crisp, Teru Thomas, and especially Tim Campbell. I am also grateful to the participants of the Oxford Population Ethics work in progress seminar as well as audiences at Umeå Universitet and the International Society for Utilitarian Studies conference at Yokohama. Funding from Riksbankens Jubileumsfond (grant M17-0372:1) is gratefully acknowledged.

NOTES

1. As Regan notes: "Moore has no theory of these concepts. He has no use for them. And in the end I agree with Moore about this too" (Regan: 2004, 211, fn 21).
2. If there could be disembodied states of happiness, then this would be just as good according to the impersonal utilitarian.
3. The objection that impersonal utilitarianism does not take personal good seriously needs to be distinguished from two other objections. First, utilitarianism is not sensitive to deontic boundaries between persons and hence does not respect the separateness of persons. Since we are only focusing on axiological issues, we will set aside these troublesome

deontic commitments. Second, total utilitarianism is concerned only with the total quantity of utility and is, accordingly, not sensitive to how utility is distributed. As long as the total quantity is the same, it is indifferent between the different ways of distributing this quantity. We will set aside this pattern-insensitivity since it can be addressed within an impersonal framework by means of suitable weighting functions as well as non-separable value functions.

4. Once two types of good are recognized as being basic, the question arises how they determine what the agent ought to do. There will then be two different types of goodness with respect to which alternatives can be evaluated, which raises the question how they can be integrated into an overall evaluation. Problems arise when there are clashes between morality and prudence, since the agent will then be subject to conflicting and irreconcilable demands. When evaluations in terms of personal good and impersonal good diverge, there will not be a univocal ordering but conflicting orderings corresponding to the different types of good. Accordingly, one will have to overcome the Sidgwickian dualism of practical reason. The fact that these different types of good are independent and basic, however, implies that there cannot be a further standpoint that subsumes them both and with respect to which conflicts can be adjudicated. Consequently, they cannot be weighed up against each other. (Here it is important to note that the conversion function is not an ethical trade-off ratio, that is, it does not tell us how to weigh up the different types of good, but instead merely represents a descriptive functional relationship between them.) Nor can they stand in a lexical priority relation or be ordered in some other way. As a result, they give rise to incommensurable requirements that cannot be integrated into a coherent ordering (cf. Bader 2015).

5. Critical-level utilitarianism (cf. Blackorby, Bossert, and Donaldson 1997; Broome 2004) and classical versions of hybrid utilitarianism are, likewise, differentiated in terms of their conversion functions. The latter but not the former function aligns the neutral level of personal good with the neutral level of impersonal good.

6. The conversion function plays a crucial role even when dealing with a 1:1 ratio, since the inputs and outputs of the function involve different units. In the same way that a 1:1 conversion ratio between two currencies does not imply that one can use the one currency in the other country, so a 1:1 ratio between units of goodness does not mean that one is dealing with types of good that can be treated as being interchangeable.

7. These objections do not apply to "empirical" versions of prioritarianism that do not consider personal good but instead empirical amounts of happiness to have diminishing marginal impersonal value. Likewise for deontic versions that consider the conversion function between values and reasons to be strictly concave.

8. At most, they differ in terms of their respective information requirements. Whereas utilitarianism requires a cardinal scale in fixed-population settings and a ratio scale in variable-population contexts, prioritarianism needs a ratio scale in fixed-population comparisons and a unit scale in variable-population contexts. Yet even this difference disappears when applying the transformations under which the representation is meant to be invariant to both the individual utilities and the prioritarian weighting function (cf. Rabinowicz 2002, 9 fn 7).

9. The situation is thus somewhat analogous to someone who recognizes aesthetic value alongside monetary value (and who considers the two to be connected insofar as things that are more beautiful have greater monetary worth) but then appreciates a beautiful painting not because of its aesthetic merits but because of its monetary value.

It is sometimes suggested that happiness is to be considered to be impersonally good because it is good for the person and that this renders the container objection ineffective. (This proposal cannot be adopted by critical-level theorists who allow that something that is good for the person, namely a worthwhile life that is below the critical level, is impersonally bad.) There are two ways of reading this suggestion, both of which are problematic. On the one hand, we should reject the idea that being good for someone is just a way of being good, so that whatever is "good for" is also "good simpliciter." Whereas this kind of entailment holds in the case of the conciliatory monistic view that treats "good for" as an empirical relativization, it does not apply in the case of hybrid theories that consider personal good and impersonal good to be two distinct types of good. On the other hand, the idea of grounding impersonal goodness in personal goodness runs into difficulties. First, if one considers good-making features to be properties of the value-bearer, and if one considers the state of affairs [x's being happy] to be good for x, then this proposal would imply that the good-maker of impersonal goodness will involve the property of being good for x, which means that [x's being happy] will not be the bearer of impersonal good but instead the state of affairs [x's being happy being good for x]. We do not end up with one state of affairs that has two types of values, but instead with different states of affairs having different values. Whereas "being happy" will be the good-maker of personal goodness, "being good for" will be the good-maker of impersonal goodness. Second, variable-population cases show that one situation can be impersonally better than another without being better for anyone, which implies that personal and impersonal good come apart. Accordingly, there is no general principle to the effect that something's being impersonally good is always grounded in being good for someone. For this reason, the suggestion does nothing to address the objectionable implications of impersonal theories in variable-population settings. Third, the suggested grounding connection does not address the objection that being concerned with impersonal good is to be concerned with the wrong thing, since persons are the proper objects of concern.

10. The case of average utilitarianism provides a helpful illustration. Whether a person is to be added depends not on how well that person's life goes, but on how the average is affected. As a result, cases can arise where a concern for goodness requires adding miserable lives that have a positive effect on the average. Such a course of action clearly cannot be recommended out of a concern for the existing persons that are unaffected, nor out of a concern for the persons being added whose lives are not worth living, but only out of a concern for an impersonal ideal that is detached from what really matters.

11. Since the critical level penalty applies at the level of impersonal good it might be more accurate to think not in terms of leakage but in terms of being paid for the total quantity of milk where one has to pay a fixed amount for each bottle.

12. Whilst personal good is frequently identified with non-moral or merely prudential good, it is worth noting that this identification is theory-driven.

13. If there were uniform over-counting that applied to all value-bearers, then the value function could be normalized so that no practical problems would result. Instead, only theoretical and intuitive concerns would be applicable.

14. This reducibility constraint is significantly stronger than the "person-affecting restriction," which only imposes a necessary condition on the betterness ordering of distributions, namely that in order for one distribution to be better than another it must be better for someone, and which is not sufficient for ruling out impersonal hybrid theories.

15. On this approach, prudential and moral evaluations do not differ in kind but in scope. Prudential evaluations are restricted to the agent in question, whereas moral evaluations are unrestricted.

16. More precisely, same-persons comparisons already involve a weak form of impartiality that requires the betterness relation to be invariant under permutations of the actual members of the domains (that is, it does not matter who in the distribution is assigned which value). Same-number comparisons, by contrast, require a strong form of impartiality, according to which the betterness relation has to be invariant under permutations of possible members of the domains (that is, it does not even matter who is in the distribution).

   Weak impartiality: $D_1 \geq D_2$ iff any permutation of $D_2 \geq$ any permutation of D_2.
   Strong impartiality: $D_1 \geq D_2$ iff the restriction to D_1 of any permutation of the universal domain $\geq$ the restriction to D_2 of any permutation of the universal domain.

17. Parfit has put forward a wide total person-affecting principle as well as wide average person-affecting principle (cf. Parfit 1984, 396–401). Moving away from a narrow to a wide principle that allows for impartiality is a relatively straightforward step that is crucial for developing a satisfactory person-affecting approach. However, the question of aggregation is an altogether different matter that does not readily admit of an extension to different-number cases. As we will see, one can only make sense of a total principle if one accepts comparativism. By contrast, an average principle is incompatible with a person-affecting approach since it violates the reducibility constraint.

18. Also cf. Regan (2004, 213, fn 25) and Arneson (2010, 735, fn 2).

19. The fact that impersonal implies impartial has the consequence that one can only make sense of agent-relativity (= partiality) within the context of personal good (cf. Bader n.d.-b).

20. The distinction between understanding impartiality in terms of perspective-invariance and in terms of perspective-independence is analogous to that between understanding objectivity in terms of invariance across observers and in terms of observer-independence (cf. Eddington 1920, 31, 82). The distinction between the invariant and the independent also plays an important role in Fine's distinction between a proposition's being true whatever the circumstances and being true regardless of the circumstances (cf. Fine 2005, 9).

21. Heyd holds that a commitment to impersonalism follows from "allowing comparisons between the welfare of two different potential beings, which is logically exactly the same as comparing the existence of a potential being with its non-existence" (Heyd 1988, 161; see also Heyd 1992, 105). This claim confuses impersonalism and impartiality. All that is required for ordering different lives is that the betterness relation be impartial. Since impartiality can be separated from impersonalism, no commitment to the latter view follows.

22. In particular, what is required is an unrestricted form of comparativism. For instance, it is not sufficient to adopt the version defended by Arrhenius and Rabinowicz (2015), which involves a failure of the accessibility principle that if D_1 is better for x than D_2, then D_1 would be better for x than D_2 if D_1 obtained.

   It might be objected that comparativism is unnecessary since it is enough that existence is good for the person. On this view one should bring a happy life into existence, not because living the happy life is better for x than non-existence, but because living the happy life is good for x and because the person is (non-comparatively) benefitted by being brought into existence (cf. Bykvist 2015). However, although a happy life has value and is good for the person living this life, this goodness is of no relevance relative to things that lack goodness, such as non-existence. Goodness operates by making things better, by providing more reasons than the alternative. In order for the goodness of option ϕ to favor ϕ over alternative ψ, the goodness of ψ must also be defined. There is only a stronger reason if there is more goodness, and this requires comparability of the options. Accordingly, in order to favor choosing one rather than the other, it must be the case that the one is better than the other. Being good is not enough. What is needed is betterness. Goodness and betterness are thus inseparable when it comes to favoring actions. In short, goodness only operates within the field of betterness.

23. This kind of theory might be thought to be unsatisfactory owing to its commitment to non-comparability. Cf. (Bader n.d.-d) for arguments to the effect that a satisfactory population ethics can (and indeed must) recognize the non-comparability of different-number cases.

REFERENCES

Arneson, Richard. 2010. "Good, Period." *Analysis* 70, no. 4: 731–744.

Arrhenius, Gustaf, and Wlodek Rabinowicz. 2015. "The Value of Existence." In *The Oxford Handbook of Value Theory*, edited by I. Hirose and J. Olson, 424–443. Oxford: Oxford University Press.

Bader, Ralf M. 2015. "Kantian Axiology and the Dualism of Practical Reason." In *The Oxford Handbook of Value Theory*, edited by Iwao Hirose and Jonas Olson, 175–201. Oxford: Oxford University Press.

Bader, Ralf M. n.d.-a. "Aggregating, Balancing, and the Separateness of Persons."

Bader, Ralf M. n.d.-b. "Personal, General, and Impersonal Good."

Bader, Ralf M. n.d.-c. "The Neutrality of Existence."

Bader, Ralf M. n.d.-d. "Person-affecting Population Ethics."

Bennett, Jonathan. 1978. "On Maximizing Happiness." In *Obligations to Future Generations*, edited by R. I. Sikora and Brian Barry, 61–73. Philadelphia: Temple University Press.

Blackorby, Charles, Walter Bossert, and David Donaldson. 1997. "Critical-Level Utilitarianism and the Population Ethics Dilemma." *Economics and Philosophy* 13: 197–230.

Broome, John. 1991. *Weighing Goods*. Oxford: Blackwell Publishers.

Broome, John. 2004. *Weighing Lives*. Oxford: Oxford University Press.

Bykvist, Krister. 2015. "Being and Wellbeing." In *Weighing and Reasoning: Themes from the Philosophy of John Broome*, edited by Iwao Hirose and Andrew Evan Reisner, 87–94. Oxford: Oxford University Press.

Eddington, Arthur. 1920. *Space, Time and Gravitation: An Outline of the General Relativity Theory*. Cambridge: Cambridge University Press.

Fine, Kit. 2005. *Modality and Tense: Philosophical Papers*. Oxford: Oxford University Press.

Heyd, David. 1998. "Procreation and Value: Can Ethics Deal with Futurity Problems?" *Philosophia* 18: 151–170.

Heyd, David. 1992. *Genethics: Moral Issues in the Creation of People*. Los Angeles and Berkeley: University of California Press.

McCarthy, David. 2006. "Utilitarianism and Prioritarianism I." *Economics and Philosophy* 22: 1–29.

McKerlie, Dennis. 1988. "Egalitarianism and the Separateness of Persons." *Canadian Journal of Philosophy* 18, no. 2: 205–226.

Moore, Andrew. and Roger. Crisp. 1996. "Welfarism in Moral Theory." *Australasian Journal of Philosophy* 74, no. 4: 598–613.

Parfit, Derek. 1984. *Reasons and Persons*. Oxford: Oxford University Press.

Rabinowicz, Wlodek. 2002. "Prioritarianism for Prospects." *Utilitas* 14, no. 1: 2–21.

Regan, Donald. 2004. "Why Am I my Brother's Keeper?" In *Reason and Value: Themes from the Moral Philosophy of Joseph Raz*," edited by R. Jay Wallace, Philip Pettit, Samuel Scheffler, and Michael Smith, 202–230. Oxford: Oxford University Press.

Rosati, Connie. 2008. "Objectivism and Relational Good." *Social Philosophy & Policy* 25: 314–349.

Sen, Amartya. 1979. "Utilitarianism and Welfarism." *The Journal of Philosophy* 76, no. 9: 463–489.

CHAPTER 12

......

SEPARABILITY AND POPULATION ETHICS

......

TERUJI THOMAS

1. INTRODUCTION

......

BELINDA wonders whether it would be morally permissible to have a child. She considers many factors: her own feelings and desires; whether the child is likely to have a good life; whether the child will have a positive or negative impact on other people who now exist, or who might exist in the future. But one thing she need not investigate is how well off the ancient Egyptians were. It would be one thing if Belinda's decision now could *change* their welfare, by enacting some kind of posthumous benefit or harm. But suppose this is not the case: the welfare of the ancient Egyptians will be unaffected, and Belinda knows it. Then their welfare is simply irrelevant to Belinda's choice. She thinks so, anyway.[1]

The principle I will call *separability* (or, more specifically, *Population Separability*), generalizes this thought. It holds, a bit roughly, that if some people's welfare is unaffected by a choice, then it is irrelevant what their welfare actually is. One aim of this chapter is to examine what can be said in favor of this principle. The second aim is to explain the consequences of separability when combined with a few other principles, especially in light of the Repugnant Conclusion.

But why care about separability? There are several reasons.

The first is that separability is simple, plausible, and yet powerful. As I will explain, there is a train of thought that leads from separability to a version of total utilitarianism, and though one can get off the train at various places along the way, it is not obvious where one *should* get off. This argument for total utilitarianism is one of the best positive arguments in population ethics.

Whether or not the argument just mentioned is sound, it is certainly methodologically useful. If we are to avoid total utilitarianism, we must reject some of the premises.

Which ones, and what alternatives can we offer? Can we adequately explain the case of Belinda if we deny separability? In this paper, I am mainly going to stick with separability, and explore what options we have then. Quite a few chapters in this volume discuss views compatible with separability. Nils Holtug and Matthew Adler discuss prioritarianism; Walter Bossert discusses critical level utilitarianism; Erik Carlson discusses non-Archimedean theories; Ralf Bader and Wlodek Rabinowicz discuss theories that (in quite different ways) deny the principle that one of two options must be at least as good as the other. It turns out that all of these theories correspond to denying specific premises in the argument for total utilitarianism.

This story about total utilitarianism is closely related to the project of Broome (1991; 2004), and even more directly to that of Blackorby, Bossert, and Donaldson (2005). While referring to relevant parts of these excellent books, I've chosen an approach that differs from and complements theirs in important ways. In particular, they take on certain "completeness" and "continuity" assumptions early on, which gives them easy access to methods pioneered by Debreu (1959; 1960), Gorman (1968), Harsanyi (1955), and others. Part of what I am explaining is that we can do pretty well without those assumptions.[2] This is not of merely technical interest, because denying these assumptions leads precisely to some of the variations on total utilitarianism I mentioned above.

Finally, there are some general reasons to be interested in separability, within and beyond population ethics. Principles of the same type occur in many different settings. They are often implicit in the use of "ceteris paribus" comparisons; more interestingly, they play a key role in measurement theory, the mathematics of numerical representation.[3] Total utilitarians—and many others—assume that lifetime welfare can be quantified at least in the sense that it can be added up. So, too, we sometimes think of adding up welfare at different times, or—to escape momentarily from the normative—adding up lengths or weights. This kind of structure emerges from separability principles. This chapter provides a gateway to the study of these very general issues.

Here is an outline of the chapter. In Section 2, I explain the general notion of separability. In Section 3, I specialize to population ethics, giving examples of theories that satisfy separability, and others that don't. In Section 4, I give two arguments for separability (one of them new), and also explain some ways these arguments could be resisted. In Section 5, I explain the main mathematical result, that separability (along with some relatively uncontroversial assumptions) implies that the value of a population can be represented in "total utility" form (construed in a way that is compatible with both utilitarianism and prioritarianism). In Section 6, I explore how the resulting views generalize total utilitarianism, and, in particular, the possibilities that they leave open for avoiding the Repugnant Conclusion. An important theme here is the usefulness of simple formal models to generate examples. Section 7 sums up.

2. SEPARABILITY IN GENERAL

2.1. The Definition

Let me begin by explaining the general notion of separability, since it is important even beyond population ethics. The general setting is one in which some objects being evaluated can vary in two respects. Separability means that, given only that two objects are alike in the first respect, their relative value depends only on what each of them is like in the second respect. Other names for separability and its close cousins are "independence" and "monotonicity."

At this point it is important to distinguish the "ordinal" from the "cardinal" conception of value. On the ordinal conception, the value facts consist in a ranking of evaluands. Thus the "relative value" of two objects x and y is just a matter of whether x is better than y, worse than y, exactly as good as y, or none of the above.[4] In contrast, on a cardinal conception, there are also facts about *how much* better x is than y; their relative value includes an answer to this "how much" question. The standard notion of separability involves only ordinal facts, and that will be my main focus in this chapter. However, the cardinal conception of value will make some important cameos.

Although my initial characterization of separability will suffice for many purposes, it will help to have a more formal definition as well. A claim of separability involves three sets X, A, and B; each x in X determines an element $a(x)$ of A and an element $b(x)$ of B. I will sometimes refer to the elements of X as "the Xs," and so on. For the sake of illustration, suppose that meals are being evaluated, and each meal involves one food and one drink. Then the Xs could be meals, the As foods, and the Bs drinks. The Xs are the objects being evaluated, and it will follow from the principle below that the value of each x depends only on $a(x)$ and $b(x)$. Thus, the value of a meal depends only on the food and the drink, and not, say, on the cutlery. We can capture the ordinal facts about Xs using the relation "at least as good as." I will abbreviate this relation as $\succsim_X$, and assume it is a *preorder* – a reflexive, transitive binary relation.[5]

> *Separability:* The Bs are separable from the As (when it comes to evaluating the Xs) if and only if the following condition holds. Given x_1, y_1, x_2, y_2 in X, such that $a(x_1) = a(y_1), a(x_2) = a(y_2), b(x_1) = b(x_2)$, and $b(y_1) = b(y_2)$, we have $x_1 \succsim_X y_1$ if and only if $x_2 \succsim_X y_2$.

In contrast, a cardinal notion of separability would say at the end that x_1 is better than y_1 *to the same degree* that x_2 is better than y_2.

Example 1. Suppose we are evaluating meals, and each meal x consists of a food $a(x)$ and a drink $b(x)$. A burger and beer (x_1) is better than a burger and tea (y_1). If drinks were separable from foods, we could then conclude that cake and beer (x_2) is better than cake and tea (y_2). But obviously cake and tea is better than cake and beer, so separability fails.[6]

Example 2. Someone who really likes beer might think that meals with beer are invariably better than meals with tea. Nonetheless, he might admit that while burger and beer is *much* better than burger and tea, cake and beer is *only a little* better than cake and tea. Given only that two meals have the same food, he can tell which one is better by looking at the beverages—ordinal separability holds—but he cannot tell *how much* better—cardinal separability fails.

2.2. Ceteris Paribus Comparisons and Contributory Value

There is another, completely equivalent way of formulating Separability. The Bs are separable from the As if and only if there is a binary relation $\succsim_B$ on the Bs such that, if $a(x) = a(y)$, then $x \succsim_X y$ if and only if $b(x) \succsim_B b(y)$.

If—as is usually assumed in this context—there is some element of A that can occur in combination with every element of B, then separability completely determines the relation $\succsim_B$, and it is a preorder.[7] It is sometimes called the "conditional" preorder, and can be interpreted as the relation "at least as good, ceteris paribus." Indeed, a ceteris paribus comparison typically presupposes some form of separability: the comparison is claimed to be true given only *that* other factors are held fixed, independent of *how* they are fixed.[8]

It is also natural to say that the conditional preorder $\succsim_B$ reflects the value that the Bs *contribute* to the Xs. On the other hand, sometimes the Bs may have *intrinsic* value, value in themselves rather than as components of Xs. In that case there is a further question about whether their contributory value matches their intrinsic value: is it better, ceteris paribus, for an X to have component b_1 rather than b_2 if and only if b_1 is intrinsically better than b_2? It is at least tempting to say "yes," and to use separability and ceteris paribus comparisons as heuristics for determining what sorts of things have intrinsic value, and how much.[9] But at bottom separability is a formal condition on the evaluation of the Xs, while questions of intrinsic value are substantive questions about the Bs.

2.3. Organic Unities

It is sometimes said that separability rules out "pattern goods," "organic unities," "holistic value," or "interaction effects" between the As and the Bs. In Example 1 above, the value of each meal depends only on the food and the beverage, but even so it intuitively depends on the interaction of these two factors. A meal is an organic unity: it has value that does not just reside in its parts, taken separately. This intuitively explains why separability fails.

This is a useful way of thinking, and we can even take the failure of separability as a way of making precise what "holistic value" and so forth means. But it is worth bearing in mind the distinction between cardinal and ordinal value. In Example 2 the failure of cardinal separability suggests that meals have holistic value, even though ordinal separability holds.

3. Separability in Population Axiology

With this background, let me turn to population axiology. I should first set out my basic framework and terminology. I will assume that each possible world of interest contains only finitely many people, and assigns each of them a welfare level. I assume that welfare levels are preordered by what I will call "individual value"; worlds are preordered by their "overall value." As a matter of bookkeeping, I stipulate that people who do not exist in a world do not have welfare levels there, although everything I say will be compatible with the controversial idea that non-existence registers somewhere on the scale of individual value.

Each world determines a welfare distribution, by which I mean a set of people (those who exist in the given world) and a welfare level for each of them. So, when I say that two worlds have the same welfare distribution, I mean for one thing that they contain the same people. More generally, for any property F of people, each world determines a welfare distribution over the Fs, by which I mean, precisely, a set of people who are Fs and a welfare level for each of them.[10]

For the most part I will assume that the overall value of a world depends only on the welfare distribution. This is often called the principle of

> *Pareto Indifference*: If two worlds have the same welfare distribution, then they are equally good.

Most discussions of population axiology take Pareto Indifference for granted. It also follows from the principle of Population Separability I will state below. It is worth noting in advance how Pareto Indifference is related to the thought that separability denies the importance of patterns. Once we specify which people have which welfare levels, it doesn't matter which people exist at the same time or within the same society. Therefore, the pattern of welfare at a time or within a society does not matter. The only sort of pattern that can matter is the pattern of welfare across all people at all times.

3.1. Population Separability

Here is the specific separability principle which is my main concern:

> *Population Separability*: Let F be any property of people. Then, when it comes to evaluating worlds, the welfare distribution over the non-Fs is separable from the welfare distribution over the Fs.[11]

If Population Separability is true according to some theory of population axiology, then I will just say that the theory is separable. In the motivating example from Section 1, we could take the F to be the property of *being an ancient Egyptian*. The claim is then that, given only that worlds W_1 and W_2 agree about who the ancient Egyptians were and how well off they were, one can correctly rank these worlds based only on which *other* people exist and how well off they are in each one.

In the rest of this section I give some examples illustrating Population Separability.

3.2. Average Utilitarianism and Total Utilitarianism

Total utilitarianism, as I will understand it, presupposes that we can represent welfare levels by real numbers, or "utilities," in an appropriate way. The main claim is that one world is better than another if and only if its inhabitants have greater total utility. In contrast, average utilitarianism ranks worlds by average utility.

Total utilitarianism satisfies Population Separability. The total utility of a world is the total utility of the Fs plus the total utility of the non-Fs in that world. Given only that two worlds agree as to the welfare distribution over the Fs, then one is at least as good as the other if and only if it gives the non-Fs higher total utility.

But average utilitarianism does not satisfy Population Separability. Indeed, the motivating example of the ancient Egyptians I mentioned in Section 1 was originally used as an objection against average utilitarianism, and as such has often been considered damning. As Parfit put McMahan's point, "If the Ancient Egyptians had a very high quality of life, it is more likely to be bad to have a child now. It is more likely that this child's birth will lower the average quality of the lives that are ever lived. But research in Egyptology cannot be relevant to our decision whether to have children" (Parfit 1984, 420).

As another example, average utilitarianism agrees with intuition that any world of good lives (hence positive average utility) is better than any world of bad lives (hence negative average utility). But it holds that *adding* good lives sometimes make things worse than adding bad lives. (Arrhenius [2000] calls this the "Sadistic Conclusion.") The combination of the two judgments violates Population Separability. Of course, in this example it is really the second judgment which is objectionable, not the failure of separability per se.

3.3. Prioritarianism and Egalitarianism

Prioritarianism and egalitarianism both differ from utilitarianism in giving extra weight to the welfare of people who are badly off (and/or less weight to the welfare of those who are well off). However, according to prioritarianism, the extra weight depends on how badly off the person is in absolute terms, whereas according to egalitarianism, the extra weight depends on how badly off the person is relative to the other people who exist.[12]

As this suggests, egalitarianism but not prioritarianism gives relevance to the "pattern" of welfare levels within a world, or, to put it another way, posits interaction effects between the welfare of different people. This gives egalitarians distinctive reasons to deny Population Separability (Broome, 2015). However, they need not do so: it could be that patterns of inequality matter in a way that violates only the cardinal and not the standard ordinal version of Population Separability.[13]

Meanwhile, prioritarians can accept Population Separability. These "total prioritarians," like total utilitarians, effectively evaluate each world by adding up what we might call the utility contributed by each person. But this utility is different from the utilitarian's: it incorporates the extra weight that the prioritarian grants to the badly off.

When discussing egalitarianism, it is reasonable to ask, "Equality among whom?" Given Pareto Indifference, what matters must be equality among all people at all times, rather than equality among people at each time or within each society, or even within the same galaxy. Because of this, the point about ancient Egyptians seems to be just as damning to non-separable forms of egalitarianism as it was to average utilitarianism. However, since egalitarianism may be less objectionable than average utilitarianism in other ways (for example vis-à-vis the Sadistic Conclusion), I will consider it a live option.

3.4. The Value of Humanity

Here is an example due to Erik Carlson (1998, 290–291). Consider a world with two epochs, Past and Future. Consider two ways the second epoch could turn out. In Future 1, there are very many fairly good lives. In Future 2, there are relatively few lives, all very good. Suppose that what happens in Past is fixed. Would it be better for Future to turn out like Future 1 or Future 2? Carlson says that the answer to this question plausibly depends on what happened in Past. If *no one* lived in Past, then Future 1 would make things better overall than Future 2 would; but if there have already been lots of very good lives, then Future 2 would make things better overall than Future 1 would. This violates Population Separability.

There are a few different ways to reproduce Carlson's judgments. He himself seems to have in mind one of the "variable value" views (Hurka 1983; Ng 1989) that are similar to total utilitarianism for small populations and similar to average utilitarianism for large populations. Such views help if, on grounds of total utility alone, Future 1 would be better than Future 2. Given an empty past, and therefore a small population overall, this comparison of total utility could be decisive. On the other hand, if there were many people in the past, then the comparison of average utility would be more relevant. As long as the people in the past were at least as well off on average as those in Future 1, Future 2 will lead to higher average utility.

Unfortunately, since variable value views are similar to average utilitarianism when it comes to large populations, they have similar defects. Perhaps a more promising route is to modify total utilitarianism by positing a "value of humanity," a bonus for worlds with more than some minimum number of people. (The bonus might increase gradually with the population size, and then level off.) This would work if, on grounds of total utility alone, Future 2 would be better than Future 1, but, given an empty past, Future 1 would result in a better world than Future 2 because it would activate the bonus. A nice feature of this approach is that it seems to be compatible with Belinda's view about the ancient Egyptians (cf. Broome 2004, 197). Belinda can take it for granted that, whatever the welfare of the ancient Egyptians, there will have existed many billions of people. So, she can take it for granted that the value of humanity does not favor any of her options over others.

In what follows, when I consider examples of non-separable theories, I will mainly focus on egalitarianism and theories that posit a value of humanity, without implying that these theories exhaust the possibilities.

4. ARGUMENTS FOR SEPARABILITY

Now let me turn to two arguments for Population Separability. Whether or not these arguments are entirely compelling, they at least point out some of the issues with which non-separable theories have to cope.

4.1. The Argument from Egyptology

This is essentially the argument sketched in the introduction. Intuitively, the welfare of the ancient Egyptians is irrelevant to the relative value of Belinda's options. I will call this the "anti-Egyptology intuition." By extension, the welfare of unaffected people is always irrelevant: Population Separability holds. However, it's not clear whether intuition extends so far. Is having unaffected welfare the only relevant feature of the ancient Egyptians? The anti-Egyptology intuition gains strength from the fact that the ancient Egyptians lived long ago, and their lives are broadly isolated from ours. Could that be relevant too?

If in doubt, we can pursue a more complicated and more rigorous version of the argument. In outline, we first claim that intuition directly supports Population Separability in some restricted range of cases; then we use Pareto Indifference, and possibly other principles, to extend the range of application. The main issue is in formulating the restricted version of Population Separability. The best-known principle of this kind is "Independence of the Utilities of the Dead," as formulated in Blackorby, Bossert, and Donaldson (1995; 2005). A little roughly, it endorses Population Separability as long as the Fs are all dead at the time of evaluation. In reconstructing their argument, I will instead consider a temporally neutral principle, based on the idea of a "divided world" (Parfit 1997). I will say that a world is divided with respect to the property F if the Fs are spatiotemporally, socially, and/or causally isolated from the non-Fs (I leave it open exactly how "isolation" is to be understood). For example, the Fs and the non-Fs might be confined to distant galaxies. Intuitions like the one about ancient Egyptians plausibly support

> *Population Separability for Divided Worlds (PSDW)*: Population Separability applies to divided worlds. More precisely, when evaluating worlds that are divided with respect to some property F, the welfare distribution over the non-Fs is separable from the welfare distribution over the Fs.

We can now argue from PSDW and Pareto Indifference to Population Separability. The rough idea is that, according to Pareto Indifference, the fact that a world is divided is ultimately irrelevant: only the welfare distribution matters. Thus, if Population Separability applies to divided worlds, it must apply to all worlds.

To make this rigorous, we need one further premise, a "domain condition" to the effect that there are plenty of divided worlds. Specifically, for every property F and world W, assume that there is a world W^F with the same welfare distribution as W, but in which the people who are F in W are isolated from the ones who are not F in W. Note that the people who are F in W need not be F in W^F. Because of this, W^F need not be divided with respect to the property of being F. Rather, it is divided with respect to the property of *being F in W*.[14]

Now, let me say that worlds W_1, W_2, W_3, W_4 are in "standard configuration" with respect to the property F if and only if the following relations hold: W_1 and W_2 agree about the welfare distribution over the Fs, as do W_3 and W_4, while W_1 and W_3 agree as to the welfare distribution over the non-Fs, as do W_2 and W_4. The claim to be proved is that, given four worlds in standard configuration, W_1 is at least as good as W_2 if and only if W_3 is at least as good as W_4.

By Pareto Indifference, each of these worlds W_i is exactly as good as its divided counterpart W_i^F. So it suffices to consider the latter instead: it suffices to show that W_1^F is at least as good as W_2^F if and only if W_3^F is at least as good as W_4^F. And this follows from PSDW *if* there is some property G such that the worlds $W_1^F, W_2^F, W_3^F, W_4^F$ are in standard configuration with respect to G and such that each of these worlds is divided with respect to G. As the reader may verify, one such G is the property of *being F in at least one of* W_1, W_2, W_3, W_4.

4.2. Three Objections

Let me briefly consider three types of objection to the argument above.

The first type of objection claims that the domain condition is incorrect. For example, if F is the property of being Donald Trump, perhaps there is no possible world with the same welfare distribution as the actual world, but in which Donald Trump is causally isolated from everyone else. To some extent, one can respond to this kind of worry by weakening the notion of isolation, or by bringing in some supplementary assumptions, or by invoking a sufficiently permissive notion of possibility.

The second type of objection undermines PSDW, by identifying further restrictions on the worlds to which Population Separability intuitively applies. For example, "value of humanity" views (Section 3.4) claim that it is relevant whether the worlds contain many people. If so, the type of argument I gave at best supports Population Separability for worlds with large populations. Broome (2004, 197) suggests this is enough to be getting on with, since our own world is large. Even so, we should take care if we wish to apply mathematical results that assume Population Separability in general.

A third objection claims that the anti-Egyptology intuition is really about what we ought to do, or what reasons for action we can have. So even if Population Separability fails, perhaps we can understand the link between axiology and right action in a way that renders the welfare of the ancient Egyptians irrelevant to the latter. Specifically, Carlson (1998, 290) suggests that a consequentialist might evaluate the causal consequences of each action, rather than the world as a whole that the action brings about. A related and slightly more popular view holds that it is the value of the future, rather than the world as a whole, that is relevant to right action. Here are two separability-related objections to the latter view, although similar considerations apply to causal consequentialism as well.[15] First, if this modification of consequentialism is actually effective, evaluating futures must often lead to different results than evaluating whole worlds. But then it must often require us to choose worse worlds over better ones, even in cases of full knowledge. This deprives consequentialism of much of its initial plausibility.[16] Second, a focus on the future threatens temporal inconsistency when separability fails. The rough idea is that one's aims change in implausible ways as time elapses and some parts of a holistic unity move from the future to the past. This and related problems are pressed by Hurka (1982) especially against future-oriented average utilitarianism, and underlies the argument of Rabinowicz (1989) that future-oriented consequentialism is "self-defeating," that is, it results in certain kinds of collective-action dilemmas.

4.3. The Argument from Anteriority

My second argument for Population Separability has the advantage of being purely axiological. It does not depend, at least not overtly, on intuitions about what we ought to do. On the other hand, it assumes that we can evaluate not only worlds, but "lotteries," situations in which different possible worlds have some probability of being realized. Each such lottery determines a "prospect" for each person: a probability of obtaining each welfare level, including a probability of non-existence. I will appeal to two principles concerning the evaluation of lotteries.

> *Simple Dominance:*[17] Suppose that W_1, W_2, W_3 are worlds. Then W_1 is at least as good as W_2 if and only if a lottery yielding W_1 or W_3 with equal probability is at least as good as one yielding W_2 or W_3 with equal probability.

Simple Dominance is itself a kind of separability principle. Suppose we imagine that we are literally comparing coin-tosses, with one world eventuating on heads and another on tails. Simple Dominance tells us that the outcomes on heads are separable from the outcomes on tails.

The second premise is:

> *Anteriority*: If each person faces the same prospect in lottery L_1 as in lottery L_2, then L_1 and L_2 are equally good.

Anteriority extends Pareto Indifference from worlds to lotteries.[18] Like Pareto Indifference, it says that one scenario cannot be better than another unless it makes a difference for someone, where here "making a difference" is understood in terms of altering someone's prospect. I will say a little more about how to interpret Anteriority after I give the argument from Simple Dominance and Anteriority to Population Separability.

To make that argument, besides Simple Dominance and Anteriority I will again need a domain condition. This time I assume that, for any property F and world W, there is a world W^F which contains all and only the people who are Fs in W, and in which they have the same welfare as in W. For brevity let me write $\succsim$ for "at least as good as," $\sim$ for "exactly as good as," and $[W_1, W_2]$ for a lottery that yields W_1 or W_3 with equal probability. I will also resort to "iff" to mean "if and only if." Now, suppose that W_1, W_2, W_3, W_4 are in standard configuration with respect to F. As a result, we can take $W_1^F = W_2^F$, $W_3^F = W_4^F$, $W_1^{\neg F} = W_3^{\neg F}$, and $W_2^{\neg F} = W_4^{\neg F}$. The domain condition also guarantees that there is a possible world W_0 with no people. By Simple Dominance,

$$W_1 \succsim W_2 \text{ if and only if } [W_1, W_0] \succsim [W_2, W_0].$$

Each person faces the same prospect under $[W_1, W_0]$ as under $[W_1^{\neg F}, W_1^F]$, so Anteriority tells us that $[W_1, W_0] \sim [W_1^{\neg F}, W_1^F]$, and similarly $[W_2, W_0] \sim [W_2^{\neg F}, W_2^F]$. Therefore

$$[W_1, W_0] \succsim [W_2, W_0] \text{ if and only if } [W_1^{\neg F}, W_1^F] \succsim [W_2^{\neg F}, W_2^F].$$

Finally, since $W_1^F = W_2^F$, Simple Dominance tells us that

$$[W_1^{\neg F}, W_1^F] \succsim [W_2^{\neg F}, W_2^F] \text{ if and only if } W_1^{\neg F} \succsim W_2^{\neg F}.$$

Stringing together the displayed biconditionals, we find that $W_1 \succsim W_2$ iff $W_1^{\neg F} \succsim W_2^{\neg F}$. By parallel reasoning, $W_3 \succsim W_4$ iff $W_3^{\neg F} \succsim W_4^{\neg F}$. Since $W_1^{\neg F} = W_3^{\neg F}$ and $W_2^{\neg F} = W_4^{\neg F}$, we find the desired biconditional $W_1 \succsim W_2$ iff $W_3 \succsim W_4$.[19]

How can advocates of non-separable theories respond to this argument? Again, one could call into question the domain condition used in the argument. More interestingly, egalitarians can naturally reject Anteriority, even while accepting Pareto Indifference. The classic example of this is given by Myerson (1981) but see also Broome (1991, 185).

Suppose there are only two people, Ann and Bob. If a coin lands heads, then both Ann and Bob will get one unit of welfare. If the coin lands tails, then they both get zero. That is the first lottery, L. In the second lottery, L', Ann gets 1 and Bob gets 0 on heads, and Ann gets 0 and Bob gets 1 on tails. According to Anteriority, these two lotteries must be equally good. But an egalitarian may well say that L is better, because, whatever the outcome, there will be perfect equality.[20]

A similar example shows why someone who thinks there is a value of humanity might deny Anteriority. For concreteness, suppose the view is just like total utilitarianism except that worlds get a bonus if some people rather than no people exist. Modify Myerson's example, replacing 0 by non-existence. Then L' may come out better than L, because, whatever the outcome, someone is sure to exist.

However, there is a different way of understanding the argument from Anteriority which offers an olive branch to these non-separable theories. Pareto Indifference can be seen as ruling out goods that are unrelated to what is good for people. Alternatively, though, it can be seen as partially *characterizing* a particularly interesting kind or dimension of value, and focusing our attention on it: value that is "personal," valuable for people (cf. Bader in this volume). Anteriority might be interpreted in the same way, as an extension of this characterization.[21] If so, the argument from Anteriority is an argument that personal value satisfies Population Separability, even if all-things considered value does not. Thus, the fact that egalitarian and "value of humanity" views naturally reject Anteriority (and thence Population Separability) just shows that they are not theories of personal value. They posit "impersonal" values, like the value of equality and the value of humanity. People who endorse such views can still take an interest in Population Separability as a principle about personal value.

On the other hand, see Goodsell (2021) for a general objection to Anteriority (and implicitly to Population Separability) related to the St Petersburg paradox.

5. FROM SEPARABILITY TO ADDITIVITY

5.1. The Additivity Theorem

It's time to explain the main mathematical result about Population Separability. Here is the informal statement, which I will go on to make more precise; I sketch the proof in Appendix A.

> *The Additivity Theorem*:[22] Assume a rich domain of possible worlds, that the identities of people are not evaluatively significant, and that the value of worlds depends positively on the welfare of the people in them. Then Population Separability holds if and only if there is a utility function—a way of quantifying welfare—satisfying
>
> *Additivity*: One welfare level is at least as good as another just in case it has at least as great utility, and one world is at least as good as another just in case it has at least as great *total* utility.

Moreover, any two such utility functions agree about which differences in the total utility of worlds are greater than which others.

The theorem tells us that theories satisfying Population Separability have a structure very similar to that of total utilitarianism and total prioritarianism. (One could introduce complications to rule out prioritarianism; see Section 5.4.) Total utilitarianism (Section 3.2) represents welfare levels by real numbers, and evaluates worlds by summing them up. The association of real numbers to welfare levels is the utility function that appears in the Additivity Theorem. Total prioritarians (Section 3.3) use a different utility function which, compared to the utilitarian's, gives extra weight to the badly off. (It is worth emphasizing that "utility function" can mean different things, and my usage here is not standard.) Theories that satisfy Population Separability generalize these two. The main source of generality is that the utility functions need not have real numbers as values; I will explain the alternative starting in Section 5.5.

The last claim of the theorem deserves some comment. Insofar as the value of a world corresponds to its total utility, *differences* in total utility might be interpreted as measuring *how much* worlds differ in value. In other words, any utility function can be interpreted as encoding a cardinal conception of overall value. From this point of view, the last claim of the theorem says that, even if Population Separability does not determine an entirely *unique* utility function,[23] any two utility functions agree on certain cardinal facts. Such facts are therefore implicit in any theory that satisfies Population Separability (and the other premises of the theorem).

Of course, if we *already* have a cardinal conception of value, then it is an open question how these conceptions relate: it is an open question how differences in utility relate to differences in value as antecedently understood. One view, though, is that our everyday cardinal conception of value is at best underdetermined or ambiguous; the Additivity Theorem gives us one way to make it determinate and unambiguous.[24] In any case, it is a common practice in measurement theory to use separability principles to derive cardinal facts from ordinal facts, rather than taking them as primitive.[25] It partly explains why we formulate separability itself in purely ordinal terms.

Now I will spell out exactly what the premises of the theorem are, and, most importantly, the general notion of "utility" I will use.

5.2. "A Rich Domain of Possible Worlds"

The simplest way to spell out this premise is through the following two assumptions:

Infinity: There are infinitely many possible individuals.

Rectangular Field: For any finite set of possible people, and any logically possible assignment of welfare levels to those people, it is possible for exactly those people to exist with exactly those welfare levels.

There are some delicate questions about whether or in what sense these assumptions are true. Rectangular Field is particularly debatable. For example, perhaps you could not exist without your parents having existed. Since such issues are orthogonal to the ones I'm interested in exploring here, I'll just say two brief things. First, I'm articulating Infinity and Rectangular Field only as simple and *sufficiently* strong background assumptions; they are obviously not necessary for Additivity. Second, I'm sympathetic to the idea of evaluating at least some metaphysically impossible worlds. It seems unproblematic to say that it would be better for me to be alone in the universe and happy than for me to be alone in the universe and miserable, whether or not it is metaphysically possible for me to be alone in the universe. Similarly, it seems possible to evaluate the possibilities demanded by Rectangular Field even if they are merely logical possibilities. This strikes me as the right way to understand domain conditions of this kind, including the ones I discussed in Section 4.

5.3. "The Identities of People are not Evaluatively Significant"

The simplest way to spell out this idea is as follows:

> *Welfarist Anonymity*: If two worlds agree about how many people get each welfare level, then they are equally good.

Note that Welfarist Anonymity, like Population Separability, implies Pareto Indifference: the latter says that pairs of worlds in which *the same* people get each welfare level are equally good. Person-affecting views often deny Welfarist Anonymity while accepting Pareto Indifference. Such views face difficulties like the non-identity problem (Parfit 1984, Ch. 16) which I need not examine here (but see Roberts in this volume). All I claim is that Welfarist Anonymity expresses a natural kind of impartiality. It is clearly a necessary condition for Additivity.

5.4. "The Value of Worlds Depends Positively on the Welfare of the People in Them"

Recall that Population Separability entails Pareto Indifference: the value of a world is determined by the welfare of the people in it. We should expect something more: at least in simple cases, higher welfare makes the world better. There are many ways of articulating such a principle, but the following one suits my purposes well.

> *One-Person Reduction*: For any person S, one world containing only S is at least as good as another if and only if it is at least as good for S.

Note that a cardinal version of One-Person Reduction would say that the first world is better than the second *to the extent that* it is better for *S*. Total utilitarianism is usually construed as making such a claim, whereas total prioritarianism denies it. But the Additivity Theorem does not distinguish between these two theories, since it does not presuppose a cardinal conception of value.

5.5. "Utility"

A typical way of quantifying welfare is to assign a utility, understood as a real number, to each welfare level. However, there is nothing sacrosanct about real numbers. Instead, I take utilities to be abstract quantities with the right kind of structure to serve a quantitative theory of value. To make sense of Additivity, we just need to be able to add up and compare utilities. Sometimes we may also want to compare *differences* in utility, so I will require that we can subtract utilities from each other. Given these requirements, we can speak of *zero* utility, corresponding to the difference between any level of utility and itself. We can then also classify utilities as positive, negative, or neutral, by comparing them to zero. We can talk about one utility being twice as large as another, and more generally multiply a given utility by an integer: $2x = x + x$ and so on. In this way, we obtain lot of what we'd want from a quantitative theory of value.

I will call a *utility space* a set $\mathbb{V}$ whose elements can be added, subtracted, and compared in a well-behaved way.[26] A prime example is the set of real numbers with the usual addition and subtraction operations and the usual ordering, and I will give several other examples in Section 5.6. But here is the precise definition. A utility space is a set $\mathbb{V}$ with a binary operation $+$ which, like ordinary addition, is commutative, associative, and unital;[27] an inverse operation $-$;[28] and a partial ordering $\geq$.[29] Finally, I require that adding a larger increment results in a larger total:

$$x \geq y \text{ if and only if } z + x \geq z + y.$$

In summary, the main claim of the Additivity Theorem is that if Infinity, Rectangular Field, Welfarist Anonymity, and One-Person Reduction hold, then Population Separability is equivalent to the existence of a function from welfare levels into some utility space, satisfying Additivity.

5.6. Examples of Utility Spaces

Having completed my explication of the Additivity Theorem, let me give some examples of utility spaces. In Section 6, I will show how these can be used to formulate some theories of population ethics.

It is useful to organize the examples by comparing them to the most commonly used utility space, the real numbers. A utility space may consist of *some* but not *all* real numbers: the set of integers is one example. And even if a utility space does not *consist* of real numbers, it may be possible to *embed* it in the real numbers: that is, it may be possible to map its elements to real numbers in a way that is compatible with their ordering and the operations of addition and subtraction.[30] Given such an embedding, we can always think about utility levels in terms of the corresponding real numbers; we have not achieved any new generality. But not all utility spaces can be so embedded. Here are two necessary and jointly sufficient conditions:

Completeness: If x and y are utilities, then $x \geq y$ or $y \geq x$.

Archimedean Condition:[31] If x and y are positive utilities, then, for some natural number n, $n\,x \geq y$.

The result, in other words, is

Hölder's Theorem: A utility space can be embedded in the real numbers if and only if it satisfies Completeness and the Archimedean Condition.

For a proof see Krantz et al. (1971, §2.2.5). The main idea of the theorem, including the "Archimedean" Condition, goes back to Eudoxus of Cnidus's theory of proportions in the fourth century BC, expounded in Book V of Euclid's *Elements*.

The following examples illustrate, for one thing, how utility spaces can violate Completeness and the Archimedean Condition. All of them take the utility space to consist of ordered pairs of real numbers, with addition defined component-wise: $(a,b)+(c,d)=(a+c,b+d)$. They differ only in how these pairs are partially ordered.

Example 3. The *lexicographic* partial order is the one such that $(a,b) \geq (c,d)$ if and only if, as real numbers, $a > c$ or else $a = c$ and $b \geq d$. The resulting utility space satisfies Completeness but not the Archimedean Condition, for although $(0,1)$ is positive, no positive multiple of it is greater than $(1,0)$.

Example 4. The *strong Paretian* partial order holds that $(a,b) \geq (c,d)$ if and only if $a \geq c$ and $b \geq d$. The resulting utility space satisfies neither the Archimedean Condition nor Completeness. Although $(1,0)$ and $(0,1)$ are both positive, they are mutually incomparable, and no positive multiple of one is greater than the other.

Example 5. The *weak Paretian* partial order, in contrast, is the one such that $(a,b) \geq (c,d)$ if and only if, as real numbers, either $a > c$ and $b > d$ or $a = c$ and $b = d$. The resulting utility space satisfies the Archimedean Condition but not Completeness. Here $(1,0)$ and $(0,1)$ are incomparable, but neither is positive.

Example 6. The *degenerate* partial order holds that $(a,b) \geq (c,d)$ if and only if $a = c$ and $b \geq d$. The resulting utility space satisfies the Archimedean Condition, but not completeness.

Although utility spaces can be large and complicated, these examples are typical in that they illustrate the two main ways in which utilities can behave differently from real numbers.

6. Abstract Total Views and the Repugnant Conclusion

I will say that an *abstract total view* consists of a utility space $\mathbb{V}$ and a utility function satisfying Additivity.[32] In this section I aim to give the reader a sense of the range of these views, by surveying the different ways in which they can avoid the Repugnant Conclusion.

I will understand the Repugnant Conclusion to be the following claim:

> *The Repugnant Conclusion*: For any world whose population consists of very good lives, there is a better world whose population consists of lives that are barely worth living.

An abstract total view will entail the Repugnant Conclusion if it has the following two features in common with total utilitarianism, as standardly construed:

> *Reality*: The utility space is the set of real numbers.
>
> *Weak Mere Addition*: Adding lives that are worth living does not make things worse—that is, the utility of such lives is not negative.

Given Reality, Weak Mere Addition means that both very good lives and lives barely worth living must have positive real numbers as utilities. The total utility of a sufficiently large population of lives barely worth living will inevitably exceed that of any given population of very good lives.

For this derivation of the Repugnant Conclusion to go through, we do not quite need Reality: it suffices that the utility space can be embedded in the real numbers. And we know from Section 5.6 that $\mathbb{V}$ can be embedded in the real numbers if and only if Completeness and the Archimedean Condition hold. We can therefore categorize strategies for avoiding the Repugnant Conclusion according to which combination of Weak Mere Addition, Completeness, and the Archimedean Condition they deny. I will now sketch each of these strategies in turn, connecting them to the broader literature.

6.1. Denying Weak Mere Addition: Positive Critical Level Views

The first basic strategy is to deny Weak Mere Addition. This allows that lives that are barely worth living have negative utility. As a result, populations of lives that are barely worth living get *worse* as they get larger. This blocks the Repugnant Conclusion, regardless of whether we deny Completeness or the Archimedean Condition. Note, however, that it leads to the Sadistic Conclusion.

If there is a level of welfare that gets zero utility, then this level is called "the critical level." On the kind of view under consideration, the critical level (if there is one) must correspond to lives that are better than barely worth living. In that sense, the critical level is positive from the point of view of individual value. Thus, views in this class are often called "positive critical level" views. (There might not, however, be a critical level in the stated sense, either because all welfare levels get negative utility, or because, although some welfare levels have positive utility and others negative utility, no welfare level gets precisely zero utility.)

Views such as this are discussed by Bossert in this volume, and are recommended by Blackorby, Bossert, and Donaldson (2005). Broome (2004) defends a closely related view, in which the critical level is vague; on a natural interpretation, this makes the Repugnant Conclusion indeterminate rather than determinately true or determinately false. (Broome himself puts things a slightly different way; see his Section 14.4 for discussion.)

6.2. Denying the Archimedean Condition: Lexical Total Views

The second strategy denies the Archimedean Condition. In doing so we can still maintain Weak Mere Addition and Completeness, so that lives worth living have positive utility. Denying the Archimedean Condition means that there will be positive utilities x and y such that $y \geq nx$ for all natural numbers n. For example, we can use the lexicographic utility space from Example 3, with $x = (0,1)$ and $y = (1,0)$. If we associate y with the welfare of very good lives and x with the welfare of lives that are barely worth living, then we find that, although adding lives that are barely worth living increases the value of a world, nonetheless, no number of lives that are barely worth living would be better than a world consisting of only very good lives.

This is quite an extreme conclusion. It can be softened a little if we also deny Completeness (see the chapter by Chang in this volume). It can then turn out that large populations of lives that are barely worth living are typically incomparable to small populations of very good lives. For example, a version of this view might use the "strong Paretian" utility space of Example 4, with $x = (0,1)$ and $y = (1,1)$.

This non-Archimedean or "lexical" view is the sort of view discussed by Carlson in this volume.

6.3. Denying Completeness: Neutral Range Views

The third general strategy accepts Weak Mere Addition but claims that lives that are barely worth living have utilities incomparable to zero. Thus, adding one to a population makes things neither better nor worse. This strategy obviously requires us to deny Completeness.

The key issues for these views are the *range* of incomparability and its *interpretation*. On the first count, is the utility of even very good lives incomparable to zero? What about very bad lives? On the second, is the "incomparability" a matter of parity, incommensurability, or some more radical failure of evaluative comparisons? I will not discuss the second of these issues, but here are some examples to illustrate the first.

We could use the weak Paretian utility space of Example 5. Thinking of welfare levels as indexed by a real number t, the corresponding utilities could be pairs of the form $(t+1, t-1)$. Then the welfare levels between $t=-1$ and $t=1$ would have utilities incomparable to 0; this is the "neutral range" or "critical band" of welfare. Note that while adding a life in the neutral range yields a population that is incomparable to the original, adding a life is always better than adding one at a lower welfare level. This kind of view is discussed by Rabinowicz in this volume.

As a more extreme example, the neutral range might be infinite in one or both directions. For instance, consider the degenerate utility space of Example 6. The utilities of welfare levels might be of the form $(1, t)$. Then all of these utilities are incomparable to 0. On this view, two worlds will be comparable if and only if they have the same number of people, in which case they are ranked by total utility. This is one way of understanding the "person-affecting" utilitarian views discussed by Bader in this volume.

7. CONCLUSION

I considered two arguments for Population Separability. Although they are not decisive, I suggested that they at least support Population Separability as a principle about personal value. I then explained how Population Separability, with some supplementary premises, allows the value of worlds to be represented by total utility. The resulting "abstract total views" generalize total utilitarianism and total prioritarianism, and I highlighted three conditions that together entail the Repugnant Conclusion. Several approaches to population axiology prominent in the literature can be understood as denying one or more of these three conditions while maintaining Population Separability. Simple examples of utility spaces can be used to understand their structure.

APPENDIX: PROOF OF THE ADDITIVITY THEOREM

In this Appendix, I outline the proof of the Additivity Theorem, explaining the main construction but omitting detailed verifications. I will write $\succsim$ for the relation "at least as good as" on possible worlds, and $\sim$ for "exactly as good as."

It is clear that, if Additivity holds, then Population Separability follows: if W_1 and W_2 agree as to the welfare of the Fs, then $W_1 \succsim W_2$ iff W_1 gives greater total utility to the non-F s; this criterion does not depend on the welfare of the F s.

Conversely, assuming Population Separability, we have first to construct a utility space and then a utility function. Note that ~ is an equivalence relation; let V_0 be the set of indifference classes of worlds. We can define a partial order on V_0: writing $[W]$ for the equivalence class of W, $[W_1] \geq [W_2]$ iff $W_1 \succsim W_2$. Now we define an addition operation on V_0. For any two worlds W_1 and W_2, choose a world $W_1 * W_2$ with the following properties: there is a one-to-one correspondence between some of the people in $W_1 * W_2$ and all of the people in W_1, and a one-to one correspondence between the rest of the people in $W_1 * W_2$ and all of the people in W_2, such that corresponding people have the same welfare levels. Such a world exists by Infinity and Rectangular Domain. It is straightforward to check, using Population Separability and Welfarist Anonymity, that $[W_1 * W_2]$ depends only on the equivalence classes $[W_1]$ and $[W_2]$. Defining $[W_1] + [W_2] = [W_1 * W_2]$, Welfarist Anonymity entails that + is a commutative, associative operation, and Population Separability entails that $[W_1] + [W_2] \geq [W_1] + [W_3]$ iff $[W_2] \geq [W_3]$. Thus, V_0 is *almost* a utility space: the only thing lacking is the possibility of subtraction. However, one can expand V_0 to a utility space V in exactly the way in which one expands the natural numbers to the integers, for which subtraction is always defined. Elements of V can be represented by formal differences $[W_1] - [W_2]$, governed by the rule that $[W_1] - [W_2] \geq [W_3] - [W_4]$ iff $[W_1] + [W_4] \geq [W_2] + [W_3]$. (If W_0 is an empty world, we can identify any $[W]$ in V_0 with the difference $[W] - [W_0]$.)

Finally, if x is a welfare level, we can define its utility $u(x)$ as an element of V: $u(x) = [W]$ for any world W containing one person with welfare x and no one else. It follows from this definition that, for any world W, $[W]$ equals the total utility of W. Thus, one world is at least as good as another if and only if it has at least as great total utility. It also follows from One-Person Reduction that $u(x) \geq u(y)$ if and only if x is at least as good a welfare level as y.

NOTES

1. The example of the ancient Egyptians comes from Parfit (1984, 420), and the point originally from McMahan (1981, 115).
2. The methods I emphasize are thus more closely related to those of Wakker (1986) and Pivato (2014), although even these authors assume completeness. (Pivato allows for some incompleteness to handle infinite populations, a subject I will not touch on here.)
3. The standard reference is Krantz et al. (1971). They and some other authors call separability "independence."
4. Some will want to refine the category "none of the above" further, to distinguish (for example) parity and incomparability; see Chang in this volume. In this chapter I will be silent about how to interpret "none of the above," and will adopt "incomparability" as a generic name to cover this category of value relations (or non-relations!).

5. Reflexive: $x \succsim_X x$. Transitive: if $x \succsim_X y$ and $y \succsim_X z$ then $x \succsim_X z$. The relations "better than" and "exactly as good as" can easily be defined in terms of "at least as good as," which is the reason to treat it as the main value relation.

6. I adapted the example from Hansson (1996).

7. We can define $\succsim_B$ to be the relation such that $b_1 \succsim_B b_2$ iff $x \succsim_X y$ for all x, y in X with $a(x) = a(y)$, $b(x) = b_1$, and $b(y) = b_2$.

8. See Kagan (1988) and Oddie (2001) for salutary discussions of the need for separability and various pitfalls. Sometimes, admittedly, "ceteris paribus" is used in a less literal way, to mean something like "in normal cases" or even "intrinsically." Such uses don't presuppose separability. See Van Benthem, Girard, and Roy (2009) for a discussion and formalization of different types of ceteris paribus comparisons.

9. Oddie in particular proposes to use separability (or a related principle of "additivity") as a "heuristic tool" and "regulative ideal" (2001, 330–331).

10. Throughout I think of properties in an abundant sense, as corresponding to *arbitrary* selections for each possible world of a subset of the people who exist in that world.

11. There are many versions of this principle in the literature, involving the words "separability" or "independence"; another name, at least in the fixed population setting, is "elimination of indifferent individuals" (e.g., Arrow 1977 and Maskin 1978). The only novel feature of my formulation is that I consider all properties F, whereas other treatments typically consider world-independent subsets of the set of all possible people. This amounts to considering only those F such that, if it is possible that S exists and is F, then it is necessary that, if S exists, S is F. Given the background assumptions I will make in Section 5, there is no real difference between these ways of doing things, but using all properties is much more natural: for example, the property of being an ancient Egyptian is not, I think, of the special kind. This issue aside, Population Separability is an application to population ethics of "strong separability" (see, e.g., Broome 1991, following Debreu 1960). It is essentially the same as the "existence independence" of Blackorby, Bossert, and Donaldson (2005), and the separability axiom of Pivato (2014), in the variable population application of his framework. Broome's (2004) "separability of persons" is also essentially a special case of Population Separability.

12. See Parfit (1997), as well as the chapters by Adler and Holtug in this volume.

13. See McCarthy (2015) for an extended treatment of this point, in the context of fixed-population egalitarianism, and understanding cardinal facts in terms of expected utility theory.

14. The reason for doing things this way can be appreciated in terms of the property F of *being Donald Trump and not isolated from everyone else*. Given that Donald Trump is the sole F in W, W^F is required to be a world in which Donald Trump is isolated from everyone else, not a world in which, incoherently, the sole F is isolated from everyone else.

15. The significance of causal and/or future-oriented consequentialism vis-à-vis separability was first noted by Broad (1914). He influentially rejected both of these kinds of consequentialism precisely because they do not respect organic unities. For a map of this terrain see Carlson (1995, Ch. 4), who himself appears to agree with Broad. For some problems with causal consequentialism unrelated to separability, see Sosa (1993, 101) and Sartorio (2009).

16. This point is basically the one in Broad (1914, 314–315). As an example unrelated to separability, future-oriented consequentialism holds that we cannot have even a prima facie reason to avoid enacting posthumous harms.

17. This is a version of the relatively uncontroversial "stochastic dominance" or "monotonicity" principle in decision theory. Unusually, this version says something about the case in which W_1 and W_2 are incomparable.

18. There is a more familiar "ex ante" version of Pareto Indifference that applies to lotteries: it says that two lotteries are equally good if they give each person prospects that are equally good. The problem with this principle is that it is not clear whether one can compare prospects in terms of individual value when they include chances of non-existence. If one can't, then Pareto Indifference does not tell us anything about lotteries in which it is uncertain which people exist. Anteriority does not have this problem, since it does involve the evaluation of prospects.

19. Although I have not seen exactly this argument in the literature, it is inspired by Proposition 4.8 in McCarthy, Mikkola, and Thomas (2020). It is also closely related to the theorem on "cross-cutting separability" in Broome (1991, 70), following Gorman (1968), although the methods are quite different. The "cross-cutting" terminology comes from imagining each lottery as a table of welfare levels, with each column corresponding to an outcome of the lottery, and each row corresponding to a person. Rows cut across columns, and vice versa.

20. A different kind of egalitarian might deny Simple Dominance instead of Anteriority; see Broome (1991) following Diamond (1967).

21. I propose a more complete formal characterization of personal value in Thomas (2016, Ch. 3), based on McCarthy, Mikkola, and Thomas (2020). Of course, a formal characterization cannot settle whether we are talking about personal or impersonal value in Bader's metaphysical sense.

22. There are many variants on this result in the literature. The closest matches are Theorem 1.1 in Wakker (1986) and (especially) Theorem 1 in Pivato (2014). The analogous result in Blackorby, Bossert, and Donaldson (2005) is Theorem 6.10. In Broome (1991), the formally stated analogue is the first separability theorem (70, following Debreu (1960)), although the whole argument for critical level utilitarianism in Broome (1991; 2004) is cut from the same cloth.

23. Given one utility function we could always multiply it by (say) 12 to get another one that would work just as well: this is akin to measuring height in inches rather than feet. Besides, we could always replace one utility space by an isomorphic one. Nonetheless, it is possible to pick out a "universal" utility function that is unique up to isomorphism; see e.g. Pivato (2014, Theorem 1). If one requires that utilities be real numbers, then the utility function is unique up to rescaling; see Krantz et al. (1971, 2.2.5).

24. See Broome (2004, 90), Greaves (2017) for thoughts along these lines, in the context of expected utility theory.

25. See Krantz et al. (1971). The best-known example is expected utility theory, which (on one interpretation) derives cardinal facts about the value of outcomes from ordinal facts about the value of lotteries, via independence or the "sure thing" principle, which are essentially principles of separability. So, one can ask how the cardinal facts derived using expected utility theory relate to those derived from Population Separability.

26. A more standard mathematical name for a utility space is "partially ordered abelian group." Their structure has been studied mathematically, with classical results by Hölder, which I discuss below, and Hahn, later developed by Hausner and Wendel (1952), Clifford (1954), and in maximum generality by Conrad (1953). (Unfortunately, I cannot read Hölder and Hahn in the original.)

27. Commutative: $x + y = y + x$. Associative: $(x + y) + z = x + (y + z)$. Unital: there is an element 0 such that $x + 0 = x$.

28. Inverse: $x + (-x) = 0$.

29. A partial ordering is a preorder that is anti-symmetric: if $x \geq y$ and $y \geq x$ then $x = y$. This reflects the thought that two things have the same utility if they are equally good.

30. That is, an embedding is a function f such that $f(x + y) = f(x) + f(y)$, and $f(x) \geq f(y)$ if and only if $x \geq y$.

31. Although the version of the Archimedean Condition I state here is fairly standard, there are many variants which are equivalent given Completeness, and it is not clear which is normatively more natural in the absence of Completeness.

32. This class generalizes what Blackorby, Bossert, and Donaldson (1995; 2005) call "critical level generalised utilitarianism" primarily in not requiring utilities to be real numbers. As I mentioned earlier, it includes not only total utilitarianism but a standard form of prioritarianism.

REFERENCES

Arrhenius, Gustaf. 2000. "An Impossibility Theorem for Welfarist Axiologies." *Economics and Philosophy* 16, no. 2: 247–266.

Arrow, Kenneth. J. 1977. "Extended Sympathy and the Possibility of Social Choice." *The American Economic Review* 67, no. 1: 219–225.

Blackorby, Charles, Walter Bossert, and David Donaldson. 1995. "Intertemporal Population Ethics: Critical-Level Utilitarian Principles." *Econometrica* 63, no. 6: 1303–1320.

Blackorby, Charles, Walter Bossert, and David Donaldson. 2005. *Population Issues in Social-Choice Theory, Welfare Economics and Ethics*. New York: Cambridge University Press.

Broad, C. D. 1914. "The Doctrine of Consequences in Ethics." *International Journal of Ethics* 24, no. 3: 293–320.

Broome, John. 1991. *Weighing Goods: Equality, Uncertainty and Time*. Oxford: Wiley-Blackwell.

Broome, John. 2004. *Weighing Lives*. Oxford: Oxford University Press.

Broome, John. 2015. "Equality versus Priority: A Useful Distinction." *Economics and Philosophy* 31, no. 2: 219–228.

Carlson, Erik. 1995. *Consequentialism Reconsidered*. Dordrecht: Kluwer Academic.

Carlson, Erik. 1998. "Mere Addition and Two Trilemmas of Population Ethics." *Economics and Philosophy* 14, no. 2: 283–306.

Clifford, A. H. 1954. "Note on Hahn's Theorem on Ordered Abelian Groups." *Proceedings of the American Mathematical Society* 5, no. 6: 860–863.

Conrad, Paul F. 1953. "Embedding Theorems for Abelian Groups with Valuations." *American Journal of Mathematics* 75, no. 1: 1–29.

Debreu, Gerard. 1959. *Theory of Value: An Axiomatic Analysis of Economic Equilibrium*. Oxford: Wiley.

Debreu, Gerard. 1960. "Topological Methods in Cardinal Utility Theory." In *Mathematical Methods in the Social Sciences*, edited by K. Arrow, S. Karlin, and P. Suppes, 16–26. Stanford, CA: Stanford University Press, 1959.

Diamond, Peter A. 1967. "Cardinal Welfare, Individualistic Ethics, and Interpersonal Comparison of Utility: Comment." *The Journal of Political Economy* 75, no. 5: 765–766.

Goodsell, Zachary. 2021. "A St Petersburg Paradox for Risky Welfare Aggregation." *Analysis*. doi.org/10.1093/analys/anaa079

Gorman, W. M. 1968. "The Structure of Utility Functions." *The Review of Economic Studies* 35, no. 4: 367–390.

Greaves, Hilary. 2017. "A Reconsideration of the Harsanyi-Sen-Weymark Debate on Utilitarianism." *Utilitas* 29: 175–213.

Hansson, Sven Ove. 1996. "What Is Ceteris Paribus Preference?" *Journal of Philosophical Logic* 25, no. 3: 307–332.

Harsanyi, John C. 1955. "Cardinal Welfare, Individualistic Ethics, and Interpersonal Comparisons of Utility." *Journal of Political Economy* 63, no. 4: 309–321.

Hausner, M. and J. G. Wendel. 1952. "Ordered Vector Spaces." *Proceedings of the American Mathematical Society* 3, no. 6: 977–982.

Hurka, Thomas. 1983. "Value and Population Size." *Ethics* 93, no. 3: 496–507.

Hurka, Thomas. 1982. "More Average Utilitarianisms." *Analysis* 42, no. 3: 115–119.

Kagan, Shelly. 1988. "The Additive Fallacy." *Ethics* 99, no. 1: 5–31.

Krantz, David H., R. Duncan Luce, Patrick Suppes, and Amos Tversky. 1971. *Foundations of Measurement, Volume 1*. New York: Academic Press.

Maskin, Eric. 1978. "A Theorem on Utilitarianism." *The Review of Economic Studies* 45, no. 1: 93–96.

McCarthy, David. 2015. "Distributive Equality." *Mind* 124: 1045–1109.

McCarthy, David, Kalle Mikkola, and Teruji Thomas. 2020. "Utilitarianism with and without Expected Utility." *Journal of Mathematical Economics* 87: 77–113.

McMahan, Jeff. 1981. "Problems of Population Theory." *Ethics* 92, no. 1: 96–127.

Myerson, Roger. B. 1981. "Utilitarianism, Egalitarianism, and the Timing Effect in Social Choice Problems." *Econometrica: Journal of the Econometric Society* 49, no. 4: 883–897.

Ng, Yew-Kwang. 1989. "What Should We Do about Future Generations?" *Economics and Philosophy* 5, no. 2: 235–253.

Oddie, Graham. 2001. "Axiological Atomism." *Australasian Journal of Philosophy* 79, no. 3: 313–332.

Parfit, Derek. 1984. *Reasons and Persons*. Oxford: Oxford University Press.

Parfit, Derek. 1997. "Equality and Priority." *Ratio* 10, no. 3: 202–221.

Pivato, Marcus. 2014. "Additive Representation of Separable Preferences over Infinite Products." *Theory and Decision* 77, no. 1: 31–83.

Rabinowicz, Wlodek. 1989. "Act-Utilitarian Prisoner's Dilemmas." *Theoria* 55, no. 1: 1–44.

Sartorio, Carolina. 2009. "Causation and Ethics." In *The Oxford Handbook of Causation*, edited by H. Beebee, C. Hitchcock, and P. Menzies, 575–591. Oxford: Oxford University Press.

Sosa, David. 1993. "Consequences of Consequentialism." *Mind* 102, no. 405: 101–122.

Thomas, Teruji. 2016. "Topics in Population Ethics." PhD diss., University of Oxford.

Van Benthem, Johan, Patrick Girard, and Olivier Roy. 2009. "Everything Else Being Equal: A Modal Logic for Ceteris Paribus Preferences." *Journal of Philosophical Logic* 38, no. 1: 83–125.

Wakker, Peter. 1986. "The Repetitions Approach to Characterize Cardinal Utility." *Theory and Decision* 20, no. 1: 33–40.

CHAPTER 13

··

EVALUATIVE UNCERTAINTY AND POPULATION ETHICS

··

KRISTER BYKVIST

1. INTRODUCTION

··

ONE obvious problem with applying theories of population ethics to pressing practical problems, such as climate change, is that we are not certain which theory to apply.[1]
Indeed, this uncertainty seems mandatory, since the many paradoxes of population
ethics show that it is impossible to consistently accept all our pet principles about the
assessment of population changes.[2] Since climate change and many other pressing real-
life problems require an urgent response, we need to think hard about how to act under
this kind of moral uncertainty.

A possible way forward is to sidestep the thorny issue of which of the conflicting
principles to drop, and instead develop a normative approach that provides guidance
to agents who are uncertain about which principles to accept and which to reject. This
chapter will sketch the contours of such an approach. The main aim is to show that the
paradoxes of population ethics and the resulting uncertainty need not paralyze our
decision-making.

I will assume that the decision-maker is interested in the *value* of population change,
and that the question is what it is *rational* for such an agent to do given her interest in the
value of population change and her credences (degrees of belief) in different theories
or hypotheses about the value of such changes. The alternative to this account is to construct a *moral* theory that makes moral rightness depend on the agent's credence in
various evaluative hypotheses. This is the path taken by Michael Zimmerman, who has
developed a version of this theory, which he calls "The Prospective View."[3] I will choose
the first option here, partly because it makes the discussion more manageable, and
partly because it enables us to sidestep certain problems that afflict the second option.

More specifically, my aim is to see how far we can go by applying standard decision
theoretical tools to agents who are evaluatively uncertain and who care only about the

value of population changes. Of course, few (if any) real agents care *only* about this kind of value, but it is a useful idealization. Once we know how to deal with these agents, we can extend the theory so that it applies to agents who care about other values too. In fact, this assumption is not too far-fetched for those agents, individuals or collectives, who have been asked, in some governmental capacity, to evaluate population change and decide on certain policy decisions on the basis of such evaluations.

It is important to note that this choice of normative theorizing does not make the suggested proposal void of any *moral* significance, since what is rational for people who care about population value is certainly also something morally significant. It tells you what a certain kind of morally virtuous person, namely, a person who cares only about the values of population change, would do. Furthermore, even on Zimmerman's alternative view, what you morally ought to do is to choose "that option that it would be most reasonable to choose in light of your evidence, were you morally conscientious," and he acknowledges that this crucially hinges on working out "the general conditions for rational decision-making."[4] It is thus likely that what Zimmerman calls the morally right option will coincide with the rational option for agents who care about the values of population changes and whose beliefs are based on evidence, at least for those cases in which only these values are at stake. So, the discussion in this chapter will be of interest even for those who follow Zimmerman in defining moral ought in terms of the agent's evidence.

Finally, two simplifying assumptions. To keep the focus on evaluative uncertainty and make the discussion more manageable, I will assume throughout this chapter that there is *no empirical uncertainty* in the cases to be discussed. Of course, this is highly unrealistic, but it is fairly straightforward to extend the rationality principles discussed here so that they take into account both empirical and evaluative uncertainty. I shall also assume a *static* framework, in which we do not need to worry about problems of dynamic choice (e.g., how to coordinate present and future decisions, how to avoid money-pumps, and how to be dynamically consistent). Again, this is a highly unrealistic assumption, but dynamic choice is a challenge for many rationality principles, and not just some of the ones presented here, and it would take us beyond the scope this chapter to dip into the extensive debate about the rationality of dynamic choice.

2. DEFLATIONARY ACCOUNTS: OBVIOUS AND EASY SOLUTIONS?

One reaction to the challenge of evaluative uncertainty would be to downplay its significance and claim that there are obvious and easy solutions. For example, one could insist that the only thing to say about evaluative uncertainty is that it is morally right for the agent to bring about the population change that is optimal in terms of *actual* value. Even if the agent has very little confidence (or perhaps none at all) in the true hypothesis about the values of population changes, the agent should nevertheless choose the option that is optimal according to this hypothesis. Now, as an account of what is morally obligatory in an *objective* sense this approach might be plausible, since this kind of moral obligation depends on objective facts rather than the agent's credences. But as an account of what is morally obligatory in a subjective sense it is much less plausible, since this kind of moral obligation is supposed to be sensitive to the agent's subjective perspective, which may include credences over different evaluative hypotheses and preferences for bringing about value. As an account of rational action, it is simply a non-starter, since rational choice, in the sense of "rational" that is prominent in standard decision theory, has to do with what one should do, *given one's beliefs and preferences*. This means that one's action, or the intention behind it, has to cohere in some sense with one's current beliefs (credences) and one's preferences, including one's beliefs about value and preference for bringing about value. An account that totally ignored one's current beliefs and preferences would thus not qualify as a theory of rational decision-making in the sense relevant for this discussion.

Another deflationary account, "my favorite theory" as it has been dubbed, tells one to act on the theory one has *most* credence in.[5] No weight is given to theories that one has less credence in. If one has most credence in total utilitarianism, according to which the value of a population equals the sum total of individual well-being, then one should maximize total individual well-being, even though one also has credence in other alternative value hypotheses. This account at least falls in the ballpark of rational decision-making, since one's current beliefs and preferences will have a say. Nevertheless, it is clearly flawed as a theory of rational decision-making, for the following reasons.

First of all, the approach does not give you any advice when you do not have a favorite theory to begin with. This can happen because of any of the following reasons:

(a) your credences split evenly between many different theories; in this case there is no theory you have *most* credence in;

(b) your credences are not well-defined for all theories; for some pair of theories you can neither say that one is more probable than the other, nor that they are equally probable;

(c) you have not considered whole theories, only different hypotheses about the particular values at stake in the specific situation.

Second, it is not sufficiently sensitive to avoidable evaluative risks, as the example in Table 13.1 brings out.

You can choose between two policies A and B, and you have credence in two different theories, T1 and T2, but slightly more credence in T1 than in T2. According to "my favorite theory," you are permitted to choose policy B (since it is tied with A) even though you can avoid the evaluative risk of bringing about a very bad outcome by choosing A instead.

As an example, consider an agent who has more credence in person-affecting utilitarianism, according to which what matters is only whether we make people better or

Table 13.1 Case 1		
Alternatives	T1 credence = 0.6	T2 credence = 0.4
Policy A	Good	Good
Policy B	Exactly as good as A	Bad

worse off, than in critical-level utilitarianism, according to which the value of an out-come equals (the average well-being minus c) multiplied by the number of people, where c is the critical level and is set above well-being neutrality.[6] Policy B would make people have many more children, but the children would have lives that are barely worth living. The well-being of all other people would not be affected (or the losses for some would be exactly compensated for by the gains for others). Policy A is the status quo, where all people have a high level of well-being. One version of person-affecting utilitarianism would say that the outcome of A is as good as that of B (since no one is affected for the worse), and critical-level utilitarianism would say that the outcome of A is better than that of B, since B contains extra people whose well-being is below the critical level (we assume).

But saying that it is rationally permissible to choose policy B seems wrong, since in this situation policy A *dominates* policy B, in the sense that choosing A guarantees that the outcome will be *at least as good* as that of B, and it is irrational to choose a dominated option (when the probability of a theory does not depend on which action you choose).

Now, some of these defects can be remedied by a more sophisticated version of "my favorite theory," but no matter how sophisticated it is made, it will still have problems with cases where there are no well-defined credences.[7] For example, if we change Case 1 so that the agent does not have any well-defined probabilities for the theories, "my favourite theory" will no longer give any advice, which is very implausible, since A still dominates B.

Furthermore, "my favourite theory" is very sensitive to how we individuate theories. Both hedonistic utilitarianism and non-hedonistic person-affecting utilitarianism will agree that A is as good as B if we assume that the different values are perfectly correlated here. But if we split the credences between these two versions of utilitarianism so that they get 0.3 each, then A is right and B is wrong, for now the critical-level theory is the favorite theory. If we just count both versions as one theory, then both A and B are right. In this case, it might seem clear that we should distinguish between the two versions of utilitarianism. But note that there is an infinite number of critical-level theories to choose between—one for each possible level—and many of them agree on the values of A and B. If the agent splits the credence between two of these versions, so that each get 0.2 credence, then the utilitarian theories call the shots again. Of course, for each of the utilitarian theories we can split the evidence between further versions (assuming they give the same verdict in the case at hand), so now each utilitarian theory has 0.15

credence, and the critical-level theories will call the shots again. And so on. It is not clear how to find a plausible non-arbitrary partition.[8]

3. Dominance Reasoning Applied to Evaluative Uncertainty

There are many paradoxes of population ethics. Here I will present one that will be instructive for how to apply dominance reasoning about rational choice to evaluative uncertainty. The starting point is the common contrastive judgment that we make the world better by making *existing* people happy, but we do not make the world better by making *extra* happy people, where "not make the world better" is read as "make a difference to the world that does not change its value." (We will come back to an alternative reading of "not make the world better" later.) The second assumption is the popular Pareto principle, according to which it is better to make everyone at least as well off and someone better off. Indeed, we can consider a more restricted version that says there is an improvement if everyone becomes not just better off but also *equally* well off. Finally, we assume that the value ordering is coherent in the sense that if x is better than y, and y is as good as z, then x is better than z (transitivity). The case that generates the inconsistency is this:[9]

The Mere Addition Case

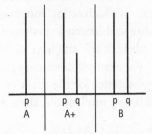

Here "p" and "q" can either be seen as picking out individual lives or populations. This very abstractly depicted case can be seen as a case of

(a) *individual reproductive choice*: a couple (p) can decide to have a child (q) and A is status quo and A+ and B are the outcomes of two possible ways of raising this child;

(b) *family planning policy*: the politicians can give tax benefits for parents and A is status quo (p is the current generation) and A+ and B are the outcomes of two possible ways of implementing a parental tax benefits policy (q are the future children of p);

(c) *extinction risk*: A is the outcome of not preventing a natural disaster that extinguishes all human life abruptly and painlessly, (so p is the current generation) and A+ and B are the outcomes of two ways of preventing this disaster (q is the future generation).

Here is how the inconsistency is generated:

1. A+ is as good as A (since a mere addition of a happy person does not affect value);
2. B is better than A+ (since B is a Pareto-improvement relative to A+);
3. B is as good as A (again, since a mere addition does not affect the value);
4. B must be better than A (since if B is better than A+, and A+ is as good as A, then B is better than A);
5. But 4 contradicts 3, since A and B cannot both have the same value and different value.

Now if we realize that our judgments are inconsistent in this way, we should stop being sure about each of them. What I will show now is that we do not need to flat out reject any of the principles that created the paradox in order to get some action guidance. We only need to consider some of the following alternative principles ("a mere addition" means "an addition of people with positive well-being, where the addition does not affect the lifetime well-being of anyone else or cause the creation of some other people"):

1. *Pareto*: It is better to make everyone at least as well off and someone better off (at least if everyone thereby becomes equally well off).
2. *Indifferent Mere Addition*: A mere addition does not affect value.
3. *Better Mere Addition*: A mere addition is *better*.
4. *Incomparable Mere Addition*: A mere addition is *incomparable* (not better, not worse, not equally as a good as).

As for the agent, I shall assume that the agent cares about the *value* of population changes in the sense that she prefers more value to less, is indifferent between equal values. More exactly, in this section, I shall assume that, for all value hypotheses V, the agent prefers the outcome x under hypothesis V to outcome y under the same hypothesis iff x is better than y, according to V; and the agent is indifferent between x under V and y under the same hypothesis iff x is equally as good as y, according to V.[10] This means that I do not here assume that we can compare values *across* evaluative hypotheses: the value of x under V is not assumed to be comparable with the value of y under some different hypothesis V'. In fact, I assume only ordinal comparability of value within each hypothesis; we only need to be able to say that, under V, x is better or worse or equally as good as y (when they are comparable in value). Finally, no well-defined probabilities or credences are required in this section. These assumptions will be relaxed later on.

As for principles of rationality, the following dominance principle for rational choice under evaluative uncertainty is assumed, according to which:

x *dominates* y iff x's outcome is preferred to y's, for some evaluative hypothesis, and x's outcome is preferred or indifferent to y's, for all other evaluative hypothesis.

x is rational, if it dominates all alternatives.

x is irrational, if it is dominated by some alternative.[11]

Table 13.2 Case 2

Alternatives	V1	V2	V3
A	1	1	1
A+	2	1	1
B	3	2	1

Table 13.3 Case 3

Alternatives	V1	V2	V3	V4	V5	V6
A	1	1	1	–	–	–
A+	2	1	1	1	1	–
B	3	2	1	2	1	–

We need to assume the usual caveat for dominance principles that the agent's credence in the alternative hypotheses is independent of her actions.[12] This dominance principle should be uncontroversial, at least if one accepts the corresponding principle for empirical uncertainty, where states of nature replace evaluative hypothesis.

Now consider the case in Table 13.2.

Of the principles listed above, V1 satisfies only Better Mere Addition and Pareto, V2 satisfies only Pareto, and V3 satisfies only Indifferent Mere Addition. The difference between V2 and V3 is that V2 accepts that a mere addition is sometimes better, for B is better than A (perhaps because the additional person has a sufficiently high level of well-being in B, and B has a more equal distribution of well-being than A+).

If the agent is uncertain about which of these hypotheses is true (and does not consider any others), it is clear what she rationally should do. Since B dominates both A+ and A, the dominance principle will tell her to choose B, given that the alternatives are A and/or A+, and to choose A+, given that the only alternative is A.

Now, this assumes that she understands "a mere addition makes no difference" as "a mere addition is indifferent in value." However, there is an alternative understanding, according to which it means "a mere addition is *incomparable* in value." What happens if the agent also considers this possibility? More exactly, what happens if we add the hypotheses V4, V5, and V6 (Table 13.3)?

V4 satisfies Pareto and Incomparable Mere Addition (so A+ is incomparable to A and B is incomparable to A). V5 and V6 satisfy only Incomparable Mere Addition. The difference between V5 and V6 is that V6 sees incomparability between all alternatives, not just between A and A+.

Now, in this situation B no longer dominates A+ and A, so the standard dominance principle will not help us here. However, there is a close cousin to this principle that can be applied, namely the following extended dominance principle:

x *dominates** y iff x's outcome is preferred to y's, for some evaluative hypothesis, and y's *outcome is not preferred to* x's, for any other evaluative hypothesis.

x is rational, if it dominates* all alternatives.

x is irrational, if some other action dominates* x and all other alternatives.[13]

According to the extended dominance principle, B dominates* both A+ and A, so it will tell the agent to choose B, given that the alternative options are A and/or A+, and to choose A+, given that the only alternative option is A.

So far, I have not questioned the principle about value coherence, according to which it holds that if x is better than y and y is as good as z, then x is better than z. But we can in fact even let the agent consider a hypothesis according to which this principle is false, and still use dominance reasoning. Suppose the agent considers V*, which says that A+ is equally as good as A, B is better than A+, and B is as good as A. Adding V* to the set of considered hypotheses in Case 2 does not change the fact that B dominates* both A and A+.[14]

So far so good when it comes to rational action guidance. We have shown that there is always a rational choice, in the sense of a dominating* action, if the agent considers V1 to V6, and V*. In fact, there is always a dominating* action, if the agent considers V1 together with any subset of V2 to V6 and V*.

To put it in biblical terms, it is uniquely rational to "Be fruitful and multiply, and fill the earth" by a mere addition of happy people, if your evaluative hypotheses are V1 together with any subset of V2 to V6 and V*. That is some significant action-guidance for agents who have not made up their minds about Indifferent Mere Addition, Better Mere Addition, Incomparable Mere Addition, Pareto, and the coherence of value. Paradoxes of population ethics need not paralyze normative decision-making even if the evaluative uncertainty is pretty extensive.

Furthermore, since A+ will always dominate* A given that V1 is one of the considered hypotheses, the so-called *strong asymmetry* does not hold for rational action under this kind of evaluative uncertainty: we have rational reason to add happy people to the world, and not just reason not to create unhappy people.[15]

Unfortunately, but not surprisingly, dominance reasoning is not always sufficient. What explains why dominance reasoning works for the cases we have discussed is that all considered value hypotheses are *non-decreasing* over the sequence A, A+, and B: no hypothesis says that things become worse when we go from one option to a subsequent one in this sequence. But this is not always true. For example, if we add hypotheses, according to which a mere addition at least sometimes makes things *worse*, dominance reasoning is not applicable. Table 13.4 shows one such case.

B no longer dominates* A+ and A, so dominance reasoning will not help here. However, A+ still dominates* A so A+ is the rational action given these two options. But this is not always true, as the case in Table 13.5 shows.

Table 13.4 Case 4

Alternatives	V1	V2	V3	V4	V5	V6	V7
A	1	1	1	–	–	–	1
A+	2	1	1	1	1	–	1
B	3	2	1	2	1	–	-1

Here B fails to dominate* A+ and A, and A+ fails to dominate* A. Dominance reasoning does not help at all here. This is where we reach the limits of dominance reasoning. Now, one could argue that the evaluation that B is worse than A is pretty weird. After all, the only difference between A and B is that B contains an extra happy person who is as exactly as happy as the people in A. So, we have more well-being, perfect equality, and no one is affected for the worse. How can B then be worse than A? One option is to assume some form of *axiological pessimism*, according to which each added life will always contain some pain or suffering which makes the world worse, even if overall the life is worth living.[16] This is not an especially attractive view, but it is not one to which all agents can justifiably assign zero credence. If one holds this pessimism as a live option, then dominance reasoning is not enough.

Other population paradoxes also show the limits of dominance reasoning. For example, the case that generates Parfit's famous Mere Addition Paradox (here in a truncated version) will not be solved by applying dominance principles.[17]

Parfit's Mere Addition Paradox Case

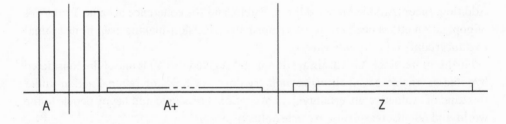

Table 13.5 Case 5

Alternatives	V1	V2	V3	V4	V5	V6	V8
A	1	1	1	–	–	–	1
A+	2	1	1	1	1	–	-1
B	3	2	1	2	1	–	0

Table 13.6 Case 6			
Alternatives	V1	V2	V3
A	1	1	1
A+	2	-1	1
Z	3	0	0

Intuitively, A+ as at least as good as A, and Z is better than A+. But this entails that Z is better than A, which seems false.[18] Indeed, it is plausible to say that Z is *worse* than A. More specifically, the principles that generate the paradox are the following (plus the coherence of value):

Mere Addition, at least in the weak version that a mere addition of a life worth living makes things *at least as good* as they would have been otherwise.
Non-Anti Egalitarianism: increasing both total and average well-being while making the well-being distribution more equal must count as an improvement.
Avoidance of the Repugnant Conclusion: a vast population with lives barely worth living is not better (in fact, worse) than a much smaller population with lives of very high well-being.

According to any evaluative hypothesis that is consistent and values A over Z, some move from one alternative to the next in this sequence must make things worse. But if the agent considers any of these hypotheses there will be no dominating* option. Table 13.6 gives an illustration.

4. WHAT TO DO WHEN DOMINANCE REASONING IS NOT APPLICABLE?

One very restrictive and pessimistic option would be to say that rationality is *silent* on these cases because we cannot make value comparisons across value hypotheses. If such inter-hypothetical comparisons cannot be made, there are no preferences that can latch on to them, so an agent's value-based preferences cannot provide any guidance in non-dominance cases.

Now, it is true that rationality would be silent if no intertheoretical comparisons were allowed and rational choice had to be based exclusively on value-based preferences. But it would not have to be silent if the agent were allowed some *latitude* when forming preferences: she only needs to make sure that her preferences line up with the evaluations given by the considered hypotheses, and that the resulting preferences are coherent (transitive, asymmetric). More exactly, if a considered hypothesis V1 values outcome x over y, then the agent prefers (x, V1), the outcome that would be the case if x were realized and V1 true, to (y, V1), the outcome that would be the case, if y were realized and V1 true; and if a considered hypothesis V1 values x and y equally, then the agent is indifferent between (x, V1) and (y, V1). For all outcomes that involve different hypotheses, that is, all outcomes of the form (A, V1) and (B, V2), where V1 is not identical to V2, the agent is free to form any preferences (including indifference), on the condition that they do not thereby create an incoherent preference ordering (a violation of transitivity, for example).

Obviously, these optional preferences would not be based on value considerations, so the agent we are imagining here cannot be said to be exclusively concerned with values. Some other non-evaluative factor would have to ground these optional preferences. So, what we have in mind is an agent with *value-constrained* preferences. What is rational for this agent to do will depend on both her evaluative and her non-evaluative preferences.[19]

To give an example, consider Case 6 above. An agent with value-constrained preferences facing this case must have these preference rankings (from the best to the worse in descending order):

(Z, V1)	(A, V2)	(A, V3), (A+, V3)
(A+, V1)	(Z, V2)	(Z, V3)
(A, V1)	(A+, V2)	

For any pair of items from different columns, the agent is free to form any preference as long as the resulting total preference ranking is coherent.

To decide what is rational for this agent to do, we only need to take a few pages from standard decision theory for agents with a complete (non-cardinal) preference ordering. More on this later. The important point to make here is that even if it is impossible to make intertheoretical comparisons of value, we can still decide what is rational to do for value-constrained agents who are evaluatively uncertain.

Now, to insist that we can *never* make comparisons of value across different value hypotheses is in fact not especially plausible. After all, we often do say things like "speciesism assigns less value to animals than Peter Singer's impartial view does," or "extreme perfectionism, which claims that happiness has only neutral value, assigns less value to happiness than hedonism does." All such claims would be false if we could never make comparisons across evaluative theories or hypotheses. But it is one thing to say that we can make them, another to say *how* we can make them. There are three main accounts.

Structuralist Accounts. According to structuralist accounts, intertheoretical comparisons should be made only with reference to structural features of the theories' value relations (such as the values of the best option and worst option) or of its numerical representation (such as the mean, sum, or spread of value).[20] One version is the 0-1 rule that claims that what is top-ranked according to one theory has the same value as what is top-ranked according to another theory and what is bottom-ranked, according to one theory, has the same value as what is bottom-ranked, according to another.[21]

Common Ground Accounts. According to these accounts, different theories are assumed to agree in their judgments about some alternatives. For example, one could assume that there are "cases in which, for some pair of options, we know that the difference between their values is the same according to both ethical theories."[22] The idea is then to use that difference to define a unit of value that is comparable across both theories.

Universal Scale Accounts. According to universal scale accounts, intertheoretical comparisons are true in virtue of the fact that there is some theory-independent scale that is the same across different theories.[23] Each theory plots alternatives to this universal scale, but there is no need to assume that they plot the same alternatives to the same values in the scale. Nor do we need to assume that different theories' top-ranked (or bottom-ranked) alternatives are plotted to the same value in the universal scale. In these two respects, universal scale accounts are superior to structuralist and common ground accounts.

Different versions of the universal scale account provide different accounts of what exactly this shared universal scale amounts to.[24] One version, which I think has a lot going for it, assumes that the universal scale is an *ordered structure of value magnitudes.*[25] According to this account of intertheoretical comparisons of value, claims such as "the value of x, according to one theory, is greater than the value of y, according to another" are thus taken literally, as referring to value magnitudes. These value magnitudes differ both from the objects that have value—the value magnitude bearers—and the numbers we may use to represent value relations. These magnitudes can be ordered and also "combined" (concatenated). On this view, to measure value is to assign numbers to the *values* of objects, not to the valuable objects, and to show a correspondence between two value magnitudes' standing in a certain relation (e.g., one being a greater value than the other) and the assigned numbers' standing in a certain relation (e.g., 2 being a greater number than 1).[26]

In all these respects, value magnitudes are analogous to abstract empirical magnitudes, such as lengths and masses, posited by magnitude realists in the philosophy of science. These magnitudes can also be ordered and combined. For example, 2 kg is a greater mass than 1 kg, and the concatenation of 1 kg and 1 kg is 2 kg. On this view, to measure length is to assign numbers to the *lengths* of objects, not to the lengthy objects, and to show a correspondence between two length magnitudes' standing in a certain relation (one being a greater length than the other) and the assigned numbers' standing in a certain relation (2 being a greater number than 1).[27]

For my discussion, there is no need to take a stand on which approach is best (but there are independent reasons to accept realism about value magnitudes). As I will show, rational decision-making under evaluative uncertainty is possible no matter which approach we go for, including the minimal value-constrained preference account. The idea is to "divide and conquer": to apply different rationality principles to different cases, depending on the facts about the agent's credences and the specific kind of comparability her value-constrained preferences allows for. In the following, I will give a short presentation of the main types of cases and, for each type, an application to population ethics.[28]

4.1 No Well-Defined Credences, Ordinal Full Comparability

Suppose the agent considers the value hypotheses for Parfit's Mere Addition Paradox Case shown in Table 13.7.

Here the agent considers four different value hypotheses that conform to different principles that are not jointly consistent: Better Mere Addition, Indifferent Mere Addition, Non-Anti Egalitarianism, and Avoidance of RC.

This is how the hypotheses are supposed to fare in relation to these principles:

V1 satisfies Better Mere Addition, Non-Anti Egalitarianism, but not Avoidance of RC.

V2 satisfies Indifferent Mere Addition, Non-Anti Egalitarianism, but not Avoidance of RC or Better Mere Addition.

V3 satisfies Indifferent Mere Addition, but not Non-Anti Egalitarianism, Avoidance of RC, or Better Mere Addition.

V4 satisfies Non-Anti Egalitarianism and Avoidance of RC, but not Better and Indifferent Mere Addition (perhaps when the inequality is sufficiently great).

V5 satisfies Indifferent Mere Addition and Avoidance of RC, but not Non-Anti Egalitarianism.

Since we have full ordinal comparability, we can apply Maximin (choose the action that maximizes the least preferred possible outcome) or, better, Leximin (choose the action that maximizes the least preferred possible outcome, and in case of a tie in the least preferred possible outcomes, choose the possible outcome which maximizes second to least

Table 13.7 Case 7

Alternatives	V1	V2	V3	V4	V5
A	1	1	1	1	1
A+	2	1	1	-1	1
Z	3	2	1	0	0

preferred possible outcome, and so on). In this case, Leximin says that the agent should choose A, since it maximizes the least preferred possible outcome. (The least preferred possible outcome for A is 1, for B, -1 and for Z, -2.)

4.2. Well-Defined Credences, Ordinal Full Comparability

Suppose that we have a variation of Parfit's Mere Addition Paradox Case (see Table 13.8).

V1 violates Better Mere Addition, Indifferent Mere Addition, but satisfies Non-Anti Egalitarianism and Avoidance of RC.

V2 violates Better Mere Addition, Indifferent Mere Addition, but satisfies Avoidance of RC and Non-Anti Egalitarianism.

V3 satisfies Indifferent Mere Addition and Non-Anti Egalitarianism, but violates Better Mere Addition, and Avoidance of RC.

Here Leximin seems too restricted, since it judges A and Z as equally rational. But this is to ignore the fact that A provides a higher probability of achieving value 2 and the same probability of achieving at least the value 1. A principle that takes this fact into account is the *Stochastic Dominance Principle*, which states that it is rational to choose an alternative that stochastically dominates all other alternatives, and that it is irrational to choose an alternative that is stochastically dominated by some alternative.[29] An alternative x *stochastically dominates* another alternative y iff:

(a) for any value v, the probability that x is at least as valuable as v is equal to or greater than the probability that y is at least as valuable as v, and

(b) for some value v, the probability that x is at least as valuable as v is greater than the probability that y is at least as valuable as v.

That A stochastically dominates both A+ and Z is easily seen if one considers Table 13.9.

Table 13.8 Case 8			
Alternatives	V1 Credence = 1/3	V2 Credence = 1/3	V3 Credence = 1/3
A	2	2	1
A+	0	0	1
Z	1	1	2

Table 13.9 Probability distribution for the
values in Case 8

Alternatives	0	1	2
A	1	1	2/3
A+	1	1/3	0
Z	1	1	1/3

In this case, the Stochastic Dominance Principle tells us that the rational action is A and that the irrational actions are A+ and Z. Does this show that this principle tends to favor not adding extra people to the world? No, it all depends on the considered theories and their probabilities. For example, Table 13.10 shows that the Stochastic Dominance Principle can favor adding extra people; indeed, in this case it favors realizing the Z-population:

V1 satisfies both Better Mere Addition and Non-Anti Egalitarianism, but violates Avoidance of RC.

V2 satisfies Better Mere Addition but violates Non-Anti Egalitarianism and Avoidance of RC.

V3 satisfies Indifferent Mere Addition but violates Non-Anti Egalitarianism, Better Mere Addition, and Avoidance of RC.

Table 13.11 shows that Z stochastically dominates both A and A+ and hence that it is rational to realize Z and irrational to choose either A or A+.

4.3. Well-Defined Credence, Cardinal Full Comparability

Here we assume that we can compare value differences across theories. More precisely, all theories can be represented by the same interval scale. In this setting we can take out

Table 13.10 Case 9

Alternatives	V1 Credence = 1/3	V2 Credence = 1/3	V3 Credence = 1/3
A	0	1	1
A+	1	2	1
Z	2	2	1

Table 13.11 Probability distribution for the values in Case 9

Alternatives	0	1	2
A	1	1	0
A+	1	1	1/3
Z	1	1	2/3

another tool from the decision theorists' toolbox: *the expected value principle (EVP)*.[30] According to EVP, the expected value of an alternative is the sum of the values assigned by each value hypothesis weighted by the credences for each hypothesis. The rational action would then be the one that brings about the alternative with the greatest expected value. Now we are in a position to make trade-offs between theories that depend on both how much value the theories assign to the alternatives and the credences we have in these theories.

Let us first look at the implications of EVP for The Mere Addition Case, in which the alternatives are A and A+. As Hilary Greaves and Toby Ord have shown, if the agent only considers theories that do not assign a fixed negative value to adding one additional person, then no matter what non-zero credence the agent has in these theories, EVP will rank A+ above A, when A is sufficiently large, and this holds even when the mere addition lowers the overall average.[31] The reason for this is that as A gets larger, the additional value of adding one person, A+, is either a fixed positive amount, as for instance the Total View would say, or it tends to zero, as for instance the Average View would say. In other words, theories that assign a fixed positive amount, such as the Total View, will become the "effective" theories that "swamp" all other theories when the base population is sufficiently large. The rational option thus becomes the one that is highest ranked by the Total View.

If the theories the agent considers all satisfy Pareto, we will also get the further result that B will come out as having an expected value that is at least as great as the value of A and of A+. So, B will be the rational option in these cases.

This "swamping" argument has some limitations, however. First, it is unclear whether the base populations that are big enough for this "swamping effect" to occur are *realistic*.[32] If the effects are practically impossible to occur in realistic settings, one might think that this implication of EVP is less troubling.

Second, if the agent considers critical-level theories that set the level fairly high, then these theories will assign a fixed negative value to adding one additional person. Indeed, if the level is sufficiently high, these critical-level theories might be the ones doing the swamping.[33]

What does EVP say about Parfit's Mere Addition Paradox Case, where the alternatives are A, A+, and Z? A similar swamping effect will occur if only the Total View and the

Table 13.12 Case 10

Alternatives	Total view Credence = 0.01	Average view Credence = 0.99
A	100 x 10 billion	100
Z	1 x billion billion	1

Average view are considered by the agent. To see this, suppose the agent considers both total and average utilitarianism. Suppose that A contains 10 billion people and Z (and A+) contains 1 billion billion. Suppose further that the average well-being in A is 100 (very high) and the average well-being in Z is 1 (very low) (Table 13.12).

Z will have greater expected value than A (and also greater expected value than A+ since the total view and the average view agree that Z is better than A+), even if the agent's credence in the total view is very low, say 0.01, and her credence in the average view is very high, say 0.99. So, the rational option is to bring about Z.

This may seem an unattractive implication of EVP. However, note that the fact that a low high-stake theory often wins over a low-stake one, even when the latter is much more probable, cannot in general be troublesome, because it seems sensible in cases of ordinary *empirical* uncertainty to take seriously even small risks of doing something that could turn out to be very bad. For example, it is wise to lock one's bike even if the probability of its being stolen is fairly small (5%, say), since the cost of losing the bike is much greater than the very mild discomfort which always locking the bike brings about. Of course, when the credence in the high-stake theories are miniscule, then it seems odd to give so much weight to them. But this problem also applies to expected value reasoning in cases of empirical uncertainty. (Should one seriously consider the extremely far-fetched empirical possibility that one causes infinite harm?)

Some would still argue that the case above shows that EVP gives too much weight to high-stake theories, especially since favoring Z over A seems so unattractive. One option here is simply to modify the expected value approach so that it no longer has these swamping effects. Perhaps one should follow "my favorite theory" in these cases and give much more weight to the theories one takes the greatest credence in.

It is worth pointing out, however, that this swamping effect vanishes if the agent considers critical-level theories, since on the most plausible settings of critical levels the

Table 13.13 Case 11

Alternatives	Total View Credence = p	Average View Credence = q	Critical-level theory Credence = s
A	1000 x 10 billion	1000	$(1000 - c)$ x 10 billion
Z	1 x 1 billion billion	1	$(1 - c)$ x 1 billion billion

well-being of the lives in the Z-population will be below them.[34] Consider, for instance, the situation shown in Table 13.13.

Here it is no longer true that the total view will prevail despite a very low credence in it. If the critical level c is greater than 1, then Z will be overall very bad. A will be the alternative with the greatest expected value, if s, the credence in the critical-level theory, is sufficiently greater than p, the credence in the total view.

4.4. Well-Defined Credence, Full Cardinal Comparability for Some Theories, Incomparability for Others

The cases above are all cases where there is full cardinal comparability. But, as shown above, it is common for agents to consider hypotheses according to which there is incomparability in value. Consider, for example, versions of The Mere Addition Case in the previous section where we add the hypothesis that A, A+, and B are not all comparable in value. Or consider versions of Parfit's Mere Addition Paradox Case in the previous section where we add the hypothesis that A, A+, and Z are not all comparable in value. What should the agent do in these cases?

Well, here it seems sensible to follow a "clumping" approach to rational action.[35] I will first present the general idea and then apply it to the cases at hand. The general idea is this. First, calculate the expected value of the alternatives for the theories that are fully cardinally comparable. Then apply the dominance* principle, introduced in Section 3. The theories that provide fully comparable cardinal values are "clumped" together and the resulting expected value is treated as *one* evaluative possibility. To illustrate this, consider the abstract toy example shown in Table 13.14.

First V1 and V2 are clumped together and the resulting expected value is treated as one evaluative possibility (Table 13.15).

Then the extended rationality principle is applied to this new representation and we get the result that B dominates* both A and C. So, B is the rational choice here.

This was a case where the incomparability hypothesis was universal: all alternatives were deemed incomparable. What shall we do when the hypothesis deems some alternatives comparable and others incomparable? In this case, clumping does not work.

Table 13.14	Case 12		
	V1	V2	V3
Alternatives	0.3	0.6	0.1
A	1	1	-
B	2	3	-
C	3	2	-

Table 13.15 Clumped version of Case 12

Alternatives	V1–V2	V3
A	0.9	–
B	2.4	–
C	2.1	–

Table 13.16 Case 13

Alternatives	V1–V2	V3
A	0.9	0
B	2.4	1
C	2.1	–

Table 13.17 Case 14

Alternatives	V1–V2	V3
A	0.9	0
B	2.4	0
C	2.1	–

But the extended rationality principle is still applicable if the incomparability hypothesis only provides positive value judgment that does not reverse the ranking given by the clumped together hypothesis for all alternatives, as in the cases shown in Tables 13.16 and 13.17.

In both these cases, B still dominates* all alternatives and is therefore the rational choice.

Now we can go back to the mere addition cases and ask what this approach prescribes. The simple answer is that it prescribes exactly the same action, B, as long as the added incomparability hypotheses does not provide value judgments that reverse the ranking given by the clumped together value hypotheses.

5. CONCLUDING REMARKS

This completes my discussion of how to react rationally to various cases of evaluative uncertainty about population changes. What I have shown is that the paradoxes of population ethics need not paralyze rational decision-making. In order to act rationally there is no need to first decide which of the conflicting conditions to drop. This is the good news, especially since climate change and many other real-life cases that involve changing the population require an urgent response. Moreover, a more substantive conclusion is that it is hard to avoid the conclusion that it is rational in a variety of cases to add happy people to the world. Indeed, in some rather far-fetched cases evaluative views that favor adding happy people to the world will "swamp" other theories that do not favor such additions (because they give it zero weight or negative weight).

These conclusions come with a big caveat, however. Even though the rationality principles I have applied have widespread support, they have or can be doubted. This means that there is room for uncertainty about rationality principles as well. Thus, the more qualified conclusion is that, *barring uncertainty about rationality principles*, I have shown that agents can get rational guidance in a great variety of cases of evaluative uncertainty about population ethics and that agents will often be guided to add happy people to the world. How to proceed in the face of rational uncertainty is beyond the scope of this chapter. Suffice it to say that there are two main alternatives. The first is to simply say that rational uncertainty should not be taken seriously. For each situation, there is a correct answer about which actions are rational, no matter whether the agent herself is certain about this answer. The second alternative is to take seriously rational uncertainty and provide principles about how to behave when one is not certain about which principle of rationality is correct. An obvious challenge for this approach is how to deal with the potential threat of a regress: if one can be uncertain about which rationality principle to apply to a case of evaluative uncertainty, one can also be uncertain about which principle for rational uncertainty is correct, and so on. There are proposals about how to deal with this potential regress, but, again, this is not the place to deal with this complex issue.[36]

It should be noted, however, that the challenge of rational uncertainty is a problem for *everyone*, not just those who take evaluative uncertainty seriously. After all, there can be rational uncertainty without evaluative uncertainty. For example, you can be uncertain about what rationality requires of you in cases of empirical uncertainty, or in cases where you have to coordinate your present actions with your future ones. This means that we have at least reduced the problem of rational guidance under evaluative uncertainty to *one* general problem, that of rational uncertainty. That is some progress.

ACKNOWLEDGMENTS

For useful comments on earlier drafts I would like to thank Tim Campbell and Orri Stéfansson. Financial support from Swedish Research Council (grant 421-2014-1037) and Riksbankens Jubileumsfond (grant M17-0372:1) is gratefully acknowledged.

Notes

1. For the challenge of climate change, see Broome's chapter in this volume.
2. For some versions of such impossibility theorems, see the chapters by Arrhenius and Bossert in this volume.
3. Zimmerman (2008; 2014). See Bykvist (2014; 2018a) for criticisms of Zimmerman's prospective view.
4. Zimmerman (2014, 89).
5. More exactly, the label "my favorite theory" is commonly used for a theory that tells you what to do when you are uncertain about what you *morally ought* to do. Here I extend the use of the label to cover theories that tells you what to do when you care about value but are evaluatively uncertain. For one of the first presentations of this theory, see Gracely (1996).
6. For a defense of a non-utilitarian version of the person-affecting theory, see Bader's chapter in this volume. For a defense of the critical-level theory, see Bossert's chapter in this volume.
7. For a more sophisticated version of "my favorite theory," see Gustafsson and Torpman (2014).
8. For an attempt to find a non-arbitrary partition, see Gustafsson and Torpman (2014). For criticism, see MacAskill, Bykvist, and Ord (2020). For another attempt at solving the problems, see Gustafsson (2018).
9. For a presentation of this case and a demonstration of the inconsistency, see Broome (2004).
10. "Under hypothesis V" should be read as "under the supposition that V," but in this paper I want to stay neutral on whether the supposition is indicative or subjunctive. We need to take a stand on this issue only if we allow that there can be an evidential relation between the actions and the probability of V. I will ignore this complication in the following and only focus on cases where this evidential relation does not hold. Thanks to Orri Stefánsson for pointing out that I need to be clearer about this issue.
11. I assume here and in the following that we only have a *finite* number of options. If there is an infinite series of ever better options (each option dominating the previous one), it seems wrong to say that they are all irrational.
12. As Orri Stefánsson has pointed out (and which I touch upon in footnote 10), this independence claim is an idealization. It seems possible that one's action can be evidentially linked to the probability of various evaluative hypotheses. However, I will ignore this complication in the following and only consider cases where this link is missing.
13. For a defense of a similar rationality principle, see Bales, Cohen, and Handfield (2014).
14. This would no longer hold if we added the hypothesis that value is *cyclical*: A+ is better than A, B is better than A+, but A is better than B. However, rational choice might be possible even if we accept crazy hypotheses like this. Perhaps one could say that it is rational to choose B when the alternatives are A and A+ because B dominates A and A+ in terms of *maximal* elements (where a maximal element is an option that is not worse than any other option). B dominates A in this sense, since, for some hypotheses, B is maximal and A is not, and, for any other hypothesis, B and A are either both maximal or both non-maximal. The same holds for B and A+. It is likely that this principle is in need of some tweaking, however. I do not have the space here to explore this issue further but hope to come back to it in future research.
15. For discussions of the asymmetry, see McMahan (1981), Narveson (1967), and Roberts (2011).

16. For a defense of this kind of pessimism, see Benatar (2006).

17. Parfit's own presentation of the longer version of this case can be found in Parfit (1996). Arrhenius (forthcoming) presents a version of this paradox which invokes weaker and even more plausible conditions.

18. One could object to the judgment that Z is better than A+, since the difference between the better off people in A+ and those in Z is vast. However, the non-truncated version of the Mere Addition does not have such big "jumps" in well-being. Thanks to Tim Campbell for reminding me to clarify this.

19. For similar ideas, see Greaves and Ord (2017) and Hicks (2018).

20. Some structural accounts deny the possibility of making intertheoretical comparisons between different theories. They claim instead that we can "treat different theories fairly" by assigning the same value to certain positions in their respective value rankings.

21. This principle is defended by Lockhart (2000). For criticisms, see MacAskill, Bykvist, and Ord (2020).

22. Ross (2006, 764).

23. A universal scale account can be less ambitious and deny that there is a universal scale that is shared by absolutely *all* theories. It seems reasonable to deny such a scale for theories that invoke very different kinds of value (e.g., Kantian choice-worthiness and utilitarian intrinsic value). Arguably, this is not a pressing problem in the present context, since we are only considering the value of outcomes, as a function of the values of lives, which in turn is a function of lifetime well-being.

24. For a discussion of some versions, see MacAskill, Bykvist, and Ord (2020).

25. For a defense of this version, see ibid. and Bykvist (2018b).

26. This realism about value magnitudes has independent support, since value magnitudes can do a lot of useful theoretical work outside the domain of moral uncertainty. If we invoke them, we can give simple and straightforward explanations of the equivalence between betterness-talk and value-talk, cross-time comparisons, mind-world comparisons, cross-world comparisons, organic unities, value aggregation, and value measurement, and we can also provide uniform definitions of goodness, badness, and neutrality, which validates central platitudes about absolute values. See Bykvist (2021) for more on this.

27. For some recent defenders of realism about empirical magnitudes, see Perry (2015), Kim (2016), Mundy (1987), Peacocke (2015), Swoyer (1987).

28. The list of cases is not complete. For example, I do not discuss cases where we have interval scale measurability within each theory but no comparability across theories.

29. For a defense of this principle and an application to moral uncertainty for deontologists, see Tarsney (2018).

30. For a representation theorem that shows that EVP (in the context of evaluative uncertainty) follows from plausible axioms, see Riedener (2020).

31. Greaves and Ord (2017).

32. For some informed speculations about how realistic this is, see Greaves and Ord (2017).

33. This is pointed out by Greaves and Ord (2017).

34. This is pointed out in Greaves and Ord (2017).

35. Thanks to Johan Gustafsson for suggesting this approach. Something similar is suggested in Tarsney (2017, 215–219).

36. For some suggestions on how to deal with this potential regress, see MacAskill, Bykvist, and Ord (2020) and Sepielli (2013).

References

Arrhenius, Gustaf. Forthcoming. *Population Ethics: The Challenge of Future Generations.* Oxford University Press.

Bales, Adam, Daniel Cohen, and Toby Handfield. 2014. "Decision Theory for Agents with Incomplete Preferences." *Australasian Journal of Philosophy* 92: 453–470.

Benatar, David. 2006. *Better Never to Have Been.* Oxford: Clarendon Press.

Broome, John. 2004. *Weighing Lives.* Oxford: Oxford University Press.

Bykvist, Krister. 2014. "Evaluative Uncertainty and Consequentialist Environmental Ethics." In *Environmental Ethics and Consequentialism*, edited by Leonard Kahn and Avram Hiller, 122–135. London: Routledge.

Bykvist, Krister. 2018a. "Some Critical Comments on Michael Zimmerman's *Ignorance and Moral Obligation,*" *Journal of Moral Philosophy*: 15, 383–400.

Bykvist, Krister. 2018b. "Intertheoretical Comparisons of Value, Evaluative Uncertainty, and Population Ethics." Unpublished ms.

Bykvist, Krister.2021, "Taking Values Seriously." Synthese. Published on-line 15 March 2021.

Gracely, Edward J. 1996. "On the Noncomparability of Judgments Made by Different Ethical Theories." *Metaphilosophy* 27, no. 3, 327–332.

Greaves, Hilary and Toby Ord. 2017. "Moral Uncertainty about Population Axiology." *Journal of Ethics and Social Philosophy* 12, no. 2: 135–167.

Gustafsson, Johan E. 2018. "Moral Uncertainty and the Problem of Theory Individuation," unpublished ms.

Gustafsson, Johan E. and Olle Torpman. 2014. "In Defence of My Favourite Theory." *Pacific Philosophical Quarterly* 95, no. 2: 159–174.

Hicks, Amelia. 2018. "Moral Uncertainty and Value Comparison." *Oxford Studies in Metaethics* 13: 161–183.

Kim, Joongol. 2016, "What Are Quantities?" *Australasian Journal of Philosophy* 94, no. 5: 792–807.

Lockhart, Ted. 2000. *Moral Uncertainty and Its Consequences.* New York: Oxford University Pres

McAskill, William, Krister Bykvist, and Toby Ord. 2020. *Moral Uncertainty.* Oxford: Oxford University Press.

McMahan, Jefferson. 1981. "Problems of Population Theory." *Ethics* 92, no. 1: 96–127.

Mundy, Brent. 1987. "The Metaphysics of Quantity." *Philosophical Studies* 51: 29–54.

Narveson, Jan. 1967. "Utilitarianism and Future Generations." *Mind* 76: 62–72

Parfit, Derek. 1996. *Reasons and Persons.* Oxford: Oxford University Press.

Peacocke, Christopher. 2015. "Magnitudes: Metaphysics, Explanation, and Perception." In *Mind, Language and Action: Proceedings of the 36th International Wittgenstein Symposium*, edited by Annalisa Coliva, Volker Munz, and Danièle Moyal-Sharrock, 357–388. Berlin: De Gruyter.

Perry, Zee R. 2015. "Properly Extensive Quantities." *Philosophy of Science* 82, no. 5: 833–844.

Riedener, Stefan. 2020. "An Axiomatic Approach to Evaluative Uncertainty." *Philosophical Studies* 177, no. 2: 483–504.

Roberts, Melinda A. 2011. "The Asymmetry: A Solution." *Theoria* 77: 333–367.

Ross, Jacob. 2006. "Rejecting Ethical Deflationism." *Ethics* 116, no. 4: 742–768.

Sepielli, Andrew. 2013. "What to Do When You Do not Know What to Do When You Do not Know What to Do . . .." *Noûs* 48, no. 3: 521–544.

Swoyer, C. 1987. "The Metaphysics of Measurement." In *Measurement, Realism and Objectivity: Essays on Measurement in the Social and Physical Sciences,* edited by J. Forge, 235–290. Dordrecht: Reidel.

Tarsney, Christian. 2017. "Rationality and Moral Risk: A Moderate Defense of Hedging." PhD diss. University of Maryland.

Tarsney, Christian. 2018. "Moral Uncertainty for Deontologists." *Ethical Theory and Moral Practice* 21, no. 3: 505–520.

Zimmerman, Michael. 2008. *Living with Uncertainty: The Moral Significance of Ignorance.* Cambridge: Cambridge University Press.

Zimmerman, Michael. 2014. *Ignorance and Moral Obligation.* Oxford: Oxford University Press.

CHAPTER 14

···

CLAIMS ACROSS OUTCOMES AND POPULATION ETHICS

···

MATTHEW D. ADLER

1. INTRODUCTION

···

THE "person-affecting principle" (PAP) is widely discussed in the literature on population ethics. (For recent treatments see Arrhenius 2015; Fleurbaey and Voorhoeve 2015; Holtug 2010.) The principle can be formulated in various ways, for example, as follows: Outcome x is better than outcome y only if there is at least one person for whom x is better than y.[1] However formulated, the PAP is usually understood as an axiom that the moral-goodness[2] ranking of outcomes must satisfy.

Why accept such an axiom? One might do so, I suppose, merely on intuition. Alternatively, a moral deliberator might assent to the PAP because it flows naturally from a certain understanding, which she has in mind, about how to *justify* the moral-goodness ranking of outcomes. Call this understanding the "Person-Affecting Idea." The comparative moral goodness of outcomes is determined by how the outcomes compare for individuals' well-being (with individual well-being a positive contributor to moral goodness). Given any two outcomes, x and y, the fact that x is better than y for some person is a pro tanto moral consideration in favor of x; and it is the totality of these pro tanto considerations that determine whether x is morally better than, worse than, equally good as, or incomparable with y.

The "Person-Affecting Idea," as just stated, is pretty vague. In prior work, I have developed a conceptual framework, "claims across outcomes," that *precisifies* the Person-Affecting Idea (Adler 2012, especially Ch. 5; Adler 2018). The claims-across-outcomes framework fills in the details of the plausible but fuzzy idea that the comparative moral goodness of outcomes is determined by how they compare for individuals' well-beings.

My work on the claims-across-outcomes framework, to date, has focused on the fixed population case—by which I mean that the very same individuals exist in all of the outcomes being compared. In the fixed population case, the framework justifies the Pareto axioms (Pareto indifference and strong Pareto) *and* the Pigou-Dalton axiom, as well as an axiom of Anonymity. The framework thereby reveals a deep linkage between axioms that are usually seen as reflecting *distinct* ethical concerns, "efficiency" (in the case of the Pareto axioms) and "equity" (in the case of Pigou-Dalton). Adding some further, plausible, axioms, we arrive at prioritarianism.

But what about the variable population case? By this I mean that the very same individuals *don't* exist in all of the outcomes being compared.[3]

A widely held view among population ethicists is that a comparison of two outcomes as regards the well-being of some person presupposes the existence of the person in both of the outcomes.[4] If this widely held view is correct, the Person-Affecting Idea (and therewith the claims-across-outcomes framework, which precisifies that idea) is a non-starter in the variable population case.

Fortunately, the widely held view needn't be accepted. Work by Gustaf Arrhenius, Nils Holtug, and Wlodek Rabinowicz has shown that rejection of that view doesn't require weird metaphysics (for example, the weird supposition that nonexistents can have properties) (Arrhenius and Rabinowicz 2015; Holtug 2010). These insights, in turn, permit the claims-across-outcomes framework to be extended to the variable population case. That is what is undertaken here.

Section 2 reviews the claims-across-outcomes framework in the fixed population case. Section 3 extends the framework to the variable population case. It does so in a manner that meets the objection (let's call this the "metaphysical" objection) that the well-being of a life can't be compared to nonexistence. And Section 3 addresses a second, distinct objection (the "standing" objection)—that even if the metaphysical objection can be countered, persons who are potential nonexistents don't have standing to assert full claims.

Section 4 presents the axiomatic upshots of the variable-population extension— namely generalized versions of the Pareto axioms, the Pigou-Dalton axiom, and the Anonymity axiom. It discusses the relation between this axiom cluster and two types of variable-population prioritarianism: total and critical-level prioritarianism. Finally, Section 4 addresses the implications of the claims-across-outcomes framework for major topics in population ethics, in particular No Difference, Mere Addition, the Sadistic Conclusion, and the Repugnant Conclusion.

The aim of this chapter is to demonstrate how the Person-Affecting Idea can be extended to the variable population case, via the specific model of claims-across-outcomes. One then wonders: why *accept* the person-affecting account, as opposed to a non-person-affecting ("impersonal") justification of the outcome ranking? Space constraints preclude a detailed juxtaposition of person-affecting and non-person-affecting views. A few brief comments are offered in Section 4.

The chapter takes as given (which I find to be exceedingly plausible) that the moral-goodness ranking of outcomes has some significant role within morality. However, it is not necessary for purposes of the chapter for me to take a position about the specifics of that role—a controversial topic, regarding which act-consequentialists, rule-consequentialists, and non-consequentialists[5] have different views. The Person-Affecting Idea, precisified by the claims framework, is a way to justify the outcome ranking—whatever its precise role within morality may be.

I *do* assume that the moral-goodness ranking is *agent-neutral*. The outcome ranking that matters, morally, is one and the same ranking for all agents (decision-makers)—not a ranking that varies between agents.[6] Defending this position (which again I find to be exceedingly plausible) is well beyond the scope of the chapter, so once more it will be taken as given.[7]

2. CLAIMS ACROSS OUTCOMES IN THE FIXED POPULATION CASE

2.1. The Basic Apparatus

It will be useful to have some formalism to structure the discussion. There is a set O of possible outcomes[8] $\{x, y, \ldots\}$. O is ranked with respect to moral goodness. The ranking takes the form of a quasi-ordering. (See Adler 2012, 38–56). This means that the "morally at least as good" relation between outcomes is transitive, but not necessarily complete. For any two outcomes, either the first is morally at least as good as the second, or the second is morally at least as good as the first, or both, or neither. In this last case, the two outcomes are "incomparable" with respect to moral goodness.

In the remainder of the chapter, I often omit the term "moral"; but discussions of the "goodness" or "betterness" of outcomes are always meant to indicate moral goodness/betterness.

There is a set I of N individuals, $I = \{1, \ldots, N\}$, who exist in all outcomes. Let's denote the pairing of an individual and an outcome as a "history," with "$(x; i)$" denoting the history of individual i in outcome x. A history is to be understood as a possible bundle of welfare-relevant attributes (properties and relations).[9] $(x; i)$ describes all of individual i's welfare-relevant attributes in outcome x.

The set of histories can be ranked with respect to well-being, and differences between histories can also be ranked with respect to well-being. These well-being rankings, too, take the form of quasi-orderings. See Appendix for more detail.

The ranking of histories is the basis for intra- and interpersonal comparisons of well-being levels. Amy in x is at least as well off as Amy in y iff $(x; $ Amy$)$ is at least as good with respect to well-being as $(y; $ Amy$)$. Saul in x is at least as well off as Timothy in y iff $(x; $ Saul$)$ is at least as good with respect to well-being as $(y; $ Timothy$)$. (The term "iff" is shorthand for "if and only if.") Similarly, the ranking of history differences with respect to well-being is the basis for intra- and interpersonal comparisons of well-being differences.

Because the rankings of histories and of history differences are quasi-orderings, possibly incomplete, there can be incomparabilities in well-being levels and differences—as in moral goodness itself. Thus we aren't yet assuming that well-being is numerically measurable. But regardless of numerical measurability, we can define specific well-being levels by grouping together all histories that are equally good for well-being, and we can define specific well-being differences by grouping together all pairs of histories with the same well-being difference.[10] I will use upper-case symbols such as W, W^* etc. to denote well-being levels.

Pulling all this together: an outcome x can be expressed as a list of histories $[(x; 1), (x; 2), \ldots, (x; N)]$, or as the list of well-being levels of those histories $[W^1, W^2, \ldots, W^N]$, with W^1 here denoting the well-being level of $(x; 1)$ and so forth.

Now for the idea of claims-across-outcomes. (I will sometimes, for stylistic reasons, use "between" in lieu of "across," and will often simplify terminology by speaking just of "claims" except where "across outcomes" is needed for clarity or emphasis.)

A claim is a relation[11] between any given individual i, and any two outcomes x and y. That relation has one of four *valences*: Either i has a claim in favor of x over y, or a claim in favor of y over x, or a null claim, or an incomparable claim. The valence of i's claim is fixed by her comparative well-being, that is, by the well-being levels of her histories in the two outcomes. She has a claim in favor of x over y if she is better off in x than y; a claim in favor of y over x if she is better off in y than x; a null claim if she is equally well off in the two outcomes; and an incomparable claim if she is incomparably well off. Equivalently (and this will be important in the variable population generalization): she has a claim in favor of x over y if $(x; i)$ is at a higher well-being level than $(y; i)$; a claim in favor of y over x if $(y; i)$ is at a higher well-being level than $(x; i)$; a null claim if $(x; i)$ and $(y; i)$ are at the same well-being level; and an incomparable claim if $(x; i)$ and $(y; i)$ are incomparable.

Non-null claims also have a *strength*. See below for a discussion of the determination of claim strength.

The claims framework includes certain basic Rules. These provide a specific and (I hope) intuitively plausible model of how the comparative goodness of two outcomes might derive from how they compare with respect to the well-being of each individual:

The Rules

Supervenience: The comparative goodness of two outcomes depends on the claim pattern, meaning: if the pattern of claims (in terms of valence and strength) between x and y is the same as between x^* and y^*, x is at least as good as y iff x^* is at least as good as y^*.

Claims as Pro Tanto Moral Considerations: If there is a claim in favor of x over y, then x is better than y unless there is a claim in favor of y over x or an incomparable claim.[12]

Equal Balance: Given two outcomes, x and y, it is sufficient for individual i's claim to be "equally balanced" with individual j's claim that the two individuals swap well-being levels.[13] If x and y are such that all non-null claims can be grouped into pairs of equally balanced claims, then x and y are equally good.[14]

Two-Person Cases: If one person has a claim to x over y, and a second person has a claim to y over x, with everyone else having null claims, then x is better than y iff the first person's claim is stronger, and y is better than x iff the second person's claim is stronger.

Consider, now, the following axioms (constraints on the goodness ranking of outcomes):[15]

Pareto Indifference: If each person is equally well off in x as she is in y, then x and y are equally good.

Strong Pareto: If at least one person is better off in x than y, and everyone is at least as well off in x as y, then x is better than y.

Anonymity: If the pattern of well-being in x is a permutation of the pattern of well-being in y[16], then x and y are equally good.

Pigou-Dalton: Assume that x and y are related as follows. (1) One person ("Higher") is better off than a second ("Lower") in y. (2) Lower is better off in x than y, while Higher is better off in y than x, and these differences are equal in magnitude. (3) In x, Higher remains at least as well off as Lower. (4) Everyone else is equally well off in x as she is in y. Then x is better than y.

Deriving the Pareto axioms from the Rules is trivial. Pareto Indifference is an immediate implication of the equal balance rule, and Strong Pareto of the rule that claims are pro tanto moral considerations. (To be sure, it's not very surprising that a conceptual scheme designed to fill in the details of the Person-Affecting Idea will endorse the Pareto axioms. The Pareto axioms and the PAP are, typically, seen as closely aligned.)

How does Anonymity follow from the Rules? Let's say that outcomes x and y are related by a "two-person permutation" if two individuals swap well-being levels and no one else's well-being level changes. By the equal balance rule, two outcomes related by a two-person permutation are equally good. Further, it can be shown that any permutation of well-being levels can be expressed as a series of two-person permutations. That is, if the pattern of well-being in y is a permutation of the pattern in x, there is a series of outcomes $x, x^1, x^2, \ldots, x^m, y$, such that x^1 is a two-person permutation of x, x^2 a two-person permutation of $x^1, \ldots, y$ a two-person permutation of x^m. By transitivity, y must be equally good as x.

The Pigou-Dalton axiom is an equity axiom. Expressed more compactly, it says that a pure, non-rank-switching transfer of well-being from someone better off to someone worse off, leaving everyone else unaffected, is a moral improvement. It can be shown that the axiom implies a preference for a mean-preserving perfect equalization of well-being (Adler 2012, 114–124)—but the Pigou-Dalton axiom is much stronger than merely preferring perfect equalization, since it applies even if the result of the transfer is not, yet, perfect well-being equality.

The Pigou-Dalton axiom involves a two-person case. Lower has a claim in favor of x over y, Higher has a claim in favor of y over x, and everyone else has null claims. The axiom follows from the rule for two-person cases *if* Lower's claim is stronger than Higher's. Thus, we now need to say something about claim strength. What follows is a partial stipulation of how claim strength is determined.[17]

> *Claim Strength Stipulation*: (a) An individual's affirmative claim (her claim in favor of one outcome over a second) becomes stronger, ceteris paribus, as her well-being difference between the outcomes increases. (b) An individual's affirmative claim becomes stronger, ceteris paribus, as her starting point well-being level[18] decreases. (c) No non-well-being factor (for example, the individual's level of desert or responsibility) is relevant to claim strength.

The reader might be surprised by (c). Mightn't we say, for example, that more deserving individuals have stronger claims, ceteris paribus? However, allowing non-well-being factors to influence claim strength will yield a conflict with the Pareto axioms (Adler 2018; Kaplow and Shavell 2001).

Conversely, I suggest that both (a) and (b) are pretty plausible. Assume that Claudia has a claim to x over y. As the x/y difference increases, Claudia has a larger personal interest in which outcome occurs. Shouldn't the magnitude of this interest be *one* factor relevant to the strength of Claudia's claim? Assume, now, that Don has a claim to x^* over y^*; that the magnitude of Don's interest is exactly the magnitude of Claudia's; but that Don in his starting point (y^*) is better off than Claudia in hers (y)? Do we want to say that Claudia and Don have claims of exactly the same strength? After all, the *strength* of a claim is meant to capture the contribution its satisfaction makes to moral goodness. Why think that well-being levels (as opposed to well-being differences) have *no* bearing on claim strength? Shouldn't an individual's well-being level in her starting point be a *second* factor relevant to claim strength, in addition to the magnitude of her interest? Further, if well-being levels do have relevance to claim strength, surely they do so by favoring (rather than disadvantaging) those who are worse off. It would be ludicrous to conclude that Don has a stronger claim than Claudia; problematic to conclude that the claims are equal; and only fair, to those who are worse off, to conclude that Claudia's is the stronger one.

The Pigou-Dalton axiom follows immediately from the Rules together with the stipulation, just defended, regarding claim strength.[19]

Let's describe a quasi-ordering of outcomes that jointly satisfies the Pareto axioms, Anonymity, and the Pigou-Dalton axiom as a "Paretian, anonymous, PD-respecting" quasi-ordering. The claims framework serves to justify the conclusion that the moral goodness ranking should take the form of a Paretian, anonymous, and PD-respecting quasi-ordering. It lays down an argumentative path from the Person-Affecting Idea to that conclusion.

2.2. Well-Being Measurement

It's often assumed, in consequentialist ethics, that well-being is numerically measurable. More precisely, by "measurability" I mean this: there is a real-valued mathematical function $w(.)$ which assigns each history a well-being number, with $w_i(x)$ the well-being number of the history $(x; i)$, and these numbers track well-being levels and differences.[20]

Using the well-being function, each outcome translates into a list ("vector") of well-being numbers. x becomes $(w_1(x), \ldots, w_N(x))$. And the goodness ranking of outcomes can expressed in terms of a ranking of well-being vectors. x at least as good as y iff $(w_1(x), \ldots, w_N(x))$ at least as good as $(w_1(y), \ldots, w_N(y))$. Let's use the symbol "R^E" to denote the ranking of well-being vectors. Assuming measurability, then, the claims-across-outcomes framework argues that R^E should be Paretian, anonymous, and PD respecting.[21]

2.3. Prioritarianism

What is the connection between the claims-across-outcomes framework and *prioritarianism*? For simplicity I'll assume well-being measurability.

It's often assumed that prioritarianism takes the form of summing well-being numbers "plugged into" a strictly increasing and strictly concave transformation function (Adler 2012, Ch. 5). Prioritarian rankings, thus understood, are a subset within the much broader class of Paretian, anonymous, and PD-respecting rankings. A prioritarian R^E *does* satisfy Anonymity, Pigou-Dalton, and the Pareto axioms. But it also satisfies three *additional* principles: Completeness, Separability, and Continuity. Completeness rules out moral incomparability: every well-being vector is better than, worse than, or equally good as every other. Separability says that the ranking of vectors doesn't depend upon unaffected individuals. Continuity says that if one vector is better than (worse than) another, that's also true for every vector sufficiently close to the first (Adler 2012, Ch. 5; Adler 2018).

Each of these axioms can be justified on pragmatic grounds; each makes moral deliberation easier. But the claims-across-outcome framework itself doesn't argue for Completeness or Continuity; and while one *can* mount a claims-based argument for Separability, that argument is less decisive than those for Pareto, Pigou-Dalton, and Anonymity. Thus, the moral case for the additional axioms is weaker than for Pareto, Pigou-Dalton, and Anonymity—or so the proponent of the claims framework might plausibly believe. The so-called Gini or "rank-weighted" R^E is a rule that is Paretian, anonymous, and PD-respecting but violates Separability. The leximin R^E is Paretian, anonymous, and PD-respecting, and satisfies Separability but violates Continuity (Adler 2012, Ch. 5).

In short, the claims framework gets us *partway* on the justificatory route from the Person-Affecting Idea to prioritarianism. Further arguments are needed to take us all the way there.

2.4. A Contrast with Other Approaches

The notion of individual "claims" or "complaints" is a standard device in normative ethics. However, across-outcome claims have various structural differences from alternative conceptions of claims/complaints.

According to Scanlonian contractualism, we evaluate a proposed moral rule by considering each individual's reasons to reject the rule (Scanlon 1998.) In effect, as between rules, we consider the pattern of individuals' "claims-across-rules." However, the currency for Scanlonian claims is not the well-being currency used here; an individual's "reasons to reject" include but go beyond her own well-being. A second difference is that my set-up has *outcomes* as the object of individual claims, while Scanlon uses his set up to determine which *rules* are morally binding.

Contractualists might find it jarring that "their" device of deriving a moral assessment of objects by considering how the objects compare from the perspective of each individual is being employed with outcomes, not rules, as the objects. But there is nothing uniquely contractualist in the device. Indeed, before Scanlon made the device the centerpiece of *What We Owe to Each Other*, Thomas Nagel had applied it to outcomes. (See Adler 2012, Ch. 5, for a discussion of how the claims-across-outcomes concept derives from Nagel's work.)

Larry Temkin, in his work on inequality, supposes that individuals, in any possible outcome, have complaints against those who are better off. (See Adler 2012, Ch. 5, for a detailed discussion of Temkin's notion of complaints.) The pattern of complaints in x as compared to the pattern in y then determines how the outcomes compare as regards the moral value of equality. A Temkin-style complaint is a relation between two individuals that obtains (or not) within each outcome; by contrast, an across-outcome claim is a relation between an individual and two outcomes. Temkin-style complaints may well be useful in a certain understanding of moral goodness, namely one that gives intrinsic weight to equality—but they don't serve to explicate the Person-Affecting Idea. (Nor does Temkin suggest that they do.) According to the Person-Affecting Idea (and the claims-across-outcomes framework precisifying this idea), there are no pro tanto moral considerations in favor of x over y if everyone is either worse off in x than y or equally well off. Leveling down[22] does not produce even pro tanto moral good. But Temkin's framework (as he freely concedes) is such that levelling down produces pro tanto moral good. In levelling down, Temkin-style complaints disappear.

Some have suggested that individuals might have outcome-related complaints with yet a different structure—distinct from that of both across-outcome claims and Temkin-style complaints as just described. Let's call these "shortfall complaints" (Arrhenius 2009; Otsuka 2018; Parfit 2011, 226–231; Roberts, this volume). The existence and strength of such complaints depends upon the set O of outcomes. An individual has a shortfall complaint in a given outcome x if she is worse off in x than in some other outcome z in O; and, if so, the strength of that complaint takes account of her difference in well-being between z and x.

The set O might be defined in various ways. It might be, for example, all metaphysically possible outcomes; or all that are "nomically" possible (consistent with the actual laws of nature); or all outcomes being evaluated, by some deliberator, for moral goodness. The claims-across-outcomes framework is, in a sense, "relativized" to O, but only in a fairly thin sense. The output of the framework is a quasi-ordering of O—thus the relativization. But this quasi-ordering is built up from binary comparisons between outcomes that are independent of the content of O. The valence and strength of each person's claim between x and y depends upon how well off she would be in x, and how well off she would be in y—not how she would fare in some third outcome. Thus, by the supposition (see the Rules) that the comparative goodness of x and y supervenes on the claim pattern between them, this comparison must be independent of the other outcomes in O. If x is at least as good as y according to the claims-based ranking of O, then x is at least as good as y according to the ranking of any other set O* that contains both outcomes.

This independence feature fits, first, with intuitions about moral goodness. Intuitively, the moral goodness of a given outcome x depends upon its intrinsic features: what would occur, were the outcome to be actual, and not what would occur if some other (mutually exclusive) possibility, z, were to obtain instead. Thus, the *comparative* goodness of x and y depends only on the intrinsic features of x and y, not on some third possibility z. Second, the independence feature of the claims-across-outcomes framework fits (and of course is designed to fit) with the Person-Affecting Idea as I understand it. Consider that the PAP is a constraint on the ranking of two given outcomes, x and y, that takes account *only* of how individuals fare in the two. There's a tight focus on how well off each individual is in x as compared to how well off she is in y; the PAP ignores individuals' well-being in outcomes other than x and y. The same is presumably true, then, of the underlying way of thinking about moral goodness that motivates the PAP—namely, the Person-Affecting Idea.

By contrast, shortfall complaints involve a thick relativization to outcome sets. Individuals might have shortfall complaints in a given outcome relative to O that they don't have in that outcome relative to some other O*; and so the moral goodness ranking of two outcomes won't be independent of O.

It might be argued that the putative independence of the x/y ranking from the outcome set is actually in conflict with the Person-Affecting Idea, once we have a fuller understanding of the nature of well-being. How well off an individual would be, were outcome x to obtain, may depend not only upon the actual facts (the states of affairs that would be actual, were x to obtain), but the modal facts. This is certainly true, at least on non-hedonic theories of well-being.[23] However, the answer on behalf of the claims-across-outcomes framework is just that outcomes should be "thickly" specified, to include modal facts insofar as these are relevant to individuals' well-being. Assume that x and y are thickly specified in this way. Why, now, should the shortfall between individuals' well-being and how they would fare in the other outcomes in O—as opposed to their comparative well-being in x versus y—determine the comparative moral goodness of x and y?[24]

3. The Claims Framework in the Variable Population Case: Meeting the Metaphysical and Standing Objections

3.1. Well-Being Comparisons to Nonexistence: The Metaphysical Objection

Can we compare the well-being of an existing person with nonexistence? It is widely believed by philosophers of population ethics that the answer to this question is "no."[25] The "no" answer appeals to fundamental considerations regarding the nature of persons, properties, and well-being. Such an answer in turns grounds one objection to the variable-population extension of the claims-across-outcomes framework, which I've termed the metaphysical objection. Because it is *impossible* to compare the well-being of an existing person with nonexistence (in light of these fundamental considerations), it is impossible for someone who exists in outcome x but not outcome y to have a claim across the two outcomes.

There are various strands to the skepticism about well-being comparisons to nonexistence. Let me address the three most important worries. First, as is often observed in the literature on well-being, this value is *subject-relative*. That is to say: outcome x is better than y with respect to individual i's well-being just in case x is better *for i* than y. Imagine now that some person (Sally) exists in x but not y. If x is better for Sally than y, then y is worse for Sally than x—and that is absurd, because Sally doesn't exist in y.

Gustaf Arrhenius, Wlodek Rabinowicz, and Nils Holtug have proposed the following rebuttal to this strand of skepticism about well-being comparisons to nonexistence:

A triadic relation consisting in one state (having a certain life) being better for a person p than another state (nonexistence) cannot hold unless its three relata exist. Now, the states in question are abstract entities and thus can be assumed to exist even if they do not actually obtain. Consequently, the triadic relation in question can indeed hold as long as also the third relatum, person p, exists. However, if persons are concrete objects . . . a person exists only insofar as she is alive. Therefore, this relation could not hold if p weren't alive, since the third relatum, p, would then be missing. Consequently, even if it is better for p to exist than not to exist, assuming she has a life worth living, it doesn't follow that it *would have been worse for p if she did not exist*, since one of the relata, p, would then have been absent. What does follow is only that nonexistence *is* worse for her than existence (since "worse" is just the converse of "better"), but not that it *would have been* worse if she didn't exist (Arrhenius and Rabinowicz 2015, 428; see also Holtug 2010, Ch. 5).

Let me build upon the Arrhenius/Rabinowicz/Holtug analysis, with a particular focus on outcomes—the linchpin of this chapter. I fully accept that well-being is subject-relative. Outcome x is better than outcome y with respect to the well-being of i iff x is better *for* i than y. Betterness *for* does, in turn, involve a triadic relation between the concrete entity i, and the two abstracta x and y.

In general, of course, a property or relation of some person that holds true in one possible world (that would be instantiated, if that world were to obtain) needn't hold true in other worlds. For example, consider the triadic relation H between a person and two outcomes, "being taller than the average population height in each outcome." Assume that average population height in x is 5 ft 5 inches and average population height in y is 5 ft 7 inches. If Joe in outcome z is 5 ft 9 inches tall, and in z^* is 5 ft 6 inches, then Joe in z bears relation H to x and y, but Joe in z^* does not bear that relation to x and y. Indeed, if Joe in outcome x is 5 ft 9 inches, and in y is 5 ft 6 inches, then Joe in x but not y bears relation H to the two outcomes.

However, I am assuming that there is a single ranking of outcomes with respect to each individual's well-being. This is reflected in a *single* well-being ranking of the set of histories. Assume Sally exists in x and y. Then Sally is either better off in x than y, worse off in x than y, equally well off in x and y, or incomparably well off in the two. These well-being comparisons hold true simpliciter, rather than being relativized to outcomes. It is not possible that Sally is better off in x than y, relative to z, but worse off in x than y, relative to z^*.

Thus—because of the conceptual connection between intrapersonal well-being rankings and the triadic betterness-for relation—we must assume that this relation satisfies an Invariance condition. Let $Bixy$ denote the triadic relation that x is better for i than y. Invariance says: for all persons i, and for all outcomes x and y, if i exists in some outcome z and $Bixy$ holds true in outcome z ($Bixy$ would be instantiated, were z to obtain), then $Bixy$ holds true in every outcome where i exists.[26]

However, Invariance does not entail the metaphysical absurdity of ascribing properties or relations to nonexistents. If x is better with respect to individual i's well-being than y, then (by Invariance) $Bixy$ hold true in every outcome where i exists. In particular, if individual i exists in both x and y, $Bixy$ holds true in both x and y. But if i does not exist in z, $Bixy$ does not hold true in z. And if i exists in x but not y, $Bixy$ holds true in x but not in y.

In short: one can accept the truisms that (a) there is a single ranking of outcomes with respect to a person's well-being, and (b) a comparison of two outcomes with respect to someone's well-being entails a triadic betterness-for relation between the person and the two outcomes, by supposing that the requite relation holds true invariantly but *only* in the outcomes where the person exists.

A second worry about well-being comparisons to nonexistence is as follows: the *basis* for well-being comparisons consists in an individual's ordinary (non-value) attributes (properties and relations), such as her health, happiness, friendships, activities, and so on. If outcome x is better with respect to i's well-being than y, then (1) x is better *for* i than y, but further (2) this is true in virtue of individual i's attributes in x and her attributes in y. Now consider the case of comparisons to nonexistence. If i exists in x but not y, and x is better with respect to i's well-being, then (1) x is better for i than y, but further (2) this is true in virtue of the person's attributes in x and her attributes in y. But (2) is absurd, since individual i doesn't exist in y and thus can't have any attributes there.

I happily accept that the basis for well-being comparisons *among existing persons* consists in individual attributes. This is precisely what allows me to capture well-being level comparisons among existing persons in a ranking of histories. Recall that a history is nothing other than an attribute bundle. Assume that Sally exists in both x and y. Then: Sally in x is better off than Sally in y iff the history (x; Sally), Sally's bundle of attributes in x, is better as regards well-being than the history (y; Sally), Sally's bundle of attributes in y. Similarly, as discussed above, interpersonal well-being level comparisons among existing persons, and intra- and interpersonal difference comparisons among existing persons, are based upon the ranking of histories and history differences.

However, this second worry can be answered via a hybrid theory of the determinants of well-being, which says the following: (a) if individual i exists in x and y, then the basis for the betterness-for relation between i, x and y is individual i's attributes in x and her attributes in y; but (b) in the special case where i exists in x but not y, the basis for this betterness-for relation is individual i's attributes in x and the fact that i does not exist in y. Note that this hybrid analysis *doesn't* make the mistake of ascribing properties or relations to nonexistents.

A third worry about well-being comparisons to nonexistence points to the conceptual connections between well-being comparisons and comparisons of well-being levels. If x is better with respect to Keith's well-being than y, then Keith in x is better off than Keith in y or, equivalently, Keith's well-being level in x is greater than Keith's well-being level in y. Yet this is absurd if Keith doesn't exist in y.[27]

The third worry can be answered via the very same hybrid theory of the basis for the betterness-for relation that answers the second worry. If an individual exists in two outcomes, then the betterness-for relation between the individual and those two outcomes is linked to a well-being ranking of her attribute bundles in those outcomes and a comparison of her well-being levels in the two outcomes. But if an individual exists in only one of two outcomes, then the betterness-for relation is not linked to either. That is, if Keith exists in x but not y, and x is better for Keith than y, what makes this betterness-for relation true is Keith's attribute bundle in x and *the fact of his nonexistence in y* (not his attribute bundle there); and it is *not* the case that Keith in y is worse off than Keith in x, or that Keith has a well-being level in y.

One upshot of the answer to this third worry is that a well-being level can't be directly assigned to nonexistence. But it can be assigned indirectly, in the following sense: if Keith exists in x and x is equally good for Keith as nonexistence, then (indirectly) the well-being level of nonexistence is just that of the history (x; Keith). As we'll now see, this device is a key component of the variable-population extension of the claims-across-outcome framework.

3.2. The Claims Framework for the Variable Population Case

The formal set-up we'll use to handle the variable population case will build on that used for the fixed population case. There's a set O of outcomes $\{x, y, \ldots\}$. The population size in each outcome is finite. There's a set I of individuals, defined as follows: an individual is in I iff she exists in at least one outcome in O. Note that I might be infinite, even with a finite population size in each outcome. I = {1, 2, . . .}. As above, we'll use integers as the "names" of individuals.

Once more, too, we generate a set of histories of the form $(x; i)$. A history pairs an outcome with some individual who exists in that outcome. The set of histories can be ranked with respect to well-being, and differences between histories can also be ranked with respect to well-being—perhaps with some incomparability. This is no different from the fixed population case.

We add the possibility of comparisons to nonexistence. For any outcome x, in which individual i exists, and any outcome y in which she does not exist, either x is better for i than y, or worse for i than y, or equally good for i as y, or incomparably good for i as y. As per the analysis in the previous section, such comparisons are true in virtue of appropriate triadic relations that hold true invariantly in all and only the outcomes in which i exists.

The following technical assumption simplifies the extension of the claims framework to the variable population case:

> *Richness*: The outcome set O is sufficiently large ("rich") that there is at least one individual i^* and one outcome x^* such that i^* exists in x^* and x^* is equally good for i^* as not existing. For short, let's refer to any such $(x^*; i^*)$ as a "zero history."

To be clear, each zero history *is* a history in the sense we've been using throughout; individual i^* *exists* in x^*, and the history is her attribute bundle in x^*. So $(x^*; i^*)$ is *in* the set of histories, and the well-being rankings of the set of histories include $(x^*; i^*)$. There is no difficulty comparing the well-being level of this history to another, or in making difference comparisons including it—any more so than with other histories.

I will also make a Consistency assumption: each zero history is equally good for well-being as every other zero history. This is very hard to dispute.

Given Consistency, all the zero histories are at a single well-being level. Let's denote this level as W^{zero}. I'll henceforth refer to "the" zero history—but this will be a shorthand for any history that is a zero history.

With these assumptions, the strategy for extending the claims framework to the variable population case is very simple. For a given pair of outcomes x and y, I'll use the term "x-or-y person" to mean someone who exists in x, y, or both (so "or" is used inclusively). The individuals with claims between x and y are the x-or-y persons. Each claim has one of four valences (null, a claim in favor of x over y, in favor of y over x, or an incomparable claim); and every non-null claim has a strength. If an x-or-y person exists in both outcomes, then the valence of her claim depends upon her histories in both outcomes, exactly as in the fixed population case. If an x-or-y person exists in one but not both outcomes, the valence of her claim is determined by using the zero history for the outcome in which she doesn't exist.

For example, suppose that Sally exists in x but not y. Let $(x^*; \text{Julie})$ be a zero history. Then Sally's claim is valenced as follows: Sally has a claim in favor of x over y if $(x; \text{Sally})$ is at a higher well-being level than $(x^*; \text{Julie})$; Sally has a claim in favor of y

over x if $(x^*;$ Julie$)$ is at a higher well-being level than $(x;$ Sally$)$; Sally has a null claim if $(x;$ Sally$)$ and $(x^*;$ Julie$)$ are at the same well-being level (in which case $(x;$ Sally$)$ is itself a zero history); and Sally has an incomparable claim if $(x;$ Sally$)$ and $(x^*;$ Julie$)$ are incomparable.

Similarly, the strength of an individual's claim is determined by using the very same claim strength rules for the fixed population case—applying those rules to the individual's histories in both outcomes (if she exists in both), or else using her zero history for the outcome where she doesn't exist. To continue with the example from the previous paragraph: assume that Sally exists in x but not y, and has a claim in favor of x because $(x;$ Sally$)$ is ranked above $(x^*;$ Julie$)$ in the well-being ranking of histories. Then the strength of that claim will be fixed by the well-being levels of $(x;$ Sally$)$ and $(x^*;$ Julie$)$, and by the difference between them.

Having thus assigned everyone who exists in either x or y a claim (with one of four valences) and a claim strength, x and y are ranked using the very same Rules as in the fixed population case—those rules that tell us how to rank outcomes in light of the pattern of claim valence and strength.[28]

The framework set forth here meets all three strands of the metaphysical objection discussed earlier, by carefully eschewing any attribution of properties or relations to nonexistent persons. But one might note: possessing a claim across outcomes is itself a property, specifically a triadic moral relation between an individual and a pair of outcomes (i has a claim in favor of x over y, in favor of y over x, etc.) How can a nonexistent individual possess such a claim?

She doesn't. Claims are treated exactly like the triadic well-being property, betterness-for. Sally's claim to x over y is a relation between the concrete individual, Sally, and the two possible outcomes, x and y, that holds true invariantly in all and only those outcomes where Sally exists.

3.3. The Standing Objection

The claims-across-outcomes framework, as presented in the previous section, does *not* downweight the claims of individuals who might not exist (in some sense)—who are merely "potential nonexistents" (in some sense). Every person in I is eligible to have a claim between any two outcomes in O, and there is no differentiation among classes of claimants.

To see this, by way of example, imagine that Donna exists in all outcomes in O; in that sense, she is a "necessary" person. Further, Donna exists in the actual world x^{act} (one of the outcomes in O; the others are merely possible), and she exists at the present time. By contrast, Sally does not exist in x^{act}; she does not exist in all the outcomes in O; and, were the outcomes in which Sally exists to be actual, she would be in existence in the future, not at the present time. Thus, there is a three-fold difference between Donna and Sally, as regards existence: Donna is a necessary, actual, and present person, while Sally is a non-necessary, non-actual, and future person.[29]

Still, there is no downweighting of Sally's claim, as against Donna's. Suppose that x and y are outcomes in O such that Donna exists in x and y, and is better off in x. Sally also exists in x and y and, let's suppose, swaps well-being levels with Donna—so that Donna's well-being level in x is equal to Sally's in y, and vice versa. Then (on the claims framework as presented here) Donna has a claim to x over y, Sally to y over x, *and these claims have equal strength*—notwithstanding the three-fold difference in Donna's and Sally's status.

Consider, by way of a second example, two outcomes x and y such that Phyllis exists in x at well-being level W^* (a higher level than W^{zero}) and does not exist in y, while Roger exists in both outcomes, at level W^* in x and level W^{zero} in y. Thus, Phyllis is a potential nonexistent relative to this pair of outcomes (were y to obtain, she would not exist), while Roger is not a potential nonexistent in this sense (he exists regardless of which outcome obtains). Still, there is *no* downweighting of Phyllis' claim relative to Roger's. According to the claims framework as presented here, both are seen as having claims to x over y. And the strength of Phyllis' claim is exactly equal to the strength of Roger's claim.[30]

Now, it might be objected that the claims framework *should* discount the claims of those persons who are potential nonexistents (in some sense). This objection, as I mean to consider it, is distinct from the metaphysical objection: that ascribing a claim regarding outcome x to a person who doesn't exist there would make the metaphysical mistake of ascribing properties to nonexistents. The metaphysical objection was answered above, and so what's now on the table is different: the argument that it is substantively unwarranted, as a matter of the content of morality, to assign claims to certain potential nonexistents that have the full weight of other individuals' claims.

For short, I'll term this the "standing" objection to the claims framework. And I'll refer to the potential nonexistents whose claims ought to be discounted (or so it is asserted) as "downweighted claimants."

The standing objection is suggested by a recent article by Michael Otsuka. Otsuka posits that individuals whose existence is dependent upon our choices lack complaints against those choices that are as strong as the complaints of individuals who would exist regardless of what we choose. Considering a case in which Beth is made worse off by a choice that brings Ann into existence, Otsuka writes:

> Beth's coming into existence is a fait accompli. Ann's existence, by contrast, is dependent on your choice regarding whether or not to benefit Beth. The fact that Ann's existence is dependent on your choice is morally significant for the following reason. You can ensure, simply by opting to benefit Beth, that Ann will never exist. In the event that you opt to benefit Beth, Ann will be nothing more than a possible person, and never an actual person. It would, moreover, be a mistake to maintain that such a merely possible person might have any standing to complain about your failure to bring her into existence. A merely possible person is nothing more than the eternal absence of a person whose actual existence was also possible. An absence of a person is not anyone. It is no one and nothing, and so lacks any moral standing to complain. (Otsuka 2018, 195)

Otsuka thus proposes the following: "When someone's existence is choice-independent, her complaints are morally weighty.... When, by contrast, someone's existence is choice-dependent, her complaints retain moral weight. But this weight is greatly reduced in comparison" (ibid., 199).[31]

"Complaints," as Otsuka conceives them, are structurally distinct from claims-across-outcomes.[32] Still, his concerns about the standing of potential nonexistents to hold full complaints suggests a corresponding objection to the claims-across-outcomes framework.

I'll answer this objection, the standing objection, in two steps. First, certain candidate definitions of downweighted claimants are inconsistent with various neutrality constraints that the ranking of the set of outcomes O is very plausibly required to meet:

(1) *Agent neutrality.* Otsuka's article is animated by the thought that an individual whose existence is independent of an actor's choice has a stronger complaint against the actor, if the actor fails to benefit her, than if the individual's existence is dependent upon the actor's choice. The thought, concededly, has some intuitive force. But the independence or dependence of someone's existence on an actor's choice cannot be reflected in an agent-neutral outcome ranking. Assume that Pam's existence depends on agent Andy's choice, but not on agent Abel's. If the ranking of O were agent-relative, we might define Pam as a downweighted claimant in the Andy-relative ranking of O, and as a full claimant in the Abel-relative ranking of O. However, I am taking as a bedrock premise that the moral-goodness ranking is an agent-neutral one.

(2) *Actual-outcome neutrality.* The ranking of O should be actual-outcome neutral: it should not depend upon which outcome is actual and which outcomes are merely possible. Violations of actual-outcome neutrality (so-called "actualism") are notoriously problematic (Hare 2007). If the requirement of actual-outcome neutrality is to be observed, we can't define full claimants as those who actually exist and downweighted claimants as lacking actuality.

(3) *Time neutrality.* A time-relative ranking is such as to depend on which point in calendar time is the present time. (For example, outcomes might be ranked one way if the present date is July 4, 1980, and a different way if the present date is April 9, 2011.)

Defining downweighted claimants as those who do or don't exist in the past, the present, or the future yields a time-relative ranking of O. But a time-relative ranking is at odds with a plausible axiom of rational choice, namely time consistency.[33]

Second, other candidate definitions of downweighted claimants—albeit consistent with an outcome ranking that is agent-neutral, actual-outcome-neutral, and time-neutral—may still create formal difficulties, and in any event are substantively problematic. Consider, here, the proposal that individuals who exist in only one of a given pair of outcomes (x and y) have downweighted claims between them, as compared to individuals who exist in both. This can yield an intransitive outcome ranking (Adler 2012, 572–273). Further, what would justify this type of downweighting? Imagine (as above) that Phyllis exists in x at well-being level W^* and does not exist in y, while Roger exists in both outcomes, at level W^* in x and level W^{zero} in y. The claims framework *could* be amended to count Phyllis as having no claim at all between the outcomes, or a claim to *x* over *y* that is weaker than Roger's claim to *x* over *y*. But why amend the framework in this way?

Recall that a claim is a tripartite relation between an individual and two outcomes that holds true invariantly in all and only the outcomes where the individual exists. Now, the following is true: if either *x* or *y* were to obtain, Roger would be able to *lay claim* (make a statement concerning) his claim between *x* and *y*. Roger could utter or inscribe the proposition that there exists this tripartite relation between himself, *x*, and *y*, that holds true in all outcomes where he exists. By contrast, if *y* obtains, Phyllis *can't* lay claim to her claim. Phyllis, in *y*, can't make the statement that there is a relation between *x*, *y*, and Phyllis holding true in all outcomes where Phyllis exists—because Phyllis doesn't exist in *y*. (No existence, no statement.) But it is obscure why a claim-holder's ability to lay claim to his or her claim should affect its weight. The claims framework, let's remember, is a precisification of the Person-Affecting Idea. Do we believe that the moral weight of a given benefit or harm to some individual—moral weight, specifically, as an ingredient in the moral goodness of outcomes—is somehow increased by the individual's ability to use language to describe that benefit or harm?

A different proposal is that the ranking of O be agent-neutral, time-neutral, and actual-outcome neutral, but be such as to give greater weight to the claims of individuals who exist in every outcome in O (in that sense, "necessary" individuals), while downweighting the claims of others. However, everyone's existence is non-necessary relative to a sufficiently large set of possible worlds (in particular, the metaphysically possible worlds and the nomically possible worlds). If some members of I are necessary existents in O, that is only because O has been truncated (for what justifying reason?) relative to these larger sets. Both those who exist in every outcome in O, and those who exist in merely some, are potential nonexistents in the metaphysical and nomic senses. It is hard to see why the first group should have stronger claims.[34]

4. THE CLAIMS FRAMEWORK IN THE VARIABLE POPULATION CASE: AXIOMS AND IMPLICATIONS

Section 3.2 discussed how to extend the claims-across-outcomes framework to the variable population case. To recapitulate: there's a set O of outcomes, each with a finite population, and a set I of individuals containing everyone who exists in at least one of the outcomes. All *x*-or-*y* persons (those who exist in *x*, *y* or both) are assigned claims between *x* and *y*. If *i* exists in both outcomes, her histories (*x*; *i*) and (*y*; *i*) are used to determine her claim valence and strength, exactly as in the fixed population case. If *i* exists in *x* but not *y*, or vice versa, her history in the outcome where she exists, together with the zero history, is used to determine her claim valence and strength. The very same Rules as in the fixed population case are then applied to rank x versus y as a function of the pattern of claim valence and strength between the two outcomes.

We now consider the axiomatic upshots of this framework; its connection with prioritarianism; implications for major topics in population ethics; and, briefly, its merits as compared to non-person-affecting approaches.

4.1. Axioms, Measurability, and Prioritarianism

In the fixed population case, we used the procedure for assigning claim valence and strength, together with the Rules, to arrive at the Pareto, Pigou-Dalton and Anonymity axioms. Similarly, the variable-population extension of the claims framework implies generalized versions of these axioms.

For purposes of the statement of the axioms, immediately following, the term "well-being level" is used as a *shorthand*. If i exists in x, her "well-being level" in x denotes the well-being level of the history $(x; i)$, namely, what i's well-being level would be, were x to be actual. If i does not exist in x, her "well-being level" in x denotes the well-being level of the zero history.

This shorthand is used *only* to permit a less wordy statement of the axioms. In the genuine (non-shorthand) sense, an individual has a well-being level in some outcome in virtue of her history in that outcome. If individual i does not exist in x she has no genuine (non-shorthand) well-being level in x, because were x to be actual she would have no history.

The Generalized Axioms (see immediately above regarding the use of "well-being level" as a shorthand):

> *Generalized Pareto Indifference*: If each x-or-y person is at the same well-being level in x as in y, then x and y are equally good.
>
> *Generalized Strong Pareto*: If at least one x-or-y person is at a higher well-being level in x than y, and the well-being level of each x-or-y person in x is at least as high as her well-being level in y, then x is better than y.
>
> *Generalized Anonymity*: Assume that the same number of persons exist in x as in y, and that the well-being levels of the persons who exist in x are a permutation of the well-being levels of the persons who exist in y.[35] Then x and y are equally good.
>
> *Generalized Pigou-Dalton*: Assume that x and y are related as follows. (1) In outcome y, the well-being level of one x-or-y person ("Higher") is higher than that of a second ("Lower"). (2) Lower's well-being level in x is greater than her well-being level in y, while Higher's well-being level in y is greater than his well-being level in x, and these differences are equal in magnitude. (3) Higher's well-being level in x is at least as high as Lower's in x. (4) Every other x-or-y person is at the same well-being level in x as in y. Then: x is better than y.

As in the fixed population case, these axioms and the claims framework that justifies them *don't* assume well-being measurability; but it's convenient to add a measurability assumption. As before, this means that a well-being measure $w(.)$ assigns numbers to histories; these numbers track well-being levels and differences.

In population ethics, the number 0 is usually assigned to the well-being level equal to nonexistence. This is purely notational, but in any event is readily achieved by rescaling the $w(.)$ numbers. We've assumed (Consistency) that all zero histories are at the same well-being level, W^{zero}. Thus $w(.)$ must assign the same number K to every zero history. If $K \neq 0$, then we can rescale $w(.)$ by subtracting K from every well-being number. I'll henceforth assume that this rescaling has occurred.

With well-being measurability, each outcome corresponds to a vector (list) of well-being numbers. Recall that each individual in I is referred to by an integer. I= $\{1, 2, \ldots\}$. The first entry in the vector for any given outcome is the "slot" for individual 1, the second entry the "slot" for individual 2, and so forth. We can use "Ω" to indicate that an individual doesn't exist in the outcome. For example, outcome x may correspond to the vector $(\Omega, 4.5, 0, \Omega, 12, 20, \ldots)$. This indicates that individual 1 doesn't exist in x, that individual 2 exists with a history assigned well-being number 4.5, that individual 3 exists with a history assigned well-being number 0, and so forth. If I is infinite, each vector is infinite—but there are only a finite number of entries with numbers rather than "Ω."

We require a rule R^E for ordering the well-being vectors[36] that is generalized Paretian, generalized anonymous, and generalized PD-respecting. What does this look like?

Let's say that a rule R^E satisfies an axiom of Zero Critical Level if is indifferent between a given vector with M existing individuals, and a vector with $M+1$ individuals identical to the first vector except that the new person is at level 0. For example, Zero Critical Level requires indifference between $(\Omega, 6, \Omega, 7, 8, \Omega, 3, 2, \ldots)$ and $(\Omega, 6, \Omega, 7, 8, 0, 3, 2, \ldots)$.

The following can be demonstrated: a rule for ordering well-being vectors satisfies the generalized Pareto axioms, generalized Anonymity, and the generalized Pigou-Dalton axiom *if and only if* (1) it satisfies the ordinary Pareto axioms, Anonymity, and the Pigou-Dalton axiom in ranking pairs of well-being vectors in which the very same individuals exist, and (2) it satisfies Zero Critical Level. (See Appendix.)

How does a generalized Paretian, generalized anonymous, and generalized PD-respecting R^E relate to *prioritarianism*? Consider, first, "total prioritarianism." Let $g(.)$ be a strictly increasing and strictly concave transformation function, normalized so that $g(0) = 0$. Total prioritarianism assigns each vector the sum of $g(.)$-transformed well-being numbers for all the existing individuals. For example, $(4, \Omega, 5, \Omega, 2, \ldots)$ is assigned the value $g(4) + g(5) + g(2) + \ldots$. Total prioritarianism is one type of eligible R^E. Specifically, it satisfies generalized Pareto, generalized Anonymity, generalized Pigou-Dalton *plus* further axioms of completeness, continuity, and separability.[37] (See generally Holtug in this volume.)

Consider, next, "critical level" prioritarianism. A "critical level" history is identified. Let w^{crit} be the well-being number of this history. Then critical-level prioritarianism assigns each vector the sum of transformed well-being numbers, subtracting $g(w^{crit})$ for each existing individual. For example, $(4, \Omega, 5, \Omega, 2, \ldots)$ would now be assigned

$$\left[g(4) - g\left(w^{crit}\right) \right] + \left[g(5) - g\left(w^{crit}\right) \right] + \left[g(2) - g\left(w^{crit}\right) \right] + \dots . \text{ (See Holtug's and}$$

Bossert's chapters in this volume.)

If w^{crit} is 0, critical-level prioritarianism reduces to total prioritarianism. Critical-level prioritarianism with $w^{crit} \neq 0$ satisfies Pareto, Pigou-Dalton, and Anonymity in ranking pairs of well-being vectors in which the same individuals exist, but of course *doesn't* satisfy Zero Critical Level and thus doesn't satisfy all three of generalized Pareto, generalized Pigou-Dalton, and generalized Anonymity.[38]

4.2. Implications for Population Ethics

What are the implications of a generalized Paretian, generalized anonymous, and generalized PD-respecting outcome ranking (the ranking implied by the claims-across-outcomes framework) for major topics in population ethics?[39]

The first concerns what Derek Parfit calls "No Difference" (Parfit 1984, Ch. 16; Parfit 2011, 219–233). Assume that the number of individuals who exist is the same in two outcomes x and y. No Difference says: how we rank x and y depends *only* on the well-being levels of the individuals in x and their well-being levels in y. This ranking is the same regardless of whether (a) the very same individuals exist in both, or instead (b) some individuals who exist in x don't exist in y, and vice versa, or instead (c) *no one* who exists in x exists in y, and vice versa.

"No Difference" is an immediate implication of generalized Anonymity.[40]

Parfit also endorses the Mere Addition principle. Adding someone to the world with a life better than nonexistence can't make things worse (Parfit 1984, Ch. 19; see also Arrhenius forthcoming). This is an immediate implication of generalized strong Pareto. Assume that every x-or-y person but one exists in both outcomes and has the same well-being level in x as in y; and that there is one x-or-y person who only exists in x, at a well-being level above W^{zero}. Then by generalized Strong Pareto x is better than y.

Gustaf Arrhenius argues that a population axiology should avoid the "Sadistic Conclusion" (Arrhenius forthcoming). Imagine that M^* individuals are added to the population with lives worse than nonexistence, or alternatively that $M+$ individuals are added with lives better than nonexistence. ($M+$ may or may not be equal to M^*). The first option should never be better than the second. This follows from generalized strong Pareto. If x and x^* are equally good for the well-being of those who exist in both, and x^* has M^* additional individuals with lives worse than W^{zero}, x^* is worse than x. If x and $x+$ are equally good for the well-being of those who exist in both, and $x+$ has $M+$ additional individuals with lives better than W^{zero}, $x+$ is better than x. By transitivity, $x+$ is better than x^*.[41]

Arrhenius (forthcoming) also suggests that any plausible axiology will satisfy "egalitarian dominance" and "negative mere addition."[42] These, too, are satisfied by any generalized Paretian, generalized anonymous, and generalized PD-respecting ordering of outcomes.

All of the principles just mentioned follow from the combination of generalized Pareto, generalized Anonymity, and generalized Pigou-Dalton *without* an additional measurability assumption. The Repugnant Conclusion involves the notion of well-being levels "close" to nonexistence, and to express that notion most simply it will be helpful to employ well-being numbers.

> *Repugnant Conclusion*: Take any well-being vector in which every existing person (M in total) has well-being number w^{high}, which can be any positive number however large. Then for any positive well-being number w^{low}, however close to zero, there is some number M^+ such that a well-being vector with M^+ persons, all with number w^{low}, is better than the first vector.

Alas, if an R^E is generalized Paretian, generalized anonymous, and generalized PD-respecting, then the Repugnant Conclusion is true of R^E. Why? Let V be a well-being vector with M individuals at w^{high}. Pick M^+ which is large enough that $M^+ \times w^{low} > M \times w^{high}$. Let V^* be a well-being vector with M^+ individuals, M of whom are at w^{high} and the remainder of whom are at 0. Finally, let V^+ be a well-being vector with M^+ individuals at w^{low}. By generalized Pareto indifference, V^* is equally good as V. By Pigou-Dalton, V^+ is better than V^*.[43] By transitivity, V^+ is better than V.

It's well known that total prioritarianism, in particular, has the Repugnant Conclusion. By contrast, critical-level prioritarianism with the critical-level history above the zero history does not (Adler 2009, Holtug, this volume). Indeed, the main motivation for critical-level prioritarianism with a critical-level history above the zero history is to avoid the Repugnant Conclusion.[44]

4.3. Should We Accept the Claims-Across-Outcomes Framework?

The main goal of this chapter has been to flesh out a person-affecting account of variable population cases. I have shown how the claims-across-outcomes framework (a specific model of the Person-Affecting Idea) can be extended to the variable-population context, notwithstanding metaphysical and "standing" objections, and have discussed what such extension implies axiomatically for the goodness ranking of outcomes, and for important questions in population ethics.

The reader is now entitled to ask: why *accept* a person-affecting account, whether of variable- or fixed-population cases? A non-person-affecting ("impersonal") account of the moral goodness ranking is also possible, in both fixed- and variable-population cases. Note that the Person-Affecting Idea yields a *welfarist* moral goodness ranking: given two outcomes, x and y, information about the well-being level of each person in x and about the well-being level of each person in y is sufficient to determine the comparative moral goodness of the two outcomes. A non-person-affecting account might also be welfarist. In this case, it would rank x versus y by virtue of some criterion for comparing the patterns of well-being in each, with this criterion itself *not* justified in a person-affecting way. Alternatively, the non-person-affecting account might be non-welfarist—taking account both of individual well-being and of non-well-being features of outcomes.

It is well beyond the scope of this chapter to engage debates between welfarists and non-welfarists, and I'll so confine myself to some remarks (necessarily brief, given space constraints) about the relative merits of person-affecting versus non-person-affecting approaches *within* welfarism.

Consider, first, fixed-population pairs of outcomes, such that the very same individuals exist in each outcome. (Note that *all* pairs of outcomes in what I have termed a "fixed population case" are fixed-population pairs; but there can also be fixed-population pairs in a variable population case.)

Many accept the strong Pareto axiom for fixed-population pairs. This itself doesn't differentiate between person-affecting and non-person-affecting approaches. An impersonal criterion for ranking well-being patterns might turn out to satisfy the strong Pareto axiom. For example, it is often suggested that utilitarianism flows from an impersonal concern for overall well-being. Note that the utilitarian criterion, summing well-being numbers, satisfies strong Pareto. It has also been suggested that an impersonal egalitarianism might take a "moderate" form—balancing the value of overall well-being against the value of well-being equality, so as always to satisfy strong Pareto (Parfit 2000).

But there is still something problematic in a non-person-affecting rationale for a criterion that satisfies strong Pareto. What's the problem? For many, strong Pareto is not merely an axiom that the goodness ranking happens to satisfy. Rather (and more robustly) it has *justificatory priority* in deliberating about candidate goodness rankings (Adler and Holtug, 2019). The fact that a proposed ranking violates strong Pareto is (for many) a powerful, indeed decisive reason to reject the ranking. This *deliberational* role of strong Pareto is very difficult to explain in a non-person-affecting way. Rather, it just reflects an explicit or implicit acceptance of the Person-Affecting Idea. Well-being improvements for each person, and only such improvements, are the basic pro tanto moral considerations determining the comparative betterness of outcomes: that is what accounts for the justificatory priority of strong Pareto.

Now let's ask: why accept the Person-Affecting Idea for variable-population pairs of outcomes as well as fixed-population pairs? The strongest argument, it seems to me, is No Difference. Assume that the same people exist in x and y; that the pattern of well-being in x^* is the same as that in x; that the pattern of well-being in y^* is the same as that in y; and that the individuals who exist in x^* are *not* identical to those who exist in y^*. Assume that person-affecting considerations determine the x/y ranking but *don't* determine the x^*/y^* ranking. Then, it would seem, the x^*/y^* ranking might differ from the x/y ranking. But No Difference precludes this from ever happening.

In short, if person-affecting considerations determine the ranking of fixed- but not variable-population pairs of outcomes, No Difference is deeply mysterious.

On the other side of the balance sheet is the Repugnant Conclusion. One analytic result of this chapter is that the Person-Affecting Idea (as precisified by the claims framework) leads to the Repugnant Conclusion. (For a similar result, see Arrhenius 2015.) This is an unwelcome result, to be sure, but is it sufficient grounds to shift to an impersonal account of the moral goodness ranking? It seems that *no* goodness ranking, whether justified in a person-affecting or impersonal way, can *both* avoid the Repugnant Conclusion *and* satisfy all of the remaining axioms that are intuitively plausible. (See, e.g., Arrhenius, forthcoming; Greaves 2017). The Person-Affecting Idea not only explains both the justificatory priority of strong Pareto for fixed-population pairs, and No Difference, but also supports Mere Addition, the avoidance of the Sadistic Conclusion, and a concern for equity in the form of generalized Pigou-Dalton.

By my lights, these are sufficient grounds to endorse the Person-Affecting Idea, notwithstanding the Repugnant Conclusion. The reader's verdict may, of course, be different.

APPENDIX

A. The Well-Being Ranking of Histories

What follows covers both the fixed- and variable-population cases. Let O be the set of outcomes, and I the set of individuals each of whom exists in at least one of the outcomes in O. $(x; i)$ is the history of individual i in outcome x, i.e., the bundle of attributes (properties and relations) of individual i in x. Let H be the set of all histories arising from O, that is, $H = \{(x; i) \text{ s.t. } x \in O \text{ and } i \in I\}$. $H \times H$ is the set of all pairs of histories.

The ranking of histories with respect to well-being takes the form of a quasi-ordering of H, denoted $\succcurlyeq$. $(x; i) \succcurlyeq (y; j)$, with i and j distinct or identical, is to be interpreted as: history $(x; i)$ is at least as good for well-being as history $(y; j)$. The ranking of histories with respect to well-being differences takes the form of a quasi-ordering of $H \times H$, denoted $\succcurlyeq^{\text{Diff}}$. $((x; i), (y; j)) \succcurlyeq^{\text{Diff}} ((z; k), (zz, l))$, with i, j, k, l wholly or partly distinct or identical, is to be interpreted as: the difference in well-being between $(x; i)$ and $(y; j)$ is at least as large as the difference in well-being between $(z; k)$ and $(zz; l)$.

In order to embody the formal properties of well-being differences, $\succcurlyeq^{\text{Diff}}$ must not only be a quasi-ordering, but must also satisfy various axioms: Reversal, Separability, Neutrality, and Concatenation. Further, $\succcurlyeq^{\text{Diff}}$ and $\succcurlyeq$ must be related via Linkage: $(x; i) \succcurlyeq (y; j)$ iff $((x; i), (y; j)) \succcurlyeq^{\text{Diff}} ((y; j), (y; j))$. See Adler (2016) for a statement of these axioms, a fuller discussion of $\succcurlyeq$ and $\succcurlyeq^{\text{Diff}}$, and a discussion of the conditions under which these quasi-orderings are representable by a well-being measure $w(.)$.

The at-least-as-good-for-well-being relation, $\succcurlyeq$, gives rise to an equally-good-for-well-being-relation, $\sim$, and a better-for-well-being relation, $\succ$, in the normal fashion for a quasi-ordering. Similarly, $\succcurlyeq^{\text{Diff}}$ gives rise to $\sim^{\text{Diff}}$ and $\succ^{\text{Diff}}$. Each equivalence class of H with respect to $\sim$ is a well-being level, and each equivalence class of $H \times H$ with respect to $\sim^{\text{Diff}}$ is a well-being difference.

B. Generalized Axioms, Ordinary Axioms, and Zero Critical Level

In the variable-population case, a ranking R^E of well-being vectors satisfies the generalized Pareto axioms, generalized Anonymity, and generalized Pigou-Dalton iff it satisfies the ordinary Pareto axioms, Anonymity and Pigou-Dalton in ranking pairs of vectors where the very same individuals exist *and* Zero Critical Level.

(1) *The generalized axioms imply the combination of the ordinary axioms and Zero Critical Level.* This is straightforward. Each of the generalized axioms implies its ordinary counterpart. Further, generalized Pareto indifference implies Zero Critical Level.

(2) *The ordinary axioms plus Zero Critical Level imply the generalized axioms.* Each of the ordinary axioms plus Zero Critical Level implies its generalized counterpart. I will demonstrate this for Pigou-Dalton; a parallel demonstration holds for the other axioms.

Let W and W* be a pair of well-being vectors. Let (W) be the vector produced from W by replacing Ω with 0 for each person who exists in W* but not W. Similarly, let (W*) be the vector produced from W* by replacing Ω with 0 for each person who exists in W but not W*.

Note that if generalized Pigou-Dalton requires W* to be ranked better than W, ordinary Pigou-Dalton requires (W*) to be ranked better than (W). For example, let W = $(3, \Omega, 10)$ and W* = $(3, 2, 8)$, so that generalized Pigou-Dalton requires W* to be ranked better than W. (W) = $(3, 0, 10)$ and (W*) = $(3, 2, 8)$, and ordinary Pigou-Dalton requires (W*) to be ranked better than (W).

Assume now that ordinary Pigou-Dalton plus Zero Critical Level are satisfied but generalized Pigou-Dalton is not satisfied. This yields a contradiction. Suppose that there is some pair of vectors W, W* such that generalized Pigou-Dalton requires W* to be better than W, but R^E does not rank W* better than W. Ordinary Pigou-Dalton requires (W*) to be better than (W). By Zero Critical Level, (W*) is ranked equally good as W* and (W) is ranked equally good as W. By transitivity, then, it can't be the case that (W*) is ranked better than (W).

ACKNOWLEDGMENTS

Many thanks to Jacob Nebel, Hilary Greaves, Simon Knutsson, Alex Voorhoeve, and the editors of this Handbook for their comments.

NOTES

1. Parfit (2017) rejects the PAP, understood as a principle that ties the betterness of outcomes to what is better or worse for persons, and instead endorses a "wide" principle that concerns what is good or bad for persons in a noncomparative sense.
2. I am interested, throughout the chapter, in moral goodness in a comparative sense—whether one outcome is morally better than, worse than, or equally good as another. So

what I term the "moral goodness" or (more crisply) "goodness" ranking of outcomes might equally well be termed the "moral betterness" or "betterness" ranking.

3. Thus, I use the term "variable population" case to mean variation in the identities of the existing individuals in the various outcomes—which may manifest itself either as variation in the total size of the population, or as variation in the identity of existing individuals as between outcomes with the same total population size.

4. See the various sources, endorsing this view, that are cited in Arrhenius and Rabinowicz (2015), Fleurbaey and Voorhoeve (2015), and Holtug (2010, Ch. 5). See also Bader (2017) and Bykvist (2017).

5. Act-consequentialists believe that the moral permissibility of an action is directly reducible to the moral-goodness ranking of outcomes. Rule-consequentialists believe that the moral permissibility of an action depends upon its conformity to moral rules, whose status as such is reducible to the moral-goodness ranking of outcomes. Non-consequentialists who accept that the moral-goodness ranking has a significant role see the moral permissibility of an action as depending both on the moral-goodness ranking (in a direct or indirect way), and on non-consequentialist moral considerations, such as deontological side constraints. See Hooker (2000), Kagan (1998).

6. See Brown (2011), McNaughton and Rawling (1991).

7. There are important similarities between this chapter and Arrhenius (2015), which also investigates a person-affecting approach to population ethics. The novel contribution of this chapter is to do so by using the claims-across-outcomes framework.

    Bader (this volume) rejects well-being comparisons to nonexistence, and explores the form that person-affecting utilitarianism would take without such comparisons.

8. An outcome might be understood as a possible world—but since distinct possible worlds may not differ in ways that matter to anyone's well-being, it's equally good for my purposes to define an outcome as a possible state of affairs maximally specified with respect to the determinants of each individual's well-being.

9. Thus, a yet more precise designation of a given history $(x; i)$ would be "$\mathbf{a}_i(x)$," namely the attributes of i in x. However, to make the symbolism less daunting, I will employ the "$(x; i)$" notation.

10. More precisely: a well-being level is an equivalence class of histories with respect to the well-being relation, and a well-being difference is an equivalence class of pairs of histories with respect to the well-being difference relation. See Arrhenius (forthcoming) for a similar approach.

11. More precisely, each of the valences listed immediately below is a distinct type of relation between an individual and two outcomes; but as a shorthand I'll say that a claim is a relation with these four possible valences.

12. Note that this formulation is more permissive with respect to moral goodness than one which says: if there is a claim in favor of x over y, then x is morally better than y unless there is a claim in favor of y over x. Why adopt the more permissive formulation? Incomparability is sometimes understood as a supervaluation over admissible *complete* assignments of well-being levels. (See, e.g., Adler 2012.) On such a view, if x and y are incomparable with respect to i's well-being, then on some admissible assignments i is better off in x than y, and on other admissible assignments i is better off in y than x. Consider then a case in which one person is better off in x than y, and the remaining individuals have incomparable claims between x and y. In such a case, it is possible that, on every admissible assignment, at least one of these latter individuals is better off in y

than x. Yet the stricter formulation would preclude y being ranked morally better than x in this case.

13. By "swap well-being levels," I mean: individual i's well-being level in x is the same as j's in y, and vice versa.

14. The equal balance rule is stated in this form so as to avoid questions regarding the strength of incomparable claims. See note 17. Let W and W^* be two incomparable well-being levels and assume that in x individual i is at W and j is at W^*, while in y individual i is at W^* and j is at W—with everyone else holding null claims. However, one determines the strength of incomparable claims, it seems intuitively very plausible that x is equally good as y.

15. The term "Pareto" is sometimes used as the name for axioms formulated in terms of individuals' preferences, and sometimes instead to denote axioms formulated in terms of individuals' well-being. In this chapter, I use "Pareto" in the latter sense.

16. This means that there is a one-to-one correspondence between the histories in the two outcomes, mapping each history in x onto a history in y at the same well-being level.

17. The Claim Strength stipulation here suffices to derive the Pigou-Dalton axiom. It is *partial* (incomplete) in not specifying how to determine the strength of incomparable claims— a topic that can be placed to one side for purposes of this chapter. Nor does it address whether the strength of an individual's affirmative claim between x and y can depend upon the population distribution of well-being levels in those two outcomes. Precluding such dependence yields an axiom of Separability. See below, and Adler (2012, Ch. 5).

18. Her well-being level in the outcome where she is worse off.

19. The Claim Strength stipulation *is* one of the rules for the claims-across-outcomes framework (a strength rule); but so as to anticipate the extension of the framework to the variable population case, I don't group it with those that were denoted above as "the Rules" (capitalized). The Rules (capitalized) do not explain how to determine the valence and strength of individuals' claims, but instead explain how the comparative goodness of two outcomes is determined *given* the valence and strength of individuals' claims between the two.

20. History $(x; i)$ is at least as good for well-being as history $(y; j)$ iff $w_i(x) \geq w_j(y)$. The well-being difference between $(x; i)$ and $(y; j)$ is at least as large as the well-being difference between $(z; k)$ and $(zz; l)$ iff $w_i(x) - w_j(y) \geq w_k(z) - w_l(zz)$.

21. Measurability is very convenient, but restrictive because it rules out well-being incomparability. A standard way to handle incomparability, while still retaining much of the convenience of well-being numbers, is by allowing for a class of well-being functions (Adler 2012). Given space constraints, I won't discuss this generalization of measurability here.

22. By "leveling down," I mean making some worse off to go from inequality to perfect equality.

23. Here's one illustrative example. An objective-good account of well-being might suppose that friendship is a good. Note that whether someone is my friend depends in part on her disposition, on what she would do were various kinds of events to occur, not merely on what she actually does.

24. A final structural feature of the claims-across-outcome framework is that the relata for an individual's claims are pairs of outcomes, not pairs of prospects (probability distributions across outcomes). It is tempting to think that an individual's claim between two prospects depends upon her expected well-being with each, and that the pattern of such claims determines the prospect ranking; but this leads to a violation of a compelling axiom of weak stochastic dominance. Rather, in the fixed-population case, prospects should

be ranked by (1) using across-outcome claims to generate the outcome ranking and (2) synthesizing the ranking with the outcome probabilities, as per the best account of choice under uncertainty, whatever that account may be (e.g., expected utility theory). See Adler (2012, Ch. 7). If across-outcome claims can indeed be extended to the variable population case (see below, Sections 3 and 4), then the same holds true for the ranking of prospects with a variable population. Space precludes a more detailed discussion of these issues. See Voorhoeve and Fleurbaey (2016) (proposing that expected well-being is part of the currency for claims); cf. Frick (2015), Nebel (2017) (doing so for purposes of contractualist or deontological moral views).

25. See sources in Arrhenius and Rabinowicz (2015), Fleurbaey and Voorhoeve (2015), and Holtug (2010, Ch. 5). See also see Bader (2017) and Bykvist (2017).

26. Invariance also holds for the relations of being equally good for, being worse for, and being incomparably good for.

    One might wonder how Invariance can be consistent with a preference-based view of well-being. If Joanna in z prefers x to y, but in z^* prefers y to x, it seems like she *is* better off in x than y relative to z, but worse off in x than y relative to z^*. The issue can't be addressed here. I believe that Invariance can be squared with a preference view by having the preferences that determine well-being incorporated within histories (see Adler 2016).

27. Bykvist (2017) provides a lengthy critique of Arrhenius and Rabinowicz (2015). Space constraints prelude a response to Bykvist here, except the following: Bykvist's critique rests upon a premise, "Better-for entails value-for," which (as I understand it) implies that someone is better off in x than y iff she has a well-being level in both outcomes. And this is nothing other than the third worry.

28. Recall that "the Rules" do not include the rules for *determining* claim valence and strength. Once we have assigned claim valence and strength in the variable population case, as per the analysis in the text, we can then apply the Rules to rank outcomes in light of the pattern of claim valence and strength.

29. On these distinctions, see Arrhenius (forthcoming, Ch. 9).

30. It might be objected that individuals who exist in *neither x nor y are* ignored—since the approach presented here assigns claims only to those who exist in at least one of the two outcomes. But this is not a genuine downweighting, since the weight of these individuals' claims, if they were included, would be null just by virtue of the rules for assigning claim valence and strength—exactly like those who exist in one or both outcomes at W^{zero}.

31. For a similar suggestion that potential nonexistents lack complaints, see Voorhoeve and Fleurbaey (2016, 948).

32. They are shortfall complaints in the sense described in Section 2.4.

33. Roughly, intertemporal choice is *time-consistent* if the following condition is met: whenever an individual at t formulates a plan for choice at some later time t^*, she conforms at t^* to the plan, absent some occurrence in the interim the possibility of which was unforeseen at t. Assume now that the goodness ranking of O is time-relative. If the individual at t formulates her plan in light of the t-relative ranking of O, the best choice at t^* in light of the t^*-relative ranking of O may be to deviate from this plan, even absent any unforeseen occurrence between t and t^*. See McClennen (1990).

34. Further, differentiating claims in this manner will violate the formal desideratum that the ranking of a given pair of outcomes should be independent of which other outcomes may happen to belong to the set being ranked. See Section 2.4.

35. Note that in the variable population case, as in the fixed population case, each person who exists in a given outcome has a history (attribute bundle) there; nonexistents don't have histories. To say that the well-being levels in x are a permutation of those in y means, as in the fixed population case, that there is a one-to-one correspondence associating each history in x with a history in y at the same well-being level.

36. Blackorby, Bossert, and Donaldson (2005) is a magisterial formal treatment of population ethics. They suppose that each outcome is associated with a *reduced* and necessarily finite-length well-being vector, listing the well-being numbers for each person who exists in that outcome; that the ranking R of these reduced vectors is anonymous; and that the ranking of outcomes corresponds to R's ranking of their associated reduced vectors. By contrast, I have each outcome associated with a *full* and possibly infinite-length vector, with a finite number of numerical entries, and a "Ω" for each nonexistent. My R^E ranks these *full* vectors.

    However, all of Blackorby, Bossert, and Donaldson's results regarding the ranking R of reduced vectors can be readily translated to my set-up. The reduced vector corresponding to a given full vector is simply the vector dropping all the Ωs. Let **W** be a full vector, and [**W**] the corresponding reduced vector. By Generalized Anonymity, if **W** and **V** have the same reduced vector, then **W** and **V** are ranked by R^E as equally good. We can now interpret R as follows: [**W**] is ranked by R at least as good as [**W***] iff any full vector corresponding to [**W**] is ranked by R^E at least as good as any full vector corresponding to [**W***].

37. Completeness, as in the fixed population case, rules out incomparability: each vector is better than, worse than, or equally good as every other. On the continuity and separability properties of total and critical-level prioritarianism, see Blackorby, Bossert, and Donaldson (2005); Bossert (this volume). Note that these sources discuss "generalized utilitarianism"; prioritarianism is one version thereof. And, as mentioned in the immediately preceding note, their analysis focuses on the ranking of reduced vectors.

38. Specifically, it can be seen that critical-level prioritarianism with $w^{crit} \neq 0$ satisfies generalized Anonymity but not generalized Pareto Indifference, generalized Strong Pareto, or generalized Pigou-Dalton.

39. See Greaves (2017) for an excellent recent survey of population ethics.

40. Assume that the very same M individuals exist in x and y, and that x is ranked better than y. Now consider any x^* with M individuals whose well-being levels are a permutation of the well-being levels in x. And consider any y^* with M individuals whose well-being levels are a permutation of the well-being levels in y. By generalized Anonymity and transitivity, x^* is better than y^*. Similarly, if x is equally good as y then x^* is equally good as y^*, and if x is incomparably good as y then x^* is incomparably good as y^*.

41. Blackorby, Bossert, and Donaldson (2005) have a related principle, "Priority for Lives worth Living," also satisfied by any generalized Paretian, generalized anonymous, and generalized PD-respecting outcome ranking.

42. Egalitarian dominance: if two outcomes have the same population size, and welfare is equally distributed in each, at a higher level in one outcome than the second, then the first outcome is better. Negative mere addition: adding people with negative welfare makes an outcome worse.

43. More precisely, let $w^{lower} < w^{low}$ be such that $M^+ \times w^{lower} = M \times w^{high}$. Consider now V** in which there are M^+ individuals at w^{lower}. By Pigou-Dalton, V** is better than V*. By strong Pareto, V⁺ is better than V**.

44. Arrhenius et al. (2017) surveys strategies for avoiding the Repugnant Conclusion.

REFERENCES

Adler, Matthew D. 2009. "Future Generations: A Prioritarian View." *George Washington Law Review* 77: 1478–1520.

Adler, Matthew D. 2012. *Well-Being and Fair Distribution: Beyond Cost-Benefit Analysis*. New York: Oxford University Press.

Adler, Matthew D. 2016. "Extended Preferences." In *The Oxford Handbook of Well-Being and Public Policy*, edited by Matthew D. Adler and Marc Fleurbaey, 476–517. Oxford: Oxford: University Press.

Adler, Matthew D. 2018. "Prioritarianism: Room for Desert?" *Utilitas* 30: 172–197.

Adler, Matthew D., and Nils Holtug. 2019. "Prioritarianism: A Response to Critics." *Politics, Philosophy & Economics* 18: 101–144.

Arrhenius, Gustaf. 2009. "Can the Person Affecting Restriction Solve the Problems in Population Ethics?" In *Harming Future People: Ethics, Genetics, and the Nonidentity Problem*, edited by Melinda Roberts and David Wasserman, 291–316. New York: Springer.

Arrhenius, Gustaf. 2015. "The Affirmative Answer to the Existential Question and the Person Affecting Restriction." In *Weighing and Reasoning: Themes from the Philosophy of John Broome*, edited by Iwao Hirose and Andrew Reisner, 110–125. Oxford: Oxford University Press.

Arrhenius, Gustaf. Forthcoming. *Population Ethics: The Challenge of Future Generations*. Oxford: Oxford University Press.

Arrhenius, Gustaf and Wlodek Rabinowicz. "The Value of Existence." 2015. In *The Oxford Handbook of Value Theory*, edited by Iwao Hirose and Jonas Olson, 424–443. Oxford: Oxford University Press.

Arrhenius, Gustaf, Jesper Ryberg, and Torbjörn Tännsjö. 2017. "The Repugnant Conclusion." *Stanford Encyclopedia of Philosophy*.

Bader, Ralf. 2017. "The Neutrality of Existence." Working paper.

Blackorby, Charles, Walter Bossert, and David Donaldson. 2005. *Population Issues in Social Choice Theory, Welfare Economics, and Ethics*. Cambridge: Cambridge University Press.

Brown, Campbell. 2011. "Consequentialize This." *Ethics* 121: 749–771.

Bykvist, Krister. 2017. "Person-Affecting Morality and Non-Identity Cases." Working paper.

Fleurbaey, Marc, and Alex Voorhoeve. 2015. "On the Social and Personal Value of Existence." In *Weighing and Reasoning: Themes from the Philosophy of John Broome*, edited by Iwao Hirose and Andrew Reisner, 95–109. Oxford: Oxford University Press.

Frick, Johann. 2015. "Contractualism and Social Risk." *Philosophy and Public Affairs* 43: 175–223.

Greaves, Hilary. 2017. "Population Axiology." *Philosophy Compass* 12: e12442.

Hare, Casper. 2007. "Voices from Another World: Must We Respect the Interests of Persons Who do Not, and Will never, Exist?" *Ethics* 117: 498–523.

Holtug, Nils. 2010. *Persons, Interests, and Justice*. Oxford: Oxford University Press.

Hooker, Brad. 2000. *Ideal Code, Real World: A Rule-Consequentialist Theory of Morality*. Oxford: Clarendon Press.

Kagan, Shelly. 1998. *Normative Ethics*. Boulder: Westview Press.

Kaplow, Louis and Steven Shavell. 2001. "Any Non-Welfarist Method of Policy Assessment Violates the Pareto Principle." *Journal of Political Economy* 109: 281–286.

Nebel, Jacob M. 2017. "Priority, Not Equality for Possible People." *Ethics* 127: 896–911.

McClennen, Edward F. 1990. *Rationality and Dynamic Choice: Foundational Explorations.* Cambridge: Cambridge University Press.

McNaughton, David and J. Piers Rawling. 1991. "Agent-Relativity and the Doing-Happening Distinction." *Philosophical Studies* 63: 167–185.

Otsuka, Michael. 2018. "How it Makes a Moral Difference that One is Worse Off than One Could Have Been." *Politics, Philosophy and Economics* 17: 192–215.

Parfit, Derek. 1984. *Reasons and Persons.* Oxford: Oxford University Press.

Parfit, Derek. 2000. "Equality or Priority." In *The Ideal of Equality,* edited by Matthew Clayton and Andrew Williams, 81–125. Houndmills: Palgrave.

Parfit, Derek. 2011. *On What Matters,* vol. 2. Oxford: Oxford University Press.

Parfit, Derek. 2017. "Future People, the Non-Identity Problem, and Person-Affecting Principles." *Philosophy and Public Affairs* 45: 118–157.

Scanlon, T. M. 1998. *What We Owe to Each Other.* Cambridge, MA: Harvard University Press.

Voorhoeve, Alex and Marc Fleurbaey. 2016. "Priority or Equality for Possible People?" *Ethics* 126: 929–954.

CHAPTER 15

···

DOES THE REPUGNANT CONCLUSION HAVE IMPORTANT IMPLICATIONS FOR AXIOLOGY OR FOR PUBLIC POLICY?

···

MARK BUDOLFSON AND DEAN SPEARS

1. INTRODUCTION

···

POPULATION ethics is a field at the intersection of economics and ethics. A central question within population ethics is what is the correct *population axiology*, which ranks outcomes composed of different numbers of individuals with different levels of well-being. A key challenge within population axiology is how to rank outcomes in which populations differ in tradeoffs between quantity and quality—that is, how should outcomes that create more lives be weighed against outcomes that create fewer but better lives? For example, consider two possible outcomes: Population A, a population of ten billion people each of whom has the same very high quality of life, versus Population Z, a far larger population composed entirely of people whose lives are all barely worth living; assume also that other things are equal between A and Z, and thus that there are no other normatively relevant differences between A and Z.[1] If a population axiology implies that for a sufficiently large population in Z, that Z is better than A, then that axiology implies the Repugnant Conclusion.

For several decades, the population ethics literature has focused on the Repugnant Conclusion and the effort to devise a suitable axiology that escapes it (Parfit 1984).[2] Figure 15.1 illustrates how an axiology might imply an instance of the Repugnant Conclusion, and how an axiology might avoid implying it.[3]

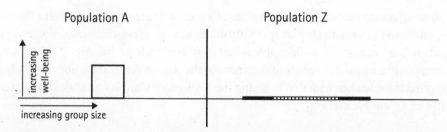

FIGURE 15.1 An instance of the Repugnant Conclusion for Total Utilitarianism: population A consists of 10 billion equally high quality lives, population Z consists of a sufficiently large population of equally barely worth living lives so that the sum total of well-being in Z is larger than in A

Total utilitarianism, which ranks populations according to their total sum of well-being, implies the Repugnant Conclusion by preferring Z to A in Figure 15.1; average utilitarianism, which ranks populations according to average well-being, avoids this specific instance by preferring A to Z, but has other undesirable implications.

Formal arguments by Ng (1989), Arrhenius (forthcoming), and others have proven that avoiding the Repugnant Conclusion is impossible without rejecting one or more other highly plausible population principles. To many, such proofs establish not only a deep challenge for axiology, but also pose an important practical problem: how can climate policy, population policy, or human development policy confidently proceed without resolving any of the central questions of population ethics, such as whether and how to avoid the Repugnant Conclusion?

Here we offer deflationary responses: first to the practical challenge, and then to the more fundamental challenge for axiology. Regarding the practical challenge, we argue that the importance of population ethics to realistic decision-making has been overstated. We provide an overview of recent literature that explores the implications for public policy of the Repugnant Conclusion and related puzzles within population ethics, and shows that there is more agreement in the implications of different population axiologies than has previously been recognized. The upshot is that uncertainty about population ethics presents no important problem for policy-making.

We then turn to more fundamental issues about axiology and describe a new series of formal proofs that undermine the idea that *any* plausible axiology could avoid the Repugnant Conclusion, including those that are assumed to avoid it in the literature. The philosophical upshot is that the Repugnant Conclusion *cannot* plausibly be avoided, and so it is a mistake to assume as a constraint on a plausible axiology that it *must* be avoided, as is assumed by most of the literature in population ethics, including by all of the fundamental impossibility theorems.

A unifying theme of both the practical and philosophical discussions is that there is more commonality in the implications of different population axiologies than has previously been recognized: in part this is because of empirical facts such as the improving trajectory of average well-being, in part this is because policy choices are coarse and constrained by feasibility, in part this is because just as policies are already evaluated for their suitability under alternative values of a statistical life or social discount rate, so too policy can be evaluated for acceptability under a range of population axiologies, and in part this is because the philosophical literature has made an important mistake by focusing only on a proper subset of instances of the Repugnant Conclusion, which has supported the mistaken idea that avoiding the Repugnant Conclusion should be a constraint on a plausible axiology.

2. EMPIRICAL DEMOGRAPHY AND FEASIBILITY CONSTRAINTS ON TIMELY, NON-COERCIVE POPULATION REDUCTION

The 2014 International Panel on Climate Change report expressed the worry that climate policy might depend importantly on population ethics and might therefore inherit the uncertainty of population axiology. The connections between population and climate take several forms. On the one hand, increases in the size of the population will lead to increases in carbon emissions; so, policy to reduce population growth might be a useful form of climate mitigation policy. On the other hand, climate change may change the size of the future population (such as by increasing early-life mortality; Geruso and Spears 2018), so population implications may change the social desirability of emissions-reduction policy. Either way, knowing what climate policy to pursue may seem to require knowing how to value increases or decreases in the size of the population. Thus, it may appear that climate change provides a clear example of how making progress on the central disagreements in population ethics is a prerequisite for confident policy-making, given the radical disagreements that are possible between axiologies like averagism and totalism when it comes to valuing changes in the size of the population (Broome 2012).[4]

In contrast, we argue that population ethics is unlikely to have much significance for policy, relying on the example of climate policy as a useful illustration. First, in this section, we note that even very ambitious population policy would be unlikely to substantially change the size of the population in the decades-long short-term that is relevant for climate mitigation policy. Climate mitigation is urgent, and in the meantime technological progress may rapidly change the environmental costs of increased population size. In Section 3, we show that even if climate change will change the size of the future population, all plausible axiologies are likely to consider decarbonization to be a policy goal as quickly as is likely to be politically feasible. These examples illustrate a more general point that uncertainty over axiology need not translate into uncertainty about policy-making.

Escaping the worst of climate change will require rapid reductions in carbon emissions over the first half of the twenty-first century. Here, *timing* is important: achieving the goals of the Paris Agreement, for example, would require carbon emissions to be essentially eliminated worldwide within the length of an average human lifespan, and to be substantially reduced even more quickly. Some people have proposed that reducing the growth of the human population would be a useful policy strategy to achieve reduction in carbon emissions. The argument is that it is an empirical fact that larger populations emit more polluting carbon all else being equal (O'Neill et al. 2012), so reducing population growth would appear to offer an effective strategy to reduce population emissions. However, populations change slowly over this timescale, and in light of this Budolfson and Spears (2021) observe that this argument overlooks two important facts from empirical demography. The first is that population growth is already slowing. The size of the population is projected to peak around 2100 (Gerland et al. 2014). This is because the world is progressing through the demographic transition, characterized by paradigm-shifting improvements in the developing world in health and human development, such as sanitation and reduced mortality rates (Coffey and Spears, 2017; Deaton 2013), leading to a subsequent fall in fertility rates. Because mortality rates have a lower bound near zero and fertility rates can also only fall so low, the uniquely rapid population growth of the mid-twentieth century—when mortality rates had fallen but fertility rates had not yet followed down—could not ever be projected to be repeated (Lam 2011). So, any fertility policy to reduce the size of the population would have the task of *accelerating* a decline in growth rates that is already underway.

The second fact is that even much-larger-than-feasible changes in fertility and mortality rates would not substantially change the size of the population over the decades-long medium-term that is relevant for climate mitigation. This is because of *population momentum*: demographers' term for changes in the size of the population that would continue to occur due to the age distribution of the population, even if fertility and mortality rates hypothetically changed to replacement levels. In short, in high-fertility countries, there are currently more young girls at each age than adult women, so their inevitable aging guarantees continued increase in the size of birth cohorts over the coming decades.

Figure 15.2 plots the UN's projection of future population size under two scenarios: the most likely path and a population momentum path. The population momentum path projects what would happen if mortality and fertility rates instantly went to replacement levels—that is, went to replacement levels starting *today*. We emphasize that the momentum path is not a policy option; it is a highly counterfactual illustration of population growth falling much faster than is actually feasible: no actual fertility policy implementable by states could plausibly cause such a large, rapid change in fertility rates. Our purpose in showing Figure 15.2 is to demonstrate that, over the coming decades relevant for climate mitigation policy, the size of the population is bounded for policy-making purposes, as even under the much-greater-reductions-than-are-feasible population momentum path there is a surprisingly small reduction in population over the coming decades, which would translate into only a small reduction in greenhouse gas emissions relative to the reductions that are needed. To see this, note that by 2050, the population would be about 9 billion people under the momentum-only path and 10 billion under the medium variant; under the O'Neill et al. (2012) elasticity estimate, this unfeasibly large population change would imply only a 10 percent reduction in

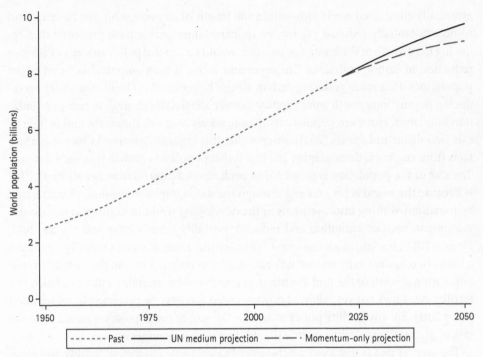

FIGURE 15.2 Two population projections are similar for coming decades

Source: UN Population Division projections

emissions from where they would otherwise be, at a time when many climate scientists argue emissions should be approaching zero. As time continues, the difference between the two projections becomes larger, but 2100 is already late in the game relative to both the policy horizon for climate mitigation and the plausible emergence of "backstop" low-emissions technology, given that the key to any decent solution to climate change is large-scale decarbonization of the economy over the next roughly fifty years.

One upshot is that it is not urgent to normatively evaluate the goodness or badness of differences in population size for climate policy-making, because if the size of the future population cannot be reduced over a timescale that matters to climate mitigation policy, then this eliminates one reason for thinking that the puzzles of population ethics are practically urgent.

A further lesson from history and demography is that policy-making to change fertility rates is neither easy nor costless in practice. Indeed, the actual history of population policies implemented by states, especially in developing countries, has involved considerable coercion and harm in some cases, as well as benefits and freedom in other contexts (Connelly 2009). With this in mind, it is important to consider the argument that population reduction is generally an undesirable policy lever—especially in the context of global problems such as climate change—because insofar as developed nations try to incentivize *non*-coercive population reduction in developing nations, the expected effect would be that (as we have observed historically) developing nations instead adopt *coercive* measures to achieve the relevant targets, and the result is that the costs of the policy greatly exceed the benefits, including in terms of human rights violations.

Another reason that it can be challenging for policy to accelerate the ongoing decline in fertility rates is that *achieved* total fertility rates often reflect *desired* total fertility rates. In other words, on average, population-level total fertility rates substantially reflect preferences. Some pregnancies are unintended, but over a childbearing career a woman who experiences an unintended pregnancy can nevertheless achieve her desired total number of children (a quantity known to population science as "ideal fertility") by reducing her subsequent fertility (such as by increasing subsequent breastfeeding or other contraceptive effort to space or avoid later pregnancies). If so, unexpected pregnancy would influence the timing and spacing of fertility but would only have a small effect on population-level average total fertility.

The empirical demography literature has long studied the important relationships between fertility intentions and fertility behavior. A classic analysis is Pritchett's (1994) examination of the results of fertility surveys, which we have updated with more recent data in Figure 15.3. Comparing across developing countries (including populations in places and times where access to modern contraceptive technology was much more limited than today), Figure 15.3 shows that ideal total fertility rates are highly correlated

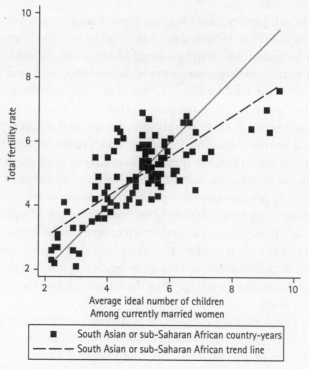

FIGURE 15.3 The correlation across populations between ideal and achieved fertility

Source: Authors' use of Demographic and Health Survey data to update Pritchett (1994)

with achieved total fertility rates. In other words, high fertility rates often happen because they are wanted.

A useful example for our purposes is the large population science literature on the extreme case of the one-child policy in China: how much of China's late-twentieth-century fertility decline was due to this policy and its implementation, rather than to economic and social changes that were also happening, at different paces, around the world? (Greenhalgh 2008). For example, a 2018 issue of the journal *Demography* contains a heated debate over this issue, with three detailed, published responses criticizing an earlier article that claimed that the one-child policy caused total fertility rates to be half-a-birth-per-woman lower than they otherwise would have been.[5] In short, many demographers who are critical of the alleged influence of the one-child policy argue that social and economic changes, qualitatively similar to trends in other developing countries, were principally responsible for China's fertility decline, operating importantly through changes in ideal fertility (Cai 2010). Babiarz, et al. (2018) have noted, for example, that China's fertility decline substantially *precedes* the 1980 introduction of the one-child policy: the total fertility rate fell from around 6 in 1970 to below 4 in 1980, which as Figure 15.3 shows was not aberrant in international comparison. The upshot for our argument is that the population science literature is far from agreed that the one-child policy had a large effect on fertility rates. In addition, no leading figure in the climate policy debate would seriously advocate a policy so coercive as a form of climate mitigation.

Around the world, fertility rates today are lower than Pritchett documented them to be in the 1980s and 1990s. What today are the highest total fertility rates are around 5 children per woman's childbearing career, in some sub-Saharan African countries. But total fertility in India, for example, is now about 2.3, and in many Latin American countries the total fertility rate has fallen below replacement. Of course, it is possible that these rates could fall even further. The important point in this context is that achieving much lower population-average total fertility rates is unlikely to be as simple as further increasing access to modern contraception, in part because investments against the HIV/AIDS epidemic have already done much to increase access to reproductive health care. Instead, if high fertility rates tend to reflect, at least in part, high fertility preferences, what policy can achieve without coercion may be limited to long-term changes in fertility preferences through education and human development. Such policy may be an important component of humanity's long-term environmental strategy but is unlikely to make a large difference to carbon emissions in the near-term decades relevant to climate mitigation, given that the key to any decent solution to climate change is large-scale decarbonization of the economy over the next roughly fifty years.

The upshot is that population momentum and other considerations create stringent feasibility constraints on the magnitude of possible non-coercive population reduction in the near term. For policy challenges like climate change that require large changes within a few decades, population reduction is therefore not well suited to serve as an important policy lever, and so uncertainty about population ethics presents no important challenge for policy-making.

3. AGREEMENT ACROSS AXIOLOGIES: CONVERGENCE ON A CORNER SOLUTION

Section 2 considered the possibility that fertility-reduction policy could be used as a form of climate mitigation policy. This section considers another possible interaction between population and climate policy. One of the possible consequences of climate change is changing the size of the future population, for example because of increasing mortality rates. If so, it may be that choosing the correct carbon mitigation policy (such as choosing an optimal tax on carbon emissions) depends on the population axiology, because the social evaluation of climate damages depends on the social evaluation of the change in the size of the population (Broome 2012).

Arrhenius et al. (2019) argue that this worry is likely to turn out not to be important in practice. The reason is that the policy-relevant set of possible climate mitigation policies (such as, e.g., the optimal 2150 decarbonization rate) is both bounded and coarse. Being *bounded* means that decarbonization cannot exceed some increasing amount each year due to political and other feasibility constraints. For example, it is likely that it is not politically feasible for the world to do anywhere near 100 percent of the mitigation that optimal policy models say we should be doing in the short and medium term. Being *coarse* means that feasibility constraints may also limit the fineness of the plausible distinctions between climate policies. For example, it may be that many political actors can only choose a broad policy such as "vigorously pursue multisectoral, rapid decarbonization as an urgent policy priority." Given these constraints, it is likely that all axiologies agree on the same climate policies into the future within this feasible set: roughly, to decarbonize as quickly as is politically feasible. In the terminology of optimization in calculus, this is called a *corner solution*: the optimum is a unique point at the boundary of the feasible set. Whether or not these features in fact describe the climate policy problem is an empirical question.

If the optimal climate mitigation policy is a corner solution, then it might not matter to policy-making what the correct population axiology is. Consider the illustrative case of average and total utilitarianism, commonly taken to be theoretical opposites in the population ethics literature. Average utilitarianism seeks to maximize average well-being; total utilitarianism seeks to maximize the total sum of well-being, the product of average well-being and the population size. It is plausible that climate damages will both decrease average well-being and will decrease the future population size, relative to a future in which there were no climate damages. Even ignoring the effect on population size, the effect of climate change on average well-being is sufficient to justify a corner solution in mitigation policy: "pursue full decarbonization in the next fifty years." Now imagine that a policy-maker realizes that instead of maximizing average well-being, she should have been maximizing total well-being. She was already pursuing the most aggressive available mitigation policy. So, the additional consideration of population size does not change the optimal action available in her choice set.

Of course, it is possible that mitigation policy-making is not so coarse. If so, different axiologies might disagree on details, such as exactly how fast to pursue decarbonization, or exactly what industries to prioritize, even if they agree on the broad outline of climate policy. It is also the case that different axiologies could agree on the optimal action while disagreeing about the comparative goodness and badness of options: for example, totalism could think that 90 percent decarbonization is much worse than 100 percent, while averaging thinks 90 percent decarbonization is only a little worse than 100 percent. Figure 15.4 illustrates this possibility with a hypothetical example. Our point is merely that if optimal feasible policy turns out to be a corner solution in a coarse set of politically feasible options, then a wide range of divergent axiologies may turn out to agree on what policy-makers should do.

Although Figure 15.4 is hypothetical and stylized, Scovronick et al. (2017) provide detailed quantitative computations that suggest that the actual case of setting optimal climate policy may have this corner solution property. They compute optimal carbon taxes for intertemporal versions of total and average utilitarianism. In both cases, the recommended mitigation policy is more ambitious that is currently being pursued, and very likely more than is politically feasible.

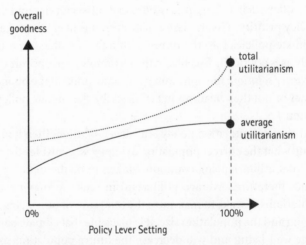

FIGURE 15.4 Total and average utilitarianism agree on what choice is best, while disagreeing on the comparative value of outcomes

4. AGREEMENT ACROSS AXIOLOGIES: CONVERGENCE GIVEN INCREASING WELL-BEING

So far, this chapter has illustrated the implications of population axiologies for policy via the example of climate policy. This section turns to policy-making outside of climate change—for example, policy intended to decrease or increase fertility rates. In short, should policy-makers seek to increase or decrease the size of the future population, or is the size of the future population irrelevant for overall social goodness?

This might initially appear to be a question on which population axiologies such as average and total utilitarianism disagree. Total utilitarianism, the conventional wisdom holds, would favor increasing the number of future well-off lives, while average utilitarianism does not seek an increase in the size of the population, separate and apart from any second-order effects on average well-being. Spears and Budolfson (2019a) observe that this conventional view is false insofar as it overlooks the fact that these population axiologies rank the goodness of the full intertemporal population: past, present, and future.

In particular, Spears and Budolfson build upon an empirical premise: average well-being will be greater among people in the future than among people in the past and should be expected to continue increasing over time. They summarize the demographic and statistical evidence for this empirical premise, rooted in the important facts of the epidemiological transition from a past world of high mortality rates to a contemporary world of low mortality, low poverty, and high literacy (Coffey and Spears 2017; Deaton 2013; Rosling 2018). More formally, this empirical premise can also be generalized and stated in axiologically neutral terms of the "equally distributed equivalent" level of well-being of a population, which allows for an axiologically neutral summary of well-being (Fleurbaey 2010).

> *Equally Distributed Equivalent*: For any population *A*, the *equally distributed equivalent* of *A*, according to a specific axiology, is the level of well-being *u* such that a population the same size as *A* in which everyone was at *u* would be ranked exactly as good as *A* by that axiology.

The concept of equally distributed equivalent generalizes the role of average well-being in a utilitarian axiology: it captures how well-off a population is, for a population of its size, according to a specific axiology. In this way, it is like the body mass index, which allows weight to be compared across people of different height. For any version of utilitarianism, the equally distributed equivalent is simply average well-being, but for other axiologies (such as versions of prioritarianism, maximin, or rank-dependent views) the equally distributed equivalent can differ from the simple average, in a way that derives from the different properties of the axiology. With this definition, we can state the Empirical Premise:

> *Empirical Premise*: The future will be better than the past: more precisely, the equally distributed equivalent well-being of the future will be greater than the equally distributed equivalent of the past (and will be greater than the critical level, if an axiology has one).

The next step is to combine the Empirical Premise with a broadly attractive axiom for population ethics, Convergence in Equivalence, which for generality and neutrality between competing axiologies uses the concept of the equally distributed equivalent. Convergence in Equivalence is accepted by a wide range of population axiologies, including total, average, variable-value, and critical-level versions of utilitarianism, prioritarianism, and egalitarianism, among many other axiologies:

> *Convergence in Equivalence*: Starting from any population A, adding a very large number of lives at an well-being level u, as the number of added lives become large, the equally distributed equivalent converges to u.

To reject Convergence in Equivalence is to hold that an arbitrarily tiny fraction of the population can be more important for social evaluation than the vast majority of the population. Convergence in Equivalence would not be accepted by some rank-dependent views, nor by Non-Archimedean axiologies or those that endorse Weak Value Superiority (Parfit 2016), such as presented by Erik Carlson in this volume; we discuss these views in the next section, and note that they have implications at least as counter-intuitive as the Repugnant Conclusion.

Convergence in Equivalence, combined with the Empirical Premise, in the context of some formal properties[6] that are generally uncontroversial even among axiologists who otherwise disagree, implies that it could be an improvement to increase the size of the future population, even in a way that makes all future people worse-off than they otherwise would be. More formally, relative to the business-as-usual size n and equally distributed equivalent well-being u of the future population, there exists $m > n$ and $v < u$ such that a population with (m, v) would be strictly better than a population with (n, u).

The intuition behind this result can be illustrated using the case of average utilitarianism, merely because average utilitarianism provides a conceptually simple illustration. Average utilitarianism wishes to maximize the average well-being among all past, present, and future people who will ever have lived. If future people will be better-off than past people, then a change that vastly increases the number of future people while slightly decreasing their well-being would increase the overall, intertemporal average.[7] Of course, it may be that another possible future would be even better: this is merely a claim relative to the business as usual. Different axiologies have different degrees of overlap in the future paths that they prefer to business as usual.

Many past and present states articulate or implement *practical population policy*, by which we mean programs or efforts to influence population-level fertility rates, such as contraception or sterilization programs, in the anti-natalist direction, or childcare subsidies and parental leave policies, in the pro-natalist direction (Connelly 2009). Given the result just noted, it is unwarranted to assume that different axiologies such as average and total utilitarianism would have radically different implications for practical population policy. We speculate that this unwarranted assumption is nevertheless widespread partly because textbook examples of population ethics often ignore the fact that practical population policy concerns future additions to the set of past and present lives which have already come to exist. In other words, the practical implications of population ethics are not about comparisons of non-overlapping populations that are merely metaphysically possible and entirely distinct, but rather are about comparisons of overlapping populations that include an unaffected base population (namely, past people and unaffected current people, who are worse-off on average than future people will be). As the next section will explore, the possibility of an unaffected base population is not merely practically important but also theoretically important for population ethics.

5. WHY THE REPUGNANT CONCLUSION SHOULD NOT CONSTRAIN THE SEARCH FOR THE CORRECT POPULATION AXIOLOGY

This section considers a final reason why some puzzles of population ethics might not pose a problem: namely, that there may be compelling arguments against a methodological requirement to avoid the Repugnant Conclusion, which would then disarm the main challenge posed by the impossibility results within population axiology, since the impossibility results all assume that the Repugnant Conclusion must be avoided.

One familiar argument for a deflationary response insists we should *endorse* the Repugnant Conclusion *even if it can be avoided by axiologies that are otherwise attractive.* The most straightforward arguments of this type are offered by Huemer (2008), Tännsjö (2002), and others: namely, that that low-positive-value lives should be recognized as socially valuable, and therefore welfarist axiology that does not do so should be off the table. This kind of argument is sometimes supplemented by the additional claim that we are misled by our intuitions about the Repugnant Conclusion because we are unable to fully appreciate how much value there is in a population with many billions of lives that are barely worth living, because we are in general unable to have reliable intuitions about cases involving very large numbers (Broome 2004; Tännsjö 2002; see also Pummer 2013 for discussion and Zuber et al. 2021). A related argument sometimes offered for endorsing the Repugnant Conclusion is that the conjunction of the principles that imply the Repugnant Conclusion is more compelling than is the intuition that the Repugnant Conclusion should be avoided. For example, several recent papers have shown that incorporation of probability and risk into population ethics point towards an additive or generalized totalist framework, with Repugnant-Conclusion-type implications (Arrhenius and Stefánsson 2018; Nebel 2019; Spears 2018; see also Broome 2004; Zuber et al. 2021). Any repugnance of the conclusion would thus be set against the attractiveness of rational decision-making under risk.

In what follows we highlight a different kind of argument against the idea that the Repugnant Conclusion must be avoided: namely, that the Repugnant Conclusion should not be avoided *because it cannot be avoided by any generalized utilitarian axiology*, or for that matter by any other axiology that we should find plausible. Here and in what follows, "generalized utilitarian axiology" is used as formally defined by Blackorby, Bossert, and Donaldson (2005) and includes all total, average, critical-level, and variable-value versions of utilitarianism, prioritarianism, and egalitarianism—not merely utilitarianism.[8] The moving parts of this argument involve, first, the observation that there are instances of the Repugnant Conclusion that cannot be avoided by average utilitarianism, and that cannot be avoided by many other axiologies that are commonly assumed to avoid the Repugnant Conclusion—thus, the Repugnant Conclusion is an implication of more axiologies than is commonly recognized; second, the articulation of a sufficient condition for being an instance of the Repugnant Conclusion that includes these instances, which are generally ignored in more simplistic formal definitions of the Repugnant Conclusion in the literature; and finally, a formal proof that exploits the improved characterization of the Repugnant Conclusion to prove that in fact *all* generalized utilitarian axiologies (and others) imply the Repugnant Conclusion when it is correctly characterized. This argument can be supplemented with an additional analysis of what the Repugnant Conclusion is most fundamentally, which then allows for more precise arguments that no plausible axiology could hope to avoid it, up to and including additional formal proofs. In the rest of this section, we explain these arguments in more detail, following their initial presentation in the philosophy literature by Budolfson and Spears 2018 and in the economics literature by Spears and Budolfson 2021.

We begin with the observation that some instances of the Repugnant Conclusion cannot be avoided by average utilitarianism and other axiologies that are commonly assumed to avoid the Repugnant Conclusion. For example, consider the three different choices in Figure 15.5, which illustrate three different kinds of choices where instances of the Repugnant Conclusion can arise.

In this figure, Choice 1 illustrates the canonical instance of the Repugnant Conclusion for total utilitarianism displayed in Figure 15.1 at the beginning of this paper, which is an implication of total utilitarianism (TU) but not of average utilitarianism (AU) nor variable-value utilitarianism (X′). However, Choice 2 and Choice 3 are instances of the Repugnant Conclusion that are implied by both AU and X′. This shows that the Repugnant Conclusion is an implication of more axiologies than is commonly recognized. Furthermore, Choice 3 shows that there are instances of the Repugnant Conclusion that are avoided by TU, despite being implications of other axiologies such

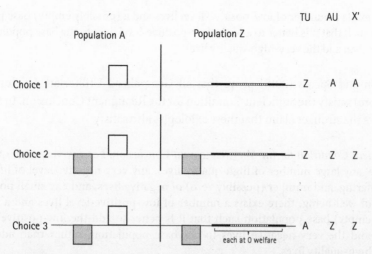

FIGURE 15.5 Different choices constitute instances of the Repugnant Conclusion for different axiologies, including not only total utilitarianism (TU), but also axiologies that are commonly assumed to avoid it such as average utilitarianism (AU) and variable-value utilitarianism (X'). A choice is an instance of the Repugnant Conclusion for a given axiology if that axiology implies that Z is better than A (noted on the right side). Note that Choice 2 and Choice 3 involve additions to a base population (grey box) unaffected by the choice of which population to add. Choice 2 is like Choice 1, except that instead of a choice between the two distinct populations A and Z described in Figure 15.1, it is instead a choice between which of those same two populations A and Z to *add* to an existing base population. Choice 3 is like Choice 2, except that in Choice 3 the lives in Z each have well-being level of zero instead of barely positive.

as AU and X' that are commonly assumed to avoid it. This shows that TU does not do worse with respect to the Repugnant Conclusion than AU or X', since it is not the case that TU implies all instances of the Repugnant conclusion, or that the instances implied by AU and X' are a proper subset of those implied by TU.[9] The population ethics literature has overlooked this phenomenon, because it has restricted its attention to instances of the Repugnant Conclusion such as Choice 1 in which there is no base population to which a chosen population is added.

So, more axiologies imply the Repugnant Conclusion than is typically acknowledged in the literature, because the literature has mistakenly ignored the importance of instances of the Repugnant Conclusion with non-zero base population such as Choice 2 and Choice 3. This raises the question of how many more axiologies imply the Repugnant Conclusion once this mistake is corrected. The next step of the argument is to articulate a sufficient condition for being an instance of the Repugnant Conclusion that includes all the instances in Figure 15.5 and others like them that may or may not include a base population to which additions are made:

Sufficient Condition for the Repugnant Conclusion: For any very high quality of life, any large number of high-quality lives, and any small positive level of well-being, there exists a number of low-positive-level lives and a (possibly empty) base population such that it is better to add the low-positive-level lives to the base population, rather than add the very-high-quality lives.

Budolfson and Spears (2018) prove that all Generalized Utilitarian Axiologies (and many more) satisfy the Sufficient Condition for the Repugnant Conclusion. In addition, they prove the stronger claim that these axiologies also satisfy:

> *Sufficient Condition for the Very Repugnant Conclusion*: For any very high quality of life, any large number of high-quality lives, any very negative level of life full of suffering, and number (possibly zero) of negative lives, and any small positive level of well-being, there exists a number of low-positive-level lives and a (possibly empty) base population such that it is better to add the low-positive-level lives and the very-negative lives to the base population, rather than add the very-high-quality lives.

It is often claimed that avoiding the Very Repugnant Conclusion should be an even stronger desideratum than avoiding the Repugnant Conclusion, because the Very Repugnant Conclusion also involves preferring to add very negative lives (Arrhenius forthcoming). The proof reveals that contrary to what has been assumed in the literature, all Generalized Utilitarian Axiologies (and many more) are also on equal footing with respect to even the Very Repugnant Conclusion.

The intuition behind the proof is that population axiologies imply the (Very) Repugnant Conclusion if they satisfy Convergence in Equivalence (stated in the previous section), together with a small number of other properties that all Generalized Utilitarian Axiologies assume are uncontroversial.[10] This is because satisfying Convergence in Equivalence means that an axiology *always cares about quantity to some non-zero extent*, whereas to avoid the Repugnant Conclusion an axiology has to deny this and insist that quantity effectively doesn't matter at least beyond some point. Convergence in Equivalence is satisfied by all Generalized Utilitarian Axiologies including total, average, and variable-value utilitarianism, and all prioritarian and egalitarian variations, as well as by many other axiologies. Thus, all of these axiologies (and more) imply instances of the (Very) Repugnant Conclusion.

Note that Convergence in Equivalence is not satisfied by rank-dependent views: maximin, for example, only cares about the worst-off person, while RDGU and Geometrism, in a way similar to maximin, care much more about some people than others. However, even rank-dependent axiologies imply an Extended Very Repugnant Conclusion, which fully retains (and arguably intensifies) the repugnant elements of Parfit's original statement of the Repugnant Conclusion. Non-Archimedean and Weak Value Superiority axiologies also do not satisfy Convergence in Equivalence. More generally, as Arrhenius (forthcoming) demonstrates, such Non-Archimedean views have striking anti-egalitarian implications. They also imply their own versions of conclusions that are repugnant. For example, in the Non-Archimedean theory explored by Carlson in this volume, each person is described by an ordered pair of superior and inferior welfare. Although Carlson does not fully specify an aggregation method (he explores totaling within category), the essence of such a view is that it must satisfy within-category Pareto, privileging superior welfare (otherwise it would not avoid Parfit's Repugnant Conclusion). On any such view, in a same-number comparison, a population in which one person has some superior welfare (such as some opera and fine dining) and many people have high inferior welfare (such as plenty of muzak and potatoes), would be worse than a population in which the well-off person instead has slightly more superior welfare (such as one more minute of opera) and the rest of the population has lives full only of highly negative inferior welfare (such as everyone's only experience, throughout their entire lives, is severe intestinal pain). This illustrates that any Non-Archimedean view will also have repugnant quantity-quality tradeoffs. Similar remarks apply to other welfarist axiologies, including rank-dependent axiologies (Budolfson and Spears 2018).

In a related vein, some authors have noted that the Repugnant Conclusion is fundamentally similar to same-number paradoxes of utilitarianism that welfarist consequentialists are prepared to accept (Cowen 1996; Ng 2013). Furthermore, even same-number axiologies (meaning social orderings that ignore the variable-number questions of population ethics) will inevitably have unintuitive implications when aggregating implications over unbounded spaces (Fleurbaey and Tungodden 2010). What these examples have in common is that, when aggregating and ranking over unbounded spaces, a factor that intuitively feels important can ultimately be outweighed by a factor that intuitively feels unimportant. Budolfson and Spears extend the observations by Cowen, Ng, and Fleurbaey and Tungodden to explain why the Repugnant Conclusion, in one form or another, is implied by every generalized utilitarian axiology and more.

These examples suggest that what is fundamental to the sort of repugnance at issue in the Repugnant Conclusion may be the mere existence of a *Large Quantity-Quality Tradeoff*. This is surely one candidate for being the main intuition behind the counter-intuitiveness of the Repugnant Conclusion. If this is the correct way to understand the nature of the Repugnant Conclusion—that is, if Large Quantity-Quality Tradeoffs are sufficient for the Repugnant Conclusion—then it follows more or less directly that any plausible welfarist axiology implies instances of the Repugnant Conclusion, since any plausible welfarist axiology must presumably endorse the possibility of significant tradeoffs.

The upshot is that the Repugnant Conclusion does not tell against any axiology, because it cannot be avoided by any plausible axiology. This provides a new argument that the methodological requirement to avoid the Repugnant Conclusion should be dropped from population ethics. If so, this has implications for axiological theory, and also provides a further reason for thinking that the Repugnant Conclusion has no policy implications, at least within the familiar welfarist approach to policy evaluation.

6. INCORPORATING POPULATION ETHICS
INTO ORDINARY POLICY ANALYSIS

For several decades, research in population ethics has focused on theoretical puzzles motivated in large part by the methodological goal of avoiding the Repugnant Conclusion. Recently, high-profile arguments have emerged that population ethics poses practical challenges to policy as well. As the discussion above indicates, we disagree: there is more convergence in the policy recommendations of competing population axiologies than is commonly understood. But what about cases in which there remains some amount of divergence?

We propose that even in these cases, population ethics can be incorporated into ordinary policy analysis without any difficulty. The method is straightforward: adopt a parameterized family of population axiologies and investigate the robustness of policy choices to alternative parameter choices. This is perhaps the most common method in actual policy analysis of representing normative uncertainty and is already routinely done for other dimensions of normative uncertainty. For example, climate policy models such as William Nordhaus' DICE and RICE models choose policy in order to maximize a (total) utilitarian policy objective (called a social welfare function in this literature) (Nordhaus 2017; 2019). This objective is broadly utilitarian but depends upon two parameters: η, which parameterizes the degree of inequality aversion (and thus the connection between consumption and well-being; mathematically, the degree of concavity of diminishing marginal well-being as a function of consumption); and ρ, which parameterizes the rate of pure time preference, according to which future well-being is discounted simply because it is in the future. Climate policy analysis routinely investigates whether recommendations hold for a *range* of values of these parameters, meaning that policy can be chosen without resolving normative uncertainty about utilitarianism and prioritarianism, what the correct intertemporal savings principle is, whether there are agent-relative permissions to give less weight to people in the far future, and so on. Similarly, health policy decisions are often investigated over a range of quantities for the value of a statistical life, or a disability-adjusted life year. Education and taxation policies are chosen that work for a variety of elasticities of taxable income. In all these cases, normative uncertainty is acknowledged and explicitly investigated in policy analysis, by parameterizing the key normative dimensions of the analysis and testing the sensitivity of optimal policy to the range of reasonable uncertainty about those dimensions.

It is straightforward to extend this method to population ethics. Consider this broad family of population axiologies: $n^{\alpha} \left[\bar{u} - c \right]$, where n is the population size and $\bar{u}$ is the equally distributed-equivalent well-being[11] (which could incorporate utilitarianism, prioritarianism, or egalitarianism). In a policy analysis, population ethics could be roughly parameterized as a critical level $c \geq 0$, and as the exponent $\alpha \in [0,1]$, where $\alpha = 0$ is averagism, $\alpha = 1$ is totalism, and values in between are variable-value forms of each of these. Many policy recommendations—such as complete decarbonization by 2150—will be uniformly recommended by all plausible values of α and c As a result, policy can be chosen that is robust to a wide range of future theoretical resolutions of the puzzles of the Repugnant Conclusion and population ethics, more broadly. In other cases, we could discover more divergence. But then by implementing this method we can learn the magnitude of that divergence and rigorously inform our decision making under normative uncertainty, in the same way we inform decisions under other kinds of normative uncertainty in ordinary policy analysis. Either way, uncertainty about population ethics does not provide an important barrier to policy-making.

ACKNOWLEDGMENTS

We acknowledge with gratitude helpful comments from Gustaf Arrhenius, Krister Bykvist, Tim Campbell, Tom Christiano, Diane Coffey, Mike Geruso, Johan Gustafsson, Vasudha Jain, Jonathan Riley, Melinda Roberts, Orri Stefánsson, Chad Van Schoelandt, Sangita Vyas, Andrew Williams, and participants in seminars at IFFS, ANU, the Paris School of Economics, and the 2019 PPE conference in New Orleans.

NOTES

1. In what follows, we will always implicitly understand this *other things are equal* condition as understood in our discussion of specific cases.
2. In contrast, a few philosophers have argued that we should endorse the Repugnant Conclusion—we outline their arguments in Section 5.
3. In figures of this type, used throughout this chapter, each box represents a group of people. The height of the box is proportional to equal per-person well-being of the group and the width is proportional to number of people; boxes are to scale unless noted otherwise.
4. "We do not know what value to set on changes in the world's population. If the population shrinks as a result of climate change, we do not know how to evaluate that change. Yet we have reason to think that changes in population may be one of the most morally significant effects of climate change. The small chance of catastrophe may be a major component in the expected value of harm caused by climate change, and the loss of population may be a major component of the badness of catastrophe. . . . So we face a particularly intractable problem of uncertainty, which prevents us from working out what we should do. Yet we have to act; climate change will not wait while we sort ourselves out" (Broome 2012, 183–185).
5. Goodkind (2017), the paper at the center of the recent debate, drew its conclusions by comparing China to Vietnam as a counterfactual. For a response based on the details and timing of China's fertility patterns, see Zhao and Zhang (2018).
6. The formal properties are "Egalitarian replication is not worse at high enough well-being," "Same-number egalitarian Pareto," and "Same-number egalitarian continuity." These are formally defined in Spears and Budolfson (2019a).

7. Although the population axiology literature accepts that population axiologies rank the full set of all lives (past, present, and future), some readers may be surprised that the past matters. Spears and Budolfson (2019a) detail preference-reversal reasons that may account for why the population ethics literature has taken this as part of the definition of a population axiology (Arrhenius forthcoming).

8. This set of axiologies is known as "generalized utilitarian" in the economics literature because they share a key property of utilitarianism: same-number anonymous additive separability.

9. In noting the existence of multiple instances of the Repugnant Conclusion, each sharing the same fundamental repugnance, we follow Parfit (2016) who enumerates many heterogenous instances of the Repugnant Conclusion, writing of "another," "a," "this," and "another version of the" Repugnant Conclusion. Anglin (1977) notes the existence of examples like Choice 2 that show that "in some cases the average principle also leads to the Repugnant Conclusion" (746).

10. Budolfson and Spears (2018) show that any transitive, anonymous population axiology that satisfies Extended Egalitarian Dominance and Convergence in Equivalence implies the (Very) Repugnant Conclusion, as stated here. Critical-level generalized utilitarianism does not satisfy these Extended Egalitarian Dominance unless it is standardized as in Broome (2004).

    Extended Egalitarian Dominance: If population A is perfectly equal-in-well-being and is of greater size than population B, and every person in A has higher positive well-being than every person in B, then A is better than B (compare Arrhenius forthcoming).

    They also define an "Extended Very Repugnant Conclusion," and show it is also implied by CLGU, maximin, and even more axiologies, including non-transitive, complete, and person-affecting axiologies, and show how even weaker conditions than Convergence in Signs can generate these implications.

11. For simplicity, the critical level is not included within the equally distributed equivalent calculation, but without loss of generality this could be accommodated in this framework.

REFERENCES

Anglin, Bill. 1977. The Repugnant Conclusion. *Canadian Journal of Philosophy* 7, no. 4: 745–754.

Arrhenius, Gustaf. Forthcoming. *Population Ethics: The Challenge of Future Generations*. Oxford: Oxford University Press.

Arrhenius, Gustaf and H. Orri Stefánsson. 2018. "Population Ethics under Risk." Working paper, Institute for Futures Studies.

Arrhenius, Gustaf, Mark Budolfson, and Dean Spears. 2021. "Does Climate Change Policy Depend Importantly on Population Ethics? Deflationary Responses to the Challenges of Population Ethics for Public Policy." In *Climate Change and Philosophy*, edited by Mark Budolfson, Tristram McPherson, and David Plunkett. Oxford: Oxford University Press.

Asheim, Geir and Stéphane Zuber. 2014. "Escaping the Repugnant Conclusion: Rank-Discounted Utilitarianism with Variable Population." *Theoretical Economics* 9: 629–650.

Babiarz, Kimberly S., Paul Ma, Grant Miller, and Shige Song, 2018. The Limits (and Human Costs) of Population Policy: Fertility Decline and Sex Selection in China under Mao. No. w25130. National Bureau of Economic Research.

Blackorby, Charles, Walter Bossert, and David Donaldson. 1995. "Intertemporal Population Ethics: Critical-Level Utilitarian Principles." *Econometrica* 63(6): 1303–1320.

Blackorby, Charles, Walter Bossert, and David J. Donaldson. 2005. *Population Issues in Social Choice Theory, Welfare Economics, and Ethics.* Cambridge: Cambridge University Press.

Blackorby, Charles and David Donaldson. 1984. "Social Criteria for Evaluating Population Change." *Journal of Public Economics* 25: 13–33.

Blackorby, Charles, Daniel Primont, and R. Robert Russell. 1998. "Separability: A Survey." In *Handbook of Utility Theory*, edited by Salvador Barbera, Peter Hammond, and Christian Seidl, 1: 49–92. Dordrecht: Kluwer.

Broome, John. 2004. *Weighing Lives.* Oxford: Oxford University Press.

Broome, John. 2012. *Climate Matters: Ethics in a Warming World.* New York: Norton.

Budolfson, Mark. 2018. "Market Failure, the Tragedy of the Commons, and Default Libertarianism in Contemporary Economics and Policy." In *The Oxford Handbook of Freedom*, edited by David Schmidtz and Carmen E. Pavel, 257–282. Oxford: Oxford University Press.

Budolfson, Mark and Dean Spears. 2018. Why the Repugnant Conclusion is Inescapable. Working paper, Princeton University Climate Futures Initiative.

Budolfson, Mark and Dean Spears. 2021. "Population Momentum, Population Ethics, and the Prospects for Fertility Policy as Climate Mitigation Policy." *Journal of Development Studies*, online first.

Budolfson, Mark and Dean Spears. 2020. "Public Policy, Consequentialism, the Environment, and Non-Human Animals." In *The Oxford Handbook of Consequentialism*, edited by Doug Portmore. Oxford: Oxford University Press.

Cai, Yong. 2010. "China's Below-Replacement Fertility: Government Policy or Socioeconomic Development?" *Population and Development Review* 36, no. 3: 419–440.

Coffey, Diane and Dean Spears. 2017. *Where India Goes: Abandoned Toilets, Stunted Development, and the Costs of Caste.* Noida: Harper Collins.

Connelly, Matthew J. 2009. *Fatal Misconception: The Struggle to Control World Population.* Cambridge, MA: Harvard University Press.

Cowen, Tyler. 1996. "What Do We Learn from the Repugnant Conclusion?" *Ethics* 106: 754–775.

Deaton, Angus. 2013. *The Great Escape.* Princeton, NJ: Princeton University Press.

Fleurbaey, Marc. 2010. "Assessing Risky Social Situations." *Journal of Political Economy* 118, no. 4: 649–680.

Fleurbaey, Marc and B. Tungodden, 2010. "The Tyranny of Non-Aggregation versus the Tyranny of Aggregation in Social Choices: A Real Dilemma." *Economic Theory* 44, no. 3: 399–414.

Gerland, Patrick, Adrian E. Raftery, Hana Ševčíková, Nan Li, Danan Gu, Thomas Spoorenberg, Leontine Alkema, Bailey K. Fosdick, Jennifer Chunn, Nevena Lalic, and Guiomar Bay. 2014. "World Population Stabilization Unlikely this Century." *Science* 346, no. 6206: 234–237.

Geruso, Michael and Dean Spears. 2018. "Heat, Humidity, and Infant Mortality in the Developing World." IZA Discussion Paper 11717.

Goodkind, Daniel. 2017. "The Astonishing Population Averted by China's Birth Restrictions: Estimates, Nightmares, and Reprogrammed Ambitions." *Demography* 54, no. 4: 1375–1400.

Greaves, Hilary. 2017. "Population Axiology." *Philosophy Compass* 12(e12442): 1–15.

Greenhalgh, Susan. 2008. *Just One Child: Science and Policy in Deng's China.* Berkeley and Los Angeles: University of California Press.

Huemer, Michael. 2008. "In Defence of Repugnance." *Mind* 117, no. 468: 899–933.

Lam, David. 2011. "How the World Survived the Population Bomb: Lessons from 50 Years of Extraordinary Demographic History." *Demography* 48, no. 4: 1231–1262.

Nebel, Jacob. 2019. "An Intrapersonal Addition Paradox." *Ethics* 129, no. 2: 309–343.

Ng, Yew-Kwang. 1989. "What Should We Do About Future Generations?: Impossibility of Parfit's Theory X." *Economics & Philosophy* 5, no. 2: 235–253.

Ng, Yew-Kwang. 2013. "Number Dampened Utilitarianism." In *The Bloomsbury Encyclopedia of Utilitarianism*, edited by J. Crimmins, 374–376. London: Bloomsbury.

Nordhaus, William. D. 2017. "Revisiting the Social Cost of Carbon." *Proceedings of the National Academy of Sciences* 114, no. 7: 1518–1523.

Nordhaus, William D. 2019. "Climate Change: The Ultimate Challenge for Economics." Nobel Prize lecture, *American Economic Review* 109(6): 1991–2014.

O'Neill, Brian C., Brant Liddle, Leiwen Jiang, Kirk R. Smith, Shonali Pachauri, Michael Dalton, and Regina Fuchs. 2012. "Demographic Change and Carbon Dioxide Emissions." *The Lancet* 380, no. 9837: 157–164.

Parfit, Derek. 1984. *Reasons and Persons*. Oxford: Oxford University Press.

Parfit, Derek. 2016. "Can We Avoid the Repugnant Conclusion?" *Theoria* 82, no. 2: 110–127.

Pritchett, Lant. 1994. "Desired Fertility and the Impact of Population Policies." *Population and Development Review* 20, no. 1: 1–55.

Pummer, Theron. 2013. "Intuitions about Large Number Cases." *Analysis* 73, no. 1: 80–98.

Roberts, Melinda A. 2015. "Population Axiology." In *The Oxford Handbook of Value Theory*, edited by Iwao Hirose and Jonas Olson, 399–423. Oxford: Oxford University Press.

Rosling, Hans. 2018. *Factfulness*. New York: Flatiron.

Scovronick, Noah, Mark B. Budolfson, Francis Dennig, Marc Fleurbaey, Asher Siebert, Robert H Socolow, Dean Spears, and Fabian Wagner. 2017. "Impact of Population Growth and Population Ethics on Climate Change Mitigation Policy." *Proceedings of the National Academy of Sciences* 114: 12338–12343.

Sider, Theodore. 1991. "Might Theory X Be a Theory of Diminishing Marginal Value?" *Analysis* 51: 265–271.

Spears, Dean. 2018. "Probabilistic Future People: Social Criteria for Evaluating Population Prospects." Working paper, University of Texas, Austin.

Spears, Dean and Mark Budolfson. 2019a. "Radical Agreement in Population Ethics—and Implications for Social Policy Analysis." Working paper, University of Vermontand University of Texas, Austin.

Spears, Dean and Mark Budolfson. 2021. "Repugnant Conclusions", *Social Choice and Welfare*, online first.

Tannsjo, Torbjörn. 2002. "Why We Ought to Accept the Repugnant Conclusion." *Utilitas* 14, no. 3: 339–359.

Zhao, Zhangwei and Guangyu Zhang. 2018. "Socioeconomic Factors Have Been the Major Driving Force of China's Fertility Changes Since the Mid-1990s." *Demography* 55, no. 2: 733–742.

Zuber, Stephane, Nikhil Venkatesh, Torbjörn Tännsjö, Christian Tarsney, H. Orri Stefansson, Katie Steele, Dean Spears, Jeff Sebo, Marcus Pivato, Toby Ord, Yew-Kwang Ng, Michal Masny, William MacAskill, Nicholas Lawson, Kevin Kuruc, Michelle Hutchinson, Johan Gustafsson, Hilary Greaves, Lisa Forsberg, Marc Fleurbaey, Diane Coffey, Susumu Cato, Clinton Castro, Tim Campbell, Marc Budolfson, John Broome, Alexander Berger, Nick Beckstead, and Geir B. Asheim. 2021. "What We Should Agree on about the Repugnant Conclusion." *Utilitas*, online first.

CHAPTER 16

··

OUR INTUITIVE GRASP
OF THE REPUGNANT
CONCLUSION

··

JOHAN E. GUSTAFSSON

CONSIDER

> *The Repugnant Conclusion*: For any possible population of at least ten billion people, all with very high quality of life, there must be some much larger imaginable population whose existence, if other things are equal, would be better, even though its members have lives barely worth living.[1]

The Repugnant Conclusion is often put in terms of a comparison between an outcome *A*—which has a large population where each member has very high well-being—and an outcome *Z*—which has a huge population where each member has positive but very low well-being. In Figure 16.1, the outcomes are represented by boxes, where the width of a box represents the size of the outcome's population and the height represents the well-being of its members. The Repugnant Conclusion says that, for every outcome like *A*, there is a better outcome like *Z*.

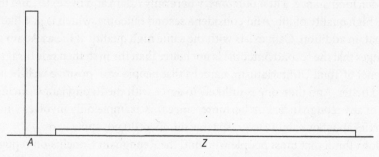

FIGURE 16.1: *A* versus *Z*

While its name is tendentious, many people do find the Repugnant Conclusion repugnant. This repugnance poses a significant challenge to views that entail the Repugnant Conclusion, such as Total Utilitarianism:[2]

> *Total Utilitarianism*: A first outcome is at least as good as a second outcome if and only if the sum total of well-being in the first is at least as great as the sum total of well-being in the second.[3]

Since the Repugnant Conclusion is counter-intuitive, we seem to have evidence that the Repugnant Conclusion is false. And, if the Repugnant Conclusion is false, then so is Total Utilitarianism.

But should we trust our intuition that the Repugnant Conclusion is repugnant? If this intuition is used as evidence against Total Utilitarianism, we should examine the reliability of this evidence. We may be able to defend Total Utilitarianism from the charge of repugnance if we can explain why this intuition is unreliable (and do so in a way that does not challenge the reliability of the intuitions that support Total Utilitarianism).

In this chapter, I will try to explain why our intuition about the Repugnant Conclusion is unreliable as evidence against Total Utilitarianism (Section 5).[4] But, before I present my proposal, I will consider some alternative explanations (Sections 2–4). These explanations, including my own, are variations of the idea that people's intuitions are misled by the very large numbers involved in the Repugnant Conclusion. Finally, I will also answer two general objections to explanations of this kind (Sections 6–7).

1. THE INTUITION OF NEUTRALITY

Before we go on, however, some words may be needed on the intended scope of these attempts to discredit our intuition. Some people reject the Repugnant Conclusion because they accept *the Intuition of Neutrality*, which says that it's axiologically neutral whether a person with a life worth living is brought into existence. This intuition is memorably captured by the slogan "We are in favor of making people happy, but neutral about making happy people."[5]

Consider, for instance, a first outcome, where only Adam and Eve exist, and they have the same high quality of life. And consider a second outcome, which is just like the first except that, in addition, Cain exists with the same high quality of life as Adam and Eve. If one judges that the second outcome is not better than the first, then one disagrees with a basic tenet of Total Utilitarianism, namely, that people with positive well-being make the world better. And then one is unlikely to agree with the Repugnant Conclusion, regardless of any repugnance. Furthermore, since this example only involves small numbers, worries about our ability to grasp large numbers do not apply here.

Yet I don't think that most people who find the Repugnant Conclusion repugnant do so because they accept the Intuition of Neutrality. If they did, there would be no need to involve large numbers in the Repugnant Conclusion to get a repugnant implication from Total Utilitarianism.

Anyway, the attempts below, by me and others, to explain the unreliability of our intuition about the Repugnant Conclusion aren't intended to cover those who reject the Repugnant Conclusion because they accept the Intuition of Neutrality. Still, these attempts may, to some extent, apply to these people too if they think that there's something additionally repugnant about the Repugnant Conclusion, on top of their not seeing any value in making happy people.

2 THE IMAGINATIVE ALIKENESS OF LARGE NUMBERS

Michael Huemer argues that our intuition about the Repugnant Conclusion is unreliable because we are unable to imaginatively differentiate between large numbers. He claims that beyond a certain level, all large numbers are imagined roughly the same.[6] So, when we compare A and Z, we imagine their population sizes the same way—that is, just as very large. Hence we compare them as follows:

A	Z
very large population	very large population
very high well-being	positive but very low well-being

If this suggestion were correct, then the main feature of Z which makes it better than A according to Total Utilitarianism (that is, the size of its population) would be lost in the comparison. And then it wouldn't be surprising if our intuitions gave us the wrong answer.[7]

Yet, in some cases with very large populations, it seems that we can take their relative sizes into account. For example, consider the comparison in Figure 16.2 between outcome A, which has a very large population, and an outcome B, which has a much larger population whose members have a slightly lower well-being.

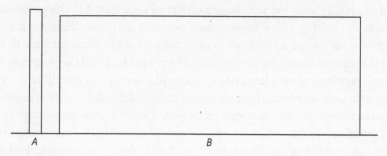

FIGURE 16.2: *A* versus *B*

In this case, I guess that most people intuitively judge that the size of the *B* population makes up for its lower level of well-being. So they judge that *B* is better than *A*.

Some people may have a clearer intuition about the corresponding outcomes with negative well-being (Figure 16.3).[8]

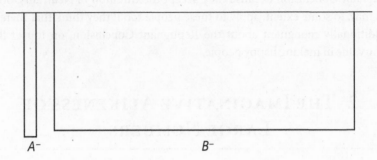

FIGURE 16.3: *A⁻* versus *B⁻*

Here, I guess that most people find *B⁻* clearly worse than *A⁻*. The fact that many fewer people suffer in *A⁻* than in *B⁻* makes up for the fact that the people in *B⁻* suffer slightly less than the people in *A⁻*. Hence it seems that, for some comparisons of very large populations, we can take their relative sizes into account.

Torbjörn Tännsjö offers a related account of how large numbers distort our intuitions, namely, that we have difficulties identifying with a large number of people. He claims that

> our actual moral sense seems to be based on identification. However, our capacity to identify with others is limited. Most of us care about our family, and those who are near and dear to us. We take less interest in our fellow countrymen but more interest in them than in people living far away from us. However, it is widely recognized that we *ought* to care about strangers. We ought to generalize our sympathy even to them. We have extra difficulties in doing so when it comes to very large numbers of people. Very large numbers *mean* very little to us. However, large numbers do matter. In the same manner that we generalize our sympathy to strangers we ought (mechanically, if necessary) to generalize our sympathy to large numbers of people, even to all the people living in Parfit's Z-world.[9]

It is hard to identify with the very large number of people in *Z*.[10] The people in *Z*, we can assume, are neither fellow countrymen nor near and dear. They are anonymous members of a very large number of people, which makes them difficult to identify with. Yet the same holds for the people in *A*. The people in *A* and the people in *Z* are all anonymous members of very large populations, so it seems that our difficulties having sympathy with large numbers of people would make it difficult for us to sympathize not only with the people in *Z* but also with those in *A*. And, if so, one would expect that we wouldn't intuitively judge one of *A* and *Z*, or one of *A⁻* and *B⁻*, as much better than the other. But those who find the Repugnant Conclusion repugnant seem to find *A* much better than *Z* and find *B⁻* much worse than *A⁻*.

3. COMPOUNDING SMALL VALUES

Huemer offers a further explanation of the unreliability of our intuition about the Repugnant Conclusion, namely, that we are bad at compounding lots of small values. Huemer claims that

> we find a tendency to underestimate the effect of compounding a small quantity. Of particular interest is our failure to appreciate how a very small value, when compounded many times, can become a great value. The thought that no amount of headache-relief would be worth a human life is an extreme instance of this mistake— as is the thought that no number of low-utility lives would be worth as much as a million high-utility lives.[11]

This proposal is based on the idea that we intuitively value the lives in a population one by one and then fail to properly compound their values to get the value of the population. There are, however, similarly repugnant cases where the compounding of the values of lives plays no role. Consider

> *The One-Person Repugnant Conclusion*: For any possible life which is at all times of a very high quality, there is a better possible life which is at all times barely worth living.[12]

The One-Person Repugnant Conclusion can be put in terms of a comparison between an A-life, a long life that is at all times of very high quality, and a Z-life, a very long life that is at all times worth living but barely so. The One-Person Repugnant Conclusion says that, for every life like the A-life, there is a better life like the Z-life. Similarly to the regular Repugnant Conclusion, it is counter-intuitive that the Z-life would be better than the A-life. In the assessment of this one-person variant of the Repugnant Conclusion, the compounding of the values of lives plays no role, since we are just comparing individual lives. Hence, even if we were unable to reliably compound small values of a large number of lives, this wouldn't explain our anti-utilitarian intuition about this one-person analog of the Repugnant Conclusion.

Nevertheless, the compounding-small-values proposal may still be able to explain the unreliability of our intuition about the One-Person Repugnant Conclusion. Any Z-life that's better than some A-life, according to utilitarianism, must be extremely long— perhaps thousands of years long. Plausibly, we are unable to grasp directly the value of such lives, because we can't intuitively imagine what living for that long would be like. So we have to make the intuitive comparison between a long A-life and an extremely long Z-life, not by intuitively valuing the whole of the Z-life, but by valuing shorter, more intuitively graspable intervals. And then we fail to properly compound the small values of these shorter parts of the Z-life.

But consider a Z-life of the same length as the longest duration of life such that we can grasp the value of that duration of life without doing any compounding. And consider a much shorter A-life with a just slightly lower sum-total of temporal well-being than the Z-life. Suppose, for instance, that the Z-life would be a year-long life that is at all times barely worth living and that the A-life would be a week-long life that is at all times of a very high quality. Then it's still counter-intuitive that the Z-life would be better than the A-life. But, in this case, we can evaluate the whole Z-life without compounding the values of any shorter segments. And then the compounding-small-values proposal doesn't work.

4. GRASPING LARGE NUMBERS

John Broome claims that

> we have no reason to trust anyone's intuitions about very large numbers, however excellent their philosophy. Even the best philosophers cannot get an intuitive grasp of, say, tens of billions of people. That is no criticism; these numbers are beyond intuition. But these philosophers ought not to think their intuition can tell them the truth about such large numbers of people.[13]

Broome's point, however, is not that we have unreliable intuitions about all principles that say something about very large populations. Broome wishes to rely on some principles that do so. For example, in his defense of Total Utilitarianism, Broome relies on

> *The Principle of Personal Good*: Take two distributions A and B that certainly have the same population. If A is equally as good as B for each member of the population, then A is equally as good as B. Also, if A is at least as good as B for each member of the population, and if A is better than B for some member of the population, then A is better than B.[14]

Since the Principle of Personal Good quantifies over all distributions (including those with very large populations), it says something about very large populations. Still, Broome wishes to rely on its intuitive plausibility.

To avoid this problem, Broome narrows his case against the reliability of our intuitions. His example of an intuition that depends on large numbers is not the Repugnant Conclusion. Instead, it's the similarly structured claim that it is better to save someone from a severe disease like AIDS than to cure any number of people from mild headaches. Broome writes:

> The intuition about AIDS mentions a fixed event A and a variable event B(n) that depends on the number of people. The fixed event is curing one person of AIDS;

the variable event is curing n people of a short mild headache. The intuition has the form: for all numbers n, A is better than $B(n)$. An intuition of this form is exposed to doubt because the goodness of $B(n)$ may increase with increasing n. It does so in this case. The intuition is that, although $B(n)$ gets better and better with increasing n, it never gets better than A, however large n might be. This sort of intuition particularly depends on our intuitive grasp of large numbers. So it is unreliable.[15]

This narrowed proposal still rules out too much, however. There are reliable intuitions of the form Broome wishes to discredit. Let, for example, A and $B(n)$ be distributions for the same population, such that

A has everyone at well-being level 3

and

$B(n)$ has everyone at well-being level $\dfrac{n}{\sqrt{1+n^2}}$

Figure 16.4 illustrates the relation between people's well-being in A and their well-being in $B(n)$.

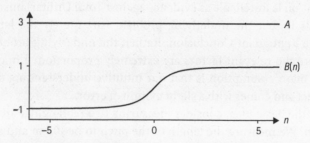

FIGURE 16.4: *A* versus *B(n)*

Plausibly, $B(n)$ gets better as n increases, because—other things being equal—it's better if everyone has a higher well-being. Similarly, it intuitively seems that, for all numbers n, A is better than $B(n)$, since everyone has a well-being of 3 in A whereas in $B(n)$ they have, for all numbers n, a well-being below 1. This intuition seems neither unreliable nor particularly dependent on our intuitive grasp of large numbers. So it seems that, if an intuition is unreliable, it's not unreliable because it has the form Broome targets.

Moreover, the Principle of Personal Good entails that A is better than $B(n)$ for all numbers n. If we have reliable intuitions about the Principle of Personal Good (as Broome claims), we should also have reliable intuitions about this logically weaker claim, which has the form Broome exposes to doubt. Hence, by his own standards, Broome's narrowed proposal also rules out too much.

It may be objected that this objection can be sidestepped if we just restrict the *n* parameter to population sizes in Broome's narrowed proposal. This move, however, cannot explain why our intuition is unreliable in the One-Person Repugnant Conclusion, since in that case the population-size parameter is fixed. Besides, the move seems ad hoc unless we can explain why our intuition can reliably grasp very large numbers of some things but not reliably grasp very large numbers of people.

5. Extreme Trade-Offs and Margins of Error

While the previous proposals seek to explain the unreliability of our intuition about the Repugnant Conclusion, I have a slightly less general aim. My aim is merely to argue that our intuition about the Repugnant Conclusion is unreliable as evidence against Total Utilitarianism.[16] So my proposal need not rule out that this intuition could be reliable as evidence against some other theories that imply the Repugnant Conclusion. I will argue that it's likely that we would have the intuition that the Repugnant Conclusion is false even if Total Utilitarianism were true. Hence, if I'm right, this intuition is unreliable as evidence against Total Utilitarianism.[17]

My diagnosis is that the underlying problem isn't merely the largeness of the numbers in the Repugnant Conclusion. Rather, the underlying problem is making trade-offs where the relevant factors are extremely proportioned in opposite ways. My proposal's main assumption is that our intuitive understanding of the relevant factors is inexact and comes with a slight margin of error.

To illustrate the basic idea, consider measuring two rectangular areas. The first is a football pitch. We measure the length of the pitch to be 105 m and its width to be 68 m. The second is a side of an extremely long and very narrow tape. We measure the length of the tape to be 3000 km and its width to be just 2 mm. We get that the area of the pitch is 7140 m^2 and that the area of the tape is 6000 m^2. So we get that the pitch has a much larger area than the tape. This conclusion, however, is only reliable if our measurement of the tape's width has a margin of error no greater than slightly below 1 mm. If our measurements are insensitive to a difference in width of just 1 mm, we can't rule out that the tape's width is 3 mm, which would make its area much larger than 7140 m^2 (it would be 9000 m^2). And then we can't rule out that the tape has a larger area than the pitch. So, even though it seems like the area of the pitch is much larger than the area of the tape and that the margin of error for the width of the tape is tiny, this tiny margin of error still makes the comparison unreliable. This is because any error in the measurement of the tape's width is multiplied by its very great length, resulting in a huge margin of error for the calculated area.

In this manner, I propose that a slight dullness in the sensitivity of our intuitive understanding of the relevant factors in an intuitive comparison can have a crucial effect on the comparison's reliability. I propose that:

our intuition about a comparative claim between x and y is unreliable as evidence against a theory T if

(i)   there is, according to T, a trade-off between two relevant factors in the comparison,

(ii) there is a possible change in one of these two factors such that the change is small enough to fall within our intuition's margin of error, and

(iii) this change would make a difference to whether the comparative claim holds according to T.

The inexactness of our intuition might result in a great mismatch between a correct theory and our intuitive judgment if some change that falls within our intuition's margin of error can make a great difference to how the theory compares the options. This, I will argue, is what's going on in the case of Total Utilitarianism and the Repugnant Conclusion.

A clarification of clause (i) may be needed. The point of this clause is merely to allow that our intuition can be reliably guided by dominance considerations even when the respects in which the options differ fall within our intuition's margin of error. When one option is superior in all relevant respects, we don't need to take the exact magnitude of this superiority into account in order to rely on dominance considerations. And, if so, our intuition's margin of error for this magnitude doesn't matter as long we grasp the dominance.

One class of comparisons that seem to fulfil clauses (i)–(iii) given a theory T are comparisons between two options such that T evaluates the options by the product of two factors F and G and one option is very little F and very much G and the other option is much F and little G. In comparisons of this kind, there's a straightforward explanation of why our intuition is unreliable. The problem is that, when options are evaluated by the product of F and G and one option has very little F and very much G, then very small variations in factor F will have a very large effect on the product of F and G. Hence a very small change in factor F may change which option has the greatest product of F and G. But, since our intuition is inexact, our intuition may plausibly be insensitive to this small change in factor F. Thus, due to the inexactness in our intuitive understanding of this factor, our intuition might deviate from T in these cases. This inexactness, however, does not rule out that our intuition reliably tracks T in cases without this kind of extreme trade-offs.

In the Repugnant Conclusion, there are, according to Total Utilitarianism, two factors opposed in this way. We must compare the high well-being and few people in A—that is, few relative to the size of the population in Z—with the very low positive well-being and huge number of people in Z. So we have two options with alternately very much and very little of two relevant factors such that Total Utilitarianism evaluates the options by the product of these factors. Note that, for every outcome Z with lives that are barely worth living such that Total Utilitarianism evaluates Z as better than A, there is an outcome Z' which is just like Z except that people in Z' have a slightly lower but still positive well-being and Total Utilitarianism evaluates Z' as worse than A.[18] The people in Z and Z' have very similar well-being, and they all have lives that are barely worth living. And, when we intuitively compare Z and Z' to A, our intuition isn't sensitive enough to take into account the small difference between the lives in Z and those in Z'. Since we cannot intuitively take into account the exact level of well-being in Z (which is crucial for Total Utilitarianism's evaluation of A and Z), it seems that our intuition in this case is unreliable as evidence against Total Utilitarianism.[19]

(Note that I do not claim that we can't reliably take the difference in the level of well-being between Z and Z' into account when we compare them with each other, because that comparison is a simple case of dominance without trade-offs.)

With my proposal, there's no need to claim that our intuitive thinking departs from Total Utilitarianism—for example, by failing to compound small values. On my proposal, our intuition may very well be guided by Total Utilitarianism. But there is a slight margin of error in our intuitive judgment of the parameters of this principle, which gets greatly amplified in cases where the principle evaluates an option by the product of two parameters such that one is a very small quantity and the other is a very large quantity.

It may be objected that my proposal would seem to predict that our intuitive evaluations of A and Z should be thoroughly equivocal, whereas there's widespread agreement that, intuitively, Z is not better than A (and very little agreement that, intuitively, Z is better than A). That is, my proposal fails to explain the observed systematicity in the alleged unreliability of our intuition about the Repugnant Conclusion.

There is, however, an erroneous assumption behind this objection. The unreliability in our intuitions need not result in equivocal judgments. In cases where our intuitions are unreliable, our judgments may have a bias in a certain direction. So far, I have only offered an account of some circumstances where our intuitions are unreliable, rather than an account of what intuitive judgments we make under those circumstances. I do think, however, that there is an explanation of the systematicity in our intuitive judgments in these cases.

Note that, in the cases we have discussed, our intuitive judgment always seems to disregard the part of an alternative's good or bad features which would, according to my account, be within our intuition's margin of error. This suggests that, when we have trouble getting an exact intuitive grasp of a certain feature, we only take into account the amount of that feature which we clearly grasp is there. Even though we have no exact grasp of the amount of well-being in an imagined life in A, we can still clearly grasp that it's at least above a fairly high amount. So, to a significant extent, we take the high quality of the lives in A into account. Yet, when we assess Z, there's no positive amount of well-being such that we can clearly grasp that there is at least that amount of well-being in an imagined life in Z. This is because the positive but very small amount of well-being in those lives is within our intuition's margin of error. So we fail to take into account the positive quality of the lives in Z.[20]

Note that this systematicity explanation still allows that we can make reliable judgments in some comparisons where the differences in the relevant factors fall within our margin of error. In cases where there are no trade-offs between the relevant factors, our intuition can still be reliably guided by dominance considerations. So we can reliably judge with the help of dominance considerations that, other things being equal, tiny improvements to people's lives make the world better and that the addition of barely good lives also make the world better. Likewise, we can reliably judge with the help of dominance considerations that, other things being equal, tiny detriments to people's lives make the world worse and that the addition of barely bad lives also make the world worse.

It may next be objected that my proposal seems a little ad hoc if it only explains the unreliability of our intuition about the Repugnant Conclusion.[21] Fortunately, the proposal also explains many other cases where otherwise intuitive theories yield counter-intuitive implications. A further counter-intuitive implication of Total Utilitarianism is

> *Hangnails for Torture*: For any excruciatingly painful torture session lasting for at least two years to be experienced by one person, there is some large number of minute-long very mildly annoying hangnail pains, each to be experienced by a separate person, that is, other things equal, worse.[22]

Here, we have another case where the options score alternately very high and very low in terms of two factors. We have a great loss in well-being for just one person—that is, the torture lasting at least two years—compared to a very small loss in well-being for a very large number of people—that is, the minute-long hangnail pains. And, since utilitarianism evaluates the badness of these options by the product of these factors, this is an instance of an extreme trade-off between morally relevant factors such that clauses (i)–(iii) hold. Hence my proposal also applies to our intuition about Hangnails for Torture.[23]

My proposal also explains why our intuition about the One-Person Repugnant Conclusion is unreliable as evidence against utilitarianism. In this case, we compare a very long life of very high quality to a much longer life with a barely positive quality. Since utilitarianism evaluates these lives by the product of their quality and their length, we have an instance of the problematic form of extreme trade-offs between morally relevant factors. So my proposal also applies to our intuition about the One-Person Repugnant Conclusion.[24]

Furthermore, my proposal does not rule out the reliability of our intuition about the Principle of Personal Good, which utilitarians typically rely on to motivate their view. If, given the same population, a first distribution strongly dominates a second distribution in the sense that the first is at least as good for everyone and better for someone than the second, then there is no relevant better-making factor according to Total Utilitarianism in which the second distribution beats the first. So, my proposal does not entail that our intuition about the Principle of Personal Good is unreliable as evidence in favor of Total Utilitarianism.

And, unlike the imaginative-alikeness proposal, my proposal doesn't rule out that we have reliable intuitions about the comparisons of A and B and of A^- and B^-. In these comparisons, there are trade-offs between population sizes and well-being levels, but these trade-offs aren't extreme; no small change in either population sizes or well-being levels would change that B is better than A or that B^- is worse than A^- according to Total Utilitarianism.

6. IMAGINING VERY MANY LIVES

Finally, we shall consider two general objections to this kind of defense of Total Utilitarianism. The first comes from Derek Parfit, who responds to the worry that we might have trouble imagining the relevant populations in the Repugnant Conclusion. He claims that:

> We can imagine what it would be for someone's life to be barely worth living. And we can imagine what it would be for there to be many people with such lives. In order to imagine Z, we merely have to imagine that there would be *very* many. This we can do.[25]

Yet it's not merely the population in Z that may be arbitrarily large; the population in A may be so too. If the population in A is sufficiently large, it would have to contain very many people. But, in that case, the Z population would have to be imagined as being much more numerous than as being very many. Because, otherwise, our imagination wouldn't do justice to the much larger size of the Z population compared to the A population, which is the main advantage of Z according to Total Utilitarianism. Hence it's insufficient to just be able to imagine Z as an outcome with very many lives barely worth living. We have to be able to take into account how much larger the Z population is when the A population is huge.[26]

Moreover, even if we only consider cases where the A population consists of just ten billion people, there's another problem with Parfit's reply. The sum total of well-being for a population of ten billion people with a very high quality of life is very large. Hence, even on Total Utilitarianism, there are outcomes that are worse than A but which still contain very many lives barely worth living. So, if we can only imagine Z as an outcome with very many lives barely worth living, we can't be sure that we imagine an outcome that is better than A according to Total Utilitarianism.

7. THE EXTRAPOLATION ARGUMENT

The second general objection comes from Theron Pummer. He argues that, in order to defend counter-intuitive principles involving large numbers (like the Repugnant Conclusion), it's not enough to show that we have unreliable intuitions about large-number cases. He claims that, even if we do have unreliable intuitions about large-number cases, we can extrapolate from small-number cases where our intuitions are reliable. Instead of the Repugnant Conclusion, however, he focuses on the similarly structured Hangnails for Torture.

Pummer claims that we normally have reason to believe something if we have reason to believe that it would seem true under ideal circumstances. He argues that, if we had reliable intuitions about large-number cases, we would find Hangnails for Torture counter-intuitive. That is, he argues in favor of

(1) If we could relevantly imagine any number of mild hangnail pains, we would have the intuition that there is *no* number of such pains such that it is worse than two years of excruciating torture.

rather than

(2) If we could relevantly imagine any number of mild hangnail pains, we would have the intuition that there is *some* number of such pains such that it is worse than two years of excruciating torture.[27]

For the Extrapolation Argument, Pummer introduces a variable version of Hangnails for Torture, where the number of years with hangnail pains is given by a variable:

The Variable Claim: Two years of excruciating torture is worse than X years of very mildly annoying hangnail pains (each a minute long), other things being equal.[28]

Pummer holds that we do not become less confident in the variable claim the larger we imagine X to be and that this counts in favor of (1) rather than (2).

The Extrapolation Argument runs as follows:

(3) If (2) were true, and thus if (1) were false, then we would become less confident in the Variable Claim, the larger we imagine X to be.
(4) We do not become less confident in the Variable Claim, the larger we imagine X to be.

So, Pummer concludes, (1) is true and (2) is false.[29]

While we might also question (4), I will argue that (3) is false.[30] For small values of X (which are the ones Pummer extrapolates from), I don't think that, if (2) were true, we would become less confident in the Variable Claim as X increases. To see why, consider first the utilitarian principle that the value of an option is proportional to that option's sum total of well-being. According to this principle, the torture is much worse than the hangnails for all relatively small values of X. So, even if utilitarianism and thus Hangnails for Torture were true, the value of the hangnails would never get close to the value of the torture for all small values of X. Now, let us assume, following Pummer, that we have reliable intuitions about small-number cases. Then we would plausibly remain fully confident in the Variable Claim for all relatively small values of X even if utilitarianism and Hangnails for Torture were true. This is because we wouldn't merely evaluate the torture as worse than the hangnails, we would evaluate the torture as *much* worse than the hangnails for all relatively small values of X. Hence, if utilitarianism were true, then, even allowing for a wide margin of error, we would plausibly remain fully confident in the Variable Claim for all relatively small values of X. And the same would hold for any theory that evaluates torture and hangnails in roughly the same way as utilitarianism.

But, if (2) were true, it seems that some theory would be true that evaluates torture and hangnails in roughly the same way as utilitarianism. And then we have that if (2) were true, we wouldn't become less confident in the Variable Claim, the larger we imagine X to be. Thus (3) seems false. Hence the Extrapolation Argument is unconvincing.

Summing up, I have argued that the intuition that the Repugnant Conclusion is repugnant is unreliable as evidence against Total Utilitarianism. My explanation is that our intuitive understanding of the morally relevant factors is inexact and comes with a slight margin of error, which makes our intuitive judgments unreliable in cases with extreme trade-offs between these factors. Given Total Utilitarianism, the Repugnant Conclusion involves an extreme trade-off of this kind. Therefore, if Total Utilitarianism is true, our intuition about the Repugnant Conclusion is unreliable. So this intuition is unreliable as evidence against Total Utilitarianism.

ACKNOWLEDGMENTS

I wish to thank Tim Campbell for especially helpful comments. I also wish to thank Gustav Alexandrie, Gustaf Arrhenius, Campbell Brown, Krister Bykvist, Roger Crisp, Marc Fleurbaey, Johan Jacobsson, Martin Peterson, Douglas W. Portmore, Theron Pummer, Wlodek Rabinowicz, Daniel Ramöller, Jussi Suikkanen, Folke Tersman, Nicolas Olsson-Yaouzis, and the audiences at the Population Ethics Workshop, Eindhoven University of Technology, March 26, 2013; at the Higher Seminar in Practical Philosophy, Stockholm University, September 10, 2013; and at ISUS XIII 2014, Yokohama National University, August 21, 2014, for valuable comments.

NOTES

1. Parfit (1984, 388). Parfit's (1982, 142) earlier formulation contained, in addition, the normative claim that we ought to bring about the larger population.
2. Parfit (1984, 388). Sidgwick (1907, 415–416) was the first to point out that Total Utilitarianism has this implication. Apart from his complaint that this conclusion is too exact for common-sense morality, Sidgwick (416) doesn't seem to find the Repugnant Conclusion repugnant. McTaggart (1927, 452–453) claims that many *other* moralists would find the Repugnant Conclusion repugnant, but *he* sees "no reason for supposing that repugnance in this case would be right." The alleged repugnance rests, he thinks, on a mistaken conviction. For a list

of some early sources of the Repugnant Conclusion, see Arrhenius (2000, 40n) who traces this general idea back to Whewell (1852, 237–238). But the distinction between average and total views were known long before that. Bentham was clear about the distinction and endorsed a total view; see Gustafsson (2018, 99n18). Of the classical utilitarians, it seems that only Mill would have found the Repugnant Conclusion repugnant. Mill's (1965, 756) following remarks on population growth suggest an average, rather than total, view:

> There is room in the world, no doubt, and even in old countries, for a great increase of population, supposing the arts of life to go on improving, and capital to increase. But even if innocuous, I confess I see very little reason for desiring it. The density of population necessary to enable mankind to obtain, in the greatest degree, all the advantages both of cooperation and of social intercourse, has, in all the most populous countries, been attained. A population may be too crowded, though all be amply supplied with food and raiment. [...] If the earth must lose that great portion of its pleasantness which it owes to things that the unlimited increase of wealth and population would extirpate from it, for the mere purpose of enabling it to support a larger, but not a better or a happier population, I sincerely hope, for the sake of posterity, that they will be content to be stationary, long before necessity compels them to it.

Yet some of Mill's (1972, 1414) later remarks suggest a total view:

> when I said that the general happiness is a good to the aggregate of all persons I did not mean that every human being's happiness is a good to every other human being; though I think, in a good state of society & education it would be so. I merely meant in this particular sentence to argue that since A's happiness is a good, B's a good, C's a good, &c., the sum of all these goods must be a good.

3. Here, I am following the usage in Arrhenius (2000, 39). In Broome (2004, 138), this axiological component of utilitarianism is called 'the total principle'. In Parfit (1984, 387), a similar principle is called 'the impersonal total principle'.

4. For a discussion of the reliability of our intuition about the Repugnant Conclusion from the perspective of the psychological literature, see Mogensen (forthcoming).

5. Narveson (1973, 80).

6. Huemer (2008, 908).

7. Compare Greene (2001), who similarly objects that

> the fact that we are able to more or less fully appreciate the "quality of life" benefits with [A] and unable to fully appreciate the "quantity of life" benefits that come with [Z] may cause us to overestimate the repugnance of the repugnant conclusion.

8. This is a variation of Parfit's (1984, 406) case The Two Hells, where the smaller population consists of just ten people, whereas in this variant both populations consist of at least ten billion people.

9. Tännsjö (2002, 344). Tännsjö (2020, 390–396) argues that the repugnance of the Repugnant Conclusion is debunked by the existence of instances where it is not repugnant that an outcome like Z is better than an outcome like A given a certain specification of what the lives in these outcomes are like. But this response does not work against the following strengthening of the Repugnant Conclusion (which also follows from Total Utilitarianism):

The Invariant Repugnant Conclusion: For any possible population of at least ten billion people, all with very high quality of life, there must be some much larger imaginable population with lives that are barely worth living whose existence would be better, *regardless of what these lives are like in other respects*.

10. If, instead, the objection is that very large numbers mean very little to us and hence that they all mean roughly the same thing to us, then it's essentially the same as the imaginative-alikeness objection. And then it is unsuccessful for the same reasons.

11. Huemer (2008, 909–910).

12. Parfit (1986, 169) presents a similar one-person variant of the Repugnant Conclusion. His variant, however, has the drawback of involving infinity, which is known to mislead intuition.

13. Broome (2004, 57).

14. Broome (2004, 120).

15. Broome (2004, 58–59).

16. In Gustafsson (2020), I argue that the total view is compatible with the Repugnant Conclusion, given that we accept an axiology where value bearers can differ not just in goodness (the value dimension where differences make value bearers better and worse) but also in undistinguishedness (the value dimension where differences make value bearers incomparable). That two-dimensional response to the Repugnant Conclusion is an alternative to the one suggested here. With the response presented here, we don't need the undistinguishedness dimension.

17. Let R be that we have the intuition that the Repugnant Conclusion is false, and let U be that Total Utilitarianism is true. We note that

$$P(U|R) = \frac{P(R|U)P(U)}{P(R|U)P(U) + P(R|\neg U)P(\neg U)}$$

given that $P(R) \neq 0$ and $P(U) \neq 0$. For example, suppose that $P(R|U)$ —that is, your conditional probability of R given U—is 0.8. And suppose that $P(U)$ —your prior credence in U—is 0.8. Then your posterior credence in U given R should be

$$P(U|R) = \frac{3.2}{3.2 + P(R|\neg U)}$$

At worst, if $P(R|\neg U) = 1$, we find that $P(U|R)$ will be roughly 0.76. And, if there is a chance (as seems plausible) that we wouldn't have the intuition that the Repugnant Conclusion is false even if Total Utilitarianism is false, then $P(U|R)$ will be even higher. For example, suppose additionally that $P(R|\neg U) = 0.8$. Then R should have no effect on our credence in U, that is, $P(U|R) = P(U) = 0.8$. Hence, if $P(R|U)$ is high, R cannot be reliable evidence against U.

18. I am assuming that there is no lowest possible positive level of well-being. I am assuming denseness for well-being levels rather than discreteness; see Arrhenius (2000, 163). If one gives up this assumption, one might get around my objection by imagining a Z outcome where each life has the lowest positive level of well-being. But this wouldn't help much unless we are clear about which well-being level is the lowest positive one, which seems implausible. If we don't know what the lowest positive level of well-being is like, we can't be sure that we're imagining lives with that level of well-being.

19. It may be objected that, if we allow the population in Z to be infinitely large, then it should suffice to judge that the people in Z have positive well-being in order to judge that Z with an infinite population is better than any outcome with a finite population. But, if we allow infinite populations, A could also have an infinitely large population and be infinitely good. And, if so, there wouldn't be any outcome like Z that is better than A; so, the Repugnant Conclusion wouldn't follow from Total Utilitarianism. To sidestep this issue, we can consider a weakened version of the Repugnant Conclusion where the A population must be finite. A first reply is that our intuitions about infinity are known to be unreliable. So, if our intuition that the Repugnant Conclusion is repugnant depends on crucially on cases involving infinity, then it's likely to be unreliable. A second reply is that, if there is a margin of error in our intuition, then we couldn't reliably tell whether we imagine an infinite population with barely good lives or an infinite population with barely not good lives.

20. One may be worried about the following kind of case: suppose we stipulate that each person in Z has a life that's slightly better than a life where the only conscious experience is the short-lived pleasure of a single lick of a lollipop (perhaps the people in Z get two licks rather than just one). Since we all know what it's like to lick a lollipop, this description of the case gives us a clear idea that there is at least that amount of well-being (that is, one lollipop lick's worth) in an imagined life in Z. Yet one might doubt that this will have any significant impact on our intuition about which outcome is better in this case. Note, however, that, though our might know what a life consisting of one lollipop lick would be like, you don't know what the exact well-being level (that is, the exact personal value) would be for that life. When you assess the well-being of the lives in Z, the dullness of our intuition comes in (and brings about a margin of error for the well-being level), and it does so even if you could imagine exactly what their lives would be like in all non-evaluative respects.

21. Similarly, Temkin (2012, 122) worries about a related attempt to explain away our intuitions about a version of the One-Person Repugnant Conclusion:

> To be sure, advocates of additive aggregation may continue to insist that our intuitions about such cases are not to be trusted, even for cases involving intuitively graspable numbers. So, for example, they might insist that the difference between oyster-like lives of 100, 1,000, and 10,000 years is on a trajectory that would eventually amount to a great difference, but that the slope of the trajectory is so slight that we don't intuitively notice it, or perceive its long-term implications. But though it is possible such a view is correct, it has the air of an untestable article of faith that advocates of additive aggregation are compelled to invoke to explain away our intuitions, and I doubt that many will find it sufficiently compelling to alter their judgments about such cases.

Since my proposal applies not just to the Repugnant Conclusion but to any similar structured case, it makes some predictions that are testable to some extent. It predicts that there will be a lot of otherwise plausible theories T that yield counter-intuitive implications in cases where clauses (i)–(iii) hold. Moreover, the possibility that my proposal, even if correct, wouldn't compel many to alter their judgements about the Repugnant Conclusion seems irrelevant if our aim is not popularity but truth.

22. Pummer (2013, 37). The example is a variation of examples in Temkin (1996, 179) and Rachels (1998, 73).

23. This explanation works equally well, changing what needs to be changed, for the similar lollipops-for-life case in Temkin (2012, 34).

24. It is easy to come up with more examples. Lots of counter-examples to expected-utility theory have the following structure: we have a choice between having a significant amount of money for sure and a gamble which is almost certain to give us nothing but might with a very low probability result in a huge win; see, for example, the truncated (that is, finite) version of the St. Petersburg paradox in Hájek and Nover (2006, 706). A tiny difference in the probability of the huge win will have a large effect on the expected value of the gamble. So, if there is a margin of error in our intuitive grasp of this probability, our intuition that it's better to have the significant amount for sure than to have the gamble won't be reliable as evidence against expected-utility theory. The structural similarity between the Repugnant Conclusion and the St. Petersburg paradox is noted in Cowen (2004, 83–84).

25. Parfit (1984, 389).

26. Greene (2001) similarly objects that

> Certainly we can imagine a very large number of people living such lives, but can we effectively imagine the *difference between* two very large numbers of people living such lives? This is what our task requires, and it's not at all clear that we are up to it.

27. Pummer (2013, 41). Here and elsewhere, I have changed Pummer's numbering.

28. Ibid.

29. Ibid, 42. Pummer's argument for (3) is, more or less, a restatement of (3). He writes:

> (3) seems plausible because if (2) were true and thus there were some value for X, call it *n*, such that if we imagined *n* years of mild hangnail pains we would have the intuition that together they are worse than 2 years of excruciating torture, it seems we would gradually lose confidence in the Variable Claim as our imagined value for X gets closer to *n*. This seems true even if *n* were very large; we would presumably lose at least *some* confidence as X gets larger, if (2) were true.

30. One problem with (4) is that, if you have some moral uncertainty with at least some positive credence in Total Utilitarianism, it seems that you should become slightly less confident in the Variable Claim the larger you imagine X to be.

REFERENCES

Arrhenius, Gustaf. 2000. *Future Generations: A Challenge for Moral Theory.* PhD diss., Uppsala University.

Broome, John. 2004. *Weighing Lives.* Oxford: Oxford University Press.

Cowen, Tyler. 2004. "Resolving the Repugnant Conclusion." In *The Repugnant Conclusion*, edited by Jesper Ryberg and Torbjörn Tännsjö, 81–97. Dordrecht: Kluwer.

Greene, Joshua D. 2001. "A Psychological Perspective on Nozick's Experience Machine and Parfit's Repugnant Conclusion." Presentation at the Society for Philosophy and Psychology Annual Meeting, Cincinnati, OH.

Gustafsson, Johan E. 2018. "Bentham's Binary Form of Maximizing Utilitarianism." *British Journal for the History of Philosophy* 26, no. 1: 87–109.

Gustafsson, Johan E. 2020. "Population Axiology and the Possibility of a Fourth Category of Absolute Value." *Economics and Philosophy* 36, no. 1: 81–110.

Hájek, Alan and Harris Nover. 2006. "Perplexing Expectations", *Mind* 115, no. 459: 704–720.

Huemer, Michael. 2008. "In Defence of Repugnance." *Mind* 117, no. 468: 899–933.

McTaggart, John McTaggart Ellis. 1927. *The Nature of Existence*, vol. 2. Cambridge: Cambridge University Press.

Mill, John Stuart. 1965. *Collected Works*, vol. 3, *Principles of Political Economy with Some of Their Applications to Social Philosophy: Books III–V and Appendices*, edited by V. W. Robson. Toronto: University of Toronto Press.

Mill, John Stuart. 1972. *Collected Works*, vol. 14, *The Later Letters of John Stuart Mill 1849–1873: Part III*, edited by Francis E. Mineka and Dwight N. Lindley. Toronto: University of Toronto Press.

Mogensen, Andreas. Forthcoming. "Against Large Number Scepticism." In *Essays in Honour of Derek Parfit, Volume 2: Population Ethics*, edited by Jeff McMahan, Tim Campbell, James Goodrich, and Ketan Ramakrishnan. Oxford: Oxford University Press.

Narveson, Jan. 1973. "Moral Problems of Population." *Monist* 57, no. 1: 62–86.

Parfit, Derek 1982. "Future Generations: Further Problems." *Philosophy & Public Affairs* 11, no. 2: 113–172.

Parfit, Derek. 1984. *Reasons and Persons*. Oxford: Clarendon Press.

Parfit, Derek. 1986. "Overpopulation and the Quality of Life." In *Applied Ethics*, edited by Peter Singer, 145–164. Oxford: Oxford University Press.

Pummer, Theron. 2013. "Intuitions about Large Number Cases." *Analysis* 73, no. 1: 37–46.

Rachels, Stuart. 1998. "Counterexamples to the Transitivity of *Better Than*." *Australasian Journal of Philosophy* 76, no. 1: 71–83.

Sidgwick, Henry. 1907. *The Methods of Ethics*, 7th ed. London: Macmillan.

Tännsjö, Torbjörn. 2002. "Why We Ought to Accept the Repugnant Conclusion." *Utilitas* 14, no. 3: 339–359.

Tännsjö, Torbjörn. 2020. "Why Derek Parfit Had Reasons to Accept the Repugnant Conclusion", *Utilitas* 32, no. 4: 387–397.

Temkin, Larry S. 1996. "A Continuum Argument for Intransitivity." *Philosophy & Public Affairs* 25, no. 3: 175–210.

Temkin, Larry S. 2012. *Rethinking the Good*. New York: Oxford University Press.

Whewell, William. 1852. *Lectures on the History of Moral Philosophy*. Cambridge: Cambridge University Press.

PART III

APPLICATIONS

CHAPTER 17

··

CLIMATE CHANGE AND
POPULATION ETHICS

··

JOHN BROOME

CLIMATE change will kill huge numbers of people. It will kill them through three sorts of processes. The first is the direct effects of changes in the weather. Sea levels are rising and storms are becoming more violent, so devastating floods will become more frequent. Also in this category come droughts with their consequent famines. The world's fresh water resources will diminish with the melting of glaciers. The second process is that rising temperatures will extend the range of tropical diseases. For instance, malaria is climbing higher into the African mountains. The third is the direct effect of heat, particularly in cities: heat waves kill people. Cold waves kill people too, and there will be fewer of those. But on balance the number of deaths from heat and cold will increase.

Recent detailed research from Tamma Carleton and others puts some figures on all this killing. Obviously, the number of deaths climate change will cause depends on how severe it is, and this depends on how hard the world fights against it. Various possible scenarios for the progress of climate change are set out in the "Representative Concentration Pathways" (RCPs), which have been developed by the Intergovernmental Panel on Climate Change. RCP 8.5 is a pessimistic scenario that may be thought of as business as usual; RCP 4.5 represents the result of moderately strenuous efforts to diminish climate change. Carleton et al. estimate that, in RCP 8.5, 73 deaths per year per 100,000 population will be caused by climate change in 2100.[1] That is around 7 million per year in the world as a whole. No end is predicted to all this killing; it will continue for decades. This is a catastrophe to human life on a stupendous scale. In RCP 4.5 the number is around 1.5 million deaths per year. This is still a catastrophic number, but it does show that working to slow climate change will have a very large benefit.

Besides killing people, climate change will affect the population of the world. Of course, killing people directly affects the world's population in a sense: at a time after they have been killed, the world contains fewer people than it would have contained had they survived. But I do not mean that. That is an effect on the world's population at a particular time: the time after the killing. I am speaking of the world's *timeless* population. By this I mean all the people who exist at some time in history. The timeless population includes Julius Caesar, me, and all the people who are yet to be born. Killing a person does not remove her from the timeless population.

But although the killing done by climate change does not directly reduce the timeless population, it does affect the timeless population less directly. For one thing, when a young person is killed, all the children she would later have had, if she had lived, and all their descendants, are removed from the timeless population. Also, think of this. Vast numbers of people are going to have to migrate across the world as some areas become uninhabitable. In Bangladesh, ten million people live within one metre of sea level, measured vertically. When the sea level rises one metre, those people will have to go somewhere else. So there will be vast movements of population, and migrations on that scale do not happen without an effect on the size of the population. Climate change will add to the population, or subtract from it. I shall not even predict in which direction the population will be affected—up or down—but I predict it will change.

Moreover, I predict the change will be large. Even if the effect on immediate numbers is small, it is likely to be perpetuated. There does not appear to be a stabilizing mechanism in human demography that, after some change, returns the population to what it would have been had the change not occurred. A few extra people at one time means some extra people in each generation through the future. This adds up to a large number altogether.

Decisions have to be made about our response to climate change. Climate change can be slowed, but only at a cost. We shall have to stop using energy in our profligate way. We shall not be able to travel around so much, and people who live in hot places will not be able to have such cool houses. These are reductions in our well-being. The question arises: How much effort should we be willing to give up for the sake of slowing climate change? What costs should we bear?

That depends on the benefits to be gained. What are those? One clear benefit is that vast numbers of people's lives will be saved in the future. But what about the change in the size of the world's future population? If slowing climate change increases the population, more people will exist than otherwise would have. Should we count that as a benefit? Or perhaps as a bad thing? If, conversely, the population is decreased, is that a good thing or a bad thing? These are questions that need to be answered if we are to judge properly what costs should be borne in order to reduce climate change. These are questions for population ethics. Philosophers have discovered that they are very difficult to answer. Their difficulty stands in the way of making sound, justifiable decisions about our correct response to climate change.

But maybe we can escape the difficulty. Many people share an intuition that suggests changes in population are neither good nor bad, and can simply be ignored in decision-making. I call this the "intuition of neutrality," and come to it next.

1. The Intuition of Neutrality

Would an increase in the future population be good or bad? The instinctive answer of very many people is "Neither." We value the benefit that can be brought to existing people by extending their lives. But we think the lives of new people added to the population are no added benefit beyond that. Nor do we think they are a bad thing. We think they are neutral. Likewise, we would also regard a diminution in the future population as also neutral.

You might think you have an easy explanation of this instinct. You might think it is obviously not a good thing to have extra people, because we have enough people in the world already. Each new person makes demands on the earth's resources, leaving less for the rest of us. So, on average, each new person diminishes the lifetime well-being of the rest of us. This harm a new person does to existing people may well outweigh the lifetime well-being of the new person herself. For this reason we should not be pleased to have new people in the world.

That seems plausible. But now you have to explain why you are in favor of keeping alive the people we already have. Most of us are in favor of that, and as a society we put a lot of effort into it. I have taken it for granted that saving people's lives in the future by slowing climate change is a benefit. If the demands on resources made by new people outweigh the good enjoyed by those new people, the same must on average be true of existing people too. Each year, each person who continues to live requires resources, and the resources she uses are not available for the rest of us. We should be happy to be rid of people, rather than work so hard to keep them alive. But we do not think like that. Our instinct is to make a great difference in value between the lives of new people and existing people. We are in favor of prolonging the lives of existing people, but we are not in favor of creating new lives. Recognizing the shortage of resources does not explain why we make this difference.

I think the source of our instinct is simply that we think the lifetime well-being of a person who is added to the world is in itself ethically neutral—to use a vague expression that I shall soon tighten up. It is neither a good thing nor a bad thing. We recognize that adding a new person may be good or bad for existing people; a new person may bring enjoyment to her family and to other people and she may also bring harm to other people by her demands on resources. We count these benefits and harms in favor of this person's existence or against it. But the goodness of the person's own life does not count ethically.

Our moral instinct is to care about people, and to care about making people's lives go well. This is caring for the people there are; we want their lives to go better. We have no natural interest in having more people about. A famous remark of Jan Narveson's puts it succinctly: "We are in favour of making people happy, but neutral about making happy people."[2] I think that is our commonest intuition. I call it "the intuition of neutrality." If it is correct, it relieves us of a heavy burden in our decision-making about climate change.

In judging what we should do, we can ignore the consequences for the world's population because they are neither good nor bad. But sadly, I shall argue that this intuition is mistaken.

2. HUMAN EXTINCTION

Before that, we should recognize that many people also have a contrary intuition about the extinction of humanity.

We need to take extinction seriously. Climate change creates a real possibility of it. Climate science is still unclear about all the complex feedback mechanisms that affect the world's climate. For example, around the fringes of the Arctic Ocean, lots of methane is locked up with water in compounds called "clathrates." Global warming could possibly break down the clathrates and release their methane into the air. Since methane is a powerful greenhouse gas the result could be a runaway cycle of more and more warming. This is only one of several potentially dangerous feedbacks. Science cannot rule out warming of five or ten degrees or even more. And if there is extreme warming, we cannot be sure the human species will survive it.

No doubt extinction is very unlikely. But unlikely events can be crucially important in decision-making, if they are very bad. Think about the lifeboats on a ship. Very few ships sink or are engulfed in fire, so their lifeboats are very rarely needed. But if they are needed, and if there are none on board, the consequences would be dreadfully bad. For this reason, ships should carry lifeboats, despite the cost and despite the fact that they are very unlikely to be used. They constitute a sort of insurance. Unlikely but very bad possibilities need to be insured against. The economist Martin Weitzman argued for many years that the possibility of a catastrophe (not necessarily extinction) is the main reason why we should take strong action against climate change:[3] it is like the need for lifeboats on a ship.

But we need insurance only for bad events. Would the extinction of humanity be bad? It is merely an extreme decrease in the world's population, and the intuition of neutrality suggests that increases and decreases in population are not bad. However, many people, including many who are attracted by the intuition of neutrality, have a contrary intuition about extinction. They think that extinction would be very bad indeed. So we have a conflict of intuitions. This is enough to show that we should not accept them without question. The intuition of neutrality needs some careful analysis.

3. TERMINOLOGY AND INTERPRETATION

First, what does "ethically neutral" mean? The term might have various interpretations. To say that doing something is ethically neutral could mean it is not the case that you ought to do it, and also not the case that you ought not to do it. This may be called a "normative" or "deontic" interpretation of "ethically neutral," but it is not the interpretation I shall adopt. Instead, I shall interpret the term evaluatively. When I say something is ethically neutral, I shall always mean it is neither good nor bad. The connection between the evaluative and the normative is contentious, and not a subject for this chapter. In this chapter, I shall concentrate on goodness only. (I use the word "value" as a synonym for "goodness.")

I shall identify the goodness of adding a person to the world with the goodness of the state of affairs that results from adding the person: that is to say, with the goodness of having an extra person in the world. This identification may be disputed. It is an application of a debatable view I call "consequentialism,"[4] but I do not need to debate it in this chapter. I am really interested in the goodness of states of affairs, and not in the goodness of actions such as adding a person. So, I interpret the neutrality intuition to be the view that the presence of an extra person in the world is neither good nor bad. More precisely: a world that contains an extra person is neither better nor worse than a world that does not contain her but is the same in other respects. Nevertheless, I shall continue to speak loosely of the goodness of adding a person, just because it is a convenient expression. I assume it is the same as the goodness of the resulting state of affairs. But if I am wrong about that, it is the goodness of the state of affairs that I really mean to refer to.

These points of interpretation mean that I am treating the intuition of neutrality as an intuition about the goodness of states of affairs. That may misrepresent it. For example, our common intuition may be fundamentally normative, and not about goodness at all. If that is so, it will not damage the conclusion of this paper. I shall eventually conclude that the neutrality intuition, interpreted my way, has to be rejected. If it is not our common intuition in the first place, no matter. However, I at least find the intuition very attractive, even when it is interpreted in my evaluative way. So, I think it is worth the trouble of showing that it is ultimately mistaken.

The intuition is that adding a person to the population is ethically neutral, understood to mean that a world that contains an extra person is neither better nor worse than a world that does not contain her. It follows that a world that does not contain this person is neither better nor worse than a world that does. I can express this by saying that subtracting a person from the population is also ethically neutral. By "subtracting" I mean not bringing into existence a person who would otherwise have existed. I do not mean removing from the population a person who already exists; that would be killing. As I mean it, to say subtracting is ethically neutral is just another way of saying that adding is ethically neutral.

The intuition of neutrality is not merely an intuition we happen to have. It is deeply embedded in the way we think about value and the way we form our moral judgments. We generally simply ignore the effects of our actions on the world's population, even when the effects are perfectly predictable. This can only be because of the intuition that they are ethically neutral. If the intuition turns out to be incorrect, it will make a huge difference to the way we should make our ordinary judgments.

4. A Difficulty for the Intuition

It is only the neutrality intuition that saves us from having to undertake the extraordinarily difficult job of evaluating the changes in population that climate change will cause. Only this intuition allows us to be confident even that climate change is a bad thing; without it, it might turn out that its effect on population outweighs the badness of all the killing it will do. But I am sorry to say I am going to argue that the neutrality intuition cannot be sustained. It has to be abandoned, however painful that might be. At least, it has to be abandoned if it is interpreted in terms of goodness. It may have a defensible interpretation in normative terms, but it has no place in *evaluations* of climate change or anything else.

To make my argument, I am going to concentrate on a stripped-down example. It will be implausible in some respects. Philosophy often requires implausible examples. I want to concentrate on just one thing: the value of having a single extra person in the population. To do that, I want to exclude from the example all complicating factors, which might affect value in other ways. So I shall compare two alternative possible states of affairs that are the same in all respects, except that in one of them a person exists who does not exist in the other.

Figure 17.1 illustrates the problem. One thing we shall obviously have to take into account in assessing the value of having a new person is how well off that person is. We shall certainly be interested in her lifetime well-being. So I have shown her lifetime well-being, and other people's too, in the diagram. It is measured vertically. The diagram shows two alternatives, A and B. In A the extra person does not exist; in B she does. Everyone apart from the added person is left equally as well off by this person's existence.

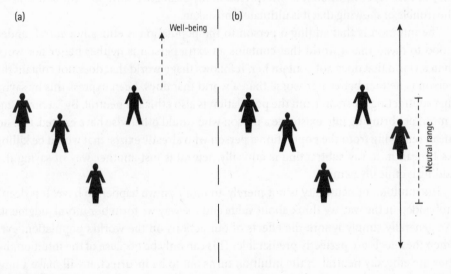

FIGURE 17.1

That is implausible, of course. One would expect her parents to be affected, if no one else. But that is my implausible simplifying assumption. I shall consider different possible levels for the extra person's well-being.

Our intuition of neutrality is that adding the person is ethically neutral. This intuition is to some extent independent of her level of well-being; there is not just one level of well-being of which we think intuitively that adding a person at that level is ethically neutral. To be sure, we do not think this of every level. We think it is a bad thing if a person lives a poor life, full of suffering. We are not neutral about adding a person whose life is like that; we are against it. Conversely, some people may think it is a good thing if a person lives an extremely good life; they are not neutral about adding a person at an extremely high standard of living. But for a wide range of levels of lifetime well-being between a bad life and a very good life, we intuitively think that adding a person at that level is neutral. The intuition is that there is a neutral *range*: a range of levels of well-being such that adding a person whose well-being is in that range is ethically neutral. The range may extend upwards to infinity, but in Figure 17.1 I have shown a finite neutral range.

Adding a person whose well-being is in the neutral range is neither better nor worse than not adding her. That is my definition of neutrality. We may naturally suppose, that if adding her is neither better nor worse than not adding her, it is equally as good as not adding her. But if there is a neutral·range, that cannot be so. Figure 17.2 shows why not. Compare B with A. The only difference is that in B a person exists who does not exist in A. This person lives within the neutral range. So if adding a person in the neutral range is equally as good as not adding her, then B is equally as good as A. For the same reason, A is equally as good as C. It follows that B is equally as good as C. But actually B is not equally as good as C. B and C are easy to compare in value, because they both contain the same population of five people. B is plainly better than C, since it is better for the fifth person and equally as good for everyone else.

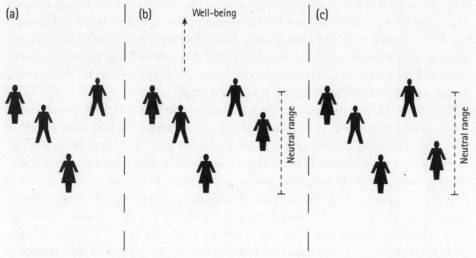

(a)   (b)   Well-being   (c)

FIGURE 17.2

So if we interpret ethical neutrality as equality of goodness, we will derive a false conclusion from the intuition of neutrality. Indeed, if neutrality is understood as equality of goodness, there can be at most one neutral level: one level of well-being such that adding a person at that level is neutral. (This level may depend on the context; it may depend on how big the existing population is and how well off the people are.) Adding a person with a well-being above that level would be a good thing, and adding a person with a well-being below that level would be a bad thing. But the neutrality intuition is that adding a person is neutral as a general rule, and certainly not just at a single level of well-being. If we are to sustain the intuition, we shall have to understand neutrality differently.

5. GREEDY NEUTRALITY

It is easy to find a way to understand it that is at first more plausible. We are used to the idea that sometimes two things are incommensurate in value: neither is better than the other and yet they are also not equally good. The classic example is Sartre's student, who was faced with a choice of staying in France to look after his mother, who desperately needed him, or of escaping to Britain to join the Free French Forces and fight for France.[5] These two options would realize very different values—so different that, plausibly, they could not be precisely weighed against each other. Plausibly therefore, neither of the options was better than the other, yet they were not equally good either.

So the resource we need is available. We simply do not assume that if neither of two options is better than the either, the two are equally good. Neutrality is being neither better nor worse, but it is not necessarily being equally good. Our intuition is that adding a person is neither better nor worse than not adding her. So long as we do not suppose it is equally as good as not adding her, the problem I mentioned does not appear. Equality of goodness is a transitive relation, but the relation of being neither better nor worse is not. So, we cannot derive a corresponding false conclusion. In Figure 17.2, we can say that B is neither better nor worse than A, and that A is neither better nor worse than C, and that B is better than C. That makes good sense of this example, so for this example we can sustain the intuition that there is a neutral range.

However, a different difficulty arises. It is illustrated in Figure 17.3.[6] B is made out of A by adding a person within the neutral range. We are supposing that addition within this range is ethically neutral. That is to say, under our present interpretation, B is neither better nor worse than A. In particular it is not worse than A. Now compare B and C. These options contain the very same people as each other. So comparing their goodness does not pose the sort of problem we are up against in comparisons involving different populations. The difference between them is that in C one man is worse off and one woman is better off than in B. I ask you to assume C is better than B. That is to say, you are to think that in C I have pushed the woman's well-being up by more than enough to balance the man's loss. I am not asking you to be a utilitarian about this. All I ask is that

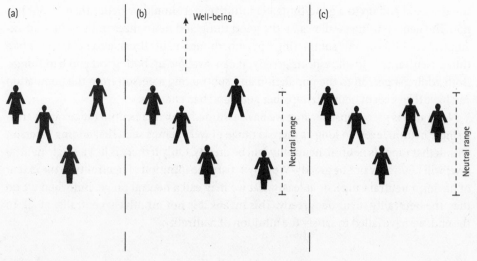

FIGURE 17.3

you allow it to be possible for a distribution of well-being like *C* to be better than one like *B*, and you assume I have done enough to make this the case. I have designed the example so that you will like it if you have egalitarian tendencies. For example, the worst-off person is better off in *C* than in *B*. I hope almost everyone who is not sceptical about the idea of goodness altogether will be willing to assume *C* is better than *B*. Since *B* is not worse than *A*, it follows that *C* is not worse than *A*.

But now compare *A* and *C*. These two options differ in two respects. First, one man is worse off in *C* than *A*. For instance, we may suppose his life is shorter in *C*; he lives eighty years in *A* and sixty in *C*, say. *C* is unequivocally worse than *A* in this respect. Second, *C* contains an extra person, whose well-being is in the neutral range. In this respect, *C* is neither better nor worse than *A*. That is the intuition we are working on: that adding a person is neutral. So, *C* is worse than *A* in one respect, and neither better nor worse in the other respect. Intuitively, therefore, *C* must on balance be worse than *A*. In going from *A* to *C* we have one bad thing and one neutral thing. A bad thing plus a neutral thing must add up to a bad thing.

However, we have actually concluded the opposite, that *C* is not worse than *A*. In going from *A* to *C*, although adding the extra woman is a neutral thing, it has managed to cancel out the bad thing that is the harm done to the man. We have found that our neutrality is *greedy*. Although neutral in itself, it is able to swallow up bad things and neutralize them. With a different example, I could equally well show how adding a person, though neutral, can cancel out good things too. Intuitively, neutrality should not behave like that; it should not be greedy.

Look at the same example in reverse. Imagine moving from *C* to *A*. This involves subtracting a person from the population. In going from *C* to *A* two things are changed. First, one person is benefited, the man. This is unequivocally a good thing. Second, one person is subtracted, the woman. This is a neutral thing. A good thing plus a neutral thing should add up to a good thing. So intuitively, A should be better than C. But it is not. The neutral thing swallows up the good thing and neutralizes it. In a different example, I could show how subtracting a person, though neutral, can also neutralize a bad thing. Neutrality is in all respects greedy; it can swallow up both good and bad things. Both adding a person to the population and subtracting a person from the population can have the effect of neutralizing other good and bad changes.

Neutrality is greedy just because we have assumed there is a neutral range rather than a single neutral level. So long as there is range of well-beings such that adding a person within that range is neutral, neutrality will be greedy. Only if there is just a single neutral level will neutrality not be greedy. We may satisfy the intuition of neutrality to the extent of having a neutral range, or at least what we may call a neutral range. But when we do that, the neutrality turns out greedy. This means it is not intuitively neutrality at all. In the end, we have failed to satisfy the intuition of neutrality.

6. The End of the Intuition

The problem is not just that greedy neutrality is intuitively unsatisfactory. Much more serious is that, if neutrality is greedy, it cannot do the work we need from it. Remember it was the intuition of neutrality that apparently justified us in ignoring population effects when assessing some of the practical problems I described. Take climate change. As I explained, it will kill huge numbers of people, and that is a dreadfully bad thing. For this reason alone, if no other, it seems clear we should think climate change will be terribly bad. But it will also undoubtedly alter the size of the population either upwards or downwards. The intuition is that this effect will be ethically neutral. For that reason, we think it safe to ignore the population change when we evaluate climate change. Since climate change will do clear and unequivocal harm in killing so many people, we conclude it is bad. The intuition of neutrality was supposed to let us maintain that conclusion.

However, we now know that, even if changing the population is ethically neutral, it has the sort of neutrality that is greedy. So, it is quite possible for it to swallow up the badness of killing people. The net effect of climate change may turn out neutral, and not bad after all. It may turn out neutral so long as it changes the population, whether upwards or downwards. I am not saying the change in population will certainly cancel out the badness of killing. That depends on the figures.[7] It depends on how many people are killed, and how that number compares with the change in the population. It depends on how much harm is done to the people by being killed, and by how good are the lives that are added to the population (or how good the lives that are subtracted would have been). It also depends on the width of the neutral range.

Think of it this way. If there is a neutral range, distributions containing different populations are not always commensurate in value. The wider the neutral range, the greater the scope for incommensurateness. If two distributions differ only slightly in their population, the scope will be small. But if they differ a lot, there will be a great deal of incommensurateness. So the more two distributions differ in their populations, the less likely they are to be commensurate in value. That is to say, the more likely are their good features and bad features to be swallowed up by the greediness of neutrality.

I said earlier that we can expect changes in population to be perpetuated; they will last for ever. For that reason, we can expect them to be large. The change in population caused by climate change will probably be large, whichever direction it goes in. Therefore, if this change is neutral, I think we have to expect its neutrality to swallow up the bad effects of climate change. We shall be forced to conclude that climate change is probably not bad, but neutral.

I think this is absurd. It spells the end of the neutrality intuition, interpreted in terms of goodness. This intuition simply cannot be fitted into a coherent account of goodness without leading to an absurd conclusion. However strong the intuition may be, we have to grit our teeth and give it up. We can no longer assume that, as a general rule, adding a person to the population is neither better nor worse than not adding her. Generally, it will be either better or worse. There can at most be only one neutral level of well-being, not a neutral range.

7. A HARD CONCLUSION

The intuition has to go. Abandoning it will save us from the absurdity I mentioned, but it will not make things easy for us. It takes us out of the frying pan into the fire. It was only the neutrality intuition that allowed us to ignore all the effects of climate change on population. If the neutrality intuition goes, we cannot ignore those effects. We shall have to take them into account when we assess the goodness of an action or policy, and we shall have to remember they can be expected to be large. This will call for extraordinary adjustments to our beliefs about goodness. We shall have to make a serious effort to predict their effect on population, and to assign a value to those effects. We shall have to take seriously the difficult philosophical discipline of population ethics.

In many cases, the factor we typically ignore—population—is likely to turn out the most important of all. And at present we are not in a position to make sound judgments about its value, since our theory of the value of population is in an underdeveloped state. We are not even clear whether adding to the population should be counted as good or bad. Many of our present views are seriously at risk of being quite wrong. For example, we have no right to assume climate change will be bad just because it will kill so many millions of people. Perhaps its effects on population will be so beneficial as to cancel out this badness.

This—the fire—is almost as uncomfortable as the frying pan. Must our moral judgments be overturned in this radical way?

Is there any alternative left? So far as judgments of goodness are concerned, I see only one more possibility: to discount future well-being. We might suppose well-being that comes later in time is less valuable than well-being that comes earlier. We might assume its value decreases exponentially at some modest, constant rate. Under that assumption, well-being that comes a few centuries from now will count for virtually nothing compared with present well-being. Since the effects of our actions on population will mostly develop over a very long time, discounting will very much diminish their importance in our judgments of goodness.

However, it is very hard to believe discounting is the right solution to our difficulty. For one thing, it is an opportunistic solution; it is not essentially connected to the difficulty's source. The source is changes in population; the solution is supposed to be the passage of time. These two are only contingently connected. If the world's population was to change unnaturally rapidly, discounting would offer no solution at all, but we would still have the same unease about the way population enters our judgments of goodness.

Secondly, it is any case incredible that later well-being is less valuable than earlier well-being. Suppose it is so, and suppose the rate of discount is enough to serve our purpose of diminishing significantly the value of a change in population. Then the killing of thousands during Caesar's Gallic Wars was a hugely worse event than the killing of millions during the two World Wars—the later killings are so much discounted compared with the earlier ones. That is incredible.

I think most people who favor discounting would refuse to accept this implication of it, because they discount later times compared with earlier ones only in the future, not in the past. This bias gives them a relativist theory of goodness: it means that the value of one event compared with another depends on the time when the valuation is made. From the perspective of a time before Caesar, Caesar's wars were indeed worse that the World Wars, but from the perspective of the present they are not worse.

Relativism brings its own problems. Suppose one of the acts that is available to you will bring about better consequences than any other, and suppose on that account you ought to do this act. Suppose you do. When your act is evaluated from the perspective of a later time, it may turn out to have had much worse consequences than the alternative acts you could have done. So from the later perspective it might turn out you ought not to have done it. This might happen, not because something unexpected occurs or some new information becomes available, but simply because values differ when assessed from the later perspective. It may turn out you should undo your previous act if you can, even though you originally acted exactly as you ought. Moreover, at the time you acted, you may have known all this. You may have calculated the value your act would have from the future perspective and seen that from the future perspective it would have much worse consequences than the alternatives. Nevertheless, according to relativism, from your present perspective, you still ought to do it, because from that perspective it has the best consequences. That is most implausible.

In sum, discounting is incredible unless it is combined with relativism, and relativism is itself most implausible. Discounting is not a plausible way out of our difficulty. I can see no other way out, so far as judgments of goodness are concerned. We shall have to include the value of population in all our judgments and be prepared to revise our judgments radically.

However, the intuition of neutrality may be able to survive in a different guise and give us some practical relief from the difficulty. In so far as it is an intuition about goodness, it has to go. But at least part of it may be normative rather than evaluative. It might be partly an intuition about our moral responsibilities, rather than about goodness.

Think about a couple who might have a child. Our intuition is that their having a child is neither better nor worse than their not having one. But we now know this intuition is mistaken except in the special case where the child happens to live at exactly the single neutral level. So if the couple have a child, that will generally be either better or worse than their not having a one. Suppose it is better. Then the couple are in a position to make the world better by having a child. But even so, we might think they have no moral responsibility to do so. We might think they are doing nothing wrong if they choose not to. This normative conclusion about rightness and wrongness may be part of what the neutrality intuition is pointing to.

Possibly the intuition might be given a coherent interpretation in these normative terms. And possibly it may apply to grand issues such as climate change as well as to a couple's decision about a child. Climate change will be very good or very bad because of its effect on population. But possibly we may have no moral responsibility towards population, and we may be entitled to ignore the goodness or badness of this effect.

NOTES

1. Carleton et al., "Valuing the Global Mortality Consequences of Climate Change," 33.
2. Narveson, "Moral Problems of population."
3. Weitzman, "On Modeling and Interpreting the Economics of Catastrophic Climate Change"; Wagner and Weitzman, *Climate Shock*.
4. My own use of this term is not the commonest. For mine, see *Weighing Lives*, 41–42.
5. Sartre, "The Humanism of Existentialism."
6. This example is a version of Derek Parfit's "mere addition paradox"; see his *Reasons and Persons*, chapter 19.
7. An example of the figures appears in my "Loosening the betterness ordering of lives" in this volume, 149–50.

REFERENCES

Broome, John. 2004. *Weighing Lives*. Oxford: Oxford University Press.
Broome, John. 2021. "Loosening the betterness ordering of lives: a reply to Rabinowicz." This volume, pp. 142–56.
Carleton, Tamma, Michael Delgado, Michael Greenstone, Trevor Houser, Solomon Hsiang, Andrew Hultgren, Amir Jina, Robert Kopp, Kelly McCusker, Ishan Nath, James Rising, Ashwin Rode, Hee Kwon Seo, Justin Simcock, Arvid Viaene, Jiacan Yuan, and Alice Zhang.

2020. "Valuing the Global Mortality Consequences of Climate Change Accounting for Adaptation Costs and Benefits." NBER Working Paper Series 27599.

Narveson, Jan. 1973. "Moral Problems of Population." *The Monist* 57: 62–66.

Parfit, Derek. 1984. *Reasons and Persons*. Oxford: Oxford University Press.

Sartre, Jean-Paul. 1986. "The Humanism of Existentialism." In *Essays in Existentialism*, 31–62. New York: Citadel Press.

Wagner, Gernot, and Martin Weitzman. 2015. *Climate Shock: The Economic Consequences of a Hotter Planet*. Princeton, NJ: Princeton University Press.

Weitzman, Martin L. 2009. "On Modeling and Interpreting the Economics of Catastrophic Climate Change." *Review of Economics and Statistics* 91: 1–19.

CHAPTER 18

EGALITARIAN JUSTICE, POPULATION SIZE, AND PARENTS' RESPONSIBILITY FOR THE COSTS OF CHILDREN

SERENA OLSARETTI

1. INTRODUCTION

MANY policies egalitarians favor distribute the costs and benefits of children in different ways between parents and society at large. Two examples include parental leave programmes defended in the name of gender justice and the provision of publicly funded schools justified by equal opportunity for children. By so doing, these policies influence people's choices of whether to have children and how many to have, and so, indirectly, a society's population size. The latter, in turn, affects the way and the extent to which a society can provide benefits for its citizens, as a society's socio-economic and political institutions can, under different conditions, gain or conversely be put under strain depending on how large its population is and as a result of changes in both the overall size and the age-distribution of its population.

In light of these facts, egalitarian theorists of justice need to address some questions they have thus far mostly neglected by assuming that the principles they formulate apply to a group of individuals whose creation and size are taken as given.[1] This chapter identifies and discusses two such questions, which I call the *Numbers Question* and the *Parental Justice Question*. These are, respectively, the question of what egalitarian justice has to say about how large the population size of a just society may or should be, and the question of what egalitarian justice requires vis-à-vis the distribution of the costs and benefits of children between parents and non-parents. More specifically, this chapter asks whether we should adopt a view about parental justice that can, under certain conditions, help provide an answer to the Numbers Question. On this view, under certain conditions, people's choices to have children are, in one important respect, on a par with consumption choices and other lifestyle choices which egalitarian justice requires individuals to internalize the costs of. Egalitarian justice may then have implications for how many children individuals may have compatibly with justice.

To be sure, the Parental Justice Question is not the only question egalitarian theorists of justice face if they are to address the Numbers Question satisfactorily. Since factors other than fertility rates directly affect a society's population size—most importantly, longevity and migration—a complete account of egalitarian justice and population size should also include a treatment of what egalitarian justice requires vis-à-vis the distribution of the costs and benefits of longevity among different individuals and age-groups, and with regard to migration. What is more, such an account should consider how the answers it provides to these sets of questions as well as to the question of parental justice fit with each other. While egalitarian theorists have paid plenty of attention in recent years to questions of justice and migration, these discussions do not ask, for example, whether the available justifications of a state's right to exclude potential immigrants are consistent with the endorsement of pro-natalist policies or even merely of the widely held view that citizens have a duty to not only include, but to share the costs of, new members added through procreation.[2] Yet such an analysis is needed and promises to cast fresh light on the ethics of migration.[3] Similarly, a complete account of egalitarian justice and population size must ask how parental justice considerations are related to the view egalitarians should take about paying for the costs of an increasingly ageing population—another question that has received scanty attention among philosophers.[4] Egalitarians should ask, for example, whether their views on who should pay for the growing costs of the pension system in ageing societies are consistent with their stance on who should pay for the costs of children. Holding that all elderly citizens are entitled to the same pension benefits regardless of whether they are parents or not may commit us to a system in which the costs of children are shared among all citizens, regardless of whether they are parents or not: since a universal pension system socializes the benefits of children, justice to parents may demand that the costs of children be socialized, too.[5] While this chapter's discussion does not tackle these questions head on, it is hoped that it can help lay the bases for addressing them by advancing debates on parental justice and bringing to view the connection between those and an account of egalitarian justice and population size.

There are two further main sets of questions that a full account of egalitarian justice and population size must take a stance on, and which the discussion that follows makes some assumptions about. So, before proceeding, it is important to mention them.

The first set of questions concerns procreative or reproductive rights and duties, that is, questions about the grounds, nature, and scope of individuals' rights and duties concerning their creation of new persons. There is a wealth of contributions in various areas of ethics on the vast array of complex issues regarding procreative rights and duties.[6] Some political philosophers who take an interest in the family, too, have recently contributed to these debates, focusing especially on whether individuals' interests in parenting ground their right to parent their own biological child and the right to bring new children into the world.[7] While this chapter does not take up directly questions about procreative rights and duties, any treatment of either parental justice or of justice and population size must make some assumptions about, and can have implications for, individuals' procreative rights and duties, so it is appropriate to spell out here three things the discussion that follows assumes in this regard. The first is that individuals have a moral right to choose whether or not to procreate, where the right in question includes at least both a liberty right and a claim right against interference.[8] Second, this chapter also assumes that individuals' right to procreative choice (at least the liberty right) is, like all other rights, not unrestricted or unlimited. In particular, it is constrained by the duties that would-be procreators have toward those whom they would bring into existence, and by some rights of third parties, including at least the equal procreative choice rights of all others. Third, the discussion that follows is open to the possibility, that, additionally, the liberty right to procreative choice is also constrained, specifically, by the considerations of egalitarian justice that are under discussion, that is, of parental justice, and concerning population size. Indeed, the view of parental justice this chapter spends most time scrutinizing makes precisely that claim, and this chapter's criticism of that view does not take it to task on that score. But, it bears emphasizing here, people's procreative rights are supposed to have independent justification from those considerations, even if the latter were thought to justifiably constrain them.[9]

There is a second set of questions which the discussion of this chapter has implications for and makes some assumptions about. These are questions concerning justice between generations, both overlapping and non-overlapping. The question of parental justice has necessarily an intergenerational dimension insofar as it asks how the costs of the creation and rearing of successive generation(s) should be distributed among members of each preceding generations and/or across different generations. As for the Numbers Question, it is especially salient in an intergenerational context, as many of the costs of changes in population size are borne by later generations (Dworkin 2004). Inevitably, then, in answering the Parental Justice Question and the Numbers Question, we are also taking a stance on some issues concerning justice between generations. This chapter's discussion assumes that members of earlier generations do have obligations of justice vis-à-vis individuals of later, both overlapping and non-overlapping, generations. It is agnostic, however, on whether these are obligations to ensure that they are equally well off as members of earlier generations, or merely above a specified threshold of advantage. Similarly, this chapter does not make assumptions outright on whether all ways in which members of earlier generations affect the level of advantage of members of later generations are morally on a par. Indeed, whether earlier generations' consumption, production, and procreative choices could be said to be similarly unjust when they result in worsening the situation of later generations is one of the questions which this chapter's discussion shows needs addressing and contributes to answering.

This chapter proceeds as follows. After making a case for the importance of addressing the Numbers and the Parental Justice Questions (in Sections 2 and 3, respectively), the chapter introduces an answer to the Parental Justice question, the Parental Provision view, that can have implications for the Numbers Question (Section 4). It then subjects that view to close critical scrutiny (Sections 5 and 6). While the chapter argues that Parental Provision is ultimately indefensible and that it cannot offer a plausible answer to the Numbers Question, this chapter's discussion of the Parental Justice Question and its relation to the Numbers Question, as well as the critique of Parental Provision, allow us to learn some important lessons about the responsibility of parents and population size.

2. The Numbers Question

Over the last half-century concerns about overpopulation or population pressure have been voiced, now and again and with varying degrees of urgency, by several moral philosophers; more recently, in light of a more widely acknowledged awareness of the pressing challenges presented by climate change and the threat which a growing population presents for meeting those challenges, the case for viewing population policies and procreative decisions as the proper object of ethical evaluation has gained new currency.[10] While during this same period of time a small but thriving area of moral philosophy has identified and grappled with a wealth of complex questions that arise around our moral evaluation of states of affairs once we acknowledge that how many people will exist (and their identity) depends on choices we make and the policies we adopt,[11] political philosophers, including theorists of egalitarian justice, have mostly abstained from addressing questions about population size.

To better understand both the possible reasons for this neglect and why this neglect is unjustified, it is helpful to distinguish between three different ways in which questions about population size might be thought to be relevant from the standpoint of egalitarian justice.

Questions of population size arise, first of all, in the context of attempts to determine what the *optimum population size* is; where the idea of an optimum population size, though in principle susceptible to different understandings, is most readily associated with that of a population size that is *best* from the point of view of impersonal goodness; and, more specifically still, from the point of view of (total or average) utility maximization.[12] Since theorists of egalitarian justice are not committed to utility maximization, discussions of optimum population size thus understood need not exercise them. However, some egalitarians could take interest in *distribution-sensitive* variants of this idea of optimum population size. In particular, *maximizing egalitarians* could view the maximization of *equal* utility or welfare as desirable, and hence ask what the population size is for which maximal equally distributed welfare can be secured.[13] Alternatively, or additionally, some egalitarians—*telic egalitarians*—view equality as being itself impersonally valuable, thus regarding equal states of affairs as (at least in one way) better than unequal ones; they may also view equal states of affairs with more equally well-off people and hence a greater number of relationships of equality as (at least in one way) better than other equal states of affairs with fewer people and fewer relationships of equality. Telic egalitarians would then think of the optimum population size (or range of population sizes) as the size(s) of the population at which equality is realized and its value is best promoted.[14]

While some contemporary egalitarians are telic egalitarians and/or maximizing egalitarians, many of them are neither of these things.[15] Instead, many egalitarian theorists of justice think of equality's demands as grounded in, and arising only in the context of, certain kinds of actual or potential relations between individuals who make reciprocal claims on one another, where these claims do not include that to being maximally well off. These theorists of egalitarian justice will then conceive of concerns about optimum population size of the kind just identified as extraneous to their views and may be tempted to conclude that insofar as we are committed to satisfying the demands of distributive justice—as opposed to promoting the impersonal values of utility and/or equality—questions about population size do not arise at all. (For an explicit endorsement of this sort of position, see Roemer 1996, 153.)

This conclusion, however, would be unjustified. Even assuming, as this chapter will do from now on, that egalitarian theorists need not be concerned with questions of optimum population size as identified above, there are two reasons why they should address the Numbers Question. (These correspond to the remaining two of the three different ways, announced earlier in this section, in which questions about population size are significant from the standpoint of egalitarian justice.)

Before mentioning these reasons, it is worth emphasizing that these are reasons, not merely to take population size into account when fleshing out the implications of determinate principles of justice in given contexts—as it is obvious enough that we must do in order to work out, for example, what constitutes a person's fair share of resources given that she is one of x many claimants, or in order to know how much the current generation must save in order to satisfy the requirements of the just savings principles. The considerations that follow are, more fundamentally, reasons to take population size into account *when formulating the principles of justice themselves*, and, more specifically, so as to be able to formulate *determinate* principles of egalitarian justice.[16] It is also worth noting here that the reasons provided below why egalitarian theorists should address the Numbers Question are reasons to address a dynamic version of that question, that is, one which asks what egalitarian justice has to say about how large the population size of a just society may or should *come to* be. In other words, as far as egalitarian justice is concerned, the proper object of egalitarian justice considerations are population size *changes*.

With these remarks in mind, here are the two reasons why the Numbers Questions is important—indeed, unavoidable—for egalitarian theorists: while the first points to the fact that egalitarian justice considerations have a bearing on *how we should respond to population size changes*, the second points to the fact that egalitarian justice considerations may bear on *whether we should bring about* some rather than other population size changes.[17]

First, all theorists of justice, including egalitarian ones, need to take a stance on how justice requires that the costs and benefits of population size changes be distributed across different generations, both overlapping and non-overlapping. Does justice between members of overlapping generations require that they share equally the costs and benefits of increases or decreases in population size, or should those costs and benefits be distributed so that the less well-off generation is benefited more, for example? Moreover, we must ask: Are earlier generations' obligations to save for non-overlapping future generations fixed assuming a steady-state population size, or do they fluctuate in line with whatever decreasing or increasing population size would be necessary to secure future individuals' ability to maintain the same level of advantage as members of the earlier generation? An answer to these questions is an integral part of a theory of intergenerational justice and is needed in order for the principles of justice between age groups and those of justice toward future generations to be complete; without an answer to these questions, we could not fully spell out, even in principle, what the obligations of intergenerational justice are.

Second, since population size changes are ones which we have some (collective) control over, and since how large the population is affects what claims of egalitarian justice everyone has, or the size of individuals' fair shares, the question arises whether egalitarian justice considerations tell in favor of the population size being smaller or greater. To take the simplest case as illustration: if justice demands that everyone who will ever live receive $1/nth$ of the value of the external resources (including natural resources and some of the resources societies produce), the—relative and, in many cases, absolute—size of each person's share of resources varies depending, among other things, on how large the n is. Other things being equal—in particular, holding constant the amount of resources available—the larger that n, the smaller each person's share, both relative and absolute. When things are not equal, an increase in the number of people, while it decreases a person's relative share, can increase the size of each person's absolute share—as happens for example if a larger number of people, through cooperation, by innovating and through their productive activities, results in a larger overall stock of resources becoming available for distribution. The question arises, then, whether egalitarians think that the n may be as large, or as small, as *it in fact happens* to be at any given time, and that accordingly, the size of people's egalitarian shares may fluctuate freely in line with changes in the fertility rate; or whether, by contrast, considerations of egalitarian justice tell in favor of constraints or targets on the size of people's fair shares, and therefore, on how large the pool of claimants of fair shares should be. By way of analogy, consider our views about production, saving, or consumption: we may think that egalitarian justice tells in favor of increasing (sustainable) productive activities so that everyone's shares are improved, at least up to a certain point; that it places us under some duties to save; and that it condemns engaging in consumption activities that result in the worsening of others' shares of a valuable resource (for example, their share of clean air). Shouldn't egalitarians think the same about procreation?

3. THE PARENTAL JUSTICE QUESTION

Just as egalitarian theories of justice are incomplete without addressing the Numbers Question, so they are incomplete without an answer to the Parental Justice Question, or the question of how the costs and benefits of children should be distributed between parents and society at large, and whether parents, by virtue of having and/or rearing children, should bear special liability for their costs.[18] To see this, it is helpful to keep in mind two important distinctions regarding what the costs of children include.[19] First, the "costs of children" include the costs of *care* (the time, energy and material resources needed to bring up children from needy infants into increasingly less dependent and more autonomous persons) and the costs of added (adult) members (added members, for short), that is, the costs people will create as adults, including the costs involved in meeting whatever claims of justice the new persons will make *once they are grown up*. (Of course, some the costs of children could be seen as a part of each individual's life-time share. But the relevant point here is that the costs of children go beyond the costs of care.) Second, the costs of children (both of care and of added members) include the "justice-based costs of children," that is, costs that must be borne in order to fulfil the justice-based claims of children both as children and as adults. That is, they include the costs required to provide the care that children as children have a claim to (according to our favored account of what rights children have) and the costs needed to meet the claims to a fair share which adults are entitled to.

With these points in mind, we can formulate the Parental Justice Question that is of interest here with greater precision: What does egalitarian justice have to say about the distribution of *at least* the *justice-based* costs of children, both of care and of added adult members? Specifically, should those costs be shared equally among all citizens, including non-parents, or should parents internalize (some, most or all of) them? With these points in mind we can also appreciate the centrality of the question of parental justice to our theory of justice: without an answer to the question of parental justice, a theory is incomplete in two crucial ways that are of interest here. (It is incomplete, and it matters, in other ways, too. See Olsaretti 2013; 2017; 2018.)

First, because the question of parental justice is also a question about who should bear the costs of added members, theories of distributive justice, including egalitarians ones, that do not address the question of parental justice fail to specify who, as a matter of justice, owes any of the benefits that our theory of justice says people are entitled to. In other words, we need an answer to the Parental Justice Question in order to know *who bears the obligation* to provide individuals with their fair shares: do all citizens bear these obligations, and do so equally, or do these obligations fall only, or mostly, on each person's parents?

Second, and less obviously, the answer to the Parental Justice Question informs *what* people's claims of egalitarian justice are claims to, or *what constitutes* individuals' *fair shares*. This is because our view of Parental Justice informs who and how many others

Table 18.1 Socialization (with no positive externalities)

Time	Total	NP	P	C	GC
t1	60	30	30		
t2	60	20	20	20	
t3	60	15	15	15	15

Table 18.2 Parental Provision (with no positive externalities)

Time	Total	NP	P	C	GC
t1	60	30	30		
t2	60	30	0	30	
t3	60	30	0	0	30

are legitimate bearers of competing claims on given resources, such that heeding their claim to a fair share is *constitutive of what our fair share is*. Consider this simple case: if we believe that egalitarian justice requires that the costs of children be fully shared among fellow citizens, we may view as compatible with justice a situation in which people's relative and absolute fair lifetime shares decrease as parents add new members to the initial population (see Table 18.1[20]). By contrast, if we hold a view of Parental Justice (*Parental Provision*) on which individuals other than parents[21] have an immunity against having their fair lifetime shares *worsened* as a result of others' choices to add new members to the population, then everyone's lifetime fair shares, including that of newcomers, would not, compatibly with justice, diminish in line with an expansion in the numbers of new members; if it did so, this would be an *unjust* encroachment on or infringement of people's claims to their fair lifetime shares (see Table 18.2). Parents alone, on this view, bear liability for the costs of children; in this simple example, they must, in the name of justice, pass on all their resources to their children in order to meet children's claims of justice *and* respect non-parents' claims to their fair share.

Defenders of Parental Provision[22] have formulated this view of parental justice as part and parcel of a certain kind of egalitarian theory of justice, namely, one which recognizes that under certain conditions people's claims of egalitarian justice should reflect their responsibility for their choices and ambitions, and that such claims must not be justified by reference to conceptions of the good that not all reasonable people share. Given these assumptions, the case for Parental Provision seems straightforward. With reference to the simple example above, two defenders of Parental Provision, Hillel Steiner and Peter Vallentyne, remark:

Suppose that one agent, A, . . . intentionally uses up 20 of his units of value, and is left with 10 units. He cannot now plausibly claim that each person has a right to an equal share of the remaining 40 units—that is, that he, like his contemporary, is now entitled to 20 (40/20) units. The right to an equal share is not, after all, a right to an ongoing equal share. It is a right to an equal initial share . . . Suppose now that, instead of using up 20 units, A intentionally procreates an additional (adult) agent. Again, it would be implausible for A to claim that he, like the two others, is now entitled to 20 (60/3) units). (Steiner and Vallentyne 2009: 67–68)

So, the reasoning goes, since egalitarian justice requires that, generally, people be held responsible for the negative consequences, for others, of their choices, and since we may not invoke, as a reason for exempting parenting from this responsibility requirement, considerations about the special value of parenting as opposed to other lifestyle choices people make, it seems fair to the non-parent to require the parent to internalize all the costs of having the child. Non-parents should be, so to speak, buffered from the net negative effects of others' procreative choices.[23]

4. THE RELEVANCE OF PARENTAL JUSTICE FOR THE NUMBERS QUESTION

Just like theorists of egalitarian justice have mostly neglected the Numbers Question, so they have, with only a few exceptions just mentioned and to be discussed shortly, also ignored the Parental Justice Question. It is noteworthy here that how we answer the Parental Justice Question can have implications for our evaluation of population size changes, so addressing this question can—and, arguably, it should—provide egalitarian theorists with at least part of an answer to the Numbers Question.

To see the connection between the two questions under discussion, it is important to bear in mind that, while the Parental Justice question is a question about how justice requires that the costs and benefits of children be distributed, it can have implications for whether (procreative) parents may bring children into existence in the first place, and hence, for how large the population is, on the assumption that we are asking what justice ideally requires, that is, assuming strict compliance with the demands of parental justice under discussion, as well as the satisfaction of other just background conditions. In particular, we assume, crucially, that those who choose to parent can do so freely; and that they are not at the short end of independently unjust, for example, gender or socio-economic, inequalities. Because the focus is on what justice ideally requires, we ask what parental justice demands not only regarding the distribution of the costs and benefits of children who already exist, but also about whether those costs (and benefits) may (or should) be created in the first place, and assuming that prospective parents may not act contrary to, and would generally not be excused if they failed to act in line with, the demands of parental justice.

With this point in mind, it should be apparent how a certain view of parental justice—the Parental Provision view mentioned above—can have implications about population size changes. On the Parental Provision view, as already mentioned, egalitarian justice requires that people's fair shares not be negatively affected as a result of others' free choices, including the choice to have children; under certain conditions, that is, those under which socializing or externalizing the costs of children (including the justice-based costs of added members) would result in a net worsening of non-parents' fair shares, parents would either have to fully internalize those costs or refrain from having children. The conditions under which children would constitute net negative externalities for non-parents include conditions in which resources are essentially scarce, that is, it is impossible to increase their supply, and/or increasing their supply would have morally adverse consequences such as, for example, disastrous consequences for our ecosystem. Under these conditions, according to Parental Provision, justice demands of parents that they internalize the costs of children; given that they would be unlikely to be able to do so compatibly with fulfilling their children's claims to their fair shares, prospective parents would be bound by justice to not have children.[24]

So, although in principle Parental Provision is compatible with population growth, even substantial population growth, in reality, given certain empirical assumptions, it can recommend limited population growth, and arguably, in the world as we know it, an endorsement of Parental Provision would provide support for anti-natalism.[25] Environmentalists who are concerned about overpopulation may be drawn to some version of Parental Provision for this reason. So, for example, Thomas Young endorses a version of Parental Provision on which prospective parents, in order to procreate permissibly, would have to fully internalize their children's lifetime carbon footprint, and other environmentalists' arguments to the effect that procreation is morally on a par with conspicuous consumption, and hence impermissible, share with Parental Provision commitment to the claim that it is impermissible foreseeably to worsen others' situation by bringing new people into existence. Procreation is not special in this regard; it is a form of harmful and wrongful activity by dint of its (unintended but foreseeable) negative effects on third parties.[26]

The version of Parental Provision egalitarian theorists of justice offer and under discussion in what follows is different from these environmentalist variants of it along at least two dimensions which it is important to notice. First, environmentalists do not necessarily commit to Parental Provision on the grounds of *egalitarian justice*, or even justice *tout court*: it is possible to view children as net negative externalities, and procreation as harmful, by reference to a view of what third parties are owed that makes no reference to claims over resources (for example, by reference to a commitment not to breach their rights to bodily integrity, or their interest in solitude), or by reference to impersonal standards (so, for example, if we were average utilitarians, we could think of procreators as acting wrongly if they are responsible for bringing into the existence either too few or too many children relative to the optimum population size as identified by average utilitarianism).[27] Second, environmentalists' versions of Parental

Provision appeal to the interests or rights or justice-based claims of not only procreators' contemporaries but also—and in fact, mainly—future people's. By contrast, the version of Parental Provision defended by egalitarian theorists of justice appeals to the claims of egalitarian justice of the procreators' contemporaries. It is important to notice these points, since these different versions of Parental Provision face different challenges and have different strengths. It is an advantage of the egalitarian justice Parental Provision view under discussion here, for example, that it eschews appeal both to what is owed to future people and to the axiological commitments involved in discussions of optimum population size mentioned earlier, which have been shown to lead to hard-to-escape paradoxes.[28]

The egalitarian justice version of Parental Provision should also be distinguished from a structurally analogous argument which appeals to considerations of justice not between parents and non-parents, but between different states or peoples. On the latter view, under certain conditions, states are held liable for the costs of the fertility policies they support, as it would be unjust to other states which have adopted different demographic policies to share those costs (Rawls 1999; see also Barry 2005). So, for example, John Rawls notes, suppose two peoples start off with equal resources and an equal population size, and one of them chooses to support extensive female market participation, resulting in smaller families and a zero-growth population which make possible a higher level of wealth, while the other adopts generous parental leave policies and does not promote female market participation, ending up with large families and a fast growing population, which leads to a lower level of wealth. It would be unjust to the now wealthier, less populous people to redistribute some of their wealth to the less well-off state, just as it would be unjust to redistribute wealth from a more productive state to one that is less wealthy as a result of its operating more leisure-supporting norms and institutions.

This justice-based argument for states' duties to internalize the costs of their demographic policies may, like the Parental Provision view, also attract environmentalists' support.[29] Here, again, procreation is not special, in the sense that an actor's (in this case, a state's) worsening others' situation by creating larger numbers of individuals is deemed to be no different from its negatively affecting others in other ways: given just background conditions, whether a country pollutes more because it is more populous or because it uses fossil fuels to produce energy, for example, are to be treated on a par in terms of the country's liability for being above its fair share of emissions targets. Although some of the considerations that support Parental Provision may also figure in this argument for states' liabilities for their demographic trends, the analysis of Parental Provision that follows does not straightforwardly extend to this argument, as Parental Provision is concerned with the obligations of *egalitarian* justice that bind *individuals* to one another, and the state-focused argument at stake is committed neither to egalitarian justice nor to individuals as the bearers of claims and obligations of justice.

Parental Provision, then, while being a view about parental justice, can provide a crucial normative premise in an argument for constraints on population growth. The possibility of extrapolating our answer, or part of it, to the Numbers Question from our answer to the Parental Justice Question is a hitherto underexplored possibility, and one that is of interest for two reasons. First, as was mentioned earlier, the appeal to Parental Provision allows us to generate limits to permissible procreation by appealing to *considerations of justice toward our contemporaries*, that is, to contemporary non-parents, who have claims to having their fair shares respected, or not negatively affected, by other people's procreative choices. If Parental Provision were defensible, it would provide a way of generating some conclusions about population size that seem intuitively plausible in an intergenerational context, but without appealing to the rights of, or the duties toward, future generations.[30] Second, Parental Provision allows us to accommodate an important conviction about the normative significance of responsibility for our view of what justice requires regarding constraints on population size. Since under just background conditions specific people—parents—are responsible for the population size's being what it is, it seems appropriate that our view about what egalitarian justice requires concerning population size take account of that fact, rather than viewing parents' rights and obligations as fully derivative of independent considerations about the desirable population size.

5. ASSESSING PARENTAL PROVISION:
OBLIGATIONS OF JUSTICE

Despite its apparent credentials, the Parental Provision view is not, I now argue, the right way for us to address questions about population size.[31] By way of preamble, recall, from Section 3, how assumptions about the fair distribution of the costs and benefits of children undergird both claims we ordinarily make about who bears *obligations of justice*, and about *what counts as people's fair shares*. (It is in virtue of these facts, it was noted, that the question of parental justice is central to the formulation of a theory of egalitarian justice.) This section and the next show that the Parental Provision view has implausible implications about both these central aspects of a theory of egalitarian justice that incorporated Parental Provision as an answer to the question of parental justice.

Consider, first, what Parental Provision entails about who has *obligations of egalitarian justice*, including obligations of intergenerational justice, that is, who has the obligations to confer fair shares on contemporary and future citizens. Given that, as was mentioned earlier, Parental Provision is committed to buffering non-parents from the net negative effects of people's choices to have children, and given that asking non-parents to help provide newcomers with their fair share, both as children and as adults, can, under some conditions, constitute such a net negative effect, an implication of Parental Provision, applied consistently, is that, *as a matter of ideal justice*, each one of us has a claim to being provided with our fair share, not against her fellow citizens, but against only her own parents. Correlatively, each one of us does not have obligations of justice to provide for any fellow citizens' fair share, but only for our own children's: respect for justice does not require that we share our fate with fellow citizens by sharing our resources with them, but on the contrary, it is thought to require that our share not be diminished in order to give our fellow citizens *their* fair share.

To be clear, it is important to distinguish the claim just made from two other claims which I am *not* making. I do not suggest that the Parental Provision view does not hold that everyone has *some* justice-relevant obligations. For notice, first, that it is consistent with Parental Provision to hold that we all have duties to uphold and support institutions that ensure that those who bear obligations of justice discharge them. Proponents of Parental Provision can hold that we have a duty to support the institutions that ensure that those who owe our fellow citizens their fair shares (i.e., our fellow citizens' parents), fulfil those obligations. But notice that these duties, like the duties we have to uphold institutions that enforce the private law or the criminal law, are not themselves obligations of egalitarian justice. So, to point to the fact that all citizens of a society governed by the demands of Parental Provision do have these duties does not contradict the point I am making.

Nor, secondly, am I suggesting that the Parental Provision view can be accused of *harshness* or *neglect of children*, in the sense that it must deny that we have *any* obligations to our fellow citizens, both while they are children and once they are adults, to meet their claims of justice under any conditions. The Parental provision view is consistent with holding that we do have those obligations under *non-ideal* conditions, that is, when the parents of our fellow citizens are unable to internalize the costs of having children. In these cases, proponents of Parental Provision can argue that everyone, including non-parents, have obligations (owed to the children involved) to step in to discharge those obligations. But note that these obligations are a last, undesirable resort that are triggered in a non-ideal context: they amount to an injustice to non-parents that arises in order to avoid what is presumed to be an even greater injustice to children.[32]

My claim, then, is that a society governed by Parental Provision is not a society in which citizens are bound by obligations of egalitarian justice to one another. Parental provision implies that the contrary is true—that non-parents must *not be* held, ideally, to any such obligations. Moreover, note that this would be true not only of the obligations toward their contemporary fellow citizens, but also toward future citizens: Parental Provision seems to commit us to the view that future citizens are not the responsibility of non-parents, but ideally, only the responsibility of their parents. To see this, imagine a scenario in which successive generations do not overlap, but instead, as soon as the parent and the non-parent die, the child that the parent decided to procreate is born, fully formed, and that the child lays a claim, at that point, to his fair share of resources. Here, just like in the normal case in which parents and children overlap, according to Parental Provision, the obligation to provide the new person with her fair share falls on the parent: the non-parent should not see his share disturbed by the new person's coming into existence. In other words, future generations are, in an important sense, negative externalities for *today's non-parents*, so non-parents can justifiably claim that only parents should bear the costs of future persons. The sense in which future generations are a negative externality for previous generations' non-parents is the following: non-parents' having to forgo depleting today's resources *for the sake* of future persons

Table 18.3 Socialization (with no positive externalities) of future generations' claims (Note: S1 and S2 here represent different possible scenarios, not two consecutive time periods)

Time	Total	NP1	P1	C
S1—No next generation	60	30	30	
S2—Next generation	60	20	20	20

leaves today's non-parents worse off *on balance*, as a result of the fact that there will be future persons, than they would be if future generations did not come into existence.[33] Table 18.3 illustrates this.

So, Parental Provision implies that—once again, ideally—only parents have obligations of distributive justice toward future people, such as the obligation to leave enough and as good for others, or to contribute toward just savings. That Parental Provision has these implications regarding the bearers of justice obligations is problematic for two reasons.

First, this seems like an intuitively unappealing consequence of taking the commitment to holding individuals responsible for the consequences of their choices too far. The Parental Provision view starts with a claim that seems eminently plausible in other contexts, for example, in contexts in which people incur avoidable gambles in order to pursue gain or consume expensive goods. In these contexts, it seems reasonable that others should not have to bear the net negative externalities of people's choices. But applying this principle to the choice of having and rearing children leads us to a view that abandons a core commitment of egalitarian justice, namely, the commitment that citizens should share each other's fate (Rawls 1972, 102).

Second, these implications of Parental Provision seem particularly troubling if our reasons for endorsing the view in the first place are, at least in part, that we are moved by a concern with intergenerational justice. In the context of a concern with intergenerational justice, we have especially strong reasons to want to be able to say that it is incumbent on all of us today—not just on those of us who contribute, by having children, to *there being* future generations—to bear some costs so that future generations' life prospects are either no worse than ours or at least not below a specified threshold. Meeting the challenges we face when we consider the prospects of future generations, such as, crucially, the challenge to halt climate change, the cooperation of all, non-parents as well as parents, is needed. The defender of Parental Provision who is concerned with climate change now faces a curious problem: his target is to show that procreation is morally on a par (at least in the respects the environmentalist is interested in) with conspicuous consumption, or "eco-gluttony", so if we want to condemn the latter—as he assumes we should—then we should also condemn the former (Young 2001). But what he ends up committing to is the claim that there is nothing wrong with eco-gluttony if those indulging in it are non-parents. This seems like too high a price to pay for being able to justify limits on population growth.

6. Assessing Parental Provision: Fair shares

The Parental Provision view also yields implausible implications with regard to what constitutes individuals' fair shares. Here, as with the question of who holds obligations of justice, Parental Provision defenders have wrongly assumed that it is possible to adopt it while retaining standardly held views about people's fair share claims: they have failed to notice that adopting Parental Provision has more far-reaching implications than first appears, and, in particular, that taking seriously the rationale behind Parental Provision—namely, that justice requires that we be buffered from the net negative costs of others' procreative choices—commits us to a radical rethinking of what constitutes people's fair shares.

To see this, it is helpful to note that any account of fair shares presupposes a view about what are the *objects* of people's fair shares. These are *what* people lay claims to— for example, raw natural resources, opportunities to obtain positions of advantage, or income and wealth. Now, notice what egalitarian theorists of justice standardly assume with regard to the object of people's fair shares. Most or all of what is up for distribution is not manna from heaven, or raw natural resources whose value is not dependent on others' labour; instead, they are the fruits of *on-going social cooperation*. Moreover, as many people have pointed out (Anderson 1999; Bubeck 1995; Folbre 1994; 2008; Rawls 2005), social cooperation is a process which requires *social reproduction*, that is, people's having and rearing new generations so as to sustain that society's socio-economic and political institutions. Since the object of people's fair shares are largely fruits of social cooperation, which in turns requires social reproduction, people's claims to their fair shares is effectively a claim to sharing the benefits of children, or what some people refer to as the "public goods" produced by parents' having and rearing children (Folbre 1994; George 1987). Theories of egalitarian justice assume, in other words, that individuals have claims of justice to sharing the benefits of children.

This assumption is intuitively plausible, but notice, now, what the defender of Parental Provision would be affirming if he endorsed it: where the object of people's fair shares are the fruits of social cooperation, non-parents' complaint is a complaint that the non-parents are entitled to internalizing the benefits of people's having and rearing children. Accordingly, non-parents' complaint that children constitute "negative externalities" is really a complaint that parents' contributing *this number* (and/or quality) *of children* is not *as beneficial* as their contributing a lower number (and/or better quality) of children. This complaint is importantly different from that which Parental Provision defenders offer support for: when they motivate their view using examples like the one mentioned earlier (see Tables 18.1 and 18.2), which make it appear as though the object of people's fair shares are given in the absence of people's having and rearing children, the case for Parental Provision appears to be a strong one. After all, if what non-parents lay a claim to is what they had prior to anyone's having children, or would have but for the fact that someone chooses to have children,[34] then non-parents' case against sharing the costs of the new arrivals may seem defensible. But this case for Parental Provision does not carry over to cases where the object of people's fair shares are the fruits of social co-operation. Non-parents have no claim to being benefited by others' having and raising children, and no complaint against being benefited less rather than more by parents. Whether or not children are negative externalities relative to a situation in which children are positive externalities—or, as we should now reformulate the point, *greater* positive externalities than they are under the scenario in question—may then not be what grounds the complaint of non-parents.

Parental Provision defenders, then, may only make the complaint they want to make on non-parents' behalf—that is, that it would be unjust to non-parents to allow parents to make create net negative externalities for them—if parents' having and rearing children worsened the share which non-parents would have in *the absence of* parents' having and rearing children. The relevant baseline for evaluating non-parents' claims, then, is a situation in which non-parents reap neither the benefits nor the costs of parents' having and rearing children. But now notice that the view of people's (including non-parents') fair shares that is compatible with this is excessively undemanding: parents would rarely contribute a net negative externality by adding new members to the population, compared to a situation in which non-parents do not internalize any of the benefits of children. Far from providing an intuitively compelling answer to the Numbers Question, the Parental Provision view would thus likely license relatively unconstrained population growth.

So, while egalitarian theorists of justice have good reasons to address both the Numbers Question and the Parental Justice Question, and also have good reasons to address them together, they should resist the Parental Provision view. While it is undeniable that procreative choices, like consumption and savings choices, can greatly affect third parties, and involve the production of benefits and burdens which can be shared in different ways between parents and society at large, thus being susceptible to moral evaluation and giving rise to questions of justice, there are also some important ways in which procreation is different from these other ways of affecting others. Parents affect others by creating the very bearers of claims and obligations of egalitarian justice. As this chapter has shown, this means that our views about what claims and obligations people have and our view of parental justice are intimately related. More specifically, it means that any complaint which third parties may move against parents' producing too many or too few children presupposes that everyone is entitled to share the benefits of children. An altogether different view of parental justice from Parental Provision—one which viewed parents and non-parents as engaged in a cooperative scheme—could justify the sharing of the benefits of children, but it would also justify the sharing of their costs, at least under many conditions, as demanded by justice.

Acknowledgments

Previous versions of this paper were presented at the Society for Applied Philosophy Annual Conference in Belfast in 2016, the *New Scholarship in Population Ethics* conference at the Duke University Law School in April 2017, the Family Justice Work-in-Progress Workshop at the Universitat Pompeu Fabra in May 2017, and at the Institute for Futures Studies Seminar in June 2017. Many thanks to members of the audiences at these events, to Paul Bou-Habib, Elizabeth Finneron-Burns, Tim Meijers, and Julia Mosquera for their comments on versions of this paper, and to Paula Casal and Andrew Williams for discussions. This project has received funding from the European Research Council (ERC) under the European Union's Horizon 2020 Research and Innovation programme (Grant Agreement Number: 648610; Grant Acronym: Family Justice).

Notes

1. This chapter talks about liberal egalitarian justice, or egalitarian justice for short, to refer to the family of views defended by contemporary political philosophers who affirm that individuals have claims both to equal liberties and to a fair share of socio-economic goods. Except where indicated, the discussion that follows remains agnostic over whether a principle of comparative or non-comparative equality (priority) determines what counts as a fair share of socio-economic goods, and over what the currency of egalitarian justice is (welfare, resources, capabilities, or some combination of these). Some of the points raised in the following discussion may apply to some non-egalitarian theories, but this possibility is not explored here.

2. An exception is Michael Blake's brief discussion of this issue in his article on the state's right to exclude. See Blake (2013).

3. For brief treatments of the relation between our views on parental justice and on migration, see Casal (1999) and George (1993). There has been more discussion of the relation between the morality of procreation and that of immigration, especially by environmentalist philosophers and social scientists. Some discussions of overpopulation and climate change by environmentalists and social scientists are concerned with the challenges raised by migration as well as of high fertility rates. See, for example, Bayles (1980); Cafaro (2012); de la Croix and Gosseries (2006); Heyward (2012); and McKibben (1998); for a brief mention of pro-natalist and pro-immigration policies as being potentially on a par, see also Mulgan (2006, 98). Recently, a few political philosophers have started paying attention to the potential similarities of the ethical issues raised by procreation and migration. See Bou-Habib (2019); Brezger and Cassee (2016); Ferracioli (2018); and Mejiers (2016).

4. See Longman (2004) for the challenges raised by the increasing age-dependency ratio. For some philosophical treatment of this issue, see Daniels (1988) and McKerlie (2012). With regard to sharing the costs of pensions, specifically, see Schoakkert and Van Parijs (2003).

5. Olsaretti (2013). Some arguments for this conclusion are found in George (1987). These philosophical arguments may give some support to, but are importantly different from,

actual public policy proposals for a special pension system for parents. For the latter, see Burgraff (1993) and Sinn (2005).

6. Three important book-length treatments of some of these issues are those by Allen Buchanan et al. (2000); David Heyd (1992); and Melinda Roberts (1998). Central edited collections include Archard and Benatar (2010); Baylis and McLeod (2016); Hannan, Brennan, and Vernon (2015); and Harris and Holm (2000). See also chapters 25 and 26 of this volume.

7. For example, Brake (2010) and Gheaus (2012).

8. What counts as interference is not discussed here, but it is clear that it includes at least coercive interference and interference aimed at making it prohibitively costly or difficult for people to have children. For discussion of the ethical aspects of different types of population controls, see Bayles (1979) and Hickey, Rieder, and Earl (2016). It is a further question whether individuals have claims to access assisted reproductive technologies, and to having them be subsidized. On this issue see Burley (1998).

9. The position assumed here, then, is fundamentally different from that defended by utilitarians. For a defence of a sophisticated utilitarian position on procreative rights, see Mulgan (2006).

10. See Bayles (1980); Barry (1989); Casal and Williams (1995); Ehrlich (1968); Hardin (1993); Heyd (1992); and Sen (1976). More recent contributions include Conly (2015); Dasgupta (2004); Kates (2004); MacIver (2016); Overall (2012). The concern is not new, and in the late eighteenth and the nineteenth century, in particular, worries about population animated Thomas Malthus's (1798) and John Stuart Mill's (1848) work on the subject.

11. The work of Derek Parfit (1984) has sparked off and contributed greatly to this area of moral philosophy, which is the subject of most chapters of this volume. For an early, important discussion of utilitarianism and population size, see Narveson (1973).

12. See Atkinson (2012) and Dasgupta (2005). As Heyd (1992) argues, the idea of optimum population can be interpreted in other ways, as it can be understood, abstractly, as referring to "the population size and/or density at which the value of some other normatively selected variable is maximized" (146). That variable can but need not be utility.

13. A view of this kind is perhaps held by Christiano (2007).

14. See Arrhenius (2013) and Temkin (1993). On Arrhenius's positive egalitarianism, it matters *how many relations of equality* exist, and a larger equal population is better, from the point of view of equality, than a smaller equal population. Mosquera (2017) critically examines different versions of telic egalitarianism and argues that the pattern of relations of equality and inequality, not only their aggregation, matters.

15. For discussion of telic and non-telic egalitarianism, see Nagel (1991); O'Neill (2008); and Parfit (1997).

16. In other words, to say that egalitarian theorists of justice have reasons to address the Numbers Question is not to say merely that they need assumptions about population size as empirical premises of arguments about public policies in which egalitarian principles provide the normative premise (or, as Heyd puts it, "relevant background data"; 1992, 42). Instead, addressing the Numbers Question, so it is argued in what follows, is necessary for developing the normative premises themselves.

17. So, in principle, the first question could arise *even if* and independently of whether we can affect population size changes ourselves. Others have noted that theorists of justice should address the Numbers Question. See Gosseries (2009); Heyd (1992); and Mejiers (2017). Barry 1998 is one of the few contributions by theorists of justice that explicitly takes

a stance on, but does not defend, the view that justice has implications about how large the population of the just society should be.

18. Three things should be noticed here. First, "parents" here refers to "procreative parents", and the fact that parents create children whose costs need meeting is of crucial importance in the discussion that follows. Second, although parents' having and rearing children also generally produces benefits, since the focus in what follows is on cases where they produce *net* costs, the just distribution of those costs is what is at stake. Third, it bears noticing that the discussion of parental justice is not over *whether* the costs of children should be met, but, over assuming they *must be met*, *who* should bear them. It is assumed throughout, then, that children's claims will be met, and the focus is on who should, in the name of justice, bear the costs of meeting them.

19. What the costs of children include depends on what our normative concerns are. See Olsaretti (2018).

20. In these tables, *t1 t2*, and t3 refer to different time periods (each coinciding with a new generation's coming into existence); the letters P, NP, and C refer to parent, nonparent, and child; the numbers refer to the value of resources that justice regulates the distribution of, and express the lifetime share of individuals *as identified at a particular time*. (For simplicity's sake, the tables assume that a person has only one parent.)

21. We could think that this immunity is shared by *some* parents whose reproductive choices are not net negative externalities—for example, parents who choose to have one child. The discussion that follows, however, assumes that we are focusing on the claims of all non-parents against all parents. For further discussion of this issue see Olsaretti (2013).

22. Defenders of different versions of Parental Provision include Ackerman (1980); Casal and Williams (1995; 2004); Rakowski (1993); and Steiner and Vallentyne (2009). Robert Taylor (2009) also seems to endorse a version of it. The term "Parental Provision" is Casal's and Williams.

23. Notice that *net* negative effects are what non-parents would have a claim of justice to be buffered from. A view that held parents to the obligation to non-parents to internalize the costs of children, even when non-parents are benefited overall by parents' having and raising children, would lack plausibility. For development of this point, see Olsaretti (2017).

24. Depending on what the costs of children are which parents would be required to internalize, the scenario under which these conditions obtain would be different. It may be impossible for parents to accumulate, during their lifetimes, enough material resources to give their children their fair lifetime children; similarly, assuming the costs of children include their lifetime environmental costs, it would be impossible for parents to restrict their own lifetime carbon footprint to the requisite level. See Young (2001).

25. As Bruce Ackerman remarks, "'Harmony' does not require any particular quantitative limit on the size of the next generation. If, for example, there are a million people on our spaceship and a million grants if manna in our new world, we may, if we think it good, have *two* million children so long as we embark upon an investment strategy that will yield at least two million grains of manna for distribution at the time when our children come of age. Harmony is not the same thing as zero population growth" (1980, 218).

26. Young (2001). Casal (1999) rejects the socialization view on environmentalist grounds. See also Hickey, Rieder, and Earl (2016) and MacIver (2015) for arguments that procreation under certain conditions should be considered harmful to third parties.

27. Arguably, John Stuart Mill's was of this kind. In *On Liberty*, he seemed to endorse a version of Parental Provision when he noted that "[I]n a country either over-peopled or threatened with being so, to produce children, beyond a very small number, with the effect of reducing the reward of labour by their competition, is a serious offence against all who live by the remuneration of their labour. . . . The laws which . . . forbid marriage unless the parties can show that they have the means of supporting a family, do not exceed the legitimate powers of the State . . . Such laws are interferences of the State to prohibit a mischievous act—an act injurious to others" (Mill 1978, 107).

28. These are the subject of Part I of this volume.

29. This argument should be distinguished from a purely forward-looking argument for state liability for its population policy, which could, like with some environmentalist versions of Parental Provision, be grounded in impersonalist standards of value. See the discussion of these views by Heyward (2012).

30. In this respect, the argument at hand resembles arguments like those of Anca Gheaus (2016) and Joseph Mazor (2010), which attempt to generate duties to confer benefits on future generations and (in Gheaus case) constrain population growth by appeal to duties toward contemporaries (one's own children, in Gheaus case and one's fellow citizens, in Mazor's case).

31. The discussion in this and the next section draws on Olsaretti (2017). That paper also focuses on critically assessing the claim that allowing for parents to worsen others' situation would be wrongful because it would reflect, or create, a distributive *inequality* between contemporary parents and non-parents.

32. Casal and Williams (1995, Section 7) explicitly endorse this position.

33. That future generations cannot benefit earlier ones is a point often made in discussions of intergenerational justice. See, for example, Barry (1977).

34. Proponents of Parental Provision do not make it clear whether they use a historical or a counterfactual baseline, perhaps because the examples they use to motivate their views are ones in which these two baselines coincide.

REFERENCES

Ackerman, Bruce. 1980. *Social Justice in the Liberal State*. New Haven, CT: Yale University Press.

Anderson, Elizabeth. 1999. "What Is the Point of Equality?". *Ethics* 109, no.2: 287–337.

Archard, David and David Benatar, eds. 2010. *Procreation and Parenthood: The Ethics of Bearing and Rearing Children*. Oxford: Oxford University Press.

Arrhenius, Gustaf. 2013. "Egalitarian Concerns and Population Change." In *Inequalities in Health: Concepts, Measures and Ethics*, edited by Nir Eyal, 74–92. Oxford: Oxford University Press.

Atkinson, Anthony. 2014. "Optimum Population, Welfare Economics and Inequality." In *Is the Planet Full?*, edited by I. Goldin, 23–45. Oxford: Oxford University Press.

Barry, Brian. 1977. "Justice between Generations." In *Law, Morality and Society*, edited by P. Hacker and J. Raz, 268–284. Oxford: Clarendon Press.

Barry, Brian. 2005. *Why Social Justice Matters*. Cambridge: Polity.

Bayles, Michael. 1979. "Limits to a Right to Procreate." In *Having Children: Philosophical and Legal Reflections on Parenthood*, edited by Onora O'Neill and William Ruddick, 12–24. Oxford: Oxford University Press.

Bayles, Michael. 1980. *Morality and Population Policy*. Tuscaloosa: University of Alabama Press.

Baylis, Francoise and Carolyn McLeod. 2016. *Family-Making: Contemporary Ethical Challenges.* Oxford: Oxford University Press.

Blake, Michael. 2013. "Immigration, Jurisdiction, and Exclusion." *Philosophy & Public Affairs* 41, no. 2: 103–130.

Brake, Elizabeth 2010. "Willing Parents: A Voluntarist Account of Parental Role Obligations." In *Procreation and Parenthood: The Ethics of Bearing and Rearing Children*, edited by David Archard and David Benatar, 151–177. Oxford: Oxford University Press.

Brezger, Jan and Andreas Cassee. 2016. "Debate: Immigrants and Newcomers by Birth." *Journal of Political Philosophy* 24, no. 3: 367–378.

Bou-Habib, Paul. 2019 The Case for Replacement Migration. *Journal of Political Philosophy* 27, no1: 67-86.

Bubeck, Diemut E. 1995. *Care, Gender and Justice*. Oxford: Oxford University Press.

Buchanan, Allen, Dan W. Brock, Norman Daniels, and Daniel Wikler. 2000. *From Chance to Choice: Genetics and Justice*. Cambridge: Cambridge University Press.

Burgraff, Shirley P. 1993. "How Should the Costs of Childrearing Be Distributed?" *Challenge* 36, no. 5: 48–55.

Burley, Justine C. 1998. "The Price of Eggs: Who Should Bear the Costs of Fertility Treatments?" In *The Future of Human Reproduction: Ethics, Choice and Regulation*, edited by John Harris and Soren Holm, 127–149. Oxford: Clarendon Press.

Cafaro, Philip. 2012. "Climate Ethics and Population Policy." *WIREs Climate Change* 3: 45–61.

Casal, Paula. 1999. "Environmentalism, Procreation, and the Principle of Fairness." *Public Affairs Quarterly* 13: 363–337.

Casal, Paula and A. Williams. 1995. "Rights, Equality and Procreation." *Analyse & Kritik* 17: 93–108.

Casal, Paula and Andrew Williams. 2004. "Equality of Resources and Procreative Justice." In *Dworkin and His Critics*, edited by Justine Burley, 150–169. Malden, MA: Blackwell.

Christiano, Thomas. 2007. "A Foundation for Egalitarianism". In *Egalitarianism. New Essays on the Nature and Value of Equality*, edited by Nils Holtung and Kasper Lippert-Rasmussen. Oxford: Clarendon Press.

Conly, Sarah. 2015. *One Child. Do We Have a Right to More?* Oxford: Oxford University Press.

Daniels, Norman. 1988. *Am I My Parents' Keeper?* Oxford: Oxford University Press.

Dasgupta, Partha. 2005. "Regarding Optimum Population." *Journal of Political Philosophy* 13, no. 4: 414–442.

de la Croix, David and Axel. Gosseries. 2006. Procreation, Migration and Tradable Quotas. CORE Discussion Paper No. 2006/98.

Dworkin, Ronald. 2004. "Ronald Dworkin Replies." In *Dworkin and His Critics*, edited by Justine Burley, 339–395. Oxford: Blackwell.

Ehrlich, Paul. 1968. *The Population Bomb*. Cuthogue, NY: Buccaneer Books.

Ferracioli, Luara. 2018. "Citizenship for Children: By Soil, by Blood, or by Paternalism?" *Philosophical Studies* 175, no. 11: 2859–2877.

Folbre, Nancy. 1994. Children as Public Goods. *The American Economic Review* 84, 2: 86–90.

Folbre, Nancy. 2008. *Valuing Children: Rethinking the Economics of the Family*. Cambridge, MA: Harvard University Press.

George, Rolf. 1987. "Who Should Bear the Costs of Children?" *Public Affairs Quarterly* 1: 1–42.

George, Rolf. 1993. "On the External Benefits of Children." In *Kindred Matters: Rethinking the Philosophy of the Family*, edited by Diana Tietjens Mejers, Kenneth Kipnis, and Cornelius F. Murphy Jr. Ithaca, NY: Cornell University Press.

Gheaus, Anca. 2012. "The Right to Parent One's Biological Baby." *Journal of Political Philosophy* 20, no. 4: 432–455.

Gheaus, Anca. 2016. "The Right to Parent and Duties Concerning Future Generations." *Journal of Political Philosophy* 24, no. 4: 487–508.

Gosseries, Axel. 2009. Three Models of Intergenerational Reciprocity. In *Intergenerational Justice*, edited by Axel Gosseries and Lukas H. Meyer, 119–146. Oxford: Oxford University Press.

Hannan, S., S. Brennan, and R. Vernon, eds. 2015. *Permissible Progeny?* Oxford: Oxford University Press.

Hardin, G. 1993. *Living within Limits*. Oxford: Oxford University Press.

Harris, J and S. Holm, eds. 2000. *The Future of Human Reproduction*. Oxford: Oxford University Press

Heyd, David. 1992. *Genethics: Moral Issues in the Creation of People*. Berkeley and Los Angeles: University of California Press.

Heyward, Clare. 2012. "A Growing Problem? Dealing with Population Increases in Climate Justice." *Ethical Perspectives* 19, no. 4: 703–732.

Hickey, Colin, Travis N. Rieder, and Jake Earl. 2016. "Population Engineering and the Fight against Climate Change." *Social Theory and Practice* 42, no. 4: 845–870.

Kates, Carol A. 2004. "Reproductive Liberty and Overpopulation." *Environmental Values* 31: 51–79.

Longman, Philip. 2004. *The Empty Cradle: How Falling Birthrates Threaten World Prosperity (And What to Do About It)*. Cambridge, MA: Basic Books.

Malthus, Thomas. 1798. *An Essay on the Principle of Population*.

MacIver, Corey. 2015. "Procreation or Appropriation?" In *Permissible Progeny? The Morality of Procreation and Parenting*, edited by Sarah Hannan, Samantha Brennan, and Richard. Vernon, 107–128. Oxford: Oxford University Press.

Mazor, J. 2010. "Liberal Justice, Future People, and Natural Resource." *Conservation* 38, no. 4: 380–408.

McKerlie, Dennis. 2012. *Justice Between the Young and the Old*. Oxford: Oxford University Press.

McKibben, Bill. 1998. *Maybe One*. London: Transworld Publishers.

Meijers, Tim. 2016. "Justice in Procreation: Five Essays on Population Size, Parenthood and New Arrivals." PhD diss., Université Catholique de Louvain.

Mejiers, Tim. 2017. "Citizens in Appropriate Numbers: Evaluating Five Claims about Justice and Population Size." *Canadian Journal of Philosophy* 47, nos. 2–3: 246–268.

Mill, John Stuart. 1848. *Principles of Political Economy*.

Mill, John Stuart. 1978. *On Liberty*. Indianopolis: Hackett.

Mosquera, Julia. 2017. "An Egalitarian Argument Against Reducing Deprivation." *Ethical Theory and Moral Practice* 20, no. 5: 957–968.

Mulgan, Tim. 2006. *Future People*. Oxford: Clarendon Press.

Nagel, Thomas. 1991. *Equality and Partiality*. Oxford: Oxford University Press.

Narveson, Jan. 1973. "Moral Problems of Population." *The Monist* 57, no. 1: 62–86.

Olsaretti, Serena. 2013. "Children as Public Goods?" *Philosophy & Public Affairs* 41: 226–258.

Olsaretti, Serena. 2017. "Children as Negative Externalities?" *Politics, Philosophy and Economics* 16, no. 2: 152–163.

Olsaretti, Serena. 2018. "The Costs of Children." In *The Routledge Handbook on the Philosophy of Childhood and Children*, edited by Gideon Calder, Anca Gheaus, and Jurgen De Wispelaere, 339–350. New York: Routledge.

O'Neill, Martin. 2008. "What Should Egalitarians Believe?" *Philosophy & Public Affairs* 36, no. 2: 119–156.

Overall, Christine. 2012. *Why Have Children? The Ethical Debate.* Cambridge, MA: MIT Press.

Parfit, Derek. 1984. *Reasons and Persons.* Oxford: Oxford University Press.

Parfit, Derek. 1997. "Equality or Priority." *Ratio* 10, no. 3: 202–221.

Rakowski, Eric. 1993. *Equal Justice.* Oxford: Clarendon Press.

Rawls, John. 1972. *A Theory of Justice.* Oxford: Oxford University Press.

Rawls, John. 1999. *The Law of Peoples.* Cambridge, MA: Harvard University Press.

Rawls, John. 2005. *Political Liberalism: Expanded Edition.* New York: Columbia University Press.

Roberts, Melinda. 1998. *Child versus Childmaker: Future Persons and Present Duties in Ethics and Law.* Lanham, MA: Rowman & Littlefield.

Roemer, John. 1996. *Egalitarian Perspectives: Essays in Philosophical Economics.* Cambridge: Cambridge University Press.

Schokkaert, Erik and Phillipe Van Parijs. 2003. "Social Justice and the Reform of Europe's Pension Systems." *Journal of European Social Policy* 13, no. 3: 245–263.

Sen, Amartya. 1976. "Fertility and Coercion." *University of Chicago Law Review* 63, no. 3: 1035–1061.

Sinn, Hans-Werner 2005. "Europe's Demographic Deficit: A Plea for a Child Pension System." *De Economist* 153: 1–45.

Steiner, Hillel and Peter Vallentyne. 2009. "Libertarian Theories of Intergenerational Justice." In *Intergenerational Justice*, edited by Axel Gosseries and Lukas Meyer. Oxford: Oxford University Press.

Taylor, Robert S. 2009. Children as Projects and Persons: A Liberal Antinomy. *Social Theory and Practice* 35: 555–576.

Temkin, Larry. 1993. *Inequality.* Oxford: Oxford University Press.

Young, Thomas. 2001. "Overconsumption and Procreation: Are they Morally Equivalent?" *Journal of Applied Philosophy* 18, no. 2: 183–191.

CHAPTER 19

....

OVERPOPULATION AND INDIVIDUAL RESPONSIBILITY

....

SARAH CONLY

1. INTRODUCTION: AM I RESPONSIBLE?

....

WE can take it as a given that anthropogenic climate change is real and will have dev-astating effects on many people in the near future and in the far future. Most people accept that rising population is one of the major causes of climate change: "The bigger the global population the faster we hit the ecological buffers, the smaller the population the lower the pressure on ecological resources" (Jackson 2011, 45); "The biggest impact a U.S. citizen can have on global environment problems, such as climate change, is having fewer children" (Biello 2011). We have had a net increase of population of a billion over the last twelve years (United Nations Department of Economic and Social Affairs 2017, 1) and even if we limit our emissions per person, continued population growth anything like what we have had so far will mean that emissions overall continue to grow. While the individual fertility rate in many areas has dropped, the global fertility rate has not dropped enough, which is why, as we know, the United Nations predicts that we will have a population of 9.7 billion by the year 2050 and 11.2 billion by the year 2100 (United Nations Department of Economic and Social Affairs 2017, 1). Even if we act on the Kyoto Accord, the Paris Accord, and almost any accord likely to be reached, an increase in pop-ulation of approximately 4 billion seems almost certain to offset that. We ought, then, to have fewer children, and insofar as voluntary efforts are unlikely to be sufficient, I have argued that appropriate government coercion to reduce population growth is permis-sible (Conly 2016).

Yet even those who agree that our present practices are likely to be disastrous have, for the most part, insisted that any reduction in how many children we have has got to be voluntary. The state does not have the right, it is maintained, to force people to have fewer children through the use of coercive regulations. Even if the coercion used is relatively mild—no invasive physical procedures, no forced abortions or sterilizations, but merely the financial fines we use to discourage other sorts of behavior—many people object that this is simply going too far.

Why? The reasons for this reluctance are probably various, but I will focus on one major one here: the fact that each person's child contributes only a small increment to overpopulation. It is not simply that we think reproduction is too personal an issue for outsiders to interfere with, even if that interference is simply financial pressure. It is true that we do think it is a personal issue, and that we do think that outsiders should interfere only for very good reasons. We typically think all operations of the body are very personal, and interfere only for great need, but we do interfere when we need to—such as when we lock a dangerous person's body in prison, thereby interfering in his sex life and every other operation of his body, or when we tell you, an innocent person, that you have to get a vaccination if you want to go to public school. Reproduction is a particularly significant bodily operation for all kinds of reasons, but again, I think most people would agree with interference if there is significant harm in the offing and only interference will prevent that. This isn't going to come up if we are thinking of a single birth in the real world, but let us imagine an unreal world circumstance. If, say, I were planning to have a child whose birth were to immediately cause the annihilation of the world, I think not only would no one claim I had a right to have that child, but that no one would object to my being prevented from having that child by the threat of a fine. (How one would collect such a fine following the annihilation of the world is something of a puzzle, I admit—perhaps you would have to convince me of a fine due in the afterlife.) The point is that if the birth of my prospective child, whom we may call Damien, were going to have these annihilating results, society would feel justified in stopping me from having him. Our respect for personal reproductive liberty is great, but not so great that we would refrain if destruction were an inevitable consequence of a given act of procreation. Most, I expect, would be willing to use even harsh physical means to stop me, but those who might hesitate to do that would at least be willing to accept non-physical means of coercion to stop me.

Why not use such methods in this world, then? Again, there may be more than one consideration that causes us to hesitate to interfere, even when environmental destruction is looming, but one big reason is presumably that no one is about to give birth to Damien the Destructor. Instead, each of us gives birth to one ordinary baby, and the collective result of all our procreation is the destruction that Damien would have brought about. That is, each of us contributes only a small increment to the growth in population that will be destructive. And while we feel justified in preventing a single individual from doing a single act that will result in great harm, we hesitate to prevent many individuals each of whose individual effect is a minor part of the great harm, even though the overall effect will be absolutely destructive.[1]

This, I think, is a common view: the average person who has a child in today's world has done nothing blameworthy, even if that person is aware of climate change, is aware that population growth inevitably exacerbates climate change, and furthermore has easy access to contraception and is free to use that. Walter Sinnott-Armstrong (2005) has provided a philosophical argument for this common perception, not about child-birth specifically but about climate change in general. In his account, no one person who emits greenhouse gases even for a frivolous reason—a joyride in his convertible—contributes decisively to climate change, and thus no one person who acts in this way is morally responsible for climate change, and thus no one individual who acts in this way has done anything that is morally wrong. Similarly, while the lifelong impact of having a child is much greater than an individual's driving for fun, the greater the population is, the smaller the increment one contributes by having a child, and certainly no one child is necessary or sufficient for the environmental destruction overpopulation will wreak. If we are not morally responsible for the emissions we produce when joyriding, we are not morally responsible for the contribution our children make to overpopulation.

2. DOES IT MATTER WHETHER WE HAVE INDIVIDUAL MORAL RESPONSIBILITY?

Even if it were true that no one individual who willingly contributes to climate change has any moral responsibility for that, it wouldn't follow that government action to con-strain people from acting this way would be unjustified (nor does Sinnott-Armstrong suggest this). Some will argue that in the absence of individual moral responsibility there is still a collective responsibility—the group as a whole may have acted morally wrongly even if no individual among that group did. This helps justify state action to avoid the harm, whatever individual responsibility may be. Even without bringing in the collective, one may say that an individual has a "forward-looking" responsibility to bring about a better situation—making joyriding illegal, say, or at least getting internal combustion engines banned. One's duties are not fulfilled simply by avoiding a harm: we each of us have a duty to try to bring about social change, and should turn our sense of responsibility to future actions.[2]

These are reasonable arguments. In a practical sense, however, they may not be arguments that will spur action. First, the metaphysics of collective responsibility are difficult, to say the least. And what a sense of collective responsibility will do for us, in the absence of a sense of individual moral responsibility, though, may be limited. As to the second argument, what constraints can be justified by the sense that we should go out and fight for better practices is not clear. While as a society we may be happy enough to prevent individuals from doing a harm, we often aren't happy to put *much* pressure on them simply to do good. While the exact line between harming and simply failing to participate in an effort to do good is not easy to draw, many people think they have an intuitive grasp of it, and if, consistent with Sinnott-Armstrong's argument, we believe that individuals who contribute to climate change are doing no harm, it may seem to follow that any pressure placed on them is pressure to make a sacrifice simply in order to do good for others. Presumably how willing we are to be forced to do good to others varies with societies; since the United States is a huge cause of climate change, however, its social sense of appropriateness is practically pertinent, and here I think notions of collective responsibility and forward-looking responsibility to make things better may not be enough to prompt a recognition of duty. If it seems to people that they are not being told to refrain from harming others but rather to engage in a charitable effort, they are likely to feel that their duty is one that it is relatively easy to override, and furthermore one that should remain a matter of conscience, not state action. After all, they aren't harming anyone! We are essentially telling them to refrain from having an unsustainable number of children as part of a charitable endeavor, like giving to Oxfam. We appreciate it if you give to Oxfam! But apparently we do not, as a society, think that people should be forced by the state to engage in charitable behaviors simply because a lot of good will be accomplished that way, in the way that we do think you can be forced to refrain from harming.

This doesn't mean state coercion couldn't be effective even in the absence of a sense that one is morally responsible for the harm so of overpopulation. For such a policy to work, though, in the absence of a sense of individual moral responsibility we would need a number of things. One might try to develop green virtues: relatively unreflective disinclinations for anti-environmental acts even when those acts aren't harmful or wrong (Jamieson 2007; Sandler 2010). This, though, has its drawbacks: it's not so easy to see how we might instill such an unreasoning disposition, and such a disposition, once instilled, might prove hard to change when we need it to (Driver 2005). Or we might try to instill an overwhelming sense that we have not only a prima face obligation to obey the law but perhaps an overriding obligation to obey the law. In that case, any doubt we have about the actual fairness of the law would become moot: we would obey the law because it is the law. We might believe in such obedience because we think we have an implicit contract with others to obey the law, or because we think that disobeying the law would lead to the destruction of the country, or perhaps because we simply feel we have a duty of gratitude to obey the laws of the state that raised us, right or wrong.[3] Such respect for the law qua law strikes me as fairly rare, though, and that is a good thing. Typically, we adjust our obedience to the law in some proportion to the degree that we think the law is justified—laws perceived as unjustified are more likely to be broken, all things being equal. Or, failing such a slavish obedience to the law qua law we could use punishments severe and pervasive enough that they would stop even actions that a person wants to take and that he thinks are in themselves morally acceptable. Such weighty sanctions, too, are expensive, both in a financial sense (detection and prosecution not being cheap) and in a psychological sense, since those who are caught breaking such laws would greatly suffer (and even those who refrain from breaking the law in light of the severity of the sanctions will suffer from that).

A sense that there is no individual moral responsibility for incremental harms, then, has a great effect: while we can still justify government action to coordinate efforts to avoid the collective harm that overpopulation brings, such regulations will become more painful all around to effect.

3. INDIVIDUAL RESPONSIBILITY FOR INCREMENTAL HARM

Given this, it is fortunate that we do have an individual moral duty to refrain from actions that contribute an increment to a great harm. We have, each individual, a moral duty to refrain from having more children than the environment can bear (and for that matter from joyriding, although the effect of that is naturally much smaller) and if we fail in that duty we are morally responsible for the wrong we do. We each are morally responsible for contributing an increment to a harm that consists of many small increments, even when our own contribution is neither necessary nor sufficient for that harm to occur.

Consider, to begin with, *Murder on the Orient Express* (Christie 2004). In this famous Agatha Christie mystery, twelve people together stab and kill a man; that is, each person stabs the man once and the collective effect is his death. For what it is worth, he is a bad man; he has kidnapped and murdered a child and subsequently avoided imprisonment, committing not only a gross injustice but also materially harming the twelve people who perpetrate the killing, and the murder is implicitly seen (by Hercule Poirot) as justified. However, we may imagine that in fact that death is not justified, and in fact constitutes wrongful murder. Let us imagine, too, that each of the twelve contributes an equal amount of damage. Let us imagine that no one of these blows is either sufficient or necessary to bring about the death of the man in question—if any one of the people in question had refrained, death would still have occurred. Let us imagine, too, that there is no Kagan-esque tipping point, a single blow that, in concert with those before it, causes the death, and after which the blows inflict no further harm. (Kagan 2011). All play an equal role. If this is too difficult to imagine when it comes to blows from a knife which would typically be administered (as they were in the *Orient Express*) seriatim, we can substitute twelve portions of poison administered all at once, no single one sufficient and no single one necessary.[4] Are all the twelve of those involved morally responsible for the death? Of course. They have committed murder. Such a death may be justified or it may not, but the twelve who stab the victim are all bear responsibility for the outcome. None can plead that his own individual act was no more than assault, even though, in isolation, it would not have killed. If such a plea were correct, no criminal would ever act in isolation, but would just take on as many co-assassins, co-thieves, co-assailants, or whatever was needed to reduce his own action from a serious one to a minor one.

All are equally culpable because causal responsibility and moral responsibility are not the same thing and do not work in the same way. Causal responsibility may indeed be divided amongst the various causes, or in this case perpetrators. If you and I each cart off half of a treasure, we are each causally responsible for one half its disappearance. Without you, half of it would remain. Without me, half of it would remain. Our moral responsibility does not get divided in the same way, however, because the allocation of moral responsibility is not a zero-sum game. The fact that we share the moral responsibility does not mean that each of us bears less than she would if she had acted alone. It is because moral responsibility may be shared by any number of people without lessening the individual moral responsibility of any one person that no one doubts that each of the twelve on the Orient Express is 100 percent guilty of murder, even though any one of them is only 1/12th causally responsible for the death.

Sinnott-Armstrong agrees that indeed you are morally responsible if you are part of a group that together intend to do harm, even if your own contribution to the intended action is neither sufficient nor necessary to its occurrence (297, 303). Thus, he agrees that if he and a group of friends intentionally push someone's car off a cliff (with that someone inside) each of them has done something morally wrong, and each of their actions has caused harm, even though no one person's own contribution was either necessary or sufficient for the occurrence of the harm (297). When it comes to joyriding, however, he, in common with all of us whose individual actions result in climate change, has no intention whatsoever of contributing to climate change: that it happens is irrelevant to his plan of enjoying an afternoon of needless driving.[5] He does not intend it as an end in itself, he does not intend it as a means to some other end. Since he has no intention of harming the environment, he has no culpable intention, and thus the presence of a culpable intention cannot make his action harmful or make him morally culpable.

However, we should pause here. If all those in the group are morally responsible for their actions, and for the effect of those actions, because they acted with a certain frame of mind, then being one of those who bring about an effect while having a particular frame of mind can, at least in some circumstances, produce moral responsibility, and in the case of a bad act, moral culpability.[6] Those who jointly push the car over the cliff, or those who kill the man on the Orient Express, did individual actions that were in themselves harmless, but because of a culpable intent, these actions become blameworthy. The question is whether the intention to do a wrong act is the only frame of mind that can turn an action that is harmless in itself into an act that bears a moral load.

In explaining the joyrider's innocence Sinnott-Armstrong seems to rely on the difference between an intention and a foreseen consequence. In the first case, one intends, aims at, hopes for, desires, a certain thing to happen, either for its own sake or as a means to a distinct end. A foreseen consequence, on the other hand, merely requires that a person believes something will result from his action (or inaction). In the case of the joyrider, the driver foresees that his action, in concert with other more or less identical actions, will cause climate change. One might be indifferent to a foreseen consequence, so that it plays no role in one's decision to act, or one might very much regret it, but feel that action is nonetheless required because the intended consequence is important enough that it outweighs the unfortunate consequence one foresees as its concomitant.

This psychological difference, between intending an outcome and merely foreseeing its occurrence, is often taken to produce a serious moral difference between actions: an action that is morally wrong when the outcome is intended may not be wrong if the outcome is merely foreseen. This distinction is used in just war theory: while it is accepted that one should not intentionally kill civilians, it is seen as permissible in some circumstances to act where one foresees the civilians will be killed. So, the general should not target a civilian area, but is morally permitted to bomb a munitions factory even though he foresees that some civilians will be killed as a result. He doesn't want them to be killed, but it is impossible to avoid this if the factory is to be destroyed, and (we will assume) the destruction of the factory is the best way to prosecute a just war.

However, even if we accept that in some cases the agent's merely foreseeing, rather than intending, an outcome removes any blameworthiness for that outcome, it doesn't always do this. It all depends on the circumstances: what is it that is foreseen? And what is the goal whose accomplishment is so important that the ancillary harm that is foreseen is justified? A foreseen consequence is not a get-out-of-jail-free card: the fact that one does not intend a harm does not mean one is never to blame for acting in a way that brings it about.

Consider the general: what if, instead of pursuing a necessary step in a just war, he is dropping his bombs because it is his son's birthday and his son loves to see bombs going off? The general doesn't intend anyone to get hurt: that is not the goal of his action. However, this particular location is one that offers a great vantage point from which to see the explosions. The general's intention is to please his son, and the killing of civilians is neither an end nor a means to that (even the son doesn't particularly want people to die—he just wants to see a fabulous display of firepower). No one would argue that the fact that the harm here is merely foreseen rather than intended means it is not blame-worthy. Whether a person who foresees the harm he is doing for the sake of some rel-atively frivolous end is as guilty as the person who intends a death for an insufficient reason is not a question I will enter into here: the point is that the moral difference be-tween the two is not as great as some seem to think. Acting on an intent to harm may or not be culpable, depending on the reasons for holding that intention (self-defense vs. wanting to remove a romantic rival) and actions taken in light of a foreseen harm may or may not be culpable, depending on the reason for that action. A person can be justly blamed for acting when he merely foresees the harm his action will cause.

How does this affect our evaluation of the person who plays only an incremental role in causing a great harm? Just as a person who intends an unjust harm does not miti-gate his moral culpability by taking in co-conspirators, even if he does thereby lessen his causal responsibility, a person who foresees harm and culpably allows it for some insufficient reason does not mitigate his responsibility by being one of a group. Just as each of the twelve persons on the Orient Express is morally guilty of the harm to which they only incrementally contributed, no matter how insufficient or unnecessary their individual stab may have been, so is each of a group whose joint action causes an unin-tended but foreseen harm morally responsible for that harm. The general who foresees deaths as a result of his birthday display cannot mitigate his guilt, or the harm of his action, by finding a lot of equally cold-hearted party planners who will join him in drop-ping the bombs that have such devastating, however unintended, effect. The point is that attempts to "divide" the wrongfulness between a larger number of people in a way that means each person's individual moral responsibility is less just doesn't work.

The ways in which we can either excuse or blame action in light of a foreseen conse-quence explains a few things that some might find puzzling. For one thing, it explains the variation in the blameworthiness of different instances of foreseen harm. The very same harm might be excusable or not, depending on the intended goal of the action that caused the harm. As we've seen, when General McMahon bombs the city as part of a necessary, proportional, and so on prosecution of a just war, his action is justified. When General Shrekli bombs the city just so his son may enjoy the fireworks, his action is culpable. Sinnott-Armstrong argued that the principle "we have a moral obligation not to expel greenhouse gases into the atmosphere" can't be right because if we accept it, it would be wrong to boil water, since that, too, involves the emissions of greenhouse gases (293). In fact, it might well be wrong to boil water if we were doing that just for fun, but typically boiling water has a very different rationale, one which may justify the emissions that it causes (Hiller 2011: 356).

Say a subsistence farmer needs to boil water to make it drinkable and has no alternative potable water sources. That farmer has moral responsibility for his incremental contribution to GHG emissions by burning a fire on which to boil his water, but in his case his action, even in light of the foreseen consequence of GHG emissions, is excused by the fact that he must do this to live. He's responsible for his contribution to climate change, but he has not acted culpably. He does not intend to harm (even incrementally) and the harm he does is excused by the fact that he does this only to subsist. Henry Shue has differentiated between luxury emissions and subsistence emissions for this reason (Shue 2010). Sometimes the harm one foresees is outweighed by the need to do whatever results in such emissions; sometimes it is not. The line between permissible and impermissible emissions is not always clear, of course. Some cases are obviously needed for life itself and others are obviously luxuries, but my boiling an egg is not obviously one or the other. I am not a subsistence level farmer, to say the least. We may well need to look at the alternatives in general when we consider our emissions—if I don't boil the egg, what will I do? Presumably this may be the path that people take when they decide that buying commercially farmed meat is simply too bad for the environment, but still allow themselves that boiled egg. It may be among the greener options when it comes to sustenance, even though it is clearly not required for life itself, as it may be for the subsistence farmer. While determining the exact differentiations between more and less justifiable emissions would involve both empirical and axiological work, the fact that not all cases of environmental harm are equally unjustified seems clear.[7]

Considering the blameworthiness of action in light of foreseen consequences also allows us to differentiate between those who perform the same action at very different times. Consider the difference between the joyrider of today and the joyrider of 1927—Lord Peter Wimsey in his twelve-cylinder Daimler. Lord Peter did not and could not have foreseen climate change and thus could not have foreseen that driving unnecessarily fast through English villages would make a person morally responsible for its occurrence. While he might be held culpable for endangering English village pedestrians, we cannot blame him for the environmental effect of his frolicsome driving.

This is not to say that failing to foresee a harm always gets one off the hook. There are cases were a person or a group fails to foresee a harm but should have foreseen it—cases we generally think of as negligence. Say that General Shrekli does not foresee that dropping his bombs as entertainment will cause deaths, because he simply never thinks about it. Human cost just doesn't enter his mind. While we can let Lord Peter Wimsey off the hook for his joyriding, someone who easily could have known and should have thought about the harm his act might cause is blameworthy. The consequence is not foreseen, but is foreseeable, which puts the emitter/bomber in the same category as those who foresee the harm but proceed to go ahead and cause it without due justification.

In sum: if we can hold all participants responsible for a bad outcome when they intend that outcome, even if the participation of no one of them is necessary or sufficient for that outcome, the same logic applies when we are speaking of foreseen consequences. Just as actions taken out of an intention to harm may or may not be culpable, depending on the reasons for that intention, actions taken in light of a foreseen harm may be culpable, depending on the reason for taking that action even given the foreseen harm. When it comes to environmental destruction, a person needs a really good reason for taking the action that contributes to it to justify that action. Survival (the subsistence farmer) is a sufficiently good reason: we generally believe that when your life is at stake you are not culpable for taking an action to save that life even when you foresee it will do great harm to others. Actions that are taken merely to augment lives that are already easy and enjoyable, however, aren't justified even when they produce only individually small increments of a very great harm to others.

Even if our procreating has only a very small effect on the overall number of people, and is in itself neither necessary nor sufficient to do significant harm, as individuals we have a moral duty to refrain from procreating an excessive amount, because we either know or should know that collectively that does significant harm to others. Inasmuch as ought implies can, of course, those who are unable to refrain from having too many children are not culpable. Those who have no access to contraception, or, who, even where contraception is available, do not have the social or political power to use it when they want, are excused. Their inability, on the other hand, gives us an added duty: we should not only refrain ourselves from having too many children but help supply others the wherewithal to do that.

4. How Many is Too Many?

I have spoken so far of excessive procreation without discussing what exactly constitutes an excessive number. I have argued that the harm you do (that is, the increment you contribute to an overall harm) may be excusable according to the reason for doing that harm, and that one reason for doing harm that is typically taken to excuse that harm is to save one's own life. This isn't generally pertinent to the problem of unsustainable procreation: seldom, if ever, do we have a child in order to save our own lives. Sometimes we may have a child in the hope of saving someone else, as when parents have a second sibling so as to use part of the second child's body to save their first child. And it is argued that subsistence farmers may need a great number of children to help them, and as indeed may those who are not farmers but who are simply very poor. Of course, both these practices are controversial, to say the least. Some object to having a second child when that is motivated by the desire to help a first child, typically by using the second child's bone marrow or such without consent. Even more fraught, to my mind, is the ethics of having children so they may serve as unpaid laborers from an early age, typically going without the education that might help them break this cycle. (In some of these latter cases, it is true, contraception is not available so there is really no choice involved, and hence no culpability.) However, let us concede that there are cases where having a child is necessary to save a life, and let us say, for purposes of argument, that having a child in order to save a life is justified, despite the contribution it makes to global population. What about the rest of us, who have access to contraception and whose lives don't depend on having children? Can we differentiate among those whose offspring would contribute to overpopulation, and if we can, what conclusion would we draw about what is permissible for different people to do?

Consider a difficult case. Say that I am, again, in possession of contraception, and under no political or social pressure to have a child. It is easy for me to avoid childbearing, so as we typically gauge responsibility I am responsible for what I choose to do. As I decide whether or not to have a child, I realize that failing to procreate would be a cost to me: I want to have children, and I want, for whatever reason, to produce them biologically. At the same time, I foresee that there is an imminent danger of global overpopulation. We may stipulate, for purposes of argument, that if we all confine ourselves at present to producing only one child the problem will be solved: the population will (eventually) stop growing and then will decline, and at some point society can allow couples to reproduce themselves by having two children. And we may imagine a scenario in which if some people have more than one child, we can only reach a satisfactory population if some of us have none. Now, in this situation I foresee that many people will continue to produce, as we might put it, more than their share—many more children than one. At this point, I may see that the only way to avoid overpopulation is for some of us to have no children at all, to compensate for the excess procreation of others. In such a case, do I do wrong in having even one child?

This is a question of what to do in what is sometimes called non-ideal circumstances— where some people fail to comply with a behavior that, if universally adhered to, would produce a satisfactory conclusion. Part of the reason this issue is difficult is that answering the moral question as to whether in such a case it is permissible to go ahead and have that one child depends on a further empirical question. What would the costs be to the individual of having no child at all? We cannot claim that it is impossible in general to live a minimally decent life without children, in the way it is generally impossible to live a minimally decent life without food, health, shelter, and so forth. After all, just as we know that just as there are many happy families who have only one child, there are many happy individuals and couples who have no children at all. On the other hand, it is much easier to understand someone feeling truly bereft at having no children than to imagine someone equally bereft at having only one child rather than two or more. A person who wants to engage in all the various activities of childrearing can do that with one child, so the difference between one and none is much greater than the difference between one and two or even more. Is this heightened sense of loss relevant? Yes, because in looking at the acceptability of intending harm and the acceptability of acting in light of a foreseen consequence we saw that whether the harm in question is morally justified depends on the reasons for inflicting (in the first case) and allowing (in the second) the harm. That the action causes a great benefit to offset the harm it also does may not be sufficient to justify the harm, but then, again, it may, depending on the circumstance. Thus, as we recall, the general who foresees that dropping the bomb will cause civilian deaths but proceeds because bombing the factory is a necessary step in a just war is not morally culpable, whereas the general who foresees that dropping the bomb will cause deaths but proceeds because dropping them on the city affords a good view for his son's birthday party is morally culpable. When it comes to climate change, I have argued that the person who joyrides (in the contemporary world) is culpable, whereas the person who emits GHGs in order simply to subsist is not culpable, because the gain to the two individuals is very different. In each case, the reason for the action makes a difference as to whether foreseeing the harm it will do is culpable. So, some of what determines the culpability of having even one child when one foresees that that is one incremental ingredient of overpopulation is the good that will accrue to the individual, or the costs that will be avoided by that individual, if she has that child. This is the empirical question to which I don't know the answer: how much of a burden would it be not to have a child? The obvious answer is that that will depend on the individuals involved, and the question is whether the cost to the individual could ever be enough to offset the harm of his or her contribution to climate change and the other environmental costs of overpopulation.

Some may argue that we needn't actually answer this question. Their argument would be that the person who wants to have single child need not feel any compunction about doing that if the only reason not to do it arises from other people's misbehavior. If those who have too many children could have refrained, but didn't because they are, for example, self-indulgent, conspicuous consumers who have children just to show that they can afford it, we may think it is quite unfair for the conscientious person to refrain from having any just to make up for their selfishness. The argument is that it would be different if no one was acting in a blameworthy way—if the conscientious person was in a position where she needed to "make up" for other people's excess procreation because they, through no fault of their own, couldn't help but have so many children. In the latter case, we might regard our conscientious person as correct in feeling herself truly bound—an unfortunate concatenation of circumstances has thrown a responsibility her way. If others are to blame, however, it seems quite unfair if she has to sacrifice her chance to have even one child to make up for the irresponsibility they have shown.

Sadly, this issue of fairness, while relevant in assessing the character of the overproducers, does not affect one's responsibility for acting given that the unfairness is occurring. The conscientious person is in a position where she needs to think about what will happen next: about who will be harmed, not about why this happened. I agree with Julia Driver when she writes that "(d)ecision-making that insists on conformity to ideal standards is 'practically' untenable" (Driver 2005, 257). Driver discusses the United States' failure to sign up to the Kyoto Accord on the grounds that other countries are not doing their fair share, but the principle remains the same with population: "to refuse to act in the face of partial compliance shows an inappropriate disregard of the good to be achieved by one's compliance" (ibid., 259–260). Or, as might be said in the case of one's obligation to have no more than one child, acting in the face of partial compliance shows an inappropriate disregard of the harm to be avoided by one's compliance. If there is an obligation to help put out a life-endangering fire when that fire was caused by lightening, the same obligation exists if that fire was started by arson.

So, it is possible in some circumstances that we may have moral responsibility, and will act culpably, if we have even one child. It depends on what the costs to us are of not having the child, and on what the costs to others are if all of us have a child when we know that others are having so many that those, in combination with the single children of the conscientious, will cause environmental disaster. Thus, it might be that government coercion to stop many of us from having even one child might be acceptable. Ideally, of course, government intervention would stop other people from having more than their fair share, so that all of us who want to might have one, but if that were not possible (say, the conscientious nation has no power over the nation of over-producers) we might have to accept that very bitter pill. Of course, we hope that it does not come to this! If it does, we will then have to revisit the question of costs and benefits, to see what we may do when we foresee a harm.

5. CONCLUSION

We have moral responsibility for actions which we foresee will contribute an increment to an effect. If that effect is harm, and the actions that produce it do not justify that harm, we are morally responsible for doing a wrong thing, even if our own individual action was neither necessary nor sufficient for that harmful effect. Just as all the members of a group that intend an unjustified harm are guilty for having produced that harm, even if their individual contribution was neither sufficient nor necessary for its occurrence, so are all the members of a group who foresee an unjustified harmful consequence responsible for that consequence.

Such a recognition is not in itself sufficient to persuade all concerned to have only a sustainable number of children, which current numbers would suggest to be no more than one (Conly 2016). People are not motivated exclusively be the desire to do what is morally right, as most of us have noticed by now. How strong that motivation is, and whether it will override others, depends in a given case on many things; we vary according to our general moral conscientiousness, according to how significant we believe a particular moral duty is, according to how costly we find it to act in accordance with a particular moral duty, and no doubt other things. We will need government regulation, which may range from providing incentives to have fewer children to creating weaker or stronger disincentives. But having a sense that we are indeed acting in a blameworthy manner when we have children without regard for the effect that has on others can make government regulation to discourage that much more effective. We need both. "Continued rapid global population growth is inevitable for the next few decades but whether it continues in the longer term will be determined by the investments made and the policy frameworks constructed by countries and the international community" (Royal Society 2012, 45). And, I would add, our recognition of our duty.

Notes

1. Well, even one child has a serious environmental impact (Nolt 2010; 2011). But probably no single child causes overwhelming environmental destruction, and even if one child were somehow the tipping point (Kagan 2011) (difficult to ascertain, since so many births are simultaneous) we would have no way of knowing which, or at present even assigning probability of a given child's being that one.
2. See Poel et al. (2012) for a thorough discussion of such responses.
3. All found in the *Crito*, as Socrates explains his refusal to flee his death sentence.
4. See Conly (2016, 96–98) for related discussion.
5. *Chacun à son goût.*
6. "Frame of mind" is an intentionally vague phrase, intending to collect a set of psychological elements including beliefs and desires.
7. I have benefited here from conversations with Atticus Carnell.

References

Biello, David. 2011. "Human Population Reaches 7 Billion: How Did This Happen, and Can It Go On?" *Scientific American*, October 28. https://www.scientificamerican.com/article/human-population-reaches-seven-billion/

Christie, Agatha. 2004. *Murder on the Orient Express*. New York: Berkeley Books.

Conly, Sarah. 2016. *One Child: Do We Have a Right to More?* New York: Oxford University Press.

Driver, Julia. 2005. "Ideal Decision-Making and Green Virtues." In *Perspectives on Climate Change: Science, Economics, Politics, Ethics*, edited by Walter Sinnott-Armstrong and Richard B. Howarth, 249–264. Oxford: Elsevier.

Hiller, Avram. 2011. "Climate Change and Individual Responsibility." *The Monist* 94, no. 3: 349–368.

Jackson, Tim. 2011. *Prosperity without Growth*. Washington, DC: Earthscan.

Jamieson, Dale. 2007. "When Utilitarians Should Be Virtue Theorists." *Utilitas* 19, no. 2: 160–183.

Kagan, Shelly. 2011. "Do I Make a Difference," *Philosophy & Public Affairs* 39: 105–141.

Nolt, John. 2010. "Greenhouse Gas Emission and the Domination of Posterity." In *The Ethics of Global Climate Change*, edited by Denis Arnold, 60–76. Cambridge University Press, Cambridge.

Nolt, John. 2011. "How Harmful Are the Average American's Greenhouse Gas Emissions?" *Ethics, Policy, and Environment*, 14: 3–10.

Poel, Ibo van de, Jessica Nihlen Fahlquist, Neelke Doorn, Sjoerd Zwart, and Lambèr Royakkers. 2012. "The Problem of Many Hands: Climate Change as an Example." *Science and Engineering Ethics* 18: 49–67.

Royal Society. 2012. *People and the Planet*. London: Royal Society Science Policy Centre.

Sandler, Ronald. 2010. "Ethical Theory and the Problem of Inconsequentialism: Why Environmental Ethicists Should Be Virtue-Oriented Ethicists." *Journal of Agricultural and Environmental Ethics* 23: 167–183.

Shue, Henry. 2010. "Subsistence Emissions and Luxury Emissions." In *Climate Ethics*, edited by Stephen Gardiner, Simon Caney, and Dale Jamison, 200–214. Oxford: Oxford University Press.

Sinnott-Armstrong, Walter. "It's Not My Fault: Global Warming and Individual Moral Responsibility." In *Perspectives on Climate Change: Science, Economics, Politics, Ethics*, edited by Walter Sinnott-Armstrong and Richard B. Howarth, 293–315. Oxford: Elsevier.

United Nations Department of Economic and Social Affairs/Population Division. 2017. *World Population Prospects: The 2017 Revision*. New York.

CHAPTER 20

....

OPTIMUM
POPULATION SIZE

....

HILARY GREAVES

1. INTRODUCTION

....

THIS chapter focuses on the question of optimal human population size: how many people it is best to have alive on Earth at a given time.

To answer this question, we need to know two things. First, we need to know which logically possible states of affairs are better than which others.[1] That is the issue studied by population axiology and discussed in Part I of this volume (for an article-length survey, see also Greaves 2017). Second, we need to know which logically possible states of affairs are achievable. For example, we cannot in practice have a population of a quadrillion humans, all living lives of untold bliss, on Earth simultaneously. Our exercise is one of optimization subject to real-world constraints. There is a non-trivial task of working out the real-world implications, for the question of optimum population, of any given theory of population axiology.

To keep the task to a manageable size, in this chapter I will limit my focus in two significant ways. First, I seek only to work out the implications of a given theory of population axiology for the question of optimum population, rather than also to assess the plausibility of any such theory as an evaluative thesis. Second, while one could in principle examine the real-world implications of any population axiology that can coherently be formulated, I will focus mainly on totalism. According to totalism, the goodness of a state of affairs is given by total well-being (summed across all persons who exist in that state of affairs). Many of the considerations I will survey, however, are also relevant in the context of other axiologies (cf. n.23). In addition, Section 2 will also include some explicit analysis of the implications of some forms of averagism.

One aspect of the literature on optimum population comes from economics and focuses on abstract formal models. These models are helpful for seeing the relationships between the various relevant considerations, but they do not by themselves settle quantitative questions of optimum population size, or even the binary question of which side of the optimum a "business as usual" population trajectory sits.

The more quantitative questions have practical relevance: once we have worked out on which side of the optimum a "business as usual" population trajectory sits (and the marginal value of approaching nearer to the optimum), there are things that we can do to try to influence that trajectory. Some such interventions, especially the more coercive, are arguably morally impermissible. But at least some interventions are morally permissible by any reasonable lights. For one thing, there is a continuum between coercion and mild incentives, and clearly some incentive mechanisms are permissible. For another, some interventions take the form of simply *facilitating* higher or lower fertility (through, respectively, fertility treatment and contraceptive services).[2]

During the long history of discussion of the quantitative questions, there have been concerns both about overpopulation, and about underpopulation.[3] Over at least the past fifty years, however, overpopulation concerns have been far more common, with large population sizes and/or high population growth rates being associated with political instability, environmental degradation, climate change, and slower economic growth, as well as simply low levels of per-capita well-being due to overcrowding and thin spreading of resources.[4] This has led to several prominent calls for deliberate action to reduce population size and/or growth rate (for example, Meadows et al. 1972; Union of Concerned Scientists 1992; Royal Society 2012, 102; UNFPA 2012, 10–12; 2013, 15, 23–25).

There are both static and dynamic elements to this population debate. The static question is that of optimal population *size* at a given time; the dynamic question is that of optimal population *growth rate*. Some of the "overpopulation" concerns relate specifically to high growth rates, rather than to high sizes. Again, mainly for simplicity, in this chapter I focus on static considerations.[5]

The structure of the chapter is as follows.

Section 2 focuses on the abstract models of optimum population that have been developed in the economics literature. Here, I distinguish between intratemporal and intertemporal versions of the question of optimum population. Section 2.1 discusses the intratemporal question, inter alia introducing the notion of a production function to model the relationship between population size and quantity of goods produced. Section 2.2 discusses the intertemporal question; it outlines how a more complex production function (taking capital stock as well as population size as argument) can model the question of optimum population path in the intertemporal context. A central result in the intertemporal case is that, under plausible assumptions, the optimum population size tends to a finite asymptote in the infinite-time limit.

Section 3 discusses overpopulation concerns, and the related arguments that deliberate attempts to reduce population size or slow population growth are warranted. Here I focus on two arguments that are of particular interest from the point of view of totalism. Section 3.1 discusses the claim that population size is anyway limited by external factors, so that we face a simple choice between reducing the birth rate or facing an increased death rate. Section 3.2 discusses the claim that too high a population in the short term would be short-sighted by the lights of totalism, since it would reduce the earth's "carrying capacity," thereby enforcing smaller populations in the longer run. I find both arguments to be inconclusive.

Section 4 summarizes.

2. ECONOMIC MODELS OF OPTIMUM POPULATION

Distinguish between *momentary* and *temporally complete* states of affairs. A momentary state of affairs represents how the world is going at some particular time; a temporally complete state of affairs represents a whole history of the world.

Correspondingly, the question of optimum population size has an intratemporal and an intertemporal version.[6] Ultimately, our practical interest must be in the intertemporal question. But consideration of the intratemporal case can at least be a useful warm-up exercise. Sections 2.1 and 2.2 consider these two questions respectively.

2.1. The Intratemporal Case

The intratemporal question is: which population size at a given time leads to the *intrinsically* best momentary state of affairs at that time, that is, ignoring the knock-on effects of population size at this time for well-being at subsequent times?

A preliminary remark: it is not obvious that a betterness ranking of *momentary* (rather than temporally complete) states of affairs even makes sense. There are two reasons one might suspect that it does not make sense. First, on most or all substantive theories of well-being, it is delicate at best whether and how the relevant facts about an individual's life can be indexed to times. For one example, conscious experiences arguably supervene on temporally extended processes, rather than on instantaneous states. But even if (in response to that worry) "momentary" states of affairs are taken to have some finite temporal duration, it is unclear how to assign even approximate temporal locations to instances of desire-satisfaction (Bradley 2016; Bramble 2018; Brink 1997; Bykvist 2015; Parfit 1984, 112; Purves 2017). Second, *if* any betterness ranking of instantaneous states of affairs would ultimately have to be derived from a ranking of temporally complete states of affairs, the exercise may presuppose temporal separability, and temporal separability may be false (Broome 2004, Ch. 7).

For the purposes of this chapter, I will simply assume that (one way or another) the exercise does make sense, and in particular that the economists' standard way of carrying out the exercise is by and large defensible, whatever precisely its theoretical foundation is. This assumption seems reasonable, since it is hard to believe that such locutions as "things will be better in 2050 if we take steps now to cut pollution" make no sense at all.

Pressing forward, then: to rank population sizes with respect to (welfarist) betterness in the purely intratemporal sense, the key empirical input is how well-being (at a time) depends on population size (at that time). This in turn depends on many things that themselves vary from one time to another, including, but not limited to: the state of knowledge, social organization and the natural environment, and the stock of productive capital (such as tools and machines). However, there are some broad qualitative results that hold for any plausible configuration of these background variables.[7] Sections 2.1.1–2.1.3 survey these results.

2.1.1. *Abstract analysis*

At the most abstract level, we ignore the mediating roles of resources and production, and simply consider average individual well-being w as a function of population size N. In general, one expects this function $w(N)$ to have something like an inverted U-shape. At very low population sizes, well-being per capita is low because the population size is too small to take advantage of economies of scale: at the extreme, the society has its work cut out simply trying to gather produce enough food to feed its members, and cannot support any of the more specialist occupations (manufacturing, printing, advanced medicine, education, etc.) that are required for more than a subsistence standard of living. Similarly, but for different reasons, well-being per capita is also low when the population size is very high: in this case well-being is constrained by overcrowding, pollution, and resource shortages, and even in purely economic terms there are "diseconomies of scale". (Beyond a certain point, a factory cannot produce twice as much output even given twice as much labor and capital, since its operations will start to become constrained by, "for example" (for consistency with stylistic choices made elsewhere in the chapter), shortages of land and difficulties of waste disposal.) Somewhere in between, average well-being reaches a maximum.[8]

Which population size is *optimal* of course depends not only on how average well-being varies as a function of population size, but also on which is the correct population axiology. Here, what we need is a "momentary population axiology": that is, a betterness ranking of all conceivable momentary states of affairs, rather than the rankings of temporally complete states of affairs that the literature on population axiology usually discusses. There is, however, an obvious way to define momentary analogues of the usual menu of population axiologies. For example, momentary averagism and momentary totalism, respectively, say that the value of a momentary state of affairs is given by the average (respectively the sum) of momentary well-being, averaged (respectively summed) across all people who exist at the time in question.[9]

In terms of our function $w(N)$, the optimum population according to momentary averagism, N^*_{av}, is obvious: it is simply the point at which $w(N)$ reaches its maximum.

The case of momentary totalism is only slightly more complicated. The optimum population size according to momentary totalism, N^*_{tot}, is the one that maximizes the area of the rectangle that we get by joining a point on the graph to both the vertical and horizontal axes. Given our assumptions about the shape of the graph, it follows that N^*_{tot} is (i) higher than N^*_{av}, but (ii) finite (see Figure 20.1).

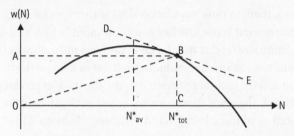

FIGURE 20.1 Optimum population sizes according to momentary averagism and momentary totalism, for a typical function $w(N)$. The averagist optimum N^*_{av} is the population size at which the function $w(N)$ reaches its maximum. The totalist optimum N^*_{tot} is such that the area of the rectangle $OABC$ is greater than that of any other rectangle whose bottom left corner is O and whose top right corner lies on the graph of $w(N)$; it is characterized by the fact that the slope of the tangent line DE is equal in magnitude (and opposite in sign) to that of the line OB (that is, $w(N^*_{tot}) = -N^*_{tot}.w'(N^*_{tot})$, where $w'(N)$ is the slope of the graph).

It is worth noting the relationship of this result to the Repugnant Conclusion. Setting aside the issue of empirical constraints, and provided the well-being scale has the structure of the real numbers,[10] totalism notoriously implies the so-called Repugnant Conclusion: that for any state of affairs and for any positive well-being level $\varepsilon > 0$, there exists a better (sufficiently large-population) state of affairs in which no individual has a well-being level greater than ε ("barely worth living") (see e.g. Parfit 1984, 388; Greaves 2017, 3; and Part I of this volume). In assessing the extent to which this counterintuitive implication furnishes evidence against totalism, it may be important to note the distinction between this "theoretical Repugnant Conclusion" and a "practical Repugnant Conclusion" (Huemer 2008, 930). The latter would be the conclusion that for any given feasible state of affairs and any $\varepsilon > 0$, there is a better feasible state of affairs (i.e., satisfying actual empirical constraints) in which no-one has a well-being level greater than ε. Arguably, the latter is more counterintuitive, and more unacceptable, than the former. We can see from Figure 20.1, though, that totalism does *not* imply the *practical* Repugnant Conclusion, unless quite special and empirically unrealistic assumptions are made about the shape of the graph $w(N)$.

2.1.2. *Fixed Resources*

The connection between population size and average well-being is of course not brute: it is mediated by what we might broadly term "resources." That is, the *reason* why average well-being varies with population size is that the latter affects what quantity of such things as land, bread, fuel, double-glazing, and education each person is able to "consume," and this consumption level in turn affects the person's well-being level.

Instead of simply taking the function $w(N)$ as given, therefore, let us (with slight abuse of notation) consider the function $w(c)$, giving individual well-being as a function of individual consumption.[11] We assume that $w(c)$ (i) is everywhere increasing, (ii) is concave (that is, the graph becomes less steep as c increases), and (iii) crosses the horizontal axis at some positive value c_0 of c (Figure 20.2). Assumption (i) means that more consumption is always better for the individual. Assumption (ii) adds that there are diminishing marginal returns of consumption to well-being: that is, a given amount of additional consumption increases well-being by a smaller amount when the recipient starts from a higher consumption level than when the recipient starts from a lower consumption level. Assumption (iii) adds that for consumption levels below c_0, life is sufficiently miserable that well-being is negative (life is "worth not living"). All of these assumptions are standard, and generally reasonable.

Suppose (unrealistically) that the total amount of resources available for consumption is some fixed quantity R, independent of population size—as if such resources were simply given as "manna from heaven." It is well recognized that if well-being is the *same* function of consumption for each individual, and satisfies assumptions (i) and (ii) above, then *for any given population size N*, the arrangement that maximizes total (and hence average) well-being distributes resources equally among those N people.[12] But what, in this case, would be the optimum population size?[13]

The answer according to momentary averagism is again obvious. Given our assumptions that total consumption is fixed and that well-being is a strictly increasing function of consumption, a smaller population (with equally distributed resources and hence equality of individual well-being) always has a higher individual well-being level than a larger population. The optimal population size is 1.

As for momentary totalism: elementary calculus shows that total well-being is maximized when the per-capita consumption level c is such that $w(c) = cw'(c)$. In graphical terms, this corresponds to the point at which a tangent to the graph intersects the origin (point A in Figure 20.2). Having established this optimal consumption level

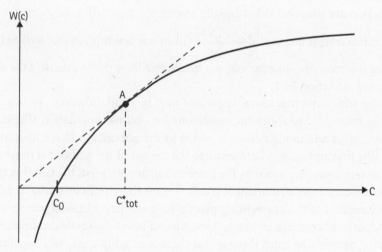

FIGURE 20.2 A well-being function $w(c)$ that is (i) everywhere increasing and (ii) everywhere concave, with (iii) a positive horizontal intercept c_0.

c_{tot}^{*}, the optimal population size (given the total available resources) is simply whatever population size allows each person to have the consumption level c_{tot}^{*} (that is, $N_{tot}^{*} = \dfrac{R}{c_{tot}^{*}}$).[14]

It is instructive to compare the relationship of this model to the "practical Repugnant Conclusion." As before, there is no reason to suspect that the optimal situation will correspond to a per-capita well-being level that is close to zero. However, the graph does illustrate that the optimal per-capita *consumption* level c_{tot}^{*} is unlikely to be more than a few times larger than the "zero well-being" consumption level c_0 (Dasgupta 1969, 307). (For example, with the utility function as drawn, c_{tot}^{*} is between two and three times c_0.)[15] *If* intuition says that the optimum must be a situation in which each person can enjoy a consumption level *many times* this "zero level," this is a counterintuitive result; it is unclear, however, whether the antecedent is true.

2.1.3. *Produced Resources*

While total supply is more-or-less independent of population size for some special resources (perhaps land), that is of course not true in general. Almost all resources are in some relevant sense produced by human labor, so that the total amount of the resource increases as population size increases.

To model this, economists use a production function. In the simplest nontrivial version of this model, this is a function whose single argument is the population size N, and whose value $F(N)$ is the total amount of goods produced. In Section 2.1.2, we were in effect assuming that the value of this "function" was simply a constant, R. More plausibly, though, F is such that average output per head $\left(\dfrac{F(N)}{N} \right)$ is low at low populations, rises to a maximum, and decreases again at sufficiently high populations as diseconomies of scale start to set in. For the intratemporal optimum, all of the outputs of production are simply divided equally among the population for consumption, so that per capita consumption is also $\dfrac{F(N)}{N}$. Given our assumption that well-being is an increasing function of consumption, at a qualitative level this is precisely the situation we discussed in Section 2.1.1.

With the additional theoretical apparatus of F in hand, however, we can now say something more precise about the conditions for optimal population size according to totalism. If an additional person is added to the population, three relevant things happen. The first and second both relate to the impact of the additional person on the amount of resources consumed by the pre-existing people. First, the fact that the additional person consumes an amount of goods c means that c must be subtracted from the total consumption of the pre-existing people. Second, the additional person increases total production; her marginal product must be *added* to the total consumption of the pre-existing people. The third thing is that there is an additional (and hopefully positive) contribution to total well-being, given by the added person's well-being level. At the optimum, these three contributions to total well-being must balance, so that that the net effect of adding or subtracting a marginal person to/from the population is zero.[16] Which numerical value this entails for the optimum population depends, of course, on both the utility function and the production function; it is difficult to say more at any abstract level.[17]

2.2. The Intertemporal Case

The models in the preceding subsection ask only for the optimal *momentary* state of affairs, and (further) evaluate this without regard to the effects of population at one time for the possibilities available for population sizes and well-being levels at later times. But ultimately, of course, what we seek is the optimal *temporally complete* state of affairs, from big bang (or anyway from the present day) to heat death.

This means that seeking the optimal momentary state in Section 2.1's sense might be myopic. Activities at one time can have both positive and negative effects on the possibilities for well-being at later times. The optimal momentary state of affairs at t *ignoring effects on later times* can therefore easily fail to be part of the optimal *path* (where a "path" is an assignment of momentary states of affairs to times), just as rational prudential behavior for a temporally extended individual very rarely coincides with maximization of prudential value realized in the present moment alone.

In particular: in the intertemporal case, it will in general be optimal for the population at t not to consume everything it produces, but to dedicate some of its output to enhancing future production possibilities. In addition, a society might well decide not to produce as much as it possibly could, if that would lead to environmental degradation that would prove disadvantageous at later times.

2.2.1. *Dasgupta's Model*

The simplest model of these considerations treats all effects of one time on later times as being mediated by a single variable called "capital." According to the simple model, (i) capital increases whenever there is an excess of production over consumption (and hence "saving"), and (ii) the production possibilities at t are determined by the population size at t *together with* the capital stock at t; meanwhile, (iii) well-being depends, as before, on consumption alone.

This model is most intuitive in a highly simplified scenario in which (1) there are no issues of knowledge accumulation or environmental degradation, and (2) only one type of good is produced, which can be either consumed immediately, or reinvested to enhance the production possibilities at future times. For example, the model is a reasonably good fit to a simple farming scenario, in which rice (for instance) can be either consumed this year, or used as seed for next year's crop. Capital, in this example, would simply be the quantity of seed grain possessed by the community.

The exercise, in this simple model, is to rank the feasible paths (K, C, N) in terms of overall betterness, where:

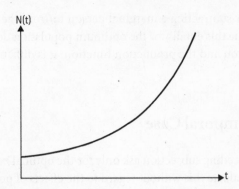

FIGURE 20.3 Exponential population growth

- K is total capital stock, C is total consumption, and N is population size;
- Each of these variables is itself a function of time;
- Feasibility is constrained by a production function $F(K,N)$, specifying how much can be produced per unit time with a given amount of capital and population size.

Dasgupta (1969) investigates this exercise, assuming a time-discounted totalist axiology. This axiology takes goodness to be given by a double sum. First, for each time, we sum total momentary well-being at that time. Second, we perform a *weighted* sum across times, in which earlier times are in general weighted more heavily than later times (this differential weighting is the time discounting).[18]

Dasgupta then considers two types of production function. The first embodies constant returns to scale: that is, multiplying both of the inputs to production (K and N) by a common amount has the result of multiplying output by that same factor.[19] In this case, Dasgupta shows that the optimum path involves (inter alia) a constant proportional population growth rate, so that (if in addition this rate happens to be positive) population size increases exponentially, without limit (Figure 20.3).

As this last result illustrates, this "constant returns to scale" model is completely unrealistic as a model of the *global* economy, *for all time*, constrained to a finite planet. Production functions that are more realistic for large population sizes involve decreasing returns to scale.[20] For this case, Dasgupta shows that the optimum path tends to a state of constant population size N^* (Figure 20.4); the numerical value of the size in question is determined by the production function, the utility function and the discount rate.[21]

2.2.2. *Connections between the Intertemporal and Intratemporal Analyses*

Since (or insofar as) our practical interest is in the intertemporal question, the different question of which momentary state is optimal *in the purely intratemporal sense*, and thus the analysis in Section 2.1, might initially seem irrelevant. However, now that we have seen that (under certain conditions) the optimal population path tends to a constant-population steady state, it seems reasonable to conjecture that this eventual steady state

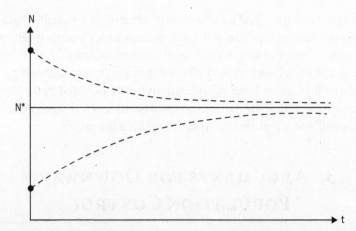

FIGURE 20.4 Optimal population paths when the production function exhibits decreasing returns to scale. In this case, there is an optimal long-run population size N^* (corresponding to the solid line); unless the initial population size happens already to coincide with this optimum, the optimal path (dotted line) is one on which population size gradually tends towards the long-run optimum.

on the optimal path will be identical to the optimal momentary state in an appropriately chosen intratemporal analysis.

If so, then many features of the intratemporal analysis will be relevant to the intertemporal case after all. In particular, it can be shown that in the optimal path's asymptotic steady state, the ratio of the average per-capita consumption rate c to the "zero well-being" consumption rate c_0 is exactly as in the fixed-resources intratemporal model discussed in Section 2.1.2 (Dasgupta 1969, 307; see also n. 15).

2.2.3 *Limitations of Dasgupta's model*

Two limitations of Dasgupta's modeling exercise are worth noting.

First: the results surveyed in Section 2.2.1 do not by themselves say anything about the *numerical value* of (in particular) the optimum long-run population size for planet Earth. As we noted, the model does yield quantitative predictions for the optimal population size *given* specifications of the production function, well-being function, and discount rate. But empirical inputs, together with reasonably complicated analysis of those inputs, are required to determine what a plausible production function might be. The contribution of the model itself is to supply conditionals of the form "*if* the production function, utility function, and discount rate are thus-and-so, *then* the optimum population trajectory is such-and-such," and (relatedly) to focus debate onto the crucial question of what the real-world production function (etc.) is (cf. n. 17).

Second: it is also unclear to what extent the simple models that Dasgupta analyses are able *even in principle* to capture the full range of considerations that are involved in real-world debates about optimum population size. As we will see below, some of those are straightforwardly economic concerns about the finitude of fixed natural inputs to production (e.g., land area), and hence are relatively straightforwardly captured by the adoption of a production function that exhibits diminishing marginal returns to scale. But others concern ways in which short-term overproduction and/or overpopulation could damage the planet, and ways in which future progress in technology might enlarge the possibilities. These latter considerations can be captured in the simple model only insofar as the quality of the environment and the state of technology can be counted as part of "capital," and it is unclear to what extent this is the case.[22]

3. ARGUMENTS FOR DOWNWARD POPULATION CONTROL

Suppose we have some model, akin to that of Section 2.2.1 or otherwise, that predicts a particular shape for the optimal population path. The crucial question for practical purposes is how the population path that we would expect history to follow under a "business as usual" scenario—that is, a scenario in which no deliberate action is taken to influence the population path in either an upward or a downward direction—relates to this optimal path. As I have noted (Section 2.2.3), the model itself does not immediately answer that question.

On this issue, the dominant concern in modern times (i) concerns population *sizes* rather than growth rates, and (ii) holds that under business as usual the population will grow too large, so that *downward* population control, in the form of deliberate attempts to reduce birth rates, is warranted.

Many commonly heard arguments for this latter conclusion presuppose that the objective is to maximize some notion of average well-being, and are therefore of limited interest to those who reject averagist population axiologies. In Sections 3.1 and 3.2, however, I will discuss two notable exceptions. In particular, the evaluative assumptions of the arguments I will discuss are consistent with totalism.[23]

3.1. Ultimate Carrying Capacity and the Threat of Increased Death Rate

The first argument appeals to the notion of carrying capacity, a concept from ecology. In simple models of population ecology, one assumes that there is simply a maximum population size (for a given species) that a given environment is physically capable of supporting. This maximum is then defined as the environment's "carrying capacity" for the species in question.[24] (There is also a more complex notion of carrying capacity that acknowledges the possibility of a population's temporarily "overshooting" its carrying capacity: carrying capacity is then defined to be as the maximum population size that can be sustained *without damaging the environment's ability to support the same species in the future*. The argument discussed here can also be couched in terms of this more complex notion.)

One possibility, then, is that human population size is in danger of crashing into the Earth's carrying capacity in this simple sense. If there is such a hard cap to population size, then any birth rate trajectory that would otherwise have taken the population above this cap must instead result in increases to the death rate. But the latter process would by highly likely to involve large amounts of suffering (via, e.g., widespread famine or war). Every plausible population axiology, including totalism, will agree that given a choice between restricting population size via restraint on the birth rate on the one hand, or restricting to the same population size via increases to the death rate along with the associated suffering, the former option is better.

This line of thought is often taken to justify calls for (1) downward population control, (2) in our lifetimes.[25] However, clearly it does not follow, from the mere fact (or claim[26]) that there is *some* limit to population size, that a "business as usual" population trajectory would reach that limit within any given timeframe. The latter depends on the quantitative details of (i) what the carrying capacity is, and (ii) what the "business as usual" population trajectory is. We take up these two issues in turn.

First, then: many authors have attempted to estimate the Earth's carrying capacity for humans. A notable feature of this literature, however, is the lack of anything approaching consensus. Cohen (1995, Ch. 11 and Appendix 3), for instance, surveys sixty-five such estimates, half of which lie in the range 5–14 billion, but a further third of which are above 20 billion.

This spread of estimates would be less significant if, as is sometimes assumed, the "business as usual" trajectory were one of never-ending exponential population increase. This assumption was reasonable in the 1960s, since the history of population size up to that time did indeed follow a pattern of exponential-like population growth, in particular since the onset of the industrial revolution (Figure 20.5a). And it is easy to see how that assumption led to neo-Malthusian alarm. For example, if population had continued to grow from its 1965 level at 2 percent per annum, the population size in 2100 and 2200 would have been (respectively) 48 billion and 350 billion. These figures are higher than all but 10 (respectively, all but 4) of the sixty-five estimates surveyed by Cohen. *If* this were the business as usual scenario, then—given the time delays involved in altering population size via birth rate reduction, and assuming that at least the upper estimates in Cohen's survey are not too conservative—it would indeed seem sensible to start population-reduction measures now.

This, however, leads us to the second issue. As is now well recognized, plausible "business as usual" population trajectories are not ones of constant-rate exponential growth; the 1960s growth rate of 2 percent per annum turned out to be a high point. Worldwide, the population growth rate steadily decreased during the period 1970–2015, reaching 1.2 percent per annum by 2015 (Figure 20.5b).

Historical data and future estimates regarding fertility rates are perhaps still more revealing. First, a definition: The *net reproduction rate* (NRR), for a given region A at a given time t, is the average number of daughters a woman would bear over the course of

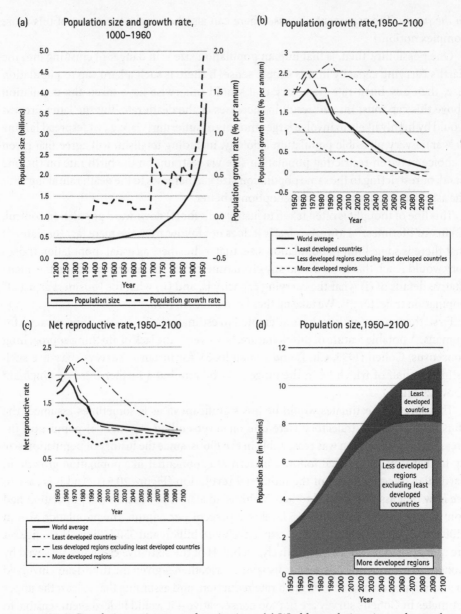

FIGURE 20.5 Population estimates and projections. (a) World population size and growth rate 1200–1960. (b) Population growth rate, 1950–2100. (c) Net reproduction rate (NRR), 1950–2100. (d) Population size, 1950–2100.

Source for Figure 20.5a: PBL Netherlands Environmental Assessment Agency, 2010.
Source for Figures 20.5b–d: United Nations, 2017.

her life if at every age, she bore the number of daughters that was average for women of that age across A at t, and was subject to the mortality rate for women of that age in A at t. A constant NRR of one, therefore, corresponds to a situation in which each generation of women exactly replaces itself in terms of numbers, and therefore leads eventually to constant population size, if fertility and mortality rates remain unchanged. Of course, if a country has a preponderance of younger over older people (as is typical in less developed countries), population will tend to increase for several decades even if the NRR is one, as new babies are born to reproductive-age couples faster than people die; this is (one aspect of) the phenomenon of "population momentum."[27]

As for the data: the worldwide NRR fell from 1.7 to 1.1 over the period 1960–2015, and the NRR for more developed regions fell over the same period from 1.2 to 0.8 (Figure 20.5c). These data suggest that a correct extrapolation of "current trends" into the future would see world population stabilize and even decline within a few generations. This suggestion indeed seems to be borne out by the UN's latest population projections, according to which worldwide population size is near-stabilized by 2100 (Figure 20.5d). On these projections, the average worldwide growth rate will have fallen to 0.1 percent by 2100, with the average growth rate excluding the least developed countries negative by that date (Figure 20.5b).[28]

These data and predictions are also readily comprehensible from a theoretical perspective. The theory of the demographic transition holds that as a country modernizes, its death rate falls before a corresponding fall in the birth rate. This predicts and explains high population growth rates *for a limited period of time* during the transition, but it does not predict that those growth rates will continue indefinitely (see, for example, Weeks 2008, 81–91).

For our purposes, the key upshot of all this is that it is not at all clear that there would be any collision between population trajectory and carrying capacity, even without deliberate downward population control, given the actual demographic trends.

To be clear: I am not asserting that there is *no* danger of such a collision. My claim is only that for such collision to be a high-probability prospect any time at all soon, carrying capacity would need to be at the lower end of the range of extant estimates. Therefore, the case for urgent action cannot be made without tangling with the details of those estimates. In particular, we should then note that many of the more conservative estimates tend to be relatively pessimistic about technical progress, assuming that key variables (such as food production per unit land area, or population density) cannot conceivably rise more than a few times their actual values at the author's time of writing, while technological optimists dispute this.[29]

3.2 Short-Term Overpopulation, Environmental Degradation, and Long-Term Carrying Capacity

The second totalist-compatible argument for population reduction I will survey appeals to the idea that too high a population in the short to medium term might be myopic. More precisely: recall that the totalist seeks to maximize total welfare *across all time*, and not merely total welfare *now* or *during the next generation*. As a result, anything that significantly reduces either future carrying capacity, or future average well-being (or both), is likely to be of negative value on balance by totalist lights, even if it increases the total amount of welfare realized during (say) the next thirty years.

The claim then is that under a "business as usual" path, population sizes will soon be (or perhaps already are) above the level that would optimize the combination of future carrying capacity and/or future average well-being, for reasons of environmental degradation.[30]

The key objection to this claim (and, more generally, to any claim that environmental degradation due to high population is an indicator that the population size is "in overshoot" *and therefore above optimal*) involves the "Boserupian account of innovation."

To understand this account, note first that (as all discussants agree) carrying capacity *for humans* is not a time-invariant matter: it is relative to level of technological sophistication, and therefore tends to rise over time. Throughout recent(ish) history, for instance, carrying capacity has increased dramatically as, for example, food production systems have become vastly more sophisticated.

The key question then is the direction of causation between population increase and technological progress, at each stage of this process.

According to those who advocate limiting population at any given time to carrying capacity at that time—that is, avoiding "overshoot"—the relevant technological developments have exogenous causes, and merely permit an otherwise-temporary population increase to become permanent. If that were true, the optimal strategy would presumably be to wait for the developments in question to occur, and *only then* to increase population towards the new, higher carrying capacity.

According to Boserupians, in contrast, necessity is the mother of invention: it is precisely the problems involved in temporary overshoot that *cause* a community to develop and/or adopt more sophisticated technologies, thus raising the carrying capacity to something above the existing population size. Boserup (1976) argues convincingly for this latter direction of causation in the case of the history of agriculture in Europe, from hunter-gatherer systems capable of sustaining only very low population densities, through to advanced agricultural systems supporting cities.[31]

Note that a Boserupian account of innovation would not support *ignoring* concerns about sustainability, and simply allowing population to increase *without giving any thought to* the resulting overshoots. That course would indeed lead to population crashes post-overshoot, and also would involve lesser technological progress. What the Boserupian account does suggest (though) is that it would in general be a mistake to infer, from environmental degradation, that deliberate population control is the best response, so as to keep population within the existing carrying capacity. Had the agriculturalists of Europe taken that latter course, we might still have the agricultural systems, lifestyles and population densities of 4500BC; we would surgically have removed the spur to progress, rather than progressing. According to the Boserupian account, then, in general one *expects* to encounter temporary overshoot and related problems of environmental degradation, as part of the natural course of things *on even the optimal trajectory*.

Inter alia, the Boserupian theory, insofar as it is correct, threatens to undermine the argument for population reduction with which I began this section, as follows. It may be true that for reasons of environmental degradation, higher short-term populations would, *other things being equal*, reduce long-term total well-being. But, according to the Boserupian theory, other relevant things would not be equal: the higher short-term population would accelerate technological progress in ways that tend to increase carrying capacity, and this latter effect may more than offset any decrease in carrying capacity due to environmental degradation.

I say only "*threatens* to undermine," and "*may* more than offset." Which of the two factors (environmental degradation or overshoot-fuelled technological progress) is more significant in a given case depends both on how serious the environmental degradation is, and on how great the prospects for technological improvement are. On the latter question in particular, as I noted above, there is a wide range of views, with optimists inclined to think that plausible technological development will easily increase carrying capacity enough to keep pace with business-as-usual population growth, and pessimists taking the opposite view. Since this disagreement in general concerns credences regarding progress from technological developments whose details are not yet envisaged, it seems to be largely a matter of differences in intellectual temperament, and somewhat intractable to resolve by appeal to hard evidence and/or rational argument.[32]

4. SUMMARY

This chapter has examined the question of optimum population size and (relatedly) whether a "business as usual" trajectory would take us above or below the optimal population-size path. These questions are decision-relevant not only for population policies whose explicit aim is to influence the population size, but also for the many other policies that foreseeably affect population size.

Which population size is optimal (under given empirical conditions) clearly depends on which population axiology is correct. In this chapter, for the most part I have restricted attention to the implications of a totalist axiology.

Section 2 surveyed abstract economic models, first of optimum population size in a purely intratemporal sense (Section 2.1), and then of the optimum population path through time (Section 2.2), given a simple model of how population size at one time affects the background conditions at later times. While highly abstract, these models allow us to represent, inter alia, the ideas that most resources for consumption are in some relevant sense produced by people, that production typically exhibits diminishing returns to scale at sufficiently large population sizes, and that saving at earlier times facilitates supporting a larger population at later times. The most sophisticated such model I surveyed, that of Dasgupta (1969), suggests an optimal population path that gradually tends to some finite asymptote, presumably interpretable as the optimal population size from an intratemporal perspective, given optimal capital stocks, and once all possible technological progress has taken place. While Dasgupta's model does not involve any explicit representation of the state of the environment or technological progress—two matters that are key to the more applied discussion of optimum population in the twentieth and twenty-first centuries—it is perhaps a close enough approximation to be helpful in organizing thoughts. What no such abstract model can do, by itself, is supply quantitative answers to questions about optimal population size, since the models quite appropriately contain several free parameters.

In Section 3, I surveyed two of the more important arguments for the claim that deliberate attempts to reduce the birth rate are warranted because the population trajectory under a "business as usual" scenario is (now and/or in the near future) above the optimal population path. One distinctive feature of these arguments—and one reason I have singled them out as being among the more important—is that, in terms of population-axiological assumptions, these arguments are compatible even with totalism. The first argument centers around the idea that a "business as usual" trajectory is on a collision course with carrying capacity, so that we face a simple choice between reducing the birth rate or experiencing an increase in the death rate. The second centers around the idea that overpopulation in the short term is reducing the Earth's long-term carrying capacity.

I found both arguments to be far from conclusive. In reply to the first argument, I noted that (i) a plausible "business as usual" population path is not one of constant-rate exponential growth, but rather has population growth rates dropping to near-zero, or even below zero, within a few generations; (ii) it is not at all clear that the relevant carrying capacity, taking into account plausible technological progress, will be low enough at any point in time to collide with these more plausible population paths. In response to the second, I noted that the Boserupian account of innovation explains why some degree of population overshoot and environmental degradation would be expected even on the optimal population path, and why it might be that even if overshoot-induced environmental degradation reduces future carrying capacity *other things being equal*, it might increase future carrying capacity *in fact*.

In both cases, my conclusion is only that it is *unclear* whether or not a business as usual trajectory would take population sizes above the optimal path (in significant part, because it is unclear what degree of technological optimism vs. pessimism is appropriate). I therefore close with the cliché that resolution of this question (if possible at all) would require further careful, unbiased research. The cliché is however perhaps more interesting than usual, since most participants in the population debate either take it to be obvious that business as usual would involve above-optimum population sizes, or regard public discussion of optimum population size as morally inappropriate.

ACKNOWLEDGMENTS

Funding from Riksbankens Jubileumsfond (grant M17-0372:1) is gratefully acknowledged.

Notes

1. As is standard in the literature on population axiology, I will discuss only betterness *with respect to welfare*, without denying (or affirming) that non-welfarist considerations may also be relevant to all-things-considered betterness.

2. This is worth emphasizing, since it goes against a consensus that prevailed for a sustained period following the 1994 Cairo Conference on Population and Development. During this period, discussion of deliberate attempts to *influence* (rather than respond to) population size was somewhat taboo (Coole 2013, Section 5). More recently, however, official governmental and intergovernmental documents have once again begun to countenance taking action to influence population sizes.

    Coercive population control is criticized by, for example, Dixon-Mueller (1993) and by Echegaray and Saperstein (2010). It is defended by Hardin (1968; 1974). Warwick (1990) and Cohen (1995) offer relatively neutral discussions of the variety of possible population-control measures. For the politics and content of the "Cairo Consensus" in general, see, for example, Halfon (2007).

3. See Cohen (1995, 5–8) for a brief historical sketch. Post-1900, concerns about under-population due to falling birth rates, at either the global or national level, are expressed by, for example, Carr-Saunders 1935; Charles 1936; Harrod 1939; Lorimer, Winston, and Kiser 1940 (cited by Gottlieb 1945). For related reasons, explicitly pro-natalist population policies have been adopted in recent decades in several developed countries (Kramer 2014). Ord (2012) is agnostic.

4. Often two or more of these concerns are interlinked: for example, overpopulation might lead to political instability *because* it first leads to diminished well-being and/or environmental degradation. For such relatively broad discussions, see, for example, Ehrlich (1971); Keynes (1919); Meadows (1972); US National Security Council (1974). Specifically on political instability, see, for example, Homer-Dixon and Blitt (1998); Robertson (2012, Ch. 4). On climate change, see, for example, Bongaarts (1992); Casey and Galor (2017); O'Neill (2000); O'Neill et al. (2010); O'Neill et al. (2012); Spears (2015).

5. The other reasons (besides simplicity) are: (1) the dominant neo-Malthusian concerns are primarily about static rather than dynamic issues; (2) from a long-run point of view the static considerations are arguably more significant (Gottlieb 1945, Section IV). Kolk (this volume) includes more discussion of dynamic considerations.

6. Since the topic is the number of people alive at a given time, rather than the number of people who ever live, we might more strictly label the topic *momentary* population size, rather than population size *simpliciter*. I will use the unqualified term throughout for elegance of exposition.

7. At least for the sake of conceptual clarity, it seems worthwhile to recognize these results. One might however be skeptical of the usefulness *in practice* of the concept of optimum population, given the complicated dependence on background variables. Gottlieb (1945) discusses (and rejects) this skepticism.

8. The relationship between population size and momentary average well-being is discussed at greater length by Kolk (this volume).

9. The early economic literature on the theory of optimum population almost universally assumes momentary averagism (Cannan 1918, Ch. 4; Cannan 1929, 81; Gottlieb 1945; Robbins 2003; Wicksell 1979, 146; Wolfe 1926, 93; 1936, 246). Totalism is recognized and

explicitly advocated by Sidgwick (1907, 415–416); its application in economic models is developed by Meade (1955, Ch. 6) and Dasgupta (1969).

10. More precisely: provided the well-being scale has the Archimedean property. See, for example, Carlson (2007, 4; 2018, sections 3 and 4); Thomas (2018, esp. Section 6).

11. It is far from obvious that the notion of consumption is flexible enough to accommodate all determinants of well-being. Be this as it may, for tractability (and following standard practice in economics), in this chapter I simply press ahead with developing a simple model based on the assumption that well-being depends on "consumption" alone.

    The function I write $w(c)$ is akin to what economists would call a "utility function," and would normally write $u(c)$. However, the term "utility" is often taken to mean specifically a representation of *preferences*, rather than of what is *good* for the individual. Since the two can (arguably) come apart and our interest here is in the latter, I stick to the terminology of "well-being" rather than "utility."

12. This is intuitive: in any unequal arrangement, one could increase total (and average) well-being by transferring a sufficiently small quantity of resources from a richer to a poorer individual, since the amount of well-being lost by the richer individual would (given the above assumptions) be smaller than the amount of well-being gained by the poorer person.

13. This question of optimal population size given fixed total resources, identical individual well-being functions that depend on consumption only, and no intertemporal considerations is what Blackorby, Bossert, and Donaldson (2005, 287) term the "pure population problem."

14. Here I assume that population size can be modeled by a continuous parameter. This is a good approximation at large population sizes.

15. In more detail: for example, to bring c_0 closer to zero while holding c^*_{tot} fixed, given our other assumptions about the shape of the utility function, we would have to put something akin to a "kink" in the graph of $u(c)$ at or close to c_0.

    If we assume (as is common in the economics literature) a well-being function of the "isoelastic" or "constant relative risk aversion" form $w(c) = \frac{c^{1-\eta}}{1-\eta} + \alpha$, then we can say something more precise: the relationship between c^*_{tot} and c_0 is then given by $c^*_{tot} = \eta^{\frac{1}{\eta-1}} c_0$. Since the coefficient $\eta^{\frac{1}{\eta-1}}$ takes on values between 1.5 and 2.25 for values of η in the plausible range 1.5-4, this supports the conclusion that c^*_{tot} cannot be many times higher than c_0.

16. In symbols, and again assuming a continuous model (cf. fn. 14), the condition is that $w\left(\frac{F(N)}{N}\right) = w'\left(\frac{F(N)}{N}\right)\left(\frac{F(N)}{N} - \frac{d}{dN}F(N)\right)$. Dasgupta (1969) dubs this formula "The Meade rule," crediting Meade (1955) with the reasoning behind it.

17. The numbers can of course be crunched for particular specifications of the production and utility functions, but the results are not especially illuminating. For example, if $w(c) = Pc^{0.5} - R$ and $F(N) = QN^{0.5}$ (where P, Q, and R are real-valued constants), the optimum population N^* is given by $N^* = \left(\frac{3PQ^{0.5}}{4R}\right)^4$. If the values of P, Q, and R happen to be such that $\frac{PQ^{0.5}}{R} = 6300$ (respectively, 420, 70, 11), this gives an optimum population of around 500 trillion (respectively, 10 billion, 8 million, 5 thousand).

18. In symbols, assuming that at each time there is perfect interpersonal equality of consumption, this amounts to: $V^\rho_{tot} = \int dt \cdot e^{-\rho t} \cdot N(t) \cdot w\left(\frac{C(t)}{N(t)}\right)$, where ρ is the discount rate on well-being. In the special case when $\rho=0$, this reduces to the undiscounted totalist formula $V_{tot} = \int dt \cdot N(t) \cdot w\left(\frac{C(t)}{N(t)}\right)$.

    A non-zero discount rate on future well-being is controversial (see, for example, Greaves 2017, Section 7, and references therein). In its defense in the present context, the following two points are worth noting. (1) The assumption is made mainly for mathematical tractability. One can gain illumination on the undiscounted case by considering the more general discounted case first, and then considering the limit $\rho \to 0$. (2) A small discount rate can be used (within an expected value approach) to account for possibilities of extinction, so that employing a discounted value function need not involve the arguably objectionable assumption that future well-being intrinsically matters less (Dasgupta 1969, 308; Stern 2007, 46–47).

19. In symbols: $F(mK, mN) = mF(K, N)$.

20. That is to say, multiplying both of the inputs to production (K and L) by a common amount has the result of multiplying output by *less* than that factor: $F(mK, mL) < mF(K, L)$.

21. In the interests of brevity, my report of Dasgupta's results omits a number of subtleties. For the full details, see Dasgupta (1969), especially theorems 2.3 and 3.3 and surrounding discussion.

22. The literature on growth theory contains various more disaggregated models, including many that explicitly model technical progress (as in the Solow and Ramsey-Cass-Koopmans models—see, for example, Romer (2012, Chs. 1 and 2)), and some that explicitly represent various factors of environment quality separately from produced capital (Freeman, Herriges and Kling 2014, Chs. 4 and 8). But, as far as I know, no such model has been applied to the question of optimum population.

23. Note that totalist-compatible arguments for downward population control are of quite general interest, since totalism tends to favor larger population sizes than any other seriously proposed population axiology.

24. See the discussion of "the logistic equation" in, for example, Vandermeer and Goldberg (2013, Ch. 1, esp. 16). This equation is a reasonably good fit to population dynamics in artificial environments for some non-human species, for example, the growth of in vitro bacteria cultures (Vandermeer 1969).

   Dhondt (1988) is a helpful review of the multiplicity of ways in which "carrying capacity" can be and has been defined. Pulliom and Haddad (1994) focus on the application to human populations in particular.

25. Witness, for example, Population Matters (2016): "Indefinite population growth being physically impossible, it must stop at some point: either sooner, through fewer births by contraception and humane, pro-active population policy; or later, through more deaths by famine, disease, war, or environmental collapse; or some combination of these."

26. Most commentators accept this relatively modest claim. A notable apparent exception is Julian Simon (1998, e.g. 580–581). Elsewhere in the same publication, however, Simon sums up his own claim as being (merely) that "there is no *known* ultimate limit to population growth" (ibid., 78; emphasis added).

27. See Weeks (2008, Ch. 6) for more discussion of the concept of the net reproductive rate and related fertility measures. On population momentum, see ibid. 339–340.

28. Data for the periods 1950–2015 and 2015–2100 are from the UN's historical estimates and "medium variant" projection respectively (United Nations 2017). The "more developed regions" are stipulated to be all of Europe and North America, plus Australia, New Zealand, and Japan. The "least developed countries" are stipulated to be a particular subset of countries outside those regions (ibid., p. vii). Another helpful overview of the relevant demographic facts is Roser, Ritchie, and Ortiz-Ospina (2013).

29. For concreteness, here is one example. Meadows et al. (1972, figure 10) assume a maximum conceivable food productivity per unit land area of four times the average at their time of

writing, leading to a minimum requirement of 0.1 hectares of arable land per person fed. Simon (1998, 100–101), writing twenty-six years later, reports an (actual) example of high-tech commercially viable farming producing enough food for 500–1000 people per 0.4 hectares, that is, 125–250 times the cap assumed by Meadows et al.

30. This argument is hinted at by (for example) Population Matters, who write: "Environmental degradation, including climate change and resource depletion, is steadily reducing the number of people the Earth can indefinitely sustain" (2016).

31. It is easy to see how the Boserupian mechanism can be mediated by economic incentives: as a resource becomes more scarce, its price rises. This generates powerful incentives, both for producers and consumers, to shift towards usage patterns that are more efficient with respect to use of the scarce resource.

    More recently, the Boserupian perspective is advocated in particular by Julian Simon, who writes for example that "high fertility leads to resource problems which then lead to solutions to the problems *which usually leave humanity better off than if the problems had not arisen*" (1998, 75–76; emphasis added).

32. This dispute at times degenerates into interdisciplinary mud-slinging. For example, responding to the suggestion that technological progress will render present trends of increase in both standards of living and population consistent with carrying capacity, pessimists Daily and Ehrlich remark that "this assertion represents a level of optimism held primarily by non-scientists" (1992, 763); it is clear from the context that the intended implication is derogatory. Optimist Julian Simon (1998) responds that scientists who are experts in the closest-to-relevant field often tend to be peculiarly ill-placed to estimate future progress, as their expertise in present technological limits psychologically blinds them to the possibility of the as-yet-unthinkable.

References

Blackorby, Charles, Walter Bossert, and David Donaldson. 2005. *Population Issues in Social Choice Theory, Welfare Economics, and Ethics*. Cambridge: Cambridge University Press.

Bongaarts, John. 1992. "Population Growth and Global Warming." *Population and Development Review*, 18, no. 2: 299–319.

Boserup, Ester. 1976. "Environment, Population, and Technology in Primitive Societies." *Population and Development Review* 2, no. 1: 21–36.

Bradley, Ben. 2016. "Well–Being at a Time." *Philosophical Exchange* 45, no. 1: 1–13.

Bramble, Ben. 2018. *The Passing of Temporal Well-Being*. London: Routledge.

Brink, David O. 1997. "Rational Egoism and the Separateness of Persons." In *Reading Parfit*, edited by Jonathan Dancy, 96–134. Oxford: Blackwell.

Broome, John. 2004. *Weighing Lives*. Oxford: Oxford University Press.

Bykvist, Krister. 2015. "Value and Time." In *The Oxford Handbook of Value Theory*, edited by Iwao Hirose and Jonas Olson, 118–135. New York: Oxford University Press.

Cannan, Edwin. 1918. *Wealth: A Brief Explanation of the Causes of Economic Welfare*. London: P. S. King.

Cannan, Edwin. 1929. *A Review of Economic Theory*. London: P. S. King.

Carr-Saunders, Alexander M. 1935. *Eugenics in the Light of Population Trends: The Galton Lecture delivered before the Eugenics Society on February 16th, 1935*. Published in *The Eugenics Review* 27, no. 1: 11–20.

Carlson, Erik. 2007. "Higher Values and Non-Archimedean Additivity." *Theoria* 73, no. 1: 3–27.

Casey, Gregory and Oded Galor. 2017. "Is Faster Economic Growth Compatible with Reductions in Carbon Emissions? The Role of Diminished Population Growth." *Environmental Research Letters* 12, no. 1: 1–8.

Charles, Enid. 1936. *The Menace of Under-Population: A Biological Study of the Decline of Population Growth.* London: Watts & Co.

Cohen, Joel E. 1995. *How Many People Can the Earth Support?* New York and London: Norton.

Coole, Diana. 2013. "Too Many Bodies? The Return and Disavowal of the Population Question." *Environmental Politics* 22, no. 2: 195–215.

Daily, Gretchen C., and Paul R. Ehrlich. 1992. "Population, Sustainability, and Earth's Carrying Capacity." *BioScience* 42, no. 10: 761–771.

Dasgupta, Partha. 1969. "On the Concept of Optimum Population." *The Review of Economic Studies* 36, no. 3: 295–318.

Dhondt, André A. 1988. "Carrying Capacity: A Confusing Concept." *Acta Oecologica* 9, no. 4: 337–346.

Dixon-Mueller, Ruth. 1993. *Population Policy and Women's Rights: Transforming Reproductive Choice.* Westport, CT and London: Praeger.

Echegaray, Jacqueline Nolley and Shira Saperstein. 2010. "Reproductive Rights are Human Rights." In *A Pivotal Moment: Population, Justice, and the Environmental Challenge*, edited by Laurei Mazur, 341–352. Washington, DC: Island Press.

Ehrlich, Paul R. 1971. *The Population Bomb.* Cutchogue, NY: Buccaneer Books.

Freeman, A. Myrick., Joseph A. Herriges, and Catherine L. Kling, 2014. *The Measurement of Environmental and Resource Values.* Oxford: RFF Press.

Gottlieb, Manuel. 1945. "The Theory of Optimum Population for a Closed Economy." *Journal of Political Economy* 53, no. 4: 289–316.

Greaves, Hilary. 2017. "Population Axiology." *Philosophy Compass* 12, no. 11. doi:10.1111/phc3.12442

Halfon, Saul. 2007. *The Cairo Consensus: Demographic Surveys, Women's Empowerment, and Regime Change in Population Policy.* Lanham, MD: Lexington Books.

Hardin, Garrett. 1968. "The Tragedy of the Commons." *Science* 162, no. 3859: 1243–1248.

Hardin, Garrett. 1974. "Living on a Lifeboat." *BioScience* 24, no. 10: 561–568.

Harrod, Roy F. 1939. "Modern Population Trends." *The Manchester School of Economic and Social Studies* 10: 1–20.

Homer-Dixon, Thomas and Jessica Blitt. 1998. *Ecoviolence: Links Among Environment, Population and Security.* Lanham, MD and Oxford: Rowman & Littlefield.

Huemer, Michael. 2008. "In Defence of Repugnance." *Mind* 117, no. 468: 899–933.

Keynes, John Maynard. 1919. *The Economic Consequences of the Peace.* London: Macmillan.

Kramer, Steven Philip. 2014. *The Other Population Crisis: What Governments Can Do about Falling Birth Rates.* Baltimore, MD: John Hopkins University Press.

Lorimer, Frank, Ellen Winston, and Louise K. Kiser. 1940. *Foundations of American Population Policy.* New York and London: Harper.

Meade, James E. 1955. *Trade and Welfare.* London: Oxford University Press.

Meadows, Donella H., Dennis L. Meadows, Jørgen Randers, and William W. Behrens. 1972. *The Limits to Growth: A Report for the Club of Rome's Project on the Predicament of Mankind.* New York: Universe Books.

O'Neill, Brian C. 2000. "Cairo and Climate Change: A Win-Win Opportunity." *Global Environmental Change* 10, no. 2: 93–96.

O'Neill, Brian C., Michael Dalton, Regina Fuchs, Leiwen Jiang, Shonali Pachauri, and Katarina Zigova. 2010. "Global Demographic Trends and Future Carbon Emissions." *Proceedings of the National Academy of Sciences* 107, no. 41: 17521–17526.

O'Neill, Brian C., Brant Liddle, Leiwen Jiang, Kirk R. Smith, Shonali Pachauri, Michael Dalton, and Regina Fuchs. 2012. "Demographic Change and Carbon Dioxide Emissions." *The Lancet* 380, no. 9837: 157–164.

Ord, Toby. 2014. "Overpopulation or Underpopulation?" In *Is the Planet Full?*, edited by Ian Goldin, 46–60. Oxford: Oxford University Press.

Parfit, Derek. 1984. *Reasons and Persons*. Oxford: Clarendon Press.

PBL Netherlands Environmental Assessment Agency. 2010. *History Database of the Global Environment: Basic driving factors: Population*, http://themasites.pbl.nl/tridion/en/themasites/hyde/basicdrivingfactors/population/index-2.html.

Population Matters. 2016. "Population Policy and the Environment: Joint International Position Statement," https://www.populationmatters.org/documents/position_statement.pdf.

Pulliom, H. Ronald and Nick M. Haddad. 1994. "Address of the Past President: Human Population Growth and the Carrying Capacity Concept." *Bulletin of the Ecological Society of America* 75, no. 3: 141–157.

Purves, Duncan 2017. "Desire Satisfaction, Death, and Time." *Canadian Journal of Philosophy* 47, no. 6: 799–819.

Robbins, Lionel. 2003. "The Optimum Theory of Population." In *London Essays in Economics: In Honour of Edwin Cannan*, edited by Hugh Dalton and T. E. Gregory, 103–136. London: Routledge.

Robertson, Thomas. 2012. *The Malthusian Moment: Global Population Growth and the Birth of American Environmentalism*. New Brunswick and London: Rutgers University Press.

Romer, David. 2012. *Advanced Macroeconomics*. 4th ed. New York: McGraw-Hill.

Roser, Max, Hannah Ritchie, and Esteban Ortiz-Ospina. 2013. "World Population Growth." *Our World in Data*, https://ourworldindata.org/world-population-growth.

Royal Society. 2012. *People and the Planet*. London: Royal Society Science Policy Centre.

Sidgwick, Henry. 1907. *The Methods of Ethics*. 7th ed. London: Macmillan.

Simon, Julian. 1998. *The Ultimate Resource 2*. Rev. ed. Princeton, NJ: Princeton University Press.

Spears, Dean. 2015. "Smaller Human Population in 2100 Could Importantly Reduce the Risk of Climate Catastrophe." *Proceedings of the National Academy of Sciences* 112, no. 18: E2270.

Stern, Nicholas. 2007. *The Economics of Climate Change: The Stern Review*. Cambridge: Cambridge University Press.

United Nations, Department of Economic and Social Affairs, Population Division. 2017. *World Population Prospects: The 2017 Revision*, vol. 1: *Comprehensive Tables*. ST/ESA/SER.A/399.

UNFPA 2012. *Population Matters for Sustainable Development*. New York.

UNFPA 2013. *Population Dynamics in the Post-2015 Development Agenda*. New York.

Union of Concerned Scientists. 1992. "World Scientists' Warning to Humanity," https://www.ucsusa.org/sites/default/files/attach/2017/11/World%20Scientists%27%20Warning%20to%20Humanity%201992.pdf.

US National Security Council. 1974. *National Security Study Memorandum 200*. Available at https://www.nixonlibrary.gov/virtuallibrary/documents/nssm/nssm_200.pdf.

Vandermeer, John H. 1969. "The Competitive Structure of Communities: An Experimental Approach with Protozoa." *Ecology* 50, no. 3: 362–371.

Vandermeer, John H. and Deborah Goldberg. 2013. *Population Ecology: First Principles*. 2nd ed. Princeton, NJ: Princeton University Press.

Warwick, Donald P. 1990. "The Ethics of Population Control." In *Population Policy: Contemporary Issues*, edited by Godfrey Roberts, 21–37. New York; London: Praeger.

Weeks, John R. 2008. *Population: An Introduction to Concepts and Issues*. Belmont: Thomson Wadsworth.

Wicksell Knut. 1979. "The Theory of Population, Its Composition and Changes." In *The Theoretical Contributions of Knut Wicksell*, edited by Steinar Strøm and Björn Thalberg, 123–151. London: Macmillan.

Wolfe, Albert B. 1926. "The Optimum Size of Population." In *The Evolution of Population Theory*, edited by Johannes Overbeek, 90–97 Westport, CT: Greenwood Press, 1977.

Wolfe, Albert B. 1936. "The Theory of Optimum Population." *The Annals of the American Academy of Political and Social Science* 188, no. 1: 243–249.

CHAPTER 21

DEMOGRAPHIC THEORY AND POPULATION ETHICS

MARTIN KOLK

1. INTRODUCTION

POPULATION ethics is concerned with demography in the sense that the analytical objects of interest are populations.[1] However, demographic theory, which explores theoretically when, how, and why populations grow, based on empirically observed patterns, has until now played only a minor role in population ethics. Similarly, debates about population dynamics among demographers have seldom been concerned with ideas and concepts in population ethics.

In this chapter, I will give a brief outline of how population size, population growth, and welfare mutually affect each other. I will discuss how population growth responds to welfare, as welfare is an important concept in population ethics. I will discuss population homeostasis (the dynamics of a system which maintains a population at a steady population size), with a focus on resource dependent homeostatic mechanisms. I will discuss both negative relationships between population size and welfare, and refer to such relationships as "Malthusian" (after Thomas Malthus), and positive relationships between population size and welfare and refer to them as "Boserupian" (after the economist Ester Boserup). I will then consider four implications of population homeostasis for population ethics. First, Malthusian assumptions about average welfare declining with increasing population size are sometimes implicit in the population ethics discourse, and ethicists may want to explore alternative assumptions, one of which I shall discuss in detail below.[2] Second, a nuanced understanding of demographic theory may help to understand if the imagined scenarios featured in thought experiments commonly used in the arguments presented by population ethicists are unlikely, or even nearly impossible empirically. If an ethical theory produces paradoxes and implausible conclusions that are unlikely given demographic theory, they may be less of a concern (both practically and theoretically) than other implications that are empirically more likely given demographic theory. Third, demographic theory suggests that human extinction from gradual processes is highly unlikely, and that therefore those concerned with mitigating extinction risk should consider focusing on risks from sudden discrete events. Fourth, demographic theory may also inform population ethicists if certain population scenarios are plausible only in the short term, or if they are plausible over longer time scales. One type of scenario that I will consider in this area, and that has been a topic of concern among some population ethicists, involves increasing intergenerational inequality (Arrhenius and Mosquera forthcoming; Caney 2014). Finally, I will discuss demographic theory in relation to historical and future demographic change.

Before proceeding, it will be useful to set out some background assumptions. One important assumption concerns my use of the term "welfare." Although an individual's welfare is arguably not the same as her living standard or the wage that she earns, for the purpose of my discussion I will use the average wage, or living standard, in the population as a proxy for average welfare. An individual's resources are predictive of individual behavior, and as such have explanatory power for a demographic system (for example the theoretical relationships described in this chapter). However, unlike average welfare, total welfare (the product of average welfare and population size) is not a dimension that explains why individuals in a society act the way they do, at least for the models that I will discuss. Thus, in this chapter I will focus mostly on the average welfare of a population, and how it relates to population size and population growth.

I will assume that the populations in my examples are homogenous in the sense that the average welfare (wage, living standard) is the same as the welfare (wage, living standard) of any individual in the population. Throughout this chapter, the time perspective will be comparatively large and encompass multiple generations of humans. When I use the term "long-term" I refer to at least 3 or more generations, a longer perspective than what is assumed in most governmental and scientific projections of population size. The determinants of population growth, mortality, and fertility in a shorter time perspective are different and are not the focus of this chapter.

Finally, it is important to note that demographic theory is descriptive, not normative or evaluative. It is concerned with empirical phenomena such as births and deaths that are easy to measure and define across widely different contexts and times. It is concerned with describing populations as systems in which population change and population size are endogenously related, and finding empirical patterns in how and why populations change. Population equilibriums in demographic theory are therefore different from calculations of optimal population size, which are explicitly evaluative, and which usually aim to find the population size that maximizes (either average or total) welfare.[3] However, demographic theory may still be used to inform population ethics. For example, inquiries into optimal population size at a time, as well as projections of cumulative welfare across a large number of generations, will (assuming certain real-world constraints) have to make assumptions about how population size at a time is related to welfare, how welfare is related to population growth, and how population size at a time is related to population growth at later times. Demographic theory can help inform these assumptions.

2. Exponential Growth, Economic Demography and Population Homeostasis

A fundamental characteristic of human populations is that they grow and decline exponentially. This creates the potential for very quick growth and decline over multiple generations. Most populations will, given favourable circumstances, quickly expand at such a quick rate that when one shifts to a longer time perspective, there must be some other factor (e.g., shortage of resources, or an awareness that the population needs to be regulated) holding back growth. For example, the French-speaking population in Quebec had population growth rates from natural growth of around 2 percent for several centuries that increased the population several hundred times starting from the seventeenth century (Charbonneau et al. 2000).[4]

That population size eventually stabilizes after a period of growth is a phenomenon that is repeatedly observed in both animal and human populations. This realization goes back to Malthus and served as inspiration for what Darwin called the "struggle for existence." Like exponential growth, *negative* exponential growth is also powerful in that it can decrease population very quickly. Even a population in which no individual ever dies would quickly stop increasing if each woman gave birth to less than two children over her (infinite) life, as each new generation would be smaller than the previous one.[5] For example, a population in which each woman gives birth to only one child would stabilize at twice the original size in a population where there are no deaths.[6]

Any fast-growing human population will stop growing rapidly at some point due to the nature of exponential growth. A world population growth rate of 2.2 percent was observed in the 1960s. If this rate were held constant for a population (such as Earth's) for 500 years, the population would be 53,143 times larger than at the beginning of the 500-year period.[7] Clearly, this would not *actually* happen. Although populations can sustain such growth over the short term, such growth rates inevitably come to an end. A useful interpretation of the demographic transition, the shift from a high fertility-high mortality society, to a society with reduced mortality and consequently high population growth, to a low fertility-low mortality society, can be seen as an inescapable outcome of a process in which exogenous factors such as improved technology reduce mortality permanently. The demographic transition is then a (homeostatic) way for a society to regain population balance and escape unsustainable population growth (Wilson and Airey, 1999). A demography theorist's definition of "overpopulation" can be said to be the population size for which population growth turns negative.

In a homeostatic population model, population growth must be related in some way to population size. That populations are bounded by available resources and that human population growth is positive when resources are abundant and negative when resources are scarce were key insights of Malthus in the eighteenth century.[8] A Malthusian relationship is central in ecological models applicable to all species, and there is clear evidence that such mechanisms regulate population size in historical agricultural and hunter-gatherer societies (Lee 1987). This is an example of population homeostasis, in which population growth responds to population size, in this case through a positive association between resource availability and population growth and a negative association between resource availability and population size.[9]

3. Boserupian Relationships

Although a Malthusian model has explanatory power, it cannot explain how human population size has increased from millions to billions in the last few thousand years. In the last 10,000 years the global population has not only grown exponentially, but the growth rate itself has until recently grown exponentially (Livi-Bacci 2007). This seems to imply that there must have been some development of human culture that has allowed an increasingly large population size over time, breaking a strict population homeostasis.

It is plausible that an increasing population size or density can also be associated with *increasing* average welfare and population growth.[10] Higher population density encourages specialization, which can be an efficient way to organize labour, encouraging higher human capital. Higher population density may also increase the demand for new technology.[11] Transportation, communication, and access to ideas would also increase with population density. Similarly, if novel ideas and innovations appear largely by chance, more people implies more novel ideas and innovation. A larger population can also maintain more knowledge at a given time (Ghirlanda, Enquist, and Perc 2010; Lehmann, Aoki, and Feldman 2011). Throughout the nineteenth century, political economists criticized Malthus and suggested that increasing population pressure might stimulate innovation that could counter diminishing returns (Hutchinson 1967, 152–202).[12] The economist Ester Boserup examined the relationship between population density and innovation in Sub-Saharan Africa (Boserup 1965; 1981), and found that higher population density on average increased the adoption of better agricultural techniques and technology, and increased both average welfare and population growth.

To illustrate both Boserupian (a positive dependency between welfare and population growth) and Malthusian relationships (a negative dependency), consider the population of medieval Europe. This population varied by around 50 million inhabitants between 1000 and 1500 CE (Livi-Bacci 1999). If, during this time, the population had instead been over 700 million, similar to what it was in the 2010s, average welfare would have been very low. If, however, the population had been only 10,000, it seems clear that it would not have been able to maintain the specialization and technology that Europe had during the Middle Ages, and that all the existing spare land and abundant resources would have been of relatively little use. With such a low population size, average welfare would also have been low. A higher average living standard (welfare) and

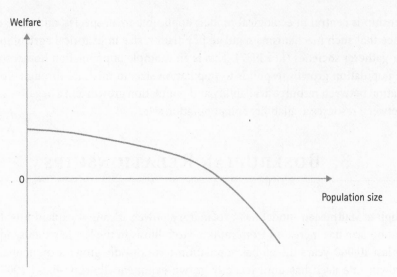

FIGURE 21.1 Malthusian relationship between population size and welfare

plausibly higher population growth would lie somewhere in between the two extremes just considered (10,000 and 700 million). Accounts of the economic and demographic history of Europe in the Middle Ages (e.g., Livi-Bacci 1999) suggest that Europe was close to its maximum population size given available resources around 1340, before the plague reduced the population. The large population size in Europe before the plague resulted in that much sub-standard land and labour-intensive cultivation. Average living standards would have been higher at a lower population density. This implies that for some hypothetical population, between 50 million and 10,000 people, the average living standard (welfare) would have been higher than at either 50 million or 10,000, though exactly at what size is very hard to estimate. It also implies that at the lower bound of that population range, we should over time expect an increasing population size and high average welfare, while at the upper bound (and above) we should expect the opposite.

4. Combining Malthusian and Boserupian Relationships

A homeostatic Malthusian model in which population growth is negatively correlated with population size, and in which population growth is high at low population size, and negative at higher population sizes, is illustrated in Figures 21.1–3. A key assumption of a Malthusian model is that higher population size is associated with lower average welfare (Figure 21.1). The relationship between average welfare and population growth is assumed to be positive as vital rates (births and deaths) respond to greater abundance of resources (Figure 21.2). This gives a negative relationship between population size

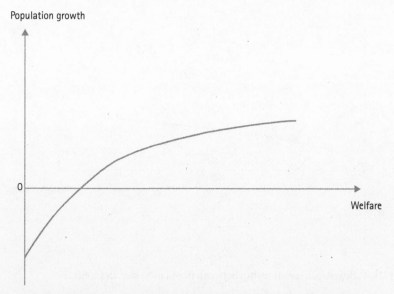

FIGURE 21.2 Malthusian relationship between welfare and population growth

and population growth (Figure 21.3). The point at which population growth is about 0 is the equilibrium population size, around which a population would oscillate. In an animal population this would be the carrying capacity of the population, and this is also one possible equilibrium for human populations. Technological growth can be seen as an exogenous process which would gradually shift the line in Figure 21.3 upwards, resulting in a period of population growth, followed by oscillation around a new higher

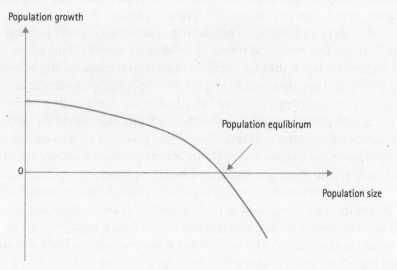

FIGURE 21.3 Relationship between population size and population growth in a Malthusian model

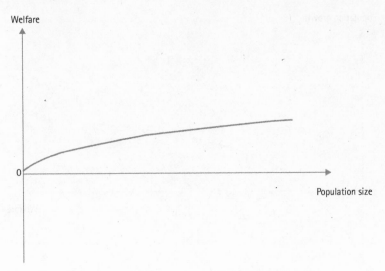

FIGURE 21.4 Boserupian relationship between population size and welfare

equilibrium population size. Moreover, both industrial and pre-industrial human populations may regulate reproduction through a Malthusian relationship that would not necessarily result in a population on the brink of population collapse where average welfare (wages) are close to a subsistence minimum. This was likely the case in pre-industrial Europe as, for example, marriages responded negatively to increasing population size and decreasing average welfare.

It is, as discussed earlier, likely that for some population levels an increasing population or higher population density would increase average welfare. If such a Boserupian relationship holds for any population size (as in Figure 21.4) this would create a Boserupian model with population size increasing toward infinity. Suppose, on the other hand, that such a Boserupian relationship is dominant at lower population sizes (Figure 21.4), but that ecological pressures result in a negative (Malthusian) relationship at higher population sizes (as in Figure 21.1). Then the relationship between population growth and population size would instead be roughly curvilinear as in Figure 21.5.[13] This figure illustrates a combined Malthusian and Boserupian relationship at a given technological level, but it is possible that such processes would also increase the equilibrium population size over time. Boserupian processes such as increased intensification of land or adaptation spurred by increasing population density may stimulate technological growth and allow higher and higher equilibrium population sizes. It is easy to construct such a model in which population size will increase forever. However, given the nature of exponential population growth, a population cannot increase infinitely, and at some point each new individual must have a negative effect on the average welfare in a population. This implies that at some population size the relationship between population and average welfare must turn negative, and one would obtain a relationship roughly like that described in Figure 21.5. Like a Malthusian model, such

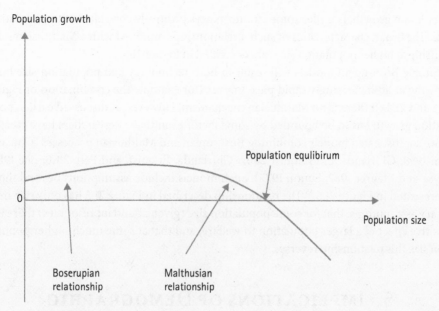

FIGURE 21.5 Combined Boserupian and Malthusian relationship between population growth and population size

a combined Boserupian-Malthusian model has an equilibrium population size around which the population would eventually oscillate. However, unlike a Malthusian model, the combined Boserupian-Malthusian model implies that at lower population sizes, increasing population size would increase population growth.

Researchers have demonstrated that in historical European populations a larger population decreased wages as in Figure 21.1 (Galloway 1988; Lee and Anderson 2002). Researchers have also found that lower (real) wages reduced population growth as in Figure 21.2 (e.g., Bengtsson, Campbell, and Lee 2003; Lee 1987; Tsuya, Feng, Alter, and Lee 2010). In preindustrial populations, it is clear that the relationship between population and welfare was Malthusian (as in Figure 21.3), and for most of human history it seems clear that human population size was regulated by resource-dependent homeostatic mechanisms (Lee 1987).[14] However, equally striking is the great, though gradual, increase in global population size over time. The rapid increase in population size during and after the industrial revolution is particularly striking.

One possible explanation for this rapid increase is that technological growth is exogenous, that human innovation increased largely independent of population size or density, and that this increase in technology resulted in increased productivity, allowing higher population size. Such a relationship could be illustrated by exogenous shifts to the right in the curve shown in Figure 21.3, allowing higher and higher equilibrium population sizes. However, both theory and empirical evidence (e.g., Boserup 1965) suggest that a growing population size itself could stimulate adoption of innovative behavior, thereby increasing average welfare. If this is the case, technology, and by extension population growth, is under some circumstances positively correlated with population size. The broad characteristics of such a relationship combined with a Malthusian relationship at higher population sizes are described in Figure 21.5.

Simple Boserupian models will result in both technology and population size both growing at an increasingly rapid pace forever (for example the combination of Figure 21.2 and 21.4) if there is no Malthusian mechanism. However, as discussed earlier, population growth has to be bounded by some factor eventually. Researchers have created more sophisticated models combining Boserupian and Malthusian processes (Chu and Tsai 1998; Ghirlanda and Enquist 2007; Ghirlanda, Enquist, and Perc 2010; Lee 1986; Pryor and Maurer 1982; Simon 1977). Such models include assumptions beyond those represented in Figure 21.5.[15] The relationship described in Figure 21.5 has only two necessary assumptions: that for some population size (given abundant resources) there is a positive effect of a larger population to welfare, and that at some much higher population size this relationship reverses.

5. Implications of Demographic Theory for Population Ethics

Above I discussed how population growth and population size mutually affect each other according to demographic theory. In this section, I consider four implications of such relationships for population ethics.

The first implication concerns population ethicists' reliance on Malthusian assumptions. There is a (sometimes implicit) tradition in population ethics of assuming a negative relationship between average welfare and population size, following a Malthusian perspective.[16] Sometimes the assumption is made only for the purpose of illustrating a theoretical point. However, arguments are sometimes driven by the assumption. Moreover, even when the assumption is adopted only for the purpose of illustration, this may reinforce belief in the assumption.

Broadly, one can distinguish two different approaches in population ethics when reasoning about the effect of population size on average welfare. The first approach, exemplified by Parfit (1984), Arrhenius (2011), and Broome (1996), compares hypothetical populations, and often the analytical treatment allows both a positive relationship between population size and welfare, as well as a negative relationship. However, typically the framing and examples assume a negative relationship. An example of this can be found in Parfit (1984). He considers a scenario in which the population of Earth expands in the next generation, driving the average welfare level down. A reason for the implicit Malthusian assumption is that the opposite case, of average welfare increasing with population size, does not involve trade-offs between population size and average welfare, which is a crucial feature in Parfit's discussion of many issues in population ethics. The second approach, illustrated by Dasgupta (1998), involves creating explicit models to calculate average welfare based on population size. Such models typically make and motivate Malthusian relationships between average welfare and population size.

The exclusive focus on Malthusian assumptions is problematic insofar as there are alternative assumptions and perspectives (e.g., Boserupian) that one could assume. This suggests that having a thorough understanding of demographic theory, and *both* Malthusian and non-Malthusian perspectives in population ethics, may clarify implicit assumptions in population ethics and may open up new avenues of research. Population ethicists should not be too confident in the assumption that, in any real-world scenario, expanding the population would drive down average welfare.

The second implication concerns the likelihood of the scenarios that are described in thought experiments intended to elicit intuitions about the comparative goodness of different populations. If a certain population axiology, or ethical theory, entails some implausible conclusion, for example that a very large population with lives only barely worth living would be very good, or better than a smaller population with much higher average welfare, then this may seem like a powerful objection to the theory. However, if the existence of such a large population is very unlikely given demographic theory, then the fact that the theory has such an implausible implication may be less of a concern than other theoretical implications regarding populations that are empirically more likely to exist given demographic theory. This point may be relevant for what we should do when we are uncertain which ethical theory is the true one. It may be that we should give more credence, or perhaps more weight, to theories that produce paradoxes or implausible conclusions only in far out (but logically possible) cases than to theories that generate paradoxes or implausible conclusions in scenarios that are more likely given demographic theory. (See, e.g., Bykvist in this volume.)

Insofar as thought experiments comparing different populations are to have application in the real world, the shape of the function between population size and welfare is relevant. As we saw, a common assumption in thought experiments is a Malthusian relationship between high population size and lower welfare. In many cases researchers also assume a monotonic Malthusian relationship for any population size, and present examples with the highest welfare in populations with only a single individual. A Malthusian population equilibrium where the population size is close to subsistence levels is probably what Parfit (1984) had in mind when he described a very large population with very low welfare (lives barely worth living) in his illustration of the "Repugnant Conclusion." He illustrates this relationship with a figure representing different populations, a smaller population with very high average welfare, and a much larger population with very low welfare. This figure conveys the same relationship between population size and average welfare as the relationship represented in Figure 21.1 (Parfit 1984, 388).

However, demographic theory suggests that a population consisting of many "lives not worth living" is an unstable and short-term deviation from a population equilibrium.[17] According to demographic theory, population size will revert to intermediate equilibrium size in cases with very high and very low welfare. In a Malthusian model, the inevitable result of adding individuals when average welfare is very low will be negative future population growth. Enormous populations with either negative welfare or very low positive welfare are thus unsustainable. The scenario that Parfit describes is highly unlikely from the standpoint of demographic theory.[18] The objection against certain theories, such as total utilitarianism, that they imply the Repugnant Conclusion may therefore be less powerful than it initially seems, and we may give less weight to this objection when deciding what credence to assign to theories like total utilitarianism in contexts involving evaluative and normative uncertainty.

Demographic theory suggests that a population with high fertility preferences will move toward a situation with high population size, and low welfare. The equilibrium population size that results is higher, and average (as well as total) welfare is lower, than optimal population size derived from average (or total) view of the value of welfare. Thus, for populations with high fertility preferences, given unlimited reproductive rights, resource availability will regulate eventual population size.

A third implication of demographic theory concerns extinction risk. Resource-dependent homeostatic models imply that a population collapse, or drastic and rapid decrease in population size, results in strong population growth following the collapse. A temporary exogenous change in population size can therefore be quickly recovered from. Effects of population reduction on welfare are therefore also short-term. In addition, we know of the human past that absolute extinction of a population in a region is rare, consistent with demographic theory.[19] Resource-dependent homeostatic models are central in basic ecological models of other species (Sibly and Hone 2002), though there are also ecological examples of inverse relationships for low population densities (Courchamp, Clutton-Brock, and Grenfell 1999). This has implications for assessing the risk of total population extinction, a topic of interest to population ethicists (e.g., Broome 2010). If the welfare of future populations is not (or is only slightly) discounted, and if total (rather than average) welfare determines the value of a population, then human extinction entails a massive value loss. However, if homeostatic population models are correct, population extinctions are highly unlikely, at least where such extinctions would result from gradual processes such as climate change or environmental degradation. This excludes sudden discrete catastrophic impacts that kill an entire population at once, such as a gigantic asteroid impact. Those concerned about human extinction risk may therefore have reason to focus more on extinction risk from such sudden discrete events, as well as events caused by factors exogenous to the models discussed in this chapter.

Finally, homeostatic population models also have implications for intergenerational justice, and in particular for intergenerational inequality, which is an issue in population ethics (Arrhenius and Mosquera forthcoming; Temkin, 1993). If population size and welfare are both likely to revert to equilibrium levels, this may reduce intergenerational inequality, or at least the size of the welfare gap between the best-off and worst-off generations. For example, rather than a steady increase or decrease in the average welfare of successive generations over long periods of time, population size and average welfare would instead oscillate between different equilibrium points and different levels of average welfare. Given homeostatic population models, intergenerational inequality may be less of a concern from a long-term perspective, at least in *one important respect*, insofar as the oscillation between different levels of average welfare across generations would constrain the size of the welfare gap between the best- and worst-off generations.

On the other hand, oscillation between different average welfare levels across generations would seem to guarantee some level of welfare inequality between different generations. It might also result in an outcome that is worse, with respect to intergenerational inequality, than a hypothetical outcome in which welfare reaches a high level and remains at that level over a long period of time. In any case, homeostatic population models are relevant to what we should think the pattern of intergenerational inequality will look like over the long term.

Changes in the age structure of a population also have relevance for intergenerational justice, and more generally for *intertemporal* population ethics. Populations change through births and deaths, but births add very young people, while people that die are often older (or very young). As such, changes to both the birth rate and the death rate will change the age structure, the proportion of individuals at different ages. Similarly, only some people in a population give birth (individuals that are neither very young nor very old), and the proportion of people in childbearing years will determine how many children are born. A consequence of this is that the proportion of young and old people is unlikely to ever be stable, even if in the long run birth rates and death rates are stable. In other words, all changes in births and deaths will also change the proportion of young and old individuals. Moreover, because humans are productive in the middle of their life and young and old individuals require more care, societies redistribute a large amount of resources across individuals' life courses (e.g., from people in the middle of life to younger and older individuals) in both pre-industrial and contemporary societies (Gurven and Kaplan 2006; Lee and Mason 2011; Kolk 2021). Intergenerational (as well as intragenerational) justice may be at least partly related to age structure and life course flows of resources. For example, age structure and life course flows of resources are important for discussions of sustainability of pension systems in contemporary societies, as well as the value of having more children in low fertility societies (e.g., Cigno and Werding 2007; Gál, Vanhuysse, and Vargha 2018).

6. The Regulation of Population Size in Historical, Modern, and Future Societies

In the previous sections, I gave a brief overview of how population size might interact with population growth and technology at a theoretical level. I also discussed four implications of such models for population ethics. Below I will apply this discussion in relation to empirical research on historical and contemporary populations.

Theorists agree that in pre-historic human societies resource availability regulated population size. The very low global population growth rates during the last 50,000 years, with the exception of the last two centuries, is strong evidence for such an assumption. However, we have close to no empirical evidence regarding how actual populations developed in the distant past, although historical agricultural societies and hunter-gatherer populations in the recent past serve as examples of how such populations might have looked. Complicating such inquiries is that even populations that must have had relatively stable population sizes in the past, experienced explosive population growth at the time of contact with Europeans (e.g., the Polynesians on Tikopia [Firth 1936], and the !Kung people [Howell 1979]).

Studies using quantitative data for historical agricultural societies relating population growth to economic variables (Galloway, 1988; Lee, 1987), as well as in-depth studies of societal institutions in pre-industrial populations (Drixler, 2013; Firth, 1965) find that populations respond to resources in a Malthusian fashion. Studies on pre-industrial Europe find that Malthusian relationships were substantial, but that they weakened considerably and disappeared during and after the industrial revolution (or at least were dwarfed by other societal changes). In order for a population to respond in a Malthusian homeostatic way to changing resources, population size must affect welfare (more people causes lower wages), and welfare must affect population growth (higher wages causes higher fertility and survival) (Lee 1985). In pre-industrial Europe, the former effect was much stronger than the latter, but combined they were important enough to determine long-run population dynamics. As explanatory factors for changes in population in the short term, such dynamics had weak explanatory power. Nevertheless, a consistent pressure downwards on population growth when population size was above its long-term trend (and vice-versa) was an inescapable determinant of long-term population developments (Lee 1985; 1987).

When analyzing the relationship between welfare and population growth in contemporary societies, it is important to keep in mind that while homeostatic tendencies may not explain short-term population trends, they may still be important for long-term developments. The demographic transition, for example, might *appear* to be inconsistent with homeostatic resource regulation relative to certain shorter time scales in which there isn't a clear Malthusian relationship between income variation and demographic rates (Coale and Watkins 1986); however such a relationship might appear on a longer time scale. Gradual technological development can either be interpreted as exogenous increases of equilibrium level between population and population growth, or as an endogenous process in which larger population sizes contributed to population growth.

Malthus wrote about different "checks" on population. Preventive checks regulate fertility and entry to sexual unions (age at marriage), and positive checks are related to catastrophic mortality and disease related to shortages of resources. The Northwest European marriage pattern has been described as Malthusian in that when economic resources were plentiful men and women marred earlier and the proportion of those who never married decreased. This has been described as the most important way in which demographic rates were related to resources in for example pre-industrial England (Wrigley and Schofield 1981). Mortality rates also increased when resources decreased. However, perhaps the most important determinant of population variation was epidemic disease largely exogenous to population size, of which the Black Death in fourteenth-century Eurasia is the most well-known case. The role of sudden and unpredictable mortality, and fertility which responded positively to a reduction in population size (and negatively to increases in population size) suggests that fertility was regulating populations in more predictable ways than mortality (Livi-Bacci 2007).

However, after and during the industrial revolution the traditional relationship between economic growth (and average welfare) and population growth changed dramatically. For the first time, the rate of technological and economic growth, and the increase in living standards (average welfare) outpaced population growth (though population growth was still higher than ever). As both average welfare and population growth increased simultaneously, and at an increasing pace until the 1960s, a broad Malthusian homeostatic interpretation of this period is not possible. This is one reason that factors other than macro-level trends in welfare have dominated explanations of trends in and determinants of mortality, fertility, and marriage, in the social sciences for contemporary societies. It is not possible to understand the fertility transition, the great decline in fertility in the nineteenth and twentieth centuries, in Malthusian terms, as welfare increased greatly at the same time as fertility fell (the opposite of what a Malthusian model predicts). However, the fertility transition can be interpreted in broader homeostatic terms as a way for a population to regain population balance (and as a response to very high population growth due to falling mortality).

Today, most people live in societies where the vast majority of mortality takes place at post-reproductive ages (United Nations Population Division 2017). In such a context, fertility is the dominant determinant of population growth. Mortality after age 45 is not at all related to the Net Reproductive Rate (NRR), or generational replacement. When mortality during and before reproductive ages is low, the difference in population growth between the fertility levels which maintains a stable population (just above two children per woman) and levels of fertility in high-fertility societies is very substantial. Furthermore, in many populations in the world today the fertility rates are lower than replacement level fertility, and roughly half of the world population between 2010 and 2015 lived in countries with a Total Fertility Rate (TFR) that implied long-term population decline (United Nations Population Division 2015). As such, fertility dynamics are clearly the major determinant of population dynamics in contemporary and future societies. From the individual perspective, it seems clear that people could, if they wanted, have more surviving children than they choose to have (though this may affect their individual welfare negatively). This seems to be the case for most people in the world today. This suggests that individual agency and childbearing preferences are the primary determinants of future population size. Individuals on average seem to, at some level, coordinate their fertility decisions with expectations of other aspects of life, and on average choose fewer children as they judge that the economic, personal, or societal costs of higher childbearing are undesirable. Whether global fertility levels will converge at a level that is above or below replacement levels seems critical for future population dynamics and the future of human population systems.

Overall, contemporary societies are still characterized by great variance in fertility, both across and within countries. With respect to welfare and fertility, there are many patterns that coexist that may appear contradictory. When examining how population level fertility is affected by the economy and business cycle the relationship is pro-cyclical, meaning that fertility tends to increase in times of economic expansion and decrease in times of recession (Sobotka, Skirbekk, and Philipov 2011). At the same time, there is a robust cross-sectional association where countries with high fertility have lower wealth, though this relationship may reverse at very high levels of national wealth (Myrskylä, Kohler, and Billari 2009). Within pre-industrial societies, wealthy individuals traditionally have had higher fertility than poorer individuals have had. This trend partly reversed during industrialization and during the twentieth century. During these times, in many societies the relationship between individual wealth and fertility was negative (Skirbekk 2008). However, there is increasing evidence that in some high-income contemporary societies we once again see a positive wealth-fertility association where richer individuals have more children (see, e.g., Andersson 2000; Jalovaara et al. 2019; Kolk 2019; Kolk and Barclay 2019).

How fertility will respond to welfare is critical for understanding the future of human population systems. At large population sizes, it seems inevitable that a broadly Malthusian link between welfare and population growth must exist, i.e., that at some point population size will reduce population growth and cap population size. From what we know about human population systems and estimates of the carrying capacity of Earth this will most likely be achieved without catastrophic drastic population change. Instead, gradually, humans will choose to have fewer children when they face resource constraints (cf. Cohen 1996). While a large number of children today might be affordable given how much richer we are today than in the past, children are still very costly as a share of parents' income (Kolk 2021). Economists have suggested that the relative opportunity costs of having children have increased with increasing investment in education, and that this can explain declines in fertility (Becker and Lewis 1974). If, globally, people eventually desire fewer children than what is necessary for replacement at current or future higher levels of development, then a shrinking and not an expanding population will be an important determinant of population size and average welfare. Under such circumstances, Boserupian relationships will be more relevant than Malthusian ones for the relation between welfare and population growth.

To explain current fertility variation within and across populations remains a challenge to contemporary demographers, though from the empirical observations discussed above it is still possible to draw inferences for the future. The most straightforward conclusion is that if fertility remains above the replacement rate, the human population will at some point encounter resource limits that will bound the size of human populations.[20] At population sizes close to these limits welfare will be lower. Population growth in all societies has often, during certain periods, had population growth rates of at least 1 percent, given socioeconomic circumstances that are harsher than what contemporary individuals face. Such population growth rates are impossible in the medium to long range, given the nature of exponential growth. Therefore, if future fertility levels remain above replacement rates, some homeostatic mechanism is a necessity. We can also be largely certain that any such mechanism will be related to fertility, as any increases mortality will not substantively affect population growth.[21] We are also unlikely to run out of the resources that make human life possible (Cohen 1996), so the homeostatic mechanism regulating population is almost certain to be human welfare. At some point a continuously growing population will be treated as an unacceptable trade-off against a higher quality of life.

If humans will desire fewer children than what is necessary to maintain population size, minimum population sizes required for maintaining current technological levels will become a more important determinant for any relationship between population size and population growth. If highly developed future societies will tend to be characterized by below replacement level fertility preferences, the amount of government-induced transfers from non-parents toward parents might be one of the most important determinants of future population size and growth. If future populations will be shrinking, and the relationship between population size and welfare is primarily Boserupian, population decline will reduce future welfare.

7. CONCLUSIONS

In this chapter, I discussed both theoretical as well as empirical evidence for the claim that population size and population growth are endogenously related. The broad theories relating welfare with population change might have weak short-term predictive power but are almost certain to be important over longer time perspectives. As population ethics often takes a long-term perspective, understanding and engaging with demographic theory may be very productive. Even very general models of how population change responds to welfare, and vice versa, may change analytical models in applied population ethics substantially. The broad Malthusian and Boserupian relationships described in this chapter are a useful starting point. Demographic theory provides a framework for thinking about how population change, population size, and welfare are related.

I provided four concrete examples of the potential usefulness of demographic theory for population ethics. First, a more nuanced discussion of possible positive (Boserupian) as well as negative (Malthusian) effects of additional people on welfare can inform population ethics. While many population ethicists worry about the negative effects on average welfare of increasing population size, growth, and concentration, consistent with Malthusian models, there is far less discussion of the possible positive effects of increasing population size, growth, and concentration on average welfare, consistent with Boserupian models.[22] Second, predications from demographic theory may help population ethicists evaluate different scenarios as more or less empirically and theoretically plausible for actual human populations. This would be particularly useful when population ethics is applied to contemporary policy concerns, but it may also be useful when considering how much weight to give to a particular theory under conditions of evaluative or normative uncertainty. For example, I argued that the scenario that Parfit describes, in which steadily increasing population size over the long term leads to an extremely large population in which average welfare is extremely low, is very unlikely as it is inconsistent with homeostatic population models. Third, I argued that from the standpoint of demographic theory, absolute human extinction resulting from gradual processes such as resource depletion or climate change is a very unlikely occurrence. Those concerned with reducing extinction risk may therefore have more reason to focus on sudden discrete catastrophic events. Fourth, I argued that homeostatic population models are relevant for how we think about intergenerational inequality over the long term. Rather than steady increases or decreases in the average welfare and population size of successive generations, it is more likely that population size and average welfare will oscillate around different levels of some equilibrium welfare.

While certain insights from demographic discourse are largely absent from debates in population ethics, the opposite is also true. That is, many insights from population ethics are largely absent in demographic discourses. This is particularly true regarding perspectives on future generations and intergenerational issues, many of which are central in economic demography, but seldom considered in the ways population ethicists approach these issues. Deeper engagement with demographers and population ethicists on these issues may provide new insights.

Acknowledgments

I want to thank Tim Campbell for helpful comments and edits. Financial support from from Riksbankens Jubileumsfond (grant M17-0372:1 and P17-0330:1) is gratefully acknowledged.

Notes

1. Throughout this text I will use the term "population" and "population size" to refer to the number of living individuals at a single time. The geographical area or definition will be left unspecified, and I will occasionally use "population density" and "population size" interchangeably as for a certain (closed) area—such as Earth—the two concepts are identical.
2. See also Dasgupta and Dasgupta (this volume), as well as Dasgupta (1998).
3. For discussion of optimal population size, see Greaves (this volume).
4. Natural growth refers to population changes arising from births and deaths, not taking migration into account.
5. Demographers use the concept of Net Reproductive Rate (NRR), which is typically defined from only a female perspective, and is the average number of surviving daughters of

a woman, at a given a level of mortality and fertility of the woman. If the NRR is larger than 1 a population will grow, and if it is smaller than 1 it will shrink. For example, an NRR of 1 would arise if women on average gave birth to two children, there is a sex ratio of 0.5, and no woman dies before the end of her childbearing age.

6. Such a population can be represented by a geometric series representing a population when every new generation is half the size of the previous one. An NRR of 0.5 then gives a geometric series with a sum of 2 where the coefficient before each exponent is 1, and the base of the exponential term is 0.5.

7. After 2,000 years there would only be enough matter on Earth for 1 gram per person.

8. However, the idea of a positive relationship between the number of people and wealth were common in many societies long before Malthus, and this idea was part of a broader scientific discourse in eighteenth-century Europe (Hutchinson 1967).

9. One example of a stable population equilibrium is when all individuals are living at subsistence level, but it is possible that the function between welfare and population growth is different, and that for example societies would regulate reproduction so that a population equilibrium would take place at welfare levels above the subsistence minimum.

10. Note that throughout this chapter I will treat population density and population size as analogous concepts. In the short-term populations will likely resort to migration when facing resource constraints, but in the longer run the destination population will face similar demographic pressures. At equilibrium population density and population size can then be treated as analogously. Most obviously Earth itself is for the foreseeable future a closed population system, in which population density and population size are identical. However, migration remains an important practical concern when attempting to test population theories using empirical data.

11. When using technology throughout the article it is defined in very broad terms as any cultural institution, idea, capital investment, or way of life, which is associated with productivity. As such, it also reflects institutional and cultural change broadly and not only technical engineering inventions.

12. Thomas Sadler in 1830, Friedrich List in 1841, and John McChulloch in 1846, all clearly and forcefully argued that better innovation and better agricultural techniques could and would be applied to counter diminishing returns (Hutchinson 1967).

13. It is not necessary to make any assumptions about the functional form of the relationships in any of Figures 21.1–5 except that below some population level, an additional person increases welfare monotonically, and at above that population level there is instead a monotonic decline for each additional person. It also seems reasonable that population growth is above 0 for a very tiny population (though this is not necessary, there are examples on animal species that face extinction if population size falls below a certain level; a famous historical case is the North American passenger pigeon). There must also be some population level for which population growth turns negative, as the model would otherwise predict a population size that would move toward infinity.

14. Similar relationships underpin ecological models on animals where similar strong effects between resources and population growth are observed (Lee 1987; Sibly and Hone 2002).

15. Examples of such additional assumptions in the models are: population sizes necessary to maintain technology, technological knowledge gradually lost over time, and technological growth is made possible from any surplus of resources above what is necessary for pure subsistence.

16. See, for example, the following quotations from population ethicists. In the quote below by Parfit (1984) he (a) takes a Malthusian relationship as an empirical fact in some contemporaneous societies, and (b) then after first qualifying that a Malthusian relationship might not apply everywhere (in two sentences), (c) proceeds to discuss the Malthusian case and implications of such a relationship (over fifty-nine pages):

The effect of population growth on existing people—My couple assume that the existence of an extra child would not on balance be worse for other people. In many countries, in many periods, this has been true. But in many other periods it has not been true. In these periods, if there had been more people, people would have been worse off. This is now true in many countries. In these countries, if the population grows, the quality of life will be lower than it would be if the population did not grow. These are the cases that I shall discuss. (Parfit 1984, 382)

The quotation below is the basis of a thought experiment introducing optimal population from Arrhenius and Campbell (2017):

If the current generation continues to consume resources at the expense of future generations, and the population increases significantly, this could lead to an enormous population—ten billion people per generation—in which most people's lives are barely worth living. Suppose we could instead create a smaller population—around one billion people per generation—with very good lives. Which population would be better?

17. They will be unstable if "lives not worth living" are defined as truly dreadful lives where resources are insufficient for subsistence needs. If one also considers many lives not worth living where people have meager but not completely insufficient resources, a Malthusian model may instead predict a population where nearly all lives would be considered not worth living.
18. As he acknowledges (1984, 388).
19. By "absolute extinction," I mean that the population in an area declines to 0, through vital rates alone, without outmigration, cultural assimilation, or replacement by other populations in the same area. While dramatic, seemingly non-recoverable, population reductions are common, complete extinction appears rare. Famous examples such as the Norse population on Greenland where abandoned through migration, and only a few (very inhospitable) Polynesian islands appear to ever have been abandoned, or even more speculatively population died out. Examples of such islands are the Auckland, Kermadec, Norfolk, and Pitcairns islands, which all at some point were depopulated, though this likely took place through migration.
20. Even wild hypothetical scenarios such as those involving interplanar travel do not change such boundaries fundamentally (Hardin 1959).
21. For example, the great famines of the twentieth century such as in China in the early 1960s and in Bengal in the 1940s had relatively little effect on long- and medium-term population developments.
22. An exception can be found in Greaves (this volume).

References

Andersson, Gunnar. 2000. "The Impact of Labour-Force Participation on Childbearing Behavior: Pro-Cyclical Fertility in Sweden During the 1980s and the 1990s." *European Journal of Population* 16, no. 4: 293–333.

Arrhenius, Gustaf. 2011. "The Impossibility of a Satisfactory Population Ethics." In *Descriptive and Normative Approaches to Human Behavior*, edited by Ehtibar. N. Dzhafarov and Lacey Perry, 1–26. Singapore: World Scientific.

Arrhenius, Gustaf and Tim Campbell. 2017. "The Problem of Optimal Population Size." In *International Panel on Social Progress, Vol. 1: Rethinking Society*, edited by Marc Fleurbay, 64. Cambridge: Cambridge University Press.

Arrhenius, Gustaf and Julia Mosquera. Forthcoming. "Positive Egalitarianism Reconsidered." *Utilitas*.

Becker, Gary, and Gregg Lewis. 1974. "Interaction between Quantity and Quality of Children." In *Economics of the Family: Marriage, Children, and Human Capital*, edited by Theodore W. Schultz, 81–90. Cambridge, MA: National Bureau of Economic Research.

Bengtsson, Tommy, Cameron Campbell, and James. Z. Lee. 2003. *Life under Pressure: Mortality and Living Standards in Europe and Asia, 1700–1900*. Cambridge, MA: MIT Press.

Boserup, Ester. 1965. *The Conditions of Agricultural Growth: The Economics of Agrarian Change under Population Pressure*. London: Allen and Unwin.

Boserup, Ester. 1981. *Population and Technology*. Oxford: Blackwell.

Broome, John. 1996. "The Welfare Economics of Population." *Oxford Economic Papers* 48, no. 2: 177–193.

Broome, John. 2010. "The Most Important Thing about Climate Change." In *Public Policy: Why Ethics Matters*, edited by Jonathan Boston, Andrew Bradstock, and David Eng, 101–116. Canberra: ANU E Press.

Caney, Simon. 2014. "Climate Change, Intergenerational Equity and the Social Discount Rate." *Politics, Philosophy, and Economics* 3, no. 4: 320–342.

Charbonneau, Hubert, Bertrand Desjardins, Jacques Légaré, and Hubert Denis. 2000. "The Population of the St-Lawrence Valley, 1608–1760." In *A Population History of North America*, edited by Michael Robert Haines and Richard H. Steckel, 99–142. Cambridge: Cambridge University Press.

Chu, C.Y. Cyrus, and Yao-Chou Tsai. 1998. "Productivity, Investment in Infrastructure and Population Size: Formalizing the Theory of Ester Boserup." In *Increasing Returns and Economic Analysis*, edited by Kenneth J. Arrow, Yew-Kwang Ng, and Xiaokai Yang, 90–107. Basingstoke: Springer.

Cigno, Alessandro, and Martin Werding. 2007. *Children and Pensions*. Cambridge, MA: MIT Press.

Coale, Ansley J., and Susan Cotts Watkins. 1986. *The Decline of Fertility in Europe: The Revised Proceedings of a Conference on the Princeton European Fertility Project*. Princeton, NJ: Princeton University Press.

Cohen, Joel E. 1996. *How Many People Can the Earth Support?* New York: Norton.

Courchamp, Franck, Tim Clutton-Brock, and Bryan Grenfell. 1999. "Inverse Density Dependence and the Allee Effect." *Trends in Ecology and Evolution* 14, no. 10: 405–410.

Dasgupta, Partha. 1998. "Population, Consumption and Resources: Ethical Issues." *Ecological Economics* 24, no. 2: 139–152.

Drixler, Fabian Franz. 2013. *Mabiki: Infanticide and Population Growth in Eastern Japan, 1660–1950*. Berkeley and Los Angeles: University of California Press.

Firth, Raymond. 1936. *We, the Tikopia*. London: George Allen and Unwin.

Firth, Raymond. 1965. *Primitive Polynesian Economy*. London: Archon Books.

Gál, Róbert Iván, Pieter Vanhuysse, and Lili Vargha. 2018. "Pro-Elderly Welfare States within Child-Oriented Societies." *Journal of European Public Policy* 25, no. 6: 944–958.

Galloway, Patrick R. 1988. "Basic Patterns in Annual Variations in Fertility, Nuptiality, Mortality, and Prices in Pre-Industrial Europe." *Population Studies* 42, no. 2: 275–303.

Ghirlanda, Stefano, and Magnus Enquist. 2007. "Cumulative Culture and Explosive Demographic Transitions." *Quality and Quantity* 41, no. 4: 591–600.

Ghirlanda, S., M. Enquist, and M. Perc. 2010. "Sustainability of Culture-Driven Population Dynamics." *Theoretical Population Biology* 77, no. 3: 181–188.

Gurven, Michael, and Hillard Kaplan. 2006. "Determinants of Time Allocation across the Lifespan." *Human Nature: An Interdisciplinary Biosocial Perspective* 17, no. 1: 1.

Hardin, Garrett. 1959. "Interstellar Migration and the Population Problem." *Journal of Heredity* 50, no. 2: 68–70.

Howell, Nancy. 1979. *Demography of the Dobe!Kung.* New York: Academic Press.

Hutchinson, Edward. P. 1967. *The Population Debate: The Development of Conflicting Theories up to 1900.* Boston, MA: Houghton Mifflin.

Jalovaara, Marika, Gerda Neyer, Gunnar Andersson, Johan Dahlberg, Lars Dommermuth, Peter Fallesen, and Trude Lappegård. 2019. "Education, Gender, and Cohort Fertility in the Nordic Countries." *European Journal of Population* 35: 563–586.

Kolk, Martin. 2019. "The Relationship between Lifecourse Accumulated Income and Childbearing of Swedish Men and Women Born 1940–1970." *Stockholm Research Reports in Demography* no 19: 1–38.

Kolk, Martin. 2021. "Government Transfers to Parents and Population Policy in a Global Perspective: An Economic Demographic Perspective." *Journal of Development Studies*, 57, no. 9: 1483–1498.

Kolk, Martin, and Kieron Barclay. 2019. "Cognitive Ability and Fertility among Swedish Men Born 1951–1967: Evidence from Military Conscription Registers." *Proceedings of the Royal Society B: Biological Sciences* 286, no. 1902: 20190359.

Lee, Ronald. 1985. "Population Homeostasis and English Demographic History." *The Journal of Interdisciplinary History* 15, no. 4: 635–660.

Lee, Ronald. 1986. "Malthus and Boserup: A Dynamic Synthesis." In *The State of Population Theory: Forward from Malthus,* edited by D. A. Coleman and R. S. Schofield, 96–130. Oxford: Blackwell.

Lee, Ronald. 1987. "Population Dynamics of Humans and Other Animals." *Demography* 24, no. 4: 443–465.

Lee, Ronald, and Michael Anderson. 2002. "Malthus in State Space: Macro Economic-Demographic Relations in English History, 1540 to 1870." *Journal of Population Economics* 15, no. 2: 195–220.

Lee, Ronald, and Andrew. Mason. 2011. *Population Aging and the Generational Economy: A Global Perspective.* Cheltenham: Edward Elgar.

Lehmann, Laurent, Kenichi Aoki, and Marcus W Feldman. 2011. "On the Number of Independent Cultural Traits Carried by Individuals and Populations." *Philosophical Transactions of the Royal Society B: Biological Sciences* 366, no. 1563: 424–435.

Livi-Bacci, Massimo. 1999. *The Population of Europe: A History.* Malden, MA: Blackwell.

Livi-Bacci, Massimo. 2007. *A Concise History of World Population.* Oxford: Blackwell.

Myrskylä, Mikko, Hans-Peter Kohler, and Francesco C Billari. 2009. "Advances in Development Reverse Fertility Declines." *Nature* 460, no. 7256: 741–743.

Parfit, Derek. 1984. *Reasons and Persons.* Oxford: Clarendon Press.

Pryor, Frederic L, and Stephen B Maurer. 1982. "On Induced Economic Change in Precapitalist Societies." *Journal of Development Economics* 10, no. 3: 325–353.

Sibly, Richard M, and Jim Hone. 2002. "Population Growth Rate and Its Determinants: An Overview." *Philosophical Transactions of the Royal Society B: Biological Sciences* 357, no. 1425: 1153–1170.

Simon, Julian, L. 1977. *The Economics of Population Growth.* Princeton, NJ: Princeton University Press.

Skirbekk, Vegard. 2008. "Fertility Trends by Social Status." *Demographic Research* 18, no. 5: 145–180.

Sobotka, Tomáš, Vegard Skirbekk, and Dimiter Philipov. 2011. "Economic Recession and Fertility in the Developed World." *Population and Development Review* 37, no. 2: 267–306.

Temkin, Larry. 1993. *Inequality.* New York: Oxford University Press.

Tsuya, Noriko, Wang Feng, George Alter, and James Z Lee, eds. 2010. *Prudence and Pressure.* Cambridge, MA: MIT Press.

United Nations Population Division. 2015. *World Fertility Report 2015—Data Booklet.* New York: United Nations.

United Nations Population Division. 2017. *World Mortality Report 2017.* New York: United Nations.

Wilson, Chris, and Pauline Airey. 1999. "How Can a Homeostatic Perspective Enhance Demographic Transition Theory?" *Population Studies* 53, no. 2: 117–128.

Wrigley, Edward Anthony, and Roger S. Schofield. 1981. *The Population History of England 1541–1871: A Reconstruction.* London: Arnold.

....

CHAPTER 22

POPULATION OVERSHOOT

....

AISHA DASGUPTA AND PARTHA DASGUPTA

1. MOTIVATION

....

EHRLICH and Holdren (1971) introduced the metaphor, I=PAT, to draw attention to the significance of the biosphere's carrying capacity for population ethics. The authors traced the *i*mpact of human activities on the Earth system to *p*opulation, *a*ffluence (read, per capita consumption of goods and services), and the character of *t*echnology in use (including institutions and social capital). Because our impact on the biosphere is proportional to the demands we make of it, and because those demands increase with our economic activity, we can assume our impact on the biosphere increases with economic activity. But it means that even though today's poorest societies can be expected in time to display fertility transitions, it is no reason to think that humanity's demands for the biosphere's goods and services will cease to exceed its ability to supply them (see below). That is why it is a mistake to ignore the Ehrlich-Holdren observation that the biosphere responds to the demands we make of it, not to changes in the demands we make of it (e.g., those that accompany declines in fertility rates), nor to changes in the rate of change in the demands we make of it (those that accompany declines in the rate of growth of the global population).[1]

Humanity's impact on the biosphere leaves traces. Studying biogeochemical signs in sediments and ice from the past several millennia, Waters et al. (2016) tracked the human-induced evolution of soil nitrogen and phosphorus from those deposits. The authors reported that the now-famous figure of the hockey stick that characterizes time series of carbon concentration in the atmosphere is also displayed by time series of a wide class of global biogeochemical signatures. These display a flat trend over millennia until some 250 years ago, when they begin a slow increase, which continues until the middle of the twentieth century, when they display a sharp and continuing rise. Waters et al. proposed that mid-twentieth century should be regarded as the time we entered the Anthropocene.[2]

Their reading is consistent with macroeconomic statistics. World population in 1950 was about 2.5 billion and global output of final goods and services a little over 8.7 trillion international dollars (at 2011 prices). The average person in the world was poor (annual income was only somewhat in excess of 3,500 international dollars). Since then, the world has prospered beyond recognition. Life expectancy at birth in 1950 was 45, today it is a little over 70. World output of final goods and services is (at 2011 prices) above 110 trillion international dollars, meaning that at a population size of 7.5 billion, world income per capita is now more than 15,000 international dollars. A more than twelve-fold increase in global output in a sixty-five-year period helps to explain not only the stresses that the biosphere has been subjected to in recent decades (MEA 2005a–d), but it also hints at the possibility that humanity's demand for the biosphere's goods and services has for some time exceeded its ability to supply them on a sustainable basis.

That possibility has been given quantitative expression. In a review of the state of the biosphere, WWF (2008) reported that although the global demand for ecological goods and services in the 1960s was less than supply, it exceeded supply in the early years of the present century by 50 percent. The figure is based on the idea of "global ecological footprint," which is the surface area of biologically productive land and sea needed to supply the resources we consume (food, fibres, wood, water) and to assimilate the waste we produce (materials, gases) on a sustainable basis. The Global Footprint Network (GFN) updates its estimates of the global ecological footprint on a regular basis. A footprint in excess of 1 means demand for ecological services exceeds their supply. By GFN's reckoning, maintaining the world's average living standard at the level reached some ten years ago (roughly 12,000 international dollars) would have required 1.5 Earths. It is now evident that the enormous gains humanity has enjoyed in the past sixty-five years have been at the expense of a diminished biosphere we are leaving behind for our descendants.[3]

What of future population? Figure 22.1, taken from UNPD (2017), shows world population projections by region from year 2015 to year 2100. The figure shows that, with the significant exceptions of Asia and Africa, population would appear to have stabilized in the rest of world when taken as an aggregate.[4] Asia's population is projected to grow from the current figure of approximately 4.1 billion to a little over 5 billion in mid-century and then taper to a little under 5 billion. In sharp contrast, Africa's population is projected to rise from its current 1 billion to 4 billion. Global population in 2100 is projected to be 11.2 billion. A global population of 11.2 billion would be expected to make vastly greater demands on the biosphere than today's population of 7.5 billion, and most certainly than a population of 2.5 billion (global population in 1950). And the reason the demands are most likely to be a lot greater is that with economic growth the per capita impact on the biosphere can be predicted to be larger.

In this chapter we offer one broad class of reasons for the overshoot in humanity's demand for the biosphere' goods and services relative to its ability to supply them on a sustainable basis. To put it figuratively, we are "eating into" the biosphere. The biosphere has the capacity to regenerate itself, which is why it is commonly modeled as a

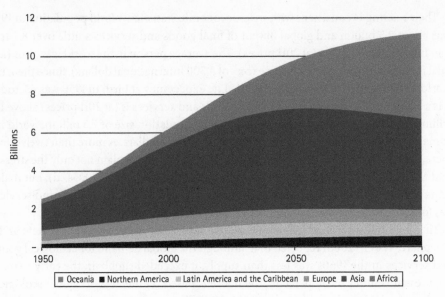

FIGURE 22.1 Total population by region, 1950–2100

Source: United Nations, Department of Economic and Social Affairs, Population Division (2019),
World Population Prospects: The 2019 Revision (New York: United Nations).

gigantic renewable natural resource. But if demand for its products exceeds its ability to supply them year to year, the socio-ecological system will eventually break. That is why environmental scientists today speak of tipping points separating distinct productivity regimes of the Earth system.

It is useful to decompose the factors making up our demands from the biosphere into population size and per capita demand, which is what Ehrlich and Holdren did in their paper. For the most part, though, we will keep technology aside and comment only at the end on the prospects of technology coming to humanity's aid in reducing the overshoot in global demand. In this chapter the focus is on demographic matters. Section 2 studies some important factors underlying what can only be called "population overshoot." We report on the way the desire for children has been estimated by demographers and argue that they overstate *informed* desire. The factors affecting expressed preferences for family size also point to "consumption overshoot" in countries that are today wealthy.[5] We package the factors under the familiar notion of "externalities." In Section 3 we make use of the estimate of humanity's current ecological footprint to ask how many people Earth can support at a reasonable standard of living. The data we use are cruder than are usual even in the social sciences. They are crude because the subject of our paper—the global population-consumption-environment nexus—has had very little quantitative airing among demographers and economists, and none from philosophers. Our aim here is to develop techniques of analysis that may prove useful when the study of socio-ecological processes becomes more common. Because the data are so crude, we do not even engage in exercises that uncover the sensitivity of our findings to the numerical assumptions on which they are built. The numbers we reach are meant to be illustrative, nothing more.

2. THE DESIRE FOR CHILDREN

2.1. Rich and Poor: Consumption and Population

People have children for many reasons. The mix of motivations depends on the customs and institutions we inherit, as well as on our character and circumstances. That children are valuable in themselves is emotionally so compelling that it may seem too obvious to require acknowledgment, but social anthropologists have shown that children are not just valuable to us because of the innate desire we have to bear and rear them, but also because they represent the fulfilment of tradition and religious dictates, and because they are the clearest avenue open to self-transcendence. A common refrain, that our children are priceless, is an expression of how innately valuable they are to us.

2.1.1. *Population in the Poor World*

In places where formal institutions are underdeveloped, children also substitute for other assets, and are thus valuable also for the benefits they bring to their parents. This is most apparent in the poorest regions of the world. Children serve as security in old age in places that have neither pension schemes nor adequate capital and land markets. They are also a source of labor in households possessing few labor-saving devices. Children mind their siblings, tend domestic animals, pick berries and herbs, collect firewood, draw water, and help with cooking. (In South Asia children have been observed to work in household production from age six.) Children in poor countries are valued by their parents both as capital and as producer goods.

Those childhood activities are so unfamiliar today in the West that they direct us to study the mix of motivations governing procreation by contrasting rich regions from poor regions. There are notable exceptions, but broadly speaking fertility and mortality rates are high and health status and education attainments are low in poor countries, whereas the corresponding statistics in rich countries read the other way. Table 22.1, which presents a snap shot (roughly, the period 2014–2015), speaks to that by displaying data published by international organizations, where the two categories, "rich" and "poor," are defined in terms of GDP per capita. Countries have been known to make a transition from one category to the other (that's what economic development is usually taken to mean); moreover, the bulk of the world's population and a majority of the world's poorest people live in neither rich nor poor countries, and international statistics say there are enormously rich people in poor countries. It nevertheless pays to study sharp contrasts, as in Table 22.1.

Table 22.1 Social statistics from rich and poor regions (2014–2015)

	Rich	Poor
Population (millions)	1,420	620
GDP per capita (international dollars)	41,000	1,570
Total fertility rate*	1.7	4.9
Under-5 mortality rate (per 1,000)	7	76
Life expectancy at birth (years)	80	60
Youth literacy	100	68
Civil liberties	high	low
Political liberties	high	low
Government corruption	low	high

Source: World Bank (2016), UNPD (2015), Freedom House (2017)

*Total fertility rate (TFR) is the number of births that a woman expects to have during her reproductive years. The number 2.1 is usually taken to be the TFR that, over the long run would lead to a stable population.

Scholars have shown that differences in Table 22.1 between the rich and poor worlds are traceable to differences in institutions, beliefs, and social norms of behavior. Kinship structure, marriage practices, and rules of inheritance vary across the world. The implied line of thinking says that causality shouldn't be traced to differences in income or wealth. It is not that fertility and mortality rates are high and health status and education attainments are low in poor regions *because* people there are poor, it is that very low incomes go hand in hand with those features of life. The variables are mutually determined over time.[6]

Table 22.1 is a snapshot. It says as compared to people in rich countries, those in societies that are poor receive far less basic education, have many more children, die a lot younger, enjoy fewer political and civil liberties, and suffer from greater failure in governance. There is no suggestion that poor societies will remain poor, nor that rich countries may not find their place reversed in the long run. Regional differences in fertility, education, and output per capita were slight until the start of the Early Modern era (roughly, 1500 CE). Global aggregates of earlier eras look much the same as their regional aggregates.[7] Figure 22.1 reveals that at least for population, regional aggregates will continue to diverge.

Caldwell (1982) drew on an idea that is suggested by Table 22.1, that the intergenerational transfer of wealth is from parents to children in rich countries but from children to parents in poor societies. The suggestion has been easier to confirm in rich countries, where the rate of investment in children's education has been found to be as high as 6–7 percent of GDP (Haveman and Wolfe 1995). Because a vast range of activities in poor societies are undertaken outside the institution of markets, it is especially hard to identify the direction in which resources there flow across the generations. Nevertheless, the Caldwell-hypothesis has been questioned for poor societies. Studies have found that even there the direction is from the old to the young (Lee 2000; 2007). Further investigations may find hidden transfers from the young to the old in poor societies that confirm Caldwell's thesis, but as of now it would seem that throughout the world inter-generational resource transfers are made by the old to the young.

2.1.2. The Case of Africa

Taken as a region, sub-Saharan Africa has long been regarded as special, even among poor regions (Bledsoe et al. 1994; Bongaarts and Casterline 2013; Goody 1976; Fortes 1978). Figure 22.1 confirms that the continent is an outlier in regard to population. In an early review of fertility intentions Cochrane and Farid (1989) noted that both the urban and rural, the educated and uneducated in sub-Saharan Africa have more, and want more, children than their counterparts in other less-developed regions. Even young women there expressed a desire for an average of 2.6 more children than women in the Middle East, 2.8 more than women in North Africa, and 3.6 to 3.7 more than women in Latin America and Asia. Updated versions of these figures are available, but it is worth considering the data from the mid-1980s because the income gap between Africa and the rest of the developing world was smaller at that time than it is now.

The idea of wealth-in-children has been developed by anthropologists to reflect the additional status and other social advantages that are conferred on women in some African societies by having children (Guyer and Eno Belinga 1995). There is a formal resemblance here to Veblen's account of status in an entirely different context, which was conspicuous consumption in the Gilded Age in America (Veblen 1925). In the context of wealth-in-children, desired fertility is higher than it would have been otherwise because of the competition among households fueled by the desire for status. It leads to a collective loss in well-being among those making fertility decisions.

Communal land tenure of the lineage social structure in sub-Saharan Africa has offered yet another inducement for men to procreate: a greater amount of land can be claimed by a larger family. In addition, conjugal bonds are frequently weak, so fathers often do not bear their fair share of costs of siring a child. Anthropologists have observed that the unit of African society is a woman and her children, rather than parents and their children. Frequently, there is no common budget for the man and woman. Descent in sub-Saharan Africa is, for the most part, patrilineal and residence is patrilocal (exceptions are the Akan of Ghana and the Chewa of Malawi). That depresses women's voices; and because women bear a disproportionate amount of the costs of reproduction, it raises fertility rate. Patrilineality, weak conjugal bonds, communal land tenure, and a strong kinship support system of children, taken together, have been a broad characteristic of the region. In principle they provide a powerful stimulus to fertility. Admittedly, patrilineality and patrilocality are features of the northern parts of the Indian sub-continent also. But conjugal bonds are substantially greater there. Moreover, as agricultural land is not communally held, large family sizes lead to fragmentation of landholdings. In contrast, large families in sub-Saharan Africa are (or, at least were, until recently) rewarded by a greater share of land belonging to the lineage or clan.[8] Figure

22.1 and Table 22.1 tell us that the cost of the enormous increase in population that an extremely poor Africa is projected to experience in the coming decades will be an enormous burden on Africans themselves.

2.1.3. *Consumption in the Rich World*

In sharp contrast is the rich world. Table 22.1 reports that the 1.4 billion people living in the World Bank's list of high-income countries enjoy a per capita income of 41,000 (international) dollars. Total income therefore sums to 57 trillion dollars. Global income today is about 110 trillion international dollars. If, as a crude approximation, we take consumption to be proportional to income, consumption in the richest 18 percent of the world's population (1.4 billion/7.5 billion) is more than 50 percent of world consumption (57 trillion/110 trillion). If economic development is to be sustainable, resource intensive consumption patterns in rich countries have to adjust substantially. In contrast, sub-Saharan Africa, a region inhabited by about 13 percent of the world's population, enjoys only 3 percent of the world's output of final goods and services. If population size and its increase is the significant social problem besetting the worlds' poorest region, it is high consumption in the world's rich countries that is currently responsible for a global ecological footprint well in excess of 1.

2.1.4. *Positive and Normative Reasoning*

Economists and historians have offered explanations for demographic trends (Rosenzweig and Stark 1997) and the evolution of consumption tastes (Trentmann 2016). They have commonly avoided moral theories in their studies. In contrast, philosophical discourses on population and consumption have been built on normative reasoning, directed at four questions: (1) What are the nature, ground, and limits of parental responsibility for existing children? (2) Does producing a child interfere with the rights of children the couple already have? (3) Do individuals have a duty not to have children who are likely to experience lives that will be bad for them? Do they have a duty to procreate if the children they create would likely to enjoy lives that will be good for them? (4) How should one value possible populations so as to decide which would be best?

One way to contrast the two disciplinary approaches is to say, in the case of population, that the economic demographer's task is to explain Table 22.1, while the aim in population ethics is to produce a normative theory that one could use to evaluate the behavior patterns that give rise to Table 22.1 and prescribe better ones. Question (4), which stands in sharp contrast to those that demographers study, is at the heart of "population axiology," which attempts to uncover the ethics involved in what Parfit (1984, 356) called Different Numbers Choices. We do not pursue that line of enquiry here.[9]

2.2. Two Classes of Externalities

Processes driving the balance between population size and our demand for the biosphere's goods and services harbor *externalities*, which are the unaccounted-for consequences for others of actions taken by one or more persons. The qualifier "unaccounted-for" means that the consequences in question follow without prior engagement with those who are affected.

The way we have formulated the notion of externalities could appear odd, on grounds that our actions inevitably have consequences for future generations, who by the nature of things cannot engage with us. In fact, future people engage with us constantly, albeit indirectly. Parents care about their children and know that they in turn will care about their children. By recursion, thoughtful parents take the well-being of their descendants into account when choosing the rates at which they save for their children and invest in them. Intergenerational engagement would be imperfect if parents choose without adequate concern for their children (e.g., if they discount the future well-being of their children at overly high rates). Externalities across the generations would be rampant in that case. We ignore that line of analysis here. Our aim is to study systematic reasons why choices made even by thoughtful parents do not reflect adequate engagement with *others*' descendants. As they are symptoms of institutional failure, externalities cannot be eliminated entirely, but can be reduced greatly by considered collective action. That is why reasoned reproductive decisions at the individual level can nevertheless result in collective failure.

One class of externalities arising from household consumption and reproduction decisions is traceable to open access resources: *the commons*. They have been much noted and studied by environmental economists (e.g., Baumol and Oates 1975). The institutional failures that give rise to those externalities owe their origin to an absence of appropriate property rights to Nature's goods and services. By property rights we mean not only private rights, but communitarian and public rights too. One reason rights over the biosphere are difficult to define, let alone to enforce, is that Nature is constantly on the move (the wind blows, particulates diffuse, rivers flow, fish swim, birds and insects fly, and even earthworms are known to travel undetected). No one can contain the atmosphere they befoul. That means the price paid by someone for environmental services (that's the private cost) is less than the cost borne by all (that's the social cost). Modern patterns of consumption, relying as they do on long distance trade, are especially prone to being underpriced. That provides people with an incentive to consume too much. To cite a familiar example, in cases involving the global environment, such as the atmosphere as a sink for our carbon emissions, the damage an individual suffers from her own emissions is negligible even though the damage to all from the climate change that arises from everyone's emissions is large and positive. From the collective point of view there is excessive use of the atmosphere as a carbon sink.

The other category of externalities we study here has been less studied in the literature. Its source is the *social-embeddedness* of our preferences. Our desire for having children, for example, is in part influenced by the number of children others have. No doubt a single household cannot much influence others, but the aggregate effect of all households on one another is not negligible. We show that the social embeddedness of household preferences, the resulting behavior can be called "conformist," can lead to high fertility even when the same preference structure sustains low fertility that households would prefer. Either situation—high fertility (allied to low educational attainment of children) or low fertility (allied to high educational attainment of children)—can sustain itself by its own bootstrap. Fertility transitions can be interpreted as moves from one equilibrium to the other.

Socially embedded preferences also influence consumption behavior. Like reproductive behavior, they take two forms. Our urge to compete with others (Veblen's "conspicuous consumption"; Veblen 1925) is one form. (It's the counterpart to the "wealth-in-children" notion we noted earlier.) The other form arises from our desire to conform with others (Douglas and Isherwood 1979). Both forms give rise to consumption externalities. We should conclude that the psychological cost to a person of a collective adjustment in consumption is likely to be much less than it would be if she were to adjust consumption unilaterally. The aggregate cost of collective adjustment could even be negative.

Externalities arising from our use of the commons and from the social-embeddedness of our preferences differ in their internal structures. The problem of choice in the use of open access resources resembles the well-known Prisoners' Dilemma. In contrast, socially embedded preferences give rise to Coordination Games. The latter class of externalities can be, and has been, turned by communities to their advantage by coordinating behavior (e.g., through an appeal to social norms). The former class in contrast requires, at least over the global commons, more traditional policy measures such as environmental regulations.

2.3. Reproductive Rights

The 1994 International Conference on Population and Development reaffirmed the language of rights in the sphere of family planning and reproductive health. The widely noted publication that reported the Conference's conclusions stated:

> Reproductive rights . . . rest on the recognition of the basic right of all couples and individuals to decide freely and responsibly the number, spacing, and timing of their children, and to have information and means to do so, and the right to attain the highest standards of sexual and reproductive health. (UNFPA 1995: Ch. 7, Section 3)

The qualifier, "responsibly," could be read as requiring couples to take into account the adverse environmental externalities their reproductive decisions may give rise to; but that would probably be a stretch. Certainly, writings affirming the UN declaration have interpreted the passage and its intent more narrowly. For example, the fundamental right of individuals "to decide freely and for themselves whether, when, and how many children to have" is central to the vision and goals of *Family Planning 2020* (FP2020). It is also pivotal in the reproductive health indicators of the United Nations' Sustainable Development Goals.

It is useful to study the relationship between "externalities" and "rights." First, to insist that the rights of individuals and couples to decide freely the number of children they produce trump all competing interests is to play down the rights of all those (most especially, perhaps, future people) who suffer from the environmental externalities that accompany additions to the population.[10] Secondly, UNFPA's statement ignores the latent need among those who do not want family planning now but would want it if others among their peer group were using modern contraceptives.

That family planning services bring in their wake many benefits (health, education, income, women's empowerment) to those who make use of them has been documented repeatedly in recent years.[11] Our focus on externalities points to the fact that they bring benefits to others as well. Those additional benefits should be included in the design of social policies. Below we show that indicators currently in use by governments and NGOs of the value of family planning services underestimate it.

Policies for curbing adverse reproductive externalities can in principle take several forms. Education, especially female education, is one route; many argue it is the most effective route (Lutz et al. 2014). But that can take time, and female education is not the only factor driving fertility.[12] Another tool involves demonstrative persuasion, which can be attempted through community discussions on the need for behavioral change. The agency of persuasion could be the community, NGOs, or the state. A further tool is taxation, which permits people to choose as they wish, but at a price. Although taxation as a device for curbing environmental externalities is familiar in wealthy countries, it is not an available tool for reducing the demand for children in poor countries, where the poorest households are most often the ones that have the highest demand.

There are thus a variety of policy tools available for reducing fertility where fertility rates are above replacement levels. The tools differ in terms of the extent to which the right to self-determination is compromised. None are likely to prove uncontroversial. The issues remain unsettled.

2.4. Socially Embedded Preferences and Conformism

That children are a parental end (and not just a means toward other parental goals) provides a potentially powerful mechanism by which reasoned fertility decisions at the level of every household could lead to an unsatisfactory outcome from the perspectives of all households. It arises from the possibility that traditional practice is perpetuated by conformity. Reproductive decisions are not only a private matter; they are subject to social mores, which in turn are influenced by both family experiences and the cultural milieu. But social mores are shaped by the behavior of all. There is circularity in this, which we can unravel by supposing that household preference structures are socially embedded. Behavior is conformist when the family size each household desires is positively related to the average family size in the community (Dasgupta 1993, Ch. 12).[13]

Whatever the basis of conformism, there would be practices encouraging high fertility that no household would unilaterally desire to break. Such practices could have had a rationale in the past, when mortality rates were high, population densities were low, natural resources were aplenty, the threat of extermination from outside attack was large, and mobility was restricted. But practices can survive even when their original purposes have disappeared. One reason they can survive is that if all others continue to follow the practice and aim at large family sizes, no conformist household would on its own wish to deviate from the practice; however, if all other households were to restrict their fertility rates, every household would wish to restrict its fertility rate as well. Conformism can thus be a reason for the existence of multiple social equilibria. A society could get embedded in a self-sustaining mode of behavior characterized by high fertility and low educational attainment, even when there is another potentially self-sustaining mode of behavior characterized by low fertility and high educational attainment, and which is preferred by all.

Socially embedded preferences for children are drawn in Figure 22.2. The curve ABCDE is the representative household's desired number of children, plotted against the average number of children per household (the horizontal axis). The curve is upward sloping and intersects the 45° line OF at three points: B, C, D. Each is a social equilibrium, at TFRs n_1, n_2, and n_3 respectively. To interpret ABCDE with concrete numbers, imagine that each household regards 5 to be the ideal number of children if all other households have 5 children (n_3 on the horizontal axis)); 4 to be the ideal number if all others have 4 (n_2); and 2 to be the ideal number if all others have 2 (n_1). Imagine now that each household prefers the outcome where all households have 2 children. It can nevertheless be that their society is stuck in a situation where each household has 5 children. It can get stuck because no household would have a reason to deviate from 5 if all other households have 5; which is another way of saying that 5 is a self-enforcing choice. It is

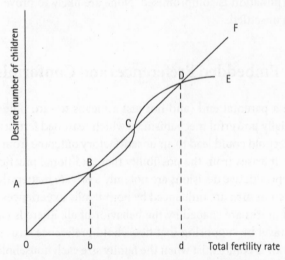

FIGURE 22.2 Conformist preferences for children. The curve ABCDE shows a representative woman's desired number of children as a function of the average number of births per woman in the population. B and D are stable equilibria, C is unstable.

easy to confirm that both 2 and 5 are stable equilibria, in that a small deviation from 2 (respectively, 5) would in time return to a situation where each household chooses 2 (respectively, 5). It follows that 5 would be just as tenacious a TFR as 2.[14]

That does not mean society would be stuck at 5 forever. As always, people differ in the extent of their absorption of traditional practice. There would inevitably be those who, for one reason or another, experiment, take risks, and refrain from joining the crowd. They are the tradition breakers, and they often lead the way. Educated women are among the first to make the move toward smaller families.[15] A possibly even stronger pathway is the influence that newspapers, radio, television, and now the internet play in transmitting information about other lifestyles. The idea here is that the media could be a vehicle by which conformism increasingly becomes based on the behavior of a wider population than the local community (the peer group widens). And that disrupts behavior.[16]

There have been a number of studies on fertility that point to choices that are guided in part by attention to others. In her highly original work on demographic change in Western Europe over the period 1870–1960, Watkins (1990) showed that differences in fertility and nuptiality within each country declined. She also found that in 1870, before the large-scale declines in marital fertility had begun in most areas of Western Europe, demographic behavior differed considerably within countries. Differences among provinces within a country were high even while differences within provinces were low. Spatial behavioral clumps suggest the importance of the influence of local communities on behavior. In 1960 differences within each country were considerably less than in 1870. Watkins explained this in terms of increases in the geographical reach national governments enjoyed over the ninety years in question. The growth of national languages could have been the medium through which reproductive behavior was able to spread.

Watkins' was a historical study. Jensen and Oster (2009) in contrast have studied a natural experiment. They found that state level fertility rates declined in step following staggered introductions of cable TV in Indian states.[17]

It is a feature of historical studies of the diffusion of behavior across space and time that they don't necessarily identify the fundamentals on which the diffusion process is built. They also differ from one another in terms of the transmission mechanism. The behavioral fundamentals (or "drivers," as some would call them) could be knowledge acquisition, they could be pure mimicry, they could be what Cleland and Wilson (1987) called "ideation," they could be the advent of modernity, they could be the desire to belong to one's (possibly expanding) group, they could be the force of celebrity culture, and so on. These fundamentals are not unrelated, but they are not the same. Regarding transmission mechanisms, it could be that people observe successful behavior and copy it, it could be that the language in which newspapers are read spreads, it could be that people discuss and debate among themselves, and so forth.

The model in Figure 22.2 is built on the common structure of all such diffusion processes. Leaving aside the virtue of parsimony, studying the common structure offers the advantage that we are able to analyze the resting (i.e., equilibrium) points of a wide variety of diffusion processes without having to identify the processes themselves. Our model is analytical, not a historical narrative. It assumes that fertility preferences are socially embedded, but it doesn't specify the reasons households are influenced by the behavior of others. Being analytical, the model is able to entertain counterfactuals. It allows us to ask how a household's behavior would differ if the social parameters underlying the curve ABCDE were to be otherwise. That's a necessary exercise in policy analysis, because policies can be used to shift the curve ABCDE (therefore the equilibrium points n_1, n_2, and n_3) as well as influence the beliefs on the basis of which households act. The common structure also tells us that fertility transitions can be interpreted as disequilibrium phenomena (Dasgupta 2002), where practices change slowly in response to gradual changes in the social environment, until a tipping point is reached from which society transits rapidly to a new stable equilibrium, say from high fertility to low fertility.

Socially embedded preference structures don't entail multiplicity of equilibria. We could have also drawn the curve ABCDE in Figure 22.2 that it intersects the 45° line OF at a single point. We are interested in multiple equilibria because there is empirical evidence that societies support a multiplicity of stable fertility choices (e.g., n_1 and n_3). Historical studies of the diffusion of fertility behavior point to that (Watkins 1990). Fertility transitions are an expression of the phenomenon.

2.5. Unmet Need, Desired Family Size, and the UN's Sustainable Development Goals

UNFPA (1995) took it that family planning and reproductive health policies should address "unmet need", meaning that they should be made to serve women aged 15–49 who want to stop or delay child-bearing but are not using modern forms of contraception (Bradley et al. 2012; Alkema et al. 2013). Although the idea of "unmet need" could appear straightforward, it has in practice proved to be complex and has been interpreted in different ways over the years. It is currently measured using more than fifteen survey questions, including questions on contraceptive use, fertility intentions, pregnancies, postpartum amenorreah, sexual activity, birth history, and menstruation. Women's reported fertility intentions are inferred from such questions as: "Now, I have some questions about the future. Would you like to have a(nother) child or would you prefer not to have (any more) children?" That is followed by a question on how long the woman wants to wait should she have responded to the previous question that she does want a(nother) child.[18]

There are deep problems here. Unmet need as calculated from responses to survey questions is based on the respondents' expressed wants for children. The need for family planning is then inferred. But in matters of life and death resource needs assume an independent status; they even serve as the basis on which commodity rights are founded. A statement of the form "person A needs commodity X" can be regarded as tantamount to a challenge to imagine an alternative future in which A escapes harm without X

(Wiggins 1987, 22). Expressed wants or desires for children, which are used for calculating a woman's unmet need for family planning, may not adequately convey her true need for family planning, that is, for her own best interests. A poor woman, suffering from iron deficiency and living in a setting where she is more or less obliged to have sex, has a need for contraception for her own benefit that could remain undetected in her responses to questions on her expressed wants for children. To infer needs solely from wants is therefore to undervalue the significance of family planning. Moreover, none of the survey questions is conditioned on the behavior of others. As we see below, that too is limiting.

Closely related is the notion of "ideal family size," which is obtained from answers to the following question: "If you could go back to the time when you did not have any children and could choose exactly the number of children to have in your whole life, how many would that be?"

There are dangers of biases in responses to the question at the basis of ideal family size, but the need for family planning programs to have quantitative estimates of it is clear enough. Notice though that the questionnaire does not ask of someone what her desire would be if the prevailing fertility practices of others were different. In fact, there is no mention of the prevailing fertility rate. As respondents are not invited to disclose their conditional desires, it is most likely they disclose their ideal family size on the assumption that fertility will remain at its prevailing rate. A direct way to discover socially embedded preferences would be to reconstruct the questionnaires by asking a series of conditional questions, which we collapse here for convenience into one:

> If you could go back to the time when you did not have any children and could choose exactly the number of children to have in your whole life, how many would that be, assuming everyone else in your community had n children over their whole life?

The survey could pose the conditional question in an ascending order of n, say from 0 to 10 (thus 11 conditional questions in total). The example in Figure 22.2 imagines that the answers to $n = 2$, 4, and 5 are, respectively, 2, 4, and 5. It also imagines that answers to the questions in which $n = 0$, 1, 3, 6–10, respectively, differ from 0, 1, 3, 6–10; which is why the latter numbers are not social equilibria. No doubt responding to a string of conditional questions would tax respondents, but to not ask them is to misread fertility desires.[19]

Fabic et al. (2015) defined "total demand" for modern contraception to be the number of women who want to delay or limit child-bearing (i.e., the sum of contraceptive users and women with unmet need). The role of family planning, the authors argued, is to supply that demand. The suggestion is that the success of family planning should be measured by the ratio of family planning users to the total demand. The United Nations have adopted this measure in their Sustainable Development Goal 3.7.1. It is known as "demand for family planning met with modern contraceptive methods," or "demand satisfied" for short. Formally, if X is the number of women between 15–49 who are users of modern contraceptives, Y is the number of women with unmet need, and Z is total demand for modern contraception, then $Z = X+Y$ and the UN's "demand satisfied" is $X/Z = X/(X+Y)$.

Reproductive rights are at the heart of X/Z, which is its attraction. The indicator reflects voluntarism, rights and equity, informed choice, and the imperative of satisfying individuals' and couples' own choices with regard to the timing and number of children. But there are problems. The use of X/Z as the measure of success could create perverse incentives among program managers. A program's performance would improve if more women were to declare that they want to get pregnant. So long as women want many children, Y (unmet need) remains small, and therefore Z (total demand) is only marginally greater than X (the number of modern contraceptive users). The country scores well in the indicator "demand satisfied" and appears not to need further family planning programming. The success could mask a situation where contraceptive use is low and stagnant and high fertility rates persist. This is demonstrated in Figure 22.3, which presents two examples. They have identical levels of demand for family planning met with modern contraceptive methods. However, the first example is characterized by higher use of modern methods. The second example is characterized by very low use of contraception and a significant proportion of women who are considered to have no need because of preferences for large families, and this example would likely have high fertility rates. Moreover, as we saw in Section 2.4, fertility preferences, which contribute to the measurement of Y, are themselves influenced by the behavior of others. Y could therefore be small in a society that harbors another equilibrium in which Y is large.

The concept of reproductive rights, as currently framed, undervalues family planning. There are collective benefits to be enjoyed if members of a community are enabled to alter their fertility desires in a coordinated manner. Family planning can help to bring

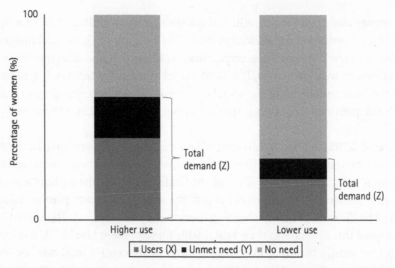

FIGURE 22.3 Two examples with identical levels of demand for family planning met with modern contraceptive methods

about changes in such social norms. Our analysis doesn't run against rights as a plank for family planning; it expands the sphere in which rights are acknowledged, protected, and promoted.[20]

3. HOW MANY PEOPLE CAN EARTH SUPPORT IN COMFORT?

We have argued that the processes that have led to an overshoot in our demands on the biosphere are triggered by environmental and reproductive externalities. Below we present evidence which suggests that a global population of 11.2 billion (Figure 22.1) at standards of living hoped for under the UN's Sustainable Development Goals would probably damage the biosphere to such an extent that the Goals would not be maintainable. Suppose then that by some miracle human society is able to eliminate the externalities. Suppose too that socio-economic inequalities are ironed out. Given current and prospective technological possibilities, what can we say about global population numbers that the biosphere can support sustainably at a comfortable living standard? In order to obtain sharp answers without technicalities, we confine ourselves to a world that is deterministic.

Economic possibilities are circumscribed by the biosphere. When thinking of the global economy, it is useful to regard the biosphere as a gigantic renewable natural resource. Fisheries are proto-typical examples of such resources. We observe next that human labor and ingenuity can be (and are!) applied to produced capital (machines and equipment) and the biosphere to produce output for consumption. That output is usually called GDP. However, other things equal, labor's contribution to output diminishes with increasing numbers. So, even though a larger population would produce more, there would be less to go round per person despite the larger output. Of course, other things are not equal: produced capital can be accumulated to counter the diminishing contribution of greater numbers of people to production. But produced capital is also subject to diminishing returns (accumulating tractors indefinitely would not contribute to further agricultural production). Therefore, balances among the various factors of production should exist. In this chapter we first select a standard of living that could be deemed to be comfortable. We then estimate the global population that could be supported by the biosphere at that living standard on a sustainable basis. But we first need an account of the biosphere in its role as a capital asset.

3.1. Ecosystem Services

The term "biosphere" is an all-encompassing construct. Although we will think of it as a gigantic renewable natural resource, it is in fact a mosaic of renewable natural resources.

Agricultural land, forests, watersheds, fisheries, fresh water sources, estuaries, wetlands, the oceans, and the atmosphere are some of the interlocking constituents of the biosphere. We will refer to them generically as "ecosystems" and, so as to draw attention to populations of species in their habitats, we will speak of them also, more narrowly, as "biological communities."[21]

Ecosystems combine the abiotic environment with biological communities (plants, animals, fungi, and microorganisms) that form functional units. Individual actors in ecosystems include organisms that pollinate, decompose, filter, transport, re-distribute, scavenge, fix gases, and so on. Nearly all organisms that help to produce those services are hidden from view (a gram of soil may contain as many as 10 billion bacterial cells), which is why they are almost always missing from popular discourses on the environment. But their activities enable ecosystems to maintain a genetic library, preserve and regenerate soil, fix nitrogen and carbon, recycle nutrients, control floods, mitigate droughts, filter pollutants, assimilate waste, pollinate crops, operate the hydrological cycle, and maintain the gaseous composition of the atmosphere.

Ecosystems differ in composition and extent. They can be defined as ranging from the communities and interactions of organisms in your mouth or those in the canopy of a rain forest to all those in Earth's oceans. The processes governing them differ in complexity and speed. There are systems that turn over in minutes, there are others whose rhythmic time extends to hundreds of years. Some ecosystems are extensive ("biomes," such as the African Savannah), there are those that cover regions (river basins) and many involve clusters of villages (micro-watersheds), while others are confined to the level of a single village (the village pond). In each example there is an element of indivisibility. Divide an ecosystem into parts by creating barriers, and the sum of the productivity of the parts will typically be found to be lower than the productivity of the whole, other things equal (Sodhi, Brook, and Bradshaw 2009). The mobility of biological populations is a reason (Section 2.2). Safe corridors, for example, enable migratory species to survive.

Ecosystems can regenerate but suffer deterioration (worse, exhaustion) when human expropriation exceeds the rates at which they are able to supply us with goods and services or when they are converted directly into produced capital. That is why ecosystems can be thought of as renewable natural resources. Population extinctions disrupt essential ecosystem services. In tropical forests dung beetles play an essential role in recycling nutrients. Excessive hunting of mammals in the forests has been found to be a cause of local elimination of dung dependent beetles (Brook, Sodhi, and Bradshaw 2008). When subject to excessive stress, once flourishing ecosystems (e.g., biologically rich estuaries) flip into unproductive states (dead zones). The stress could be occasioned by an invasion of foreign species or substance (as in the above example), it could be owing to loss of population diversity, it could be triggered by the demise of a dominant species, and so on. Ehrlich and Ehrlich (1981) likened the pathways by which an ecosystem can be tipped out of a stable regime into an unproductive state to a flying aircraft from which rivets are removed, one at a time. The probability that it will crash increases very slowly at first, but then at some unspecifiable number rises sharply to 1.

Erosion of the biosphere usually goes unrecorded in official economic statistics because GDP does not record depreciation of capital assets. Destroy an open woodland so as to build a shopping mall, and the national accounts will record the increase in produced capital (the shopping mall is an investment), but not the disinvestment in what we may called "natural capital." The example is a commonplace. Even while industrial output increased by a multiple of 40 during the twentieth century, the use of energy increased by a multiple of 16, methane-producing cattle population grew in pace with human population, fish catch increased by a multiple of 35 and carbon and sulfur dioxide emissions rose by more than 10. It has been estimated that 25–30 percent of the 130 billion metric tons of carbon that are harnessed annually by terrestrial photosynthesis is appropriated for human use (Haberl et al. 2007). Although the rise in the concentration of atmospheric carbon receives much the greater public attention, MEA (2005a–d) reported that fifteen of the twenty-four ecosystems the authors had reviewed world-wide were either degraded or are being exploited at unsustainable rates.

Current extinction rates of species in various orders have been estimated to be 100–1,000 times higher than their average rate (about 1 per million species per year) over the past several million years (Sodhi, Brook, and Bradshaw 2009). The figures are reached from field studies of the decline in numbers of specific groups of mammals, insects, and birds, and from empirically drawn relationships between the number of species in an area and the size of the area. But the relationships are known to vary substantially among communities and habitats, which is why, as the range shows, there are great uncertainties in the estimates. Despite the uncertainties, the figures put the scale of humanity's presence on the Earth system in perspective.

The statistics we have just summarized for sketching humanity's recent doings differs sharply from the one that has been on offer in a string of recent books, in which intellectuals have re-drawn our attention to the remarkable gains in the standard of living humanity has enjoyed over the past century (Micklethwait and Wooldridge 2000; Pinker 2018; Ridley 2010). The authors have collated data on growth in scientific knowledge and the accumulation of produced capital and human capital and argued that humanity has never had it so good. But with the exception of rising carbon concentration in the atmosphere, trends in the state of the biosphere accompanying those advances have gone unnoted by the authors. The problem is, global climate change is but one of a myriad of environmental problems we face today. And because it is amenable to technological solutions (innovating with cheap non-carbon sources of energy and, more speculatively, firing sulfur particulates into the stratosphere to reflect sunlight back to space; Pinker 2018), it is not representative. Global climate change attracts attention among intellectuals and the reading public not only because it is a grave problem, but also because it is possible to imagine meeting it by using the familiar economics of commodity taxation, regulation, and resource pricing without having to forego growth in living standards in rich countries. The literature on the economics of climate change (e.g., Stern 2006) has even encouraged the thought that with but little investment in clean energy sources (say 2 percent of world GDP) we can enjoy indefinite growth in the world's output of final goods and services (global GDP).

And that's a thought to be resisted. At least as grave a danger facing humanity is the unprecedented rate of species extinctions now taking place. Continued extinctions will damage the biosphere irreparably, and that cannot be prevented by technological fixes. Politics has intervened to prevent even the relatively small global investment that experts suggest is required to stall climate change. Thus, we should expect the problem of species extinctions to remain off the table, at least until citizens take the matter seriously.[22]

3.2. The Biosphere as a Capital Stock

We assume that people apply their labor to produced capital (machines and equipment) and the biosphere's goods and services to produce an all-purpose commodity that can be consumed. Our idea is to choose a living standard deemed to be comfortable and identify the state of the biosphere that can sustain humanity at that standard on an indefinite basis.[23]

For the purposes of illustration, we use the figure of 20,000 international dollars at today's prices. As the figure falls in the range of per capita incomes in the World Bank's list of upper middle-income countries, we use it to represent an acceptable standard of living.[24]

As of now we have little quantitative knowledge of the biosphere's dynamics when viewed in the aggregate: we don't know the G-function. But we know that expanding our stock of produced capital would very likely have environmental consequences. So, with both pairs of hands proverbially tied behind our backs we now regard K to be an aggregate measure of the biosphere and produced capital.

Let Q be aggregate output. If global population is N and φ the proportion of N in production, we assume that

$$Q = K^{(1-\rho)}[\varphi N]^{\rho}, \quad 0 \leq \rho < 1, \, 0 < \varphi < 1 \tag{1}$$

We now stop K in its tracks and estimate $K^{(1-\rho)}$ (eq. (1)) on the basis of the current size of the world economy. Stopping K in its tracks amounts to imposing a quota on what the human population is permitted to take from the biosphere.

The latter thought is not outlandish. Quotas are applied routinely to fisheries and forestry, and for access to potable water in dry regions. The recent international agreement to limit the rise in mean global temperature to 1.5°C above what it was in pre-industrial times is tantamount to the use of quotas in emissions. That said, we realize that applying the idea on the biosphere as whole is a leap of faith in the ability, not to mention willingness, of international organizations to reduce the ecological footprint to a sustainable size. But we have found no other way to estimate the size of the global population Earth can support at reasonable comfort. Wilson (2016) has made an impassioned plea to leave half of Earth free of human encroachment, but we follow a somewhat different, and much blunter, route to identify a sustainable socio-ecological state of affairs.

The data being utterly crude, we confine ourselves to pen-on-paper computations. We assume that the value of the world's production of final good and services draws proportionately on ecosystem services at all levels.[25] World output is currently about 120 trillion international dollars. Using the model of production in equation (1), we therefore have

$$K^{1-\rho}\left[\varphi N\right]^{\rho} = 120 \text{ trillion (international) dollars} \tag{2}$$

World population is currently 7.8 billion. The global dependency ratio, that is, the ratio of the sum of the number of people below age 15 and above age 65 to the number of people between 15 and 65, is today about 1.6:1. Thus $\varphi = 1/2.6$, and so $\varphi N = 3$ billion. A huge empirical literature in economics suggests that as a rounded figure, $\rho = 0.5$ is not unreasonable.

Equation (2) then says

$$K^{0.5} = 120 \times 10^{12} / \left(3 \times 10^{9}\right)^{0.5} \text{ dollars per producer}^{0.5}$$
$$\approx 2.2 \text{ billion dollars per producer}^{0.5} \tag{3}$$

Having calibrated our model of global production, we compute the sustainable population size. Let N^{*} denote the size of the sustainable global population. To err on the conservative side of GFN's most recent estimate of 1.6, we assume the current global ecological footprint is 1.5. That means if the biosphere and the stock of produced capital were stopped on their tracks, their sustainable value would be $K/1.5$, which we denote by K^{*}. Using equation (3),

$$(K^{*})^{0.5} \approx 1.8 \text{ billion dollars per producer}^{0.5} \tag{4}$$

Using equations (2)–(3), we have

$$(K^{*})^{0.5}\left(\varphi N^{*}\right)^{0.5} = \left(1.8 \times 10^{9}\right)\left(\varphi N^{*}\right)^{0.5} = \left(20 \times 10^{3}\right)N^{*} \tag{5}$$

But $\varphi = 1/2.6$. From equation (4) it follows that

$$N^{*} = 3.32 \text{ billion} \tag{6}$$

This was global population about sixty years ago (Figure 22.1); so, we are not staring at a figure from the distant past.

The figure is revealing. The global population today is 7.8 billion and per capita consumption is 16,000 international dollars. Our estimate, with all the caveats we have stressed, says that if humanity were to find ways to husband the biosphere in a sustainable manner and to bring about economic equality, the population Earth could support at a living standard of 20,000 international dollars is approximately 3.3 billion. It is a simple matter to conduct the exercise with alternative figures. We resist doing that.

Our decision to study how many people Earth can support in comfort in a *stationary state* was forced on us because of lack of data. We know that the biosphere can be thought to be a gigantic renewable natural resource, but we know next to nothing about the parameters that define its dynamics. So, we have taken the desperate steps of freezing the biosphere and all other capital assets on their tracks and of calibrating the model by using estimates of our global ecological footprint. The idea that society can lock so complex an object as the Earth system on its tracks is wholly beyond belief, but it's the only move we have had available to us for finding a way through a horrible maze. The population figure we have reached (3.3 billion) on the basis of the calibration are not attainable, but we have presented them only to show how far off humanity is from where we should probably now be. Our aim has been to explore a mode of analysis, nothing more.

3.3. Technology and Institutions

When communities face exceptional resource stress (droughts and pests are only two causes), they can be expected to seek new practices and fashion new institutions. If migration to better locations is a possibility, communities can be expected to try that if all else fails. We shouldn't imagine people taking impending disasters lying down. Boserup (1965) collated evidence from agrarian societies to argue that resource stress generates societal responses that not only fend off disaster but can even lead to prosperity. Exceptional scarcities may raise exceptional "problems," but as the saying goes today, they offer exceptional "opportunities" as well. Boserup's work countered a widespread fear in the early 1960s that our capacity to produce food was being overtaken by growth in human numbers. She saw population growth as a spur to innovations. The Green Revolution that came soon after her publication matched her narrative. Population was dropped from public discourse even as Boserup came to be seen as a counterpoint to Malthus.

Boserup's case studies were about "organic economies" (Wrigley 2004), where not only food but also raw materials are either animal or vegetable in origin. Inevitably, there was sample bias in her choice of examples. Societies that hadn't made the cut would have disappeared or moved to blend themselves among communities that survived; they would be absent from such records as those that Boserup studied. In a study of a modern-day society, Turner and Ali (1996) put together the contrasting concerns of Malthus and Boserup by demonstrating that in the face of rising population and a deteriorating resource base, small farmers in Bangladesh expanded production by intensifying agriculture practices (introducing multiple cropping and collectively strengthening drainage systems and flood and storm defenses). The farmers haven't been able to thrive, they still live in poverty, but they staved off collapse (they haven't abandoned their villages *en masse* for cities), at least for now. Studies with a similar flavor for agricultural prospects in Africa have been summarized by Christiaensen (2017).

If Boserup is a counterpoint to Malthus, Jared Diamond is a natural counterpoint to Boserup. Techniques for reading archaeological records have improved since the 1960s. In a series of case studies drawn from early-to-middle second millennium CE, Diamond

(2005) found that a number of societies that had deforested their land had been able to develop successful forest management practices and population measures, but that in contrast there were others, most notoriously Easter Island, that had failed to develop successful management practices, and had collapsed as a result. Diamond also found a common pattern in past collapses: population growth that followed access to an abundant resource base made people intensify the means of food production (irrigation, terracing, double-cropping) and expand into marginal land. Growing populations led to a mining of the resource base, which in turn left communities vulnerable to climatic variations, as there was little room left for either mistakes or bad luck.

PNAS (2012) contains a Special Feature on historical collapses. Contributors reported twelve studies of past societies that had faced environmental stress. Seven were found to have suffered severe transformation, while five overcame them through changes in their practices. Butzer (2012) reported the ways in which a number of societies in fourteenth- to eighteenth-century Western Europe displayed resilience by coping with environmental stresses through innovation and agricultural intensification. Like Diamond, he concluded that collapse is rarely abrupt.

That collapse is rarely abrupt suggests that socio-ecological systems are not brittle, but that on facing continual stress they become less resilient to withstanding shocks and surprises. In a study of European Neolithic societies that began some 9,000 years ago, Downey, Randall Haas, and Shennan (2016) found that the introduction of agriculture spurred population growth, but societies in many cases experienced demographic instability and, ultimately, collapse. The authors also uncovered evidence of warning signs of eventual population collapse, reflected in decreasing resilience in socio-ecological systems. Scheffer (2016) has given further support to the thesis by reporting that there had been warning signs of reduced resilience prior to the great drought in the late 1270s that destroyed the communities that had built the iconic alcove sites of Mesa Verde.

Inevitably, these studies have been about societies with tight geographical boundaries. A community that failed because of population overshoot or bad resource-management practices no doubt destroyed their natural resource base, but it was their *local* resource base they destroyed; societies until modern times were incapable of affecting the Earth system as a whole. Matters are different today. Our presence is so dominant that the biosphere is no longer as modular as it was until recently. Disturbance in one location today gets transmitted to other parts in short order. Movements of people and trade in goods have created a transmission mechanism with a long and quick reach. The mechanism's medium has, however, remained the same. Nature is mobile: the wind blows, rivers flow, the oceans circulate, and birds and insects fly. We weaken the Antarctica ice sheet without ever going there; fish in the North Sea eat micro-plastic originating in markets in the Bahamas; phosphorus discharge from farms in Minnesota contributes to a deadening of the Gulf of Mexico; emissions of black carbon from kitchens in the Indian sub-continent affect the circulation patterns of the Monsoons; the Green Revolution's demand for water, fertilizers, and pesticides pollutes the rivers and ground waters of the Indo-Gangetic Plain; and so on.

Economic historians of the Industrial Revolution point to the role institutions played in creating incentives for entrepreneurs to find ways to work round natural resource constraints. The rate at which we are able to reduce our dependence on natural resources has to exceed the growth rate of humanity's consumption level. Otherwise, our ecological footprint will not decline. The footprint currently exceeds 1 and is continuing to increase. We can be sanguine about the character of technological advances and consumption patterns we correspondingly adopt only if we personally experience the scarcity value of the biosphere, that is, if we have to pay for its use. Understandably, entrepreneurs economize on the expensive factors of production, not the cheap ones. So long as the biosphere's goods and services remain under-priced, technological advances can be expected to be rapacious in their use. Moreover, technological advances that are patently good can have side-effects that are not benign. The tightening of links that bind the biosphere together has meant that economizing on the use of one resource is frequently at the expense of a greater reliance on some other resource (e.g., sinks for our waste products). The ability to use fossil-based energy at large scales has transformed lives for the better, but it has created the unintended consequence of global climate change. Bulldozers and chainsaws enable people to deforest land at rates that would have been unimaginable 250 years ago, and modern fishing technology devastates large swathes of sea beds in a manner unthinkable in the past. If technological progress is our hope, it has either to come allied with elimination of environmental externalities or be directed by public investment in research and development (R&D).

The recent focus on global climate change has led us, even if imperceptibly, to concentrate on technological solutions. But climate change is not paradigmatic of environmental problems. Contaminating the oceans with materials in all probability requires collective behavioral change in parallel with R&D that is moved by public concerns. Restoration and conservation measures are ways by which we can reduce the global ecological footprint. Creating safe zones for migratory species is another needed measure. Reducing waste is yet another. Advances in bio-technology would raise ecosystem productivity, but the advances would be successful only if they don't have large, unintended adverse consequences for the biosphere. Moreover, irreversible losses, arising say from biological extinctions, would act as constraints on the biosphere's ability to recover. Social moves toward consumption and production practices that make smaller demands on the biosphere would be a more direct approach to reducing our impact on the Earth system. A complementary approach involves investment in family planning as well as information programs that shift fertility norms toward smaller families. That's the basis on which we have conducted our numerical exercise on how many people Earth can support in comfort.[26]

ACKNOWLEDGMENTS

The views expressed in this paper are entirely those of the authors and do not necessarily reflect the views of the Foreign, Commonwealth, and Development Office, UK.

For their most helpful comments on a previous draft, we are grateful to Krister Bykvist, Tim Campbell, John Cleland, Rachel Friedman, and Robert Solow.

NOTES

1. The "PAT" in I = PAT may appear to be a product of P, A, and T, but it is not. There is no sense in which "technology" can multiple with the product of population and affluence. The equation should be read as a metaphor, nothing more.
2. The term "Anthropocene" was popularized by Crutzen and Stoermer (2000) to mark a new epoch of human domination of the Earth system. The Anthropocene Working Group has proposed that the immediate postwar years should be regarded as the start of the Anthropocene. See Voosen (2016).
3. For pioneering work on the idea of ecological footprint, see Rees and Wackernagel (1994). Wakernagel, who founded the Global Footprint Network (www.footprintnetwork.org/public), was a lead author of WWF (2008).
4. Some countries have even experienced a population shrinkage in recent decades.
5. Our analysis borrows from Dasgupta and Dasgupta (2017).
6. Dasgupta (1993) contains a survey of these issues.
7. The classic on this is Maddison (2001), who provided estimates of expectancy of life at birth, population size, and output from 1 CE until year 1998 in various regions of the world.
8. The claim that households' access to natural resources increase with their size provides an inducement to procreate is proved formally in Dasgupta (2019).
9. The essays in the theoretical section of the current volume explore population axiology. Dasgupta (2019) is a monograph-length treatment of the subject.
10. Sen (1982) likens the emission of persistent pollutants to torturing future people. The clash between reproductive rights and adverse environmental externalities allied to new births is at its most striking under his reading.
11. See, for example, Bongaarts (2016), Canning and Schultz (2012), Cleland et al. (2006), Debpuur et al. (2002), Koenig et al. (1992), Miller and Babiarz (2016), Sonfield et al. (2013), and Tsui et al. (2010).
12. World Bank (2012) reported that in 2010 the proportion of people who completed primary education was, in India 96 percent, in Pakistan 67 percent, and in Bangladesh, 65 percent. Total fertility rates (TFRs) in those countries were 2.6, 3.4, and 2.2, respectively. It should also be noted that in Bangladesh non-governmental organizations at work on social matters have a far more extensive reach than in India and Pakistan. Reproductive behavior is not mono-causal.
13. Douglas and Isherwood (1979) offered reasons for regarding consumption as an expression of social engagement. Taken literally, that would appear odd, but what the authors were pointing to is that a meal taken alone is a different activity from a meal taken communally. Fads and fashion may be short-run expressions of social engagement, what Douglas and Isherwood showed is that our need to belong is deep and enduring and expresses itself in a wide variety of ways. We rely on one another for safety, consolation, information, companionship, and governance. Much of our actions are undertaken in a social setting, and all our actions are influenced in part by attention to others. In the text we apply that framework to reproductive decisions.

14. Formally, we are studying Nash equilibria in a coordination game (Dasgupta 1993). It can be shown that the social equilibrium in which each household has four children (n_2) is unstable. It would take us far afield to explain why, but see Dasgupta (2002) for the reason.

15. Farooq et al. (1987) is an early study that spoke to the phenomenon in West Africa. Lutz et al. (2014) is a collection of essays on the effect of education on fertility behavior. Interactions between the elite and the general public can be a vehicle by which fertility behavior among the poor changes.

16. The media are increasingly used to such end. For example, the Development Media International runs media campaigns aimed at changing behavior.

17. For a wide-ranging discussion of the role of societal norms on fertility behavior, see Bongaarts and Watkins (1996).

18. Casterline and Sinding (2000) discuss ways in which the measure of unmet need can be used to inform family planning policies.

19. Because people's preferences differ, we should expect the responses to differ but discover that each individual's preferred number of children is an increasing function of n. That would reveal socially embedded preferences.

20. Some moral philosophers would argue that the evaluation of family planning programs should include the quality of lives that will not be lived on account of the programs. Space forbids us from discussing those further considerations.

21. Tilman (1982) remains an excellent introduction to the processes by which competition among organisms for resources gives rise to the structure of biological communities.

22. The really hard problem in the political economy of global climate change involves using the latter's features to frame the way we should explore prospects of international agreements. Barrett (2003) and Barrett and Dannenberg (2012) are incisive studies on this.

23. Our calculations here are a refinement of Dasgupta and Dasgupta (2017), who assumed that people are mere consumers. Here we assume that humans are born not only with a mouth, but also hands and a brain.

24. We are not conducting an optimization exercise, for that would require additional features in the model, such as a social objective function. On this, see Dasgupta (2019).

25. This would be an incorrect assumption in non-stationary states, because it ignores differences among sectors in the value that labor adds to production of output.

26. Dasgupta (2021) contains a more detailed study of these issues.

REFERENCES

Alkema, Leontine, Vladimira. Kantorava, Clare Menozzi, and Ann Biddlecom. 2013. "National, Regional, and Global Rates and Trends in Contraceptive Prevalence and Unmet Need for Family Planning Between 1990 and 2015: A Systematic and Comprehensive Analysis." *Lancet* 381: 1642–1652.

Barrett, Scott. 2003. *Environment and Statecraft: The Strategy of Environmental Treaty Making*. Oxford: Oxford University Press.

Barrett, Scott and Astrid Dannenberg. 2012. "Climate Negotiations Under Scientific Uncertainty." *Proceedings of the National Academy of Science* 109, no. 43: 17372–17376.

Baumol, William J. and Wallace E. Oates. 1975. *The Theory of Environmental Policy*. Englewood Cliffs, NJ: Prentice Hall.

Bongaarts, John. 2016. "Slow Down Population Growth." *Nature* 530: 409–412.

Bongaarts, John and John Casterline. 2013. "Fertility Transition: Is Sub-Saharan Africa Different?" *Population and Development Review* 38, no. 1: 153–168.

Bongaarts, John and Susan Cotts Watkins. 1996. "Social Interactions and Contemporary Transitions." *Population and Development Review* 22, no. 4: 639–682.

Boserup, Ester. 1965. *The Conditions of Agricultural Growth: The Economics of Agrarian Change Under Population Pressure*. London: Allen & Unwin.

Bradley, Sarah E. K., Trevor N. Croft, Joy D. Fishel, and Charles F. Westoff. 2012. "Revising Unmet Need for Family Planning." In *DHS Analytical Studies No. 25*, edited by Bryant Robey. Calverton. MD: ICE International.

Brook, Barry W., Navjot S. Sodhi, and Corey J. A. Bradshaw. 2008. "Synergies Among Extinction Drivers Under Global Change." *Trends in Ecology and Evolution* 23, no. 8: 453–460.

Butzer, Karl W. 2012. "Collapse: Environment and Society." *Proceedings of the National Academy of Science* 109, no. 10: 3632–3639.

Caldwell, John C. 1982. *The Theory of Fertility Decline*. New York: Academic Press.

Canning, David and T. Paul Schultz. 2012. "The Economic Consequences of Reproductive Health and Family Planning." *Lancet* 380: 165–171.

Casterline, John B. and Steven W. Sinding. 2000. "Unmet Need for Family Planning in Developing Countries: Implications for Population Policy." *Population and Development Review* 26, no. 1: 691–723.

Christiaensen, Luc. 2017. "Agriculture in Africa: Telling Myths from Facts." *Food Policy* 67 (February): 1–11.

Cleland, John, Stan Bernstein, Alex Ezeh, Anibal. Faundes, Anna Glasier, and Jolene Innis. 2006. "Family Planning: The Unfinished Agenda." *Lancet* 368, no. 9549: 1810–1827.

Cleland, John and Christopher Wilson. 1987. "Demand Theories of the Fertility Transition: An Iconoclastic View." *Population Studies* 44, no. 1: 5–30.

Cochrane, Susan H. and Samir M. Farid. 1989. *Fertility in Sub-Saharan Africa: Analysis and Explanation*. World Bank Discussion Paper No. 43. Washington, DC: World Bank.

Crutzen, Paul J. and Eugene F. Stoermer. 2000. "The Anthropocene." *Global Change Newsletter* 41: 17–18.

Dasgupta, Aisha and Partha Dasgupta. 2017. "Socially Embedded Preferences, Environmental Externalities, and Reproductive Rights." *Population and Development Review* 43, no. 3: 405–441.

Dasgupta, Partha. 1993. *An Inquiry into Well-Being and Destitution*. Oxford: Clarendon Press.

Dasgupta, Partha. 2002. "A Model of Fertility Transition." In *Economic Theory for the Environment: Essays in Honour of Karl-Goran Maler*, edited by Bengt Kristrom, Partha Dasgupta, and Karl -Gustaf Lofgren, 118–128. Cheltenham: Edward Elgar.

Dasgupta, Partha. 2019. *Time and the Generations: Population Ethics on a Diminishing Planet*. New York: Columbia University Press.

Dasgupta, Partha. 2021. *The Economics of Biodiversity: The Dasgupta Review*. London: HM Treasury.

Debpuur, Cornelius, James F. Phillips, Elizabeth F. Jackson, Alex Nazzar, Pierre Nigom, and Fred N. Binka. 2002. "The Impact of the Navrongo Project on Contraceptive Knowledge and Use, Reproductive Preferences, and Fertility." *Studies in Family Planning* 33, no. 2: 141–164.

Diamond, Jared 2005. *Collapse: How Societies Choose to Fail or Survive*. London: Allen Lane.

Douglas, Mary and Baron Isherwood. 1979. *The World of Goods: Towards an Anthropology of Consumption*. New York: Basic Books.

Downey, Sean S., Randall Haas Jr., and Stephan J. Shennan. 2016. "European Neolithic Societies Showed Early Warning of Population Collapse." *Proceedings of the National Academy of Science* 113, no. 35: 9751–9756.

Ehrlich, Paul R. and Anne H. Ehrlich. 1981. *Extinction: The Causes and Consequences of the Disappearance of Species.* New York, NY: Random House.

Ehrlich, Paul R. and John P. Holdren. 1971. "Impact of Population Growth." *Science* 171, no. 3977: 1212–1217.

Fabic, Madeleine Short, Yoonjoung Choi, John Bongaarts, Jacqueline E. Darroch, John A. Ross, John Stover, Amy O. Tsui, Jagdish Upadhyay, and Ellen Starbird. 2015. "Meeting Demand for Family Planning Within a Generation." *Lancet* 385, no. 9981: 1928–1931.

Farooq, Ghazi, I. I. Ekanem, and Sina Ojelade. 1987. "Family Size Preferences and Fertility in South-Western Nigeria." In *Sex Roles, Population and Development in West Africa*, edited by C. Oppong, 75–85. London: James Currey.

Fortes, Meyer. 1978. "Parenthood, Marriage and Fertility in West Africa." *Journal of Development Studies* 14: 121–149.

Freedom House. 2017. *Freedom in the World 2017*, https://freedomhouse.org/report/freedom-world/freedom-world-2017.

Goody, Jack. 1976. *Production and Reproduction.* Cambridge: Cambridge University Press.

Guyer, Jane I. and Samuel M. Eno Belinga. 1995. "Wealth in People as Wealth in Knowledge: Accumulation and Composition in Equatorial Africa." *Journal of African History*, 36, no. 1: 91–110.

Haberl, Helmut, K.-Heinz Erb, Fridolin Krasmann, Veronika Gaube, Alberte Bondeau, Christoph Plutzer, Simone Gingrich, Wolfgang Lucht, and Marina Fisher-Kowalski. 2007. "Quantifying and Mapping the Human Appropriation of Net primary Production in Earth's Terrestrial Ecosystems." *Proceedings of the National Academy of Science* 104, no. 31: 12942–12947.

Haveman, Robert and Barbara Wolf. 1995. "The Determinants of Children's Attainments: A Review of Methods and Findings." *Journal of Economic Literature* 33, no. 4: 1829–1878.

Jensen, Robert and Emily Oster. 2009. "The Power of TV: Cable Television and Women's Status in India." *Quarterly Journal of Economics* 124, no. 3: 1057–1094.

Koenig, Michale A., Ubaidur Rob, Mehrab Ali Khan, J. Chakraborty, and Vincent Fauveau. 1992. "Contraceptive Use in Matlab, Bangladesh in 1990: Levels, Trends and Explanations." *Studies in Family Planning* 23, no. 6: 352–364.

Lee, Ronald D. 2000. "Intergenerational Transfers and the Economic Life Cycle: A Cross-cultural Perspective." In *Sharing the Wealth: Demographic Change and Economic Transfers Between Generations*, edited by Andrew Mason and Georges, 17–56. Tapines. Oxford: Oxford University Press.

Lee, Ronald D. 2007. "Demographic Change, Welfare, and Intergenerational Transfers: A Global Overview." In *Age, Generations and the Social Contract: The Demographic Challenge Facing the Welfare State*, edited by Jacques Veron, Sophie Pennec, and Jacques, 17–44. Legare. Amsterdam: Springer.

Lutz, Wolfgang, William.P. Butz, and K.C. Samir, eds. 2014. *World Population and Human Capital in the Twenty-First Century.* Oxford: Oxford University Press.

Maddison, Angus. 2001. *The World Economy: A Millennial Perspective.* Paris: OECD.

MEA (Millennium Ecosystem Assessment). 2005a. *Ecosystems and Human Well-Being*, vol. 1: *Current State and Trends*, edited by Rashid Hassan, Robert Scholes, and Neville Ash. Washington, DC: Island Press.

MEA (Millennium Ecosystem Assessment). 2005b. *Ecosystems and Human Well-Being*, vol. 2: *Scenarios*, edited by Stephen R. Carpenter, Prabhu L. Pingali, Eelena Bennet, and Monika B. Zurek. Washington, DC: Island Press.

MEA (Millennium Ecosystem Assessment). 2005c. *Ecosystems and Human Well-Being*, vol. 3: *Policy Responses*, edited by Kanchan Chopra, Rik Leemans, Pushpam Kumar, and Henk Simons. Washington, DC: Island Press.

MEA (Millennium Ecosystem Assessment). 2005d. *Ecosystems and Human Well-Being*, vol. 4: *Multiscale Assessments*, edited by Doris Capistrano, Cristian Samper, Marcus J. Lee, and Ciara Randsepp-Hearne. Washington, DC: Island Press.

Micklethwait, John and Adrian Wooldridge. 2000. *A Future Perfect: The Challenge and Promise of Globalization*. New York: Random House.

Miller, Grant and Kimberly S. Babiarz. 2016. "Family Planning Program Effects: Evidence from Microdata." *Population and Development Review* 42, no. 1: 7–26.

Parfit, Derek. 1984. *Reasons and Persons*. Oxford: Oxford University Press.

Pinker, Steven. 2018. *Enlightenment Now: The Case for Reason, Science, Humanism, and Progress*. New York: Allen Lane.

PNAS. 2012. "Special Feature: Critical Perspectives on Historical Collapse." *Proceedings of the National Academy of Science* 109, no. 10: 3632–3681.

Rees, William E. and Mathis Wackernagel. 1994. "Ecological Footprints and Appropriated Carrying Capacity: Measuring the Natural Capital Requirements of the Human Economy." In *Investing in Natural Capital: The Ecological Economics Appropriate for Sustainability*, edited by AnnMari Jansson, Monica Hammer, Carl Folke, and Robert Costanza, 362–391. Washington, DC: Island Press.

Ridley, Matt. 2010. *The Rational Optimist: How Prosperity Evolves*. London: 4th Estate.

Rosenzweig, Mark R. and Oded Stark, eds. 1997. *Handbook of Population and Family Economics*. Amsterdam: North Holland.

Scheffer, Martin 2016. "Anticipating Societal Collapse: Hints from the Stone Age." *Proceedings of the National Academy of Science* 113, no. 35.

Sen, Amartya. 1982. "Approaches to the Choice of Discount Rates in Social Benefit-Cost Analysis." In *Discounting for Time and Risk in Energy Policy*, edited by Robert C. Lind, 325–353. Baltimore, MD: The Johns Hopkins University Press.

Sodhi, Navjot S., Barry W. Brook, and Corey J. A. Bradshaw. 2009. "Causes and Consequences of Species Extinctions." In *The Princeton Guide to Ecology*, edited by Simon A. Levin, Stephen R. Carpenter, H. Charles J. Godfray, Ann P. Kinzig, Michael Loreau, Jonathan B. Losos, Brian Walker, and David S. Wilcove, 514–520. Princeton, NJ: Princeton University Press.

Sonfield, Adam Kinsey Hasstedt, Megan. L. Kavanaugh, and Ragnar Anderson. 2013. *The Social and Economic Benefits of Women's Ability to Determine Whether and When to Have Children*. New York: Guttmacher Institute.

Stern, Nicholas H. 2006. *The Stern Review of the Economics of Climate Change*. Cambridge: Cambridge University Press.

Tilman, David. 1982. *Resource Competition and Community Structure*. Princeton, NJ: Princeton University Press.

Trentmann, Frank. 2016. *Empire of things: How We Became a World of Consumers, from the Fifteenth Century to the Twenty-first*. London: Allen Lane.

Tsui, Amy. O., Raegan McDonald-Mosley, and Anne E. Burke. 2010. "Family Planning and the Burden of Unintended Pregnancies." *Epidemiological Reviews* 32, no. 1: 152–174.

Turner, B. L. and A. M. S. Ali. 1996. "Induced Intensification: Agricultural Change in Bangladesh with Implications for Malthus and Boserup." *Proceedings of the National Academy of Sciences* 93, no. 25: 12984–14991.

UNFPA. 1995. *Programme of Action of the International Conference on Population and Development.* New York: United Nations Population Fund.

UNDP. 2015. *Work for Human Development.* New York: United Nations Development Programme.

UNPD. 2017. *World Population Prospects.* New York: United Nations Population Division.

Veblen, Thorstein. 1925. *The Theory of the Leisure Class: An Economic Study of Institutions.* Repr. London: George Allen & Unwin.

Voosen, Paul. 2016. "Anthropocene Pinned Down to Post War Period." *Science* 353, no. 6302: 852–853.

Waters, Colin Neil, Jan Zalasiewicz, C. P. Summerhayes, Anthony D. Barnosky, Clement Poirier, Agnieszka Galuszka, Alejandro Cerreta, Matt Edgeworth, Erle C. Ellis, Catherine Jeandel, Reinhold Leinfelder, John R. McNeill, Will Steffen, Jaia Syritski, Davor Vidas, Michael Wagreich, Mark Williams, An Zhisheng, Jacques Grineveld, Eric Odada, Naomi Oreskes, and Alexander P. Wolfe. 2016. "The Anthropocene is Functionally and Stratigraphically Distinct from the Holocene." *Science* 351, no. 6269: 1–10.

Watkins, Susan Cotts. 1990. "From Local to National Communities: The Transformation of Demographic Regions in Western Europe 1870–1960." *Population and Development Review* 16, no. 2: 241–272.

Wiggins, David. 1987. "Claims of Need." In *Needs, Values, Truth,* edited by David Wiggins, 1–58. Oxford: Basil Blackwell.

Wilson, Edward O. 2016. *Half-Earth: Our Planet's Fight for Life.* New York: Liveright Publishing Corporation.

World Bank. 2012. *Gender Equality and Development.* Washington, DC: World Bank.

World Bank. 2016. *Development Goals in an Era of Demographic Change.* Washington, DC: World Bank.

Wrigley, E. A. 2004. *Poverty, Progress, and Population.* Cambridge: Cambridge University Press.

WWF (World Wildlife Fund). 2008. *Living Planet Report 2008.* Gland: WWF International.

CHAPTER 23

··

CREATING PEOPLE AND
SAVING PEOPLE

··

JEFF MCMAHAN

1. DEPENDENT PEOPLE

··

SUPPOSE that whatever one does a new person will come into existence. But one can determine who this person will be by either doing or not doing act A.

Dependent People
A: P_1 will later exist and live to 80 P_2 will never exist
Not A: P_1 will never exist P_2 will later exist and live to 60

P1 will exist only if one does A; P2 will exist only if one does not do A. We can say that they are *dependent people* relative to act A. Suppose that each of them would be highly and equally well off while they were alive, that there is no cost to doing A, and that the effects that the existence of one of these people would have on the lives of others would be neither better nor worse, overall, than the effects of the existence of the other. Because a life that is well worth living that lasts eighty years is better than an otherwise comparable life that ends after sixty years, it seems that the outcome in which P_1 comes into existence is better than that in which P_2 comes into existence. And if one outcome is better than another, there is a reason, from an impartial point of view, to prefer it and to bring it about if one can—though this reason might of course be outweighed by some other conflicting reason. In this case, however, there are no other relevant differences between doing A and not doing A. It seems, therefore, that in *Dependent People*, one has an unopposed reason, and seemingly a moral reason, to do A.

The choice between doing A and not doing A is what Derek Parfit calls a "Same Number Choice."[1] Although different people would exist in the different outcomes of the choice, the same number of people would exist in each outcome. Parfit suggests that Same Number Choices should be evaluated by reference to

This chapter draws heavily on, and in many places coincides with, my earlier article, "Causing People to Exist and Saving People's Lives," *Journal of Ethics* 17, nos. 1–2 (2013): 5–35.

The Same Number Quality Claim
If in either of two possible outcomes the same number of people would ever live, it would be worse if those who live are worse off, or have a lower quality of life, than those who would have lived.[2]

This principle implies the intuitive view that it is better to do A than not. Although it is concerned solely with the comparative evaluation of outcomes, it is directly relevant to what we have reason to do, provided that we understand "good," "bad," "better," and "worse" in what Parfit calls the reason-implying sense.[3]

To describe certain relevant features of this choice, it will be helpful to introduce both some assumptions and some further terms. Although this is controversial, I will assume that it cannot be better or worse for a person to be caused to exist. This is because "better for" and "worse for" are essentially comparative. The claim that to cause a person to exist would be better for that person thus entails that it would be worse for that person never to exist. But nothing can be worse, or bad, for someone who never exists. People who never exist cannot be victims of misfortune or the beneficiaries of good fortune. There is, however, a corresponding claim that does make sense. It is coherent, and plausible, to claim that to cause a person to exist is *good* for that person when the intrinsically good elements of the person's life more than compensate for the intrinsically bad elements. Because the claim is only that this would be good for the person and not that it would be better for the person, there is no implication that it would be bad, or worse, for this person never to exist.[4]

Because causing a person to exist can be good or bad for that person, it also makes sense to apply the terms "benefit" and "harm" to instances of causing people to exist. If causing a person to exist is good for that person, it is convenient and perspicuous to say that causing that person to exist benefits him or her. Similarly, causing a person to exist harms that person if it is bad for him or her because the intrinsically bad aspects of the life are not offset by the good.

I will use the terms "existential benefit" and "existential harm" to refer to benefits and harms brought about by acts that are a necessary part of the cause of the existence of the subjects of those benefits are harms. Existential benefits and harms contrast with *ordinary* benefits and harms, which are conferred or inflicted on individuals who exist, or will or may exist, independently of the act that causes or constitutes the benefit or harm. I will here refer to people whose existence is independent of whether some act is done as "independent people" relative to that act. Independent people divide into two subsets. Those who exist at the time some act is done are "existing people" relative to that act. It is common to refer to the other subset of independent people—those who neither exist nor have existed at the time an act is done—as "future people." But not all those who might exist in the future and whose existence is independent of some particular act will in fact exist. Consider a person who does not exist but may exist in the future whose future existence is independent of whether I do act *a* now. That person is an independent person relative to act *a*. But this person's existence may depend on whether some different act will be done later, either by me or by someone else. It would therefore be misleading to refer to this person as a *future* person. For want of a better word, I will refer to such a person as an "unconditional person" relative to act *a*, since *a* is not a condition of the person's existence. These various terms—dependent, independent, existing, unconditional—can also be applied to individuals, such as animals or infants, who are not persons.

Existential benefits and harms are usually noncomparative, in the sense that they are good or bad, but not better or worse, for their subjects. But there are exceptions, as in the following example.

Same Dependent Person
One must choose one of three options. One can
(1) cause a person, P, to exist with a life that will last eighty years,
(2) cause the same person to exist with a life that will end after sixty years, or
(3) not cause anyone to exist.

Either option for causing P to exist would confer an existential benefit on him, since in either case his life would, we may assume, be well worth living. But the first option would confer a greater existential benefit on him than the second option would.[5] While neither of these existential benefits would be better for him than never existing at all, the greater existential benefit *would* be better for him than the lesser existential benefit. Correlatively, the lesser existential benefit would be worse for him than the greater. Some existential benefits and harms are, therefore, not merely good or bad for people but also better or worse for them, at least in relation to other outcomes in which those same people would exist. Yet existential benefits that have this comparative dimension are relatively rare. This is because changes in the conditions that cause a person to exist that affect the character of the life that is thereby created also tend to result in the existence of a *different person* from the one who would have existed in the absence of those changes. This is the essence of what Parfit calls the *Non-Identity Problem*.[6]

In contrast to existential benefits and harms, ordinary benefits and harms are always comparative, in that they are better or worse for those on whom they are conferred or inflicted. Normally a benefit will be better for the one who receives it. But it is possible for a benefit to be both better and worse for the one who receives it, depending on the alternative with which it is compared. One might, for example, do what makes an individual better off than she *was* yet worse off than she *would have been* had one conferred a greater benefit instead. The benefit one confers is thus better for the beneficiary than the conferral of no benefit but worse for the beneficiary than the conferral of a greater benefit. Similar remarks apply to ordinary harms. The important point is that ordinary benefits and harms are always better or worse, or better *and* worse, for the beneficiary or victim than some alternative in which the beneficiary or victim would have existed but would not have had that particular benefit or harm. Later, on the assumption that all ordinary benefits and harms are comparative whereas, because of the Non-Identity Problem, virtually all existential benefits and harms are noncomparative, I will refer mainly to comparative and noncomparative benefits and harms rather than to ordinary and existential benefits and harms.

2. UNCONDITIONAL PEOPLE AND DEPENDENT PEOPLE

Suppose next that, in *Unconditional or Dependent*, one can do either B or C but not both. If one does C, a person, P_U, who does not exist now but will later exist independently of what one does, will live to eighty rather than to sixty. That is, doing C now will prevent this future person from dying when he is sixty, thereby enabling him to live to eighty. The possible outcomes of one's choice are these:

B: P_1 will later exist P_2 will never exist P_U will later exist
    and live to eighty   and live to sixty

C: P_1 will never exist P_2 will later exist P_U will later exist
                                        and live to sixty   and live to eighty

Doing B would confer a greater existential benefit on one person rather than allowing a lesser existential benefit to go to another person. Doing C would confer an ordinary benefit comparable in magnitude to the difference between the two existential benefits.

If one does B, that will make it the case that a person will exist and live to eighty rather than that a person will exist and live to sixty. The same will be true if one does C. The difference is that if one does B, the person who will live to eighty (P_1) will be a different person from the person who would have lived to be sixty (P_2), whereas if one does C, the person who will live to eighty and the person who would have lived to sixty will be the same person. Because of this, the failure to do C will be worse for that person. But the failure to do B will not be worse for the person who will exist and live to sixty. Indeed, the failure to do B will not be worse for anyone who ever lives.

According to Parfit's *No-Difference View*, this difference between B and C is insignificant.[7] None of the people whose existence or longevity would be determined by the choice between B and C now exists. Whether one does B or C, two new people will exist. It is therefore a Same Number Choice. If one does B, a person will later exist who will live to be eighty and another will exist who will live to be sixty. The same will be true if one does C. It makes no difference, according to Parfit, that doing B would be worse for one person and better for no one, while doing C would be better for one person and worse for no one.

Described that way, however, the difference seems to matter. But Parfit presents an example, the Medical Programs case, to show that intuitively it does not matter.[8] In that example—revised so that the bad effect is, as in my examples, a shorter life span—one of two medical programs must be canceled. If Preconception Testing is canceled, 1,000 children will later exist and live to sixty rather than 1,000 different children who would live to eighty. If Pregnancy Testing is canceled, 1,000 children will be born in the future who will live to sixty but who would have lived to eighty had Pregnancy Testing been preserved. Cancelation of either program, therefore, will result in the future existence of 1000 children who will live to sixty rather than 1,000 children who would have lived to eighty. Assume that the effects on other people would be equal. Many people share Parfit's intuition that, if there are no other relevant differences, it does not matter which program is canceled. This intuition might be supported by the fact that, if only 999 instances of life to sixty rather than eighty could be prevented by Pregnancy Testing while 1,000 could be prevented by Preconception Testing, it seems that it would be *better* to cancel Pregnancy Testing, even though there would be 999 people for whom that would be worse.

Unconditional or Dependent is modeled on the Medical Programs case. The only possibly significant difference is that in the Medical Programs case the number of people in each outcome is greater. (It might be thought significant that Pregnancy Testing involves medical treatment of fetuses while doing C extends the life of an adult. But the benefit of Pregnancy Testing spans an entire life and it could be stipulated that C operates causally while the beneficiary (P_U) is a fetus, so that the increased longevity is, as in Pregnancy Testing, a consequence of what is done to a fetus.) It seems, therefore, that those who agree with Parfit that it makes no difference which program is canceled should also accept that it makes no difference in *Unconditional or Dependent* whether one does B or C. When there is literally *no difference* evaluatively between two acts or outcomes, those acts or outcomes are evaluatively equivalent. According to the No-Difference View, therefore, doing B and doing C are *equally good*. This judgment is, like Parfit's intuitive judgment in the Medical Programs case, not implausible. (See, however, the final paragraph in Section 5, below.)

3. UNCONDITIONAL PEOPLE AND EXISTING PEOPLE

Suppose that, in *Unconditional or Existing*, one can do either D or E but not both. If one does E, an existing person, P_E, will live to eighty rather than to sixty, while a different person, P_U, who will exist in the future independently of the choice between D and E, will live to sixty rather than eighty. The possible outcomes of one's choice are these:

D: P_U will later exist and live to eighty P_E will live to sixty
E: P_U will later exist and live to sixty P_E will live to eighty

In this case, one can either prevent an unconditional person from dying at sixty or prevent an existing person from dying at sixty. In order for the options to be as similar as possible, assume that the only difference in the relation that one bears to the two people is that P_E exists at the time one must act. One has no more knowledge of P_E than one has of P_U, since one has no knowledge of either apart from the fact that one exists now while the other does not but will exist later. Thus, at the time at which one must choose whether to do D or E, P_E might be a late-term fetus or infant, or he or she might be sixty and close to death. If one knew at the time at which one had to make the choice that P_E was then on the verge of death, that might make it seem more important to do E.[9] But I want to exclude that possible reason for thinking that it would be better to do E rather than D. The difference I want to highlight is simply that between a presently existing person and a person who does not now exist but will in the future. Hence the stipulation that all that one knows is that if one does E, that will cause P_E to live to be eighty rather than die at sixty, while if one does D, that will cause P_U to live to be eighty rather than die at sixty. This is of course consistent with the earlier stipulation that the act that extends a person's life from sixty to eighty years could operate causally at any point in the person's life. While most ways of extending a person's life count as saving the person's life, I will in general refer to "extending" rather than "saving" both to avoid any possible positive associations that the term "saving" might have and to allow for the possibility that there are ways of extending a person's life that do not count as saving it.

Unconditional or Existing is what Parfit calls a "Same People Choice": all and only the same people exist in both outcomes. It is a choice between bestowing an ordinary benefit on one person and bestowing an equal ordinary benefit on another person. The only question is whether it matters that one of these people exists at the time one must choose while the other will exist only later.

Many people find it intuitively plausible to suppose that doing D and doing E are equally good. Many people also believe that it is permissible to do either. To suppose that it matters more to extend P_E's life than to extend the life of P_U by the same amount would be relevantly similar to supposing that it matters more to extend the life of a person who is physically proximate than to do the same for a person who is farther away, when this difference in spatial proximity is the *only* difference in the way one is related to them. As Parfit observes, "remoteness in time has, in itself, no more significance than remoteness in space."[10]

4. EXISTING PEOPLE AND DEPENDENT PEOPLE

Suppose that, in *Existing or Dependent*, one can do either F or G but not both. The possible outcomes of one's choice are these:

F: P_1 will later exist P_2 will never exist P_E will live to sixty
     and live to eighty

G: P_1 will never exist P_2 will later exist P_E will live to eighty
                                          and live to sixty

This is a Same Number Choice, since whether one chooses to do F or G, the same number of people will ever exist. Indeed, even if there is the third option of doing neither F nor G, one still faces a Same Number Choice provided that in exercising that third option one does not cause a further individual to exist. Furthermore, when applied to the choice between F and G, the No-Difference View implies that it is morally irrelevant that there is someone for whom the failure to do G would be worse whereas there is no one for whom the failure to do F would be worse.

But I suspect that in this choice, many people would find this difference to be intuitively morally significant. They would think that it is better, in effect, to extend the life of an existing person than to ensure that a person who will have a longer life comes into existence rather than a person who would have a shorter life. And they would think that, given the choice, one ought to extend the life of the existing person—that is, that it would be wrong to allow an existing person to die when he could live an additional twenty years, in order instead to do what would cause a longer-lived person to come into existence rather than a different, shorter-lived person. This is my own untutored intuitive response. Many people, I suspect, would have the same view even if the example were altered so that doing G would enable P_E to live only to seventy rather than eighty.

But now there is a problem. I have suggested, in discussing *Unconditional or Dependent*, which is a smaller-scale version of Parfit's Medical Programs case, that

(1) causing a person to exist who would live to eighty rather than allowing a different person to exist who would live to sixty matters as much, or is equally good, as
(2) extending the future life of an unconditional person from sixty years to eighty years, if other things are equal.

I have also suggested, in discussing *Unconditional or Existing*, that

(2) extending the future life of an unconditional person from sixty to eighty years matters as much, or is equally good, as
(3) extending the life of an existing person from sixty years to eighty years, if other things are equal.

If these judgments are correct, then, assuming that the relations "matters as much as" and "equally good as" are transitive, it follows that, in *Existing or Dependent*,

(1) causing a person to exist who would live to eighty rather than allowing a different person to exist who would live to sixty

matters as much, or is equally good, as

(3) extending the life of an existing person from sixty years to eighty years.

Although this conclusion is implied by the No-Difference View, it is, I suggested, intuitively implausible. It seems to matter more to save the life of an existing person than to cause a longer-lived dependent person to exist rather than allow a different, shorter-lived dependent person to exist instead. (In the remainder of the text, I will often use the following shorthand descriptions of the three choices of action stated immediately above: (1) "cause a longer-lived person to exist," (2) "extend an unconditional person's life," and (3) "extend an existing person's life.")

One might object that these inferences cannot be drawn from the discrete pairwise comparisons I have made—doing (1) with doing (2), doing (2) with doing (3), and doing (3) with doing (1)—since comparisons between acts may be affected by which other acts are possible. The relevant question is whether the problem cited in the previous paragraph arises when all three acts are possible, as follows:

X: P_1 will exist and live to eighty P_2 will never exist P_U will later live to sixty P_E will live to sixty

Y: P_1 will never exist P_2 will exist and live to sixty P_U will later live to eighty P_E will live to sixty

Z: P_1 will never exist P_2 will exist and live to sixty P_U will later live to sixty P_E will live to eighty

It seems that the same reasoning applies even when it is possible to do any one of the three acts. It seems intuitively plausible that doing X and doing Y are equally good, that doing Y and doing Z are equally good, but that doing Z is better than doing X. So, the problem I identified remains.

Because the choice between causing a longer-lived person to exist and extending an existing person's life is a Same Number Choice, the claim that these options are equally good is directly implied both by Parfit's Same Number Quality Claim and by his No-Difference View. But if we intuitively find that causing a longer-lived person to exist is not as good, or does not matter as much, as extending an existing person's life, cases such as *Existing or Dependent* challenge both of Parfit's claims. If we considered only *Existing or Dependent*, intuition might prompt us to reject both these claims. But I have argued that the claim that causing a longer-lived person to exist is as good as extending an existing person's life is entailed by the conjunction of two plausible claims: namely, that causing a longer-lived person to exist is equally good as extending an unconditional person's life, and that extending an unconditional person's life is equally good as extending an existing person's life. It seems, therefore, that if we are to reject the claim that causing a longer-lived person to exist is equally good as extending an existing person's life, we must also deny either that causing a longer-lived person to exist is equally good as extending an unconditional person's life or that extending an unconditional person's life is equally good as extending an existing person's life.

It seems implausible to deny the latter. For the *only* difference between extending an unconditional person's life and extending that of an existing person is that the existing person exists at the time when one must choose between the two acts, while the unconditional person does not. One might, of course, claim that coexistence in time, even for a very brief period, is a special relation that provides grounds for legitimate partiality toward an existing person (a suggestion that Derek Parfit once made to me in conversation). But that expands the notion of a *special* relation to the point of vacuity. And, in any case, the distinction between an existing person and an unconditional person is in this instance a matter of whether they exist at the time at which one must choose between extending the life of one and extending that of the other. That leaves it open that one might *later* overlap in time with the unconditional person, in which case one could anticipate being "specially" related through coexistence to the unconditional person as well as to the existing person.

5. Is There an Asymmetry Between Comparative and Noncomparative Benefits?

The other option is to deny that causing a longer-lived person to exist is as good as extending an unconditional person's life—so that in *Unconditional or Dependent*, it is better to do C than to do B. Recall, however, that *Unconditional or Dependent* is just the Medical Programs case writ small and that the intuition that Parfit hopes to elicit from the latter supports the No-Difference View. Thus, to deny that causing a longer-lived person to exist is as good as extending an unconditional person's life is tantamount to affirming that there *is* a relevant difference between the two medical programs and thus is also tantamount to rejecting the No-Difference View.

One might base this denial on the claim that existential benefits matter less than ordinary benefits so that the reason to confer an existential benefit is weaker than the reason to confer an equivalent ordinary benefit, if other things are equal. Some philosophers in fact claim that the conferral of existential benefits does not make the outcome better and that there is no moral reason to confer them. (Some even deny that there can be existential benefits.) There is intuitive support for this claim in the common belief that the expectation that a person would have a life worth living does not by itself provide any reason to cause that person to exist. This belief constitutes one half of the view sometimes referred to as the *Asymmetry*, the other half of which is that the expectation that a person would have a life in which the intrinsically bad elements outweigh the good *does* provide a moral reason *not* to cause that person to exist.

The idea that benefits matter less if they are existential is, however, challenged by Same Dependent Person. The benefit of the longer life for P is an existential benefit, but it seems a mistake to discount it. For it seems that to cause P to exist with the life that will last eighty years (henceforth "cause P-80 to exist") rather than to cause P to exist with the life that will last for only sixty years (henceforth "cause P-60 to exist") matters just as much as enabling an unconditional person to live for eighty years rather than sixty, which in turn matters just as much as enabling an existing person to live for eighty rather than sixty years.

There is, however, a question about what the relevant comparison is here. What exactly is the analogue in the case of an existing person of causing P-80 to exist? Or the analogue of causing P-60 to exist? If causing P-80 to exist is, as I suggested, like *enabling* an existing person to live to eighty rather than sixty, then causing P-60 to exist should be like *failing to enable* an existing person to live to eighty rather than sixty. This assumes that the default in the case of the existing person—that is, what would happen with no intervention—is living to sixty. But if one causes P-60 to exist, one has *caused* him to live to sixty rather than causing him to live to eighty. But *causing* an *existing* person to live to sixty rather than to eighty could be an instance of *killing* - for example, killing the person rather than either allowing him to die or saving him. If the appropriate comparison with causing P-60 to exist rather than causing P-80 to exist is killing an existing person at sixty, then it seems plausible to suppose that the existential benefits in Same Dependent Person must be discounted. For causing P-60 to exist rather than P-80 does seem less bad than killing an existing person at sixty.

It seems, however, that neither failing to enable an existing person to live to eighty rather than sixty nor killing an existing person at sixty is precisely analogous to causing P-60 to exist rather than P-80. This is because the "defaults," or what would happen in the absence of intervention, are different in the three cases. The implied default in failing to enable a person to live to eighty rather than sixty is that the person will live to sixty. And the implied default in causing a person to live to sixty rather than eighty is that the person will live to eighty. What the default is determines the nature of one's agency—for example, whether one causes or allows a person to die. And the nature of the agency affects the morality of the action. But in Same Dependent Person, there is no single implied default. There are two possible alternatives to causing P-60 to exist: causing P-80 to exist and not causing P to exist at all. Of these, the latter is the natural default, for it best captures the idea of one's doing nothing, or not intervening at all. Because there is no option of allowing it to be the case that an existing person never exists, there can be no unique parallel in the case of an existing person to causing P-60 to exist or to causing P-80 to exist. It therefore seems impossible to test for the intuitive plausibility of discounting existential benefits in Same Dependent Person by comparing the options in that case with parallel options involving an existing person.

Suppose, however, that one causes P-60 to exist. Putting aside issues of agency, the absence of the additional twenty years of good life that P could have had—that is, the absence of that additional existential benefit—seems to matter just as much as the absence in an existing person's life of an ordinary benefit of an additional twenty years that were possible for him. This seems to be because in this case the existential benefit, unlike most existential benefits but like most ordinary benefits, has a comparative dimension. P's getting the sixty-year life is *worse for* him than getting the eighty-year life. Perhaps the relevant difference between types of benefit is not between existential benefits and ordinary benefits but between benefits with a comparative dimension and those that are essentially noncomparative. A moral asymmetry between equivalent comparative and noncomparative benefits would explain why, in *Existing or Dependent,* causing a longer-lived person to exist does not matter as much as extending an existing person's life. For the benefits of the former act are noncomparative whereas those of the latter are comparative. It would also explain why, in Same Dependent Person, causing P to exist with a life to eighty rather than a life to sixty seems to matter as much as extending the life of an unconditional person. For, although the benefit of a life to eighty is an existential benefit, it is also comparative in relation to the alternative in which P would live only to sixty (though it is also noncomparative in relation to the third option of not causing P to exist).

That there is a moral asymmetry between comparative and noncomparative benefits is suggested by the conjunction of two common beliefs: (1) there is always *a* reason to benefit an existing person provided the beneficiary does not deserve *not* to be benefited and there would be no cost to anyone in providing the benefit, and (2) the "negative claim" of the view that I referred to earlier as the Asymmetry, according to which the fact that person would have a life worth living does not provide any reason to cause that person to exist. This pair of beliefs, however, suggests that the asymmetry between comparative and noncomparative benefits is extremely strong. The Asymmetry, in particular, seems to presuppose that there is *no* reason to confer noncomparative benefits.

Yet the idea that noncomparative benefits do not matter at all may seem to have the counterintuitive implication that it is generally bad, in practice, to cause people to exist, for example by having children. For if we think, as most people do, that noncomparative harms do matter, and if causing people to exist always involves the infliction of noncomparative harms (since all lives unavoidably contain suffering), then it seems that for it to be permissible to cause a person to exist, doing so must have good effects that outweigh the noncomparative harms. But if noncomparative harms matter while noncomparative benefits do not, so that noncomparative benefits cannot offset corresponding noncomparative harms, it seems that it can be permissible to cause a person to exist only if the ordinary, comparative benefits (that is, benefits to existing and unconditional individuals) of doing so are sufficient to outweigh the noncomparative harms—which to most of us is a highly counterintuitive claim.

Yet the Asymmetry does not imply that there is such a presumption against causing people to exist. There are two distinct ways in which in which a noncomparative benefit might matter. First, that causing a person to exist would confer a noncomparative benefit on that person might provide a reason for causing that person to exist. Since the benefit might weigh in our deliberations in this way, I will say that it might have "reason-giving weight." Second, this same noncomparative benefit might also weigh against the noncomparative harm that inevitably occurs when a person is caused to exist. Most people believe, for example, that the fact that a person would experience suffering if she were caused to exist provides a reason not to cause her to exist. But they also accept that the suffering can be offset by corresponding noncomparative benefits, making it overall permissible to cause people to exist despite the suffering these people will have to endure. I will say that noncomparative benefits have "offsetting weight" if they can weigh against and counterbalance or offset noncomparative harms.

The Asymmetry is, thus, the claim that whereas noncomparative harms have reason-giving weight, in that they provide reasons not to cause people to exist, noncomparative benefits do not (at least just on their own). But this is compatible with the claim that noncomparative benefits have offsetting weight. And this is in fact what most people seem to believe. They believe (1) that the expectation that causing a person to exist would benefit that person in many ways provides no reason to cause her to exist, (2) that the expectation that causing a person to exist would harm her in various ways provides a reason not to cause her to exist, but (3) that the potential benefits can offset the harms, so that the reason not to cause a person to exist can be and normally is outweighed or overridden by the prospect of those benefits.

Still, the claim that noncomparative benefits have no reason-giving weight is implausible. Other intuitions—for example, the intuition that in Dependent People there is a reason to cause a longer-lived person to exist rather than allow a shorter-lived person to exist— suggest that noncomparative benefits must have *some* reason-giving weight. I will discuss these intuitions in subsequent sections. For the moment I will assume that there is a general asymmetry between comparative and noncomparative benefits, while acknowledging that there are some cases, such as Dependent People, in which noncomparative benefits seem to have some reason-giving weight, as well as other cases in which comparative benefits have little or no reason-giving weight. (An example of the latter might be a choice between saving the life of a newly existent fetus and allowing the fetus to die, when no one else's interests would be affected. For discussion, see pages 542–543 below.).

Even a comparatively slight asymmetry between comparative and noncomparative benefits would undermine the simple argument I presented earlier for the intuitively problematic conclusion that in *Existing or Dependent*, causing a longer-lived person to exist matters as much as extending an existing person's life. For if there is an asymmetry between comparative and noncomparative benefits, that would imply that it is better, or matters more, to extend an unconditional person's life than to cause a longer-lived person to exist. Then, whether extending an unconditional person's life matters as much as or less than extending an existing person's life, it follows that extending an existing person's life matters more than causing a longer-lived person, rather than a different, shorter-lived person, to exist, if other things are equal.

It is worth emphasizing the precise nature of the suggested asymmetry. The benefits that would be discounted are those that altogether lack a comparative dimension. They therefore do not include those ordinary benefits to which I referred earlier that are not better for those who receive them—namely, those benefits that exclude a greater a benefit. Such ordinary benefits do have a comparative dimension, as they are worse for those who receive them than receiving a greater benefit would be. The only benefits that are fully noncomparative are existential benefits. Of course, as Same Dependent Person shows, not all existential benefits are noncomparative. Thus, the suggestion is that existential benefits that lack a comparative dimension, which include the great majority of existential benefits, matter less than equivalent ordinary benefits and less than equivalent existential benefits with a comparative dimension.

Here is a further test of our intuitions about the significance of comparative and noncomparative benefits. In Same Dependent Person, both the benefits one might confer are existential benefits, but both have a comparative dimension. Consider next a parallel choice in which the benefits one might confer are existential benefits of the same magnitude as those in Same Dependent Person but without a comparative dimension. Recall the first case we considered, Dependent People, in which P_2, who will live to sixty, will come into existence unless one causes P_1, who will live to eighty, to exist instead. We can alter this case so that the default—that is, what will happen if one does not act—is not that P_2 will exist but that no one will come into existence. This yields:

Different Dependent People
One must choose one of three options. One can
(1) cause P_1, who will live to eighty, to exist;
(2) cause P_2, who will live to sixty, to exist; or
(3) not cause anyone to exist.

This case is like Same Dependent Person except that the person with the longer life and the person with the shorter life are different people rather than the same person. Because in each case there is the option of not causing anyone to exist, these are both Different Number Choices.

Suppose that in this case one causes P_2 to exist. And suppose that in Same Dependent Person one causes P-60 to exist. Both these choices seem worse than the alternative in which a person would have existed and lived to eighty. But are they equally bad? In *Different Dependent People*, one confers a lesser noncomparative benefit. In Same Dependent Person one confers an equivalently lesser comparative benefit (comparative at least in relation to one of the options). If there is an asymmetry between comparative and noncomparative benefits, the conferral of the lesser benefit should matter less in Different Dependent People. And this may seem intuitively plausible if we consider the thoughts available to the people in the outcomes of the two choices. In Same Dependent Person, P can reflect that causing him to exist with the sixty-year life was *worse for him* than causing him to exist with the eighty-year life. But in Different Dependent People, the corresponding thought to which P_2 is entitled is only that causing him to exist with a sixty-year life was *good for him*. These facts provide some intuitive support for the idea that the failure to confer a greater noncomparative benefit is less bad than the failure to confer an equivalently greater comparative benefit.

If one finds the idea that there is an asymmetry between comparative and non-comparative benefits plausible, one may wonder whether there is a corresponding asymmetry between comparative and noncomparative harms. That seems unlikely. While many might find it acceptable to suppose that noncomparative benefits do not matter at all, it is wholly implausible to suppose that noncomparative harms do not matter at all. If that were true, there would be no reason not to cause a person to exist whose life would contain nothing but agony. This leaves it open whether there might be a lesser asymmetry between comparative and noncomparative harms. But if there is, it is unlikely to be as significant as that which might plausibly be supposed to exist between comparative and noncomparative benefits. That is, if noncomparative harms matter less at all, they cannot matter less to the extent that one might find acceptable in the case of noncomparative benefits. I will return to this.

That the asymmetry I have suggested is only between comparative and non-comparative benefits, and not between comparative and noncomparative harms, shows that the suggestion is not equivalent to the claim that independent people—that is, existing and unconditional people—matter more than dependent people. Some philosophers have sought to defend the view that while our choices must be constrained by respect for the rights and well-being of independent people, the possible well-being of dependent people—those whose existence depends on the outcome of our choice—does not matter at all. Others have argued that, while the well-being of dependent people has some weight, it matters less than the well-being of independent people. The suggestion I have made, in contrast, is about benefits only, not about the distinction between independent and dependent people more generally. It is therefore compatible with the view that harms caused by causing dependent people to exist matter as much, or nearly as much, as equivalent harms inflicted on independent people. And it holds that some benefits conferred by causing dependent people to exist—namely, those with a comparative dimension, such as those that might be conferred in Same Dependent Person—can matter, at least in some ways, as much as equivalent benefits conferred on independent people.

To claim that there is an asymmetry between comparative and noncomparative benefits is to deny the No-Difference View. To defend the asymmetry, therefore, one must respond to Parfit's main argument for the No-Difference View, which appeals to the Medical Programs case. One must, in particular, explain why most of us seem to share Parfit's intuition about that case—namely, that there is no moral difference between the cancelation of Preconception Testing and the cancelation of Pregnancy Testing. Many of us have this intuition even though the benefits provided by Preconception Testing are noncomparative while the equivalent benefits provided by Pregnancy Testing are comparative, so that the cancelation of Pregnancy Testing, but not the cancelation of Preconception Testing, would be worse for the children who would later die at sixty rather than eighty.

I think there are two features of Pregnancy Testing that explain why we tend not to distinguish intuitively between canceling it and canceling Preconception Testing. One is that the children affected by the cancelation of Pregnancy Testing are unconditional people, not existing people. While coexistence during some period of time may have no more moral significance than coexistence in some region of space, existing people tend nevertheless to be more vivid to us emotionally than people who will exist later, perhaps only after we have ceased to exist (just as people who are spatially proximate tend to be more vivid to us than people who are spatially remote). This led me to wonder, some years ago, whether Parfit had deliberately made the children affected by the cancelation of Pregnancy Testing unconditional rather than existing people because this would more reliably elicit intuitions favorable to the No-Difference View. When I asked him about this, he conceded that he had.[11]

The second feature of Pregnancy Testing that I think affects our intuitions is that the immediate victims of the cancelation of the program are fetuses. It is true, of course, that the bad effect that they will suffer—death at sixty rather than at eighty—will occur when they are adults. But the immediate bad effect of the cancelation of Pregnancy Testing—the failure to detect and cure the maternal condition that will otherwise cause them to die at sixty—occurs when these individuals are fetuses. And this, I think, affects our intuitions. We can see this if we consider a different medical program: Postnatal Testing. Postnatal Testing would screen millions of 30-year-olds and predictably detect in 1,000 of them the precursor of a condition that would cause them to die at sixty rather than being able to live to eighty. Those in whom the precursor was found would be treated, thereby preventing them from developing the condition and dying at sixty. I suspect that if the Medical Programs case had consisted in a choice between the cancelation of Preconception Testing and the cancelation of Postnatal Testing, Parfit could not have been confident about eliciting intuitions supportive of the No-Difference View. Many people, I suspect, might think that the cancelation of Preconception Testing, or even of Prenatal Testing, would be less objectionable than the cancelation of Postnatal Testing. One might defend the claim that the reason not to cancel Prenatal Testing is weaker than the reason not to cancel Postnatal Testing by appealing to two claims. The first is that, whereas a 30-year-old would be strongly psychologically connected to herself at 60, a fetus would be psychologically almost entirely unrelated to herself at 60. The fetus therefore has at most only a weak present interest in what will happen to the 60-year-old it will become. The second claim is that, if the life the fetus would have without the treatment would, from the beginning, be different from the life she would have with the treatment, there may be no time in the life without the treatment when it would be egoistically rational for her to regret not having had the longer, alternative possible life.[12]

6. Choices between Greater and Lesser Benefits, and Choices between Some Benefits and None

Even though there are cases in which noncomparative benefits seem clearly to have reason-giving weight, it may seem that these are all cases involving a choice between conferring greater noncomparative benefits rather than lesser ones. In Dependent People, for example, there is a reason to cause P_1 to exist rather than to allow P_2 to come into existence instead. That the noncomparative benefits in P_1's life would be greater constitutes a reason to cause P_1 to exist rather than P_2. But in Different Dependent People, it may seem that there is a reason to cause P_1 to exist *only* if one decides to cause *someone* to exist—that is, only when the alternative is to cause P_2 to exist. Most people do seem to think that noncomparative benefits have reason-giving weight only in this rather peculiar way—namely, that they provide a reason to cause a person to exist when the alternative is to cause or allow someone else to exist who would be worse off, but not when the alternative is that no new person will come into existence. Thus, although most people believe that in Different Dependent People there is a reason to cause P_1 to exist *rather than to cause P_2 to exist*, they also think that there is *no* reason to cause P_1 to exist *rather than not to cause anyone to exist*. It seems, that is, that most people accept that noncomparative benefits have reason-giving weight *only conditionally*—only if someone is going to come into existence, either because that is unavoidable (as in Dependent People) or because one has *decided* to cause someone to exist (as one might in Different Dependent People).

Similarly, most people believe that in Same Dependent Person, there is no reason to cause P to exist but that, *if* one decides to cause him to exist, one ought, other things being equal, to cause him to exist with the life that will last eighty years rather than the life that will last only sixty years. In this case, the benefit of causing him to exist with either life is comparative in relation to causing him to exist with the other life, but noncomparative in relation to not causing him to exist at all.

But these beliefs are puzzling. Suppose that, as the common view suggests, there is initially no reason in Different Dependent People to cause either P_1 or P_2 to exist. But if one decides, arbitrarily, or on a whim, to cause someone to exist, the common view implies that that decision somehow creates a reason to cause P_1 to exist. The noncomparative benefit to P_1 does not matter when the alternative is that no noncomparative benefit will be conferred. But that benefit to P_1 *does* matter if an arbitrary decision makes it the case that the alternative is the conferral of a lesser noncomparative benefit on a different person. But how can a decision made simply on a whim create a *reason* that did not exist antecedently to cause P_1 to exist? More generally, how can noncomparative benefits have reason-giving weight in choices between greater and lesser benefits, but not in choices between some benefits and none?[13] If there is no reason to bestow a noncomparative benefit on its own, how can there be a reason to bestow it rather than a lesser benefit?

These cases in which noncomparative benefits seem to have reason-giving weight when the alternative is to bestow a lesser noncomparative benefit but not when the alternative is to bestow no benefit at all are quite unlike a superficially similar case of Parfit's in which one can save one of a person's arms at significant cost to oneself, do nothing, or save both that person's arms at the same cost to oneself.[14] Parfit claims that it can be permissible to save neither arm, but that if one decides to help this person, one must save both arms rather than only one. As in Different Dependent People, the requirement to bestow the greater benefit is conditional on a decision to confer *some* benefit. But despite the fact that it is permissible to bestow neither benefit in Parfit's case, this is not because there is no reason to bestow either rather than neither. There is a strong reason to bestow each benefit rather than no benefit. It is just that that reason can be overridden by the cost to the agent.

Jonathan Glover also once observed that a policy of picking the best apples does not entail that one has a reason to pick as many as possible.[15] That is clearly true, since the reason for picking apples is instrumental and there is a limit to the instrumental value of apples. What he could not have said is that having a reason to pick the best apples does not entail that one has a reason to pick apples. If one had *no* reason to pick apples, one would have no reason to pick better rather than worse apples.

The common assumption that noncomparative benefits have reason-giving weight in choices between greater and lesser benefits but not in choices between some benefits and none may imply an absurd conclusion. Consider two choices, one between a greater and a lesser noncomparative benefit, the other between a noncomparative benefit equivalent to the greater benefit in the first choice and no such benefit at all. The first of these choices can simply be the original Dependent People:

A: P_1 will exist and live to eighty P_2 will never exist
Not A: P_1 will never exist P_2 will later exist and live to sixty

The second choice can be called *Dependent Person*:

A*: P_1 will exist and live to eighty P_2 will never exist
Not A*: P_1 will never exist P_2 will never exist

In this case, the choice is between causing P_1 to exist and no new person coming into existence. Suppose that Dependent Person is like Dependent People in that there is no cost to doing A* and that the effects of doing A* on existing and unconditional people would be neither better nor worse overall than the effects of not doing A*. Suppose further that P_1 in *Dependent Person* would enjoy the same high quality of life that he would enjoy in *Dependent People*. P_1's life would be the same in all relevant respects in each case. The only difference between the cases is that, in *Dependent People*, the alternative to P_1's existing is that P_2 will exist instead, whereas in *Dependent Person* the alternative to P_1's existing is that no new person will come into existence. Our concern here is with a comparison between doing an act when the alternative is a certain specific outcome and doing the same act when the alternative is a different specific outcome. I will therefore refer to the comparison between these two choices as the *Same Act Comparison*.

In Dependent People, it is better to do A than not to do A—that is, it is better to cause P_1 to exist than to allow P_2 to exist instead. Most people, it seems, accept this. In contrast, most people deny that in Dependent Person it is better to do A* than not to do A*. They deny that there is a moral reason to cause P_1 to exist rather than not to cause anyone to exist. (This denial is of course one of the two claims that together constitute the Asymmetry.)

Yet the actual consequence of doing A and the actual consequence of doing A* are equivalent in all morally significant respects. There is no relevant difference between the existence of P_1 in *Dependent People* and the existence of P_1 in *Dependent Person*. But if doing A and doing A* result in morally equivalent states of the world, and not doing A is worse than doing A, it seems to follow that not doing A must also be worse than doing A*. Most people believe, however, that not doing A* is not worse than doing A*. But if not doing A* is *not* worse than doing A*, yet not doing A *is* worse than doing A*, it seems to follow that not doing A is worse than not doing A*—that is, that allowing P_2 to exist is worse than causing no one to exist. But that is false. It is not worse, if other things are equal, to allow a person to exist and live for sixty years with a high quality of life than not to cause any person to exist at all.

If this argument is correct, it seems that we should accept either that it is *not* better to do A than not to do A, or that it *is* better to do A* than not to do A*. For if, for example, it is better to do A* than not to do A*, the *Same Act Comparison* does not then imply the absurd claim that it is worse to allow P_2 to exist than not to cause anyone to exist. For if doing A* is equivalent in its results to doing A, and if doing A is better than not doing A, so that doing A* is better than not doing A, and if doing A* is better than not doing A*, then nothing at all follows about the relation between not doing A* and not doing A. Both are worse than doing either A or doing A*, but nothing follows about whether one is worse than the other.

Of the two options, it seems more plausible to accept that doing A* is better than not doing A*. For it is plausible to suppose that noncomparative benefits have *some* reason-giving weight in *all* contexts, even if they do not have the same reason-giving weight as equivalent comparative benefits. That this is plausible is supported by common sense intuitions about the prospect of human extinction. Most of us believe that the extinction of the human species would be the worst of those possible tragedies that have more than a negligible probability of actually occurring. The badness of extinction can of course be explained in part by the effects on the members of the final generation, and in part by the retroactive diminution of the meaning or significance of acts done by members of previous generations in the expectation that they were contributing to efforts that would continue indefinitely into the future. But there seems intuitively to be much more to the badness of extinction than this. As long as extinction can be deferred, human life, and posthuman life, can continue indefinitely, with unimaginable numbers of people enjoying the goods of life, which might in time become vastly superior to the goods accessible to human beings thus far, just as the goods accessible to us are vastly superior to those that were accessible to our remote evolutionary ancestors. To most of us, it is appalling to think that instead of this incalculable number of people enjoying these incalculable benefits, there might instead be only the emptiness of a world devoid of consciousness.[16]

To accept that noncomparative benefits have reason-giving weight even in choices between some benefits and none—that is, to accept that there is a reason to cause people to exist if their lives would be worth living—is not to accept any particular view about what weight noncomparative benefits have in relation to that of equivalent comparative benefits. Even so, to acknowledge that they have any reason-giving weight at all is to raise certain difficult problems, as I will indicate in Section 8.

7. OBJECTIONS TO THE ARGUMENT BASED ON THE *SAME ACT COMPARISON*

It is therefore worth considering what might be said against the argument I have given on the basis of the *Same Act Comparison*. One obvious objection is that my claim that doing A and doing A* are equally good ignores an essential dimension of the evaluation of the two acts. For I appealed only to the actual outcomes of those acts—the existence of P_1 in the case of doing A and in the case of doing A*. But this fails to consider what would happen in each case if the act were not done. And that is clearly relevant to how good it is that each act is done. Suppose that if A were not done, a million people would die, whereas not doing A* would have no effect on whether anyone would die. If A and A* are both done, the only way in which the world differs after each act from the way it was before is that it contains one more person. But clearly it does not follow that in these circumstances, doing A and doing A* are equally good.

As we have seen, it seems that most people accept that doing A is better than not doing A but deny that doing A* is better than not doing A*. These evaluations suggest that most people accept that it is better to do A than to do A*, considering each choice in isolation from the other and taking into account what would happen if each act were not done. But is this common view actually defensible? I have noted that the actual consequences of doing A and of doing A* are relevantly equivalent. Thus, if it is better or more important to do A than to do A*, that must be because of what would have happened if each had not been done. That is, doing A must be better than doing A* because the alternative to doing A would be worse than the alternative to doing A*. But to accept that is to directly embrace the absurd conclusion I drew from the *Same Act Comparison*—namely, that allowing P_2 to exist is worse than not causing anyone to exist. This first objection to the argument based on the *Same Act Comparison* therefore fails.

A second objection is that there is a fundamental difference between Dependent People and Dependent Person that prevents us from drawing any conclusions from the comparison between them, at least until further work is done in moral theory. This difference is that Dependent People is a Same Number Choice while Dependent Person is a Different Number Choice. According to Parfit, conclusions we might draw about Same Number Choices cannot be straightforwardly extrapolated to Different Number Choices. He argues in *Reasons and Persons* that we must find a principle, *Theory X*, that implies the Same Number Quality Claim and is compatible with the No-Difference View but also applies to Different Number Choices.[17] Yet he has thus far been unable to find Theory X and, so far as I am aware, no one else has succeeded where he has failed.

One reason why Different Number Choices are so much more problematic than Same Number Choices is obvious. When the number of people in the different possible outcomes of a choice is the same, the standard measures of how well off the people in the different outcomes are coincide. For example, an increase in total well-being is also a corresponding increase in average well-being. Thus, when the Same Number Quality Claim, which applies only in Same Number Choices, says that an outcome in which people are worse off is worse, there is no uncertainty about which of the possible outcomes is the one in which people are worse off, even though there are different people in the different outcomes. (It is perhaps worth noting that certain other principles could conflict with the Same Number Quality Claim. Distributional principles, such as principles of equality or priority, which could imply that an outcome that is worse according to the Same Number Quality Claim is actually better.) Yet when there are differences in the number of people in the different possible outcomes, standard measures of collective well-being may diverge. It may no longer be obvious or uncontroversial which group is worse off. For this reason, principles such as the Same Number Quality Claim, which seem highly plausible when applied to Same Number Choices, such as Dependent People, cease to have any clear application in Different Number Choices, such as Dependent Person. Furthermore, outcomes with different numbers of people tend to be less precisely comparable than outcomes with the same number of people.

Yet it seems that these ought not to be significant problems in a simple Different Number Choice such as Dependent Person, in which all relevant factors are the same in the two possible outcomes except that in one there is an additional person who will have a life that is well worth living and will last for eighty years. If we accept that Dependent People shows that noncomparative benefits matter and have reason-giving weight, then the presumption must be that they have reason-giving weight in Dependent Person as well. An explanation is required of why the additional noncomparative benefits to P_1 provide a reason to cause him to exist instead of P_2 while the possibility of conferring equivalent noncomparative benefits on him provides no reason to cause him to exist if the alternative is that no new person will exist.

We can, of course, imagine circumstances in which there would be a reason to cause P_1 to exist in Dependent People but not in Dependent Person. If, for example, everyone in the world had the same level of well-being that P_1 would have, it might be objectionable on grounds of equality to allow P_2 to come into existence. Hence there could be a reason to prevent that by causing P_1 to exist instead, even if there were no reason to cause him to exist in Dependent Person, when the outcome of the choice would have no effect on equality. This would support our intuition in Dependent People without implying that it would be better to cause P_1 to exist in Dependent Person. Yet while this would support our intuitive belief, it would not explain it in a plausible way. For the suggestion here is that the reason to do A is not that P_1 would benefit more from existence than P_2 would, but that the existence of P_2 would be *bad*, for reasons of equality. Furthermore, reasons of equality do not provide a general justification for doing A rather than not doing A. If, for example, everyone in the world had the level of well-being that P_2 would have, reasons of equality might imply that it would be better not to do A, and indeed not to do A* either.

It seems, therefore, that the fact that Dependent People is a Same Number Choice while Dependent Person is a Different Number Choice provides no obvious reason to deny that whatever explains why in most circumstances it is better to do A than not to do A also justifies and explains the claim that in most circumstances it is better to do A* than not to do A*. In particular, it provides no reason to suppose that in Dependent Person, which is an extremely simple Different Number Choice, the outcome in which P_1 exists is not the one in which people are better off. It certainly provides no reason to think that this outcome is the one in which people are worse off.

There is, however, one further type of objection to the argument I developed on the basis of the *Same Act Comparison* that seems quite powerful. This type of objection consists of challenges to the precision of the relations that I have claimed hold between the various acts. For example, one of the premises in the argument I gave is that doing A* is not better than not doing A*, hence not doing A* is not worse than doing A*. As Parfit points out, "not worse than" is sometimes an *imprecise* relation.[18] If the most that can be claimed is that not doing A* is *imprecisely not worse than* doing A*, it does not follow that not doing A* is at least *equally good* as doing A*. In that case, the fact that not doing A* is not worse than A*, which is better than not doing A, may not entail that not doing A* is better than not doing A.

A further objection of this type is that there is no warrant for the precision in my earlier claim that doing A is equally good as doing A*. The most that is warranted, one might argue, is the imprecise claim that neither doing A nor doing A* is better or worse than doing the other. If that is correct, then the claim that not doing A is worse than doing A does not entail that not doing A is worse than doing A*. For it seems possible, because of the imprecision in the comparisons, that not doing A is worse than doing A, that doing A* is neither better nor worse than doing A, and yet that not doing A is not worse than not doing A*. In short, if there is no basis for the claim that not doing A is worse than doing A*, then even if not doing A* is not worse than doing A*, it does not follow that not doing A (that is, allowing P_2 to exist) is worse than not doing A* (not causing anyone to exist).

I am uncertain whether there is imprecision in these relations that are asserted to obtain in the premises of the argument based on the *Same Act Comparison*. But even if there is, the challenge remains to explain how it could be that noncomparative benefits have reason-giving weight in choices between greater and lesser benefits but not in choices between some benefits and none. Given that noncomparative benefits clearly do have reason-giving weight in choices between greater and lesser benefits (such as Dependent People), the presumption seems to be that they also have reason-giving weight in choices between some benefits and none—that is, that there is a reason to confer noncomparative benefits by causing people to exist even when the alternative is not to cause anyone to exist. That presumption stands unless one can find a good reason to believe that noncomparative benefits have reason-giving weight in choices between greater and lesser benefits but not in choices between some benefits and none.

8. CHOICES BETWEEN CAUSING PEOPLE TO EXIST AND SAVING PEOPLE'S LIVES

It may help to review the overall argument to this point. If, as virtually everyone believes, it is permissible to have a child in the absence of some unusual reason not to, then noncomparative benefits seem to have full offsetting weight—that is, they weigh against and offset corresponding noncomparative harms in the same way that comparative benefits weigh against and offset comparative harms. Many people, of course, believe that there is a moral asymmetry between comparative benefits and comparative harms, in that for it to be permissible to harm a person without her consent in the process of bestowing a benefit on her, the benefit must significantly outweigh the harm (that is, the benefit must be good for her by significantly more than the harm would be bad for her). Those who accept this view about comparative benefits and harms may accept a similar view about noncomparative benefits and harms.

Dependent People supports the view that noncomparative benefits have reason-giving weight as well as offsetting weight. When we initially consider the *Same Act Comparison*, however, our intuitions may suggest that while noncomparative benefits have reason-giving weight in choices, such as that in Dependent People, between bestowing a greater benefit and bestowing a lesser benefit, they do not have reason-giving weight in choices between bestowing a great noncomparative benefit and not bestowing any such benefit at all—that is, in choices between causing a person to exist and not causing anyone to exist. Although I developed an argument to show that that view is mistaken, it may be that the argument fails because of the imprecision of the comparative evaluations that constitute its premises. Yet even if that particular argument fails, it nevertheless seems arbitrary to suppose that noncomparative benefits have reason-giving weight in choices between greater and lesser benefits but not in choices between some benefits and none.

Assuming that noncomparative benefits have reason-giving weight in at least some choices, do they have the same weight as equivalent comparative benefits? The No-Difference View asserts that they do, though Parfit's discussion of that view is confined to Same Number Choices, which are choices between greater and lesser benefits. I suggested, however, on the basis of *Existing or Dependent*, that it is intuitively plausible to suppose that noncomparative benefits have less reason-giving weight than equivalent comparative benefits.

Our intuitive reluctance to accept that noncomparative benefits have reason-giving weight in choices between some benefits and none suggests a further possible view, which is worth noting. According to this view, noncomparative benefits have discounted reason-giving weight in choices between greater and lesser benefits. Hence in *Existing or Dependent*, it is better to confer the comparative benefit of an additional twenty years of life on an existing person than it is to confer a greater noncomparative benefit by causing a person to exist who will live twenty years longer than a different person who would otherwise come into existence. Yet in choices between some benefits and none, noncomparative benefits are discounted *even more* than they are in choices between greater and lesser benefits. Hence the reason to do A in Dependent People might be stronger than the reason to do A* in Dependent Person, despite the fact that doing A would confer a lesser net noncomparative benefit than doing A* would.

Irrespective of whether we think that noncomparative benefits have less reason-giving weight in choices between some benefits and none, it is, as I have suggested, difficult to see how they could have *no* reason-giving weight in such choices when they do have *some* reason-giving weight in choices between greater and lesser benefits. Yet if it is conceded that they have reason-giving weight in choices between causing a person to exist and not causing anyone to exist, various problems arise. For the reason to confer noncomparative benefits by causing people to exist can conflict with reasons to confer comparative benefits on existing people, or with reasons to prevent existing people from losing comparative benefits, or even with reasons not to cause or allow existing people to suffer comparative harms.

This problem is most acute if we accept the No-Difference View, which implies that there is no moral asymmetry between comparative and noncomparative benefits. The No-Difference View does not, of course, directly imply that there is *any* reason to confer noncomparative benefits by causing people to exist when otherwise no new person would come into existence (that is, in choices between some benefits and none). But Parfit defends the No-Difference View by reference to Same Number Choices such as the Medical Programs case, of which *Unconditional or Dependent* is an analogue, and he assumes that it will be implied by Theory X, which will extend the Same Number Quality Claim so that it will apply to Different Number Choices. So Parfit assumes that even in Different Number Choices, the fact that an outcome is worse for a particular person makes no difference, and this is tantamount to assuming that there is no moral asymmetry between comparative and noncomparative benefits, or between comparative and noncomparative harms.

Suppose, then, that one must choose between causing a person to exist and saving an existing person's life. Suppose, for example, that one can either cause a person to exist who would live to be sixty or save the life of a twenty-year-old, enabling him to live to eighty. The first of these options would confer a great noncomparative benefit, while the second would confer an equivalent comparative benefit. Everyone, I assume, would accept that the second option is better, and that one has a stronger moral reason to save the existing person than to cause a person to exist. While the No-Difference View does not imply the contrary claim, it does deny that the intuition that everyone has about this choice can be defended on the ground that the failure to save the existing person would be *worse* for that person, or on the ground that there would be a *victim* of the failure to save the person but not of the failure to cause a person to exist.[19]

This problem is mitigated but not eliminated if we reject the No-Difference View and instead accept that the reason-giving weight of noncomparative benefits is discounted relative to that of equivalent comparative benefits. According to this view, it is better in the case just presented to save the existing person than to cause a person to exist. But if the numbers were different, this view too would imply that it is better to cause a person to exist. Suppose, for example, that the person one might cause to exist would live for eighty years while the person one might save would live only two more years. In that case, unless the discounting factor is exceedingly high, even a view that discounts the reason-giving weight of noncomparative benefits should imply that it is better to cause the person to exist than to save the existing person. This remains true even if noncomparative benefits are *doubly* discounted, once for being noncomparative and again because the alternative to causing them is that there will be no noncomparative benefits at all. This problem arises for *any* view that concedes that there is a reason to confer noncomparative benefits by causing a person to exist even when the alternative is not to cause anyone to exist.

Parfit has suggested that even a wholly impersonal moral theory can recognize one respect in which it is better, other things being equal, to save a person's life than to bestow an equivalent benefit by causing a person to exist.[20] This is that the benefit conferred in the first way would go to a population with fewer people than the benefit conferred in the second way, since the second way would expand the size of the population. When a benefit of a fixed size goes to a population with fewer people, it makes people better off on average than it would if it went to a population with more people. This may matter even if it is a mistake to suppose that in general one ought to maximize average well-being. This claim is limited, of course, to choices between saving a person in a given population and causing a person to exist who would be a member of that same population. But in practice these are the important choices and in any case one could claim that the relevant population is the set of all the people who ever live.

While I think this point is correct, it seems to have little significance in a choice between saving one person and causing one person to exist. The difference that such a choice would make to the level of well-being per person in a world as highly populated as ours is negligible. And the difference it would make if the relevant population is all the people who ever live is less than negligible.

Before concluding, I will mention one further set of problems raised by the claim that noncomparative benefits have reason-giving weight even in choices between some benefits and none. Suppose that one can do either of the following acts but not both:

A*: Cause an individual to exist who will live for eighty years with a life well worth living

H: Save a different individual's life immediately after he has begun to exist, thereby enabling him to life for eighty years with a life well worth living

Almost everyone believes that we begin to exist prior to birth. Most people seem to believe that we begin to exist at conception, though others believe that we come into existence when significant cell differentiation occurs, when twinning ceases to be possible, when brain activity begins, or when the capacity for consciousness first appears. All such views imply that we begin to exist with no psychological capacities or with extremely rudimentary psychological capacities.

If one does A*, one will confer a great noncomparative benefit. If one does H, one will confer an equivalent comparative benefit. If comparative benefits have substantially more reason-giving weight than equivalent noncomparative benefits have in some-or-none choices, as the previous choice between saving a person and causing a person to exist suggests, it would be much better to do H, and one's reason to do H would be much stronger than one's reason to do A*. But if we are wholly unconscious, or only dimly conscious, when we begin to exist (and for a considerable time after that), it may seem that failing to save a zygote or embryo is not much worse, or not worse at all, than failing to cause a person to exist. After all, around two-thirds of naturally conceived human embryos die spontaneously in the first few months of pregnancy, yet no scientifically advanced society has devoted more than a trifling amount of effort or resources to trying to prevent these many deaths from occurring. And one might ask oneself whether from one's present perspective one can find any relevant difference between the possibility that one might not have been caused to exist and the possibility that one might have died immediately after beginning to exist. These reflections may suggest that noncomparative benefits matter almost as much as equivalent comparative benefits.

But this would be a mistaken inference. The truth is instead that equivalent comparative benefits do not always have equivalent weight. In particular, given that we begin to exist with rudimentary psychological capacities, or no psychological capacities at all, the benefit that an embryo or fetus receives in having its life saved must be heavily discounted for the weakness of the psychological relations it bears to itself in the future. I cannot elaborate on this suggestion here, though I have defended it at length elsewhere.[21] The point is that the comparative benefit one bestows in saving the life of a fetus has substantially less weight than a *lesser* comparative benefit one might bestow in saving the life of a twenty-year-old. Hence even if causing an individual to exist matters almost as much as saving the life of an individual who has just begun to exist, that is compatible with the fact that causing an individual to exist matters substantially less than saving the life of an older child or adult.

This does, however, leave a residual problem, at least for those who believe that abortion can be permissible in a wide range of cases, including relatively late in pregnancy. No one supposes that the comparative benefit to a fetus of saving its life could matter *less* than an equivalent noncomparative benefit that could be produced by causing a person to exist. Thus, if noncomparative benefits have significant reason-giving weight in some-or-none choices, there must also be a significant reason to save the life of a fetus, and, assuming there is an asymmetry between doing harm and allowing harm to occur, an even more significant reason not to kill a fetus via abortion.[22] Defenders of abortion must presumably claim that the benefit to the fetus of being enabled or allowed to continue to live is outweighed in most cases by conflicting considerations. But this is tantamount to conceding that this comparative benefit has relatively little weight, which in turn implies that an equivalent noncomparative benefitscannot have more weight, and presumably has even less.

While this may seem intuitively plausible, it has to be reconciled with the reasons we have discussed for accepting that noncomparative benefits have significant weight. Consider, for example, the following variant of *Unconditional or Dependent*:

B: P_1 will later exist P_2 will never exist P_U will later exist
     and live to eighty   and live to sixty
C*: P_1 will never exist P_2 will later exist P_U will later exist
                                            and live to forty   and live to sixty-two

If noncomparative benefits have relatively little weight compared with equivalent comparative benefits, one's reason to do C* could be stronger than one's reason to do B. I find that difficult to accept.

The case just cited is, however, one that tests for the reason-giving weight of noncomparative benefits in a choice between greater and lesser benefits. I suggested earlier in this section that it is possible that noncomparative benefits have greater reason-giving weight in choices between greater and lesser benefits than in choices between some benefits and none. If that is the case, and if, for the reasons I indicated in the discussion of abortion immediately above, the choice of whether to have an abortion is relevantly like a choice between some benefits and none, then the reason to do B could be stronger than the reason to do C* without that having any implication about the strength of the reason not to have an abortion.

One final problem worth noting is that the claim that there is a general reason to confer noncomparative benefits by causing people to exist not only implies that in some cases it can be better to cause people to exist than to save people's lives but also seems to imply, in other cases, what Parfit calls the *Repugnant Conclusion* (though Parfit has well-known arguments that lead to that conclusion even without the assumption that there is a general reason to cause people to exist if their lives would be worth living).[23] So the implications of the claim that noncomparative benefits have reason-giving weight in choices between some benefits and none include some that virtually everyone will find counterintuitive.

This is a depressing point on which to conclude, though perhaps not *disappointing*, as I had no real hope of solving any of the problems in this area of moral theory when I began. Problems in the morality of causing people to exist seem to me the most difficult and intractable of all the problems of which I am aware in normative and practical ethics. They suggest that it is a real possibility that any moral theory that is both complete and coherent will have implications that are intuitively intolerable. It is these problems, therefore, rather than arguments in metaethics about the queerness of objective values, the connections between normativity and motivation, and so on, that seem to me to pose the greatest challenge to realism in ethics.

ACKNOWLEDGMENTS

I am extremely grateful to Todd May, Melinda Roberts, Yu-Ting Su, Victor Tadros, and Rivka Weinberg for generous written comments on an earlier draft of this essay. I owe an even greater debt to Tim Campbell, who gave me extensive comments on the penultimate draft and helped me to see how extremely unclear the previously published version of this essay was. My greatest debt is to Derek Parfit, who not only gave me two sets of detailed and illuminating written comments on earlier drafts but also discussed them with me at length on several occasions.

NOTES

1. Derek Parfit, *Reasons and Persons* (Oxford: Oxford University Press, 1984), 356. I have argued elsewhere that in practice it is unlikely that there are any Same Number Choices (bearing in mind that this category does not include Same People Choices). But we can ignore this here, for when one knows that one's choice will ultimately affect the number of people who will exist but not whether it will increase or decrease that number, that choice

may in practice be treated as a Same Number Choice. See Jeff McMahan, "Preventing the Existence of People with Disabilities," in *Quality of Life and Human Difference: Genetic Testing, Health Care, and Disability*, edited by David Wasserman, Jerome Bickenbach, and Robert Wachbroit (New York: Cambridge University Press, 2005), 146.

2. Ibid., 360.

3. Derek Parfit, *On What Matters* (New York: Oxford University Press, 2011), 1:38.

4. Compare Jeff McMahan, "Problems of Population Theory," *Ethics* 92 (1981): 105. Also on this page I consider, but reject, the suggestion that although it makes no sense to say of a person who never exists that never existing is worse for him, it does make sense to say of an *existing* person that never existing would have been worse for him.

5. The act that would cause P to exist with a life lasting only sixty years might itself cause P's death at sixty or it might simply cause P to exist in conditions in which his life would end at sixty without itself causing those conditions. I put this distinction aside here.

6. Parfit, *Reasons and Persons*, 359.

7. Ibid., 366–371. The No-Difference View is, in effect, the view that the Non-Identity Problem makes no moral difference.

8. Ibid.

9. Todd May and Derek Parfit independently offered this observation. May thinks that it would be more important to save the existing person if he were on the verge of death at the time one had to choose between D and E. Although this view exerts some intuitive pull on me, I am unsure what to think of it.

10. Parfit, *Reasons and Persons*, 357.

11. Personal communication, March 20, 2012.

12. These claims are elaborated and defended in my paper, "'It Might Have Been!': What Matters in Alternative Possible Lives" (unpublished).

13. Compare McMahan, "Wrongful Life: Paradoxes in the Morality of Causing People to Exist," in John Harris, ed., *Bioethics* (Oxford: Oxford University Press, 2001), section III.

14. Derek Parfit, "Future Generations: Further Problems," *Philosophy and Public Affairs* 11 (1982): 131

15. Jonathan Glover, *Causing Death and Saving Lives* (Harmondsworth: Penguin, 1977), 69.

16. Our intuitions about extinction seem to include not only beliefs about the importance of the quantity and quality of human life but also beliefs about the importance of life persisting *over time*. See Jeff McMahan, "The End of the Future," *London Review of Books*, July 1, 1982.

17. Parfit, *Reasons and Persons*, 370.

18. Derek Parfit, "Towards Theory X: Part One" (unpublished manuscript).

19. In conversation, Parfit has said that he expects that Theory X will *not* imply that it is as good to enable a person to have sixty years of good life by causing him to exist as it is to enable a person to have sixty more years of good life by saving him. What he denies is that this can be explained by the idea that benefits have greater weight if their absence would be worse for someone.

20. In his comments on this essay.

21. Jeff McMahan, *The Ethics of Killing: Problems at the Margins of Life* (New York: Oxford University Press, 2002), Chs. 1, 2, and 4.

22. For an extended, closely argued discussion of these and related issues, see Melinda A. Roberts, *Abortion and the Significance of Merely Possible Persons* (Dordrecht: Springer, 2010).

23. Parfit, *Reasons and Persons*, Chs. 17 and 19.

CHAPTER 24

··

ANIMAL POPULATION ETHICS

··

AXEL GOSSERIES AND TIM MEIJERS

1. INTRODUCTION

··

CLAIMS about the desirable size and composition of animal populations are part of our daily lives. Nature conservationists worry about wild animal populations when they attract our attention to the sixth mass species extinction, the need not to drop below minimum viable populations, the rise of so-called invasive species, and the decline of common birds. Serious farmers know the minimum herd size needed for them to make a living and the maximum herd size that their land can sustainably feed. They can tell you about the size of insect populations that their crops can stand or the size of predator populations that their herd can take. Hunters claim that they are needed to regulate wild animal populations in the absence of large wild predators. Starving villagers on the edge of national parks have an idea about how much we should preserve wild species. Some vegans and vegetarians are aware of what the generalization of their dietary requirements would mean for the size and composition of domestic and wild animal populations. The collapse of livestock populations could free space for wild animals. But the substitution of pastures with non-organic monocultures could also increase insect mortality and habitat loss for wild birds. Interventionist animal ethicists suggest that we may have to drastically reduce the population of wild predators, given the suffering they inflict on other animals. Heritage activists believe that preserving animal breeds is as important as the conservation of natural biodiversity.[1] Public authorities expect citizens to contribute to keeping pet populations under control through sterilization while fighting pests such as rats and mosquitoes, the latter being a major source of human mortality. These are not marginal issues, given our planet's massive number of animals and given the extent of animal species diversity and biomass involved.

Population axiology is concerned with what makes one population better than another. In contrast, *population ethics* is concerned with how we ought to *act* to affect a population's size or composition. Whether an outcome is better than another does not automatically tell us how we should act, as other considerations may matter. In principle, population axiology could rank populations independently of the ethical assessment of the actions that brought them about, albeit in a pro tanto manner. Here, we will understand animal population ethics in a *broad sense*, that is, as an approach bringing ethics and axiology together. Animal population ethics thus encompasses both animal ethics issues in the strict sense that are relevant for those concerned with population—that is, most animal ethics issues—*and* animal population axiology—that is, the branch of population ethics which is concerned with evaluating and raking different non-human animal populations. We need both population size and composition assessments as well as assessments of the *means* of bringing about a population of a given size and composition in order to form an overall judgment of what we ought to do in particular cases where our decision will affect population.

Besides being interesting as such, there are at least three reasons why we should explore *animal* population ethics. First, *animal ethicists* could gain from insight from animal population axiology. Actually, how we treat animals is often motivated by population concerns. We may permit catching one species of fish while forbidding catching another, not because we think that individual members of the latter species are more valuable than members of the former, but in order not to let the stocks of a species drop below viable levels. In other cases, such as for vegetarian or vegan motives, we may decide not to interact in certain ways with animals anymore (e.g., stop eating them), without considering the population impacts of such decisions.

We interact with wild and domestic animals in many ways: we eat their meat, drink their milk, dress with their wool, take advantage of their strength to carry us, use them as allies against pests, consume drugs or cosmetics that have been tested on them, enjoy their company as pets, and so on. We kill them, inflict suffering on them, exploit them, and so on. In assessing these interactions, impacts on animal demography may matter. Should we prefer a small population of happy cows to a much larger one of slightly less happy ones (leaving *how* these two states of affair came about out of the picture)? Then, as a second step, what (if anything) does this tell us about the moral acceptability of bringing such states about, that is, bringing cows into existence and/or inflicting harm on them?

The second reason for looking into animal population ethics—in particular, animal population axiology—concerns *human population axiology*. Because of the way in which we tend to look at animals—rightly or wrongly—we may feel freer to look at animal population axiology with a fresh eye, which could potentially inform our views on human population axiology. Moreover, thinking about animal populations forces us to carefully consider whether it makes sense to assess human populations independently of their interactions with animal populations. For instance, certain human populations may be realizable only at the cost of a radical reduction of the size of animal populations. We might want to conclude that the population we should be concerned with axiologically speaking encompasses all sentient beings.

For instance, population axiology has tended to focus more on size than on composition, that is, more on absolute size than on relative sizes of groups within the total population.[2] And yet, we do express concern in various contexts about the composition of human populations: certain age pyramids can be deemed trickier to handle by pension schemes or health care systems, higher degrees of social and ethnic mixing may be judged preferable in school and housing policy, extreme linguistic diversity without a *lingua franca* may be considered challenging for democratic deliberation, and so on. We might worry about these imbalances for welfare related reasons (e.g., the impact on welfare of an ageing society), or because we attach value to diversity for its own sake (e.g., species diversity in the case of animals, or ethnic, cultural, or linguistic diversity in the case of humans). Consider massively sex-unequal cattle populations—consisting almost entirely of females. Axiologically, is this sex-biased composition problematic independently of how it was brought about (typically through sex-biased slaughtering practices) and of what other effects it might have? The same arises in the case of "missing girls" in human populations: is a male-heavy population less desirable than a more sex-balanced population?[3] Can this be assessed independently of how it was brought about (e.g., through female infanticide) and of what other effects it might have?

The third reason for looking into animal population ethics concerns *human population ethicists*. The way in which we articulate animal population axiology and ethics might shed light, *analogically*, on how we should articulate human population axiology and ethics. It is possible that we are experiencing human over-population globally, given the pressure we put on natural resources as well on other species. And yet, while debates about animal under- or over-population are common, debates about human over-population are more controversial. Why is this? Here are two possible explanations. On the one hand, philosophers face significant meta-ethical challenges when settling on what kind of populations are better than others, axiologically speaking. On the other hand, some non-philosophers may be under the impression that while the idea of human over-population is plausible, *any* policy aimed at reaching a given population target would necessarily be ethically problematic.[4]

In contrast, debates about desirable animal population size might seem less problematic. Axiology for non-human animal populations isn't philosophically easier to work out than axiology for human populations. However, in the case of non-human animals, the means to reach a given demographic goal still appear—often mistakenly so—unproblematic to many. Animal population management through pet sterilization, male-female cattle segregation, the slaughtering of farm animals, and fencing off areas to preserve vulnerable wild animal species, continue to appear uncontroversial to many. Importantly, we are neither suggesting that such means should also be considered for human populations, nor implying that they are morally acceptable for animals.

Our general goal in this chapter is to explore questions about the connections between animal population ethics (in the broad sense defined above) and human population ethics (in the same broad sense). Is there something *special* about animal population ethics compared to human population ethics, for example, in terms of its theoretical assumptions or its implications for various real-world problems, such as dealing with overpopulation and/or underpopulation? Or are human and animal population ethics more or less continuous with each other? Should we look at these two fields in isolation, or can we gain a better understanding of the issues in each field by looking at issues that arise in the other? The chapter focuses on four specific hypotheses concerning the relation between animal population ethics and human population ethics. In Sections 2–5 we critically examine each of these four hypotheses. Section 6 concludes.

2. Multispecies Population Axiology

Here is a first hypothesis to consider:

> *HYP1*: Animal population ethics shows that we require a *multispecies* population axiology.

Consider first a view that holds that only humans count, morally and evaluatively speaking. Such a view has no need for a multispecies population axiology, since it implies that the only basic value bearers are of one species—*Homo sapiens*. Of course, even if we accept such a view, we might want to assess the desirable population size of other species, from the strict perspective of human well-being. A reduction in mosquito populations and an increase in dragonfly populations might benefit humans even if the members of these non-human species have only instrumental value.

Consider next the view that non-human animals also have some intrinsic and positive value. In that case, our population axiology should grant positive value to members of more than one species. Our position on the desirable relative sizes of the populations of different species will then depend on our answers to at least the following two questions:

(1) Should we adopt a *speciesist* account of moral status, that is, of the weights to be attached to the existence and/or well-being of individuals composing the populations at stake?
(2) Do inter-species *relationships* change our obligations in an axiologically relevant way?

2.1. Speciesism

Establishing the moral status of members of the respective human and non-human species will face the usual problems in interspecies ethics.[5] Notably, one very hard challenge is to propose a theory that does not necessarily grant the same moral worth to a dragonfly as to a human being, and that avoids *both* ascribing differences in moral worth on the basis of morally irrelevant features *and* threatening the idea of basic equal moral value *within* the human species.[6] Now, in order to answer our first question—Should we adopt a speciesist account of moral status?—consider two partly interrelated versions of speciesism in turn.

According to *standard* speciesism,[7] some individuals have higher moral status by virtue of their mere species-membership, regardless of their actual capacities or well-being. It denies that moral worth derives from some of an individual's capacities, or well-being, only.[8] There are humans with capacities above or below the average capacities of humans. If we compare a chimp with a human person in an irreversible coma, a standard speciesist who holds that humans have higher moral status than chimps regardless of their individual capacities would grant a higher moral value to the human's life than to the chimp's. As a result, a speciesist multi-species axiology is likely to look different from a non-speciesist one. Note that even someone rejecting speciesism at the theoretical level may endorse a heuristic of attaching different moral worth to individuals from different species if—and insofar as—species membership is a reliable *proxy* for a capacity that one thinks confers higher moral status.

The second type of speciesism worth considering is what could be referred to as *ontological* speciesism. It holds that animal species *as species* have a moral importance irreducible to the aggregated moral value of their individual members—as if the worth of the British people were not reducible to the value of all British citizens together. The precise axiological implications of ontological speciesism are complex to work out. For instance, does it entail that a world with more species diversity is a better world?[9] If valuing individual human beings does not necessarily entail that a larger human population is better, valuing species per se does not necessarily entail that a larger number of species is better.

Like standard speciesism, ontological speciesism has implications for the way in which value members of the species at stake. However, these implications differ. For ontological speciesists, a focus on individual birds *does not* fully capture what is bad about the disappearance of the last dodo or the last Java lapwing on Earth. Ontological speciesists are likely to disvalue species *extinction* while this is not necessarily the case for standard speciesists. The latter ascribe axiological importance to membership in one species or another without necessarily ascribing value to species as entities worth preserving. Ontological speciesists are also likely to *instrumentally* value members of endangered animal species more than members of species that are not endangered.[10] Similarly, they will disvalue the existence of individual animals that are predators of endangered species and value the existence of individual members of a species that tend to be the prey of endangered species.

These are of course pro tanto claims. Ontological speciesism does not entail that the death of individual members of a given species is irrelevant as such, or that the concern for species extinction should always prevail over the concern for, for example, individual suffering. Ontological speciesists do not claim that a species matters *more* than its individual members. They merely claim that a species' value is partly *independent* from the aggregate value of its members. If we can show that carnivorous species generate unacceptable net suffering for individuals, ontological speciesists do not necessarily need to oppose species extinction out of interventionist concerns for such species.[11] Other issues are less clear. For instance, should ontological speciesists consider it worse for an animal population to go extinct rather than never to have existed? Can the creation of a new sheep breed compensate for the extinction of an old one? Is a population with more species diversity better, other things being equal? Ontological speciesism alone does not answer these questions.

To sum up, our axiology will vary depending on whether we are speciesist or not. For a *standard* speciesist, the test case is two individuals from two different species with similar morally relevant capacities and with the same welfare; the standard speciesist will claim that one of these individuals can contribute more to the overall goodness of the population merely in virtue of its species membership. The contrary position holds that species membership per se is axiologically irrelevant. For an *ontological* speciesist, the test case is two individuals with similar morally relevant capacities, one of which belongs to a more valuable species, where this value is irreducible to the values of the individual members. The ontological speciesist might claim that the existence of one of these individuals contributes more to the goodness of the population because it is a member of a axiologically more important species. The contrary position holds that species itself does not have irreducible value.

2.2. Relationships and Obligations

Besides exploring the implications of speciesism, we have to consider the nature of inter-species *relationships*. By this, we refer to relationships among animals (commensalism, predation, etc.) as well as between humans and animals. Besides the moral worth of the members of different species, the nature of the relationship between them matters as well. Consider a comparison between mosquitoes and bees. One could claim that bees have an intrinsic moral worth *slightly* greater than that of mosquitoes, say based on relevant capacities. However, the instrumental value of bees to humans is vastly greater than that of mosquitoes. Thus, it is not only the moral worth of individual animals, but also the nature of the relationship between the animal species and humans (and between different non-human animal species) that matters when assessing desirable relative population sizes of different species.

This brings us to a second point: theorists disagree about whether we have special obligations to particular animals, and—if so—what kind of relationships ground or trigger them.[12] Consider *domestication*. When we domesticate animals, we select features that also turn them more dependent on us, being selected for their docility.[13] Since we have made these domestic animals more dependent on us, our duties to them might be stronger than duties to wild animals. Alternatively, domestic animals can be seen as participants in a cooperative scheme.[14] We may owe more to a domestic goat that provides us with milk every day than to a feral goat that lives on the wild cliffs of an island. Of course, these claims could be challenged. Wild animals might be very vulnerable too and they might provide us with services equivalent to those of domestic animals sometimes, while remaining wild. Be that as it may, it remains plausible that our obligations toward domestic animals might differ from our obligations toward wild animals. From this, it doesn't follow that we have *no* duties toward wild animals, for example, duties to alleviate animal suffering in the wild.

Now, here is a third point. If we accept the idea that we have different obligations based on the different relationships that we have with animals, this might have interesting implications for population ethics. Imagine a population constituted of wild and domestic horses. One question for population axiology is whether it is better, non-instrumentally speaking, to have a larger proportion of domestic animals and a smaller proportion of wild ones. Such an assessment may have to do with how we make a trade-off between different values, that is, whether we give more value to the fact that domestic animals are likely to have more well-being (e.g., suffer less from hunger and thirst if properly taken care of), or the fact that wild animals are able to live freer from human interference.[15]

Besides this well-being versus freedom-from-dependency-to-humans distinction—and possible trade-off—another dimension worth noticing is that the claim that domestic animals are less likely to suffer from hunger necessarily rests on the assumption that there are differential obligations toward domestic and wild animals *and* that people will effectively act upon them. Perhaps this would not be the case if humans had the ability and duty to feed all hungry and thirsty animals, regardless of whether they are domesticated or not. Note as well that the duty to feed animals might be seen as a burden on human populations. This might be relevant to analyzing the value of the composition of the total population of sentient beings consisting of both non-humans and human animals. This illustrates how difficult it is to separate the axiological assessment of population composition from the assessment of ethical duties toward animals.

So, a complete multi-species population axiology has to take a position on each of several questions: What is the relative worth of different species? Does species diversity have intrinsic value? What is the instrumental value of a species for other species? What do we do when a given course of action is harmful for one species and beneficial for another? How will the individual members of the species flourish? The last of these depends both on external circumstances and on the moral claims of individuals to have their well-being protected. What seems clear is that, insofar as non-human animals have any moral value at all, the assessment of the total population consisting of both humans and non-human animals needs to be multispecies. This affirms HYP1.

We have seen that a population axiology can be multi-species in different senses. It can assign different values to members of different species, for example, based on welfare levels or capacities of individual members of each species, or for purely speciesist reasons. It can also value a species as a whole, over and above the sum of the values it assigns to the individual members of the species. By focusing on animal ethics, we have also seen how a complete population axiology might care about the composition of the overall population consisting of both humans and non-humans and how it might care about the relationships between different species within the overall population.

3. A LIFE NOT WORTH LIVING?

A second possible hypothesis about what renders animal population ethics special is the following:

> HYP2: Animal population axiology is special compared with human population axiology because a significant amount of non-human animal beings have lives *not worth living*.

Let us first discuss the possible *implications* of this claim before discussing the claim's *plausibility*.

What are the possible *implications* of HYP2? Population axiology notoriously faces impossibility theorems. One way out is to assume that creating new individuals with positive well-being albeit below a certain threshold of well-being worsens the state of the world. So, let us assume that a significant part of the Earth's animal population is composed of beings of this kind. In that case, critical-level utilitarianism[16] (or any other threshold-based view of the kind just mentioned) entails that it would have been better if these animals had not existed, even if they are harmless to human beings.

There may be a pro tanto case for improving the living conditions or genetic makeup of below-threshold animals. There might even be reason to exterminate these species so that their members cannot reproduce further individuals below the threshold, unless one holds an ontological speciesist view granting a very significant value to species preservation, including for such below-threshold species. We would of course have to identify which features render a species a good candidate for extinction out of welfare concern, for example by looking at the cause of suffering ("is it human-caused or not?"), whether it is avoidable, and what the costs of avoiding such suffering would be.

What is the *plausibility* of HYP2? Ng (1995) supports it. Although some individual animals may have positive levels of welfare "for any such a fortunate individual, there are dozens or thousands of other less fortunate individuals that are either starved to death or physically hunted down and eaten, most of them well before they are mature enough to mate."[17] Given that mating is one of the few pleasures for some species, he continues:

> Thus, a typical individual is destined to starvation, capture, or struggling unsuccessfully for mating. It is difficult to imagine a positive welfare for such a life. Thus, while a mathematical proof is impossible, reason requires us to accept that, in all probabilities, the welfare level of an individual (affective) sentient that fails to survive to have successful mating is negative. It follows that, if we can reduce the number of such miserable individuals, other things being equal, we can increase the level of overall welfare.[18]

In order to determine which species detract from overall welfare, we would have to know for instance whether the lives of domestic animals are in general better than those of wild ones, whether the lives of top predators are better than those of their preys, whether the lives of higher vertebrates are better than those of invertebrates and lower vertebrates,[19] whether the lives of species with low birthrates are better than those of species with high birthrates (*K* vs. *r* strategies).[20] An interesting complication comes from the food chain problem. Imagine that there is a species whose members lead lives definitely worth living, but which depends for their survival on the existence of another species whose members lead lives definitely not worth living. Multispecies animal population ethics will have to be able to say whether the existence of both species is overall better than the nonexistence of both.

In assessing the plausibility of the claim that animals tend to have lives not worth living, there are at least two sources of complexity to consider. Here is the first one. We might hold the view that most chimpanzees have lives worth living, that most moles have lives worth not living, and that sponges have lives of neutral value because they are unable to experience pleasure or pain. This suggests that there are actually *three*—rather than two—groups of animal species to consider. And only the members of one of these three groups have, generally speaking, lives *worth not living*, lives that involve *net negative welfare*.[21]

The second source of complexity has to do with more radical approaches[22] that focus on instances of negative welfare, as opposed to *net* negative welfare over a being's life. Imagine that we hold the view that it is preferable not to bring people into existence if they would experience *some* harm. This view assumes an asymmetric concern for pain and pleasure (or bads and goods). It does not allow for benefits to compensate for harms in genesis choices, because the absence of pain is good (even if not good *for someone*), whereas the absence of pleasure is not bad unless it is bad for someone. Coming into existence is always a harm, because all lives contain some pain, while the absence of pleasure is not bad for a nonexistent entity. Hence, it is always better never to have been. So, even if a being's life were overall way above the threshold of a life worth living, the fact that it involves *some* suffering renders it worse than nonexistence. If this is true, a smaller population will always be preferable to a larger one, even for beings that have a life definitely worth living according to other views.

For anyone endorsing such an asymmetric concern for harm, the factual assumption that animals would less often have a life worth living than humans would make no significant difference. In both human and animal cases, the mere fact of experiencing *some* suffering would render it preferable not to bring these beings into existence. Hence, while HYP2 has some plausibility, its factual assumption is irrelevant for those who hold views that do not care about *net* well-being levels.

4. ANIMAL SPECIES EXTINCTION

We are currently experiencing both continuing human population growth and a mass extinction of non-human animal species.[23] Extinction is an extreme case of population decline. It entails the disappearance of the last living and reproducible tokens of a species-type.[24] Our concern is twofold. First, we consider whether extinction of a species is more problematic than the mere aggregation of the deaths of each of its members. When trying to identify what is distinctively bad and/or wrong about *extinction*, we need to identify something that sets it apart from the sum of badness of the death of the individual members of the species. Intuitively, the death of the estimated 1,800 remaining panda bears in the wild seems worse than the death of 1,800 individuals of another species of similar moral standing (say, ordinary brown bears of which there are more than 200,000 left). If the badness of extinction just consisted in the badness of individual deaths, then 1,800 panda deaths (leading to the extinction of the species) and 1,800 brown bear deaths (not leading to extinction) should be roughly equally bad, assuming that these animals generally have similar levels of well-being. Ontological speciesists will deny this.

Second, we want to know whether there is something special about human extinction, compared with the extinction of non-human animal species (and conversely). Here is our hypothesis:

> *HYP3*: The reasons why non-human species extinction is bad or wrong differ significantly from those that render human extinction bad or wrong.

There are various reasons to worry about extinction. First, we may worry about the disappearance of features supported or instantiated by the members of a species, such as specific forms of intelligence, ways of connecting ourselves to the world, and so on, independently of the impact of such losses for beings of moral relevance. We can think about the hunting abilities of barn owls, the migration skills of arctic terns, the echolocation skills of bats, the social skills of great apes, the sense of responsibility of humans, and so on.

Second, we may worry about human-*induced* extinction as a particularly egregious moral crime. Let us call this the "respect for nature" argument. Dworkin writes that "we tend to treat distinct animal species (though not individual animals) as sacred" and that "we consider it some kind of cosmic shame when a species that nature has developed ceases, through human actions, to exist."[25] The badness and wrongness of human-induced animal species extinction on such a view rests with the disrespect for the sanctity of nature expressed by humanity in making this species go extinct.[26] This assumes that human-induced extinction would be worse than non-human-induced extinction, and that the extinction of a wild species is worse than that of a domestic breed.

The "skill disappearance" and "respect for nature" arguments provide us with two illustrations of non-individual-affecting concerns[27] for species extinction.[28] Such considerations are among those that ontological speciesists may support. Before we leave non-individual-affecting arguments aside, let us consider a third consideration that points at what may render human extinction special in a non-individual-affecting way: *the extinction of valuers would entail the end of value.* According to some meta-ethical views, value does not exist mind-independently. Heyd, for example, argues that when we bring future generations into existence, we are not just bringing valuable entities into existence; by engendering children, we reproduce the circumstances under which value exists: "[T]he existence of valuers (for whom things might be good) is, as we shall claim throughout this book, a necessary condition for anything being of value."[29]

What is necessary for things to have value, one might argue, is that there are creatures who value. If, without humans, there is *nothing* of value by lack of *valuers* (who could be benefited), the extinction of humankind would differ from that of other animal species: with humanity, value itself would end. This idea is not completely implausible, although some may deny it. Brian Barry seems to share such a position when he discusses how to compare different states (beautiful or ugly) of the world from which humans are absent. He writes:

> I have to say that the whole question [of comparing these two worlds] strikes me as ridiculous. In what possible sense could the universe be a better or a worse place on one supposition rather than the other? It seems to me an abuse of our language to assume that the word "good" still has application when applied to such a context.[30]

So, if one either defends the idea that humans are the only objects of moral value, or the idea that the continued existence of value *itself* is conditional on there being *valuers*, and if human beings are the only species that values, the end of mankind would entail the end of value. The "ifs" here are important. Not all would agree that value depends on there being valuers. If we care, for example, about minimizing suffering, we could argue that the absence of suffering is better than the presence of suffering, even if there are no valuers—that is, even if there is no one capable of appreciating the absence of suffering as better than its presence.[31] One may argue that the well-being of individual animals— or perhaps the flourishing of the species—matters *even if* there are no humans.

Besides the non-individual-affecting set of concerns for species extinction, another group of concerns lumps together those of an "individual-affecting" type. They correspond to worries about the impact of extinction *on individuals*.[32] This comes in two subcategories. We might care about the nonexistence of future individuals that is caused by extinction. Additionally, we might care about the impact of the extinction on *existing*—or even past—beings. Concern for existing beings will be our focus here.[33] One might be concerned about the *intra*-species impact of extinction, that is, the impact of extinction on the last members of the species that goes extinct. We might also be concerned about the impact of extinction on the members of other species.

If we focus on the well-being of those humans who live through the process of extinction (i.e., the last generation), there are two worries that one may have about human extinction. If no new children are born, an aging population faces the absence of young people. In this case, people would have to rely on members of their own age group (and/or on robots and animals) both for keeping society and the economy going and for care-work, which may become increasingly difficult as they come closer to the end of their lives.[34] In other words, because people age and because old age entails some forms of inabilities and dependencies, we depend on the existence of new people for the provision of our needs. This problem might be absent in an ageless society in which people would remain able to preserve all the skills of their prime until the very last day of their life.

However, an additional difficulty would still obtain in such an ageless society: several philosophers have argued that the preservation of a horizon of indefinite continuation of humankind is essential to preserve the meaningfulness of our life.[35] Many of the projects in which we engage would be far less valuable if they were not to continue in the future. Let us thus label the two concerns discussed above *dependency* and *meaninglessness*.[36]

Do these two concerns (dependency and meaninglessness) arise in the case of non-human animal species extinction too? Regarding dependency, we can conjecture that intra-species dependency is often lower in non-human animal populations while inter-species dependency is stronger for specialized carnivorous animal species than for omnivorous humans. The intra-species question is whether animal societies are such that older animals tend to depend on young ones for their survival to the same extent that humans do. For issues of dependency to arise, we would have to identify societies of non-human animals with high life expectancy in which young-to-old cooperation takes a significant place. If such societies exist, the impact of extinction on their existing members may be similar to the impact of human extinction on existing humans.

Moreover, if we broaden and revert the notion of dependency to include our need *to care for* our descendants, for example, as parents (as opposed to the need to *care for* our contemporaries or to the need to be *taken care of by* our descendants), then we can also claim that this feature is likely to be limited to those species who raise their offspring. If humans have a particularly strong interest in the opportunity to parent, extinction is particularly bad for members of the last generation because they will not fulfill this interest.[37] This would apply to other species with a significant interest in procreation and parenthood as well (see Section 5.2).[38] This can also apply *across* species, be it when animals rely on humans, or even between non-human species. This inverted understanding of dependency on care nicely bridges this concern with the second one, that is, meaninglessness.

Consider now this *meaninglessness* worry. We can advance at least two claims. First, if the worry is justified—as many have argued—human extinction would significantly undermine peoples' capacity to lead meaningful lives in the light of extinction. Or at least, people would suffer severe psychological trauma from the belief that humanity will end soon after their own deaths. We can then identify one way in which human extinction is distinctively bad.[39] Even though many animal species can have *future-oriented* attitudes and have an understanding of their own existence through time,[40] their life does not tend to contain—as far as we know—important life-transcending plans. Thus, insofar as the value of future generations for currently existing non-human animals depends on the latter having such life-transcending plans, a good life for currently existing non-human animals is not undermined by the absence of future generations to continue their plans and value the things they value.

Second, whenever humans develop *animal-oriented* projects that play a significant role in their lives, the meaning of their lives will be affected by the extinction of such non-human species. This is probably true for, for example, horse whisperers, dog breeders, and butterfly conservationists. If we care about the existence of some people pursuing our projects in the future, we will also care about the existence of other species whenever they are central to such projects. Again, while it seems that the meaninglessness concern is especially valid when it comes to human-animal interactions and human-human interactions, it seems less so at the intra-species level for the majority of non-human animal species. This renders animal extinction distinct from human extinction.

Our analysis suggests that HYP3 is true: the reasons why non-human species extinction is bad or wrong differ significantly from those that render human extinction bad or wrong.

5. Shaping Population

Let us assume that it is possible to formulate a given (set of) goal(s) about population size and composition. Which means are ethically acceptable to reach such goals? In order to shape population, we can work directly or indirectly on natality, mortality (longevity) or mobility (migration). Is it easier to meet moral requirements when it comes to implementing natality-related or mortality-related on non-human animal populations rather than on human ones? We concentrate on mortality and natality and the means to control them. Here is the hypothesis:

> HYP4: Relying on morality-related, mobility-related or natality-related means to shape non-human animal population is morally less problematic than using such means to shape human population.

We actually rely on natality-related, mortality-related and mobility-related means to shape animal populations. We operate mass killings of animal populations, for example, through slaughtering lambs and calves for meat or dairy consumption or hunting wild birds and mammals. We engineer natality, for example, by selecting more fertile domestic breeds, segregating males from females during part of the year or sterilizing urban cats. And we also displace animal populations, for example, when we move herds of domestic animals to summer pastures.

One way of evaluating HYP4 is to focus on rights. We tend to think that humans have certain rights which render natality-related or mortality-related population policies objectionable. These include rights to life, bodily integrity, and sexual and reproductive freedom. Controlling human mortality through killing would violate people's rights to life and bodily integrity. Controlling human natality through gender segregation would violate people's right to sexual freedom (and of course peoples' right to freedom of association more generally). Doing so through forced sterilization would violate people's right to bodily integrity and to reproduction. If we think that animals can have rights,[41] it is worth finding out whether members of at least some non-human species could hold similar rights to the ones we just mentioned. Here, we will assume that ascribing rights to animals can make sense and focus on the *content* of such rights as well as their potential *implications*.

5.1. Mortality, Killing and Letting Die

If more people die younger, this reduces human population size in two ways. It reduces the number of people alive at a given moment in time, from their death onwards. It also reduces future population size if people die before they reproduce. Killing people (i.e., shortening their life) to come closer to an axiologically preferable population size or composition is of course very problematic. Setting aside racist/genocidal ideologies, killing people has, as far as we know, never been *seriously* proposed as a way to bring the size of a human population down to a desirable size. However, for animals, killing has been proposed, sometimes because it is supposedly the most humane way to control a population (e.g., shooting deer in an overpopulated park, rather than letting them die of hunger in winter). *Letting people die* has been proposed as a policy for human population control, but the attempts to defend this have been rightfully discredited.[42] Although letting people die might sometimes be morally acceptable, it is very unlikely to be acceptable as part of an effort to control the size of a human population. This is true either because letting people die is not an *effective* way to suppress population growth (poverty and child mortality are important determinants of fertility), or—more importantly—because we tend to believe that peoples' right to life carries heavier moral weight than most demographic goals. Humans are generally thought to have a very strong—if not inviolable—right to life. At the very least, this right protects against killing. Under most understandings, it also generates at least a moral reason to assist those in need, and to ensure that each of us reaches at least a given age.

Does this hold for animals as well? Do animals have a right not to be killed, or—if not a right—are there other moral reasons to think that killing animals is impermissible? Are they also entitled to being saved if their lives are threatened by, for example, parasites or predators?[43] If animals have a right to life, we need to ask whether this right is strong enough to block the permissibility of killing or letting die as a method of bringing animal population down to the desired size. Current practices massively deny animals this right to life. For example, according to some estimates, we kill 65 billion farm animals per year.[44] Others are killed for pleasure (e.g., game hunting), pest control (rats, mice, etc.), in medical experiments or for other reasons (e.g., deer population control). When it comes to *letting die*, we seem to similarly place little value on animal lives. We let them die regularly, by failing to assist them, sometimes easing their suffering by opting for euthanasia instead. For example, we let wild animals die of weather, food shortage, parasites, and predators.[45] In practice, people act as if non-human animals lack both negative and positive rights to life. Are such acts morally permissible? We cannot possibly do justice here to the complex literature on the ethics of killing animals.[46] If we believe that animals have moral standing, and that it matters that they lead good lives (e.g., in terms of flourishing), it is clear that killing or letting die harms, and in many cases wrongs, individual animals.

Axiologically, is death worse for humans than for animals? Taking McMahan's *Time Relative Interest Account of the badness of death*[47] as a starting point, the answer is yes. McMahan argues that the badness of death for an individual—animal or human—depends on the strength of psychological unity over time: the loss of future well-being is smaller if an individual has weaker psychological links with her future self. If animals would have no future-oriented projects, no memories, and/or no sense of their own continued existence over time but only experience *in the moment*, then death might not be bad for them.[48] But, as Cochrane points out, "given that we also know that these animals are not 'stuck in the moment', but possess some future-oriented desires, we can also say that this ordinarily gives them an interest in satisfying future-oriented goods—and thus to continue life itself."[49]

But, given that human beings have, generally speaking, stronger psychological unity over time than most animals, for many humans with good lives and many years ahead of them, death is worse than for most animals. McMahan's view has the advantage of avoiding speciesism; it does not give extra weight to human interests *as* human interests.[50] This still does not tell us whether, despite being less bad, animals' deaths are trivial *enough* to ground a moral permission to kill them. Also, if we consider the indirect badness that animal death has for humans (as in the case of a dear pet), the issue is of course more complex, since it is the psychological unity *of humans* that may be relevant to assessing the overall harm resulting from the death.

If we think we have reasons to protect good animal lives, and that animals have some sense of a future, then we have at least pro tanto reasons not to kill animals for whom dying would be bad. Suppose that killing animals is at least a pro tanto wrong in most cases. Does it follow that killing or letting die to manage population-size is never justified? No, because we still need to bridge this pro tanto assessment with an all-things considered assessment in a multispecies setting. When confronted with meat-eating human societies, we may ask whether the badness of non-human animal death outweighs the benefits (if any) to humans. It is unlikely that a positive answer can be plausibly defended. But we can also consider killing non-human animals as a means of resolving conflicts between non-human species, such as between wild wolves and domestic sheep. We can even consider killing non-human animals to increase the quality of life of the other members of their species or increase the chance of survival of an endangered species (as when hunters kill sick members of a species to preserve the others).

Note a few difficulties. In case of a massive reduction of meat consumption driven by moral reasons, we can reasonably predict a collapse of many domestic animal populations that are raised for meat production. Supposing that it is possible to breed animals for meat while making their lives worth living (unlike many of the animals suffering now for meat production), we have to ask whether a population of animals with shortened but worth living lives is better than the nonexistence of that population. Note too that there might be a tension between protecting non-human animals' right to reproduce and their right to life, whenever reproduction may lead to proliferation that may in turn lead to a significant increase in mortality (e.g., through epidemics). Note as well that whether we adopt a form of ontological speciesism may be key here. For the goal of species survival may sometimes prevail upon the right to life of specific species members, in case these two goals clash.

When it comes to human beings, we generally consider killing (and often letting die as well) for the common good unacceptable. Yet, when it comes to animals, killing is often seen as acceptable. What could justify this, assuming that animals have *some* kind of right to life? Perhaps the difference concerns *facts*: maybe we tend to believe that killing animals and letting them die is unavoidable when it comes to controlling populations, whereas with human beings it is avoidable. However, very often killing is not necessary for population control. Even when it comes to pests, controlling procreation might be equally (or more) effective. If there is an alternative to killing to control a population, and if animals have a pro tanto right to life or just an interest in continued life, we have serious reasons to look at the moral costs involved in the alternatives. Let us turn to one of these alternatives, and its possible costs, now.

5.2. Natality, Gender Segregation, and Sterilization

We can influence the size of a population by changing reproductive behavior. Talking about tinkering with humans' procreative decisions is notoriously controversial, and freedom in matters of procreation is often framed in terms of human rights. Interfering with peoples' reproductive life runs against several important rights (e.g., privacy), but two stand out. First, one might think that people have a right to *reproduce*, that is, to create offspring. Second, one might think that people have a right to engage in sexual relations with others.

The sexual and reproductive lives of domestic animals are almost completely controlled by humans, and whether, when, and with whom animals have sexual intercourse is up to them to a severely limited extent. There are two ways to prevent procreation. First, there is sterilization. Second, there is gender segregation (often associated with a huge gender imbalance). These two methods relate differently to the two rights mentioned. With sterilization, animals can still engage in sexual activity but will not be able to reproduce. If males and females are kept separately, they might be able to reproduce (e.g., through artificial insemination) but are not always able to engage in sexual activity (at least not with members of the other sex).

If animals have a right to reproduce, this will have far-reaching consequences for population size, as Donaldson and Kymlicka point out. Against those who call for the extinction of domestic species, they claim—illustrating the way in which population ethics goals and means are linked—that

> their own call for extinction of domesticated species implicitly presupposes an equally systematic program of coercion and confinement in order to prevent domesticated animals from reproducing. If current practices force animals to reproduce

in ways that serve human purposes, the abolitionist/extinctionist approach involves forcing animals not to reproduce.[51]

Do animals have a right to reproduce? Let us look at the reasons why *humans* have a right to reproduce and ask if similar reasons apply to animals.

One way to defend a right to reproduce is to point to the important interests at stake in reproduction. One ground for a human being's right to reproduce is that reproduction gives access to children to *parent*.[52] And parenting children is an important part of life, at least for many of us.[53] Does this reason apply to animals as well?[54] Human parents and their children often stand in long-lasting relationships, which gives access to certain relationship goods. This is certainly not the case for all non-human animal species. In the case of dairy animals, it could be the case, but it isn't in practice, due to human intervention. The calf is usually separated from its mother from the very beginning of its life in many dairy farms, preventing them from developing a relationship. Some animals never build a relationship with their offspring at all (cuckoos and sea-turtles come to mind here), while others nurture their children briefly and then go their separate ways completely. Other species continue to live together in a family setting, and for these species it is more plausible that family life—or perhaps "herd life"—is an important interest. Elephants are a case in point: a baby is likely to live together with its mother until one of them dies. This "living together" goes beyond mere co-existence; elephants are reported to have personal relationships and display mourning behavior if a member of their pack dies. If engaging in procreation and parenthood is indeed an important part of the well-being of some individual animals, if animal well-being matters and if we can relate it somehow to the idea of significant interests, then those animals should be allowed to engage in reproduction (or, perhaps, adopt a child if this is a feasible alternative).

One might object that animals do not really get the same goods from parent–child relations as humans do: no matter how complex, say, the relationship between an elephant mother and her offspring may be, it would not cover what makes human parent–child relationships valuable. This is partly correct, although of course the interest newborn animals have in being protected by a competent parent is similar to the interest newborn humans have in being protected by a competent parent. The analogy is more difficult on the side of the parents. The interests parents have in parent-child relationships identified in the literature (non-voluntariness, paternalism, shaping of values, spontaneous love) are not easily applicable to non-human animals. For an offspring, although a parental relationship is also non-voluntarily, and the relationship is in many cases paternalistic, it does not involve the shaping of values or—depending on one's view on whether animals are capable of love—spontaneous love from the child to the parent.[55]

The differences are, then, potentially big. But this is beside the point: of course, non-human animals do not need the same things as a human being to attain well-being. The question we need to ask is whether the (relational) goods animals acquire by engaging in family life of sorts contributes significantly to *their* species-specific well-being and can be characterized as an interest on their side.

Moreover, if animals have a right to procreate, do they have a right to have *large* amounts of offspring? Is there an absolute prohibition on curtailment of procreative freedom? If we ground an interest in procreation in parenthood, it is not clear that animals have an *interest* in having large amounts of offspring. If we ground it in the value of exercising agency, we have to take into account that there are limits to free exercise of agency. If animals cannot or will not constrain reproductive behavior, the costs this will have for others might justify constraining their procreative liberty.[56]

Finally, consider whether non-human animals have a right to sexual intercourse. We can ask (i) whether they have an *interest* in sexual activity, and (ii) whether they have the capacity to act freely when it comes to choosing sexual partners. Whether animals have an *interest* in sexual activity depends on the species. Some species have intercourse in a violent way, and it is unlikely that the partner subjected to the violence is better off because if it (ducks are an example). For other species, sex may be more like consensual sex (or at least enjoyable for both partners), and it may constitute an important part of their lives. This argument has been made especially for primates held in captivity[57] and for domestic animals[58] on the grounds that the freedom to engage in sexual intercourse increases their well-being.[59]

To conclude this section, it seems plausible that certain kinds of animals have a weighty interest in sexual freedom as well as in procreation and parenthood. But, given their more limited interest and/or lesser capacity in autonomous decision-making, limiting these freedoms for their own sake (i.e., to control a population) might be less problematic than with humans. This affirms HYP4. However, we need to keep in mind whether the reasons we limit animals' freedoms stem from truly paternalistic considerations, or whether we just think it is, for example, too expensive to accommodate a growing population of non-human animals.

6. Conclusion

In this chapter, we considered whether there is something *special* about animal population ethics, that is, what—if anything—sets it apart from population axiology and ethics that focuses on human beings. Although we have not offered any straightforward answers, we have explored four main hypotheses (HYP1–4) and looked at the extent to which each of them can be supported. By doing this, the chapter aims to be a steppingstone toward a complete view of animal population ethics.

While HYP 1 and 2 point to the conclusion that animal and human population ethics might not be easy to distinguish clearly if we abandon our implicitly speciesist commitments, although HYP3 and 4 suggest more significant differences. Insofar as the difference between humans' and animals' moral status is not absolute, but a matter of degree (e.g., based on certain capacities), the difference in how (members of) different species should count when comparing different possible worlds will be difficult to draw in a precise way.

Acknowledgments

Many thanks to Bernice Bovenkerk, David de la Croix, Catia Faria, Anca Gheaus, Oscar Horta, Joachim Nieuwland, Danielle Zwarthoed as well as to the audience of the Braga CEPS Seminar (June 8, 2018) for very helpful suggestions. We are particularly grateful to Timothy Campbell for several rounds of constructive comments and excellent editorial work. Both authors contributed equally to this chapter.

Notes

1. See, for example, Horta (2018).
2. Size and composition are inter-related as composition is a matter of relative size of sub-populations within a wider population. There is some sense in which some size issues can be answered independently of composition ones, that is, independently of the size of other populations. Perhaps we can tell whether a larger parrot population is better than a slightly smaller one, if both of them are composed of happy parrots only and if average happiness is identical in both cases. In other cases, the relative sizes of sub-groups in the total population matters, for instance if we want to avoid the systematic domination of one of these groups by another. As composition also refers to the welfare of the individuals that compose it, deciding whether a larger population is better than a smaller one may depend on the size of the group of well-off or badly-off animals in it.
3. UNFPA (2012).
4. See Conly (this volume); Dasgupta and Dasgupta (this volume); Meijers (2016).
5. See, for example, Gruen (2017) or Vallentyne (2005).
6. This is the problem of marginal cases—or of overlap. See, for example, Gosseries (1998); Horta (2014); Tanner (2011).
7. For a critique of speciesism, see Singer (1979). For a defense, see Kagan (2016).
8. See, for example, Korsgaard (2004); Regan (1983).
9. We focus here on the "richness" dimension of diversity, leaving aside "evenness" and "distance". See Van Parijs (2011, Ch. 6).
10. See, for example, Hurka (1983).
11. Interventionist animal ethicists believe that humans have far-reaching obligations to intervene in nature to alleviate and prevent suffering of sentient animals.
12. Donaldson and Kymlicka (2011) argue that we have a shared "human-animal" political community, the membership of which comes with special obligations.
13. For example, Palmer (2011).
14. Donaldson and Kymlicka (2011, Ch. 2).
15. On breeding companion animals, see Dutoit and Benatar (2017).
16. Bossert (this volume).
17. Ng (1995, 270).
18. Ng (1995, 271).
19. See Ng (1995, 267).
20. r-strategists, such as ladybirds, produce a large number of offspring while investing very little in caring about them. K-strategists, such as bears, produce a small number

of offspring and invest heavily in each of them, leading to a much higher survival rate (Pianka, 1970).

21. An important question is which species fall in the sponge category, for example fish. See, for example, Balcombe (2016).

22. Benatar (2006).

23. On the badness/wrongness of human extinction, see Finneron-Burns (2017); Scheffler (2013).

24. We exclude here the possibility of Jurassic Park scenarios involving species resurrection.

25. Dworkin (1993, 75).

26. Ibid. For a critical discussion, see Rakowski (1994).

27. That is, concerns which arise not due to the effect extinction has on particular individual members of a species but on something impersonally valuable.

28. Jonas (1985) on a somewhat similar line argues that the extinction of mankind would be bad because it would mean the end of responsibility.

29. Heyd (1994, 4; see also 211–212).

30. Barry (1997, Section 5).

31. See, for example, Benatar (2006).

32. See Purves and Hale (2016).

33. On the former, one issue is whether the extinction of animal species is a loss for those who will never have experienced this species. See Zwarthoed (2016).

34. In such a society, the dependency ratio (i.e., the ratio of those who are *not* in the labor force [children, pensioners] and of those who are) will come closer and closer to 1.

35. On the importance of transgenerational communities: de-Shalit (1995), Heyd (1994); Meyer (1997); Scheffler (2013); Thompson (2009); Meijers 2021.

36. For a more detailed discussion, see Meijers (2016; 2017). Note that in one case, we depend on the existence of the next cohort because it entails the *coexistence* of different age groups whereas in the latter case, we could very well imagine preserving the meaningfulness of our projects in a world of *non-overlapping* generations, as long as there exist humans from time to time in the future, and as long as the absence of overlap does not prevent us (although it might make it more difficult!) from transmitting them what we value (a rich language, some beautiful objects, etc.).

37. See Gheaus (2016).

38. We leave aside another source of dependency between species that is not age-related, the one associated with relations of predation, commensalism, parasitism, and so on. Also, even though human beings are responsible for a significant part of species extinctions, humans may also be necessary for avoiding a significant number of further extinctions, for instance species extinctions that would result from massive events such as supervolcano eruptions or asteroid strikes, only humans (and human technology) may be able to prevent this. This is one of the ways in which other species may depend on humans.

39. See Finneron-Burns (2017); Heyd (1994, Ch. 8); Meyer (1997); and Scheffler (2013).

40. See, for example, DeGrazia (1996); Singer (1979).

41. See Feinberg (1974); Frey (1977); Regan (1983).

42. Those who embrace a neo-Malthusian lifeboat ethics argue that helping those who starve would only make the problem *worse*, because this way the global population would only continue to grow. Poorer countries, Hardin claims, should learn this the "hard way" (e.g., Hardin 1968). For excellent rebuttals of the empirical and normative claims underlying these arguments, see Gardiner (2001); Sen (2001); Shue (1980, 97–104).

43. To be sure, even if animals are not rights-bearers, they might still have an *interest* in not being killed (See Višak and Garner 2015, 3). See also McMahan (2008).
44. Višak and Garner (2015).
45. The goal of these policies is population control in some cases. In densely populated countries, deer populations living on fenced reserves cannot plausibly be seen as "wild animals," but rather as animals living in captivity but endowed with a very large cage. In such cases the distinction between killing and letting die—for example, because of a lack of food—fades as well, given that human beings placed these animals in their constrained environment.
46. See Višak (2013). For an excellent collection Višak and Garner (2015).
47. McMahan (2002, Ch. 6.1).
48. Nussbaum (2006, 384).
49. Cochrane (2015).
50. Cochrane (2015, 213).
51. Donaldson and Kymlicka (2011, 144).
52. While parenting and procreating differ, they often go together in practice. See Meijers (2020).
53. Brighouse and Swift (2014).
54. Nussbaum (2006, 396) denies that animal sterilization necessarily limits their flourishing in central aspects of life. If this is correct, there is no such right (or at best a very weak one).
55. But see Gheaus (2012).
56. Donaldson and Kymlicka (2011, 147).
57. Kasperbauer (2016) argues that primates have an interest both in sex and reproduction, but his arguments are strongest when it comes to sex and freedom to choose a sexual partner.
58. Donaldson and Kymlicka (2011).
59. Of course, there are other ways of trying to justify a right to reproduce, for example by an appeal to self-determination or a right to exercise bodily control. See, for example, Donaldson and Kymlicka (2011, 147).

References

De-Shalit, Avner. 1995. *Why Posterity Matters*. London: Routledge.

Barry, Brian. 1997. "Sustainability and Intergenerational Justice." *Theoria* 44, no. 89: 43–64.

Balcombe, Jonathan. 2016. *What a Fish Knows: The Inner Lives of Our Underwater Cousins*. New York: Scientific American/Farrar, Straus and Giroux.

Benatar, David. 2006. *Better Never to Have Been: The Harm of Coming into Existence*. Oxford: Oxford University Press.

Brighouse, Harry and Adam Swift. 2014. *Family Values: The Ethics of Parent-Child Relationships*. Princeton, NJ: Princeton University Press.

Cochrane, Alisdair. 2015. "Life, Liberty and the Pursuit of Happiness." In *The Ethics of Killing Animals*, edited by Tatjana Višak and Robert Garner, 201–204. Oxford: Oxford University Press.

DeGrazia, David. 1996. *Taking Animals Seriously: Mental Life and Moral Status*. Cambridge: Cambridge University Press.

Donaldson, Sue and Will Kymlicka. 2011. *Zoopolis*. Oxford: Oxford University Press.

Du Toit, Jessica and David Benatar. 2017. "Reproducing Companion Animals." In *Pets and People: The Ethics of Our Relationships with Companion Animals*, edited by Christine Overall, 157–171. Oxford: Oxford University Press.

Dworkin, Ronald 1993. *Life's Dominion: An Argument about Abortion, Euthanasia, and Individual Freedom*. New York: Vintage.

Feinberg, Joel. 1974. "The Rights of Animals and Unborn Generations." In *Philosophy and Environmental Crisis*, edited by William. T. Blackstone, 43–68. Athens, GA: The University of Georgia Press).

Finneron-Burns, Elizabeth. 2017. "What's Wrong with Human Extinction?" *Canadian Journal of Philosophy* 47, no. 2–3: 327–343.

Frey, Raymond. 1977. "Animal Rights." *Analysis* 37, no. 4: 186–189.

Gardiner, Stephen 2001. "The Real Tragedy of the Commons." *Philosophy & Public Affairs* 30, no. 4: 387–416.

Gosseries, Axel. 1998. "L'éthique environnementale aujourd'hui." *Revue Philosophique de Louvain* 96, no. 3: 395–426.

Gheaus, Anca. 2016. "The Right to Parent and Duties Concerning Future Generations." *Journal of Political Philosophy* 24, no. 4: 487–508.

Gheaus, Anca. 2012. "The Role of Love in Animal Ethics." *Hypatia* 27, no. 3: 583–600.

Gruen, Lori. 2017. "The Moral Status of Animals." In *Stanford Encyclopedia of Philosophy*, edited by Edward Zalta. Stanford: Stanford University Press.

Hardin, Garrett. 1968. "The Tragedy of the Commons." *Science* 162, no. 3859: 1243–1248.

Heyd, David. 1994. *Genethics: Moral Issues in the Creation of People*. Berkeley and Los Angeles: University of California Press.

Horta, Oscar. 2014. "The Scope of the Argument from Species Overlap." *Journal of Applied Philosophy* 31, no. 2: 142–154.

Horta, Oscar. 2018. "Concern for Wild Animal Suffering and Environmental Ethics: What are the Limits of the Disagreement?" *Les ateliers de l'éthique* 13, no. 1: 85–100.

Hurka, Tom. 1983. "Value and Population Size." *Ethics* 93, no. 3: 496–507.

Jonas, Hans. 1985. *The Imperative of Responsibility: In Search of an Ethics for the Technological Age*. Chicago: University of Chicago Press.

Kagan, Shelly. 2016. "What's Wrong with Speciesism?" *Journal of Applied Philosophy* 33, no. 1: 1–21.

Kasperbauer, T. J. 2016. "Should Captive Primates Have Reproductive Rights?" In *Animal Ethics in the Age of Humans*, edited by Bernice Bovenkerk and Jozef Keulartz, 279–293. Cham: Springer.

Korsgaard, Christine. 2004. "Fellow Creatures: Kantian Ethics and Our Duties to Animals." *Tanner Lectures on Human Values* 24: 77–110.

McMahan, Jeff. 2002. *The Ethics of Killing*. Oxford: Oxford University Press.

McMahan, Jeff. 2008. "Eating Animals the Nice Way." *Daedalus* 137, no. 1: 66–76.

Meijers, Tim. 2017. "Citizens in Appropriate Numbers: Evaluating Five Claims about Justice and Population Size." *Canadian Journal of Philosophy* 47, nos. 2–3: 246–268.

Meijers, Tim. 2016. "Climate Change and the Right to One Child." In *Human Rights and Sustainability*, edited by Gerhard Bos and Marcus Duwell, 181–194. London: Routledge.

Meijers, Tim. 2020. "The Value in Procreation." *Journal of Value Inquiry* 54, 627–647.

Meyer, Lukas 1997. "More Than They Have a Right to: Future People and Our Future-Oriented Projects." In *Contingent Future Persons*, edited by Nick Fotion and Jan C. Heller, 137–156. Dordrecht: Springer.

Ng, Yew-Kwang. 1995. "Towards Welfare Biology: Evolutionary Economics of Animal Consciousness and Suffering." *Biology and Philosophy* 10, no. 3: 255–285.

Nussbaum, Martha. 2006. *Frontiers of Justice: Disability, Nationality, Species Membership.* Cambridge, MA: Harvard University Press.

Palmer, Clare. 2011. "The Moral Relevance of the Distinction Between Domesticated and Wild Animals." In *The Oxford Handbook of Animal Ethics*, edited by Tom L. Beauchamp and R. G. Frey, 701–725. Oxford: Oxford University Press.

Pianka, Eric. 1970. "On r- and K-Selection." *The American Naturalist* 104, no. 940: 592–597.

Purves, Duncan and Benjamin. Hale. 2016. "Non-Identity for Non-Humans." *Ethical Theory and Moral Practice* 19, no. 5: 1165–1185.

Rakowski, Eric. 1994. "The Sanctity of Human Life." *The Yale Law Journal* 103, no. 7: 2049–2118.

Regan, Tom. 1983. *The Case for Animal Rights.* Berkeley and Los Angeles: University of California Press.

Scheffler, Samuel. 2013. *Death and the Afterlife.* Oxford: Oxford University Press.

Sen, Amartya. 2001. *Development as Freedom.* Oxford: Oxford University Press.

Shue, Henry. 1980. *Basic Rights: Subsistence, Affluence, and US Foreign Policy.* Princeton, NJ: Princeton University Press.

Singer, Peter. 1979. *Practical Ethics.* Cambridge: Cambridge University Press.

Tanner, Julia. 2011. "The Argument from Marginal Cases: Is Species a Relevant Difference?" *Croatian Journal of Philosophy* 11, no. 2: 225–235.

Thompson, Janna. 2009. *Intergenerational Justice.* London: Routledge.

Tomasik, Brian. 2015. "The Importance of Wild-Animal Suffering." *Relations: Beyond Anthropocentrism* 3: 133–152.

UNFPA. 2012. *Sex Imbalances at Birth.* Bangkok: UNFPA Asia and the Pacific Regional Office.

Vallentyne, Peter. 2005. "Of Mice and Men: Equality and Animals." *The Journal of Ethics* 9, no. 3: 403–433.

Van Parijs, Philippe. 2011. *Linguistic Justice.* Oxford: Oxford University Press.

Višak, Tatjana. 2013. *Killing Happy Animals: Explorations in Utilitarian Ethics.* Dordrecht: Springer.

Višak, Tatjana and Robert Garner, eds. 2015. *The Ethics of Killing Animals.* Oxford: Oxford University Press.

Zwarthoed, Daniele. 2016. "Should Future Generations be Content with Plastic Trees and Singing Electronic Birds?" *Journal of Agricultural and Environmental Ethics* 29, no. 2: 219–236.

CHAPTER 25

GAMETE DONATION AS A LAUDABLE MORAL MISTAKE

ELIZABETH HARMAN

1. INTRODUCTION

WE can see altruistic actions as falling into three different kinds. Some specific altruistic actions are required; other altruistic actions are such that it's morally required to do some of them—but no one of them is itself morally required; and other altruistic actions are *deeply supererogatory*, in that they are morally good things to do, they are not morally required, and it is not the case that it is morally required to do a certain amount of such things in one's life.

An example of the first kind of action is this: Anne has some medicine for which she has no use, and Bill, her acquaintance, needs the medicine to live. Anne can give it to Bill at virtually no cost to herself; she does not anticipate that she or anyone else will need it in the future. Anne is morally required to provide the medicine to Bill.[1] Actions of the second kind are ordinary charitable and helping actions. Each of us (who is not desperately needy herself) should do some things to help those less fortunate. But there is no particular form that this help must take.[2] Actions of the third kind are various. Here is a simple example. Chris is a middle-class person in the United States. He gives away half of his after-tax income to UNICEF. This particular action is not morally required. Nor is it morally required that he ever perform actions of this magnitude of giving.[3]

We typically see altruistic actions as wonderful things to do. In particular, we see the deeply supererogatory as wonderful to do. This is manifested in how we might talk to a friend or acquaintance who has just announced that she is leaning towards doing a deeply supererogatory thing. We might say, "Good for you! That's wonderful. You're going to make such a difference. If only more people would do what you're doing." This seems to be an appropriate way to respond to such an announcement.

In this chapter, I will develop and examine a view on which some deeply supereroga-tory actions are not simply wonderful things to do. While being wonderful things to do, these actions are also moral mistakes. They are actions that each person should not per-form, and they should not perform them *for moral reasons*. Nevertheless, these actions are morally permissible, and they are morally good things to do. In order to develop this more general view, I will first develop a specific view about sperm and egg dona-tion, as an instance of a deeply supererogatory action which is also a moral mistake. In discussing that view, I will draw out some general lessons about the relationship be-tween what one is morally obligated to do and what one should do, all things considered, and about the nature of moral reasons.

This paper thus has three goals:

- to develop a view about gamete donation and put it forward to be taken seriously
- to develop the more general view that many deeply supererogatory actions are moral mistakes, though they are morally permissible
- to draw out some general lessons about the relationship between *what one is mor-ally obligated to do* and *what one should do, all things considered*, and about the na-ture of moral reasons.

2. RECONCILING TWO APPARENTLY CONFLICTING ATTITUDES ABOUT GAMETE DONATION

Why might anyone think that some deeply supererogatory actions, while being won-derful things to do, are moral mistakes? To understand the moral picture I want to ex-amine, let's consider the views of a woman, whom I'll call Julie, regarding anonymous sperm and egg donation. Julie finds herself of two minds about sperm and egg donation. On the one hand, Julie thinks this:

> Every person who donates sperm or eggs is making a mistake. They are causing chil-dren to exist—their children—who will grow up completely isolated from them. They will have no relationship with these children, they will never know if these children are doing well or poorly, and they will not be available to these children if the children need anything from them. Furthermore, they are placing blind faith in strangers to raise their children well. A person should not risk her child's well-being in that way. A person should not cause her own child to be created and then have no further relationship with him. And a person should not be unavailable to her child if he might need help.

Julie's views about sperm and egg donation thus appear to be very harsh. On the other hand, she also thinks the following:

> It is wonderful that sperm and egg donation is practiced regularly in the United States. This practice makes it possible for people who are unable to conceive on their own to have children; it makes such a good difference in these peoples' lives. (These may be couples struggling with fertility problems, same-sex couples, or single women.) This practice creates loving, happy families that would not otherwise have been created. When a person is a sperm or egg donor, he or she is doing a tremendously wonderful thing for the people he or she helps to become parents.

Do Julie's thoughts contradict each other? I want to consider the idea that Julie's two reactions, though they appear to be in conflict, could both be correct. I want to examine what a view would look like on which Julie is right that donating sperm or eggs is a mistake, indeed that it is a mistake for moral reasons, but she is also right that it is a generous, wonderful thing to do for someone else, and she is right that it is wonderful that this regularly happens.[4]

3. FLESHING OUT THE VIEW

Julie's view is that, all things considered, one should not be a gamete donor.[5] In her view, there are compelling reasons against being a gamete donor: that one would be putting blind faith in strangers to raise one's child, that one would not have a relationship with one's child, and that one would be unavailable to one's child if he needs one's help. She believes that these reasons are of the right type to render this something one should not do, and no other considerations cancel or override these reasons. Her view is that the fact that donating would enable someone to have a baby is a reason in favor of the action, it is indeed a weighty reason, but it is not the kind of reason that can undermine or outweigh the existing reasons not to do it.

Nevertheless, Julie thinks that being a gamete donor is *morally good*. She thinks it is morally praiseworthy. She thinks it is wonderful that people do this, and she thinks it is wonderful of people to do it.

I suggest that we can understand Julie's view as the view that being a gamete donor is a *morally permissible moral mistake*. On this view, one should not be a gamete donor, for moral reasons, but if one does so, this is morally permissible; it is even morally good.[6]

On this view, a gamete donor's action falls into the category of the *deeply supererogatory*: these actions are morally good actions, they are not morally required, nor is it morally required to perform a certain amount of such actions in one's life. There is a particular burden involved in these actions—that one will have children from whom one will be isolated—and one is not obligated to accept any amount of such burdens to help others.[7]

How does a donor's action differ from Chris's, as we initially understood his action? Chris announces he is probably going to donate half his after-tax income. I said that an appropriate reaction of a friend would be to say, "Wow, it's wonderful that you're doing that. Good for you! If only more people would do that!"

What would be the appropriate reaction of a friend to Daria, if Daria announces that she is probably going to sign up to be an egg donor? On Julie's view, a friend should not say "Wow, it's wonderful that you're doing that. Good for you!" A friend should rather say, "I think you would be making a mistake. Think about what this would mean. You would have children out there in the world, but you would never know them. You would have no relationship with them. People you know nothing about would be raising them. And what if one day they needed your help? You would never know." At least, this is how a friend should respond if the friend cares that Daria make good choices.[8]

Let's continue to elaborate and clarify Julie's view. It might seem that Julie's view depends on an empirical psychological claim, such as this: sperm and egg donors will grow to regret their choices one day, when they realize that they have children out there in the world from whom they are isolated. If this empirical claim is true of someone, it seems it would indeed be a compelling reason against becoming an egg or sperm donor. But Julie does not make this general empirical psychological claim. Julie's view is not that donors in fact will regret their choices, though it does follow from her view (it seems) that regretting the choice would be an appropriate reaction to the fact that the choice was a mistake.[9]

One aspect of Julie's view is that it holds that there can be morally permissible mistakes. This should not be controversial, however. Morally permissible mistakes are commonplace. Suppose I took all of the money currently in my wallet, and I burned it. This would be morally permissible. But it would be a mistake: all things considered, I should not do it. For another example, I should have gone to the gym when I woke up on Monday morning. I was planning to go, but I just didn't. This was a mistake, but it wasn't morally wrong. What's more interesting about Julie's view is that she thinks that there are morally permissible mistakes that are *morally good things to do*, and she thinks that there are morally permissible mistakes in which the sources of the mistake are moral considerations—that is, there are morally permissible *moral* mistakes. I will say more about this aspect of the view later, in talking about the fourth objection I will consider to the view.

Julie's view is not simply that it is bad for the donor to be isolated from his or her children (that it makes his or her life worse), nor that it is bad for the child. She does think that there is a respect in which the donor's life is worse, and a respect in which the child's life is worse. But she does not think that either of these considerations is the heart of the matter. Julie's view is thus different from David Velleman's view.[10] Velleman argues that people have an interest in understanding themselves through understanding their genetic ancestors, and that a child isolated from a genetic parent is in that way deprived of an important route to self-understanding. There is something to what Velleman says; this is something lost to a child raised in isolation from one or both of his or her genetic parents. But Velleman draws the strong conclusion that it is morally wrong to donate

sperm or eggs, to conceive with donated gametes, or (I believe) to assist in this process in any way, such as a doctor does. But Velleman does not discuss the questions:
how seriously bad for someone is it to be cut off from this one particular route to self-
understanding, and how much can other aspects of a good life outweigh and compensate for this badness? It seems that it needn't be very bad for someone to be cut off from
this particular route to self-understanding. And it seems that other aspects of a created
child's life could greatly compensate for, and could outweigh, this downside, enough to
make the practice of donation morally permissible.[11] In light of these considerations,
Velleman's argument fails. A proponent of Julie's view can reject Velleman's argument
and conclusion for these reasons. Julie's view does not hold that sperm or egg donation
is morally wrong.

Consider the public policy implications of Velleman's view. If we became convinced of
Velleman's view, we would think that it would be better if there were fewer instances of
children being created through anonymous donations. We might think that it would in-
fringe people's rights to regulate donation. But we could be in favor of public education
programs about the downside of donation, of children being cut off from this means of
understanding themselves.[12] At least, we would *hope* that fewer children were created
through anonymous donations.

What are the public policy implications of Julie's view? Remember, in Julie's view, it is
a good thing that anonymous sperm and egg donation occurs, because it helps couples
struggling with fertility problems to have children, and it causes happy families to be
created which would not otherwise exist. Julie does not think it is a bad thing that these
donations occur. She would not be in favor of a campaign to convince people not to donate. She does not hope that fewer donations occur.[13]

How can Julie simultaneously think that donation is a mistake and also that it is
good that it occurs? In Julie's view, the weighty reasons not to donate are agent-relative
reasons. When Daria considers whether to donate, Daria has these reasons not to donate. If I am Daria's friend, and I believe I should help her to see what reasons she has,
then I should try to get her to see these reasons. But those who are sufficiently removed
from Daria, who don't care particularly about whether Daria makes the choices she
should make—these people, on Julie's view, don't have compelling reason to want Daria
to refrain from donating and indeed have a significant reason to want her to donate,
because she would be helping some people. Compare Daria with a couple who want to
use her donated eggs to create a child they would raise. On Julie's view, Daria has the
following reasons not to donate: she would be isolated from her child, she would not be
available to her child if the child needed her help, and she would be putting blind faith
in strangers to raise her child. None of these considerations apply to the couple: they
would not be isolated from their child, they would not be unavailable to their child,
and they would not be putting blind faith in anyone else to raise their child. On Julie's
view there are agent-relative reasons that a prospective donor has not to donate,[14] but
there are no parallel reasons that confront couples who seek to raise children created
via donation; and there are no parallel reasons for third parties to oppose the practice
of donation.[15]

4. OBJECTIONS TO JULIE'S VIEW

In this section, I will discuss some objections to Julie's view. Some of the objections hold that Julie's view is not *true*. Other objections hold that Julie's view is not even *coherent*.

4.1. First Objection

> "On Julie's view, a gamete donor has a special relationship with her genetic child. But this is false. The donor's relationship with the child is no different from the fertility doctor's relationship. Both played a causal role in the creation of the child. That is all."

We can see that this objection is mistaken by considering some cases in which what a donor should do is different from what a fertility doctor should do. Suppose that Ellen has decided to be an egg donor, she meets the couple to whom she is supposed to donate, and she learns that they are homophobic. Ellen thinks to herself: "Oh no! This is a terrible environment for a child. They will instill bad values. But more seriously: what if the child is gay?" Ellen should refuse to donate to this couple; it would be morally wrong for her to go forward. By contrast, suppose that Fiona is a fertility doctor who learns that a couple she is treating, using an egg donor, is homophobic. Fiona has the same thought as Ellen, but she also thinks, "I am a doctor; I will not select my patients based on their moral views." It is morally permissible for Fiona to continue to treat the couple.[16,17]

Fiona and Ellen have different moral obligations in this situation. A proponent of Julie's view could argue that part of what explains this difference is that Ellen has a special obligation to the child who would be created, while Fiona does not.

In considering this case, it is again important to recognize the *agent-relative* nature of the reasons Julie's view highlights. The donor's special reason to be concerned about the kind of home in which the child will be raised is an agent-relative reason. The donor has a special reason (and perhaps a special duty) to take an interest in the circumstances of *this child's* upbringing. But while this provides the donor a special reason to be wary of donating, it provides no reason to the prospective parents to be wary of using donation as a means of conceiving a child. Of course, all prospective parents have strong reasons to think carefully about how their children will be raised, and to think realistically about whether they can be good parents and can provide a good environment for their children. But this does not single out parents who become parents through gamete donation; it does not make gamete donation problematic in any way. Indeed, people who have chosen to conceive via donation have already settled for themselves that they want to become parents, so presumably have already settled for themselves that they believe they will be good parents.

And while these concerns may provide a special reason for a donor to be wary of donating, they do not provide any reason for disinterested others to be wary of donations occurring. Indeed, there is some reason to think that it's better that *planned parenthood* occur than that *unplanned parenthood* occur; those who plan to be parents are somewhat more likely to be good parents. Parenthood that arises out of donation is always planned parenthood.

4.2. Second Objection

"We can see that a gamete donor has no special relationship with the created child by recognizing that the created child was *meant to be* the child of the parents who will raise him. There was a *plan* to create this child, to be raised by these particular parents. Were it not for *their desire* to have a child, this child would not exist at all. Although it did not happen in the usual way, this child is literally the product of their mutual love—in that their mutual love is no doubt the basis of their desire to have a family together. And the gamete donor too had this intention. (Particularly in the case of an egg donor, for whom a recipient couple is usually settled at the time of a donation, the donor donated in order that *this couple* would have a child.)"

The second objection gets something right.[18] In fact, the second objection brings out an important and beautiful truth, which explains why there is a special moral relationship, from the moment of conception, between a child created through gamete donation and both of the parents who are intended to raise the child, even given that one or both parents have no genetic relationship to the child.

But in order to reject Julie's view, the second objector must hold not only that children of donation are meant to be with the parents who raised them—which is clearly true on one reading—but that this relationship *exhausts* the meaningful parental relationships involved in donation. While the second objector makes an excellent case—a correct case—that there *is* a special relationship between the created child and the parents who will raise him, this simply does not rule out that there is also a special relationship (perhaps less significant, but still there) with the gamete donor.

4.3. Third Objection

The third objector elaborates on the second objection:

"Not only was the child *meant to be* the child of the parents who will raise him or her, but it is morally important that he or she be *only theirs* and have no other morally significant parental relationships. After all, when two people in love want to have a child together, there is an injustice if they are unable to do so. In the case of infertility or a same-sex couple, this is a naturally arising injustice; it is not an injustice caused by the state or some people; but it is an injustice nonetheless. The process of gamete donation is redressing this injustice. But if it turns out that the created child has a morally significant relationship with its genetic parent, the donor, then an injustice remains: this couple does not get to be parents in the same way that others do. Rather, they have to contend with this other person being in the moral picture too. For reasons of justice, there is no morally significant relationship between created children and gamete donors."

I think the third objector gets something right. When two people want to become parents, they do typically want a child who is *just theirs*. It is worse for them that there be a third party, a virtual stranger to them, who has a morally significant relationship with their child. However, the objector's claim is that *because it would mean that donor-assisted reproduction does a better job of righting an injustice*, there is no morally significant relationship between donors and created children. I am not convinced that moral reasons work in this way.

4.4. Fourth Objection

"Julie's view doesn't make sense. On her view, it is a mistake to be a gamete donor—one should not be a gamete donor—because of concern for the created child. But these are *moral considerations*. So, her view is that gamete donation is *morally wrong*. But then it is not supererogatory!"

This objector relies on a natural thought, captured in this principle:

(1) If, all things considered, one should not φ, and the reasons against φ-ing—in virtue of which one should not φ—are *moral reasons*—then φ-ing is morally wrong.

While this principle is intuitively attractive, it is false. Consider Samantha, who is trying to decide between staying home to read a silly novel and going to a talk by an old classmate. The classmate would appreciate seeing Samantha in the audience, but Samantha wouldn't enjoy the talk. Let's suppose that (a) it is morally permissible for Samantha to stay home. Now, Samantha has to decide what to do. It's possible that neither of the following claims is true: (b) all things considered, Samantha should go to the talk, and (c) all things considered, Samantha should stay home. It could be that neither is true; but one of those claims could be true. (c) could be true. Or, for all we've said, (b) could be true. It could be that *both* (a) and (b) are true: it's morally permissible for Samantha to stay home, but all things considered, Samantha should go to the talk. This could be the case, even though, if (b) is true, then the *reason* that Samantha should go to the talk is a *moral reason*: it is *that her classmate would be happy to see her there* (or *that it would be loyal to her classmate to go*). What this shows is that sometimes a consideration which is properly described as a moral consideration does settle that one should do something, all things considered, without making that option morally obligatory.[19]

(Note that I do not claim that the case of gamete donation, on the moral story I told above, is analogous to Samantha's case. In Samantha's case, there is something morally *good* about the option she should, all things considered, take. In the case of gamete donation (according to the arguments I was considering), there is something morally *bad* about donation, which makes it the case that, all things considered, one should refrain from donating. There are significant differences between the nature of our reasons in the two kinds of cases.)

4.5. Fifth Objection

"An action cannot be both, on the one hand, praiseworthy and a morally good thing to do, but also, on the other hand, a mistake which is a mistake in virtue of moral considerations."

While the fourth objector doubted that Julie's view could maintain that gamete donation was *morally permissible*, the fifth objector doubts that Julie's view can maintain that gamete donation is *a morally good thing to do*. The fifth objector endorses:

(2) If, all things considered, one should not φ, and the reasons against φ-ing—in virtue of which one should not φ—are *moral reasons*—then φ-ing is not a morally good thing to do and φ-ing is not a praiseworthy thing to do.

This is a natural thought, but it is mistaken. Consider the following case. Tom has some gift cards for ice cream, which he could give to some schoolchildren. Tom has three options: go straight home, which is easiest for him; go a bit out of his way and give the coupons to some kids who live near a somewhat expensive ice cream shop, so that five kids can get free ice cream; or go a bit more out of his way and give the coupons to some other kids who live near a cheaper ice cream shop, so that ten kids can get free ice cream. Let's suppose furthermore that it's morally permissible for Tom to go home: he needn't do any good deeds today, and he doesn't owe anyone these gift cards. It's supererogatory for Tom to give the gift cards to any of the kids. Finally, let's suppose that, all things considered, Tom should take the third option: he should go out of his way to the farther school and enable ten kids to have ice cream. (Note something important here: that was a further, substantive stipulation. It is not always true that an agent should do the most good that he or she can do.[20]) Given all of these stipulations, this case provides a counterexample to (2). The counterexample is given by Tom's second option: going a bit out of his way and enabling five kids to get ice cream. All things considered, Tom shouldn't do this. The reasons against doing it, in virtue of which he shouldn't do it—that more kids would get ice cream if he went more out of his way, to the other school—are moral considerations. But, nevertheless, if Tom takes the second option he is doing a morally good thing, and he is praiseworthy. He's benefiting some kids whom he was not morally obligated to benefit.[21]

So, the fifth objection fails.

4.6. Sixth Objection

The case of Tom taking his second option is importantly morally different from the case of Dariah becoming a gamete donor. Both are doing something morally good and helping some people, though it is not what they should do, all things considered. But in Tom's case, this is because he has an alternative which is even morally better, on which he helps more people. Tom is praiseworthy for taking his second option and he'd be *more praiseworthy* if he did what he should do, all things considered. By contrast, Dariah's case may appear to raise a puzzle, which gives rise to a new objection. It may appear that, on Julie's view, while being a gamete donor is praiseworthy, there is a *morally better action*—refraining from being a gamete donor—which is not praiseworthy at all. After all, refraining from being a gamete donor does not involve *helping* anyone. It just involves continuing one's life as usual. The sixth objection is that Julie's view cannot be true because:

> (3) It cannot be the case that one action is morally praiseworthy while a morally better action is not morally praiseworthy

In this case, I am happy to concede that the objector's claim is true; I will not take issue with (3). However, I deny that Julie's view violates (3). Rather, properly understood, Julie's view holds that if Dariah considers gamete donation but then is moved by the thoughts that she would be isolated from her child, that she would be putting blind faith in strangers to raise her child, and that she would not be available to her child if her child needed her help, and Dariah refrains from donation *for these reasons*, then Dariah is praiseworthy. It's true that the praiseworthiness of Dariah for refraining does seem different from the praiseworthiness of Dariah in the case in which she donates. The kind of praiseworthiness that a person merits when she makes a sacrifice to help others is but one species of praiseworthiness. The objector might reformulate the objection by appeal to this claim:

> (4) It cannot be the case that one action is morally praiseworthy *in the special way that making a sacrifice to help others is morally praiseworthy* while a morally better action is not morally praiseworthy *in the same way*

But this claim I do deny.

4.7. Seventh Objection

The seventh objector picks up on my acknowledgment that on Julie's view, the reasons against donation, in virtue of which one should not donate, are moral reasons:

> "A child created through gamete donation wouldn't have existed at all if it weren't for the donation, so there can't be any reasons *stemming from the interests or welfare of the child* against donation."

The objector is assuming that there can't be a reason against an action, stemming from the interests of a particular person, if that person is not made worse-off than he would otherwise be by the action. This principle has some initial plausibility, but it is false. I argue elsewhere that people can be harmed by their creations, indeed impermissibly harmed, even though their lives are well worth living.[22]

It is easy to see that the objector's line of thought is deeply implausible. Suppose that Ellen is deciding whether to donate eggs to a particular couple, and then she learns that the husband is an abusive alcoholic. He's just verbally abusive, not physically abusive. It happens that Ellen has studied this topic and knows that while children of verbally abusive alcoholics experience much pain and hardship, their lives are certainly worth living. Ellen then concludes that the child she will help to create, her genetic child, will not be worse off than not having existed, so it's just fine to donate her eggs to this couple. Something has clearly gone wrong in Ellen's reasoning.

5. My Conclusions So Far

I've developed Julie's view and defended its coherence. I think it should be taken seriously as a possible view about gamete donation.

I've argued that principles (1) and (2) are false, despite their initial plausibility:

(1) If, all things considered, one should not φ, and the reasons against φ-ing— in virtue of which one should not φ—are *moral reasons*—then φ-ing is morally wrong.

(2) If, all things considered, one should not φ, and the reasons against φ-ing—in virtue of which one should not φ—are *moral reasons*—then φ-ing is not a morally good thing to do and φ-ing is not a praiseworthy thing to do.

In the face of learning that (1) is false, we might worry about how we can understand the relationship between *what is morally wrong* and *what one should not do, all things considered*. Do they have nothing to do with each other? We need not go so far. For example, I have not challenged the claim that morality is overriding; I do endorse:

Morality is overriding: If one's φ-ing is morally wrong, then one should not φ, all things considered.

But I have pointed out the following:

- When we ask, about some moral considerations against φ-ing, "Are these reasons sufficient that they win out?" this may raise either of two questions: "Is φ-ing morally wrong?" or "Is it the case that, all things considered, one should not φ?"

- Some acts should not be performed, all things considered, but are not morally wrong (such as burning the money in my wallet), and for some of these acts, the reasons in virtue of which they should not be performed are *moral reasons*.

In the next section, I will discuss two related issues about the nature of moral reasons.

6. WHAT MORAL REASONS CAN DO

One thing that emerges from our discussion so far is that the following claim is false:

(5) Moral reasons only function to determine which actions are morally permissible and which actions are morally wrong; their contribution to that issue exhausts their import.

It is easy to see that this claim is false. The mere existence of supererogatory actions undermines (5). Some actions have something to be said for them, morally, but are not morally required. For these actions, moral reasons in favor of them are doing additional work beyond rendering them morally permissible as opposed to morally wrong.

Once an agent knows that she has several morally permissible options, what is the agent's position? A naive and mistaken picture would hold that moral reasons have no further import for this agent, and that at this point she should choose which action to perform based solely on other factors, such as what is best for her. This picture would imply the following deeply unattractive view:

(6) It is never the case that a supererogatory action is the action that an agent should perform, all things considered, because of its morally good features.

The view would imply that each supererogatory option is either a mistake or is such that it is no more supported by an agent's reasons than some other option she has. (Or, unusually, we might have a supererogatory action that an agent should perform, but for reasons that have nothing to do with its morally good features.) The view implies that a person's moral reasons never win out to favor a supererogatory option above her other options. That is false.

A picture according to which moral reasons are silent after they settle which actions are morally permissible and which are morally wrong is particularly unattractive if it furthermore holds that once these are settled, the only reasons available to do any further work are *prudential* reasons. It would then turn out that every supererogatory action is a mistake—something one should not do, all things considered—for prudential reasons. (Or if a supererogatory action is not a mistake, that has nothing to do with its morally good features.) By contrast, the correct view is that sometimes, all things considered, one should perform a supererogatory act, even though that act is not the act that is *best for the agent* out of the morally permissible acts (and one should do so *because of the features that make it a morally good thing to do*).

Note that while it is a mistake to think that all supererogatory actions are mistakes, there is an interesting class of supererogatory actions that are mistakes. In the next section, I'll propose the view that many supererogatory actions are *moral mistakes*. (That is, all things considered, the agent should not have performed the action, and the reasons against acting in virtue of which this is true are *moral* reasons.) But the class of supererogatory actions that are *prudential mistakes* is also very interesting. There may even be a special kind of honor or praiseworthiness that comes with making this kind of mistake, sacrificing oneself for others to such a degree that it goes beyond what one all things considered had reason to do.[23]

What I have emphasized in rejecting (1) is that moral reasons can continue to have force *beyond* settling what is morally wrong and what is morally permissible. This is most obvious when it comes to moral reasons to do something because it would have *good consequences*. This is the classic case of the supererogatory action: there's a way one can help someone but it isn't morally required. What I have suggested, which is more controversial, is that moral reasons of a different kind can exhibit this phenomenon. Consider moral reasons *against* acting a certain way, which behave like *constraints*; these include for example reasons against lying, reasons against breaking promises, and reasons against killing. (These are not reasons against acting a certain way simply because there would be bad consequences of acting that way.) Sometimes these reasons make an action morally wrong. Sometimes these reasons are present, but they fail to make an action morally wrong. I have proposed that these reasons are not *silent* after failing to make an action morally wrong; they still have force, and they can make an action something that, all things considered, one should not do. This is the claim I deny:

> (7) A moral reason that functions in a constraint-like way only exerts force in determining whether the action in question is morally wrong. If the action is morally permissible, then there is no further import of the constraint-like reason against it.[24]

On Julie's view, the reasons against gamete donation are like this. That the agent would be isolated from her child, that she would not be available to her child if her child needed her help, and that she would be putting blind faith in strangers to raise her child, are all constraint-like reasons against being a gamete donor; but they do not make gamete donation morally wrong; nevertheless, they do make gamete donation something that, all things considered, one should not do.

7. SHOULD WE SEE OTHER SUPEREROGATORY ACTIONS AS MORALLY PERMISSIBLE MORAL MISTAKES?

Having presented and defended Julie's view, I want to turn now to consider a somewhat radical suggestion. Perhaps, appropriately understood, many deeply supererogatory actions have the character that Julie thinks gamete donation has. This is the view I want to examine: that many deeply supererogatory actions are morally permissible moral mistakes. On this view, these actions are ones that the agents, all things considered, should not perform. But nevertheless, it is morally good that agents do perform them, and it's appropriate to wish that agents would perform more of them.

Let's consider Chris again. He announces that he is probably going to donate half of his after-tax income to UNICEF. Chris is middle-class in the United States. He is not wealthy. I said at first that a friend, hearing this announcement, might reasonably react as follows: "Wow, it's wonderful that you're doing that. Good for you! If only more people would do that!" On the view I am now exploring, a friend who reacts this way is failing to be a helpful or properly engaged friend. In particular, if Chris wants to think his choice through with his friend, then what the friend owes Chris is a response more like this: "I think you would be making a mistake. Think about how hard it will be for you to live on half your income. Think about what you and your family will have to give up. Sure, I know you *could* do it. But that's a big sacrifice to make!" In fact, that's the way a lot of people would respond to Chris's announcement.[25]

Consider another type of deeply supererogatory action: risking or sacrificing one's life to save more than one other person, in an emergency situation. Someone who does this is lauded as a hero. Such a person is praiseworthy: he or she has done a wonderful thing for the people he or she has saved. But suppose it is an emergency situation with some time to ponder built in. Suppose Evan, a bystander, before rushing into a burning building with two people inside, says "I'm going to go in there!" What should Evan's friend say to him? A friend might well say, "Don't do it, don't risk your life. Think of your family."

Note that on the proposed view, the reasons that both Chris and Evan should refrain concern their special relationships to their loved ones. These, again, are *agent-relative* reasons. They are reasons that the agents should refrain from acting, but they are not reasons that third parties should wish the agents to refrain from acting. On the proposed view, risking one's own life to save two or more strangers may be a morally good thing to do but also a moral mistake: one shouldn't do it because of *moral reasons* given by one's special relationship with one's loved ones; but if one does it, one has done a praiseworthy, wonderful thing.

On the view we're considering, we should have the following attitude toward some cases of deeply supererogatory actions: it's great that someone does something like this, and it would be great if more people would. Things would be better if we could convince more people to act in these ways. However, were we to try to convince them, we would be convincing them to do what they have most reason not to do.

8. CONCLUSION

I have developed the following view about gamete donation, which I think should be taken seriously:

> Potential gamete donors have serious moral reasons against donation: they would have children from whom they would be isolated, they would be unavailable to these children if the children needed their help, and they would be putting blind faith in strangers to raise their children well. But gamete donation has such good effects—it enables people who want to become parents to be parents, and it enables families to exist that would not otherwise exist—that gamete donation is morally permissible, despite the reasons against it; in fact, it's a morally good thing to do. Nevertheless, gamete donation is a moral mistake: all things considered, one should not be a gamete donor, for moral reasons.

I have also suggested the more general view that many deeply supererogatory actions are moral mistakes, though they are morally permissible.

I have argued that these claims are false:

(1) If, all things considered, one should not φ, and the reasons against φ-ing—in virtue of which one should not φ—are *moral reasons*—then φ-ing is morally wrong.

(2) If, all things considered, one should not φ, and the reasons against φ-ing—in virtue of which one should not φ—are *moral reasons*—then φ-ing is not a morally good thing to do and φ-ing is not a praiseworthy thing to do.

Because (1) is false, the following are true:

- When we ask, about some moral considerations against φ-ing, "Are these reasons sufficient that they win out?" this may raise either of two questions: "Is φ-ing morally wrong?" or "Is it the case that, all things considered, one should not φ?"
- Some acts should not be performed, all things considered, but are not morally wrong (such as burning the money in my wallet), and for some of these acts, the reasons in virtue of which they should not be performed are *moral reasons*.

Finally, I pointed out that moral reasons have force beyond their contributions to the question which actions are morally permissible, and I claimed that even a constraint-like moral reason can continue to have force in a case in which it does not render an action morally wrong: it may nevertheless render the action something that, all things considered, the agent should not do.

ACKNOWLEDGMENTS

For comments on drafts of this paper, I thank Tyler Doggett, Elizabeth Finneron-Burns, Alexander Guerrero, Jennifer Morton, Alastair Norcross, Jonathan Quong, Laurie Shrage, Bradford Skow, Sharon Street, and audiences at the Analytic Legal Philosophy Conference; the Center for Human Values, Princeton University; New York University; Oxford University; the Pacific APA; Syracuse University; University of California, Los Angeles; University of Texas, Austin; and Yale University.

NOTES

1. I leave open that it may be permissible for Anne to ask for payment for the medicine; the point is that she is morally required to relinquish it somehow.
2. There is some disagreement about whether actions in the second category count as supererogatory; I think they do, but this doesn't matter for my purposes. Some people think that only actions in the third category are supererogatory; if they are correct, then all supererogatory actions are "deeply supererogatory" as I use the term.
3. I assume this is so, though some would disagree. See Peter Singer, "Famine, Affluence, and Morality," *Philosophy and Public Affairs* 1, no. 3 (1972): 229–243.
4. I want to set aside some issues that are not occupying Julie. First, Julie does not draw a distinction between "purely altruistic" gamete donation and paid gamete donation. In particular, Julie recognizes that someone who donates sperm or eggs for money can nevertheless truly be said to be motivated by the desire to help others. There are many paid activities which help others and have moral worth in virtue of helping others. Second, Julie believes that anonymous sperm or egg donation is a mistake because it creates children from whom the donor is ultimately isolated. She does not think that it is the physical burden of egg donation which makes it a mistake, though those burdens are real. (The donor must take hormones to stimulate egg production and must undergo an invasive egg extraction procedure.) She would have the same concern about egg donation were it as logistically easy as sperm donation. Third, Julie's concern about sperm or egg donation does not stem (at least not obviously so) from any concern that the sperm or egg donor is being exploited; her concern does not distinguish between well-off and impoverished donors.
5. I restrict the discussion to anonymous gamete donation unless explicitly stated otherwise. By "anonymous gamete donation," I mean donation in which the donor is anonymous *to the created child*, at least until the child is eighteen years old. This is compatible with some non-anonymity between the donor and the intended parents of the child.
6. A number of authors have argued that gamete donation is morally wrong, while others have argued that gamete donation is morally permissible. None of these authors has articulated a

view along the lines of Julie's view: that gamete donation is a moral mistake (one should not do it *for moral reasons*) but is not morally wrong.

Luara Ferracioli, "On the Value of Intimacy in Procreation," *Journal of Value Inquiry* 48 (2014): 349–369 argues that anonymous gamete donation is usually morally wrong because donors do not know that the recipient(s) of donation will be good parent(s).

Melissa Moschella, "Rethinking the Moral Permissibility of Gamete Donation," *Theoretical Medicine and Bioethics* 35 (2014): 421–440 argues that gamete donors have parental responsibilities they do not fulfill, and thus that gamete donation is morally wrong.

Rivka Weinberg, "The Moral Complexity of Sperm Donation" *Bioethics* 22 (2008): 166–178 argues that gamete donors have parental responsibilities for their genetic children, and that this probably makes gamete donation morally wrong.

Tim Bayne, "Gamete Donation and Paternal Responsibility," *Journal of Applied Philosophy* 20 (2003): 77–87 argues that gamete donors lack parental responsibility; or if they have it, then donation is nevertheless compatible with meeting this responsibility.

7. However, in saying this, I do not mean to suggest that the view holds that the mistake in gamete donation is merely the taking on of a particular burden.

8. Some people advocate for laws that would allow all children of gamete donation to find out the identities of their genetic parents once they are eighteen years old. An objector might hold that if such laws became widespread, then there would be little interest in the topic of my chapter: *anonymous* gamete donation. The objector's suggestion would be that the mistake present in gamete donation on Julie's view, that donors are isolated from their children, would not be present in such a legal regime. But Julie's worry would still largely remain. It would still be true for eighteen years that donors are isolated from their children, have no relationship with them, know nothing about them, and are not in a position to help them if they need help.

9. Strictly speaking, it does not follow from the claim that a certain choice is a mistake, that an agent who performs the choice should later regret it. Procreative choices in particular are often such that they were mistakes, but their agents are later reasonable in being glad to have made them. Consider a girl who chooses at age fourteen to conceive; later, in loving her child, she is glad to have conceived him and does not regret her choice, even if she understands it to have been something she should not have done. Anonymous donors are different; they do not know their children created through the donation, and they do not love them (at least, they often do not love them, or they do not love them with any knowledge of them). Still, donors could value these children, knowing that they exist, and for that reason not wish that they did not exist, and so not wish not to have donated. I discuss the *reasonable attachment to the actual* in "'I'll Be Glad I Did It' Reasoning and the Significance of Future Desires," *Philosophical Perspectives* 23 (2009): 177–199 and "Transformative Experiences and Reliance on Moral Testimony," *Res Philosophica* 92 (2015): 323–339.

10. In "The Gift of Life," *Philosophy and Public Affairs* 36, no. 3 (2008): 245–266.

11. Furthermore, there are certain burdens that can come from genetic relatedness to one's parents: parents often have misguided expectations that children will be like them and follow in their footsteps; there is something to be said for having one or two parents without such preconceptions.

12. Though one might think that even such public education programs would be problematic for similar reasons that outlawing the practice would be problematic. Imagine a publicly funded campaign aimed at convincing women not to have abortions. See Sarah Stroud, "Dworkin and *Casey* on Abortion," *Philosophy and Public Affairs* 25 (1996): 140–170.

13. It seems that Julie does have reason to hope that reproductive technology advances, in certain ways. For example, it would be wonderful if a skin cell from an adult could be transformed into a gamete and if two such gametes could be combined to create an embryo. This could enable two women in a relationship to have a child to whom both were genetically related. Similarly, two men could conceive a child to whom both were genetically related (though a surrogate would have to gestate the child). And a heterosexual couple experiencing fertility problems could conceive a child to whom both were genetically related. Reproductive technology is indeed advancing toward this goal. (See Philip Ball, "Reproduction revolution: how our skin cells might be turned into sperm and eggs," The Guardian, October 14, 2018.)

14. While Julie's view does recognize an agent-neutral reason against gamete donation—that it creates a child who lacks a relationship with her parent—her view does not see this reason as particularly weighty; it is not what makes it the case that a donor should not donate, and it is not weighty enough to mean that prospective parents should not use gamete donation to create a child, nor is it weighty enough to mean that third parties should wish that gamete donation not occur.

15. Making an adoption plan for one's child also may mean being isolated from one's child, putting blind faith in strangers to raise one's child, and being unavailable to one's child if one's child needs one's help. Should Julie think that one should not make adoption plans for one's child? No. Because there is already an existing child in such cases, there is often a compelling reason to go ahead with an adoption plan. But the considerations that move Julie do tell in favor of *open adoption* rather than closed adoption.

16. Melissa Seymour Fahmy, "On Procreative Responsibility in Assisted and Collaborative Reproduction," *Ethical Theory and Moral Practice* 16 (2013): 55–70 offers a view that would ground disagreement with my claim. Fahmy argues that doctors who facilitate gamete donation should screen prospective parents to make sure they would be good parents.

17. In saying that it would be morally permissible for the doctor to continue to provide fertility treatments to the homophobic couple, I am not making the strong claim that doctors may ignore *all* evidence that people will be bad parents. Evidence that prospective parents would be physically abusive, for example, would make it morally impermissible for a doctor to provide fertility treatment.

18. It also provides a useful contrast between children of gamete donation and children of adoption. Children of adoption were not created in order to be raised by the parents who raise them. That such children may themselves yearn for their genetic parents may make more sense than that the children of donation would do so. For children of adoption, there was presumably at one time a real possibility that they would be raised by their genetic parents. But for children of donation, there was never any possibility that they would be raised by their genetic parents. Indeed, they would not have existed but for the plan that they be raised by the parents who raise them.

19. I argue for the existence of morally permissible moral mistakes in "Morally Permissible Moral Mistakes," *Ethics* 126 (2016): 366–393 and "Morality Within the Realm of the Morally Permissible," *Oxford Studies in Normative Ethics* 5 (2015): 221–244; I discuss related issues in "There Is No Moral *Ought* and No Prudential *Ought*," in *Routledge Handbook of Practical Reason*, ed. Ruth Chang and Kurt Sylvan (London: Routledge, 2021), 438-456; and I use the notion of a morally permissible moral mistake to develop a view about the ethics of eating meat in "Eating Meat as a Morally Permissible Moral Mistake,"

in *Philosophy Comes to Dinner*, ed. Andrew Chignell, Terence Cuneo, and Matthew C. Halteman (London: Routledge, 2015), 215–231.

20. For example, suppose that you are an amateur squash player and you've worked hard in preparation for the local Y's squash tournament. While you drive to the Y for the first match, you see some volunteers picking up trash in a public park. You could stop to join them, sacrificing your chance to play in the tournament in order to improve the park. Suppose that helping in the park is the most good you could do at this moment; it's nevertheless not true that you should do so: you should drive to the Y, given how important it is to you.

21. The existence of these "second-best" supererogatory actions (such as Tom's giving the gift cards to five nearby kids) is underappreciated in discussions of the supererogatory. For example, in Terry Horgan and Mark Timmons, "Untying a Knot from the Inside Out: Reflections on the 'Paradox' of Supererogation," *Social Philosophy and Policy* 27 (2010): 29–63, the authors gloss the paradox of supererogation as arising because supererogatory actions are "morally best" (29). Similarly, Jamie Dreier, "Why Ethical Satisficing Makes Sense and Rational Satisficing Doesn't," in *Satisficing and Maximizing*, ed. Michael Byron (Cambridge: Cambridge University Press, 2004), 131–154 proposes that supererogatory actions are those that are required from the perspective of beneficence, and Douglas Portmore, "Are Moral Reasons Morally Overriding?" *Ethical Theory and Moral Practice* 11 (2008): 369–388 says "for there is a sense in which supererogatory acts are acts that agents morally ought to perform" (379). Paul McNamara, "Supererogation, Inside and Out: Toward an Adequate Scheme for Common Sense Morality," in *Oxford Studies in Normative Ethics*, ed. Mark Timmons (Oxford: Oxford University Press, 2011), 202–235 points out that sometimes a supererogatory action is not an agent's morally best option, that such an action can nevertheless be praiseworthy, and that this phenomenon is underappreciated.

22. See my "Can We Harm and Benefit in Creating?" *Philosophical Perspectives* 18 (2004), 89–113) and "Harming as Causing Harm," in *Harming Future Persons*, ed. Melinda Roberts and David Wasserman (Dordrecht: Springer, 2009), 137–154.

23. For more on prudential mistakes (things that one should not do, all things considered, such that prudential considerations explain why one should not do them), see my "There is No Moral *Ought* and No Prudential *Ought*."

24. For more on the falsity of claim (7), see section II of my "Morally Permissible Moral Mistakes."

25. Some people might respond to Chris's announcement by feeling threatened, thinking "If Chris is doing that, does that mean he thinks *I* should be doing that too?" They might try to talk him out of it to vindicate the reasonableness of their own choices. Someone who reacts for these reasons is reacting *understandably*, but he's not getting right *why* what Chris is doing is a mistake.

CHAPTER 26

DISABILITY AND POPULATION ETHICS

JULIA MOSQUERA

1. INTRODUCTION

POPULATION ethics is, broadly speaking, the discipline that aims at the evaluation of populations that vary in terms of (1) the identity, (2) the number, (3) the quality of life of the individuals that compose them, or a combination of (1) to (3).

Normative population ethics, the subfield of population ethics concerned with what populations we ought to choose, has experienced a noticeable development in the last decades. Among the reasons for this development are some of the pressing challenges of our time which have great potential to influence the life of future generations.

Applied population ethics, the subfield that applies the evaluative and normative knowledge about populations to other practical areas of philosophy, is a fruitful field of research. The ethics of disability, climate change, animal ethics, and so on are among the challenges that motivate this field. It is estimated that climate change will substantially affect populations in the future (lower quality of life in those regions most affected by rise in temperatures and/or by climate change-related natural disasters, change in their size, etc.).[1] This makes it necessary to come up with principles sensitive to these changes in the quality and composition of our future populations (see Arrhenius, Ryberg, and Tännsjö 2006; Arrhenius 2018; forthcoming; and Broome, this volume). The field of animal ethics too faces challenges that connect to population ethics. Some of the recent discussion in this field focuses for example on evaluating the goodness of non-human animal populations that live in the wild and who are exposed to high levels suffering. The discussion has proved that population dynamics resulting from different reproductive patterns are a key mechanism that determines the welfare of non-human animals who live in the wild (see Horta 2010; Mejers and Gosseries, this volume).

With respect to the ethics of disability, the story is somewhat similar. The ethics of disability focuses on, among other things, the evaluation of the lives of people with disabilities, as well as on some of the decisions that involve current and future disabled individuals. The ethics of disability raises a number of philosophically interesting questions, some of which fall directly within the scope of population ethics. First, some populations of people with disabilities have a level of well-being that is on average lower than that of other groups.[2] Second, the size of the population of people with disabilities is easily susceptible to changes for several reasons, among which are the introduction and ready availability of reproductive technologies, changes in lifestyle that lead to health conditions, the effects of climate change, and so on. These reasons make population ethics particularly interesting for the ethics of disability, and vice versa.

In fact, disability has been a recurrent source of theoretical inspiration in the population ethics literature. This literature is filled with cases that involve disability and which have motivated some of the most famous paradoxes in this field. Some examples include Derek Parfit's Two Medical Programmes (1984, 367–369); Parfit's Wrongful Life (1984, 367–368; 2011, 2: 221–222; 2017, 121); Parfit's Wretched Child (1982, 148), provided to contextualize the Procreative Asymmetry introduced first by Jan Narveson (1967, 62–72) and which would be labeled as such later on by Jeff McMahan (1981, 96–127); Kavka's Restricted Lives (1982, 103–112); and Parfit's Handicapped Child (1984, 118), which would later inspire Boonin's Wilma's case (Boonin 2014, 2). It has even been argued that the lives contained in population Z of Parfit's Repugnant Conclusion (Parfit 1984, Ch. 17) should be thought of as representing the lives of significantly disabled individuals which, despite containing a very low level of well-being, are lives worth living (Tännsjö 2004).

Given their theoretical similarities, the ethics of disability inherits some of the problems that occupy the field of population ethics. This chapter presents and reviews some of those problems. Below are three sets of questions that fall under the intersection of population ethics and disability:

(1) Procreation questions
    a. Is it wrong for parents to bring into existence a disabled child when they cannot bring a non-disabled child into existence instead?
    b. Is it wrong for parents to bring into existence a disabled child when they could bring a (different) non-disabled child into existence instead?
    c. Is a disabled person harmed by being brought into existence?
(2) Disability infliction/removal questions
    a. Is a person harmed by being inflicted with a disability, if doing so would cause her to cease to exist and bring into existence a numerically different person?
    b. Is a disabled person harmed by having her disability removed, if that would cause her to cease to exist and bring into existence a numerically different person?

(3) Numbers questions
    a. Does adding/removing a disabled person to/from a population affect the burden of disability of the population? Does the addition/removal of individuals to/from a population affect the disability of the remaining disabled individuals of that population?
    b. How does the size of the disabled population affect the badness of their disability? How does the ratio of disabled and non-disabled individuals affect the badness of disability?
    c. Does reducing the size of the disabled population improve the population in terms of the impact of disabilities? And in terms of equality?

Sets of questions (1) and (2) deal with the morality of procreation and harm, and the morality of disability infliction and removal, respectively. While these two sets of questions have received considerable attention in the literature on disability, the last set of questions, (3), which deals with disability in the context of variable population size, hasn't. In what follows, I explore each of these three sets of questions, reviewing how the literature has dealt with some of them, and adding some new insights, especially to the last set of questions.

2. Procreation Questions: Causing Disabled People to Exist

Since the 1990s, the debate about procreation and disability has mostly focused on reproductive decisions within the context of the family, such as decisions that may result in a parent having a child with a disability. Reproductive technologies make reproductive decisions more pressing in that they give more options to prospective parents, making their procreative decisions more complex and challenging.

The ethical debate has been framed around the question of whether it is wrong to choose to have a disabled child, or to fail to avoid having a disabled child and, if so, why. This debate has two main aspects. The first is a (partly) empirical aspect and it involves determining the level of well-being of people with different disabilities. The second is a normative aspect and it concerns the moral constraints on prospective parents in bearing children expected to have a disability.

Views on selection against disability range widely, from those on which prospective parents should select the child expected to have the most well-being (Savulescu and Kahane 2009) to those on which parents should not select at all (Herissone-Kelly 2006). Those in favor of selecting the child expected to have or produce the most well-being commonly appeal to the principle of Procreative Beneficence (Savulescu 2007; Savulescu and Kahane 2009). Understood broadly, this principle says that prospective parents have a significant moral reason to select the child whose life can be expected to go best in light of the relevant information available, or at least no worse than any of the others. The idea is that, other things being equal, it is better to create lives free from disability. This has been commonly referred to as the *disability-free intuition* (Barker and Wilson 2019).

Despite its plausibility, the disability-free intuition faces a challenge. The child with the disability would not have existed if the progenitor had instead chosen to have a non-disabled child. Defending the intuition that choosing or failing to avoid having a disabled child is wrong involves condemning the very decision to which the child with the disability would have owed her existence. Procreative choices of this sort are choices between non-identical individuals. This problem, known as the non-identity problem, is a challenge for the defense of the disability-free intuition.

The disability-free intuition can lead to the inference that choosing or failing to avoid having a disabled child is not only suboptimal but also wrong. In order to defend such a claim, one ought to point at where this wrong lies and what kind of wrong it is. It is common to frame the debate on selection against disability in terms of whether the presumed wrong should be understood in person-affecting or in impersonal terms.[3] If it is wrong to choose or to fail to avoid having a disabled child, is it because it causes some sort of harm to the child? Or is it, instead, wrong for impersonal reasons?

2.1. Person-Affecting and Non-Person-Affecting Arguments against Choosing Disability

Person-affecting arguments against creating a disabled child rely on the intuition that a disabled child is wronged by parents who fail to prevent her existence, even if the child has a life that is worth living. The arguments are person-affecting in the sense that the wrongness of creating the disabled child is directly explained by the impact on *that child*.

Most person-affecting arguments against the permissibility of creating a disabled child seem to rely on the idea that parents have certain specific duties related to the quality of life of their future children and that failing to fulfil those duties constitutes a wrong to their child. One of these duties is granting their future children a life not just worth living, but something beyond that. Some think that parents owe their children a life expected to have at least an average level of opportunity for well-being (Tooley 1998). Others think parents owe their children a life expected to have a minimum level of well-being that goes beyond what is necessary to make a life worth living (Kamm 2002; Steinbock and McClanrock 1994), or a life expected not to contain unusually severe hardships (Benatar 2000). And some think that what parents owe to their children is a decent chance of a good life, if it does not cost an unreasonably big burden to themselves (Glover 2006).

Finally, it has also been argued that while, by choosing the disabled child instead of the non-disabled the child, parents do not harm the resulting child, there is still a wrong done to the child, one that derives from the attitude with which the child is conceived, namely some sort of carelessness, disrespect, or insensitivity toward the child and the decision to create it (Kumar, 2003; Purdy, 1996; Roberts, 1995).

Other arguments against choosing to have a disabled child rather than a non-disabled child have focused instead on impersonal moral reasons. According to such arguments, while there is a wrong committed in choosing disability, this wrong is not directed to the disabled child. Dan Brock (2005), for example, has argued that the right choice is to bring into existence a non-disabled child for the sake of a world with less diminishment of well-being or limitation in opportunity. But perhaps the most influential impersonal defense of this position is the one provided by McMahan (2005).

McMahan reintroduces Parfit's Same Number Quality Claim (1984, 360) under the Impersonal Comparative Principle (ICP):

> *Impersonal Comparative Principle* (ICP): If in either of two possible outcomes the same number of people would ever live, it would be worse if those who live are worse off, or have a lower quality of life, than those who would have lived (McMahan 2005).

The ICP is limited in various respects. First, the principle is limited to the comparison of the value of different outcomes. Thus, it does not say what one ought to do when facing a choice to bring about one or the other of these outcomes. The principle must be coupled with a normative action-guiding principle in order to prescribe such a recommendation.

Second, and most importantly, the ICP is explicitly restricted to same number choices, that is, to choices that while involving the existence of different people do not affect the number of people who will exist. Thus, the principle is silent about, for example, any choice between causing an individual with a disability to exist and not bringing anyone into existence. It is also silent about, for example, whether it is better to create more disabled individuals rather than fewer non-disabled individuals.

The restriction of ICP to same number choices is problematic in various ways. McMahan admits this. First, he points out that there is uncertainty, and perhaps also indeterminacy regarding what counts as a same number choice which makes it hard to determine in which cases it is pertinent to apply ICP (McMahan 2005). He provides the example of a woman who is in the early stages of pregnancy and discovers that her fetus is damaged in a way that ensures that her child would be disabled. She therefore considers whether to have an abortion in order to enable herself to conceive a different, normal child instead. McMahan wonders if this decision should count as a same number choice:

> Perhaps she might treat it as such and thus be guided by the Impersonal Comparative Principle, despite the fact that, after having the abortion, she may change her mind about conceiving another child, or may be unable to conceive another child. But

what if she is considering aborting her defective foetus but is as yet undecided about whether to conceive another child? (McMahan 2005, 146)

McMahan concludes that, in cases like the above, which are common when it comes to procreative decisions that involve disability, it is unlikely that the ICP can guide our choice. There is uncertainty about whether cases like this should coun as same or as different number choices.

Moreover, McMahan argues, a simple choice that causes one person to exist rather than another at a given time will almost certainly, given enough time, affect the number of people who will exist. Causing A to exist rather than B will most likely lead to a different number of progeny than if we had caused A to exist instead of B. It would then seem that any choice that might look like a same number choice when we consider only the immediate effects, can actually turn out to be a different number choice. If McMahan's worry is grounded, it would restrict the application of the ICP to the point that its applicability may almost vanish.

McMahan suggests that same number choices are still sufficiently different from different number choices and that the considerations that apply in the former do not apply in the latter. Thus, he concludes, we can only apply the ICP in those cases in which our choice would not foreseeably affect the number of people who would exist (McMahan 2005).[4]

Even if the uncertainty worry could be left aside, ICP is subject to a further worry. Even if we knew *all* the immediate effects of our procreative actions, there are some common cases to which ICP still could not apply. Take the case of IVF. Reproductive decisions involving the use of IVF very often include alternatives that contain different numbers of individuals. IVF is used to select embryos with a low probability of carrying a genetic condition or disability. While IVF can help decrease the probability of disability, it has been shown to also increase the probability of having a multiple pregnancy due to the procedure of transferring more than one embryo into the mother's uterus in order to increase the probability of at least one of the embryos implanting (Klitzman 2016). This means that some of the families who consider the choice of undergoing IVF due to a diagnosis of disability will often face a decision between having a disabled child or, through IVF, have two or more non-disabled children.

According to McMahan, ICP could not possibly apply to these cases given that they involve different number choices. One may think this is a problem for ICP. After all, this case is not that different from the same number case in which the choice is between creating one disabled child and one non-disabled child, for which ICP would unproblematically recommend choosing the one non-disabled child. Given that the difference between these cases consists only in the addition of one non-disabled child, one may think that some sort of dominance principle would imply that the addition of one more non-disabled child makes no difference to the recommendation ICP would give in the original same number case. Unfortunately, although these kinds of procreative decisions are common, ICP is silent about them.

Given the prevalence of different number cases in the context of procreative decision-making, we need a wider principle that is capable of dealing with these cases. For such a principle to succeed, it should appeal to a more fundamental ground than ICP. A principle like ICP, Parfit argues, can only re-state our intuitions about the cases at hand, but it does so without appealing to any substantial explanation of the features that underlie the cases. Only a principle that appeals to such a more fundamental ground could also apply to different number cases (Parfit 1982, 123; 1984, 361). The search for this principle remains open and subject to some of the paradoxes and impossibility theorems in population ethics (see Arrhenius, forthcoming).

3. Disability Infliction and Removal: Causing Non-Disabled People to be Disabled and Causing Disabled People to be Non-Disabled

The section above dealt with questions about the morality of causing disabled people to exist. There is another set of interesting questions surrounding the morality of causing people to be disabled and causing disabled people to be non-disabled, and whether it is permissible to inflict or remove disability and why.

We saw that the question of whether it is permissible to cause the existence of disabled people is particularly challenging in that it involves non-identity and different number cases. The question of whether it is permissible to inflict or remove disability also involves non-identity. But although similar in some respects, these two questions can be treated separately.

3.1. Disability Infliction and Non-Identity

There has been growing philosophical attention to the question of whether it is wrong to cause or to remove disability and if so, why. Many have the intuition that inflicting disability is wrong. A common way of supporting this intuition is by appeal to the argument that inflicting disability harms the person on whom the disability is inflicted. The harm is due to the fact that the person's well-being is reduced. This intuition presupposes

> *The Standard View (of disability)*: Having a disability is—always or almost always—bad for the person who has it (in a way that non-disabilities are not).[5]

The Standard View has been a dominant position among a number of philosophers (e.g., Buchanan et al. 2000; Singer 2001; McMahan 2005; Brock 2005; Glover 2006;

Savulescu 2009; and, Kahane 2012;). Recently, the view has been challenged as a justification for the wrongness and impermissibility of inflicting disability. It has been argued that while it might be the case that inflicting disability is wrong, the welfare-based justification on which the Standard View rests is incorrect. According to some, the Standard View of disability makes a mistaken empirical assumption, namely, that disability necessarily or automatically makes you worse off (Barker and Wilson 2019; Barnes 2014; 2016; Campbell and Stramondo 2017). Some have taken this objection seriously, which has led to the rise of a spectrum of new views about the value of disability for disabled individuals.

Some have rejected the Standard View fully, claiming that disabilities do not in themselves impact overall well-being negatively. According to the Mere Difference View of disability, for example, while disabilities can be considered local bads, they are nonetheless not global bads (Barnes 2014; 2016). Local bads are, in Barnes's terminology, bads that do not compromise the overall level of well-being of an individual because—as opposed to *global* bads—disabilities are detrimental in one area of one's life but can also bring about goods in other areas of one's life that can be of high value for the person.

Views that, like the Mere Difference View, reject that disability is bad overall for the person who has it face the following challenge: If disability does not impact well-being negatively, what can explain the impermissibility of inflicting disability?[6] There are different ways of responding to this challenge.

For Barnes, the impermissibility of inflicting disability is supported by two arguments. First, becoming disabled involves the substantial transition cost of having to adapt to a newly acquired state of functioning. I have elsewhere argued that the transition costs argument cannot account for the impermissibility of inflicting disability on everyone, especially on young infants and fetuses, since there is no adaptation that a baby must undergo when she is inflicted with a disability (Mosquera 2020).[7][8]

Second, causing disability violates what Barnes calls the Principle of Non-Interference. In Barnes's words:

> You shouldn't go around making substantial changes to people's lives without their consent (even if those changes don't, on balance, make them worse off). We'd be inclined to say that Amy does something wrong if she carelessly (and permanently) turns Ben's hair from brown to blond, if she carelessly (and permanently) changes Ben's height by a few inches, and so forth. . . . We have a basic reaction that Amy shouldn't alter Ben in any of these ways without his consent–regardless of the overall effect of such alterations on Ben's well-being. (Barnes 2016, 147–148)

According to the Principle of Non-Interference, causing disability is impermissible because doing so changes the self-conception of the individual on whom the disability is inflicted without consent. For Barnes, there are certain features that determine our self-identity or conception of who we are such as our hair color or whether we are disabled or not and interfering with these features without our consent is wrong (Barnes 2014; 2016).

The background conception of personal identity on her view is "a looser sense of identity (self-conception)" as opposed to a "stricter one" (numerical identity) (Barnes 2014, 98).

The Principle of Non-Interference bases the impermissibility of disability infliction on the effect that such infliction has on the identity of individuals. Given that the infliction of a disability changes the identity (understood as self-conception) of the individuals on whom the disability is inflicted without their consent, inflicting disability is wrong. Below is a general formulation of a principle like Barnes' Principle of Non-Interference:

> *Self-Conception Impermissibility*: Other things being equal, it is impermissible to inflict disability if such infliction changes the identity (understood as self-conception) of the individual on whom the disability is inflicted.[9]

I have elsewhere argued that if the Principle of Non-Interference is based on a sense of identity understood as self-conception, then this principle cannot justify the wrongness of inflicting disability on everyone (Mosquera 2017; 2020). First, it is dubious whether children have any particular self-conception. Second, we often perform interventions (e.g., education) on children that lead to changes in their self-conception, and the fact that these interventions have this effect does not make us judge them as impermissible.

Given that changes in an individual's self-conception without the consent of that individual cannot ground the impermissibility of disability infliction in all cases in which a disability is inflicted, one may want to consider a different version of the Principle of Non-Interference that focuses on numerical non-identity as opposed to self-identity. Such a principle may be formulated in the following way:

> *Non-Identity Impermissibility*: Other things being equal, an act of disability infliction, *DI*, is impermissible if, when that act is performed on a person, x, it causes x to cease to exist and by ceasing to exist, it causes a new person with the disability, y, to be created.

The acts condemned by Non-Identity Impermissibility are structurally analogous to "killing and creation" acts. An example of such an act could be inflicting a severe disability on a person that fully removes the cognitive ability to remember, as well as other basic cognitive abilities that would otherwise allow for a sufficiently high degree of psychological connectedness across time. If a high degree of psychological connectedness is required for numerical identity, such an act would cause one person to cease to exist and would result in the creation of a numerically different person.

A principle like Self-Conception Impermissibility allows for the impermissibility of a greater number of instances of disability infliction than Non-Identity impermissibility, given that it appeals to a weaker notion of non-identity. However I have tried to show that it does so based on the wrong reasons. Non-Identity Impermissibility allows for the impermissibility of a smaller number of instances of disability infliction, but hopefully for better reasons.

While Non-Identity Impermissibility is an improvement over Self-Conception Impermissibility in that it avoids the problem of not accounting for the wrongness of inflicting disability on children, young infants, and fetuses, the principle is still unable to accommodate the impermissibility of *all* instances of disability infliction, including some instances that we might have good reasons to object to. Thus, it would seem that changes in self-conception or numerical identity cannot fully explain why inflicting disability is wrong. There are instances of disability infliction that do not involve causing individuals to cease to exist without their consent, such as the infliction of a severe physical disability, but which might still seem impermissible. For those cases, it seems inevitable that one must appeal to other grounds, for example, the probability of a negative impact on well-being or opportunities.

Finally, Campbell and Stramondo (2017) provide a view that follows this route and, at the same time, avoids having to fully commit to the Standard View, according to which disability implies a net reduction in well-being. Their view consists in weakening the Standard View; although the Standard View as such is false, they claim, there is a moral difference between causing disability and causing non-disability, and this asymmetry is not grounded in a necessary connection between disability and decreased well-being.

They propose what they call the "Probabilistic Standard View" (Stramondo and Campbell 2020), according to which disability is *likely* to be worse for a person than non-disability; that is, disability "is likely to make a person worse off than she would be without disability" due to the likelihood of a number of factors that disabilities can lead to and which support the claim that causing disability is impermissible (Stramondo and Campbell 2020). These factors include the likelihood of lower well-being, the risk of very low or negative well-being, the irreversibility of the condition, the lack of preference to be disabled, the questionable motivation in third party disability inflictors, the vulnerability to stigma and discrimination, and the social cost of being disabled (Stramondo and Campbell 2020).[10]

3.2. Disability Removal and Non-Identity

There seems to be an asymmetry between our general judgments about causing disability and removing it. We seem to have the intuition that inflicting disability is prima facie wrong and that removing it is right, other things being equal.[11]

In the previous section, we saw how changing the identities of individuals can ground the impermissibility of certain instances of disability infliction. If this can explain the impermissibility of inflicting disability, one would think that it would for the same reasons also ground the impermissibility of removing certain disabilities. This clashes with the widely shared intuition that removing disability is good. Let us elaborate further.

Take the case of removing a cognitive or intellectual disability. One of the most easily detectable genetic conditions in human fetuses is Down Syndrome. Current tests are safe for both the mother and the fetus, cheap, and reliable. The abortion rate after fetuses test positive for Down Syndrome is extremely high in Western countries. Very recently, the introduction of techniques that allow us to edit genes opened up the possibility of curing conditions like Down Syndrome.

Although still far off, if there was a therapy that could delete the extra copy of chromosome 21 (or all symptoms related to Down Syndrome), this therapy might cause a certain person to cease to exist. If there is insufficient psychological connectedness between the being with Down Syndrome and the cognitively enhanced being that emerges from the treatment, that is, if not enough psychological connections hold between them, like memories, intentions, beliefs, and desires (see, e.g., Parfit 1984, 205–207), then this case effectively eliminates one person in order to create a numerically different one.

It could perhaps be argued that there is a significant moral difference between inflicting and removing disability. One might think that while it is true that both interventions can lead to non-identity, we have good reasons to think that while disability removal is permissible, disability infliction is not. Nonetheless, non-identity makes it unsurprisingly challenging to find a person-affecting justification for the permissibility of removing certain disabilities.

Imagine now that these identity-altering interventions would become available for adults. It would be incorrect to claim that such an intervention would be in the best interest of the individual targeted by that intervention. The same intervention that would presumably make the resulting non-disabled adult well off would also make the original disabled adult on whom the intervention is performed cease to exist. So, if non-identity can ground the impermissibility of disability infliction, it could also ground the impermissibility of disability removal in cases like this.

Another related worry about disability removal is replaceability. It has been argued that total utilitarianism justifies the view that certain individuals such as very young infants are replaceable. Death, the argument goes, would not be as bad for them as it would be for adults because the psychological connectedness between the mental states of very young infants is sufficiently weak (Singer 2011, 106). According to the replaceability argument, the welfare loss incurred by the ceasing to exist of a very young infant can be compensated by the bringing into existence of a new child who is at least as well off as the child that has ceased to exist would have been.

While many would be ready to accept that removing certain disabilities is right, not so many would be willing to accept the replaceability argument.[12] But accepting the permissibility of certain identity-altering instances of disability removal would force them to accept the idea that certain disabled individuals are replaceable. This is a conclusion that not many would be ready to accept.[13]

4. Numbers Questions: Disability in the Context of Variable Population Size

Philosophers of disability have mainly focused on questions that fall under the scope of what I have called "procreation questions" and "disability infliction and removal questions." This section focuses on the third set of questions presented in the

Introduction, that is, questions about variable population size and disability. These questions are particularly interesting for several reasons.

First, and in general terms, disabled individuals are a group whose level of well-being tends to be lower than that of other groups, other things being equal. Second, the size of the disabled population is easily susceptible to variation. Among the factors that contribute to this variation in size are the implementation of new technological devices (e.g., cochlear implants), new reproductive technologies, policies that incorporate the use of new medical treatments for disabling conditions, constant changes in lifestyle (some of which have led to, e.g., an increase in obesity), and phenomena like climate change (which is believed to lead to, e.g., a wider spread of infectious diseases like Zika and Malaria among others). These factors make the size of the disabled population more easily susceptible to variation than the size of the population of other traditionally deprived groups, like the female or the black population (at least under normal circumstances or under democratically implemented measures). And they make disability particularly interesting for population ethics. But despite the obvious connection between the ethics of disability and ethical questions about variable population, issues that arise because of this connection are considerably underexplored. This chapter addresses some of these issues.

4.1. Mere Addition and Definitions of Disability

Definitions of disability have an important role in tracking disability both at the individual and at the population level. At the individual level, they are a necessary tool for identifying whether some particular individual is disabled and/or whether she belongs to a certain disability category. This is particularly useful for states to identify which individuals may be entitled to special compensation or subsidies, and to what degree they may be entitled (if the definition at hand incorporates some sort of quantitative measure of the degree of disability).

Interestingly, philosophical definitions of disability do not pay much attention to the issue of numbers, that is, to how variations in the size of the population (both of the disabled and the non-disabled people) can affect disability in that population and, more specifically, how these variations can affect *who* should count as a disabled individual. In this section I look at what some of the well-known definitions of disability imply in the context of variable population and how well those definitions are suited to deal with changes in population size.

In 2001, the International Classification of Functioning, Disability and Health, belonging to the World Health Organization's (WHO), provided a standard and widely used definition of disability:

> "Disabilities" is an umbrella term, covering impairments, activity limitations, and participation restrictions. An impairment is a *problem in body function or structure*;

an activity limitation is a difficulty encountered by an individual in executing a task or action; while a participation restriction is a problem experienced by an individual in involvement in life situations. (WHO 2001; emphasis added)

The WHO's definition—as other standard and widely used definitions of disability—distinguishes between *impairment* and *disability*. The WHO provides blindness and deafness as examples of impairments. Blindness and deafness are problems in the normal functioning of a body. A person is blind due to a problem in her visual system. A person is deaf due to a problem in her hearing system. And both blindness and deafness are impairments that will lead to disabilities, in that individuals with those conditions are not able to see or to hear, which will limit their activities and participation in everyday life.

If impairment is to be understood as a problem in one's body functioning or structure, it seems necessary to spell out first how "problem" ought to be understood in this context. One typical way of understanding it is as a deviation from the functioning of the statistical majority of the individuals of the population.[14] This interpretation of the definition suggests a comparative reading of disability; that is, the definition determines whether an individual is disabled by reference or comparison to some other individual(s) or to some of the properties of other individual(s) that, for a particular reason, are salient in that context.[15]

According to this interpretation of the WHO's definition, I am disabled if I have a problem in my body functioning or structure, which is determined by whether the statistical majority of the individuals of the population, or the average individual of the population, has that problem. If my condition is not part of the statistical majority of the population, or the average person does not have a condition like mine, according to the WHO, I have an impairment, which might eventually result in a disability.

A more recent philosophical definition of disability has been proposed by Barnes (2016). According to her view, the *Mere Difference View* of disability, a person is physically disabled in context C, *iff*:

(1) S is in some bodily state, x;
(2) The rules for making judgments about solidarity employed by the disability rights movement classify x in context C as among the physical conditions that they are seeking to promote justice for. (Barnes 2016, 46)

Interestingly, Barnes complements the above definition with a claim about numbers. She says that being a disabled person is also having a body that functions or contains traits that only a minority of bodies contain:

Being disabled is, I'll argue, a way of being a minority with respect to one's body, just as being gay is a way of being a minority with respect to sexuality. It is something that makes you different from the majority, but that difference isn't by itself a bad thing. *To be disabled is to have a minority body*, but not to have a broken or defective body. (Barnes 2016, 6)

I'll refer to the above as the *Minority Claim*. Barnes's account responds to an attempt to move the notion of disability away from some of the traditional accounts of disability, such as the impairment-based account and the medical account. Contrary to these, her account does not require a condition to be a medical problem or an impairment to count as a disability. Impairment-based accounts are normally associated with the idea that disability implies a defect or a suboptimal deviation from normal functioning that impacts disabled individuals' lives negatively. Barnes wants to rebut this belief by arguing instead that being disabled is having a body with features that only a minority of bodies have (Barnes 2016, 69). Those features are normally local bads, but not necessarily global bads. While local bads are detrimental in one area of a person's life, they can bring about goods in other areas that can be of high value for that person's life (Barnes 2016, 78–101).

There are two main components of Barnes's Minority Claim of relevance here: *bodies* and *minorities*. Barnes is not specific about what *kind* of condition "minority bodies" play in the definition of disability; that is, whether having a minority body is a necessary or sufficient condition for one to be a disabled person. There are three possible readings of the Minority Claim available, each of which specifies a different role to minority bodies (Mosquera 2017a).

> *Minority Claim*: One is a disabled person
>
>   (a) *only if* one possesses a minority body (necessary condition). If one has a nonminority body, then one cannot be disabled. But one may need something other than a minority body in order to be disabled.
>
>   (b) *if and only if* she possesses a minority body (necessary and sufficient condition)
>
>   (c) *if she possesses a minority body (sufficient condition)*. If one has a minority body then one is disabled, but one can be disabled without having a minority body.

Both readings (a) and (b) of Barnes's Minority Claim are subject to counterexamples. Reading (a)—*having a minority body is a necessary condition of being disabled*—is subject to counterexamples where an individual has a body that is not a minority body but our intuition seems to suggest that the person is disabled. Take the following case of disability in the context of variable population size:

> *Radiation*: In a world in which there is a huge explosion in a nuclear platform, a process of radiation affects the vast majority of the population. The consequences of this radiation are that everyone in the following generations will be born with a condition—condition "x"— that will make all new individuals be born without legs.[16]

Radiation is a case in which a feature that under current circumstances would be referred to as a "disability" becomes a feature held by the majority of people. In Radiation, the vast majority of people are born without legs and will continue to be born without legs for an indeterminate amount of time. Thus, in a few decades, after a great generational replacement, the majority of people in Radiation will have no legs.

A similar composition of the population could be achieved through the mere addition of legless individuals to the original population.[17] For that, one can imagine a scenario where there is a huge natality boom from which each new individual is born without legs. Call this scenario Legless Mere Addition.

It seems implausible that, because now the majority of people have no legs, this fact alone means that these people are non-disabled. After all, even if *all* were born without legs, their functioning and well-being would be drastically impacted due to this change. It seems particularly relevant that these people would lack something that would negatively affect their everyday functioning like their basic mobility.[18]

Radiation and Legless Mere Addition challenge both interpretations (a) and (b) of Barnes's definition and the WHO's definition of disability (on the assumption that it involves a comparison with statistical averages or with some reference class, as suggested above). According to these accounts, the legless people in Radiation are not disabled. Condition "x" stops being a disability the moment the next generation is composed mostly of humans with no legs. If we were able to specify the moment at which those without legs became the majority, we would be able to say that at this precise moment, being born without legs is no longer a disability. But it seems implausible that such change can make the very same individual go from disabled to non-disabled.

Every-day, real cases can also be raised as counterexamples to the definitions above. Take the case of visual impairment. Recent studies predict a significant increase in the prevalence of myopia globally, estimating that by 2050 there will be 4,758 million people with myopia in the world (49.8 percent of the world total population) (Holden et al. 2016). But despite myopia being a relatively common feature, this does not make myopia itself less of a burden. People affected by myopia cannot see perfectly at certain distances and therefore need visual help to perform fairly basic activities, like walking or driving. There are other cases to consider. People with bodies that present dysfunctional mobility represent 13 percent of the population of the United States. Although 13 percent of the population of a country is not the majority of the population, based on those numbers we can confidently say that bodies with dysfunctional mobility represent a prevalent group. I will address what I mean by "minority" below.

Obesity is nowadays one of the main causes of dysfunctional mobility. Obese people represent one third of the current population of the world. Suppose trends continue such that more than one half of the population is morbidly obese, leading to an increase in the number of obese bodies and thus bodies with reduced mobility.[19] Would this increase in the number of bodies with obesity and dysfunctional mobility make those who are now disabled due to severe obesity, non-disabled? I take it that the answer to this question is "no," or at least "not necessarily." The fact that a body belongs to the majority of a population (either in appearance, in functioning, or both) does not make the body, immediately, less disabled under most social arrangements.

A second issue with Barnes's Minority Claim relates to how the term "minority" should be understood. It is reasonable to think that when Barnes refers to "minority bodies" she does not refer to a "strict minority." A type of body that is possessed by 49.9 percent of the population, I think, would not fit with the account Barnes presents.

First, and counterintuitively, a conception like this—that accepted the 49.9 percent as a normatively significant minority for disability—would make, for example, having a male body a disability, since male bodies would be minority bodies under this account. Second, it seems plausible to think that what Barnes is referring to when talking about minority bodies is bodies that have a small presence in society, and it is this small presence—as opposed to the functioning of those bodies—that makes having one of those bodies a potential source of disability.

As I have tried to show, for definitions of disability like the WHO's or Barnes's, the addition of disabled people to the original population makes originally disabled people non-disabled. This is odd. It might be that an addition of disabled people to a population can, for example, put more pressure on society to accommodate people with that particular disability, so that the negative effects of the disability have a lesser impact on the individuals with that condition. One might claim short-sightedness to be a case like this. The more short-sighted people who are born into a population, the more pressing it becomes to accommodate them, and the more welfare can be increased by their accommodation.

Nonetheless, I suggest that one be cautious in making a causal connection between the prevalence of a condition and the degree to which society accommodates it. In the case of short-sightedness, one of the drivers (perhaps the main one) of its widespread accommodation (ready availability of glasses and even ocular surgery) can be argued to be the fact that it is an easy, non-costly accommodation. After all, glasses are relatively easy to design, manufacture, and transport. But for other disabilities, although the addition of more people with the same disability might still increase the pressure to accommodate, the fact that the disability is harder to accommodate might make it so that a simple mere addition of people with that disability will not necessarily lead to a reduction of the negative impact of that disability, or at least not so that it would make originally disabled people non-disabled.

Addition of new people is not only a challenge for the definitions presented above. Any definition of "disability" that establishes a comparison between a particular individual and a reference class will face this challenge. And given that the most common definitions of disability are comparative in this sense, most definitions of disability inherit the same problem.

Take now comparative definitions of disability that use the norm of the species as the relevant class of reference or comparison (as opposed to the average body or functioning). These definitions are also problematic in the context of variable population size and are subject to the addition problems explained above. Take the addition of genetically enhanced human beings to a population. It seems plausible that such a scenario would change the norm of the human species of the population from "non-enhanced" to "enhanced" if a sufficiently large number of them were added to the original population. Under such a scenario, previously standard "non-enhanced" human beings would count now as disabled human beings.[20]

Some will find this conclusion ridiculous. They may think it is unjustified that otherwise perfectly functional human beings will be considered disabled only because there is now a majority of human beings with higher cognitive and functional capacities. On the other hand, if the way enhanced human beings function becomes the norm and society becomes more adapted to their higher level of cognition and functionality, perhaps there is reason to think of non-enhanced human beings as "disabled" in this respect. But if we think of this case as a case of pure addition, that is, other things being equal and leaving societal design and functionality unchanged, it would seem unjustified, some would claim, to think of non-enhanced human beings as disabled.

Finally, one way of resisting the implication that the addition of enhanced human beings can make otherwise perfectly functional human beings disabled, is to argue that in such a scenario, the population of enhanced human beings would simply constitute a species different from the human species. But this solution comes with a cost. If enhancement can give rise to a new species, then so would extreme deviation in the other direction, namely in the direction of human disability. This means that many with genetic disabilities should also constitute a different, non-human species. This is a serious challenge for species-norm definitions of disability.

4.2. Disability and Equality in the Context of Variable Population Size

Within the context of disability and different number cases, another interesting question is whether changes in the size of the population of disabled and/or non-disabled people can worsen or lessen the inequality that disabilities give rise to.

This issue emerges if we think about disabilities within the context of the luck egalitarian framework of justice. Egalitarians have traditionally taken disabilities and the inequalities that these lead to as an undeniable focus of concern. The majority of both congenital and acquired disabilities give rise to inequalities that are the result of bad brute luck and, therefore, inequalities that are unfair and for which people should be compensated. This conception of inequality, commonly known as *luck egalitarianism*, is at the heart of most contemporary accounts of equality (Arneson 2001; Rawls 1972; Segall 2016; Temkin 1993).

Going back to the different number scenario, an intuitive way to reduce the inequality that stems from deprivations (like disability or poverty) is to eliminate these deprivations, either by reducing the number of deprived people in the population by eliminating their deprivation, or by preventing the existence of further deprivation which, in some cases, may lead to an increase in the number of non-deprived people.

Within the domain of poverty reduction, Nicole Hassoun (2014) has interestingly argued that adding rich people to a population does not necessarily reduce poverty. Hassoun argues that while poverty indexes have traditionally conflated the notion of the *poverty in a population* and the *population's poverty*, these two notions should come apart.[21]

Where X and Y are two different populations, saying that there is more poverty in population X than in Y means that

(1) X has more poverty than Y (that is: there is more poverty present in X than in Y)

but (1) is not equivalent to the following judgment about these *populations' poverty*:

(2) X is poorer than Y (that is: X is less wealthy overall than Y)

Given this distinction, Hassoun argues that it is not the case that merely adding rich people to a population will reduce the poverty *in that population*. While adding rich people to a population may make the population richer, this does not reduce the poverty in that population. The following axiom, which Hassoun argues the main poverty indexes in the literature violate, is meant to express this intuition.

> *Weak Population Focus*: Poverty in a population is not reduced by changes in the non-poor population which leave the distribution of goods amongst the poor unchanged. (Hassoun 2014; Hassoun and Subramanian 2012)

The intuition behind the Weak Population Focus axiom reflects an idea originally raised by Sen: "poverty is a characteristic of the poor, and therefore a reduction of the incomes of the poor must increase the measure of poverty, no matter how much the incomes of the non-poor go up at the same time" (Sen 1981, 190 as cited in Hassoun 2014, 169). Similarly, Hassoun's intuition goes, if poverty is a characteristic of the poor, merely adding rich people does not affect the poor any more than if the incomes of the rich increase (Hassoun 2014, 169). An increase in the number of rich people should not in itself reduce the poverty in a population.

An observation akin to Hassoun's can be made in the context of inequality. It could be argued that an addition of better-off people (e.g., people above the average level of well-being) doesn't necessarily make things better for the inequality of that population, in that it does not make the worst off better in any respect.

I have elsewhere tried to show that when it comes to equality, the addition of better off people does not necessarily make a population better from the point of view of inequality, referring to this conclusion as the Paradox of Deprivation Reduction and Inequality (Mosquera 2017a; 2017b). The idea is that, although it might be prima facie paradoxical, an increase in the number of better-off people, a decrease in the number of worse-off people, or a combination of both, does not necessarily lead to a decrease in inequality because it increases the number of relations of inequality that are concentrated in the worse-off.

The idea is that the way in which relations of inequality are distributed among individuals should also matter when accounting for the egalitarian value of a population.

For example, it is pro tanto worse if there are many pairwise relations of inequality all concentrated on a single individual, than if those relations are spread over different individuals. This concern introduces a relevant distinction: egalitarians qua egalitarians should care not only about the equal distribution of goods—whether there is equality of resources, welfare, and so on—but also about second order equality—a notion that refers to equality in the metadistribution of goods, or equality in the distribution of relations of inequality.[22]

To account for this intuition, I provided a principle called Distribution-Sensitive Pairwise Egalitarianism (DSP) (Mosquera 2017a, 2017b). DSP is a function between the number of relations of inequality of a population and how equally or unequally these are distributed among the individuals of that population. As opposed to what I called "aggregative pairwise comparisons of inequality" (those comparisons made on the basis of the total aggregate of relations of inequality in a population), DSP suggests a further variable for the measure of inequality; it is not just the amount of relations of inequality or equality that should matter for egalitarians, nor their size, but also how these relations of inequality are distributed. One world with the same amount of relations of equality and inequality as another is not simply better but more egalitarian if no individual has an unequal burden of them.

This "piling-up" effect captured by DSP reflects the idea of an increasing marginal significance of relations of inequality. Relations of inequality matter more the more concentrated they are, so it is worse from the point of view of equality when one person it is subject to two relations of inequality than when two people each are it is subject to one relation of inequality, other things being equal.

In Figure 26.1 below, the vertical axis measures the level of well-being of the individuals in the populations and the horizontal axis measures the size of the populations. Capital letters represent populations and low case letters represent individuals. The concentration of inequality captured by DSP is what makes B's inequality in Figure 26.1 feel in one respect more flagrant than A's inequality. And it is this unfairness that can override the value of the extra relations of equality that B, as opposed to A, contains.[23]

Concerning the relationship between disability and inequality, the lesson is that a significant reduction in the number of disabled people through, for example, genetic screening followed by abortion, or through an addition of non-disabled people to the population by selecting embryos without disability, does not necessarily make

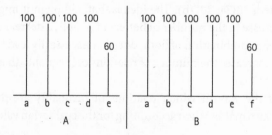

FIGURE 26.1 Concentration of pairwise inequality

inequality better. In fact, the inequality that the remaining disabled people are subject to due to their disability might increase in magnitude given that a greater number of non-disabled, better off people live in that population (Mosquera 2017a, 2017b). This observation should not be ignored by policy-makers when designing policies that may lead to the reduction of the number of disabled people or to the increase in the number of non-disabled people in a particular population.

Finally, although important, I would not claim this aspect of inequality implies that reducing the incidence of disabilities in the future is bad from the point of view of equality. The concentration or piling-up effect of relations of inequality is only one of the considerations that egalitarians should pay attention to. It ought to be decided how much weight should be assigned to those considerations as compared to other egalitarian considerations. There is room for policy-makers to implement policies of this kind without worsening the burden of inequality of already existing individuals. One such way would be, for example, to give further support to already existing disabled people making sure that their inequality gap becomes smaller than what it currently is, so that the concentration effect of this change in the composition of the population could be at least lessened.

5. Measures of Disability and Health: DALYs and Population Ethics

Finally, one may wonder whether health measures of disability can do better at the issues presented here than some of the philosophical definitions and accounts discussed in this chapter. Interestingly, one of the best-known measures of the burden of disability and/or disease, DALYs, faces problems that parallel the ones I have presented here.

The DALY (disability-adjusted life-year) is a measure used to quantify health losses from disease and disability. It has been argued that different justifications of the use of DALYs to evaluate the effectiveness of health interventions face either the non-identity problem or the variable population size problems discussed in this chapter (Campbell n.d.; Hutchinson 2019).

First, we might claim that a health intervention is effective to the extent that it improves the health states of individuals in the global population, and this extent is measured by the number of DALYs averted by the intervention. This kind of justification is subject to the non-identity problem (Hutchinson 2019, 210). Consider the case of the Zika virus. During the Zika crisis, some governments recommended delaying conception by several months to those who lived in or traveled to areas with a high risk of infection with Zika. Interventions targeted at delaying conception may have averted a large number of DALYs, but due to non-identity, these interventions cannot be said to have improved the health states of those who, as a result, were born a few months later, or of any other actual children. Thus, the use of DALYs averted to evaluate policies like this cannot be justified on the grounds that the number of DALYs averted reflects the extent to which the health states of particular individuals have improved (Campbell n.d., 6–8). Interventions that lead to the addition of new people who, for example, can be expected to live only to age eighty and be mostly free of disease and disability, would be bad given that these people would fall short of the ideal standard of health (say, eighty-seven years free of disability). Adding these people would increase the number of DALYs, thus exacerbating the global burden of disease (Hutchinson 2019, 204). This may be viewed as a problematic implication.[24]

Finally, one may argue that the goal of some policy interventions is to increase the total number of years of healthy life. The number of DALYs averted by a health intervention could be used to track the number of additional years of healthy life that exist because of the intervention. The justification could be that health policy should aim to maximize the number of years of healthy life, whether this is achieved by improving the health states of existing individuals, creating new individuals with positive health states, or by a combination of both (Hutchinson 2019, 206–207).

Although this justification avoids the problems faced by the other two, it can be said to be problematic for a different reason. It suggests that failing to add new healthy people to a population increases the number of DALYs, since there are fewer years of healthy life than there could be, and that we can avert DALYs by increasing the global population. This, again, seems odd. It is unclear how a mere increase in the total population can make an intervention more effective with respect to health.

The above are some problematic implications of the use of DALYs averted as a measure of the effectiveness of a health intervention. These implications do not mean that such a measure should be abandoned. But they do reinforce the point that the issues of population ethics discussed in this chapter are transversal to both philosophical definitions of disability and to well-known measures of their health impacts.

6. Conclusion

This chapter argued that the ethics of disability has interesting and useful implications for population ethics. I suggested that there are three main sets of questions in the realm of population ethics and disability: procreation questions, disability infliction and removal questions, and numbers questions.

Procreation questions deal with the morality of bringing disabled people into existence. The standard way of framing this issue is by asking whether it is better to bring a disabled child into existence as opposed to a non-disabled one. A standard way of approaching this question has been to look for different ways of arguing that it is better to bring the non-disabled child into existence. I have looked at some of these arguments, some of which are person-affecting and others of which are impersonal.

Disability infliction and removal questions deal with the permissibility of inflicting or removing disability. This debate has been focused on trying to provide arguments to support the judgment that inflicting disability is wrong. While some authors have appealed to the idea that disability has a net negative impact in well-being in order to argue disability infliction impermissible, others have rejected this and argued instead that the reason why it is impermissible is because it causes a disruption in identity, mainly in terms of self-conception. I have also raised the issue of disability removal and argued that those who appeal to non-identity to argue for the impermissibility of disability infliction are in trouble when it comes to defending the permissibility of disability removal. If inflicting disability is wrong mainly because it changes the identity of the individual, removing disability would have to be wrong since it would also cause a disruption in identity.

The numbers questions deal with how the evaluation of disability changes in the context of variable population size. I have argued that many philosophical definitions of disability (especially those that I refer to as "comparative") lead to opposing evaluations about whether a certain individual is disabled when applied in the context of variable population size. Given that one of the aspects of the badness of disability is inequality, I showed that evaluations about the equality of a population can, too, vary in the context of variable population size. I argued that this is something for policy-makers to take into account when designing policies that may have an impact in the incidence of disability.

Finally, measures of health that aim at determining the health impacts of certain disabilities seem to face versions of the same problems that affect philosophical accounts of disability. Both non-identity and different numbers issues seem to undermine the three most plausible justifications for the use of DALYs as a measure of the effectiveness of different health interventions aimed at averting years of life with disabilities and/ or diseases.

The ethics of disability is a particularly fruitful and interesting field for population ethics. In this chapter, I have discussed a number of issues at the intersection of these two fields. Given that the ethics of disability inherits some of the issues at the core of population ethics, solutions to the latter field will be of great benefit also for the former.

NOTES

1. On the relationship between climate change and population change, see Bommier, Lanz, and Zuber (2015); Carleton et al. (2019); Geruso & Spears (2018); WHO (2014); Mejean, Pottier, Zuber, and Fleurbaey (2017).

2. Even if *certain* disabilities do not negatively impact individual's overall well-being. I expand on this point later.

3. For a very comprehensive overview of this debate and the different positions involved in it, see Wasserman (2005). Wasserman's own position diverges from the ones commonly referred to in the debate. He rejects both the person affecting and the non-person affecting intuitions as a basis for the rejection of having to create the child expected to have a disability and argues for a different basis to evaluate procreative decisions. His view is based on the morality of prospective parents and the justifiability of the reasons for making a

decision of this kind and does not prohibit the bringing a disabled child into existence (Wasserman 2005). Given the nature of this chapter, I leave his view aside.

4. McMahan points to another challenge of a different nature for ICP. This principle can seem to be judged as prescribing a form of positive eugenics (McMahan 2005, 146). This has been known as the expressivist argument against selecting against disability (see, e.g., Wilkinson 2010). The idea is that to choose a non-disabled child over a disabled child expresses a pernicious view of disabled people. Given the scope of this chapter, I leave this issue aside.

5. The label of this view is due to Amudson (2005).

6. Assuming that inflicting disability is unarguably impermissible, which I take for granted here.

7. Or for cases in which the effects of the disability infliction become noticeable for the person very gradually, in a way akin to the effects of natural aging.

8. Further, and for similar reasons, it is possible that the transition costs argument cannot account either for the impermissibility of inflicting further disability(s) to already highly disabled individuals.

9. My own formulation.

10. The authors identify the actual lower average well-being of the group of the current disabled with three factors that are nonetheless relatively independent on the value of disabilities themselves: the transition costs of acquiring a new disability, some disabilities greatly diminishing a person's well-being in a wide range of contexts, and inaccessible and hostile social institutions and practices (Stramondo and Campbell 2020).

11. Some might not share this intuition in cases where the disability doesn't impact well-being significantly, or perhaps due to adaptation. For further discussion on the acceptability of the Asymmetry, see Barnes (2016).

12. Leaving the transition costs of adapting to non-disability, as well as other costs, aside.

13. Disability removal also raises questions about the rationality of consent to disability-removal treatments. For example, if these therapies lead to the end of one person's existence and the creation of another, under which circumstances would and should a cognitively disabled adult rationally consent to such treatment? Given the focus of this chapter, I leave these questions aside.

14. Such an interpretation has also been suggested by others. Glover suggests that impairment, in the WHO's definition of disability, could be understood as a comparison with the average person of a population (Glover 2006, 8).

15. I take this comparative element to be common to definitions of health, too. An example of this is Boorse's definition of disease, in which the concept of function is normative in that it makes assumptions about for example which aims are worthwhile. See Boorse (2011).

16. See Mosquera (2017a).

17. The term "mere" here refers to the fact that the new individuals added to the original population (1) have lives worth living, (2) affect no one else negatively, and (3) whose existence does not involve social injustice. For contrast, see Parfit's *Mere Addition* (c.f. Parfit 1984, 420).

18. Since (a) is an element of (b), any counterexample to (a) will be a counterexample to (b).

19. This is a current trend in a number of the Pacific Island countries, where globalization and rapid economic growth have led to a shift in dietary patterns and to the adoption of sedentary habits. Some of the countries with the highest prevalence rates of adult obesity in the world are found there, ranging from 50 percent to 90 percent of overweight prevalence,

and 30 percent to 80 percent of obesity prevalence, according to WHO surveys; https://www.who.int/bulletin/volumes/88/7/10-010710/en/.

20. McMahan (1996) raises a similar criticism against the species norm account understood as a basis for moral standing. In his Superchimp example (1996, 13), McMahan argues that a sufficiently large addition of genetically enhanced chimps ("superchimps") to a population of non-enhanced chimps that outweighs the number of non-enhanced chimps, would change the norm of the species of that population; the new species-norm would correspond to the capabilities of the enhanced members of population. "At that point, what counts as normal capacities for the species will have changed. The hitherto normal chimpanzees will have become abnormal or retarded [author's terminology]. According to the Species Norm Account, they will have become unfortunate, for their level of well-being will be far below the higher levels made possible by the capacities that have now become the norm for the species" (McMahan 1996, 13–14). McMahan takes this implication to be a reductio ad absurdum of species-norm accounts.

21. A similar distinction can be made between *total pairwise inequality* and *average pairwise inequality*. See Arrhenius (2013) and Mosquera (2017a).

22. If one believes that it is not only relations of inequality that egalitarians should be concerned with, but also relations of equality, therefore subscribing to Positive Egalitarianism, then one will also care about the equal distribution of relations of equality. For further elaboration on this view, see Arrhenius (2013), Mosquera 2017a), (Mosquera 2017b), and Arrhenius and Mosquera (2021).

23. For further discussion on how to weigh different egalitarian concerns, see Arrhenius and Mosquera (2021).

24. This point is also made by Arrhenius (n.d.). For further problematic implications of this justification see Campbell (n.d.).

References

Amundson, Ron. 2005. "Disability, Ideology, and Quality of Life: A Bias in Biomedical Ethics." In *Quality of Life and Human Difference*, edited by David Wasserman, Jerome Bickenbach, and Robert Wachbroit, 101–124. Cambridge: Cambridge University Press.

Arneson, Richard. 2001. "Luck and Equality, *Proceedings of the Aristotelian Society*, supp. vol. 75, 73–90. https://doi.org/10.1111/1467-8349.00079.

Arrhenius, Gustaf, Ryberg, Jesper, and Tännsjö, Torbjörn. 2006. "The Repugnant Conclusion." In *The Stanford Encyclopaedia of Philosophy*, edited by Edward N. Zalta (Spring 2017 Edition). https://plato.stanford.edu/archives/spr2017/entries/repugnant-conclusion/.

Arrhenius, Gustaf. 2013. "Egalitarian Concerns and Population Change". In *Measurement and Ethical Evaluation of Health Inequalities*, edited by Ole Frithjof Norheim, 74–91. Oxford: Oxford University Press.

Arrhenius, Gustaf. 2018. "Climate Change, Risk, and Population." In *Global Warming, Global Ethics*, edited by Narumi Yoshikawa. Shiizukobundoshobo.

Arrhenius, Gustaf. Forthcoming. *Population Ethics: The Challenge of Future Generations*. Oxford: Oxford University Press.

Arrhenius, Gustaf. n.d. "Inequality Measures and Population Change," Stockholm: Institute for Futures Studies (IFFS).

Arrhenius, Gustaf and Mosquera, Julia. 2021. "Positive Egalitarianism Reconsidered." *Utilitas*, 1–20. doi:10.1017/S0953820819000566

Barker, Mathew. J. and Wilson, Robert A. 2019. "Well-being, Disability, and Choosing Children." *Mind* 128, no. 510: 305–328.

Barnes, Elizabeth. 2016. *The Minority Body: A Theory of Disability*. Oxford: Oxford University Press.

Barnes, Elizabeth. 2014. "Valuing Disability, Causing Disability." *Ethics* 125, no. 1: 88–113.

Benatar, David. 2000. "The Wrong of Wrongful Life." *American Philosophical Quarterly* 37: 175–183.

Bommier, Anoine, Lanz, Bruno, and Zuber, Stéphane. 2015. "Models-as-Usual for Unusual Risks? On the Value of Catastrophic Climate Change." *Journal of Environmental Economics and Management* 74: 1–22.

Boonin, David. 2014. *The Non-Identity Problem and The Ethics of Future People*. Oxford: Oxford University Press.

Boorse, Christopher. 2011. "Concepts of Health and Disease." In *Handbook of the Philosophy of Science*, vol. 16, *Philosophy of Medicine*, edited by Fred Gifford, 13–64. Oxford: North Holland (Elsevier).

Brock, Daniel. 2005. "Preventing Genetically Transmitted Disabilities while Respecting Persons with Disabilities." In *Quality of Life and Human Difference: Genetic Testing, Health Care, and Disability*, edited by David Wasserman, Jerome Bickenbach, and Robert Wachbroit, 67–100. New York: Cambridge University Press.

Buchanan, Allen, Brock, Dan, Daniels, Norman, and Wikler, Daniel. 2000. *From Chance to Choice: Genetics and Justice*. Cambridge: Cambridge University Press.

Campbell, Tim. n.d. "Using DALYs to Evaluate Health Interventions: Lessons from Population Ethics." Stockholm: Institute for Futures Studies (IFFS).

Campbell, Stephen. M. and Stramondo, Joseph A. 2017. "The Complicated Relationship of Disability and Well-Being." *Kennedy Institute of Ethics Journal* 27: 151–184.

Carleton, Tamma A. Jina, Amir Delgado, Michael T., Houser, Trevor, M. Hsiang, Solomon, Hultgren, Andrew, Kopp, Robert E. McCusker, Kelly E. Nath, Ishan B., Rising, James Rode, Ashwin Seo, Hee Kwon Viaene, Arvid, Yuan Jiacan, and Zhang Alice. 2019. *Valuing the Global Mortality Consequences of Climate Change Accounting for Adaptation Costs and Benefits*, https://bfi.uchicago.edu/working-paper/valuing-the-global-mortality-consequences-of-climate-change-accounting-for-adaptation-costs-and-benefits/.

Geruso, Michael and Spears Dean. 2018. "Heat, Humidity, and Infant Mortality in the Developing World." IZA—Institute of Labor Economics, IZA DP No. 11717.

Glover, Jonathan. 2006. *Choosing Children*. Oxford: Oxford University Press.

Hassoun, Nicole. 2014. "An Aspect of Variable Population Poverty Comparisons: Does Adding a Rich Person to a Population Reduce Poverty?" *Economics and Philosophy* 30, no. 2: 163–174.

Hassoun, Nicole and Subramanian, S. 2012. "Variable Population Poverty Comparisons." *Journal of Development Economics* 98, no.2: 238–241.

Herissone-Kelly, Peter. 2006. "Procreative Beneficence and the Prospective Parent." *Journal of Medical Ethics* 32, no. 3: 166–169.

Holden, B. A. et al. 2016. "Global Prevalence of Myopia and High Myopia and Temporal Trends from 2000 through 2050." *American Academy of Ophthalmology* 123 no. 5: 1036–1042.

Horta, Oscar. 2010. "Debunking the Idyllic View of Natural Processes: Population Dynamics and Suffering in the Wild." *Telos* 17: 73–88.

Hutchinson, Michelle. 2019. "People Aren't Replaceable: Why It's Better to Extend Lives Than to Create New Ones." In *Saving People from the Harm of Death*, edited by Espen Gamlund and Carl Tollef Solberg, 203–214. Oxford: Oxford University Press.

Kahane, Guy and Savulescu, Julian. 2009. "The Welfarist Account of Disability." In *Disability and Disadvantage*, edited by Kimberley Brownlee and Adam Cureton, 15–53. Oxford: Oxford University Press.

Kahane, Guy and Savulescu, Julian. 2012. "The Concept of Harm and the Significance of Normality." *Journal of Applied Philosophy* 29: 318–332.

Kamm, Frances M. 2002. "Genes, Justice, and Obligations to Future People." *Social Philosophy and Policy* 19: 360–388.

Kavka, Gregory S. 1982. "The Paradox of Future Individuals." *Philosophy and Public Affairs* 11, no. 2: 93–112.

Klitzman, Robert. 2016. "Deciding How Many Embryos to Transfer: Ongoing Challenges and Dilemmas." *Reproductive Biomedicine & Society Online* 3: 1–15.

Kumar, Rahul 2003. "Who Can Be Wronged?" *Philosophy and Public Affairs* 31, no. 2: 99–118.

McMahan, Jeff. 1981. "Problems of Population Theory." *Ethics* 92: pp. 96–127.

McMahan, Jeff. 1996. "Cognitive Disability, Misfortune, and Justice." *Philosophy and Public Affairs* 25, no. 1: 3–35.

McMahan, Jeff. 2005. "Preventing the Existence of People with Disabilities." In *Quality of Life and Human Difference*, edited by David Wasserman, Jerome Bickenbach, and Robert Wachbroit, 142–171. Cambridge: Cambridge University Press.

Mejean, Aurélie, Pottier, Antonin Zuber, Stephane, and Fleurbaey, Marc. 2017. "Intergenerational Equity under Catastrophic Climate Change." Working paper, the Sorbonne Economics Centre.

Mosquera, Julia. 2020. "Why Inflicting Disability Is Wrong: The Mere Difference View and the Causation Based Objection." In *The Handbook of Philosophy of Disability*, edited by Adam Cureton and David Wasserman, 158–173. Oxford: Oxford University Press.

Mosquera, Julia. 2017a. "Disability, Equality, and Future Generations." PhD diss. University of Reading.

Mosquera, Julia. 2017b. "An Egalitarian Argument Against Reducing Deprivation." *Ethical Theory and Moral Practice* 20: 957–968.

Narveson, Jan. 1967. "Utilitarianism and New Generations." *Mind* 76, 62–72.

Parfit, Derek. 1982. "Future Generations: Further Problems." *Philosophy and Public Affairs* 11, no. 2, 113–172.

Parfit, Derek. 1984. *Reasons and Persons*. Oxford: Oxford University Press.

Parfit, Derek. 2011. *On What Matters: Volume Two*. Oxford: Oxford University Press.

Parfit, Derek. 2017. "Future People, the Non-Identity Problem, and Person-Affecting Principles." *Philosophy & Public Affairs* 45: 118–157.

Purdy, Laura. 1996. *Reproducing Persons: Issues in Feminist Bioethics*. Ithaca, NY: Cornell University Press, 50–74.

Rawls, John. 1972. *A Theory of Justice*. Oxford: Clarendon Press.

Roberts, Melinda A. 1995. "Present Duties and Future Persons: When Are Existence-Inducing Acts Wrong?" *Law and Philosophy* 14: 297–327.

Savulescu, Julian. 2007. "In Defence of Procreative Beneficence." *Journal of Medical Ethics* 33, no. 5: 284–288.

Savulescu, Julian and Kahane, Guy. 2009. "The Moral Obligation to Create Children with the Best Chance of the Best Life." *Bioethics* 23, no. 5: 274–90.

Segall, Shlomi. 2016. *Why Inequality Matters*. Cambridge: Cambridge University Press.

Sen, Amartya 1981. *Poverty and Famines: An Essay on Entitlement and Deprivation*. Oxford: Clarendon Press

Singer, Peter. 2011. *Practical Ethics*. 3rd edition. Cambridge: Cambridge University Press.

Steinbock, Bonnie. and McClamrock, Ron. 1994. "When Is Birth Unfair to the Child?" *Hastings Center Report* 24: 15–21.

Stramondo, Joseph A. and Stephen. M. Campbell. 2020. "Causing Disability, Causing Non-Disability: What's the Moral Difference?" In *Oxford Handbook of Philosophy and Disability*, edited by Adam Cureton, and David Wasserman, 138–157. Oxford: Oxford University Press.

Tännsjö, Torbjörn. 2002. Why We Ought to Accept the Repugnant Conclusion. *Utilitas* 14, no. 3, 339–359.

Tooley, Michael. 1998. "Value, Obligation, and the Asymmetry Question." *Bioethics* 12: 111–124.

Temkin, Larry. 1993. *Inequality*. Oxford: Oxford University Press.

Wasserman, David. 2005. "The Nonidentity Problem, Disability, and the Role of Morality of Prospective Parents." *Ethics* 116, no. 1: 132–152.

WHO. 2001. *International Classification of Functioning, Disability and Health (ICF) External Icon*. Geneva: WHO.

WHO. 2014. *Quantitative Risk Assessment of the Effects of Climate Change on Selected Causes of Death, 2030s and 2050s*. Geneva: WHO.

Wilkinson, Stephen. 2010. *Choosing Tomorrow's Children: The Ethics of Selective Reproduction*. Oxford: Oxford University Press.

INDEX

"Due to the use of para id indexing, indexed terms that span two pages (e.g., 52– 53) may, on occasion, appear on only one of those pages."

Tables and figures are indicated by *t* and *f* following the page number